Lecture Notes in Computer Science   10280

Commenced Publication in 1973
Founding and Former Series Editors:
Gerhard Goos, Juris Hartmanis, and Jan van Leeuwen

More information about this series at http://www.springer.com/series/7409

Stephanie Lackey · Jessie Chen (Eds.)

Virtual, Augmented and Mixed Reality

9th International Conference, VAMR 2017
Held as Part of HCI International 2017
Vancouver, BC, Canada, July 9–14, 2017
Proceedings

 Springer

Editors
Stephanie Lackey
Federal Solutions Division
Design Interactive, Inc.
Orlando, FL
USA

Jessie Chen
US Army Research Laboratory
Orlando, FL
USA

ISSN 0302-9743   ISSN 1611-3349   (electronic)
Lecture Notes in Computer Science
ISBN 978-3-319-57986-3   ISBN 978-3-319-57987-0   (eBook)
DOI 10.1007/978-3-319-57987-0

Library of Congress Control Number: 2017938563

LNCS Sublibrary: SL3 – Information Systems and Applications, incl. Internet/Web, and HCI

Printed on acid-free paper

This Springer imprint is published by Springer Nature
The registered company is Springer International Publishing AG
The registered company address is: Gewerbestrasse 11, 6330 Cham, Switzerland

Foreword

The 19th International Conference on Human–Computer Interaction, HCI International 2017, was held in Vancouver, Canada, during July 9–14, 2017. The event incorporated the 15 conferences/thematic areas listed on the following page.

A total of 4,340 individuals from academia, research institutes, industry, and governmental agencies from 70 countries submitted contributions, and 1,228 papers have been included in the proceedings. These papers address the latest research and development efforts and highlight the human aspects of design and use of computing systems. The papers thoroughly cover the entire field of human–computer interaction, addressing major advances in knowledge and effective use of computers in a variety of application areas. The volumes constituting the full set of the conference proceedings are listed on the following pages.

I would like to thank the program board chairs and the members of the program boards of all thematic areas and affiliated conferences for their contribution to the highest scientific quality and the overall success of the HCI International 2017 conference.

This conference would not have been possible without the continuous and unwavering support and advice of the founder, Conference General Chair Emeritus and Conference Scientific Advisor Prof. Gavriel Salvendy. For his outstanding efforts, I would like to express my appreciation to the communications chair and editor of *HCI International News*, Dr. Abbas Moallem.

April 2017   Constantine Stephanidis

HCI International 2017 Thematic Areas and Affiliated Conferences

Thematic areas:

- Human–Computer Interaction (HCI 2017)
- Human Interface and the Management of Information (HIMI 2017)

Affiliated conferences:

- 17th International Conference on Engineering Psychology and Cognitive Ergonomics (EPCE 2017)
- 11th International Conference on Universal Access in Human–Computer Interaction (UAHCI 2017)
- 9th International Conference on Virtual, Augmented and Mixed Reality (VAMR 2017)
- 9th International Conference on Cross-Cultural Design (CCD 2017)
- 9th International Conference on Social Computing and Social Media (SCSM 2017)
- 11th International Conference on Augmented Cognition (AC 2017)
- 8th International Conference on Digital Human Modeling and Applications in Health, Safety, Ergonomics and Risk Management (DHM 2017)
- 6th International Conference on Design, User Experience and Usability (DUXU 2017)
- 5th International Conference on Distributed, Ambient and Pervasive Interactions (DAPI 2017)
- 5th International Conference on Human Aspects of Information Security, Privacy and Trust (HAS 2017)
- 4th International Conference on HCI in Business, Government and Organizations (HCIBGO 2017)
- 4th International Conference on Learning and Collaboration Technologies (LCT 2017)
- Third International Conference on Human Aspects of IT for the Aged Population (ITAP 2017)

Conference Proceedings Volumes Full List

1. LNCS 10271, Human–Computer Interaction: User Interface Design, Development and Multimodality (Part I), edited by Masaaki Kurosu
2. LNCS 10272 Human–Computer Interaction: Interaction Contexts (Part II), edited by Masaaki Kurosu
3. LNCS 10273, Human Interface and the Management of Information: Information, Knowledge and Interaction Design (Part I), edited by Sakae Yamamoto
4. LNCS 10274, Human Interface and the Management of Information: Supporting Learning, Decision-Making and Collaboration (Part II), edited by Sakae Yamamoto
5. LNAI 10275, Engineering Psychology and Cognitive Ergonomics: Performance, Emotion and Situation Awareness (Part I), edited by Don Harris
6. LNAI 10276, Engineering Psychology and Cognitive Ergonomics: Cognition and Design (Part II), edited by Don Harris
7. LNCS 10277, Universal Access in Human–Computer Interaction: Design and Development Approaches and Methods (Part I), edited by Margherita Antona and Constantine Stephanidis
8. LNCS 10278, Universal Access in Human–Computer Interaction: Designing Novel Interactions (Part II), edited by Margherita Antona and Constantine Stephanidis
9. LNCS 10279, Universal Access in Human–Computer Interaction: Human and Technological Environments (Part III), edited by Margherita Antona and Constantine Stephanidis
10. LNCS 10280, Virtual, Augmented and Mixed Reality, edited by Stephanie Lackey and Jessie Y.C. Chen
11. LNCS 10281, Cross-Cultural Design, edited by Pei-Luen Patrick Rau
12. LNCS 10282, Social Computing and Social Media: Human Behavior (Part I), edited by Gabriele Meiselwitz
13. LNCS 10283, Social Computing and Social Media: Applications and Analytics (Part II), edited by Gabriele Meiselwitz
14. LNAI 10284, Augmented Cognition: Neurocognition and Machine Learning (Part I), edited by Dylan D. Schmorrow and Cali M. Fidopiastis
15. LNAI 10285, Augmented Cognition: Enhancing Cognition and Behavior in Complex Human Environments (Part II), edited by Dylan D. Schmorrow and Cali M. Fidopiastis
16. LNCS 10286, Digital Human Modeling and Applications in Health, Safety, Ergonomics and Risk Management: Ergonomics and Design (Part I), edited by Vincent G. Duffy
17. LNCS 10287, Digital Human Modeling and Applications in Health, Safety, Ergonomics and Risk Management: Health and Safety (Part II), edited by Vincent G. Duffy
18. LNCS 10288, Design, User Experience, and Usability: Theory, Methodology and Management (Part I), edited by Aaron Marcus and Wentao Wang

Virtual, Augmented, and Mixed Reality

Program Board Chair(s): **Stephanie Lackey** and **Jessie Y.C. Chen, USA**

- Sheryl Brahnam, USA
- Jesse D. Flint, USA
- Panagiotis D. Kaklis, UK
- Ben Lawson, USA
- Fotis Liarokapis, Czech Republic
- Phil Mangos, USA
- Crystal S. Maraj, USA

- Skip Rizzo, USA
- Maria Olinda Rodas, USA
- Julie N. Salcedo, USA
- Jose San Martin, Spain
- Randall Shumaker, USA
- Peter A. Smith, USA
- Marjorie A. Zielke, USA

The full list with the Program Board Chairs and the members of the Program Boards of all thematic areas and affiliated conferences is available online at:

http://www.hci.international/board-members-2017.php

HCI International 2018

The 20th International Conference on Human–Computer Interaction, HCI International 2018, will be held jointly with the affiliated conferences in Las Vegas, NV, USA, at Caesars Palace, July 15–20, 2018. It will cover a broad spectrum of themes related to human–computer interaction, including theoretical issues, methods, tools, processes, and case studies in HCI design, as well as novel interaction techniques, interfaces, and applications. The proceedings will be published by Springer. More information is available on the conference website: http://2018.hci.international/.

General Chair
Prof. Constantine Stephanidis
University of Crete and ICS-FORTH
Heraklion, Crete, Greece
E-mail: general_chair@hcii2018.org

http://2018.hci.international/

Contents

VAMR in Education and Training

Virtual Worlds and Games

User Experience in VAMR

Developing Virtual and Augmented Environments

Analytical Mapping of Linear Walk from Infinite Virtual Space to Finite Real Space

Angelos Barmpoutis[(✉)]

University of Florida, Gainesville Fl 32611, USA
angelos@digitalworlds.ufl.edu
http://research.dwi.ufl.edu/angelos

Abstract. This paper presents a framework for natural traversal of an infinite virtual path using a camera-projector augmented-reality system. In the proposed framework this problem is formulated as an optimization problem using an energy function that is based on several user-experience factors as well as topological constraints in the real and virtual space. The solution is analytically derived by minimizing the cost function with respect to the parameters of the path in the real and virtual space. The obtained optimal path has the form of a zigzag curve and is demonstrated in an interactive application for delivering stimulating slide-show presentations for on-line learning.

Keywords: Locomotion interface · Walking through virtual environments · Magic-mirror augmented reality · Optimization

1   Introduction

One common problem of human-computer interaction in virtual reality is the natural traversal of a large (potentially infinite) virtual space while being in a limited real space [7,11]. By the term "natural traversal" we imply the use of natural walking motions and gestures contrary to the use of mechanical interfaces such as joysticks and keypads. Various mechanical solutions have been proposed such as omnidirectional treadmill platforms that however restrict the position of the user within the area of the platform and typically require cumbersome and expensive installations [5,8–10,12,15,16,18,19]. Motion tracking sensors offer an alternative solution by monitoring the position and orientation of the user within a relatively larger space that could potentially expand to the limits of the available real space [17]. In the first method, the natural rolling of the user on the platform produces a direct mapping to an infinite virtual space, while in the latter solution an artificial "jump" of the camera should be introduced to overcome the limitations of the real space. An in-depth survey of locomotion interfaces for virtual reality can be found in [7].

This paper will focus on how to optimize the geometry of a virtual space by minimizing the additive movement of the virtual camera, while maximizing the use of the available real space. The problem will be formulated as an optimization problem by expressing each component as a parameter in an energy

© Springer International Publishing AG 2017
S. Lackey and J. Chen (Eds.): VAMR 2017, LNCS 10280, pp. 3–14, 2017.
DOI: 10.1007/978-3-319-57987-0_1

function, which can be minimized using optimization techniques in order to find the optimal solution for the given set of input parameters. Parametric models will be introduced for imposing constraints to the position and orientation of the user in the real space, as well as the position and orientation of the virtual camera.

The proposed optimization framework is applied to the scenario of walking an infinite linear walk while being within a small room (real space). This scenario was tested using a Microsoft Kinect sensor for tracking the real position and orientation of the user, and a conventional 2D projection surface for rendering a real-time mixed-reality visual stimulus that shows the real image of the user within a virtual environment. This setup is also known as "magic-mirror" augmented reality [4] and has been used in various applications such as education, physical therapy, and others [2–4]. In this experimental setup the constraints of the user's real position and orientation will be defined as follows: (a) the user's orientation should form an angle with the normal vector of the projection surface of 90° or less, and (b) without loss of generality the user's position should be restricted within a trapezoid area defined by the field of view of the Kinect sensor. In addition, the orientation of the virtual camera will be constrained so that it forms an angle with the virtual path trajectory of 90° or less, so that the mixed-reality rendering will depict the upcoming segment of the virtual path. All constraints will be analytically defined as parametric components of the energy function and its minimization will be performed with respect to the parameters of the path in the real and virtual space.

The obtained solution reveals the optimally designed virtual path, which takes the form of an infinite piecewise curve and corresponds to an infinite walk in a line segment defined by two points in the real space. The turning points of the virtual zigzag path are mapped to the two end points of the real line segment, and the rest of the path corresponds to linear transitions between these two points in the real space. The smoothness of the zigzag curve depends on the constraints of the virtual camera motion. The obtained result is in agreement with other empirically-derived zigzag designs of virtual paths presented in literature [13, 14].

The derived design is demonstrated in the area of on-line learning. The content of a specific lecture was obtained by a participating instructor in the form of a linear slide-show, and it was mapped along the optimally designed virtual path, obtained from the proposed energy minimization framework. More specifically, the slides were positioned to the walls of a virtual zigzag path, by placing one slide in each zigzag segment. The instructor was requested to naturally walk in this virtual slide show (i.e. the virtual path) while stepping in front of the camera-projector interface inside a typical college classroom.

The contributions of this paper are three-fold: (a) the problem of mapping an infinite virtual space to a finite real space is analytically formalized as an energy minimization problem, (b) the optimal solution is derived for the typical scenario of a Kinect-projector augmented-reality setup, and (c) the obtained solution was demonstrated and tested as a delivery mechanism of linear slideshow on-line lectures.

2   Methods

Let $\Omega \subset \mathbb{R}^3$ denote a space in the physical world that corresponds to an area of natural user computer interaction in a camera-projector system. This space is naturally bounded by either physical boundaries such as the walls of a room, or technological boundaries such as the field of view of a range camera or the area of operation of a motion sensor (Fig. 1). The location of the user is a point in this subspace, and during a user interaction session the location of the user forms a uniparametric path $p(\lambda) \in \Omega$, where λ is a scalar that represents the progression within the path.

In a "magic mirror"-type of augmented reality interaction (MMAR) the user is depicted within a potentially unlimited/unbounded virtual space. Due to the nature of this interaction, the real world topology is locally preserved in the virtual space thus forming a path $p'(\lambda) \in \mathbb{R}^3$. This means that there exists a $\delta > 0$ such that $\forall \lambda_0$ and $\epsilon > 0$,

$$|\lambda - \lambda_0| < \delta \Rightarrow \|p(\lambda) - p(\lambda_0)\| + \|p'(\lambda) - p'(\lambda_0)\| < \epsilon. \tag{1}$$

Any arbitrary path can be infinitesimally approximated by a piecewise linear function formed by an ordered set of points $\mathbf{p}_0$, $\mathbf{p}_1$, ... $\in \Omega$, where $\mathbf{p}_0 = p(\lambda_0)$, $\mathbf{p}_1 = p(\lambda_1)$, ... and $\lambda_0 < \lambda_1 < ...$ [1]. This corresponds to an equivalent approximation in the virtual space formed by the set of points $\mathbf{p}'_0$, $\mathbf{p}'_1$, ... $\in \mathbb{R}^3$, where $\mathbf{p}'_0 = p'(\lambda_0)$, $\mathbf{p}'_1 = p'(\lambda_1)$, ...

Such correspondence can be described as a mapping $\mathcal{M} : \Omega \to \mathbb{R}^3$ that maps the user, who is located in the real physical space, to the virtual space. Due to the natural limits of Ω that do not exist in the potentially unlimited virtual space, $\mathcal{M}$ does not have to be defined as a unique mapping from Ω to $\mathbb{R}^3$. Instead, a sequence of mappings $\mathcal{M}_0$, $\mathcal{M}_1$, ... can be defined for the line segments $\lambda_0 \le \lambda < \lambda_1$, $\lambda_1 \le \lambda < \lambda_2$, ... respectively. Each mapping $\mathcal{M}_i$ maps uniquely Ω to $\mathbb{R}^3$, without restricting the overall piecewise $\mathcal{M}$ to have such property, hence allowing the user to traverse an unbounded virtual linear path by interactively moving between established locations in the limited physical space.

The goal of this paper is to identify the physical locations $\mathbf{p}_i$ and corresponding mappings $\mathcal{M}_i$ that optimize the user experience while performing a walk in a large virtual space by naturally walking within a limited real space. An optimal solution is defined here as the one that offers the most natural way for the user to interact with the system. More specifically, several conditions can be defined that impose natural constraints to the solution. These constrains will ultimately be combined in the form of an energy function, the minimization of which will lead to the desired solution. This constraint-driven optimization will affect both unknown sets of variables $\mathbf{p}_i$ and $\mathcal{M}_i$ and therefore will determine the optimal shape of the physical and the corresponding virtual path respectively.

The following sections introduce constraints imposed to the length of the path, size of the physical space, direction of motion, and viewpoint of the virtual path. Each constraint will be defined analytically as a function of the unknown parameters of this model and its role and importance with regards to the user's experience will be discussed in detail.

2.1 Length Equivalency Constraint

In order to implement the basic properties of physicality in the virtual environment during the interactive traversal of the path by the user, it is essential that the implemented mappings $\mathcal{M}_i$ maintain locally proportional relationship between the length metrics of the real and virtual spaces.

$$s \left\| \mathbf{p}_i - \mathbf{p}_{i+1} \right\| = \left\| \mathcal{M}_i(\mathbf{p}_i) - \mathcal{M}_i(\mathbf{p}_{i+1}) \right\| \tag{2}$$

This property will allow one step of the user in the real space to correspond to one step in the virtual space and be experienced by the user in a natural way. In the form of an energy function that can be minimized with respect to the unknown variables $\mathbf{p}_i$ and $\mathcal{M}_i$, this constraint can be implemented as

$$f_l = \sum_i \left(s \left\| \mathbf{p}_i - \mathbf{p}_{i+1} \right\| - \left\| \mathcal{M}_i(\mathbf{p}_i) - \mathcal{M}_i(\mathbf{p}_{i+1}) \right\| \right)^2 \tag{3}$$

where s is a positive scalar. In the special case of $\mathcal{M}_i(\mathbf{x}) = s\mathbf{A}_i\mathbf{x} + \mathbf{t}_i$, where $\mathbf{A}_i$ denotes an affine transformation for the segment i with $|\mathbf{A}_i| = 1$ and $\mathbf{t} \in \mathbb{R}^3$, Eq. 3 becomes zero. In this case, the transformations $\mathbf{A}_i$ represent rotations, and $\mathbf{t}_i$ are the corresponding spatial translation vectors.

2.2 Directional Constraint

The natural body orientation of a person who walks from location $\mathbf{p}_i$ to location $\mathbf{p}_{i+1}$ can be in general assumed to be given by the vector $\mathbf{p}_{i+1} - \mathbf{p}_i$. In the case of camera-projector systems such as MMAR, the image of the user is depicted on a fixed projection surface along the physical area of interaction. Due to the nature of such interaction, the user's head orientation should be such that the user can observe the result of the interaction on the screen. Assuming that the head orientation and body orientation should form an angle of 90° or less, the following set of constraints can be formed for restricting the orientation of the segments of the path:

$$(\mathbf{p}_{i+1} - \mathbf{p}_i)^T \mathbf{n} \geq 0 \qquad \forall i \tag{4}$$

where $\mathbf{n} \in S_2$ is the normal vector of the projection surface (towards the surface). If we add together the conditions in Eq. 4 for $i = 0 \ldots k$ we obtain

$$\sum_{i=0}^{k} (\mathbf{p}_{i+1} - \mathbf{p}_i)^T \mathbf{n} \geq 0 \Rightarrow (\mathbf{p}_{k+1} - \mathbf{p}_0)^T \mathbf{n} \geq 0 \qquad \forall k, \tag{5}$$

which means that all steps in this path should be taken towards the screen or within ±90° from it, as expected.

Without loss of generality we will fix the coordinate system of the real physical space so that the x-axis is parallel to the projection surface and z-axis is
parallel to $\mathbf{n}$, i.e. $\mathbf{n} = [0, 0, 1]^T$. For simplicity we will also assume that the
path is uniformly segmented, i.e. the segments of the path are of equal length
$\|\mathbf{p}_{i+1} - \mathbf{p}_i\| = \delta p > 0$, where δp is a constant scalar. Under these assumptions,
the condition in Eq. 4 reduces to

$$\delta p \cos \phi_i \geq 0 \qquad (6)$$

where ϕ_i is the angle between $\mathbf{n}$ and the direction of the ith segment of the path.
Therefore the path can be expressed as the following series:

$$\mathbf{p}_{i+1,x} = \mathbf{p}_{i,x} + \delta p \sin \phi_i \quad and \quad \mathbf{p}_{i+1,z} = \mathbf{p}_{i,z} + \delta p \cos \phi_i \quad \forall i \quad (7)$$

$$\Rightarrow \mathbf{p}_{k,x} = \mathbf{p}_{0,x} + \delta p \sum_{i=0}^{k-1} \sin \phi_i \quad and \quad \mathbf{p}_{k,z} = \mathbf{p}_{0,z} + \delta p \sum_{i=0}^{k-1} \cos \phi_i \quad \forall k > 0 \quad (8)$$

where $\mathbf{p}_{i,x}$ and $\mathbf{p}_{i,z}$ denote the x- and z-coordinates of the location $\mathbf{p}_i$ respectively.

In the next section, Eq. 8 is combined with spatial constraints of the physical
space in order to define the shape of the optimal path in a given available space.

2.3   Space Constraint

Since Ω was defined as a bounded space, there exist C_x^{min}, C_x^{max}, C_z^{min}, and
C_z^{max} such that the respective coordinates as defined in Eq. 8 are bounded:
$C_x^{max} \geq \sum_{i=0}^{k-1} \sin \phi_i \geq C_x^{min}$ and $C_z^{max} \geq \sum_{i=0}^{k-1} \cos \phi_i \geq C_z^{min}$.

From Eq. 6 we can derive that C_z^{min} is bounded below by zero. Furthermore,
in order the limit $\lim_{k \to \infty} \sum_{i=0}^{k-1} \cos \phi_i$ to be upper bounded by C_z^{max}, the values of $\cos \phi_i$ should approach zero as the limit approaches C_z^{max}. In fact, the
boundary conditions are satisfied in the special case of $\cos \phi_i = 0 \; \forall i$, in other
words when $\phi_i = \pm \pi / 2$. This shows that the optimal path that satisfies the
aforementioned constraints is one that consists of segments that are parallel to
the projection screen.

In order to utilize the given real space to the fullest possible extend, we need
to maximize the length of the individual segments of the path $\delta p = \|\mathbf{p}_i - \mathbf{p}_{i+1}\|$,
during which the user maintains an undisrupted natural walking pattern. This
can be achieved by imposing spatial constraints to the unknown points $\mathbf{p}_i$ so
that $\mathbf{p}_i \in \partial \Omega$, where $\partial \Omega$ denotes the boundary of Ω. If the boundary $\partial \Omega$, which
is a closed curve, is expressed in the form of a function $b : \mathbb{R}^3 \to \mathbb{R}$ such that
$b(\mathbf{x}) = 0, \forall \mathbf{x} \in \partial \Omega$, the special constraint can be implemented by the following
energy function:

$$f_s = \sum_i \|\mathbf{p}_i - \mathbf{p}_{i+1}\|^2 - \lambda_i b(\mathbf{p}_i) \qquad (9)$$

where λ_i are Lagrange multipliers to ensure that $\mathbf{p}_i$ are points on the boundary
$b(\mathbf{x}) = 0$. If we substitute $\mathbf{p}_i$, and $\mathbf{p}_{i+1}$ in the above energy function with the

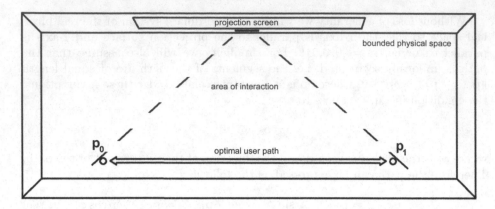

Fig. 1. The optimal path in the real space is a repetitive transition between the points p_0, p_1, $p_2 = p_0$, $p_3 = p_1$, ...

expressions in Eq. 8, we derive that $\mathbf{p}_0 \in \partial\Omega$ and $\mathbf{p}_0$ is located at that distance from the projection screen that the length of Ω along the screen is maximal and is equal to δp. Furthermore, to satisfy the boundary conditions for $\mathbf{p}_{i,x}$, the angles ϕ_i should alternate values between $\pm\pi$, for example: $\phi_i = \pi/2 \; \forall i = 0, 2, 4, \ldots$ and $\phi_i = -\pi/2 \; \forall i = 1, 3, 5, \ldots$. Therefore the optimal solution to our problem is given by: $\mathbf{p}_i = \mathbf{p}_0 + \delta p \frac{1-(-1)^i}{2}[1, 0, 0]^T$.

According to the shape of this optimal solution, the user will perform an infinite walk by walking along the projection surface and across the room between the left-most and right-most bounds back and forth as shown in the illustration in Fig. 1. As explained earlier, each of these segments of the path, although it overlaps the others within the limited real space, it corresponds to a different non-overlapping segment of an infinite virtual path. Finally, each segment maintains a distinct directionality, i.e. walking towards $\mathbf{p}_{i+1} - \mathbf{p}_i$ corresponds to a forward direction in the virtual path, while walking towards $\mathbf{p}_i - \mathbf{p}_{i+1}$ corresponds to a backwards direction along the virtual path. Therefore, the user can perform an infinite walk in either direction and is even allowed to change direction at any time during this interaction.

2.4 Virtual Model Viewpoint Constraint

The previous constraints provided an optimal solution for $\mathbf{p}_i$ that defined precisely the shape of the path in the real space. However the shape of the virtual path has yet to be determined by finding solution for the unknown mappings $\mathcal{M}_i$. As discussed earlier, the mappings are expressed in the form $\mathcal{M}_i(\mathbf{x}) = s\mathbf{A}_i\mathbf{x} + \mathbf{t}_i$.

One first requirement for the virtual path is that it should be a connected path, as described in the definition of the problem. Since the real world path is a piecewise linear function, the mappings $\mathcal{M}_i$ should also form a piecewise connected function, i.e. in the form of an energy minimization function:

$$f_c = \sum_i \|\mathcal{M}_i(\mathbf{p}_{i+1}) - \mathcal{M}_{i+1}(\mathbf{p}_{i+1})\|^2. \tag{10}$$

Equation 10 becomes zero when the virtual path is defined as a sequence of rotated and translated connected virtual path segments by setting the mapping parameters as follows:

$$\mathbf{A}_i = \mathbf{R}_i \mathbf{A}_{i-1} \tag{11}$$

$$\mathbf{t}_i = (\mathbf{I} - \mathbf{R}_i) s \mathbf{A}_{i-1} \mathbf{p}_i + \mathbf{t}_{i-1} \tag{12}$$

where $\mathbf{R}_i \in SO(3)$ is a 3×3 rotation matrix and $\mathbf{I}$ is the 3×3 identity matrix. It can be easily proven that $s\mathbf{A}_i\mathbf{p}_i + \mathbf{t}_i = s\mathbf{A}_{i-1}\mathbf{p}_i + \mathbf{t}_{i-1}$, which satisfies the above constraint.

Additionally, in MMAR the model-view matrix is chosen so that the user is depicted mirrored on the projection screen during the interaction. This mirroring does not have to maintain the perspective and size of the real space as long as it establishes an one-to-one relationship with the real space. For example a bird's eye view could be adopted as long as it is consistent during each segment of the interaction. In order to impose across-segment model-view consistency, we must establish correspondence between two consecutive path segments as follows:

$$\mathbf{M}_i \mathbf{F} s \mathbf{A}_i \mathbf{x} = \mathbf{M}_{i-1} s \mathbf{A}_{i-1} \mathbf{x} \tag{13}$$

where $\mathbf{M}_i$ and $\mathbf{M}_{i-1}$ are the model-view matrices for the ith and $i - 1^{th}$ path segments respectively, and $\mathbf{F}$ is a diagonal 3×3 matrix with diagonal $[-1\ 1\ -1]$, which implements a necessary rotation of $180°$ around y-axis. The reason for introducing $\mathbf{F}$ is to reflect the $180°$ angle between two consecutive path segments in the real physical space, as discussed in the previous section. The model-view matrices will contain all the required information to describe the camera's viewpoint from which the virtual space is observed during each path segment. By substituting $\mathbf{A}_i$ in Eq. 13 with Eq. 11 we obtain:

$$\mathbf{M}_i \mathbf{F} \mathbf{R}_i \mathbf{A}_{i-1} = \mathbf{M}_{i-1} \mathbf{A}_{i-1} \tag{14}$$

$$\Rightarrow \mathbf{M}_i = \mathbf{M}_{i-1} \mathbf{R}_i^{-1} \mathbf{F}. \tag{15}$$

Equation 15 can be used in order to define a balance between the movement of the virtual camera and the angle of the virtual path during the transition from one path segment to another. For example if we want to minimize the movement of the camera by setting $\mathbf{M}_i = \mathbf{M}_{i-1}$ so that there is no change of the model-view matrix between two segments, the angle between the path segments becomes $180°$ since $\mathbf{R}_i = \mathbf{F}$. In this case the virtual path consists of overlapping segments that match the shape of the path in the real physical space. However, such topology is problematic as it does not correspond in practice to an infinite path.

On the other hand, if we set the angle between the virtual path segments to be $0°$ by setting $\mathbf{R}_i = \mathbf{I}$, the camera moves for $180°$ since the model-view matrix is modified by $\mathbf{F}$, i.e. $\mathbf{M}_i = \mathbf{M}_{i-1} \mathbf{F}$. In this case the virtual path corresponds to a straight path without any turns. However, the user experiences large view-point transitions at the end of each path segment, which might cause discomfort (Fig. 2 left).

An optimal solution that minimizes simultaneously the camera transition and the angle between the path segments is obtained by setting $\mathbf{R}_i$ to a rotation matrix of 90° around y-axis. If the rotation matrices $\mathbf{R}_i$ maintain directionality $\forall i$, the virtual path obtains a square shape, around of which the user performs an infinite walk either clockwise or counter-clockwise depending on the directionality of the rotation matrices. However, the physical interpretation of this solution is problematic as the virtual path consists of overlapping square blocks.

On the other hand, if the rotation matrices alternate directionality, i.e. $\mathbf{R}_i = \mathbf{R}_{i-1}^T$, the virtual path obtains a zig-zag shape with a 90° angle between the path segments and a 90° rotation of the model-view matrix in each corner of the path. Although this corresponds to the optimal solution, variations can be added to each $\mathbf{R}_i$ so that they correspond to different angles $90° \pm \delta\phi$. In this case the virtual path obtains a non-uniform zig-zag shape, which could be visually more appealing, and therefore improve further the user experience (Fig. 2 right). Interestingly, this result is in agreement with other empirically-found designs in literature [13,14], which are unified and generalized by the proposed method beyond zigzag patterns as a function of the magnitude of virtual camera transitions as discussed in this section.

The next section presents a computer implementation of the proposed framework and demonstrates an application for slide-show presentation in the form of an interactive linear walk in a virtual space.

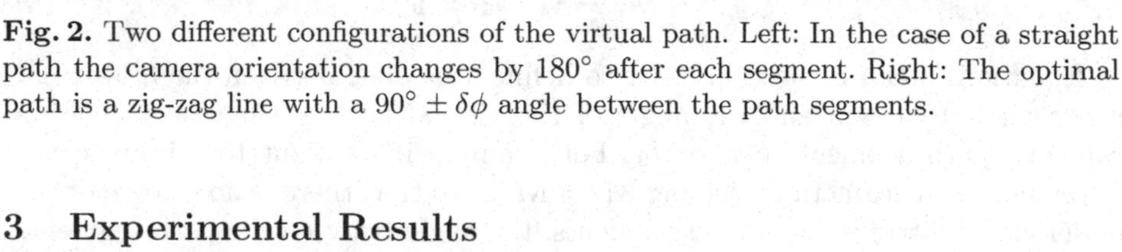

Fig. 2. Two different configurations of the virtual path. Left: In the case of a straight path the camera orientation changes by 180° after each segment. Right: The optimal path is a zig-zag line with a $90° \pm \delta\phi$ angle between the path segments.

3   Experimental Results

The proposed method was implemented using the Kinect™ sensor by Microsoft. The resolution of the depth sensor was 640 × 480 pixels at 30 frames per second and was calibrated so that it records depth in the range from 0.8 m to 4.0 m, which provided an adequate space for interaction. The implementation was developed using the Java for Kinect (J4K) application programming interface developed in [2], and it was tested on a 64-bit computer with Intel Core i7™CPU at 2.80 GHz and 8 GB RAM. This configuration enabled real-time interaction cycle with the user tracking and rendering being performed in 33 ms ($\approx$ 30 frames/second).

The Kinect sensor was installed in front of a projection surface in which the visual output of the developed MMAR system was rendered in real time. The users could move naturally within the area of interaction and see themselves inside a mixed-reality environment. Within this environment the user could walk through a virtual corridor that had the shape of a zig-zag path as recommended by the results obtained in Sect. 2. Two screen shots of the developed system are shown in Fig. 3. The RGB-D image of the user was segmented and rendered in real-time at the proper location of the virtual path. At the corner points of the zig-zag path, the user stepped onto an activation area (shown in red in Fig. 3 right), which triggered the virtual camera to move/rotate by 90° so that the next segment of the path appears within the field of view. The users could proceed as far as they wanted in this virtual path by walking naturally in the real physical space. As expected, the walk could also be performed backwards by walking naturally towards the opposite direction. An interesting observation is that the optimal zig-zag angle of 90° allows the user to observe the next segment of the path (when moving forwards), and to have a better perspective of the overall path, which may improve user experience in general. This is demonstrated in the screen shots in Fig. 3.

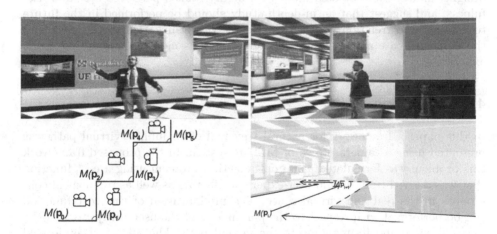

Fig. 3. Top: Two screen shots of the implemented optimal virtual path. Bottom left: The design of the implemented path. Bottom right: An overlay of the path in 3D over the above screen shot of the system.

The proposed framework for linear walk in an infinite virtual space can be used in various applications ranging from entertainment to education. In order to demonstrate the efficiency of this method, a 3D slide-show application was developed as a linear walk in a virtual space. Such interactive slide-show system can be used for generating stimulating visual output for the purposes of delivering an on-line lecture, which can be dynamically streamed in real-time or packaged as a video that can be watched on-demand. More specifically, the instructor's slides were placed as virtual posters on the walls of a zig-zag corridor, by assigning individual slides to different consecutive segments of the path (Fig. 3). The instructor could gradually "page" through the slides by naturally walking through the virtual path without the need of any type of hand-held controllers. Additional interactions were introduced to individual slides/path segments such as 3D virtual props that the user could hold, move, rotate, and scale using hand gestures.

Finally, an exploratory small-scale user testing was performed ($n = 14$, $age = 24.7 \pm 2.5$) in order to estimate the perceived ease of use and perceived usefulness of the developed lecture system with the optimally designed virtual path. The estimation was performed using the Technology Acceptance Model (TAM) questionnaire [6], which has been established in literature as a robust instrument to measure technology acceptance. The study showed that the most highly ranked subscale of the TAM model was U6: "overall useful" (average score of 1.71) with the system users to state that it extremely or quite likely to agree with this statement. Other similarly highly ranked subscales were the U2: "enhances performance" (average score of 2.0), U4: "enhances effectiveness" (average score of 2.14), and E2: "easy to do what I want" (average score of 2.14). The findings of this limited exploratory study indicate that the optimally designed model could be associated with highly ranked perceived ease and usefulness, and suggest that an in-depth study should be performed in the future to assess the correlation between the degree of optimization of the path and the perceived ease and usefulness of each design as means of measuring user's experience.

4   Conclusion

In this paper a framework for natural traversal of an infinite virtual path was presented using a camera-projector MMAR system. In the proposed framework this problem was formulated as an optimization problem using a cost function that was derived from several user-experience factors as well as topological constraints in the real and virtual space. The minimization of this cost function can be performed with respect to the parameters of the user's trajectory in the physical space and its mapping to the virtual path. The solution was derived analytically and corresponds to the optimally designed path, which is an infinite zig-zag line in the virtual space. The solution also defines the mapping from the limited real physical space to this infinite virtual path. The applications of this framework are numerous in the fields of entertainment, such as augmented reality games, education, physical therapy, interactive storytelling, and other applications that involve natural traversal of a large virtual space by walking in a bounded real physical space. The framework was demonstrated as an interactive 3D slide-show application that can be used for creating stimulating lecture presentations for on-line learning. Finally, the results of a small-scale user study were presented, which indicated high perceived usefulness and ease of use. In the future an in-depth study will be performed to assess the correlation between the degree of optimization of the path and the perceived ease and usefulness of each design as means of measuring user's experience.

References

1. Andersson, S.B.: Discrete approximations to continuous curves. In: Proceedings 2006 IEEE International Conference on Robotics and Automation, pp. 2546–2551, May 2006
2. Barmpoutis, A.: Tensor body: Real-time reconstruction of the human body and avatar synthesis from RGB-D. IEEE Trans. Cybern. **43**(5), 1347–1356 (2013)
3. Barmpoutis, A., Fox, E.J., Elsner, I., Flynn, S.: Augmented-reality environment for locomotor training in children with neurological injuries. In: Linte, C.A., Yaniv, Z., Fallavollita, P., Abolmaesumi, P., Holmes, D.R. (eds.) AE-CAI 2014. LNCS, vol. 8678, pp. 108–117. Springer, Cham (2014). doi:10.1007/978-3-319-10437-9_12
4. Blum, T., Kleeberger, V., Bichlmeier, C., Navab, N.: Mirracle: An augmented reality magic mirror system for anatomy education. In: 2012 IEEE Virtual Reality Short Papers and Posters (VRW), pp. 115–116. IEEE (2012)
5. Darken, R.P., Cockayne, W.R., Carmein, D.: The Omni-Directional Treadmill: a locomotion device for virtual worlds. In: Proceedings of the 10th annual ACM symposium on User interface software and technology, pp. 213–221. ACM (1997)
6. Davis, F.D.: Perceived usefulness, perceived ease of use, and user acceptance of information technology. Manag. Inf. Syst. Q. **13**(3), 319–340 (1989)
7. Hollerbach, J.M.: Locomotion interfaces. In: Handbook of Virtual Environments: Design, Implementation, and Applications, pp. 239–254 (2002)
8. Interrante, V., Ries, B., Anderson, L.: Seven league boots: a new metaphor for augmented locomotion through moderately large scale immersive virtual environments. In: 2007 IEEE Symposium on 3D User Interfaces, 3DUI 2007. IEEE (2007)
9. Iwata, H.: Walking about virtual environments on an infinite floor. In: 1999 IEEE Proceedings Virtual Reality, pp. 286–293. IEEE (1999)
10. Iwata, H., Yano, H., Fukushima, H., Noma, H.: Circulafloor [locomotion interface]. IEEE Comput. Graph. Appl. **25**(1), 64–67 (2005)
11. LaViola Jr., J.J., Feliz, D.A., Keefe, D.F., Zeleznik, R.C.: Hands-free multi-scale navigation in virtual environments. In: Proceedings of the 2001 Symposium on Interactive 3D Graphics, pp. 9–15. ACM (2001)
12. Medina, E., Fruland, R., Weghorst, S.: VIRTUSPHERE: walking in a human size VR hamster ball. In: Proceedings of the Human Factors and Ergonomics Society Annual Meeting, vol. 52, pp. 2102–2106. SAGE Publications, Los Angeles (2008)
13. Razzaque, S., Kohn, Z., Whitton, M.C.: Redirected walking. In: Proceedings of EUROGRAPHICS, vol. 9, pp. 105–106. Citeseer (2001)
14. Razzaque, S., Swapp, D., Slater, M., Whitton, M.C., Steed, A.: Redirected walking in place. In: EGVE, vol. 2, pp. 123–130 (2002)
15. Souman, J.L., Giordano, P.R., Schwaiger, M., Frissen, I., Thümmel, T., Ulbrich, H., Luca, A.D., Bülthoff, H.H., Ernst, M.O.: CyberWalk: enabling unconstrained omnidirectional walking through virtual environments. ACM Trans. Appl. Percept. (TAP) **8**(4), 25 (2011)
16. Souman, J.L., Giordano, P.R., Frissen, I., Luca, A.D., Ernst, M.O.: Making virtual walking real: perceptual evaluation of a new treadmill control algorithm. ACM Trans. Appl. Percept. (TAP) **7**(2), 11 (2010)

17. Templeman, J.N., Denbrook, P.S., Sibert, L.E.: Virtual locomotion: walking in place through virtual environments. Presence Teleoperators Virtual Environ. **8**(6), 598–617 (1999)
18. Williams, J.: Walk simulation apparatus for exercise and virtual reality. US Patent 7,470,218, 30 Dec 2008. https://www.google.com/patents/US7470218
19. Yoon, J., Ryu, J.: A novel locomotion interface with two 6-DOF parallel manipulators that allows human walking on various virtual terrains. Int. J. Robot. Res. **25**(7), 689–708 (2006)

Leaning-Based 360° Interfaces: Investigating Virtual Reality Navigation Interfaces with Leaning-Based-Translation and Full-Rotation

Abraham M. Hashemian[✉] and Bernhard E. Riecke

iSpace Lab, School of Interactive Arts and Technology,
Simon Fraser University,
Vancouver, Canada
{hashemia,ber1}@sfu.ca

Abstract. Despite recent advances in high quality Head-Mounted Displays (HMDs), designing locomotion interfaces for Virtual Reality (VR) is still challenging, and might contribute to unwanted side effects such as disorientation and motion sickness. To address these issues, we investigated the potentials of leaning-based 360° locomotion interfaces, which provide full-rotational motion cues (unlimited 360° rotations) for rotation, and leaning-based translational motion cues for forward/backward and sideways translation.

In this experiment we compared **joystick** with three locomotion interfaces: **Real-Rotation** (rotation control by an office swivel chair and forward/backward and sideways translations by joystick); **Swivel-Chair** (rotation control by the swivel chair and forward/backward and sideways control by leaning forward/ backward and sideways on the chair respectively); **NaviChair** (rotation control by a sit/stand stool and forward/backward and sideway control by weight shifting and leaning in the same direction, which is sensed by a Nintendo's Wii balance board pressure sensors the stool is mounted on).

We asked participants to follow an avatar in an unpredictable curvilinear path in a gamified experiment to evaluate interfaces in terms of different usability aspects, including accuracy, motion sickness, sensation of self-motion, presence, immersion, ease of use, ease of learning, engagement, enjoyment, overall preference, etc. Results did not show any significant advantages of our suggested interfaces over the joystick. But in a sense this is promising because in many aspects, the usability of the proposed interfaces was similar to the well-trained joystick. Moreover, our interfaces had slightly lower motion sickness ratings, and higher sensation of self-motion and spatial presence ratings than the joystick. However, they showed controllability issues, which resulted in significantly lower navigation accuracy (i.e., distance errors) and reduced control precision ratings, which made them less easy to use and comfortable than joystick.

We also discuss the participants' qualitative feedbacks about our interfaces, which shows their strengths and weaknesses, and guide the design of more embodied future VR locomotion interfaces.

Keywords: Virtual reality · Locomotion interface · Leaning-based interface · Motion sickness · Disorientation

© Springer International Publishing AG 2017
S. Lackey and J. Chen (Eds.): VAMR 2017, LNCS 10280, pp. 15–32, 2017.
DOI: 10.1007/978-3-319-57987-0_2

1 Introduction

Recent HMDs (including Oculus Rift and PS4 headset) use game controllers for continuous locomotion in VR games, however when using game controllers or joysticks for locomotion, because the user's body sense no physical motions corresponding to their visual locomotion cues, this conflict between visual, vestibular and proprioceptive sensory data can lead to undesirable side-effects such as spatial disorientation or motion sickness [10, 17]. In order to address these issues and reduce the sensory cues conflict, VR researchers designed many embodied locomotion interfaces, which include at least some physical motions to the user's body.

One of the fairly low-cost solutions for the natural locomotion in VR are the leaning-based locomotion interfaces, where the users lean physically to control their simulated rotational/translational velocity in the Virtual Environment (VE). VR researchers designed many leaning-based locomotion interfaces [1, 6, 16, 22, 24, 26, 31]. Typically, these interfaces use limited leaning-based motion cues to control the simulated translation and limited-rotational motion cues to control the simulated rotation. Many studies investigated the benefits of these leaning-based motion cues on user experience [2, 7, 12–14, 33]. Another fairly low-cost solution for natural locomotion in VR is called Real-Rotation, where the user rotates physically to control the simulated rotation, but uses joystick for forward/backward or sideways translation. This technique, which provides full-rotational but no-translational motion cues was investigated by many researchers such as [4, 8, 25–30, 32].

Each of these two locomotion techniques (i.e., Real-Rotation and leaning-based) have their own strengths. For example, Real-Rotation provides more natural motion cues for rotation, while leaning-based technique provides natural motion cues for translation. Therefore, it might be useful to integrate both techniques as one hybrid technique, where the user physically rotates toward the desired direction and lean to control their simulated translation. This combined technique provides full-rotational/limited-translational motion cues, which has higher fidelity than each of these two techniques to bipedal walking, which is one of the best VR navigation techniques. Therefore, we posit that our suggested technique, provides the richer vestibular/proprioceptive sensory data, which is resulted in less disorientation and motion sickness.

In the current article, we evaluate our new locomotion interfaces, which use full-rotational/leaning-based-translational motion cues, to investigate how integrating full rotational motion cues with limited translational motion cues affects the user experience. To provide a thorough evaluation of our interfaces, not only we measure the introspective data, but also we measured behavioral data including navigation distance/angular errors. The short term benefit of our study is to know if our suggested locomotion interfaces are actually worth to be used in practical applications (such as VR games) rather than joystick. The long term benefit of this study will be to better understand the strengths and weaknesses of using full rotational and limited translational motion cues in VR locomotion interfaces in terms of usability and user experience measures, which can lead us to design better VR locomotion interfaces.

2   Related Works

2.1   Full-Rotational (360° Degrees) Motion

Many researchers investigated if full-rotation of the user's body when rotating in VE help the spatial updating process – the automatic process of updating the spatial awareness of the user while navigating through the environment. However, the results are contradictory, for example, Ruddle and Lessels [28, 29] stated that actual walking is by far better than the Real-Rotation in terms of the user performance in complex tasks (i.e., navigational search task), but Riecke and colleagues [23] performed a similar study with some modifications, and reported that Real-Rotation yielded almost comparable performance to actual walking in terms of search efficiency and time.

One of the practical motivations behind the above studies is the considerable extra cost and effort, which is needed to allow for physical rotations in the VR locomotion interfaces [25], so it is also important to evaluate how physical rotations benefit other important qualities of the user experience (such as immersion, presence, motion sickness, engagement, vection, enjoyment, etc.), which we evaluated in the current study.

2.2   Leaning-Based Locomotion Interfaces

Many studies investigated if limited motion cues benefit the simulated translation within VR in terms of the sensation of self-motion (AKA vection). For example, Groen and Bles [9] showed that the whole body tilt up to 3 degrees/second amplify the vection, and Berger and colleagues [2] reported that the backward tilting on the hexapod motion platform enhance the vection intensity.

As for the leaning-based interfaces, which provide the user-generated limited motions, Riecke and colleagues [22] used a modified wheelchair for VR navigation. The user pushed the wheelchair to forward/backward (up to 8 cm) or rotate it (up to 10°) to control the simulated translation/rotation in the VR, while an elastic band - attached to the wheels - provided a force feedback to return the wheelchair to its center position. The results showed that this limited motion cues increased vection. Specially, Freiberg [7] showed that using NaviChair (a modified version of the stool chair, called Swopper) as a locomotion interface enhances the immersion, presence and enjoyment. Kruijf and colleagues [14] showed that standing leaning enhanced the vection rather than joystick and Riecke et al. [26] showed that leaning forward/backward using as a 'human joystick' metaphor increased enjoyment, engagement, vection and involvement rather than joystick.

One of the important motivations behind all these studies is the simplicity and the low-cost design of the user-generated leaning-based interfaces [12]. Therefore, if our current study shows that combining leaning-based translation with full-rotation will aggregate their benefits, it can be resulted into designing low-cost yet highly usable VR locomotion interfaces eventually.

2.3   Leaning-Based 360° Locomotion Interfaces

Few studies investigated the potentials of the full-rotational leaning-based interfaces. As an example, Marchal et al. (2011) introduced a full-rotational leaning-based loco-motion interface for VR – called Joyman - where the user stands on a trampoline, and lean their body to control the simulated velocity/direction by the angle/direction of their body respectively. The preliminary results showed that the Joyman has higher fun, pres-ence and rotation realism, but lower performance (i.e., higher navigational task comple-tion time) than joystick. However, the user should hold the Joyman handles by their hands, which reduces their ability to use their hands for other tasks (such as pointing or interacting with objects) in VR applications [1, 13, 16, 26, 33].

In 2015, Langbehn et al. used leaning to increase the velocity of forward locomotion in Walking-In-Place (WIP) techniques using four Kinect-2 around the user [15]. Not only this interface is expensive, but also like other WIP techniques it has no backward or sideway locomotion. In 2014, Harris and colleagues designed a locomotion interface – called Wii-leaning, where user stand on two Wii Balance Board and put their foot toward the desired direction to control their simulated locomotion [11]. A comparison between Wii-leaning technique with physical-rotation and WIP in pointing task showed that the angular error of Wii-leaning was less than physical-rotation but and 8 (out of 12) participants preferred Wii-leaning than the WIP.

All above full-rotational leaning-based techniques require the user to stand up, which can lead to higher fatigue, discomfort, and leg swelling rather than seated body posture in long periods of time [5]. Specifically as for the leaning-based interfaces, Riecke and colleagues reported that using seated leaning-based locomotion interfaces can be used for longer periods of time rather than standing posture due to user fatigue [26]. Moreover, based on postural instability theory of motion sickness, stronger motion sickness happens in standing body posture comparing to the seated body posture [21]. In 2007, a comparison experiment by Merhi and colleagues also reported that standing VR gamers had significantly higher motion sickness than the seated gamers [19]. As a result, we designed seated hands-free locomotion interfaces with full-rotation and leaning-based translation.

As far as the author knows, very few seated hands-free leaning-based 360° locomo-tion interfaces have designed. As an example, Nguyen-Vo et al. used a sit/stand stool for VR navigation [20], which we used as one of our interfaces for the comparison purposes. Early VR researchers (such as [6]) discussed our suggested technique as a great interface, but due to the technical issues (such as sensor accuracy and the HMD cable entanglement around the user's neck) did not implement it [12]. New technologies (such as the wireless HTC vive controller) helped us to solve these issues using a simple solution, however, by incoming wireless HMDs (e.g., wireless HTC vive HMD) in a near future, the cable entanglement won't be a problem anymore, which provides a stronger motivation for our research.

2.4 Predictions and Hypotheses

Because of the discussed studies related to the leaning-based-translational motion cues studies, we predicted that our suggested interfaces enhance the vection intensity [14, 26]; immersion, presence [7, 18] and enjoyment [7, 18, 26]. We also predicted that the full-rotational motion cues will help the spatial updating process [23], so it should improve the user performance in velocity/direction control and reduce the distance/angular error. Conversely, we predicted that the joystick can be used for longer periods of time, and also is easier to be learned and easier to be used [7, 14, 18, 26].

3 Study Methodology

The goal of this study was to evaluate four different locomotion interfaces to investigate the potentials of leaning-based 360° locomotion interfaces.

3.1 Participants

We recruited 23 participants (twelve females) SFU students with an average of 21.4 years old. We compensated the participants time by the course credit for the 90 min experiment. Participants had normal or corrected to normal vision and were informed about the potential risks of motion sickness. The local ethics board approved this research. However, because 2 participants excluded due to the technical problems and 7 participants did not finished the experiment due to the motion sickness, we used the data for the other 14 participants.

3.2 Experiment Design and Environment

Controlling velocity and direction is an important task while travelling in many applications (such as games), so we designed the whole experiment to measure how accurate the user can control their velocity and direction.

Although the velocity control is being used in most real-life applications (such as games), but this task is not assumed as an end goal in itself, and when the players are travelling, they have higher important tasks in their minds [3]. However, many VR experimental designs for evaluating locomotion interfaces only focus on the locomotion tasks, which might be resulted into an unnatural situation, and so it might not be easy to generalize their results into the real-life like applications. In order to address this issue, and design an experiment similar to a real-life like application (especially video games), we designed the whole experiment as a sci-fi game, and different phases of our experiment are designed as different levels of the game.

For example, many vection evaluation experiments start with a vection demonstration phase, which familiarizes the user with the vection using a passive locomotion approach. We gamified this phase as the beginning cut-scene of the game, when the player is moving in a volcanic island (Fig. 1) using an airplane, and reads the game story on screen.

Fig. 1. The experiment environment - A volcanic island

The game narrative happens in a futuristic sci-fi VE, where the robots fight against humans, and one of the human scientists creates a virus to disable the robots brain all together. But when the scientist come to this island - the main base of the robots - to upload the virus, robots capture and imprison him, and now the player's mission is to find, rescue and help him to upload the virus.

After 90 s, the beginning cut-scene will be finished, and the player should play the game using one of the locomotion interfaces. The experiment is a within-subject experiment, so the player plays the game four times, each time with one of the interface. The interfaces assigned to the player by the Latin square order.

3.3　Apparatus and Stimuli

Considering, video games including First Person Shooter (FPS) games can be played usually by joysticks or game controllers with three Degrees of Freedoms (DOFs) - including forward/backward, sideways and rotation, we used these DOFs for all interfaces in our experiments. The maximum forward/backward and sideways velocity was 3 m/s (fast walking speed), and pushing the chairs more than this threshold did not changed the maximum velocity. Also the maximum rotational velocity for the joystick was 30 degrees/second.

As for our interfaces (see Fig. 2), we selected joystick as the standard interface, because it is a standard locomotion interface for VR [18]. Also to understand how adding full-rotational motion cues without any translational motion cues affect the user experience, we added Real-Rotation as our second interface. To investigate how combining forward/backward and sideway translational motion cues with full-rotational motion cues affect the user experience, we added two more interfaces into our experiment conditions.

The first leaning-based 360° interface is called NaviChair –used in [20], where participants sit on a regular sit/stand stool – called Swopper Chair, which is on a Wii Balance Board, so participants can rotate physically to control simulated rotations, and also lean forward/backward and/or sideways to control simulated forward/backward and

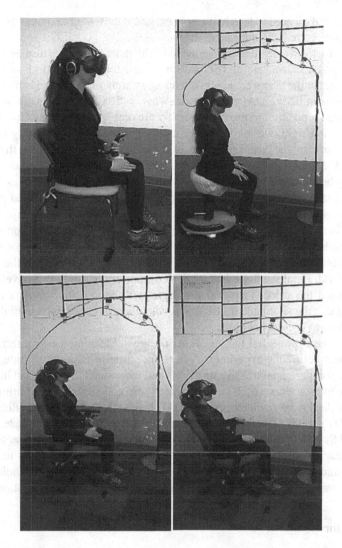

Fig. 2. Locomotion interfaces – (top-left) joystick, (top-right) NaviChair, (bottom-left) Real-Rotation, (bottom-right) Swivel-Chair

sideways translations respectively. We added NaviChair to our experiment for comparison purpose and also to have a broader understanding of shared potentials of both our leaning-based 360° interfaces.

The second and last leaning-based 360° interface is called Swivel-Chair, where the user sits on a regular office swivel chair and rotate physically to control simulated rotations, and lean the chair's backrest forward/backward to control simulated forward/backward translations respectively. This means that unlike typical human-joystick approaches (such as [14, 26]), where user lean forward to move forward in VR, in the Swivel-Chair, the user is required to sit straight to move forward with maximum velocity, and if they want to stop moving forward, they need to lean halfway back, and if they want to move backward with maximum velocity, they should lean all the way back.

The reason why we decided to use the straight seated body posture as for forward locomotion, was because leaning forward on a chair for longer periods of time might produce fatigue for the user's back, while leaning straight or backward is more comfortable for the human body. Also, to move sideways with Swivel-Chair, the user need to move their head's position to the right/left. To prevent going sideways by rotating the user's head to left/right, we used the user's neck position, by subtracting the average human head size form the position of the user's forehead position, which is the positional data of HMD. To measure the chair backrest's angle and the user's head distance from the center of the chair, we attached a HTC-vive controller to the chair's backrest.

All the joystick data (either in joystick or Real-Rotation interface) used the velocity control paradigm with linear transfer function, which means that the simulated velocity are related linearly to the deflection of the joystick. All the full-rotations interfaces (including Real-Rotation, Swivel-Chair and NaviChair) used the position control paradigm, where the direction of the user in the virtual world is the same as their direction in the real world. Finally, all the leaning-based translations (in both Swivel-Chair and NaviChair) used the velocity control paradigm with exponential transform function, which means that the simulated translational velocity are related exponentially – by the power of 1.53 – to their deflections.

We chose the exponential transfer function for the leaning-based interfaces based on a pilot study before the experiment, where six participants used our interfaces with both linear and exponential transfer functions and mentioned that they had higher accuracy over the interface control in velocities near zero and slightly less motion sickness.

As for the display, all the interfaces used HTC vive HMD, with 110° of diagonal Field Of View (FOV), 1200 * 1080 pixels resolution (per eye), and 90 Hz update rate. Real-Rotation and Swivel-Chair were designed by attaching a HTC vive controller to the backrest of a regular office swivel chair to measure the backrest's pitch and yaw to control the velocity and direction of the user respectively. We also used a curved rod to hold the HMD cable over the user's head to prevent entangling the cable around while rotation.

3.4   Procedure

After signing the consent form, and the vection demonstration phase, (discussed in Sect. 3.2) participants played the game four times with each of the four interfaces. At the end, we interviewed them to ask for their qualitative feedbacks regarding the interfaces. The game has two levels. In the first level of the game, the player practices how to control the interface. We gamified this task as a mission for the player to search for three prison cells in the environment, and then opening them by pressing the joystick button, to find and rescue the imprisoned scientist (Fig. 3-left).

Fig. 3. Experiment levels –(left) level one: Practice the interface by finding the scientist (right) level two: Following the scientist in an unpredictable path

In many games, one of the basic player's tasks is to travel on unpredictable curvilinear paths, we chose this task as for the second level task to test the player's skill with the interface. We gamified this task as where the scientist is training the player on how to follow him within areas filled with lava without being burned. A cooling energy beam coming from the scientist backpack, which protects the player from lava if the player stands on its center, where it hits the ground. The center of this energy field is always four meters behind the scientist, which means that player always need to stay behind him with this distance while following him. To help players see the environment (instead of staring at the ground to find the center of the energy beam), a green bar on the scientist backpack, shows the distance of the player from the center of the protective energy field (Fig. 3-right).

In order to help the player practice this task, the player practice this task two times at the beginning of this level. In the first practice trial, he/she need to follow the scientist in a straight path for 10 s, and in the second practice trial, they need to follow the scientist in a slightly curved path for another 10 s. Then the player need to do the same for three test trials, where each of them takes about 30 s, and the scientist walks with 2 m/s velocity, and change his direction continually with the maximum rotation speed up to 22 degrees/second.

After finishing all three test trials, the level is finished, and the player should answer the post-trial questionnaire (including 15 questions) about the interfaces. We will explain these questions at the result section.

4   Results

In this section, first we report the analysis of our quantitative data and then report the participant comments in the post-experiment interview about the interfaces as a qualitative approach. To analyze our quantitative data, we performed 1-way within-subject two-tailed ANOVA on both our behavioral and introspective measures. As for the behavioral measures, we analyzed the participant's position data to calculate their accuracy in terms of both distance and angular errors, and as for the introspective data, we analyzed their answers to 15 questions about each interface, which were a continuous rate between 0 ~ 100%.

4.1 Behavioral Results

As for the behavioral measures, considering both distance and angular error data were skewed negatively (toward zero), we converted them to logarithmic scales, and Shapiro Wilkes test showed the normality of the scaled data.

Accuracy of Each Interface. Mauchly's test showed the violation of sphericity assumption for both overall distance and angular error, so we performed the Greenhouse-Geisser correction of ANOVA, which showed no significant difference in terms of angular error. However the Greenhouse-Geisser correction of ANOVA showed that the interface has a significant effect on distance error ($F(1.55, 20.2) = 5.53$, $p = .017$, $\eta_p^2 = .298$). Tukey HSD post hoc showed that NaviChair ($M = 2.26$ m, $SD = 1.59$ m) had higher distance error than both Joystick ($M = 1.76$ m, $SD = 2.01$ m) and Real-Rotation ($M = 1.43$ m, $SD = 1.39$ m) (all $ps < .010$) (Fig. 4).

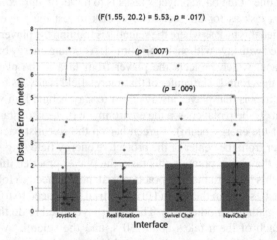

Fig. 4. Average of distance error for each interface. Dots present individual participant's mean data (CI = 95%)

Accuracy of Each Trial (Learning Effect). Beside interfaces, which affect the average distance error of participants, we also compared the overall distance error of participants for each trial. Considering the Mauchly's test showed violation of the sphericity assumption, we performed the Greenhouse-Geisser correction of ANOVA, which showed a significant effect of trials over distance error ($F(1.88, 24.4) = 3.73$, $p = .040$, $\eta_p^2 = .223$). Tukey HSD post hoc showed that the average distance error of first trial ($M = 2.14$ m, $SD = 2.17$ m) had higher distance error than the third trial ($M = 1.66$ m, $SD = 1.61$ m) ($p = .030$), which shows a learning effect. But there were no significant effect for second trial ($M = 1.89$ m, $SD = 1.85$ m) (Fig. 5).

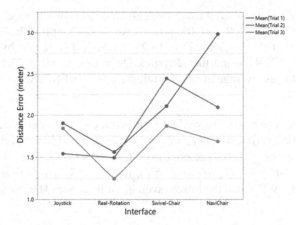

Fig. 5. The average of participant's distance errors for each interface at each trial.

4.2 Introspective Results

Shapiro Wilkes test showed that the introspective data were normal or had small violation of normality, which ANOVA is robust enough for the small normality violations. The Mauchly's test showed the violation of the sphericity assumption for all the measured variables, so we performed the Greenhouse-Geisser correction of ANOVA for all the variables, and all the significant effects have been mentioned at below sections ($p < .05$). All other results were not significant including immersion, enjoyment, learnability, and overall preference.

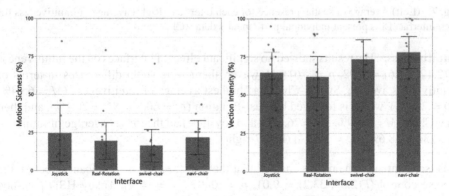

Fig. 6. (Left) Average of motion sickness for each interface (right) average of vection intensity for each interfaceDots present individual participant's data. (CI = 95%)

Motion Sickness. The results showed no significant effect of interfaces on motion sickness ($F(1.34, 17.7) = .170, p = .750$). However, swivel-chair had the lowest average of motion sickness ($M = 16.1\%, SD = 18.5\%$), which is followed by Real-Rotation ($M = 19.3\%, SD = 20.8\%$) and then NaviChair ($M = 21.4\%, SD = 19.3\%$), and joystick had the highest average of motion sickness ($M = 24.4\%, SD = 32.1\%$)   (Fig. 6-left).

Vection Intensity. The results showed no significant effect of interfaces on the vection intensity ($F(2.36, 30.6) = 3.09, p = .052$). However, NaviChair had the highest average of vection intensity ($M = 77.9\%, SD = 18.2\%$), which if followed by Swivel-Chair ($M = 73.4\%, SD = 22.4\%$), and then Joystick ($M = 64.6\%, SD = 23.6\%$), and Real-Rotation had the lowest average of vection intensity ($M = 61.8\%, SD = 23.3\%$) (Fig. 6-right).

Spatial Presence. The results showed no significant effect of interfaces on the spatial presence (being there physically) ($F(2.12, 29.6) = 2.15, p = .132$).However, NaviChair had the highest average of spatial presence ($M = 69.1\%, SD = 21.7\%$), which is followed by Swivel-Chair ($M = 65.6\%, SD = 20.5\%$), and then Real-Rotation ($M = 57.9\%, SD = 17.5\%$), and joystick had the lowest average of presence ($M = 54.6\%, SD = 21\%$) (Fig. 7-left).

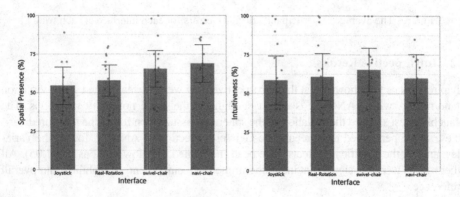

Fig. 7. (Left) Average of spatial presence for each interface (Right) average of intuitiveness for each interfaceDots present individual participant's data. (CI = 95%)

Intuitiveness. The results showed no significant effect of interfaces on the intuitiveness ($F(2.12, 27.6) = .292, p = .761$). However, there were slight differences in terms of intuitiveness average. Swivel-Chair had highest average of intuitiveness ($M = 65.4\%, SD = 24.3\%$), which is followed by Real-Rotation ($M = 60.8\%, SD = 26.1\%$), and then NaviChair ($M = 59.9\%, SD = 26.8\%$), and Joystick had the lowest average of intuitiveness ($M = 58.6\%, SD = 27.3\%$) (Fig. 7-right).

Precise Control. The results showed that the interface had a significant effect on the precise control ($F(2.55, 33.2) = 9.01, p = .0003, \eta_p^2 = .409$). Tukey HSD post-hoc showed that joystick ($M = 75, SD = 23.9$) had significantly higher precise control than both Swivel-Chair ($M = 49.8\%, SD = 29.9\%$) and NaviChair ($M = 32.3\%, SD = 18.7\%$) (all $ps < .021$). Moreover, Real-Rotation ($M = 54.8\%, SD = 20.7$) had significant higher precise control than NaviChair ($p = .046$) (Fig. 8-left).

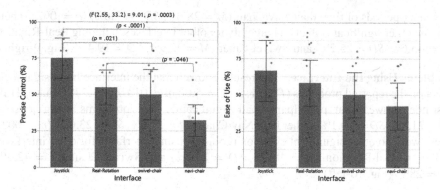

Fig. 8. (Left) Average of precise control for each interface (Right) ease of use average for each interface. Dots present individual participant's data. (CI = 95%)

Ease of Use. The results showed no significant effect of interfaces on the ease of use ($F(2.15, 28.0) = 2.09, p = .139$). However, Joystick had the highest ease of use mean ($M = 66.6\%, SD = 36.7\%$), which is followed by Real-Rotation ($M = 58.1\%, SD = 27.4\%$), and then Swivel-Chair ($M = 49.9\%, SD = 27.0\%$), and NaviChair had the lowest ease of use ($M = 42.2\%, SD = 28.0\%$) (Fig. 8-right).

Comfort. The results showed that the interface has a significant effect on the comfort ($F(1.37, 17.9) = 4.08, p = .048, \eta_p^2 = .239$). Tukey HSD post-hoc showed that joystick ($M = 71.4\%, SD = 32.3\%$) had higher comfort than NaviChair ($M = 43.3\%, SD = 28.9\%$) ($p = .010$). There were no other significant effect on comfort for other interfaces including Real-Rotation ($M = 65.1\%, SD = 28.0\%$) and Swivel-Chair ($M = 58.9\%, SD = 23.1\%$) (Fig. 9-left).

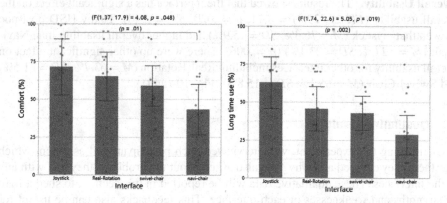

Fig. 9. (Left) Comfort mean for each interface (right) longevity mean for each interface. Dots present individual participant's data(CI = 95%)

Long Time Use (i.e., Longevity). The results showed that the interface had a significant effect on the longevity ($F(1.74, 22.6) = 5.05, p = .019, \eta_p^2 = .280$). Tukey HSD post-hoc showed that participants could imagine using joystick ($M = 62.8\%, SD = 29.6\%$)

for longer periods of time than NaviChair ($M = 28.6\%$, $SD = 22.6\%$) ($p = .002$). There were no other significant effect on longevity for other interfaces including Real-Rotation ($M = 45.6\%$, $SD = 25.2\%$) and Swivel-Chair ($M = 42.9\%$, $SD = 19.4\%$) (Fig. 9-right).

Problems Using the Interface. The results showed that the interface has a significant effect on the reported problems ($F(2.31, 30.1) = 5.00$, $p = .010$, $\eta_p^2 = .278$). Tukey HSD post-hoc showed that participants had significantly less problems using joystick ($M = 21.4\%$, $SD = 19.1\%$) rather than NaviChair ($M = 54.6\%$, $SD = 23.6\%$) ($p = .002$). There were no other significant effect on problems using interfaces for other interfaces including Real-Rotation ($M = 38.6\%$, $SD = 27.7\%$) and Swivel-Chair ($M = 42.3\%$, $SD = 28\%$) (Fig. 10-left).

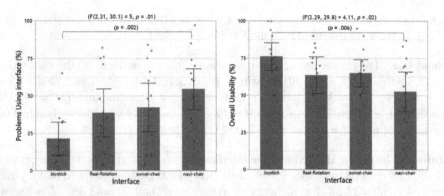

Fig. 10. (Left) Average of user problems with each interface (right) average of overall usability for each interfaceDots present individual participant's data (CI = 95%)

Overall Usability. The results showed that the interface has a significant effect on the overall usability ($F(2.29, 29.8) = 4.11$, $p = .020$, $\eta_p^2 = .240$). Tukey HSD post-hoc showed that joystick ($M = 76.3\%$, $SD = 15.9\%$) had higher overall usability than Navi-Chair ($M = 52.6\%$, $SD = 23.1\%$) ($p = .006$). There were no other significant effect on overall usability for other interfaces including Real-Rotation ($M = 63.7\%$, $SD = 21.5\%$) and Swivel-Chair ($M = 65.1\%$, $SD = 15.8\%$) (Fig. 10-right).

4.3   Qualitative Results

After finishing the experiment, we interviewed each participant and ask them which interfaces they enjoyed and why? We also asked about the problems they had with any of the interfaces. These qualitative data will be reported in this section, to shed a light on strengths and weaknesses of each interface. This feedbacks also can be useful for future improvement of the interfaces.

Joystick Feedbacks. Two (out of 14) participants enjoyed joystick over the other interfaces, because they were used to it or it was comfortable for them. However, as for the problems of joystick, some participants mentioned that joystick locomotion was not natural, and two of them mentioned that they also rotated their neck instead of rotating joystick. One participant suggested to use game controllers instead of joystick, because he were more familiar with the game controllers.

Real-Rotation Feedbacks. Five (out of 14) participants enjoyed Real-Rotation over the other interfaces, because physical rotation helped them to be immersed in the VR, but also they could precisely control their speed with joystick. However, as for the problems of Real-Rotation, four participants mentioned that it was not easy to control two interfaces (i.e., chair for rotation and joystick for translation) simultaneously, and they were disconnected from the game.

Swivel-Chair Feedbacks. Five (out of 14) participants enjoyed Swivel-Chair over the other interfaces, because it was a comfortable chair and intuitive. Four participants also mentioned that it was highly intuitive and natural, which made them highly engaged into the game. However, as for the problems of Swivel-Chair, five participants mentioned that it was not easy for them to control the speed by leaning back, so they could not control their speed precisely.

NaviChair Feedbacks. Two (out of 14) participants enjoyed NaviChair over the other interfaces, because it was comfortable for them, so engaged and immersed them into the game. However, as for the problems of NaviChair, eight participants mentioned that it was hard for them to control it accurately. One of them mentioned that it was hard to focus on the bottom of their body to navigate, another participant mentioned that due to her back problem. One participant mentioned that it was hard to stop NaviChair, and another one mentioned that it was too sensitive. Two participants mentioned that it was too loose and jumpy. Because NaviChair was over the Wii Balance Board, even its lowest height was too high for some participants, so three participants mentioned that the height of NaviChair was too high for them. One participant mentioned that NaviChair is an interesting interface for free exploration of VE but not for accurate maneuvering purposes.

5 Discussion and Conclusions

The experiment results did not confirmed many of the predicted advantages of leaning-based 360° interfaces over joystick or vice versa significantly. However, the slight difference between measured data means seems promising. For example, as we predicted about the low motion sickness of our interfaces, the motion sickness average of both Swivel-Chair and NaviChair is slightly lower than joystick. Especially, Swivel-Chair has slightly lower motion sickness average than Real-Rotation as well, which shows that adding leaning-based translation to a full-Rotational interface trends to reduce motion sickness.

Beside that, as we predicted based on the previous studies (i.e., [14, 26]), both Swivel-Chair and NaviChair had slightly higher vection intensity average than the joystick and Real-Rotation. Also as for the presence, as we predicted [7, 18], both Swivel-Chair and NaviChair had slightly higher spatial presence average than joystick and Real-Rotation.

As for the joystick advantages, as we predicted [7, 14, 18, 26], joystick showed significantly higher precise control, comfort, longevity, and overall usability than

NaviChair, but comparing to Swivel-Chair, it had only higher precise control. The results of this experiment, also rejected some of our predictions. For example, unlike our prediction about the higher accuracy of NaviChair (i.e., lower navigational distance errors) [23], it had significantly lower accuracy than both joystick and Real-Rotation.

Overall, the results suggest the potentials of leaning-based 360° interfaces, however they still have controllability issues and need to be improved in terms of precise control, ease of use, comfort, longevity, and overall usability. One of the possible explanations for our non-significant results might be because of using only 14 participants with huge between-subject variability, which can be resulted into the limited power of the test.

As for the design guidelines to improve our suggested interfaces, as mentioned in the participant's feedback section, NaviChair can be improved in many aspects (e.g., height, loose and jumpy seat, etc.). As for the Swivel-chair, participants did not mention many problems regarding the sideways controllability by their neck muscles, but instead mentioned that controlling forward/backward motion by their back muscles was not easy. Therefore, it might be useful to control both forward/backward and sideways locomotion using neck muscles, which is more accurate than the back muscles. It means that the simulated forward/backward and sideways locomotion can be controlled by moving the head forward/backward and sideways respectively.

Overall, our results suggest that using leaning-based 360° locomotion interfaces might be promising, however our interfaces need to be improved. Moreover, our experiment was a simple avatar-following task without of spatial orientation or navigational tasks, which are important tasks in many VR applications (especially games), and should be done in future experiments. Beside that, if we compare leaning-based 360° interfaces with joystick or Real-Rotation in an experiment, which needs interaction with the environment, because both our leaning-based 360° interfaces (i.e., Swivel-Chair and NaviChair) provide hands-free locomotion, the users can use their hands for natural interaction with the environment (such as pointing and shooting enemies in a FPS game by gun), which joystick and Real-Rotation have no such natural hand interaction. Such an experiment also can investigate other potentials of our suggested interfaces as a joystick for VR applications.

References

1. Beckhaus, S., Blom, K.J., Haringer, M.: Intuitive, hands-free travel interfaces for virtual environments. In: 2005 New Directions in 3D User Interfaces Workshop of IEEE VR, pp. 57–60 (2005)
2. Berger, D.R., Schulte-Pelkum, J., Bülthoff, H.H.: Simulating believable forward accelerations on a stewart motion platform. ACM Trans. Appl. Percept. 7(1), 5:1–5:27 (2010)
3. Bowman, D.A., Koller, D., Hodges, L.F.: A methodology for the evaluation of travel techniques for immersive virtual environments. Virtual Reality 3(2), 120–131 (1998)
4. Chance, S.S., Gaunet, F., Beall, A.C., Loomis, J.M.: Locomotion mode affects the updating of objects encountered during travel: The contribution of vestibular and proprioceptive inputs to path integration. Presence 7(2), 168–178 (1998)
5. Chester, M.R., Rys, M.J., Konz, S.A.: Leg swelling, comfort and fatigue when sitting, standing, and sit/standing. Int. J. Ind. Ergon. 29(5), 289–296 (2002)

6. Fairchild, K.M., Lee, B.H., Loo, J., Ng, H., Serra, L.: The heaven and earth virtual reality: Designing applications for novice users. In: Proceedings of IEEE Virtual Reality Annual International Symposium, pp. 47–53, September 1993
7. Freiberg, J.: Experience Before Construction: Immersive Virtual Reality Design Tools for Architectural Practice (MSc Thesis). Simon Fraser University, Surrey, BC, Canada (2015)
8. Grechkin, T.Y., Riecke, B.E.: Re-evaluating benefits of body-based rotational cues for maintaining orientation in virtual environments: Men benefit from real rotations, women don't. In: Proceedings of the ACM Symposium on Applied Perception, New York, 99–102 (2014)
9. Groen, E.L., Bles, W.: How to use body tilt for the simulation of linear self motion. J. Vestib. Res.: Equilib. Orientation **14**(5), 375–385 (2004)
10. Hale, K.S., Stanney, K.M., Keshavarz, B., Hecht, H., Lawson, B.D.: Visually induced motion sickness: Causes, characteristics, and countermeasures. In: Handbook of Virtual Environments: Design, Implementation, and Applications, pp. 647–698. CRC Press (2014). Second Edition
11. Harris, A., Nguyen, K., Wilson, P.T., Jackoski, M., Williams, B.: Human joystick: Wii-leaning to translate in large virtual environments. In: Proceedings of the 13th ACM SIGGRAPH International Conference on Virtual-Reality Continuum and its Applications in Industry, New York, pp. 231–234 (2014)
12. Kitson, A., Hashemian, A.M., Stepanova, K., Riecke, B.E.: Comparing Leaning-Based Motion Cueing Interfaces for Virtual Reality Locomotion (2017)
13. Kitson, A., Riecke, B.E., Hashemian, A.M., Neustaedter, C.: NaviChair: Evaluating an embodied interface using a pointing task to navigate virtual reality. In: Proceedings of the 3rd ACM Symposium on Spatial User Interaction, New York, pp. 123–126 (2015)
14. Kruijff, E., Marquardt, A., Trepkowski, C., Lindeman, R.W., Hinkenjann, A., Maiero, J., Riecke, B.E.: On Your Feet! Enhancing Self-Motion Perception in Leaning-Based Interfaces through Multisensory Stimuli (2016)
15. Langbehn, E., Eichler, T., Ghose, S., von Luck, K., Bruder, G., Steinicke, F.: Evaluation of an omnidirectional walking-in-place user interface with virtual locomotion speed scaled by forward leaning angle. In: Proceedings of the GI Workshop on Virtual and Augmented Reality (GI VR/AR), pp. 149–160 (2015)
16. LaViola Jr., J.J., Feliz, D.A., Keefe, D.F., Zeleznik, R.C.: Hands-free multi-scale navigation in virtual environments. In: Proceedings of the 2001 Symposium on Interactive 3D Graphics, New York, pp. 9–15 (2001)
17. Lawson, B.D.: Motion sickness symptomatology and origins. In: Handbook of Virtual Environments: Design, Implementation, and Applications, pp. 531–599 (2014)
18. Marchal, M., Pettré, J., Lécuyer, A.: Joyman: A human-scale joystick for navigating in virtual worlds. In: 2011 IEEE Symposium on 3D User Interfaces (3DUI), pp. 19–26, March 2011
19. Merhi, O., Faugloire, E., Flanagan, M., Stoffregen, T.A.: Motion sickness, console video games, and head-mounted displays. Hum. Factors: J. Hum. Factors Ergon. Soc. **49**(5), 920–934 (2007)
20. Nguyen-Vo, T., Riecke, B.E., Stuerzlinger, W.: Moving in a Box: Improving Spatial Orientation in Virtual Reality using Simulated Reference Frames (2017)
21. Riccio, G.E., Stoffregen, T.A.: An ecological theory of motion sickness and postural instability. Ecol. Psychol. **3**(3), 195–240 (1991)
22. Riecke, B.E.: Simple user-generated motion cueing can enhance self-motion perception (vection) in virtual reality. In: Proceedings of the ACM Symposium on Virtual Reality Software and Technology, New York, pp. 104–107 (2006)

23. Riecke, B.E., Bodenheimer, B., McNamara, T.P., Williams, B., Peng, P., Feuereissen, D.: Do we need to walk for effective virtual reality navigation? Physical rotations alone may suffice. In: Hölscher, C., Shipley, T.F., Olivetti Belardinelli, M., Bateman, J.A., Newcombe, N.S. (eds.) Spatial Cognition 2010. LNCS (LNAI), vol. 6222, pp. 234–247. Springer, Heidelberg (2010). doi:10.1007/978-3-642-14749-4_21

24. Riecke, B.E., Feuereissen, D.: To move or not to move: can active control and user-driven motion cueing enhance self-motion perception ("Vection") in virtual reality? In: Proceedings of the ACM Symposium on Applied Perception, New York, pp. 17–24 (2012)

25. Riecke, B.E., Sigurdarson, S., Milne, A.P.: Moving through virtual reality without moving? Cogn. Process. 13(1), 293–297 (2012)

26. Riecke, B.E., Trepkowski, C., Kitson, A., Kruijff, E.: Human Joystick: Enhancing Self-Motion Perception (Linear Vection) by using Upper Body Leaning for Gaming and Virtual Reality (2017)

27. Ruddle, R.A.: The effect of translational and rotational body-based information on navigation. In: Steinicke, F., Visell, Y., Campos, J., Lécuyer, A. (eds.) Human Walking in Virtual Environments, pp. 99–112. Springer, New York (2013)

28. Ruddle, R.A., Lessels, S.: For efficient navigational search, humans require full physical movement, but not a rich visual scene. Psychol. Sci. 17(6), 460–465 (2006)

29. Ruddle, R.A., Lessels, S.: The benefits of using a walking interface to navigate virtual environments. ACM Trans. Comput.-Hum. Interact. 16(1), 5:1–5:18 (2009)

30. Sigurdarson, S., Milne, A.P., Feuereissen, D., Riecke, B.E.: Can physical motions prevent disorientation in naturalistic VR? In: 2012 IEEE Virtual Reality Workshops (VRW), pp. 31–34, March 2012

31. Wang, J., Lindeman, R.W.: Silver Surfer: A system to compare isometric and elastic board interfaces for locomotion in VR. In: 2011 IEEE Symposium on 3D User Interfaces (3DUI), pp. 121–122, March 2011

32. Williams, B., Narasimham, G., McNamara, T.P., Carr, T.H., Rieser, J.J., Bodenheimer, B.: Updating orientation in large virtual environments using scaled translational gain. In: Proceedings of the 3rd Symposium on Applied Perception in Graphics and Visualization, New York, pp. 21–28 (2006)

33. Zielasko, D., Horn, S., Freitag, S., Weyers, B., Kuhlen, T.W.: Evaluation of hands-free HMD-based navigation techniques for immersive data analysis. In: 2016 IEEE Symposium on 3D User Interfaces (3DUI), pp. 113–119, March 2016

Curved Plates Positioning and Flexible Brackets Control in Virtual Shipbuilding Simulation

Cheng Huanchong[1,2(✉)], Fan Xiumin[1,2], Zhu Minghua[3], Gu Yan[1,2], and Du Jiwang[1,2]

[1] CIM Research Institute, School of Mechanical Engineering,
Shanghai Jiao Tong University, Shanghai 200240, China
hccheng@sjtu.edu.cn
[2] Shanghai Key Lab of Advanced Manufacturing Environment, Shanghai, China
[3] Jiangnan Shipyard Co., Ltd., Jiangnan, China
zhuminghua@gmail.com

Abstract. Flexible bracket system is a kind of adjustable fixture with many movable pillars and adaptive to curved plates with various sizes and shapes, thus facilitating fast and precise position or assembly of the curved plates. The purpose of this work is to simulate the control process of flexible brackets to fit different curved plates automatically in virtual environment, thus helping process engineers preview the assembly results, adjust and determine the configuration and controlling scheme of the flexible brackets. The proposed methods for flexible bracket simulation are composed of four steps. First, build a virtual environment of the shipbuilding scene. Second, calculate the pose of the digital curved plate model. Third, optimize the pose and layout of the flexible brackets to fit the curve plate. Last, calculate and optimize the control parameters of the flexible brackets. Our virtual simulation method for flexible brackets reduces the workload for pose adjustment and reconfiguration during the real assembly process, contributing higher precision and efficiency for the curved block building.

Keywords: Flexible bracket · Position · Curved plate · Shipbuilding simulation · Collision detection

1 Introduction

Block building is the most commonly applied method in ship building industry, which constructs the ship hull mainly on curved blocks. Curved plates are massively used on curved blocks during the shipbuilding process, consequently, the assembly precision of curved blocks is directly influenced by the position precision of the plates. However, curved plate has large volume, complex 3D shape and complex contour, bringing difficulties in its positioning and assembly process. Traditionally, curved plates are fixed by specific brackets, which are not reusable for plates of different shapes. When position unmatched plates on specific brackets, the shape difference is adjusted by welding or cutting the position part of the brackets. Such adjustment method cost much

© Springer International Publishing AG 2017
S. Lackey and J. Chen (Eds.): VAMR 2017, LNCS 10280, pp. 33–42, 2017.
DOI: 10.1007/978-3-319-57987-0_3

resource on time, labor and material, and its precision relies on the experiment and performance of the technicians. Therefore, traditional manual bracket adjustment method increase the shipbuilding time and still exists precision issues.

An alternative adjustment method is to use flexible bracket system, which is an adjustable fixture with several movable pillars. Flexible brackets are adaptive to curved plates with various sizes and shapes, thus facilitating fast and precise position or assembly of the curved plates. Though flexible brackets controlled by computer can realize fast position of curved plates of different shapes, it needs to simulate and plan the motion of the pillar before on-site application to check the feasibility and precision of the control scheme. As virtual CAD models of shipbuilding parts are available for visualized simulation, it is convenient to simulate the control scheme with model information under virtual environment, providing an intuitive simulation result.

In this work, a virtual simulation environment is presented for simulating the layout, positioning and digital control process of curved block building. Digital controllable models of flexible bracket and curved plates are established under the virtual simulation environment. An active plate position function is proposed to precisely adjust the brackets and plates simultaneously, which supporting the generation of the digital location and layout control scheme of the flexible brackets system. The related works have been surveyed in Sect. 2. The proposed simulation methods are illustrated in Sect. 3. The simulation results of the are shown in Sect. 4. Section 5 concludes our work and provides possible future improvements.

2   Related Works

2.1   Research on Flexible Fixture for Shipbuilding

Fixture and jigs are essential equipment for the construction of curved hull block, the quality and efficiency of ship construction depend on the assembly accuracy of the curved hull block on jigs. As one of the most important equipment in shipbuilding, how to realize its flexibility has become a focus of research all of the world.

Shipyard in japan has begun to use the tubular active jigs in the 1950's [1]. Although the tubular active jigs has many technical improvements, it still cannot fully meet the flexibility needs of modern shipyard.

The flexibility of shipbuilding is originated from the concept of "multi point forming", which is based on the characteristics of flexible and digital manufacturing of multi point forming equipment. David E. Hardt [2] in MIT has carried out the research on the flexible bracket to realize automation for more than ten years and applied to the forming experiment of thin plate parts. By using the closed loop control principle to measure the height of a base body, and thus to control the forming precision, it was an important research direction for the modern flexible bracket technology [3].

Jiangnan Shipyard has tried to make and use NC jigs for curved hull block in shipbuilding for the first time in China [4]. It proposes a new type of NC flexible jigs which kept the advantages of existing jigs. The application of flexible NC jigs could realize the fast and accurate positioning and assembling of curved block parts, to improve the quality and increase the efficiency of the construction of curved blocks.

2.2 Computer Simulation Technology in Shipbuilding

Digital manufacturing has become the main technical means in shipbuilding industry, as its characteristics of quick response, high quality, low cost and good flexibility. In the field of integrated virtual simulation of ship digital construction, shipyards of the worldwide mainly developed virtual simulation software system.

In April 2002, Samsung heavy industry launched the digital shipbuilding system development plan and developed a digital shipbuilding system in two years later [5]. This system can simulate the whole shipbuilding process from steel plate cutting to ship launching in the virtual environment.

Daewoo shipyard launched the simulation system of the construction process of the ship based on discrete time simulation kernel in 2010 [6]. Based on the previous experience of ship construction and digital technology, engineers could built a virtual shipyard in the system, which could simulate the whole shipbuilding process from steel plate cutting to ship launching [7].

Hudong Zhonghua shipyard in China developed its own enterprise information system HDS-CIMS and shell, outfitting and painting integration of ship product design system independently.

3 Method

3.1 Overview

Simulating the control process of flexible brackets to fit different curved plates automatically in virtual environment, thereby, to help process engineers to preview the assembly results, adjust and determine the configuration and controlling scheme of the flexible brackets. The major simulation process is divided into five steps:

1. Build a virtual environment of the shipbuilding scene for simulation, which contains curve plate model, flexible bracket model and related objects in workshop.
2. Calculate the pose of the digital curved plate model. An optimization algorithm is proposed to find out the position of the curved plate with the lowest barycenter.
3. According to the pose of curve plate, number and layout of the flexible brackets are automatically calculated to fit the curve plate.
4. Control the position of supporting pillars in the brackets. Real-time collision detection method is used for calculating the contact point between supporting pillar and curve plate.

3.2 Build Virtual Environment

A virtual environment close to the real environment should be built for simulation firstly. This research is based on the VRLAYOUT platform developed by Shanghai Jiao Tong University. As a general developing platform for virtual reality, VRLAYOUT supports multiple formats of 3D model import, real time interactive operation, collision detection between 3D model, etc.

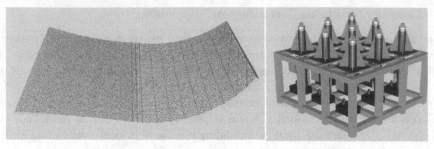

a)Triangle Mesh of Curve Plateb) 3D Modelof Flexible Brackets

Fig. 1. Import curve plate and flexible bracket 3D model

During the simulation, curved plate model, flexible brackets model and other related objects in workshop are required. 3D Model of curved plate is exported from design software TRIBON, and converted to triangle mesh model by VRLAYOUT. 3D Model of flexible bracket, split into one fixed base and nine supporting pillars, is imported to the virtual environment. Figure 1 shows the triangle mesh of curve plate and 3D model of flexible brackets imported into virtual environment.

Then other related 3D models s such as ground, cranes, processing equipment are imported into VRLAYOUT and placed according to the production site. Figure 2 shows the layout result of other related objects in virtual environment.

Fig. 2. Layout related objects in virtual environment

3.3   Calculate the Pose of Curved Plate

Due to the large weight of curved plates used in shipbuilding, it is hard to position and fix them on the flexible brackets. In the production process, the curved plates are usually positioned with the lowest barycenter to increase the stability. The barycenter of a curved plate can be estimated by triangle mesh model in virtual environment. The position with the lowest barycenter is chosen as the fixed position on flexible brackets.

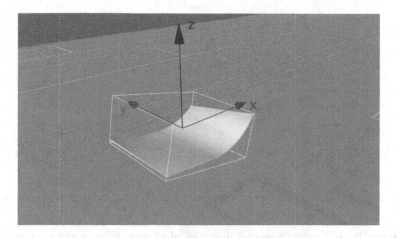

Fig. 3. WCS direction in virtual environment

Calculating the Pose of Curved Plate contains four steps:

1. Sample the Positions for Curved Plate

First, build a world coordinate system (WCS) $oxyz$. In this WCS, o is origin, $+x$ axis points to east direction, $+y$ axis points to north direction, and $+z$ axis points to up direction. Pose of curved plate in the WCS can be described by a 4×4 matrix M_q. The initial pose of curved plate is consistent with the WCS. Figure 3 shows the WCS direction in virtual environment.

As the figure shows, the height value of barycenter would change if the curved plate rotated around x axis or y axis, but would remain unchanged if rotated around z axis. Thus, the pose can be sampled by rotate the curved plate around x axis or y axis. A sample point, which can also described by a rotation matrix, is token when curved plate rotated every $1°$. M_{ix} and M_{jy} represent rotation matrix rotated around x axis and y axis. The pose matrix of curved plate $M_{qij} = M_{ix} \times M_{jy}$. In the previous formula, i and j represent the rotation angles, the value scope of which are [0,90]. For every pair (M_{ix}, M_{jy}), $i, j \in [0, 90]$, the height of barycenter H_{ij} can be calculated by the pose matrix M_{qij}. In all 8281 pairs, the pose matrix M_{qmin} can be picked out by the minimum value H_{min} in all H_{ij}.

2. Calculate Z-coordinate of the barycenter

Load the triangle mesh data file of curved plate, and traverse all triangle facets in the mesh. Every triangle facet contains 3 points, $P_i = [x_i, y_i, z_i]^T$, $i \in \{0, 1, 2, 3\}$. The normal of facet $\vec{n} = \overrightarrow{P_1 P_2} \times \overrightarrow{P_2 P_3}$. Then calculate coordinate of point in every triangle facet in WCS, $P_{iw} = P_i \times M_q$. For every triangle facet T, project the points $P_{iw}, i = \{1, 2, 3\}$ onto xoy plane to get vertical lines $P_{iw}P'_{iw}, i = \{1, 2, 3\}$. Figure 4 shows a pentahedron constructed by $P_{1w}P_{2w}P_{3w}P'_{1w}P'_{2w}P'_{3w}$. The Z-coordinate of the barycenter for this pentahedron $m_{Tz} \approx \frac{P_{1wz} + P_{2wz} + P_{2wz}}{6}$.

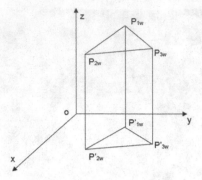

Fig. 4. A pentahedron constructed by vertexes in triangle facet and their projection points

Consider the influence of normal direction of triangle facet, a normal factor σ_T is introduced to describe the coefficient:

$$\sigma_T = \begin{cases} 1, \vec{n} \cdot \vec{oz} > 0 \\ 0, \vec{n} \cdot \vec{oz} = 0 \\ -1, \vec{n} \cdot \vec{oz} < 0 \end{cases}$$

For entire model of triangle mesh, Z-coordinate of curved plate can be calculated by $m_{qz} = \sum_1^n \sigma_{iT} m_{iTz}$.

3. Calculate the height value of barycenter

Traverse all the triangle facets of curved plate and find $P_{zmin} = \min(P_{iz})$, where P_{iz} are Z-coordinate values among all vertexes in triangle mesh. The height value of barycenter $H = m_{qz} - P_{zmin}$.

4. Calculate M_{qmin} of the curved plate

For every M_{qij}, calculate the height value of barycenter H_{ij}, traverse all pose and get M_{qmin} when the height value of barycenter gets H_{min}.

3.4   Flexible Brackets Layout

In the 3D virtual environment, the bracket pose is set at where the height of barycenter reaches the minimum value, which is denoted by M_{qmin}. All vertexes $P_i = [x_i, y_i, z_i]^T$ of the triangular meshes on the curved plates are iterated to calculate their position under the world coordinate system $P_{iw} = [x_{iw}, y_{iw}, z_{iw}]^T = P_i \times M_{qmin}$. During the iteration, the max and minimum value of x_{iw}, y_{iw} are recorded and denoted as x_{iwmax}, x_{iwmin}, y_{iwmax} and y_{iwmin} respectively. Then the minimum projection rectangle on the xoy plane of the bracket is calculated as shown in Fig. 5.

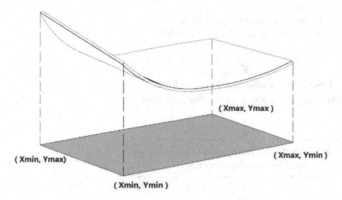

Fig. 5. The minimum projection rectangle of curved plate on xoy plane

According to the width of single bracket W_T, the total number of required brackets on both x and y direction under the world coordinate system are calculated by $Num_x = \left\lceil \frac{x_{max} - x_{min}}{W_T} \right\rceil + 1$ and $Num_y = \left\lceil \frac{y_{max} - y_{min}}{W_T} \right\rceil + 1$. Therefore, the total bracket number used on one curved block is $Num = Num_x \times Num_y$.

3.5 Moving Control of Supporting Pillars

The flexible brackets achieve their flexibility by control the height and the motion of their supporting pillars. Each pillar supports the curved plate, and the goal of the control is to adjust the height of the pillars well fit for the shape of the curved plates supported by the bracket, thus maintaining the shape of the plate during its processing. When the position of the plate is determined, the problem turns into calculating the height motion of the each supporting pillar along its moving direction.

To address the irregular shape of curved plate and supporting pillar, collision detection is used to calculate the contacting point between the end of the pillar and the plate. Intersection checking of the triangular meshes of pillar and plate models are used to check if the two objects contact with each other.

Collision detection have already been realized by VRLAYOUT, which provides an effective detection method based on triangle mesh models. The main steps to calculate the movement of each supporting pillar are as follow:

1. Generate collision model of each supporting pillar and the curved blocks. The model is generated by CDMake provided by VRLAYOUT, and its precision can be set by user.
2. Discretize the max motion path of the supporting pillar along its moving direction. The max upward motion distance is S_{max}, and the discrete step size can set by user. The pose of the supporting pillar along the upward directions denote as M_Z.

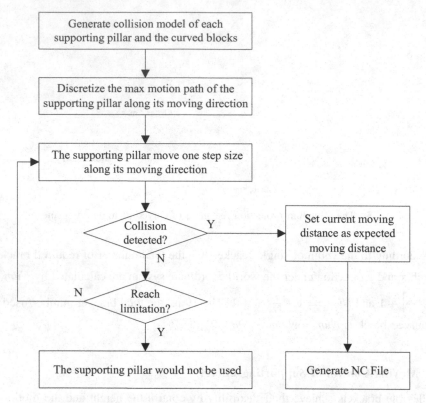

Fig. 6. Flowchart of calculating the moving distance of supporting pillars

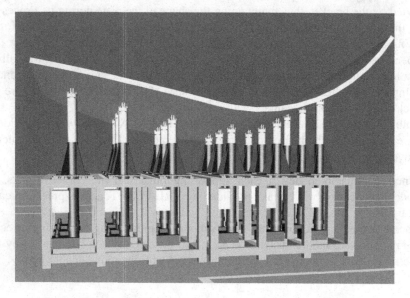

Fig. 7. The result of flexible brackets control in virtual environment

3. Collision detection is performed to determine if the pillar touches the plate, if the result is positive, then all steps are added as the moving distance, or else move to the next step.
4. If no collision detected when the supporting pillar reach the limited position, it means that the supporting pillar would not use in the positioning process, or else the supporting pillar move one step size along its moving direction. Jump to step. 3 with new M_Z and recalculate the collision status.
5. Calculate all moving distance of supporting pillars, record them and generate the NC program file used to control the flexible brackets.

Figure 6 shows the flowchart of calculating the moving distance of supporting pillars. Figure 7 shows the result of flexible brackets control in virtual environment.

4   Results

According to the research above, Flexible Brackets Control System is developed based on VRLAYOUT and concentrates on curved plates positioning in shipbuilding industry. The system has been applied on a shipbuilding corporation and archived a good result. Figure 8 shows the system used in shipbuilding process in this corporation.

In this case, calculating the pose of curved plate and controlling the movement of supporting pillars in flexible brackets help process engineers to determine the fix method and controlling scheme of the flexible brackets. The curved plate has a more precise with a triangle mesh contains about 4.5 million triangle facets. Benefited from multithread optimization, the process of calculating the pose of curved plate costs about 176 s. In flexible brackets controlling process, the collision model precision is set to 0.1 mm, and step size of supporting pillars is set to 0.05 mm to get an accurate result.

Fig. 8. The system used in shipbuilding process in corporation

The cost time is about 17 m 25 s for calculating the moving distance of 864 supporting pillars in 96 flexible brackets. The simulation contributes higher precision and lesser time cost than traditional methods.

5 Conclusions

This paper proposed a virtual simulation method of flexible bracket for curved hull block building. An implementation of the system is developed based on VRLAYOUT (interactive plant layout with VR) platform. The system proposes a pose simulation method of curved plates and flexible brackets. A collision detection based method is proposed for planning the control scheme of the flexible brackets system. The proposed system provides an interactive, precise and efficient movement planning and controlling tool for flexible bracket planning and for users from shipbuilding industry. The system has been verified and applied on a shipbuilding corporation. By replacing fixed brackets with the flexible ones, the virtual bracket simulation system demonstrates an improvement of the efficiency and reducing the test-cost for the curved-block shipbuilding process.

For further research, an algorithm for searching optimal solution can be added for calculating the pose of curved plate, which can provide more effective method to find the optimal result. The precision of collision detection model can be improved for a more accurate result.

References

1. Kang, W., Lu, C., Gao, X., et al.: Research on the industrial design method of control panel based on man-machine engineering restriction. In: The International Conference on Computer-Aided Industrial Design and, Conceptual Design. Chinese Mechanical Engineering Society, pp. 7–11 (2008)
2. Hardt, D.E., Webb, R.D., Suh, N.P.: Sheet metal die forming using closed-loop shape control. CIRP Ann. Manuf. Technol. 31(1), 165–169 (1982)
3. Walczyk, D.F., Hardt, D.E.: Design and analysis of reconfigurable discrete dies for sheet metal forming. J. Manuf. Syst. 17(6), 436–454 (1998)
4. Jun-jie, S., Yang, Y., Jian, W., et al.: Research on flexible manufacturing technology based on NC jigs for curved hull block. Nav. Archit. Ocean Eng. 32(2), 63–68 (2016)
5. Lee, K., Shin, J.G., Ryu, C.: Development of simulation-based production execution system in a shipyard a case study for a panel block assembly shop. Prod. Plann. Control 20(8), 750–768 (2009)
6. Cha, J.H., Roh, M.: Combined discrete event and discrete time simulation framework and its application to the block erection process in shipbuilding. Adv. Eng. Softw. 41(4), 656–665 (2010)
7. Cha, J.H., Park, K.P., Lee, K.Y.: Development of a simulation framework and applications to new production processes in shipyards. Comput.-Aided Des. 44(3), 241–252 (2012)

Intelligent Virtual Environment Using Artificial Neural Networks

Sandra Mateus[1(✉)] and John Branch[2]

[1] Politécnico Colombiano Jaime Isaza Cadavid, Medellín, Colombia
spmateus@elpoli.edu.co
[2] Universidad Nacional de Colombia, Medellín, Colombia
jwbranch@unal.edu.co

Abstract. This paper describes an Intelligent Virtual Environment (IVE) which incorporates Artificial Neural Networks (ANN) in the perception and reasoning of a character in this virtual environment, in order to react intelligently to some given warning signs. First, we explore different types of ANN simulated in MATLAB to understand their operation in order to choose the one that fits to our virtual environment. The environment was created with the UDK game engine and it consists of a character that moves across a working environment to identify warning signals. Later we implemented the Multi-Layer Perceptron (MLP) ANN in this environment. MLP was selected according to data obtained in several tests. This implementation was done by integrating the ANN in the state machines in the source code of the game engine to perform several operations within a controlled work environment.

Keywords: Intelligent virtual environment · Perception · Reasoning · Artificial neural network · Multi-Layer perceptron

1 Introduction

Virtual Reality is a computer technology that simulates a 3-D environment representing mostly visual experiences on a screen or a stereoscopic device. When a virtual environment incorporates Artificial Intelligence (AI), it reaches a new feature resulting in an asynchronous event distribution system. This is what distinguishes it from a conventional virtual environment. Hence its high applicability [1]. According to Whiting [2], there is an interesting dilemma for animators and designers, who are constantly creating new environments to incorporate autonomous characters. Each environment requires a complex and time-intensive work to be performed by an expert programmer because their underlying models are created to solve specific problems. This makes difficult their reutilization.

Literature reports related work on virtual environments incorporating AI. Jia and Zhenjiang [3] developed the Platform "Paladin" which uses collaborative and neuro-evolutive agents. It combines the Backpropagation Neural Networks with Evolutionary Algorithms in a 2D environment. Clement et al. [4] presented an intelligent tutoring system as an IVE for training. It allows to infer the learning objectives that the student has acquired and they evaluated it in a 3D biotechnology virtual lab. Xi and Smith [5] created a virtual environment with game technology and intelligent agents to simulate

© Springer International Publishing AG 2017
S. Lackey and J. Chen (Eds.): VAMR 2017, LNCS 10280, pp. 43–53, 2017.
DOI: 10.1007/978-3-319-57987-0_4

human emergencies. Liu et al. [6] proposed a framework for modeling virtual humans with a high level of autonomy at the behavioral and movement levels in a virtual environment. Gilbert and Forney [7] perfected a guided by an avatar in a clothing store in a 3D virtual world of Second Life tour through virtual agents using a robust variant of Artificial Intelligence Markup Language (AIML) and applied to it the Turing test.

Following the line of the related work, this paper describes an Intelligent Virtual Environment with Artificial Neural Networks. First, we explore different types of ANN. We finally selected MLP according to the data obtained in several evaluation steps. From the experiments performed, we conclude that ANN offer a good performance with low operational costs for visual effects requiring real time results and constrained to a given number of operations per cycle (this is not the case for most of the applications or Virtual Reality).

This paper is organized as follows: the concepts of perception and reasoning are discussed and the 3D virtual environment created is displayed in Sect. 2; in Sect. 3, we explain the Artificial Neural Network implemented in the virtual environment; in Sect. 4 we present the experiments and results; the paper is concluded in Sect. 5.

2   Perception and Reasoning

The Intelligent Virtual Environments must reach large capacities of complex and interactive behaviors to achieve a high level of realism [8]. This realism is based on elements that enable intelligent performance such as perception, learning, and communication through natural language and reasoning. According to the above, this paper focuses only on the perception and reasoning, cognitive and behavioral levels of a Virtual Environment.

According to Marthino et al. [9], perception is considered as all events of the virtual environment that are filtered according to the interests and location of the character. It is based on two principles: (1) A limited perception, in which a character perceives all events, but only in its associated area; and (2) An inaccurate perception, in which the character perceives the virtual environment as it is, but only receives relevant events associated with it. They also describe the reasoning as a process developed by a set of production rules which are conditions based on the model of the world, in the state of the target, the characteristic behavior and internal state information.

Given the above concepts, the character implemented in the Intelligent Virtual Environment presented in this work based its reasoning on the impact of its internal target and priority of the action to perform on the cognitive and behavioral levels.

Based on the above, a model of Intelligent Virtual Environment leaning on a game engine, which are incorporated Artificial Intelligence techniques in order to occur from a given perception with a character, a reasoning proposed proper respect to the Virtual Environment.

In this model, this can be seen as a set classifier S, which takes a set of perceptions $P_1 \ldots P_n$ and combines them to make adequate reasoning $R_1 \ldots R_n$. This reasoning to perform a certain action is supported on one of the techniques of Artificial Intelligence named in the model. So the system decides and selects an action A according to the reasoning made (Eq. 1).

$$S(\{P_1,\ R_1\}, \{P_2,\ R_2\}, \ldots \{P_n,\ R_n\}) \rightarrow A \qquad (1)$$

With this model, we want to achieve the following characteristics of an Intelligent Virtual Environment described by [10]: Decisive: any action taken by the character will be reflected in an effective plan; Real Time: The character must respond in real time to the perceptions of the environment and in the same way, adequate reason to perception form received; Ordered: That follows the proper sequence in their behavior.

Perceptions were simulated in this virtual environment and their respective actions to perform, through reasoning with AI technique, are shown in Table 1.

Table 1. Perceptions and actions that the character execute in the Virtual environment

Perception	Action run
Detects fire	Activate the fire alarm
Detects electrical risk	Turn off light switches
Detects wet floor	Call the cleaning staff
Workplace - Do not know what to do	Use the intercom for help

In Fig. 1 is shown a rendering of the Virtual Environment. The character will be interacting in environment as disclosed in Table 1 and is to this environment that the ANN will be applied as described next.

Fig. 1. Virtual environment developed with UDK

3   Intelligent Virtual Environment with Artificial Neural Network

In this section, we present the creation of an IVE for the perception and reasoning of warning signs in a work environment. We address the time constraints and computational cost in the ANN learning. In order to do this, we simulated different types of ANN and we finally chose the one requiring the least training time, which provides. Thus, we achieve a reduction of resources and time costs. Then, we adapted it to the videogames engine.

3.1   Characterization of Different Types of RNA

In this stage, we perform an exploration of the different types of ANN and we identify the type of learning. This is a key point in the development of the ANN because it implies that a processing unit can change its input/output behavior as result of the changes in the environment. Therefore, we classify some ANN according to their type of learning (Table 2).

Table 2.   ANN Classification by type of learning

ANN	Type of learning
Perceptron	Supervised
MLP (Multi-Level Perceptron)	Supervised
SOM (Self-Organizing Maps)	No supervised
LVQ (Learning Vector Quantization)	No supervised
Hopfield	No supervised
RBF (Radial Basis Function)	Hybrid

After knowing the types of ANN according to their learning, we simulated each one in MATLAB in order to understand their operation. This task was performed to choose the one that would fit to the perceptions and actions of the Virtual Environment. We also checked that this selected ANN could be implemented within the game engine. Two networks were chosen: The Radial Basis Function (RBF), and the Multi-Layer Perceptron (MLP). After making comparisons between these two networks measurements by square error, we selected the MLP due to the lower number of neurons used in the hidden layer and the error which was lower than for the RBF.

3.2   Multi-Layer Perceptron ANN (MLP)

MLP is the first ANN topology used. We present the training algorithm for a hidden layer in Fig. 2, which is an adaption of the algorithm in [11].

An MLP ANN was used with a 4-10-4 configuration (4 input neurons, 10 hidden and 4 output). We also used 80% of tickets available for training, 10% for validation and the other 10% for testing, to verify that the results given by the ANN were satisfactory if reserved; this is what is defined as the process of overfitting (Training, Validation, Testing). The confusion matrix resulting in this process showed 99.2% of correct classifications.

Figure 3, shows the point where the square error of these two variables matches. It can be found at the beginning of the network and it adapts progressively to the learning set, thus adapting itself to the problem.

```
MLP_ANN()
Selection of the number of neurons in the hidden layer
Initialization of weights W
    Do
    For (each of the data Xi) do
        To calculate the exit for the first layer
```

$$G_j = f\left(\sum_{i=1}^{N} X_i W_{hji} + W_{hjB}\right)$$

To calculate the total exit

$$F_j = f\left(\sum_{i=1}^{k} G_i W_{Oji} + W_{OjB}\right)$$

```
    EndFor
    For (each of the exit Fj for all j since 1 to M) do
        To calculate the error
```

$$\varepsilon_{Oj} = \left(Y_j - F_j\right)\left[F_j\left(1 - F_j\right)\right]$$

```
    EndFor
    While the termination condition is reached
End MLP_ANN()
```

Fig. 2. Algorithm MLP ANN

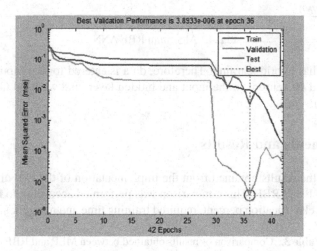

Fig. 3. Evolution of learning error of MLP ANN

This training provided satisfactory results due to the right grouping of the input data, according to the visual problem type.

3.3 Radial Basis Function ANN (RBF)

RBF is a network with Gaussian activation functions. The training algorithm for this network is an adaption of the algorithm in [11] and it is presented in Fig. 4.

RBF ANN()
    Selection of the number of neurons of the hidden layer

    Initialization of ω_i (Center of the RBF)
    Do

    For (each of the data X_i) do
       To assign X_i a θ_i(cluster) such that $\|X_i - \omega_i\|^2$ be the
           minimum between the parallel
    EndFor

    For (each cluster θ_i) do

$$\omega_i = \frac{1}{\|\theta_j\|}\Sigma_{j\in\theta_j}X_j$$

    EndFor

    While none the X_i switch cluster

    Find the variance of the data using

$$\sigma_i^2 = \frac{1}{|\theta_j|-1}\Sigma_{X=\theta_j}(X - \omega_i)^T(X - \omega_i)$$

Find the weights of the exit layer using
$$W^T = \varphi^T T$$
End RBF_ANN()

Fig. 4. Algorithm RBF ANN

This ANN has hybrid learning. Therefore, data is entered for the input and hidden layers. We used 40 neurons in the input and hidden layer, and we used Gaussian activation function.

4 Experiments and Results

We compared the results obtained from the implementation of the two different ANN topologies, MLP and RBF. This comparison was performed according to features such as the accurate classification percent, required training time and network size (Table 3).

Table 3. Comparison of results obtained between MLP and RBF

Description	MLP	RBF
Number of neurons optimal for the hidden layer	10	40
Network training time	40 s	120 s
Number of iterations made in training	42	420
Average classification rate	75%	73%
Average error	1,0416%	1,0408%

Once the results of the simulations of MLP and RBF were obtained and analyzed, it can be observed that MLP is closer to the expected results during the performed evaluation. RBF is discarded also due to its complexity in processing and implementation whiting the game engine that we used.

Besides being recognized due to its proximity in the actions to be performed, MLP is known by its quick classification of datasets. This is a desirable property in order to satisfy the constraints of the Virtual Environment to achieve the real time feature.

Later, we implemented the MLP in the state machines integrated within the source code of the game engine. The idea was to perform several operations withing a controlled work environment. The scenario describes some offices where several warning signals occur. When the result of the RNA is 1, some if the previously described signals (perceptions) is present (Fig. 5). Therefore, some action needs to be performed to address this situation (Fig. 6).

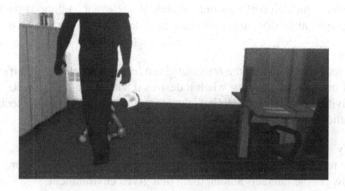

Fig. 5. Character identifying the wet floor (Perception)

Fig. 6. Character calling the cleaning staff (Action Run)

We used some qualitative and quantitative metrics [12] and some concepts suggested by [13] for the IVE performance evaluation. For the qualitative evaluation, we used the following metrics: interactivity, connectivity, adaptability and sensitivity to the context. For the quantitative evaluation, the metrics were latency and scalability.

4.1   Qualitative Evaluation

Next, we present the explanation of the qualitative metrics that we selected and adapted for the evaluation of the implemented ANN

Interactivity
This feature is related to the reduction of explicit interaction given that the system uses its intelligence, to infer from the observed the situations and needs of the character.

The interactivity in the ANN is high. The way how the calculations are arranged cause that the RNA has a high level of interactivity because when it perceives a given state in the environment, it performs immediately the relevant operations without variations in the graphical section, thus providing confidence in the performed operation.

Connectivity
This feature focuses on finding the freedom given to the character so that it can choose what type of information it wants, when it desires it and where it desires it.

Connectivity in the ANN is High. Calculations arranged within the technique are performed efficiently, at a high rate of perception.

Adaptability
This features refers to the adaptable nature of the environments. This features is mainly related to how people interacts among them in a given environment.

Adaptability in the ANN is high. Due to the way how this technique was implemented in the environment, it can be seen how it can learn to perform and adapt to it in a fast and agile way.

Sensitivity to the Context
A system is context-sensitive if it uses the context to provide relevant information or services to the user. Relevance depends on the task that the user performs.

The Sensitivity to the Context in ANN is High. The way in which perceptions are effectively identified and what decision to make in a given case makes this technique highly sensitive because it knows where it is and what it should do in specific cases.

4.2   Quantitative Evaluation

Next, we present the explanation of each one of the quantitative metrics that we selected and adapted for the evaluation of the ANN

Latency or Environment Response Time
This metric is defined as the time that takes to the environment to perform one or more tasks oriented to achieve the adaption of the character present in the environment.

The measurements in this metric were taking considering the time that takes to perform all the assigned operations (real-time execution) in a render engine with a determined number of iterations for each frame drawn on the screen. That is, if the character requests to recalculate the current technique, this is performed integrally within a single frame.

The render engines aim to reach 60 frames in one second. Each frame has a presence in screen of approximately 0.016 s (1 s/60 frames = 0.016), this the operation must be performed in a way that does not affect the frame rate per second. To demonstrate the measures of frames per second, the samples are taken while the application is running, through one of the UDK commands and it displays the data of frames per seconds and milliseconds in real time, according to the machine in the which is running.

In order to evaluate the latency, we took some samples. The ANN was run 10 times and we took samples to show how many repetitions are required to move to the next action. As few iterations required, the application is more optimized.

The ANN achieved low response time. This shows high similarity when compared to human learning. Every time the character has a perception, it must compare the initial results against the actions to be taken. If these actions are wrong, the it must recalculate the previously generated curve.

It can be seen from the sample that it does not affect the performance in frames per second. Thus, it can be said that every time a recalculation is performed, it takes between 16 and 19 ms to be performed.

In Table 4, we show a summary of the time taken to reason in each perception in order to take the appropriate action.

Table 4. Error! No text of specified style in document. Recurrent latency for RNA

Perception	Number of Repetitions	Latency (Seconds)
Detects Fire	2	40,19
Detects Electrical Risk	0	2,82
Detects wet floor	0	0,85
Workplace - Do not know what to do	0	0,75

Scalability

Scalability determines how IVE performance varies when the number of tasks to be performed increases. Its measurement is based on determining in what proportion the latency time is altered. For its measurement, Eq. 2 is defined (Eq. 2).

$$E_s = \frac{l_{max} - l_{min}}{n_{total}} \tag{2}$$

where, l_{max} and l_{min} are the maximum and minimum values of latency respectively and n_{total} is the total number of tasks. Scalability is associated with one of the following qualitative values:

- Good Scalability: When the Eq. 3 is satisfied (Eq. 3).

$$\Delta E_s = \frac{E_s current - E_s previous}{E_s previous} < 0.5 \tag{3}$$

- Deficient Scalability: When the Eq. 4 is satisfied (Eq. 4).

$$\Delta E_s = \frac{E_s current - E_s previous}{E_s previous} > 0.5 \tag{4}$$

Where E_s current is the scalability by increasing the number of tasks and E_s previous is scalability without increasing them.

For the case of ANN implemented, a good scalability was presented and given minutes/task, as can be seen in Table 5.

Table 5. Scalability in ANN

E_s current	E_s previous	E_s	Value
1,23	1,19	0,03	Good scalability

5   Conclusions

ANN have provided several contributions in different fields because they can perform diagnosis using patterns. This diagnosis helps to make more agile some procedures, for instance, in dynamic behaviors such as the ones present in work environments. In those fields where real time results are required and there is a given limit of number of operations by cycle (Which is the case in Virtual Reality Applications), Neural Networks provide high performance with low costs. That is to say, a very high level of learning and optimization can be obtained without sacrificing performance and without requiring very high technical specifications, which is ideal for its applicability in Virtual Reality.

References

1. Lozano, M.: Animación Comportamental de Personajes Inteligentes 3D basada en MINIMIN-HSP. Tesis Doctoral, Universitat de Valéncia, España (2004)
2. Whiting, J., Dinerstein, J., Egbert, P.K., Ventura, D.: Cognitive and behavioral model ensembles for autonomous virtual characters. Comput. Intell. **26**(2), 142–159 (2010)
3. Jia, L., Zhenjiang, M.: Entertainment oriented intelligent virtual environment with agent and neural networks. In: IEEE International Workshop on Haptic Audio Visual Environments and their Applications, Ottawa, Canada (2007)
4. Clemente, J., Ramirez, J., De Antonio, A.: Applying a student modeling with non-monotonic diagnosis to intelligent virtual environment for training/instruction. Expert Syst. Appl. **41**(2), 508–520 (2014). Elsevier
5. Xi, M., Smith, S.: Simulating cooperative fire evacuation training in a virtual environment using gaming technology. In: IEEE Virtual Reality 2014, Minneapolis, Minnesota, USA, pp. 139–140. IEEE (2014)
6. Liu, W., Zhou, L., Xing, W., Liu, X., Yuan, B.: Creating autonomous, perceptive and intelligent virtual humans in a real-time virtual environment. Tsinghua Sci. Technol. **16**(3), 233–240 (2011)
7. Gilbert, R., Forney, A.: Can avatars pass the Turing test? Intelligent agent perception in a 3D virtual environment. Int. J. Hum.-Comput. Stud. **73**, 30–36 (2015)

8. Cavazza, M., Lugrin, J.-L., Hartley, S., Renard, M., Nandi, A., Jacobson, J., Crooks, S.: Intelligent virtual environments for virtual reality art. Comput. Graph. **29**(6), 852–861 (2005). Elsevier

9. Martinho, C., Paiva, A., Gomes, M.: Emotions for a motion: rapid development of believable panthematic agents in intelligent virtual environments. Appl. Artif. Intell. **14**, 33–68 (2000)

10. Mang-Xian, Q., Hai-ming, Y.: Investigation and realization of multi-agent interaction behavior in intelligent virtual environment. In: International Conference on Cyberworlds. IEEE Computer Society (2008)

11. García, J., Carmona, E., Gallardo, L., González, M., Fernández, A., González, M.: Desarrollo de un sistema automático de discriminación del campo visual glaucomotoso basado en un clasificador neuro-fuzzy. En Rev. Scielo **77**(12), 669–676 (2002). Archivos de la Sociedad Española de Oftalmología

12. Restrepo, S.: Modelo de Inteligencia Ambiental basado en la integración de Redes de Sensores Inalámbricas y Agentes Inteligentes. Tesis de Maestría. Universidad Nacional de Colombia - Sede Medellín (2012)

13. Zhang, D.: Multi-agent based control of large-scale complex systems emplying distributed dynamic inference engine. Ph.D. thesis. Georgia Institute of Technology (2010)

Digital Map Table VR: Bringing an Interactive System to Virtual Reality

Gunnar Strentzsch[1], Florian van de Camp[2(✉)], and Rainer Stiefelhagen[1]

[1] Karlsruhe Institute of Technology, Karlsruhe, Germany
gunnar.strentzsch@student.kit.edu,
rainer.stiefelhagen@kit.edu
[2] Fraunhofer IOSB, Karlsruhe, Germany
florian.vandecamp@iosb.fraunhofer.de

Abstract. Virtual Reality has the potential to replace large, multi-screen systems due to cost, flexibility, and mobility. It is desireable to keep interaction concepts from existing systems in virtual reality and avoid having to recreate existing software solutions. We recreated an interactive table in virtual reality using the same software used for the hardware table and conducted a user study to compare the two systems. Users were able to complete all tasks on both systems and results show little difference regarding preference between the two systems. While only a few of the advantages of virtual reality were taken advantage of, the results are promising for virtual display environments in general.

Keywords: Virtual reality · Interaction · Touchscreens · User study

1 Introduction

1.1 Motivation for Simulating a Real Touchscreen System in Virtual Reality

The digLT is a large table surface screen allowing multi-hand, multi-finger gesture-based touch interaction with the displayed map data and other interactive elements [11,12,14,25]. Virtual reality (VR) systems using headsets have been around for a long time, [20] but recent developments have led to high quality and comparatively cheap virtual reality experiences as well as driven an increased development of new complementing interaction systems, e.g. for the recognition of the hand poses [5]. We replicated the digLT system within a virtual environment using such VR technologies, essentially simulating the current system and its capabilities virtually, which has the potential for some advantages over the existing system:

- The virtual reality enables users to work collaboratively from remote locations, their virtual presence, or telepresence [16], preserving the important modalities such as gesturing to other users, pointing at map contents, etc., or enable users to participate in situation briefings from afar without entering the workspace.

© Springer International Publishing AG 2017
S. Lackey and J. Chen (Eds.): VAMR 2017, LNCS 10280, pp. 54–71, 2017.
DOI: 10.1007/978-3-319-57987-0_5

- Given the VR systems' capabilities, display and interaction may in the future not only be replicated but also enhanced by the display of and hands-free interaction with three-dimensional data such as 3D heightmaps, entire three-dimensional building plans or a street view of an area. Also, information displayed in the room would not be bound to the location of hardware screens but could be put anywhere in the environment according to a user's choice and preference or according to user-evaluated efficiency-optimized layouts. Information needed by only a single user might be omitted from the view of other users.
- The simulation of arbitrary environments could increase the users' acceptance of the workplace, and possibly eliminate distractions posed by nearby objects which are not part of the purpose of the workspace.
- The hardware of the current digLT system is comparatively large, heavy and expensive. Replacing the large touchscreen with a virtual reality system comprised of a head mounted device (HMD) and a couple of small, lightweight sensors would increase the viability of the system for users who need lower cost, an increased mobility or quick setup of the system.

1.2   Objectives for Implementation of the VR System

To evaluate the viability of a VR system for the direct replacement of the digLT situation table, the table and its fundamental map interaction concepts are replicated in a virtual environment, using a tracked HMD display and hand recognition.

A VR system that may simulate all relevant interaction needs to put the user into a virtual environment in an immersive way, ideally mimicking reality completely. To preserve a user's perception and apply the same interaction concepts as used in the real system, it must take into account that the interaction with the system is largely body centered, regarding gestural and touch interaction with the screen, but also cooperation with other users [11]. As [18] argues, the user's ability to interact in such a way relies fundamentally on his own proprioception, an internal, mental model of his own body. Ideally, this model should be supported with the same virtually generated or passively provided sensory cues that come with having a body and interacting in reality. We implement a VR system as an exploratory prototype towards these ideal aims. It enables the user to see his own hands and feel objects touched. A digLT surface dummy is placed in co-location with a virtual representation of the digLT to passively provide haptic feedback (See Fig. 1).

Fig. 1. Usage of the 'real' digLT system and its VRLT simulation with a cloth-covered haptic surface dummy

2 Related Work

Hand Interaction with the Digital Situation Table (digLT). [6] describes the advantages of a direct hand-based interaction concept with displays in contrast to interaction in which a user needs to manipulate additional devices. The evaluation of optically well discriminable hand poses leading to a hand gesture interaction set used for the digLT system, which is robust against unintended interaction, is described. Stationary camera systems for optical hand recognition are used.

Interaction with VR Systems. [5] describes current low-cost consumer VR systems, providing a taxonomy of current hardware developments, listing input and output devices by their capabilities.

As a possible low-cost component of a room-scaled VR system, the Microsoft Kinect system has been used to demonstrate full "smooth" hand tracking including finger movement [22], but of course depends on the visibility of the hand from the sensor's perspective.

Using free-hand interaction in a head-tracking enabled VR system, [15] find that users prefer gestural interaction with objects over a controller-based approach. [7] use free-hand interaction with 3D-modelled objects visualized in a head-tracked VR system, finding that users found the interaction simple and natural, although the models displayed could not be touched. While not providing full force feedback for touched objects, [19] describes a free-hand system

using hand tracking and providing tactile feedback enabling the user to differentiate between different "textures" of virtually touched objects by shooting air
vortices at a user's skin at the point of interaction.

3 Implementation

3.1 Integration of Elements into the Virtual Environment

For an overview, please refer to Fig. 2: On the left, entities and interaction in
the real world are shown, in the middle, the method of transporting entities and
interactions from and to the virtual environment are shown, and on the right
side, the virtually simulated entities and interactions are shown. The digLT's
surface and display capabilities are grayed out since only a digLT dummy is
placed in the real world, providing a physical surface with identical dimensions
for its virtually co-located VRLT representation. Hand movement and thus touch
interaction is transported via the hand tracking device and hands are displayed
in the virtual environment, the hand interaction is detected within the virtual
environment, and a corresponding touch signal sent to the IVIG map software.
The software's map display is shown on the VRLT model's surface. The user
perceives and moves his field of view through the virtual environment via an
HMD, which is head tracked.

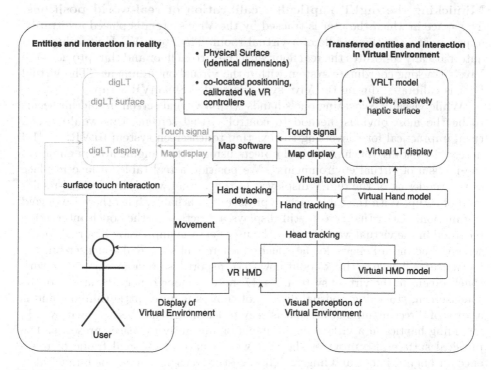

Fig. 2. Transport of interaction and perception concepts from reality to virtual reality.

Mimicking the digLT optically: the VRLT. The entire project is built within a 3D room environment set up and rendered within the game engine Unity. The environment chosen to give the user a general frame of reference (floor, walls, and ceiling of a futuristic corridor and the lighting of the environment) was taken from an example scene provided for the game engine [4]. To mimic the user's real-world digLT experience in VR, a 3D model representing the digLT optically was built for and placed in the virtual environment. This virtual situation table (VRLT) model's surface layer was programmed to display the IVIG situation table software by copying the current display of the computer running the whole system to the surface layer texture.

Due to early availability of the system and the high quality of its technological capabilities, an HTC Vive HMD system [2] was used to provide for display and navigation through the virtual environment. The Vive is sold commercially and designed for end user comfort, uses low latency head tracking for navigation through the virtual environment and provides a 110° field of view updated with 90 frames per second [24]. Thus, the Vive provides a maximally natural and efficient means of navigation. The Vive also provides a fundamental safety function of displaying boundaries of the virtually traversable world where physical obstacles in the real world are located.

Mimicking the digLT haptically: calibration of real-world positions. The space in which the user is tracked by the Vive system is placed arbitrarily, approximately in the middle of a virtual room. The SteamVR Unity plugin [1] automatically co-locates the real floor with the virtual floor and thus provides the Vive's tracking coordinate system within the virtual environment. (The virtual floor is calibrated during the Vive system's guided SteamVR setup).

While visually colocating one's hands with a virtual screen in mid-air seems to be the most obvious method to control virtual screens, this would be, in turn, impractical for converting the existing touchscreen system to VR. As [10] notes, "Physically touching virtual objects using tactile augmentation enhances the realism of virtual environments". We position a real table surface in place of the rendering of the digLT displayed in the virtual world, in a mixed-reality kind of setup. With the table surface physically touchable, but otherwise devoid of function, the virtual screen still displays a reaction to the touch interaction recorded in the virtual world so that the user gets the impression of a real touchscreen. The more believable the touchscreen resembles a real touchscreen, the less a user will have to think about how to transport his previous experience with touchscreens to the virtual system. As [17] notes, among other advantages of the touchscreen, "touching a visual display of choices requires little thinking and is a form of direct manipulation that is easy to learn". As has been shown by [13], including haptics in a virtual environment significantly increases presence. The physical surface also provides the user with a natural physical frame of reference for angling hands and fingers. Thus, gesture recognition can be mimicked as closely as possible to the existing touchscreen's gesture set. In respect to possible future conversions of touchscreen systems to VR, this is, of course, to be desired, as the conception and validation of a gesture set are not trivial (an example for the digLT gesture set conception can be found in [6], p. 60). Furthermore, the user will be less fatigued, since the surface provides rest for arms and fingers so they need not be held up constantly. The dimension of movement is reduced to lifting the arms and letting them down onto the surface, instead of having to use force to stop hand movement in the position of a merely virtual screen. As [21] found, the colocation of virtually seen objects with physical feedback also increases users performance when interacting with them. Lastly, since the recognition of intended touch interaction with the virtual screen is not actually done by touch recognition, but rather by a measurement of the user's hand positioning within a small interaction area above the screen surface, the movement to remove the hands from the interaction area can not be distinguished from movement intended for interaction. If the user lifts a hand 'upwards' and out of the interaction area, if the movement is not perfectly perpendicular to the screen surface, the hand may also unwantedly be moved 'sidewards', resulting in an unwanted sidewards interaction with the virtual screen. Providing a physical surface reduces the vertical layer size of the interaction area in which the user's hands can move and thus reduces the potential for such unwanted interaction.

Thus, the real digLT system's surface covered with a cloth was used to provide the passive haptic representation, a touchable dummy, of the virtual screen in the real world. Using the Vive system provided the possibility to use the included controllers to calibrate the virtual table's position to match the dummy's position. The controllers' virtual models match their real world dimensions.

For calibration, the VRLT model's surface position is virtually attached to the bounds of a controller. The VRLT is placed in the approximate position of the dummy by laying this controller upon the dummy's surface. Then, the second controller can be used to test the VRLT's position by holding it to the dummy's physical bounds. If the VRLT's position is off, its bounds can iteratively be matched to the digLT's bounds by moving the controller lying upon the real digLT and repeated probing. As soon as the surfaces are satisfyingly co-located, the virtual position is locked in.

Displaying a user's hands virtually: interaction with the VRLT. To provide for object manipulation, a Leap Motion controller [3] for the detection and display of the users' hands in the Virtual environment was used, providing a most direct correspondence between the physical and virtual world, practically enabling the user to interact with the virtual environment and objects naturally, as he may interact with them in the real world. The low latency and robustness of tracking, both of which have been shown to be at a reasonably high quality [23,27], provide the user with a visible hand. This may increase the sense of proprioception for his virtual body parts and enables him to have "direct contact" with virtual objects, increasing his sense of Presence.

The hands are visualized by virtual hand models following the user's tracked movements within the virtual world. By attaching the device to the front of the HMD as specified, the Leap Motion Orion plugin for Unity infers the origin of the LeapMotion's coordinate system from the position of the headset, thus no further calibration is needed. The virtual hands' position and gesture were then used to trigger interactions upon the VRLT when the user would virtually bring his hands down upon the VRLT's surface, by sending appropriate signals to the IVIG software. Since both the user's hands and their virtual counterparts, as well as the VRLT and the physical table's surface, are co-located, this could be perceived by the user much like the touch of a touch-screen. The interaction was detected within a physical margin of tolerance, a thin interactive layer or 'interaction area' above the virtual table's surface, because of the expected, but minor imprecision of both tracking systems. The physical surface also naturally prompts the user to hold his hands in poses more plainly visible to the Leap Motion system, which aids the device's capacity to detect the finger poses for the intended set of gestures.

Since the imprecisions of the Leap Motion sensor seem to largely depend on the distance of the user's hands from his body, this systematic error was offset by recalibrating the VRLT's height for each user until touching the VRLT with the virtual hands would coincide with touching the physical table's surface with the real hands. Offsetting the point of touch seen in the virtual world to the point of touch felt in the physical world intends to 'fool' the user into truly perceiving the virtual representation of his hands as his own, proprioceptively [26].

As an additional visual cue for the user, the position of the users' index fingers' fingertips was projected perpendicularly onto the table surface, where a thin vertical bar extending from the table surface to the top of the interaction layer was displayed. Also, when interaction was detected, a floating text was displayed in a position above his hands, displaying the name of the type of interaction currently detected (See Fig. 3).

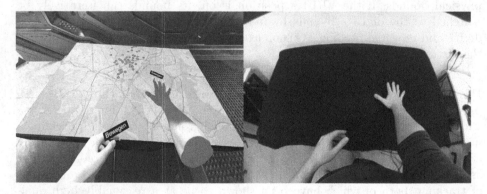

Fig. 3. User performing the map movement gesture on the VRLT. Left: VRLT and user's virtual hands in virtual environment. Right: Photographic image taken from the HTC Vive's internal camera.

Interaction Gestures. Three chosen fundamental interactions and their corresponding gesturing were implemented to mimic the digLT's interaction concept as closely as possible. Gestures were differentiated simply by discretely deciding if a finger is stretched out. The state of the finger was derived from the "finger angles", an estimate of the degree of bending of the metacarpophalangeal joints provided by the LeapMotion.

A gesture was then detected by comparing the list of currently stretched out fingers with a list of fingers that have to be stretched out for a certain gesture.

To move the map, the user puts one hand flat, with all fingers stretched out (as opposed to bent to the position they would have when the user makes a fist), onto the table's surface. The hand with all fingers stretched out is recognized by the system as the map movement gesture. Upon putting the hand within the interaction area, 'touching' it to the virtual table, the appropriate signals are sent to the IVIG software to make the map follow the hand's movement, keeping the map below the user's hand. Upon removing the hand from the surface and out of the interaction area, the interaction stops and the map is at rest again.

To initiate the zoom interaction, the original digLT's zoom gesture had to be replaced. The original zoom gesture consisted of the index and middle fingers of both hands stretched out and tilted away from each other, which was frequently tracked improperly, as either only one finger stretched out or all non-thumb fingers stretched out. Thus, the zoom interaction gesture for the VRLT was replaced by having both hands' fingers stretched out in the same way as for the move gesture. Upon entering the interaction area with two hands with stretched out fingers the IVIG software would zoom the map in if the user would move his hands closer to each other and zoom out when he would move them away from each other. As with the original IVIG software, the map would zoom in and out on its center. Removing either of the hands from the interaction area would stop interaction.

Lastly, to initiate the rotation interaction, the user places one hand with stretched out fingers as in the movement gesture and one hand with only the index finger stretched out and the other fingers clenched into a fist into the interaction area. Upon moving the hand with the stretched out finger, the map is rotated around an estimated point in the middle of the hand with the stretched out fingers by the angle that the finger is moved around the hand center relatively to its previous position. Removing the hands from the interaction area stops the movement.

The hand's recognized movement was interpolated and large jumps, indicating tracking errors, were ignored.

4   Evaluation

4.1   Hypotheses and Questions

To assess the viability of the VR system, digLT and VRLT systems were compared in multiple categories for their usability as perceived by the participants of the user study we conducted. The study covers the capability to interact with and view the map data in an efficient way, with the digLT being used as a base-line that the VR system is compared to. The fundamental hypothesis tested in each category was thus generally a variation of "H0: Users do not perceive a difference between aspects of the systems", which were tested against their alternatives, "H1: Users perceive a difference between aspects of the systems".

As a central question of this evaluation, the study's participants were asked if the system enabled them to fulfill an interaction task sets using each of the systems, as detailed below.

To further assess the quality of interaction, the study participants were asked about the differences they perceived in workload factors (as assessed by the NASA TLX subscales) as well as precision of interaction and functioning of system components.

4.2   Procedure

Preparation. Before every evaluation session, the system was set up and cal-ibrated as described in Implementation, Sect. 3. The IVIG map software was setup in the same starting state both on the machine running the virtual envi-ronment and the real digLT to display a map overlayed with information element icons (see Fig. 4).

An evaluation session consisted of seven phases, a demonstration phase, a questionnaire phase concerning demographic information, a familiarization and explanation phase, a task execution phase on one system, a questionnaire phase

Fig. 4. A typical map overlaid with information symbols, provided by the IVIG soft-ware.

concerning the previous phase, a task execution phase for the second system, and a questionnaire phase concerning the second system and a comparison of the systems, as detailed below.

Demonstration. Upon arrival, study participants were given a short explanation of the purpose and interaction capabilities of both systems in random order by the study's conductor, who curtly demonstrated their function.

Questionnaires. Following demonstration, participants were asked to begin answering a questionnaire. All questionnaires were presented on a computer using a computer mouse and a keyboard. This phase's questionnaire concerned their physiological and demographic data.

Familiarization and explanation. The participants were then asked to familiarize themselves with the systems by operating them themselves. The study's conductor explained the system's function and taught users how to optimally utilize the system for interacting with the map.

Afterwards, an explanation of the questions that would follow each of the two following task phases was given, closely following the NASA TLX instruction manual [9]. Notably, the study's conductor asked the participants to emphasize on trying to record and compare their experience of usability of the systems as precisely as possible, keeping in mind how they answered for the first tested system.

The interaction and questionnaire phases following were randomized in order to even out or omit effects of fatigue and task familiarity interfering with the evaluation.

Task set execution on first system. The study conductor then gave the participants a task set made of four stages with multiple short tasks to move, zoom and rotate the map and finally use all interaction gestures in combined tasks. In a single task, the participants were asked to update the display of the map (e.g., 'Move the information elements displayed to the upper left corner of the display area' as one of the movement tasks during the first stage). The participants were told that their execution of the task was not going to be objectively rated since the tasks' purpose was to give the participants an impression of usability. Participants indicated their completion of a task by their own assessment. To give the participants a feeling of how much time they needed to complete a task, the conductor would stop them after thirty seconds, offering once to reset the map for a single task.

Questionnaire for first system. Using the questionnaire, the participants were asked to now rate their experience, keeping in mind that the purpose of the study was a comparison between the two systems, emphasizing on the positive or negative intensity of their perceptions.

Repetition for second system and final questionnaire. After finishing the questionnaire, the second task execution phase would be started off and after the tasks' execution, the second questionnaire was done, including a final part that let the participants compare the systems to each other directly.

4.3   Participants and Demographics

The study took place in Germany, and all of the study's 28 participants were German, speaking German as their first language. 22 were male, 6 female, almost all having achieved general qualification for university entrance/being students, 9 having a university degree, 16 coming from a MINT/STEM background.

10 participants were 170–179 cm tall, 13 gave their size as 180–189 cm, 3 participants were smaller than 169 cm, 2 were taller than 190 cm.

Participants were mainly young adults and middle-aged adults, 12 aged 18–24, 10 aged 25–34, 5 aged 25–64 and 1 aged older than 75. By own assessment, none of the participants reported extreme physical or mental unfitness, extreme susceptibility to getting sick or dizzy easily, nor *"any sort of physical, mental or health impairment that might have influence on the usage of a large screen, hand-based interaction with a screen, or wearing a headbound headset that covers the eyes"*, except for sight impairments.

15 participants reported sight impairments (mostly short-sightedness), 5 of whom explicitly stated after familiarization that they preferred to evaluate the systems keeping their glasses on (including under the HMD), and 3 stating to prefer not using glasses (reporting being only mildly seeing impaired).

One participant reported having only one eye, but tested the VR system and indicated having a realistic experience. One other user had to remove his varifocals during evaluation, since it required him to change head pose to see sharply, which disabled him from using the system with his glasses on.

All of the participants reported at least a bit of experience and knowledge about technology and accessories as well as previous experience with touch-screens, 7 of the participants reported previous experience with head-mounted VR systems and 7 reported previous experience with optical body pose recognition systems.

4.4   Statistical Analysis Method

All answers were given on seven-point Likert-scales for comparative questions and nine-point Likert-scales for the TLX subscale questions, exceptions are noted. To analyze Likert-type data, i.e. qualitative ordinal scales, non-parametric methods are used.

Results are visualized as boxplots (showing median, range of values and quartiles of the collected data) overlaid with swarmplots showing all data points. To derive qualitative impressions of user tendency for the systems, the differences between the answers given on the nine point scales for the TLX subscales and the seven-point scales for all other questions are shown.

Differences are calculated by subtracting the answers for the VR system from those for the digLT system. Positive values can give the intuition of being "in favor of the VR system", negative answers "in favor of the digLT system".

Note that a "magnitude of difference" between the systems cannot be absolutely inferred from these differences since the ordinal, non-metric scaling does not provide a "fixed unit" of strength of impression across evaluation participants. E.g., two participants rating the difference between the systems "very large" and "very slight" on the frustration scale, corresponding to 4 vs. 1 point of difference in rating, may perceive the difference as equally large, but their a priori interpretation of the frustration scale may differ in its "range" or their total tolerance for frustration, depending on personal predisposition.

The significance of differences between answers for both systems is analyzed by employing the nonparametric Wilcoxon signed rank test for matched pairs [8]. The test statistic is the Z-value, analyzed for significance resulting in a p-value, which will signal significance of the H0 hypotheses when $p < 0.05$. As often done in other publications, the results were also analyzed analogously using t-testing, giving t- and p- values which were also tested for $p < 0.05$; this showed statistical significance of the differences for the same categories as the aforementioned Wilcoxon test and will thus not be reported separately.

4.5 Results and Interpretation

In this section, for each of the evaluated categories, the results, the statistical analysis and the interpretation of results are presented.

Task Fulfillment. Answers to the question, *"Did the system enable you to fulfill the tasks given to you?"*. Answer options were "Yes" or "No", answering was required. Out of the 28 participants, all answered "Yes" for the digLT system. For the VRLT system, 26 participants answered "Yes", two answered "No". Barring very specific cases, the VR system enabled the users to use the VR system in a way that resembled the digLT system closely. Depending on circumstances, the system is a viable alternative to the classical system.

Differences in NASA TLX Subscales. Using the statistical analysis on the results from Fig. 5, Table 1 shows that the hypothesis "H0: The participant's impression of [NASA TLX Subscale] is equal on both systems" is accepted for Mental Demand, Physical Demand, Temporal Demand and Frustration. It is rejected and alternative H1: "The participant's impression of [NASA TLX Subscale] differs on both systems" accepted for Performance and Effort.

The difference is significant and the effect size showing a large decrease of participants' performance for the VR system as compared to the digLT system, while the significant difference for effort shows a negligible effect size for effort differences for the VR system. For the other factors of workload, the perceived differences between VR and digLT systems are not statistically significant.

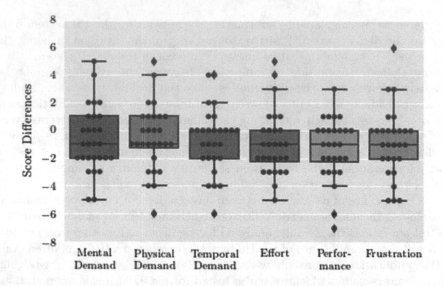

Fig. 5. NASA TLX subscales

Table 1. Statistical analysis – Wilcoxon signed rank test for matched pairs – TLX subscales

NASA TLX Subscale	Z	p	r_C
Mental Demand	−1.633	0.102	−0.102
Physical Demand	−1.195	0.232	−0.052
Temporal Demand	−1.503	0.133	−0.051
Performance	−2.860	0.004	−0.525
Effort	−2.131	0.033	0.019
Frustration	−1.880	0.060	0.067

Differences in Precision of Interaction. Using the statistical analysis on the results from Fig. 6, Table 2 shows that the hypothesis "H0: Users perceive the precision of interaction as equal" is accepted only for *Panning Precision*, and rejected in favor of the alternative hypothesis "H1: Users perceive the precision of interaction as inequal" for *Zooming Precision, Rotation Precision* and *Combined Tasks Precision*. The significant differences for the zoom and rotation interaction precisions have a small and moderate effect size showing decreased precision for the VR system; consequently, the effect size for the combined tasks precision was in between.

Differences in Functioning. Using the statistical analysis on the results from Fig. 7, Table 3 shows that the hypothesis "H0: Users perceive the functioning of the systems as equal" is rejected for all functioning categories but *graphic*

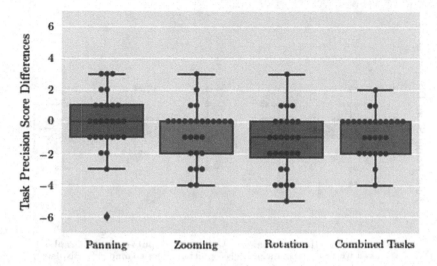

Fig. 6. Rating differences of perceived precision per task category

Table 2. Statistical analysis – Wilcoxon signed rank test for matched pairs – Precision

Precision task categories	Z	p	r_C
Panning Precision	−0.053	0.957	0.127
Zooming Precision	−2.088	0.037	−0.250
Rotation Precision	−3.256	0.001	−0.421
Combined Tasks Precision	−2.583	0.010	−0.333

display in favor its alternative hypothesis "H1: Users perceive the functioning of the systems as inequal". The differences between the functioning of the systems are significantly perceptible, mostly palpable in subcategories, as the difference in the functioning of the *system as a whole* shows a weak effect size. The strongest effect size shows for *recognition of hand movement*, showing a large proneness to erroneous behavior for the VRLT system. *Recognition of performed gesture* has a small effect size showing a performance worse on the VRLT with a small degree. *Transfer of input to the map* however seems to even function a little better on the VRLT, showing a small effect size.

4.6   Participant Comments

The participants were very excited for the innovation of the system, praising the potential of the VR system's capabilities. When participants were asked to imagine long-term use of the system, they perceive hand interaction imprecisions and detection errors as well as HMD encumbrance and image quality as the most detrimental technical hurdles.

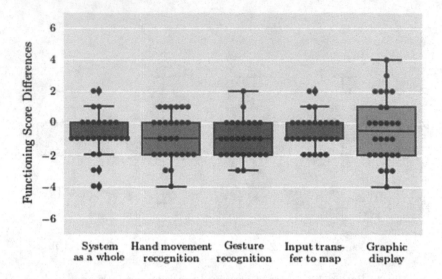

Fig. 7. Rating differences of perceived function per system component.

Table 3. Statistical analysis – Wilcoxon signed rank test for matched pairs – Functioning

System components functioning	Z	p	r_C
Errors system as a whole	−2.523	0.012	0.029
Errors hand movement recognition	−2.923	0.003	−0.733
Errors gesture recognition	−3.411	0.001	−0.132
Errors input transfer to map	−2.086	0.037	0.167
Errors graphic display	−1.103	0.270	0.018

5 Conclusion

The digLT situation table, a large touch-screen, and its map interaction concepts were replicated in a virtual environment, as directly as possible. Within the environment, the user can see his own hands and physically touch the virtual table. The table provides passive haptic feedback, enabling a proprioceptively guided, body centered interaction. The VR system is evaluated to compare the usability and with the aim of finding necessary improvements toward a system that is perceived as well as the real system.

The evaluation shows that the sensors and systems used, provide the general ability to manipulate maps using the VR system almost on par with the conventional system.

While participants find long-term use of the system problematic because of drawbacks in interaction and encumbrance, VR systems have the liking and excitement of users, who see large promises for increase of usefulness if implementations are optimized and the content displayed makes more imaginative use of the capabilities of VR technologies.

For the VR system proposed, the most directly possible optimizations may include an improved hand detection by fusion of data from the different sensors and the implementation of a more sophisticated existing hand pose detection method. An update of the interaction concept, using a more modern form of gestural interaction with the map, such as keeping the 'touched' points on the map below the user's hands and scaling, rotating and panning the map accordingly, should be evaluated in further studies. As an alternative to optical hand tracking, the use of gloves or tracked controllers may serve as suitable substitutes. The display of the user's own and other users' full body avatars or similar representations of the users' bodies may increase the perceived immersion in the environment and enable cooperation on the system, e.g. via telepresence. Lastly, the display of map data optimized for visibility in the HMD system and the use of three-dimensional map data is a viable improvement.

Using a VR system to simulate the digLT is a cost-effective alternative compared to the existing digLT system and gives the user the ability to deploy an environment providing the digLT capabilities with a much-increased mobility, as well as providing the potential to include functionality unrealizable with the actual touchscreen system.

References

1. Steamvr plugin version 1.1.1. https://www.assetstore.unity3d.com/en/#!/content/32647. Accessed 20 Dec 2016
2. Vive^{TM} – discover virtual reality beyond imagination. http://www.vive.com. Accessed 11 Jan 2016
3. Leap motion – mac & pc motion controller for games, design, virtual reality & more (2016). https://www.LeapMotion.com/. Accessed 11 Jan 2016
4. Unity – asset store (2016). https://www.assetstore.unity3d.com/. Accessed 11 Jan 2016
5. Anthes, C., García-Hernández, R.J., Wiedemann, M., Kranzlmüller, D.: State of the art of virtual reality technology. In: 2016 IEEE Aerospace Conference, pp. 1–19, March 2016. https://www.researchgate.net/publication/297760223
6. Bader, T.: Multimodale Interaktion in Multi-Display-Umgebungen, vol. 9. KIT Scientific Publishing (2014). http://www.ksp.kit.edu/9783866447608
7. Beattie, N., Horan, B., McKenzie, S.: Taking the leap with the oculus hmd and cad – plucking at thin air? Procedia Technol. **20**, 149–154 (2015). http://www.sciencedirect.com/science/article/pii/S2212017315002029
8. Cohen, B.H.: Explaining Psychological Statistics, 3 edn., pp. 739–743. Wiley, Hoboken (2008)
9. Hart, S., Staveland, L.: Nasa task load index (tlx) v1.0 users manual (1986). https://humansystems.arc.nasa.gov/groups/tlx/
10. Hoffman, H.G.: Physically touching virtual objects using tactile augmentation enhances the realism of virtual environments. In: Proceedings of the IEEE 1998 Virtual Reality Annual International Symposium (Cat. No.98CB36180), pp. 59–63 (1998)

11. Ijsselmuiden, J., Stiefelhagen, R.: Towards high-level human activity recognition through computer vision and temporal logic. In: Dillmann, R., Beyerer, J., Hanebeck, U.D., Schultz, T. (eds.) KI 2010. LNCS (LNAI), vol. 6359, pp. 426–435. Springer, Heidelberg (2010). doi:10.1007/978-3-642-16111-7_49

12. Ijsselmuiden, J., Van De Camp, F., Schick, A., Voit, M., Stiefelhagen, R.: Towards a smart control room for crisis response using visual perception of users. Poster at ISCRAM 2004 (2004)

13. Meehan, M., Insko, B., Whitton, M., Brooks Jr., F.P.: Physiological measures of presence in stressful virtual environments. ACM Trans. Graph. (TOG) 21(3), 645–652 (2002). https://www.researchgate.net/publication/2529722_Physiological_Measures_of_Presence_in_Stressful_Virtual_Environments

14. Peinsipp-Byma, E., Eck, R., Bader, T., Geisler, J.: Teamarbeit am digitalen lagetisch mit fovea-tablett®. MMI-Interaktiv Nr. 12, p. 36, April 2007. http://www.mmi-interaktiv.de/uploads/media/mmiij-vr_02.pdf

15. Pinto, J., Dias, P., Eliseu, S., Santos, B.S.: Interactive configurable virtual environment with kinect navigation and interaction. Atas do 22o Encontro Português de Computação Gráfica e Interação - SciTecIn/EPCGI 2015 (2015). http://www.isr.uc.pt/epubs/epcgi2015.pdf

16. Schloerb, D.W.: A quantitative measure of telepresence. Presence Teleoperators Virtual Environ. 4(1), 64–80 (1995)

17. Shneiderman, B.: Sparks of innovation in human-computer interaction. In: Human/Computer Interaction, Intellect Books, pp. 187–188 (1993). https://books.google.de/books?id=G0AdPjbIoVUC

18. Slater, M., Usoh, M.: Body centred interaction in immersive virtual environments. In: Artificial Life and Virtual Reality, pp. 125–148. John Wiley and Sons (1994)

19. Sodhi, R., Poupyrev, I., Glisson, M., Israr, A.: Aireal: Interactive tactile experiences in free air. ACM Trans. Graph. 32(4), 134:1–134:10 (2013). http://doi.acm.org/10.1145/2461912.2462007

20. Sutherland, I.E.: A head-mounted three dimensional display. In: Proceedings of the Fall Joint Computer Conference, AFIPS 1968, Part I, (Fall, Part I), pp. 757–764. ACM, New York, 9–11 December 1968. http://doi.acm.org/10.1145/1476589.1476686

21. Swapp, D., Pawar, V., Loscos, C.: Interaction with co-located haptic feedback in virtual reality. Virtual Reality 10(1), 24–30 (2006). http://dx.doi.org/10.1007/s10055-006-0027-5

22. Taylor, J., Bordeaux, L., Cashman, T., Corish, B., Keskin, C., Soto, E., Sweeney, D., Valentin, J., Luff, B., Topalian, A., Wood, E., Khamis, S., Kohli, P., Sharp, T., Izadi, S., Banks, R., Fitzgibbon, A., Shotton, J.: Efficient and precise interactive hand tracking through joint, continuous optimization of pose and correspondences. ACM Trans. Graph. (TOG) – Proc. ACM SIGGRAPH 2016 35, 143 (2016)

23. Tung, J.Y., Lulic, T., Gonzalez, D.A., Tran, J., Dickerson, C.R., Roy, E.A.: Evaluation of a portable markerless finger position capture device: accuracy of the leap motion controller in healthy adults. Physiol. Meas. 36(5), 1025 (2015). http://stacks.iop.org/0967-3334/36/i=5/a=1025

24. Vlachos, A.: Advanced vr rendering (2015). http://media.steampowered.com/apps/valve/2015/Alex_Vlachos_Advanced_VR_Rendering_GDC2015.pdf, https://www.youtube.com/watch?v=JO7G38_pxU4

25. Wagner, B., Eck, R., Unmssig, G., Peinsipp-Byma, E.: Interactive analysis of geodata based intelligence. In: Proceedings of SPIE 9825, 98250N, 12 May 2016. http://dx.doi.org/10.1117/12.2222534

26. Ward, J.: Observed touch. Scholarpedia **4**(3), 8251 (2009). http://www. scholarpedia.org/article/Observed_touch, revision

27. Weichert, F., Bachmann, D., Rudak, B., Fisseler, D.: Analysis of the accuracy and robustness of the leap motion controller. Sensors **13**(5), 6380 (2013). http://www.mdpi.com/1424-8220/13/5/6380

Understanding Where to Project Information on the Desk for Supporting Work with Paper and Pen

Mai Tokiwa and Kaori Fujinami[✉]

Department of Computer and Information Sciences,
Tokyo University of Agriculture and Technology,
2-24-16 Naka-cho, Koganei, Tokyo 184-8588, Japan
fujinami@cc.tuat.jp

Abstract. Paper-based work still remains in daily life, and digital information may help such paper-based work. In this paper, we assume an environment, in which a projector presents information on the desk that is used in a transcription task such as filling a form of notification of change of address to post office. We explore the effect of the distance and the direction between the transcription target (printed) and the reference information (projected) on the efficiency and effectiveness. We confirmed that presentation on the upper sides of the transcription target and the area close to the target showed better results (faster task completion and lower error rate), while worse results were observed on the lower right side that was around the dominant hands.

Keywords: Projector · Information presentation · Transcription work · Augmented Reality (AR) · Physical world

1 Introduction

In our daily life, paper-based work still remains even though work with digital documents has become popular. People often need to deal with multiple digital/paper documents to accomplish a task. In this paper, we focus on an environment, in which people work with paper and a pen by referring digital information presented onto a table from a video projector. A use case is that a high school student studies physics with an exercise book by comparing her answer on the notebook with an answer key projected on the desk and correcting wrong answers by a pen. Another scenario is that a person who wants to submit a notification of change of address to the post office writes the (paper) document by referring projected information that is aware of his/her condition. People check if presented number and written one are identical, transcript from projected information to a paper document, and so on. In such cases, gaze switching between document and information may cause problems in task efficiency and precision if it takes too much time to find desired information, as well as

© Springer International Publishing AG 2017
S. Lackey and J. Chen (Eds.): VAMR 2017, LNCS 10280, pp. 72–81, 2017.
DOI: 10.1007/978-3-319-57987-0_6

making mistakes of using incorrect information due to the limitation of human short-term memory.

In this paper, we show a result of investigation on the position of information projection on the desk for efficient and precise pen-based task. The rest of the paper is organized as follows. In Sect. 2, we briefly introduces related work of information annotation in augmented reality. Section 3 presents experiments that intend to explore the relationship between the work performance and the placement of information. In Sect. 4 discuss the result, and finally Sect. 5 concludes the paper.

2   Related Work

Augmented Reality (AR) technology presents information near physical objects or places, or connects between them using a linkage line, which allows information to be related with the physical world [1]. View management techniques have been proposed to improve the visibility of presentation in multiple labels, i.e., information, environment [2,4] and on various background, i.e., contrast, texture, etc. [3]. These work allow a system to find a position of information presentation that a user easily perceives and reads it; however, the condition in which a user is actively involved with the information has not yet been considered well. Here, "active use" is found in the use cases described above, e.g., referring and transcribing presented information, which requires tight hand-eye coordination.

3   Experiment

We investigated the relationship between the work performance and the placement of information.

3.1   Methodology

A transcription task was chosen, in which a subject was asked to transcribe the characters in a specific cell of a printed table from the projected information. Figure 1 shows a scene of this experiment. A blank paper strip is placed at a specific position on the desk, on which the instruction to the subject is presented by a video projector (a). Every time a subject clicks a mouse, a new instruction is presented, and he/she transcribes the characters at the directed cell in the printed table. The printed table is placed in the center of the desk (c). The position of the instruction slip is randomly selected from 54 positions, which are set at every $30°$ and at a distance of r (=1, 5, 10, and 20 cm) as shown in the circle of (b). A variable r represents the distance between the source of transcription, i.e., paper strip, and the target, i.e., printed table, which is defined as the distance between the point where the straight line that connects the center of the paper strip and that of the printed table intersects with the respective side (Fig. 2). The reason why we do not utilize the distance between the centers

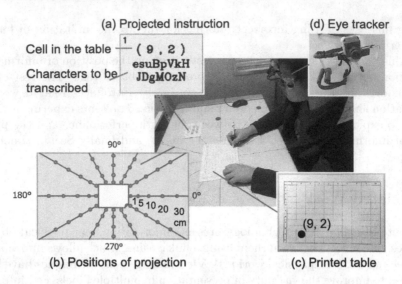

Fig. 1. A scene of an experiment

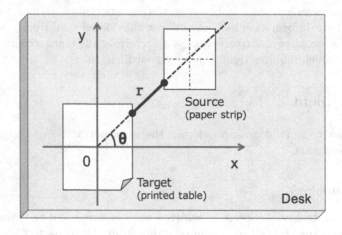

Fig. 2. The definition of r and θ.

of two rectangles as r comes from the assumption that information is directly presented on the desk, rather than overlapping on these sheets. So, r should be defined as a variable that does not depend on the size of these sheets.

One session at a particular position on the desk consists of five trials of transcription, and three sessions are performed at the position. So, one subject performs 162 (= 54 positions × 3 sessions) sessions in total. To avoid recall of known words, 15 alphabetic characters are randomly generated. Ten subjects (three men and seven women in their 20's) whose dominant hands are right participated to the experiments.

Two performance metrics are measured: (1) task completion time as an efficacy metric and (2) number of errors as an effectiveness metric. Task completion time is defined as the duration taken to complete one session, i.e., from the beginning of the first trial to the end of the fifth trial, based on the timestamps generated by mouse clicks. The number of errors includes two types of errors: incorrect position of transcription and incorrect character transcription. We counts the incorrect character transcription as what the subject cannot notice during the session and the experimenter later finds. In addition to these performance metrics, we analyze the eye movement using an eye tracker (Arrington Research Inc. View Point EyeTracker) (d). The experimenter counted the number of eye movements by watching the recorded video from the eye tracker. Also, we asked the participants about 5-most and 5-least preferred positions for the task after all trials, which is intended to understand subjective opinions.

3.2 Result

To investigate the difference of the performance by position visually, the performance metrics are averaged and represented as heat maps by interpolating spatial data using inverse distance weighting (IDW) [5]. Figures 3(a) and (b) show the task completion time and the number of errors, respectively. The heatmap overlaps with the area of the desk. The values were normalized between 0 (minimum) and 1 (maximum).

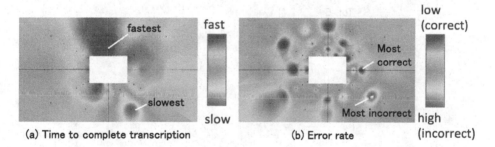

Fig. 3. Heat maps of (a) task completion time and (b) the number of errors. (Color figure online)

Average task completion time is about 73.9 s (SD: 6.6), in which the fastest and the slowest average completion times per position are 65.00 s (at 5 cm and 90°) and 100.13 s (at 20 cm and 300°), respectively. We confirmed significant difference between these positions at the level of $p < 0.05$ ($t(9) = -5.14$). By contrast, an average number of error per trial is 0.16 (SD: 0.09), ranging from 0.03 (at 10 cm and 0°) to 0.40 (at 20 cm and 330°), which do not show any significant difference ($p > 0.05$ ($t(9) = -2.01$)). Generally, presentation on the upper sides of the printed table and the one close to the target show better results (blue area in Fig. 3), while worse results are observed on the lower right side (red area in Fig. 3).

Regarding the eye movement, we could obtain data from five subjects and counted the number of eye movements. On average, 38.5 times (SD: 3.7) per session of eye movements were observed, ranging from 29.2 (at 20 cm and 270°) to 45.7 (at 1 cm and 60°); however, no clear difference in the number of eye movements was observed. Rather we found three types of gazing that may depend on individuals: (1) keeping eyes on the instruction slip during transcribing after checking the position of the target cell, (2) transcribing by looking at the instruction slip and the target cell alternatively, and (3) transcribing by gazing the target cell once he/she looked at the instruction slip.

In terms of the subjective opinions for position, we assigned scores of 5, 4, 3, 2, and 1 in ascending order of "like". Likewise, scores of $-5, -4, \ldots, -1$ were assigned in ascending order of "dislike". Figure 4 shows the preference ratings, in which the numbers in rectangle and triangle indicate the rank of "like" and "dislike", respectively. Similar to the performance metrics in Fig. 3, the lower side of the transcription target was not preferred, and upper left part was preferred instead. We consider that these performance and preference came from the characteristics of the dominance hand use.

By taking into account the fact that all subjects are right-handed, the low performance and disliked positions are generally inside or near the forearm of dominant side, i.e., closer to the body, while the preferred positions appear on the opposite side.

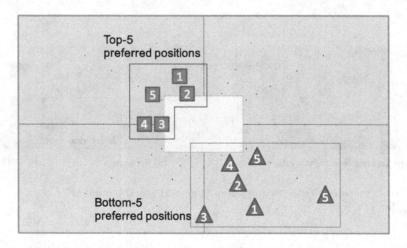

Fig. 4. Preference for the positions (5 most preferred (rectangle) and 5 least preferred (triangle) positions)

4   Discussion

4.1   Analysis of the Experimental Results

The distribution of task completion time (Fig. 3)(a) and the preference for the positions (Fig. 4) looks consistent with each other in that presentation at an upper and closer area from the target (printed table) was relatively good, while presentation at bottom-right area was not. The reason for this is that the presentation does not overlap with either the right hand holding the pen, or the left hand holding the paper for tracing the printed table when the information is presented at upper work area. Furthermore, by presenting the information at close position from the work area, we consider that the subjects could perform the transcription task with natural postures because a large head movement was not necessary to see the information.

On the other hand, the areas that were mentioned as difficult places to work and had long task completion time overlap with the right arm. Also, the subjects needed to look inside to see the information, which forced to the subjects to turn their necks and physical burden was imposed to the subjects. Thus, we consider that they felt troublesome and extra time was consumed.

The effectiveness of the presentation is measured by the number of errors. As shown in Fig. 3(b), bottom right of the desk shows large number of errors on average; however, we found large amount of user dependency. The breakdown of the errors is shown in Fig. 5, in which the confusion between "I" and "l" shares the largest portion of observed errors, followed by that of "6" and "8". By taking into account the feedback from the subjects, the experimental environment might affect the precision of the transcription. This includes low readability of fonts, low resolution of projected information, occlusion from eye tracker, and so on. As described in Sect. 3.2, the number of errors in one session is 0.40 out of 75

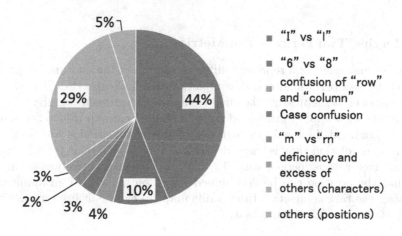

Fig. 5. The breakdown of errors.

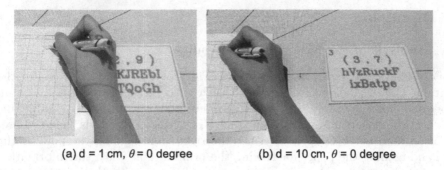

(a) d = 1 cm, θ = 0 degree   (b) d = 10 cm, θ = 0 degree

Fig. 6. Too much short distance makes overlap (a), while presentation at an adequate distance avoids overlap (b).

characters (= 15 characters × 5 trials) at most, which corresponds to 0.53% of input characters and small enough to be ignored in most applications.

As discussed above, small r was generally preferred except for the case with overlapping with the right hand; however, Fig. 3(a) implies another exceptional case. For example, the position at 1 cm and 0° shows longer task completion time than the position at 5 cm and 10 cm with the same angle (0°). As shown in Fig. 6(a), the information overlaps with the right hands when the information is presented next to the working area, 1 cm in this case. By contrast in (b), such overlap does not happen because an area enough to avoid overlapping with the information is provided. Consequently, the requirements for the system can be listed below:

– As close to the working area as possible.
– Least necessary activity of referring to the source information.
– Avoid current or predicted working area.

4.2   Merging Two Performance Metrics

The two heatmaps in Fig. 3 represent different aspects of the information presentation on the task performance; task completion time indicates the efficacy, while the number of errors represents the effectiveness of the presentation. By merging these aspects with appropriate blend ratio, a single heatmap that reflects both aspects is obtained. In Fig. 7, three types of merged heatmaps are shown, in which task completion time is merged with (a) 0.8, (b) 0.5, and (c) 0.2, and in turn, the error rate is merged with 0.2, 0.5, and 0.8, respectively. The figures mean that the position can be determined based on map (a) if an application emphasizes the task completion time, while map (c) can be utilized in case that the correctness of work is important.

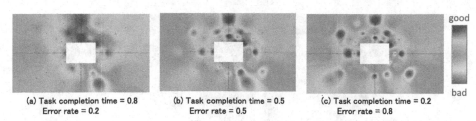

(a) Task completion time = 0.8
Error rate = 0.2

(b) Task completion time = 0.5
Error rate = 0.5

(c) Task completion time = 0.2
Error rate = 0.8

good

bad

Fig. 7. Merging two aspects of performance with different blend ratio. (Color figure online)

4.3 Applying to Other Tasks

We performed the task of transcribing specific character string at the specific position in the experiment of this study. Since this work is abstraction of transcription from reference information, we consider that the heatmap can be applied to similar work such as filling in the application form, copying the content of the booklet etc., and collation work like self-study answering.

As a constraint in the experiment for creating the heatmap, we narrowed down the type of information to a static one that the user only refers to; however, interactivity with the user is often required in real world tasks, in which presented information is operated by the user. Similar to the static information, dynamic information should also be unobtrusive by the dominant hand and presented close to the work area for referring to information necessary for work. On the other hand, the angle at which operation is easier for the user, i.e., ergonomically suitable, is unclear from the experimental results. So, the heatmap is not always possible to apply as it is. Extra experiment is needed to understand the characteristics of the presentation from this aspect.

Furthermore, the generated heatmap was specialized for right handed users. We consider that the heatmap for right handed users cannot just be flipped horizontally for left handed users. In writing characters or drawing lines from left to right, right handed people often do not bend their wrists too much (Fig. 8(a)), while we can see that left handed people tend to bend the wrist inward and surround the paper (Fig. 8(b)). We consider that there are two reasons for this specific posture:

- Make the characters that the user wrote before visible
- Natural and comfortable to warp the wrist outward in drawing a line

The area where the left hand becomes a barrier is different from the right handed person due to bending the elbow and warping the wrist outward. So, the optimal information presentation position for the left handed person is not simply symmetric about y axis. Similar to the right handed people, close distance to the target and unobtrusiveness for the dominant hand is necessary for left handed people; however, the effect of angle should be investigated carefully.

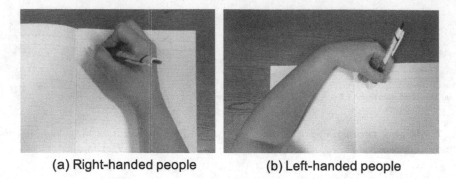

(a) Right-handed people   **(b) Left-handed people**

Fig. 8. Difference of forearm posture for those who are right-handed and left-handed in writing characters from left to right.

4.4 Integration into a System

In this paper, we obtained heatmap that shows the relationship between the position of information presentation and work efficiency as well as accuracy. Here, we describe the utilization of the map and other functional components to realize an entire system. Prior to applying the heatmap, three areas are recognized: (1) operational area in work area, (2) free space in work area, (3) the area of operational hand, i.e., dominant hand. Work area is an area where the task is carried out. In this study, work area is the transcription target. The position of operational area is considered as "hot spot" that is utilized to start searching candidate area around it from free space for information presentation. In Fig. 7, the work area is drawn as white rectangles, and the candidate areas are drawn with blue color. Free space is the area, where no object except for the target object exists. Finally, the area of the user's dominant hand is detected as dynamic obstacle that is the lowest possible area for presentation, which is drawn with yellow to red in Fig. 7. The three types of areas are overlapped with the heatmap, and free space with as high performance as possible is found. Additionally, the preference for presentation as shown in Fig. 4 can be referred in determining the position of presentation.

5 Conclusion

In this paper, we explored the suitable and unsuitable positions for information presentation on the desk through a projector; we focused on a task that contains user's active involvement with paper, i.e., transcribing characters in a specific cell of a printed table from the projected information. The position of the information presentation is represented as the distance between the edge of the transcription target and the edge of source information, and the direction of the source information from the transcription target.

In the quantitative experiment that dealt the distance (r) and the direction (θ) as variables, the task completion time and the error rate were measured as metrics for analysis, and visualized as heatmaps. Eye movement was also observed. Generally, presentation on the upper sides of the printed table and close to the target showed better results (faster task completion and lower error rate), while worse results are observed on the lower right side that was around the dominant hands. Regarding the eye movement, no particular characteristic was found. Subjective preference for the position had similar characteristics as the performance metrics, i.e., the lower side of the transcription target was not preferred, and upper left part was preferred instead.

Although the result is obtained under very limited environment, we consider it is a good starting point to design a projector-based information presentation system that supports existing paper tasks. A use case is that a high school student studies physics with an exercise book by comparing her answer on the notebook with an answer key projected on the desk and correcting wrong answers by a pen. Extra experiment is needed to understand the effect of the presentation on the user's subjective preference, especially from the ergonomic point of view.

Acknowledgment. This work was supported by a JSPS Grant-in-Aid for Scientific Research: 15K-00265.

References

1. Azuma, R., Furmanski, C.: Evaluating label placement for augmented reality view management. In: Proceedings of the 2nd IEEE/ACM International Symposium on Mixed and Augmented Reality, ISMAR 2003, pp. 66–75 (2003). http://dl.acm.org/citation.cfm?id=946248.946790
2. Bell, B., Feiner, S., Höllerer, T.: View management for virtual and augmented reality. In: Proceedings of the 14th Annual ACM Symposium on User Interface Software and Technology, pp. 101–110, UIST 2001, NY, USA (2001). http://doi.acm.org/10.1145/502348.502363
3. Leykin, A., Tuceryan, M.: Automatic determination of text readability over textured backgrounds for augmented reality systems. In: Proceedings of the 3rd IEEE/ACM International Symposium on Mixed and Augmented Reality Systems, pp. 224–230. IEEE Computer Society (2004). http://dl.acm.org/citation.cfm?id=1033719
4. Sato, M., Fujinami, K.: Nonoverlapped view management for augmented reality by tabletop projection. J. Vis. Lang. Comput. **25**(6), 891–902 (2014)
5. Shepard, D.: A two-dimensional interpolation function for irregularly-spaced data. In: Proceedings of the 1968 23rd ACM National Conference, pp. 517–524. ACM, New York (1968). http://doi.acm.org/10.1145/800186.810616

Methodology for the Estimation of Effort for a Project of Virtual Reality– A Case Study: Ennui

Francisco Torres-Guerrero[1]([✉]), Leticia Neira-Tovar[1,2], and Ignacio Martinez Garcia[2]

[1] Universidad Autónoma de Nuevo León, San Nicolás de los Garza, Mexico
franciscot@gmail.com, leticia.neira@gmail.com
[2] Ennui Studio, Monterrey, Mexico
idmg87@gmail.com

Abstract. The use of software engineering is vital to have maximum control of a development project, often these practices are not used when developing virtual reality projects. Currently there is little literature that provides advice to the estimation of project development efforts in virtual reality, this research provides a theoretical and empirical analysis resulting in a proposed methodology for estimating efforts. In order to have a more precise scenario, a case study for the company ENNUI in developing a virtual reality project on astro physics laboratory, was performed. The estimation of effort was conducted through the Delphi method, involving six experts in different evaluation processes, a final estimate was compared to the time it took to perform the requested requirement was made.

Keywords: Virtual reality · Training · Software development · User experience · Immersive technology

1 Introduction

Currently, a diverse multimedia educational purpose is used in the classroom to improve the traditional way of teaching. Most of the content is in 2D format, which can be videos, or photographic, these limited interaction with the content.

Different studies have shown that a 3D environment turns out to be more assertive however the development of a 3D application is a challenge as it often can be expensive, time consuming, with deficiencies in usability and difficult Access [1].

The use of interactive labs can be of great help to capture the attention of students in the study of science [3], and other subjects.

For development to be successful it is important to identify learning objectives, skills of students as well as educational needs [2]. It is essential that the designs contain interactive elements like physical graphics and elements to enable a user experience.

For a comprehensive educational model is important multimedia tools use a distribution of information from different cognitive style.

© Springer International Publishing AG 2017
S. Lackey and J. Chen (Eds.): VAMR 2017, LNCS 10280, pp. 82–93, 2017.
DOI: 10.1007/978-3-319-57987-0_7

A common problem in development a virtual reality project is that do not have a methodology to dimension the estimation of effort in the integration of education professionals and technologists to develop new tools of virtual reality [5, 6].

In many cases the virtual reality projects could be canceled by having a low estimate timely efforts.

This research describes a proposal for the estimation of effort in the development of 3D interactive applications for educational purposes for the area of physics that meet the technological and operational requirements exploring the Delphi methodology as a tool for information integration in building a project of virtual reality.

This article focuses on studying the design and construction of a virtual laboratory application through human interaction information to solve a problem from a virtual science lab. The student reads the practice from science book, which describes a task to perform. During the time of the activity the student can interact with laboratory instruments.

Even with the instructions, the student may neglect some details on how to solve the activity may cause an accident or damage laboratory instruments.

The result of the research includes the analysis of building a virtual tool to support a virtual laboratory.

2 Operation

All development projects should go through a process of software engineering is more common to hear this concept for administrative projects and business intelligence they are also more applicable to virtual reality projects [4].

Software engineering allows developing solutions to problems of data processing in areas such as bioinformatics, medicine, finance, economics, business intelligence and others. The software development projects in many of the occasions arise from the needs of customers, which are expressed in the requirements requested.

In a virtual reality project with a learning approach there are explicit and implicit needs. We mention that the explicit needs are those observables are literally the needs expressed by the customer, for example where the client request states that the virtual laboratory should be equal to an existing physical laboratory with detailed measures and equipment.

Implicit needs are not textually observable and rarely expressed by the customer, these are commonly interaction or usability problems.

Considering that one of the objectives of implementing an information system, is the need to represent virtually focused on learning scenarios, the software engineering is the discipline that combines all aspects of the production of an information system, its main objective is the development of methods that allow optimal construction of an information system [5].

To ensure the success of any software engineering model is necessary to perform the necessary calculations for management of resources resulting in an optimal manner.

It is prominent, the importance of development projects information systems must maintain a high degree of bidirectional communication and a strong commitment to the attachment of the agreements and schedule [6].

3 Methodology

An interactive laboratory analysis was develop into a high school physics laboratory, usingUnity 3D engine.

The instrument was test three times, allowing all items were discriminatory.

Students enter the hall in the specific time of his subject. The teacher gives introduction of the scheduled issue proceeds to give a theoretical explanation, then start the practice in the virtual laboratory, a test form was applied to know the experience.

3.1 Study Case: ENNUI

The virtual reality project is develop on the topic for learning the solar system, commonly this subject is explained using a scale models and prototypes made with some balls. This time is used: Virtual Laboratory: Solar System, By Ennui Studio.

For the creation of the solar system, the following stages of construction were generate:

Research and formulation stage. At this stage, we evaluated different concepts and references that could represent a real way the solar system around us and give an immersive experience within the environment taking as key factors - Distance between planets, size, and scales representative characteristics of each one (Fig. 1).

Fig. 1. Image that represents the solar system

3.2 Design/Whitebox Stage

For this stage basic models were generated in blender, a scale that could make a visual representation of each of the planets, each of the models were generated in FBX files and were integrated into a test scene in Unity 3d (Fig. 2).

To represent the sun, was taken as a pivot point, taking as distance ratio 1 unit of Unity in 100,000,000 km.

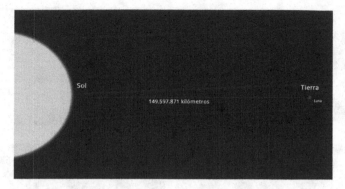

Fig. 2. Distance between Sun and Earth.

3.3 Modeling and Texturing

Within this stage the models generated for the white box are taken and 2 main elements were modified; outer layer, inner layer, atmospheric mantle (Figs. 3 and 4).

Fig. 3. Outer layer model which is assigned planet texture and material.

3.4 Core Model

Is the visual representation of the core, which is formed by a texture with transparency representative planet core 72 512 × 512 pixels to dpis, within the engine of unity, you add a shader with transparency, texture and pattern core (Figs. 5 and 6).

3.5 Effects and Lights

Within the selected effects, to generate greater investment, the following are described:
    Infinite space: For the generation of space A cubemap texture was created with a resolution of 512 × 512 pixels at 72 dpis, which is used in the skybox component of unity allowing simulation of infinite space (Fig. 7).

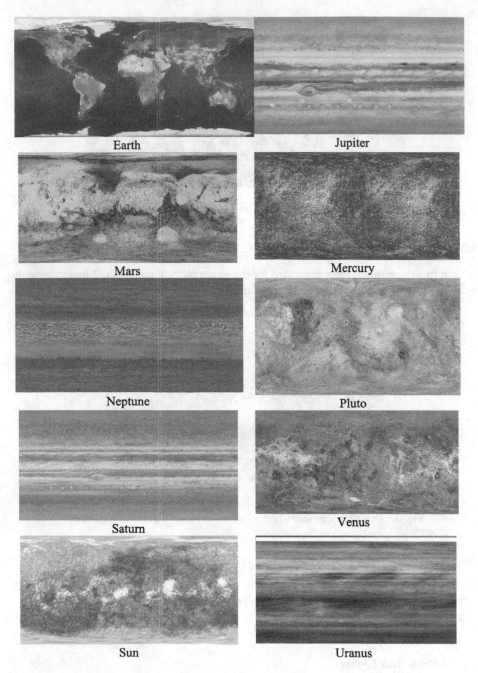

Fig. 4. For each planet its own texture is generated with a screen resolution of 72 DPI. using as a basis actual photos of each of the planets and generating adjustment substance painter.

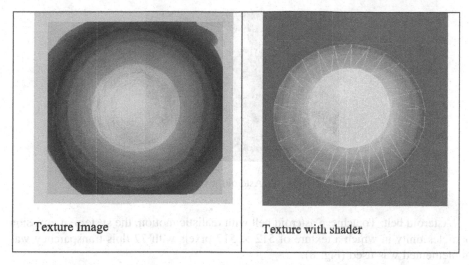

Texture Image   Texture with shader

Fig. 5. Visual representation of the core.

Mantle texture   Diffuse texture with transparent shader

Fig. 6. Atmospheric blanket - It is a primitive spherical model combined with a texture to 72 dpi resolution with transparency, which represents the planet's atmosphere creating the effect of wrapping and combined with a shader Transparent /Diffuse type.

Fig. 7. Skybox cubemap.

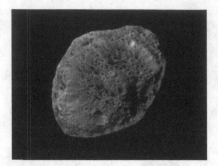

Fig. 8. Asteroid texture.

Asteroid belt: To achieve asteroid belt with realistic motion, the system of emission particles unity in which a texture of 512×512 pixels with 72 dpis transparency was implemented was used (Fig. 8).

Fig. 9. Solar Corona: Solar light emitted on the planets.

Solar System: To generate the sunlight that is projected into the planets, a component type of lights used Point Light, which can generate light emission and bounce on models that simulate the planets allowing light and shadow on the planets in the most natural way possible (Fig. 9).

Solar Corona: To assimilate the solar corona, another particle system which includes a gas texture transparent 512 × 512 pixels of 72 dpis in combination with a diffuse shader transparent, allowing to simulate the solar corona surrounding the sun was used (Fig. 9).

3.6   Animation

Using the component of unity animator, animation rotations for planets were generated allowing to simulate the rotation on its axis as well same rotation of the atmosphere and the rings of different planets (Figs. 10 and 11).

Fig. 10. Animation window

Fig. 11. Playing the created animation

3.7   Movement and Integration Controller VR

The motion controller is a script generated in c # which consists of a detector inputs such as keyboard and computer mouse, allowing mobility within the space, The motion controller is a script generated in c # which consists of a detector inputs such as keyboard and computer mouse, allowing mobility within the space, as well as being made up of 3 components camera, which allow generate the rendering in each of the VR device displays in this case the oculus rift and tracking the movement of the head (Fig. 12).

Fig. 12.   Driver image generating rendering of planets

3.8   Equipment Requirements

The classroom should have a minimum space of 25 m^2 and an optimum of 70 m^2. Free area furniture 3×3 m^2. It must have an HD projector. Augmented reality glasses oculus rift, Kinect 2.0 device.

3.9   Evaluation and Metrics

It explores the methodology used to estimate a virtual reality project focusing on astro physics laboratory. In this study we used the case of Ennui Company, which has an experience of just over 5 years, specializing in the construction of virtual reality and animation. The calculation effort estimation is managed by the Project Manager, which has the support of a technical committee.

The methodology used for the estimation is derived from the Delphi method, as prospective technique which is implemented to make predictions in regard to project implementation.

The scope of the Delphi method depends on the ability of the expert team when solving complex problems through individual questionnaires are taken where a leader moderates discussion and sets out the agreements.

The purpose is to reduce the gap between expert opinion and the group using the median of the results obtained (Fig. 13).

The Delphi method consists of different stages: problem definition, selection of experts, Development and launch of the questionnaires, and exploitation of results.

Fig. 13. Equipment in use

Delphi methodology studies allow us to make very extensive assessment or unusual topics. Because assessments are conducted in the first stage individually helps us coordinate a multifocus team, who can express their point of view from different perspectives.

You can view the problem from the following perspective, if we have a set of projects to develop $P = \{P_1 \ldots P_i\}$ size i and that $Q = \{Q_1 \ldots Q_s\}$ is a set of modules within a system size s.

Each module is developed through a joint analysis work $= \{A_1 \ldots A_t\}$, a set of development work $D = \{D_1 \ldots D_w\}$ and a set of features $F = \{F_1 \ldots F_v\}$, R_{istw}, $1 \le i \le s, 1 \le t \le w \le v$.

This allows us to express the following equation

$$R_{istw} = \{R_{11111}, \ldots R_{istwv}\}$$

We can say that a set value R expresses that the value i is one of the projects of the company, s is a module system, t is the analysis and documentation related to the module, w is the code for such v analysis It corresponds to the functionality of the code.

As we can see in the equation, the corresponding variable functionality affected by other dimensions are the project module, analysis and development.

For different functionality it corresponds a different combination of values i, s, t, w. which each will be included in the estimation of efforts.

Exchange controls is evaluated by a group of expert engineers $E = \{E_1 \ldots E_x\}$ evaluating *Tmin* minimum effort and maximum *Tmax* corresponding to the different dimensions of functionality. Is an estimate, which we can express in the following formula.

$$S_{istwx} = \{S_{111111}, \ldots S_{istwvx}\}$$

A set of exchange controls is evaluated by an expert panel where each estimated a minimum and a maximum and according to the methodology Delphi midpoint value is estimated.

$$\sum \frac{\left(\frac{T_{min}(S_{istwx})}{x} + \frac{T_{max}(S_{istwx})}{x}\right)}{2}$$

4 Results

Through the Delphi method, the estimation of effort of each of the stages of the project were consulted, each expert gave a minimum estimate and a maximum proceeded to perform descriptive statistics to calculate the mean time estimates of each expert as well as a comparison between the need for the project final time and the estimated time. At Table 1 you can see the minimum ranges in the time estimate made in hours (Tables 2 and 3).

Table 1. Estimate of minimum ranges efforts by experts.

	Expert 1	Expert 2	Expert 3	Expert 4	Expert 5	Expert 6
Requirements	56	47	53	50	49	53
Planning	15	14	16	13	15	16
Analysis	11	13	16	10	12	14
Development	95	85	90	95	89	95
QA	10	12	14	12	16	13

Table 2. Estimate ranges maximum efforts by experts.

	Expet 1	Expert 2	Expert 3	Expert 4	Expert 5	Expert 6
Requirements	76	70	80	77	78	73
Planning	20	20	22	18	20	21
Analysis	25	25	22	27	23	21
Development	110	113	133	124	135	137
QA	20	18	19	17	15	16

Table 3. Comparative table of ranks and end development time.

	Mean Mín	Mean Máx	Mean	Std Deviation	Final
Requirements	51.3	75.6	63.5	17.20	62
Planning	14.8	20.1	17.5	3.77	15
Analysis	12.6	23.83	18.25	7.89	23
Development	91.5	125.33	108.41	23.92	134
QA	12.8	17.5	15.1	3.29	15

5 Conclusion and Future Works

This research allows us to evaluate the use of the Delphi method for calculating estimates of efforts in a virtual reality project. If we look at the final column, this represents the actual time it took the technical team to implement the requested requirement, we can see that the values are between the minimum and maximum except in the development phase which was an additional 9 h than estimated which represents 8% of the maximum value.

This research allowed us a framework for estimating efforts when an implementation of a virtual reality project is required, in this case access to 6 expert support for the implementation of the Delphi method which complicates the use of the method in those had to companies where access to expert group is limited.

A work of future research could be related to the use of historical data that allow adjustment of the data as well as the creation of an intelligent system which could be accessed by other communities that are not available with a similar number of experts.

Acknowledgements. Authors want to thank to ENNUI Studios, who develop the prototype to probe the Virtual laboratory, using their experience and their equipment to develop the software.

Also thanks to Diego Flores, Marco Elizondo and Jesus Escobar, to support with the Unity images used in this work.

References

1. Barrera, S., Takahasi, H., Nakajima, M.: Hands-free navigation methods for moving through a virtual landscape. In: Proceedings of IEEE 2004 Computer Graphics International, Crete, Greece, 16–18 June 2004, pp. 388–394 (2004). ISBN 0-7695-2171-1 CGI
2. Dawson, P., Levy, R., Lyons, N.: 'Breaking the fourth wall': 3D virtual worlds as tools for knowledge repatriation in archaeology. J. Soc. Archaeol. **11**(3), 387–402 (2011)
3. Coll, C.: Psicología de la educación virtual: aprender y enseñar con las tecnologías de la información y la comunicación. Ediciones Morata (2008)
4. Vera, L., Herrera, G., Vived, E.: Virtual Reality School for Children with Learning Difficulties. In: Proceedings of the International Conference on Advances in Computer Entertainment Technology, ACE 2005, pp. 338–341 (2005)
5. Ramirez, H.: Automating AR Software Architecture Development: An authoring platform for AR projects [interview] 8 October (2012)
6. Coton, C., Shegog, R., Markham, C., Thiel, M., Peskin, M., Tortolero, S.: Creating an immersive virtual world through integration of 2D and 3D technologies to implement E-learning curricula for middle school students. In: Iskander, M., Kapila, V., Karim, M. (eds.)-Technological Developments in Education and Automation. Springer, Dordrecht (2010)

Interaction Techniques in VAMR

Evaluation of a Low Cost EMG Sensor as a Modality for Use in Virtual Reality Applications

S.N. Gieser$^{(\boxtimes)}$, Varun Kanal, and Fillia Makedon

Heracleia Human Centered Computing Laboratory,
Computer Science and Engineering Department,
University of Texas at Arlington, Arlington, TX, USA
{shawn.gieser,varunajay.kanal,makedon}@uta.edu

Abstract. Virtual Reality (VR) is becoming more accessible to everyday users. Users of VR want realistic experiences, both in how it looks and in how to interact with the environment. Electromyography (EMG) is a possible tool to use to make VR more realistic, but in the past, has been considered too expensive to be accessible to the everyday user. New low-cost EMG sensors have become available in recent years that have made this technology more available to the everyday user. In this paper, we evaluate one low-cost EMG sensor to assess its usefulness as an input modality for VR. We will do this by assessing how accurately gesture recognition can be accomplished with the data acquired from the sensor. We will compare it to gesture classification done with data obtained from a higher cost EMG system that has a much higher sampling rate. If the classification results are similar, then low-cost EMG is a valid choice as an input modality for VR.

Keywords: EMG · Gesture classification · KNN · SVM · Myo Armband · Trigno Lab

1 Introduction

Virtual Reality (VR) technology is becoming more and more accessible to everyday users. Just in the last two years, releases of multiple consumer versions of Head Mounted Displays (HMDs), such as the HTC Vive, Oculus Rift, Samsung Gear VR, Sony Playstation VR, and Google Daydream just to name a few, have increased the demand for this technology [1]. The people who use VR love how immersive the environment is and that tasks are accomplished by mimicking the motions needed to perform the task in real life [2].

VR tasks, however, sometimes do not properly mimic their real world counterpart. Once commercial example would be the game The Climb by Crytek [3]. In this game, one climbs a virtual wall using two controllers to represent their hands. Buttons are used for grabbing rocks and putting chalk on the virtual hands. In real rock climbing, one uses their hands, feet, and various muscle groups to climb a wall or rock face. There are no buttons to press to perform these tasks. Therefore, one could say that this virtual task does not have a high degree of interaction fidelity. Interaction fidelity is

© Springer International Publishing AG 2017
S. Lackey and J. Chen (Eds.): VAMR 2017, LNCS 10280, pp. 97–110, 2017.
DOI: 10.1007/978-3-319-57987-0_8

the objective degree of exactness in which real-world interactions can be reproduced in an interactive virtual environment [4].

One possible way to increase interaction fidelity is to add electromyography (EMG) as an input modality. Let us create an example task by requiring a user to push a heavy block in a virtual environment. With controllers, this task can be completed by navigating to the block, moving the controllers to the block, pressing a button to grab the block, then finally moving the controllers forward to push the block. This is a very simple list of actions to complete if this block really was heavy. With the addition of EMG, we could add one more requirement to the list of actions. In addition tomoving the controllers forward, the user would have to flex the muscles in their arms and chest. This would make the task more similar to the real world counterpart since the virtual task now requires similar muscle activation to the physical task.

In this paper, we will be evaluating a low cost, off the shelf, EMG sensor in its usefulness to classify gestures. We will be comparing the results with a full EMG system that has a higher sampling rate. If the low-cost sensor is useful in being able to classify gestures and has a similar success rate classifying gestures as the full EMG system, then it would also be useful as a modality in VR applications. We will begin by going over background information and related works, followed by our experimental setup and procedure. We will then talk about our analysis and discuss our results. Lastly we will present our conclusions and future work.

2 Related Work

There have been many different approaches for deciding how to handle input in VR. Text input has been attempted many times. Researchers have used various techniques such as speech, gloves, writing on tablets, chord keyboards, and gesture mapping [5, 6]. SteamVR uses a controller in which users point at a virtual keyboard and click which letters they want [7]. Drawing has also had various techniques applied to it. Haptic devices which have a pen or a stylus attached have been used [8]. Modern approaches however use controllers to accomplish this, such as what is used in Google Tilt Brush [9]. Others have focused on movement techniques in VR. [4] compares game movement techniques and its correlation to different levels of display fidelity. The two different movement techniques compared are keyboard input and a "human joystick" where the user's position and distance from a central point effects direction and speed of movement in a game. The two different levels of display fidelity were a one wall of a six-sided CAVE and another version using four wall of the CAVE to create a full 360-degree environment. The situations that performed the best were either high levels of both interaction and display or low interactions of both. It has also been said that developers should focus on not developing mid-fidelity or semi-natural interactions techniques that do not resemble real world interactions [10]. Commercial examples of movement techniques vary between many different options, which include, but not limited to, an omni-directional treadmill and using a controller to point at a location and "teleport" to that location [11, 12]. All ofthese various techniques represent different degrees of interaction fidelity.

Gesture classification has been done by others using EMG. Most of these studies involve expensive equipment, or equipment put together in house. Various classification techniques have been used, including K-Nearest Neighbor (KNN) [13], Support Vector Machines (SVM) [14], Dynamic Time Warping (DTW) [15], and Bayes [16]. EMG gesture classification has been used for various applications as well. It has been used as an input device for games and computers [13, 17], as well as assisting the users with motor disabilities in navigating a wheelchair [18]. EMG has also been combined with accelerometers to get increased accuracy on motions and tasks that involve movement of the hand or arm [19]. EMG has been used in VR to train amputees how to control a prosthetic device so that they can become used to controlling the device before having it attached to their body [20]. These uses of EMG data show that EMG can serve as a modality in VR. With low-cost options becoming available, can these EMG sensors, that don't have as high of a sampling rate, serve in the same capacity?

3 Experimental Setup and Procedure

In this section, we will begin by describing the equipment that was used. This will be followed by the procedure, detailing the gestures used, sensor placement on the body, and how the study was conducted.

3.1 Equipment

We acquired data from two different EMG sensors. The first one was the Myo Armband developed by Thalmic Labs [21], seen in Fig. 1 Left. It is a wireless sensor that communicates with a computer or smart phone via Bluetooth. It contains eight EMG sensors with a sampling rate of approximately 200 Hz [22]. It also has a nine axis IMU, a three-axis accelerometer, and a three-axis magnetometer, all with a sampling rate of approximately 50 Hz. For the sake of this study, all we are using is the EMG aspect of this sensor. The Myo Armband is relatively inexpensive when compared to that of medical grade EMG systems. The main issue with this sensor is that the sampling rate for the EMG sensor does not satisfy the Nyquist-Shannon Theorem. The Nyquist-Shannon Theorem states that the sampling frequency should be greater than twice the signal frequency [23]. Based off this theorem, the Myo Armband should only be able to pick up signals with a frequency of 99 Hz and lower. This then creates a potential issue, since most significant EMG activity happens in the 5 to 450 Hz range [24].

The second sensor was the Trigno Lab developed by Delsys [25], seen in Fig. 1 Right. The Trigno Lab has a number of small sensors that communicate to a base station via an RF signal. Each sensor contains an EMG sensor with a sampling rate of approximately 1926 Hz and has a three-axis accelerometer with a sampling rate of approximately 148 Hz [26]. This EMG sampling rate easily satisfies the Nyquist-Shannon Theorem since it is over four times the maximum frequency of significant EMG activity.

Two different pieces of software were used for data collection. For collecting data from the Myo Armband, we used Unity [27]. We felt that it was a more realistic

Fig. 1. (Left) The Myo Armband (image from myo.com). (Right) Delsys Trigno Lab (image from delsys.com)

approach than specialized data collection programs. Since the goal was to see if the Myo Armband would be good for VR, it made sense to use a program that had built in functionality for game design and VR. For data collection from the Trigno Lab, we used EMG Works [28], a specialized piece of software developed by Delsys.

3.2   Experimental Procedure

To assess the validity of low cost EMG sensors as a modality for VR, we will be assessing how well we can classify gestures with just EMG data. This will be useful in recognizing what a user is trying to do in a virtual environment. For this study, we used eleven gestures. These gestures were resting, wave out, wave in, fist, fingers spread, double tap, pinching, holding up a block, pretending to hold up a block, pointing, and thumbs up. All these gestures, except for double tap, can be seen in Fig. 2. Six of these gestures can be detected by the Myo Armband already, which are resting, wave out, wave in, fist, fingers spread, and double tap. As far as the authors have noticed, all other gestures are primarily classified as resting even though there is an unknown gesture reading available.

In order to get as similar readings as possible from the two different sensors, we attempted to place the sensors in the same position on the body. To do this, we first had each participant for the study place the Myo Armband on their arm following the instructions for the Myo Armband (Fig. 3 Left). These were that the armband had to be placed on the widest part of the forearm with the USB port facing towards the hand. We additionally added that the sensor logo should be facing upwards when the arm is in a supinated position. We then marked where the top and bottom of the individual pods were positioned on the arm with a red marker (Fig. 3 Center). The EMG sensors from the Trigno Lab were then placed in the areas marked (Fig. 3 Right).

There were thirty-five participants for this study. Participants were recruited through one of the introductory courses in the Computer Science Department. There were no exclusionary criteria to prevent someone from participating in this study.

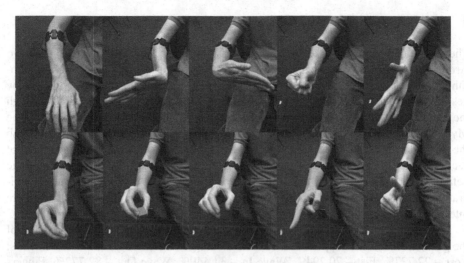

Fig. 2. The gestures used during data collection. From Top-Left to Bottom-Right: Rest, Wave out, Wave in, Fingers Spread, Pinching, Holding a Block, Pretending to hold a Block, Pointing, and Thumbs up

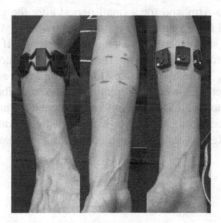

Fig. 3. (Left) Placement of the Myo Armband. (Center) Markings from where the Myo was positioned. (Right) Placement of Trigno Sensors

The order of the sensors was alternated between participants to balance the study. The participants placed the Myo armband on first so that its position on the arm can be marked. The participant then either left the Myo Armband on, or took it off so the Trigno sensors can be put on. The participants made the eleven gestures three times each. The gesture was made before being recorded. Each gesture was held and recorded for approximately 5 s. After the first set of gestures were complete, the sensors were switched. If the Myo Armband was second, it was lined back up with the markings on the arm so that it can be in the same position it was before. Then the participants repeated the same gestures as before. Overall, each participant performed sixty-six gestures, thirty-three with each sensor.

4 Analysis and Discussion

The first component we looked at was the classification algorithm built into the Myo Armband's software. We wanted to see how the Myo Armband's classification algorithm looks at gestures it can already classify and what it's results are for the new gestures we added. Table 1 shows these results. These results were acquired through the IMU sensor of the Myo Armband which has a sampling frequency of 50 Hz. The Myo Armband sends the gesture classification results with the IMU data instead of with the EMG data. These results show what the Myo Armband classified each gesture as at each time the IMU sensor acquired a sample. These results were also acquired using the default calibration setting on the Myo Armband. Even though there is a custom calibration setting available, we chose to use default settings since this is what we were interested in most.

As you can see in Table 1, the Myo Armband correctly identified a little over 50% of the gestures that it was supposed to. The individual gesture success rates are as follows: Rest – 22.727%, Fist – 70.294%, Wave In – 34.449%, Wave Out – 82.772%, Fingers Spread – 41.560%, and Double Tap – 32.380%. The classification results for Double Tap were presented differently in Table 1. For the other gestures, we showed what the Myo Armband classified each sample sent by the IMU sensor. However, Double Tap is only shown by the Myo Armband for a small period after the gesture has been completed. We examined all the classification results sent by the Myo Armband during the 5 s recording period to see if there was a Double Tap result. If there was, the whole gesture was determined to be a Double Tap. If not, we used whatever the most common classification result was. These low classification rates may have been caused by using the default calibration settings instead of creating a custom calibration profile for each participant. Using a custom calibration profile should greatly improve these results.

Looking at the added gestures, all five of them had one common element. These gestures all shared the Rest gesture as their highest classified gesture. Therefore, if you

Table 1. Myo self-classification results

Gesture made	Myo classification						
	Rest	Fist	Wave in	Wave out	Fingers spread	Double tap	Unknown
Rest	13998	0	0	0	0	0	47593
Fist	14079	44308	1735	368	1178	0	1364
Wave in	17004	13433	21106	3	1330	88	8292
Wave out	1170	5479	2187	51236	1762	66	0
Fingers spread	14947	15775	1947	4178	26227	31	0
Double tap	13252	405	216	262	416	853	0
Pinching	28788	14741	2510	6780	9552	0	0
Pick up block	35960	13877	2836	4541	4714	25	0
Pretend	34359	9634	5739	2396	10982	0	0
Pointing	48180	12375	1167	575	26	0	0
Thumbs up	36695	21144	305	0	4544	0	0

were building a classifier to support the Myo Armband, the Rest gesture can be used to determine if an additional classifier is even necessary for the current gesture or not. If the Myo Armband shows rest, then run the additional classifier. If the Myo Armband shows any other gesture, then the additional classifier would most likely not be needed in that case.

Figure 4 shows a sample of the raw data collected from the Trigno Lab and the Myo Armband. These plots show the data collected from each sensor or pod used. Two gestures are shown in the graph. The blue dashed line represents the data collected while a participant performed one of the "Pretend" gestures, and the red solid line represents one of the "Rest" gestures. These were plotted on the same graph to show the comparison of muscle activity between the two gestures. All other attempts for all gestures were plotted in this same way. One thing to note is that the Y-axis on Myo Armband graphs is not in Volts like traditional EMG data. This is because the data the Myo Armband SDK produces for the EMG sensors is unitless activation [29]. We have decided to label this "Myo Units."

Figure 5 shows a frequency analysis done on the data previously shown in Fig. 4. This was also done for all attempts for all gestures. To perform the frequency analysis, the signals obtained from both the sensors was decomposed into their individual frequencies. This was done by performing a Fast Fourier Transform (FFT) on the signal. FFT is a modification of the Direct Fourier Transform (DFT) for quicker results. The formula for DFT is:

$$Xk = \sum_{n=0}^{N-1} x_n e^{-i2\pi kn/N} \tag{1}$$

where x_n is the data sequence and X_k is the DFT. Even though the data collected from the Myo Armband was unitless, we decided to perform the frequency analysis on the data to show a comparison between two data sets.

For gesture classification, we focused on using the data collected instead of the frequency analysis. This decision was made to make it simulate as if a program or game was getting a window of data at a time. For the Trigno Lab data set, we used filtered data. The filtering process was performed in 3 steps. First, the signal was passed through a high pass filter. The corner frequency for this filter was 10 Hz. Then, the filtered signal was passed through a low pass filter with the corner frequency at 500 Hz. Finally, the signal was passed through a notch filter at 50 Hz. The resulting signal has its frequency in the range of 10 Hz to 500 Hz. This removes any low frequency and high frequency noise. The filter used for this was a zero phase shift equiripple filter. We did not filter the Myo Armband data, since the data is unitless, and the Myo Armband has a small sampling rate.

To help with classification, each senor was given a weight of 1, 0.5, or 0 based on the graphs that were generated in the style of Fig. 4. This weight was determined manually based on how different the "Non-Rest" gesture was compared to the "Rest" gesture. If the "Non-Rest" gesture's EMG signal had significantly greater and/or easily distinguishable from the "Rest" gesture, then that sensor was given a weight of 1. If there was no difference, or the "Rest" gesture showed more activity, then it was given a weight of 0. If the EMG for the "Non-Rest" gesture was greater, but not significantly

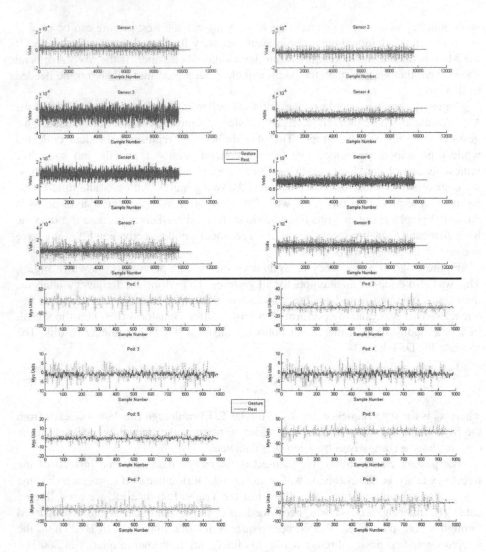

Fig. 4. Sample of the raw data collected from the Trigno Lab (Top) and the Myo Armband (Bottom) EMG sensors for the "Pretend" Gesture compared to the "Rest" Gesture

greater, then it was given a weight of 0.5. Figure 6 shows examples of how these were classified. Tables 2 and 3 show the averages of the weights given for each sensor separated by gesture.

The data was extracted from 8 pods from each sensor. The weights were used to narrow down the pods which was the most important for each sensor. The pod with the highest weight was used for classification. There were some cases where the highest weight for the pods was below 0.5, even in such cases the pod with the highest weight was used. Two classification algorithms were considered: K Nearest Neighbors (KNN) and Support Vector Machines (SVM) with a linear kernel. A 5 fold cross

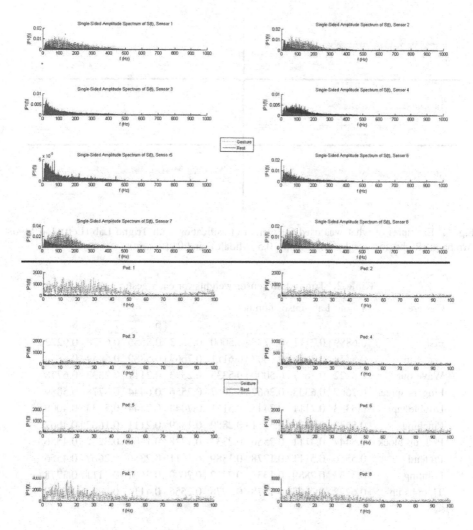

Fig. 5. Frequency analysis of data collected from Trigno Lab (Top) and Myo Armband (Bottom) EMG sensors for the "Pretend" Gesture compared to the "Rest" Gesture

validation method was used to create the model. When creating these models, we focused on the gestures "Holding a Block" and "Pretend." This was done so that we could apply this to previous work in VR. [30] shows a problem with interaction fidelity of picking up virtual blocks. One of the possible solutions was to consider other input modalities. These two gestures best represent the motions needed to pick up a block. Table 4 shows the classification results using these methods.

The results in Table 4 are not promising, which a highest classification rates on the Trigno Lab data set being 61.11% on KNN with the "Double Tap" gesture and the Myo Armband data set being 53.81% on KNN with the "Pinching" gesture. This initially led us to believe that not enough data was collected, or we did not consider enough

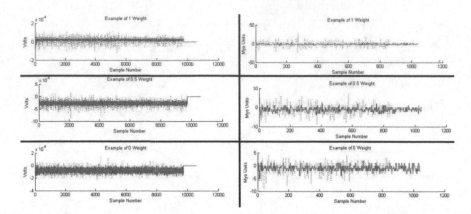

Fig. 6. Examples of what was used for weight classification with Trigno Lab (Left) and Myo Armband (Right) for weights of 1 (Top), 0.5 (Middle), and 0 (Bottom)

Table 2. Trigno Lab sensor weights for each gesture

Gesture	Trigno Lab sensor number							
	1	2	3	4	5	6	7	8
Fist	0.6889	0.7111	0.5778	0.5000	0.6333	0.8556	0.6778	0.9222
Wave in	0.5778	0.3556	0.1667	0.6111	0.7667	0.5889	0.5444	0.5889
Wave out	0.8222	0.7667	0.5000	0.5333	0.2333	0.2111	0.2333	0.6778
Fingers spread	0.7667	0.6333	0.2667	0.3667	0.2556	0.6444	0.4778	0.5889
Double tap	0.6333	0.7111	0.7444	0.5111	0.7444	0.7444	0.5333	0.4000
Pinching	0.5333	0.5333	0.3111	0.2889	0.1889	0.2111	0.1667	0.4667
Pick up block	0.5444	0.4111	0.2556	0.2333	0.1778	0.1889	0.3222	0.4556
Pretend	0.5556	0.5111	0.1778	0.1889	0.1111	0.2356	0.2667	0.4556
Pointing	0.3333	0.2889	0.1333	0.2222	0.2000	0.3667	0.3111	0.3778
Thumbs up	0.6222	0.2667	0.1778	0.2778	0.2556	0.4111	0.4222	0.6889

Table 3. Myo Armband sensor weights for each gesture

Gesture	Myo Armband sensor number							
	1	2	3	4	5	6	7	8
Fist	0.7476	0.8714	0.7667	0.7000	0.7190	0.8524	0.8714	0.8476
Wave in	0.9429	0.3952	0.2905	0.6571	0.8000	0.7190	0.7333	0.6810
Wave out	0.9857	0.9524	0.8333	0.6762	0.5190	0.5190	0.7048	0.8333
Fingers spread	0.9381	0.8238	0.5286	0.4143	0.5000	0.7952	0.8095	0.7571
Double tap	0.9476	0.9524	0.8905	0.7905	0.9095	0.9286	0.7762	0.7143
Pinching	0.8048	0.7952	0.6571	0.4000	0.5143	0.5224	0.5143	0.5810
Pick up block	0.8286	0.7381	0.5143	0.3048	0.4810	0.2714	0.4000	0.6476
Pretend	0.7714	0.6524	0.4714	0.3000	0.4095	0.4333	0.5333	0.6095
Pointing	0.5429	0.5048	0.2619	0.2095	0.4190	0.5238	0.6619	0.6333
Thumbs up	0.6810	0.5000	0.3238	0.2524	0.5714	0.6905	0.6905	0.7143

Table 4. Classification results: Filtered Trigno Lab Data and Myo Armband Raw Data

Gesture	Trigno Lab filtered data set		Myo Armband raw data set	
	KNN	SVN	KNN	SVN
Fist	50.00%	41.11%	26.67%	24.76%
Wave in	50.00%	43.33%	43.81%	45.24%
Wave out	48.89%	45.55%	40.95%	41.91%
Fingers spread	48.89%	42.22%	40.00%	39.05%
Double tap	61.11%	43.33%	41.86%	41.43%
Pinching	50.00%	41.01%	53.81%	49.05%
Pick up block	50.00%	43.33%	48.57%	50.00%
Pretend	55.56%	38.89%	49.05%	49.05%
Pointing	53.33%	36.67%	38.57%	40.47%
Thumbs up	50.00%	38.89%	41.43%	40.48%

sensors. We then started modifying our approach to classification to look at extracted features from the EMG data. There were 5 features extracted from the signal; Maximum value of the selected window, the Minimum value, the absolute Mean of the window, the Variance and the Root Mean Square (RMS) of the signal. These features are few of the common features that are used for signal analysis and have been known to be used in EMG gesture classification [31]. We used extracted features on both sets of data for comparison, even though the Myo Armband data was unitless. Table 5 shows the classification results using the extracted features.

The Trigno Lab data set performed significantly during KNN classification using extracted features instead of filtered data. SVM classification only showed a slight improvement in success rates. The Myo Armband data set, however, showed significant improvements with both classifiers. This is very interesting since the Myo

Table 5. Classification results: extracted features from Trigno Lab and Myo Armband Data

Gesture	Trigno Lab data set		Myo Armband data set	
	KNN	SVN	KNN	SVN
Fist	86.66%	41.11%	95.24%	95.24%
Wave in	94.44%	52.22%	81.43%	81.90%
Wave out	93.33%	48.89%	99.05%	98.57%
Fingers spread	90.00%	46.67%	99.05%	96.67%
Double tap	90.00%	50.00%	98.10%	98.10%
Pinching	83.33%	36.66%	86.19%	92.86%
Pick up block	75.56%	43.33%	87.62%	87.14%
Pretend	84.44%	44.44%	90.95%	92.38%
Pointing	73.33%	48.89%	77.62%	77.62%
Thumbs up	91.11%	43.33%	84.28%	85.24%

Armband data set is unitless. Even though this does look promising, further investigation is needed to explain why this result occurred. These initial results, however, do show that low-cost EMG sensors could have a place in VR and an input modality if used properly since the KNN classification results were similar between the Trigno Lab data set and the Myo Armband data set.

5 Conclusions

In this paper, we evaluated a low cost, off the shelf, EMG sensor for its potential use in VR. We decided that if this sensor can classify gestures, and we can classify gestures with a similar success rate to a sensor with a better sampling rate, then we can use it to trigger virtual interactions. We used KNN and SVM to classify the gestures. Our results show that using extracted features to classify gestures works significantly better than using raw data. Also, the classification results between the two different sensors were similar. With these results, we can conclude that, if used properly, then low-cost EMG sensors can be used in VR. We cannot fully support the use of extracted data with the Myo Armband yet until we have done further investigation.

6 Future Work

There are many future steps for this work. The first is to investigate how the extracted features affected the Myo Armband classification so much. This would help solidify our claim that this sensor is useful in VR. Also, we would need to expand the training set for our data so we can get more accurate weights. This will allow us to have a primary sensor with one or two secondary sensors to be considered as well. This will also allow us to get more accurate classification results. Lastly, we would look at to see how a custom calibration file effects the data collected, if at all.

The other major category for future work is using EMG in VR. We will expand on our previous work to improve gameplay and interaction with virtual objects [30]. This will then be expanded to future games as well. This should increase the interaction fidelity of virtual tasks. This will require user experience tests to be done to see if this does increase interaction fidelity as expected.

Acknowledgements. This work was partially supported by the NSF grant 1338118. Any opinions, findings, and conclusions or recommendations expressed in this publication are those of the author(s) and do not necessarily reflect the views of the National Science Foundation.

References

1. Market Intelligence and Consulting Institute, MIC: Development Trends of VR Head-Mounted Displays. Technical report (2016). http://www.rnrmarketresearch.com/development-trends-of-vr-head-mounted-displays-market-report.html
2. Adams, R.L.: Five reasons why virtual reality is a game-changer. Forbes (2016). http://www.forbes.com/sites/robertadams/2016/03/21/5-reasons-why-virtual-reality-is-a-game-changer/
3. The Climb. http://www.theclimbgame.com
4. McMahan, R.P., Bowman, D.A., Zielinski, D.J.: Evaluating display fidelity and interaction in a virtual reality game. IEEE Trans. Vis. Comput. Graph. **18**(4), 626–633 (2012). doi:10.1109/TVCG.2012.43
5. Bowman, D.A., Rhoton, C.J., Pinho, M.S.: Text input techniques for immersive virtual environments: an empirical comparison. Proc. Hum. Factors Ergon. Soc. Annu. Meet. **46** (26), 2154–2158 (2002). doi:10.1177/154193120204602611
6. Fels, S.S., Hinton, G.E.: Glove-talkII – a neural network interface which maps gestures to parrallel formant speech synthesizer controls. IEEE Trans. Neural Netw. **9**(1), 205–212 (1998). doi:10.1109/72.655042
7. SteamVR. http://store.steampowered.com/steamvr
8. Keefe, D.F., Zeleznik, R.C., Laidlaw, D.H.: Drawing on air: input techniques for controlled 3D line illustration. IEEE Trans. Visual Comput. Graph. **13**(5), 1067–1081 (2007). doi:10.1109/TVCG.2007.1060
9. Google Tilt Bursh. https://www.tiltbrush.com/
10. McMahan, R.P., Lai, C., Pal, S.K.: Interaction fidelity: the uncanny valley of virtual reality interactions. In: Lackey, S., Shumaker, R. (eds.) VAMR 2016. LNCS, vol. 9740, pp. 59–70. Springer, Cham (2016). doi:10.1007/978-3-319-39907-2_6
11. Virtuix Omni. http://www.virtuix.com/product/omni-package/
12. The Lab on Steam. http://store.steampowered.com/app/450390/
13. Chen, X., Wang, Z.J.: Pattern recognition of number gestures based on a wireless surface EMG system. Biomed. Signal Proc. Control **8**(2), 184–192 (2013). doi:10.1016/j.bspc.2012.08.005
14. Benatti, S., Casamassima, F., Milosevic, B., Farella, E., Schönle, P., Fateh, S., Burger, T., Huang, Q., Benini, L.: A versatile embedded platform for EMG acquisition and gesture recognition. IEEE Trans. Biomed. Circ. Syst. **9**(5), 620–630 (2015). doi:10.1109/TBCAS.2015.2476555
15. Lu, Z., Chen, X., Li, Q., Zhang, X., Zhou, P.: A hand gesture recognition framework and wearable gesture-based interaction prototype for mobile devices. IEEE Trans. Hum. Mach. Syst. **44**(2), 293–299 (2014). doi:10.1109/THMS.2014.2302794
16. Kim, J., Mastnik, S., André, E.: EMG-based hand gesture recognition for realtime biosignal interfacing. In: Proceedings of the 13th International Conference on Intelligent User Interfaces, IUI 2008. pp. 30–39. ACM Press, New York (2008). doi:10.1145/1378773.1378778
17. Wheeler, K.R., Jorgensen, C.C.: Gestures as input: neuroelectric joysticks and keyboards. IEEE Pervasive Comput. **2**(2), 56–61 (2003). doi:10.1109/MPRV.2003.1203754
18. Moon, I., Lee, M., Chu, J., Mun, M.: Wearable EMG-based HACI for electric powered wheelchair users with motor disabilities. In: Proceedings of the 2005 IEEE International Conference on Robotics and Automation, ICRA 2005, pp. 2649–2654. IEEE Press, New York (2005). doi:10.1109/ROBOT.2005.1570513

19. Zhang, X., Chen, X., Li, Y., Lantz, V., Wang, K., Yang, J.: A framework for hand Gesture recognition based on accelerometer and emg sensors. IEEE Trans. Syst. Man Cybern. – Part A: Syst. Hum. **41**(6), 1064–1076 (2011). doi:10.1109/TSMCA.2011.2116004

20. Pons, J.L., Ceres, R., Rocon, E., Levin, S., Markovitz, I., Saro, B., Reynaerts, D., Van Moorleghem, W., Bueno, L.: Virtual reality training and EMG Control of the MANUS hand prosthesis. Robotica **23**, 311–317 (2005). doi:10.1017/S026357470400133X

21. Myo Armand Technical Specifications. https://www.myo.com/techspecs

22. Myo RAW EMG Data. http://developerblog.myo.com/raw-uncut-drops-today/

23. Shannon, C.: Communication in the presence of noise. Proc. Inst. Radio Eng. **37**(1), 10–21 (1949). doi:10.1109/JRPROC.1949.232969

24. Merletti, R., Torino, P.D.: Standards for reporting EMG data. J. Electromyogr. Kinesiol. **9** (1), 3–4 (1999)

25. Trigno Lab. http://www.delsys.com/products/wireless-emg/trigno-lab/

26. Trigno Standard Sensor. http://www.delsys.com/products/emg-auxiliary-sensors/std-sensor/

27. Unity Game Engine. http://unity3d.com/

28. Delsys EMGworks Software. http://www.delsys.com/product/emgworks-software/

29. Thalmic Labs Developer Forum/General Discussion/EMG Sampling Rate. https://developer.thalmic.com/forums/topic/1945/

30. Gieser, S.N., Gentry, C., LePage, J., Makedon, F.: Comparing Objective and Subjective Metrics Between Physical and Virtual Tasks. In: Lackey, S., Shumaker, R. (eds.) VAMR 2016. LNCS, vol. 9740, pp. 3–13. Springer, Cham (2016). doi:10.1007/978-3-319-39907-2_1

31. Luppescu, G., Lowney, M., Shah, R: Classification of Hand Gestures using Surface Electromyography Signals For Upper-Limb Amputees. Technical report, Stanford University. http://cs229.stanford.edu/proj2016spr/report/040.pdf

Vitty: Virtual Touch Typing Interface
with Added Finger Buttons

Yongjae Lee and Gerard J. Kim[(✉)]

Digital Experience Laboratory, Korea University, Seoul, Korea
lyj930303@gmail.com, gjkim@korea.ac.kr

Abstract. In this paper, we propose to add individual finger buttons to a nominal interaction controller to realize a QWERTY like touch typing experience in virtual reality. The method is called Vitty, and the intuition behind it is real life typing is emulated by mapping the fingers/buttons to the appropriate sectional rows in the virtual QWERTY layout. Vitty is expected to reduce the mental and physical fatigue in the usual aiming and selecting of each small alphanumeric keys. We compare the performance and usability of Vitty to those of the typing interfaces as available with the current popular VR interaction controllers, and found that with minimal training, Vitty can be an inexpensive yet viable alternative for text input for VR.

Keywords: Virtual reality · Alphanumeric/Text input · Interaction · Controller · Performance evaluation · Usability

1 Introduction

With the innovations for affordable head mounted displays (HMD), stable sensing and high-end computer graphics, immersive virtual reality (VR) has attracted much attention lately. Aside from the reality and immersion, the virtual experience is often contingent on natural and usable interaction as well. In fact, interactive techniques for VR have long been studied, e.g. particularly for the generic tasks of navigation, object selection and manipulation [1]. However, there has not been a satisfactory solution to the task of text entry in VR due to the difficulty in tracking individual fingers and providing even a minimal haptic/tactile feedback. Moreover, its utility had been relatively low and overlooked, while today, its importance has risen significantly by the prevalence of social networking.

In this paper, we propose a simple solution: adding buttons, for each finger (except for the thumb), to the conventional interaction controller as an interface for virtual touch typing for a QWERTY style keyboard (hence, named "Vitty"). In the usual touch typing, one uses the muscle memory to reach and locate the wanted key with the eight fingers (the index to the pinky) from the home middle row. With Vitty, the same muscle memory (aided by the visual feedback) is applied to the VR interaction controller in a similar way to match the fingers to the desired keys. This way, Vitty emulates the usual method of typing while providing the important sense of haptic/tactile feedback through the

© Springer International Publishing AG 2017
S. Lackey and J. Chen (Eds.): VAMR 2017, LNCS 10280, pp. 111–119, 2017.
DOI: 10.1007/978-3-319-57987-0_9

individual buttons (See Fig. 1). We compare Vitty to the typing interface as available with the current popular VR interaction controllers.

Fig. 1. Text input for VR using Vitty: selecting the keyboard section using the ray casting with the interaction controllers then entering the individual letter with finger mapped buttons.

2   Related Work

There is a large amount of pervious work on various VR interaction techniques [2–4]. We only outline notable works in text entry for VR. The most popular and conventional way of text entry in VR setting is the "aim and shoot" style, in which a hand-held device or hand-mounted sensor is used to cast a virtual ray and select a particular key and making the final confirmation using a button (or other discrete input method) [5, 6]. A more direct method is to use a glove like device that attempts to sense individual finger movements and map them into the virtual space to realize virtual QWERTY style typing [7–9]. A slight variant is the hand-mounted but restricted set of buttons, each corresponding to an alphabetic key [10, 11]. Such a non-QWERTY method would require extensive training, however. Recently, improved external finger tracking and sensing technologies have allowed the use of bare hands, relieving the user from having to use the cumbersome glove-like hand worn device [12]. However, these sensors are still not accurate enough, often need to be installed in the environment (making the input system not self-contained) and has a limited operating range. Combined with the lack of haptic feedback, such a scheme generally has low usability.

One other interesting approach is capturing and segmenting out the imagery of a real keyboard and using hands (using a computer vision method), and blending it into the virtual scene [13]. While such an approach makes it possible to use the familiar conventional keyboard, the keyboard (on a fixed desktop location) is not fit for active usage while navigating in the VR space.

3 System Overview

The Vitty QWERTY keyboard is divided in its layout into several sections (see Fig. 2) which are first selected by the standard ray-casting technique (Fig. 1) aimed by the interaction controller, e.g. those that are equipped with sensors and few buttons for orientation/position control and discrete command input (we have used the motion controller from the HTC Vive). Each section contains 4 letters that are mapped to four different fingers as used in the normal QWERTY typing, and thus four different finger buttons attached to the controller (see Fig. 3). For instance, the letter "w" in the normal typing is to be entered by the left ring finger and similarly so by the corresponding finger button in the proposed scheme. Once the section which includes the "w" key (colored in red in Fig. 2) is selected, the individual letter input is made through the corresponding finger button, For instance, to input "w", the user points the left hand controller to the red section (in Fig. 1) and press the third button with the ring finger.

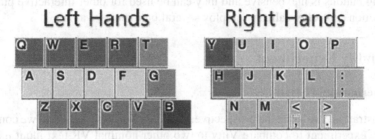

Fig. 2. The sections in the virtual QWERTY keyboard layout. For example, to input "w", the user points the left hand controller to the red section and press the third button with the ring finger. (Color figure online)

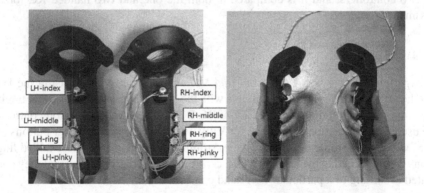

Fig. 3. Finger buttons added to HTC Vive interaction controller for QWERTY style text input.

Note that there are few exceptions. There are sections with only one letter such as those for "t", "g", "b", "y", "h" and other special keys like the space bar and backspace (see Fig. 2). The typing process is still the same; that is, select the section by ray-casting and entering the letter with the "index finger" (as so in normal typing). Such a nearly equivalent finger mapping (to QWERTY) makes the proposed method quite natural. Figure 1 shows a screen shot of the virtual keyboard interface within the virtual space. The rationales behind the proposed method are summarized as follows:

1. Using any layout other than QWERTY would require extensive training.
2. With stable tracking performance, the conventional interaction controllers have shown favourable usability for supporting general interactive tasks in the virtual space, e.g. by ray casting, joy stick, buttons and touch-pad. Adding yet another dedicated device for text entry would be prohibitive.
3. Using buttons as key input provides tactility and haptic feedback (vs. e.g. purely with ray-casting).
4. Despite the stable tracking, selecting the individual alphabetic key using ray-casting can still be difficult or tiring in comparison to the selection of the larger keyboard "section." And the successive button click is very fast, due to the same finger-to-letter mapping as the normal typing.
5. Adding buttons is inexpensive and they can be used for other interactive purposes. Interaction controllers already employ several buttons anyway.

4   Usability Experiment

4.1   Experimental Design

To demonstrate and validate the prospective advantages of Vitty as noted, we conducted a usability experiment to compare Vitty to two other nominal VR text input methods, thus, there are three test conditions as explained in Table 1; (1) ray casting one-handed, (2) ray casting two handed and (3) Vitty. The typing performance and subjective usability were measured as dependent variables. Note that Vitty is designed to be used with two controllers, and it is compared to both the one and two handed RC for fair assessments.

4.2   Test Apparatus

The experimental task was carried out in a VR environment, viewed using the HTC VIVE headset and the input made possible with the VIVE interaction controller, tracked by separate sensing modules. In the case of RC-2 and Vitty, two interaction controllers were used. The interaction controllers for Vitty were added with the finger buttons (see Fig. 3) which were implemented using the Arduino controller [14]. These added finger buttons were attached to the original VIVE controller using the Velcro so that they could be fitted according to a particular user hand comfortably.

4.3   Experimental Procedure

Nine paid subjects participated in the experiment. All the subjects had to possess a typing skill of higher than 38 words-per-minute (in English alphabets). While only subject had the prior experience of using VR equipment, none complained of any discomfort. After

Table 1. The three experimental conditions tested.

No.	Factor level	Explanation	
1	Ray casting One-handed (RC-1)	One interaction controller (held in the dominant hand) is used to select the desired key by ray casting and confirm the input by a dedicated trigger button input.	
2	Ray casting Two-handed (RC-2)	Two interaction controllers are used held in both hands. Each is used to select the desired key in the left or right part in the same manner as the one-handed aim-and-shoot.	
3	Vitty	Subsection of the keyboard is selected by ray casting with the controller, then individual key input by corresponding finger buttons. Two hands/controllers are used.	

collecting their basic background information, the subjects were briefed about the purpose of the experiment and given instructions for the experimental tasks. A short 10-minute training was given, without wearing the HMD to reduce the fatigue as much as possible, so that the subjects could be familiarized with the experimental process and three text input methods.

In the main experiment, the subject sat, wore the HMD, and held the controllers and carried out the typing task. The chair and viewing distance to the virtual keyboard were adjusted for the subject's maximum comfort. The experimental task comprised of a set of sentences (13) from the Mackenzie's "Phrase set for evaluating text entry techniques" [15] for each test treatment. Each treatment was presented in a balanced fashion using the Latin square methodology, and in each treatment the task was repeated three times.

The task started by the user pressing the "start" button, then 13 sentences would appear above the virtual keyboard for which the user was to enter. A single block (13 sentences) was finished by touching the "enter" button after entering all the sentences. Three performance indicators were measured: the task completion time, the time interval between the individual key input and the error rate (number of incorrectly input letters). The user was asked to make the entries correctly as fast as possible. After the session, the subjects filled out a usability questionnaire (see Table 2). The user rested between each treatment and the total experimental session took about 1 h.

Table 2. The usability survey questions.

Q1: Ease of use	Rate how easy it was to enter the text. 1 (very hard) ~ 7 (very easy)
Q2: Physical load	Rate the level of physical fatigue. 1 (very tiring) ~ 7 (not tiring at all)
Q2: Mental load	Rate the level of mental fatigue. 1 (very tiring) ~ 7 (not tiring at all)
Q4: Ease of learning	Rate how easy it was to learn the text entry input method. 1 (very difficult) ~ 7 (very easy)
Q5: General satisfaction	Rate how satisfied you were for the text entry input method. 1 (very unsatisfactory) ~ 7 (very satisfactory)

4.4 Results

Figure 4 shows the comparative results of the task completion time among the three tested condition. The graph shows the performance change over the three blocks so that the learning effect can be taken into consideration. In the first two blocks, there were statistically significant differences among the three input methods, with RC-2 being the fastest, followed by the RC-2, then Vitty. By the third block, however, the statistical differences were reduced to an insignificant level. As for the error rate, no statistically significant differences could be found among the three methods.

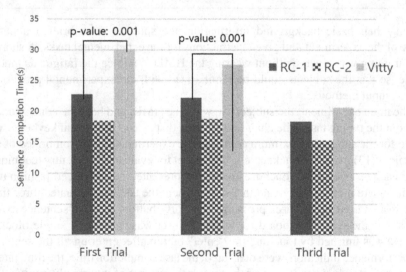

Fig. 4. Task completion times in three trial blocks for the three tested conditions (RC-1, RC-2 and Vitty). Unlike the first two blocks, the third block shows no significant difference in the performance between the conventional and Vitty.

Figure 5 shows two examples of the time taken to input two successive key inputs; one for two keys that belong to different sections (e.g. "a" then "n") and other for those that belong to the same section (e.g. "e" then "r"). For the former, we see that RC-1

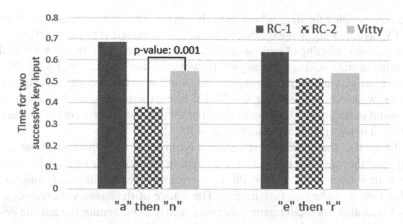

Fig. 5. Time taken for two successive key inputs, for those belonging to: (1) different sections, e.g. "a" then "n" (left) and (2) same section, e.g. "e" then "r". In the former, the RC-1 performs the best, while for the latter, RC-1 and Vitty performs at a similar level.

generally performs better than RC-1 (because of the less movement using two hands) and also Vitty (because Vitty requires a button press after ray casting to the desired section). As for the latter, Vitty shows an improvement statistically equaling the performance of RC-2.

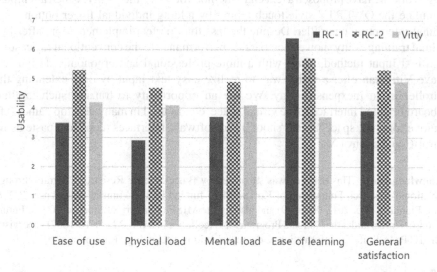

Fig. 6. Responses to the usability survey across the three text input methods. RC-2 generally showed the highest usability.

Figure 6 shows the usability survey results. In most categories, the RC-1 showed the worst usability particularly with respect to the fatigue factor (having to manage all input with just one hand). RC-2 was the rated the most usable among the three due to its familiarity and directness. One intuition behind Vitty was that real life typing could be emulated by mapping the fingers/buttons to the appropriate sectional rows in the virtual QWERTY layout. Vitty was expected to reduce the mental and physical fatigue in the usual aiming and selecting of each small alphanumeric keys, with the current less-than-perfect sensing and tracking technologies. However, while not exactly QWERTY style, using ray casting was still much simpler and familiar to the average user. Ironically, sectional row selection to emulate QWERTY like experience seem to have required some amount of training and getting used to. For this reason, its expected advantage was not sufficient to supersede the performance of RC-2.

We found that the QWERTY style touch typing was not followed all the time in actuality, and the way such users change the typing rules on their own could not be re-enacted with Vitty as in the real world. Post-briefing revealed that many subjects felt the added buttons to be less than natural. The stance of the hands with respect to the keyboard was also not totally natural because it had to be aiming toward the desired sectional row. Subjects also complained of the ray obscuring the sectional rows and made the initial selection difficult. Despite these little overlooked factors which contributed to a non-ideally recreated QWERTY typing experience, the task performance after few blocks of trials showed a promising improvements.

5   Conclusion and Future Work

In this work, we have proposed a text entry method for VR, called Vitty, which attempted to emulate the QWERTY style touch typing by adding individual finger buttons to a nominal interaction controller. Despite the less than perfect implementation, after just minimal training, Vitty showed comparable performance to the conventional ray casting based text input method. Thus, with a more professional and ergonomic design, we believe Vitty can offer a viable way to realize easy text input by only extending the controller in an inexpensive way. We see an opportunity to transfer such familiar keyboard oriented interface to the virtual space, e.g. as used in many desktop games ("f" for move forward, spacebar for "shoot") and software interfaces (copy and paste using control-C and control-V).

Acknowledgment. This research was supported by Basic Science Research Program through the National Research Foundation of Korea (NRF) funded by the Ministry of Science, ICT & Future Planning (No. 2011-0030079) and also by the MISP (Ministry of Science, ICT & Future Planning), Korea, under the National Program for Excellence in SW) (R2215-16-1007) supervised by the IITP (Institute for Information & communications Technology Promotion)

References

1. Bowman, D., Kruijff, E., LaViola Jr., J., Poupyrev, I.: 3D User Interfaces: Theory and Practice, CourseSmart eTextbook. Addison-Wesley (2004)
2. Feiner, A., Olwal, S.: The flexible pointer: an interaction technique for selection in augmented and virtual reality. In: Proceedings of the UIST 2003, pp. 81–82 (2003)

3. Poupyrev, I., Billinghurst, M., Weghorst, S., Ichikawa, T.: The go-go interaction technique: non-linear mapping for direct manipulation in VR. In: Proceedings of the 9th Annual ACM Symposium on User Interface Software and Technology, pp. 79–80. ACM (1996)

4. Thomas, B., Piekarski, W.: Glove based user interaction techniques for augmented reality in an outdoor environment. Virtual Reality **6**(3), 167–180 (2002)

5. HTC VIVE User guide. http://dl4.htc.com/web_materials/Manual/Vive/Vive_User_Guide.pdf?_ga=1.64742511.1367646068.1462853716. Accessed 10 May 2016

6. PlayStation4 User's Guide, Entering characters. http://manuals.playstation.net/document/en/ps4/basic/osk.html. Accessed 10 May 2016

7. Bowman, D., Wingrave, C., Campbell, J.M., Ly, V., Rhoton, C.: Novel uses of Pinch Gloves™ for virtual environment interaction techniques. Virtual Reality **6**(3), 122–129 (2002)

8. Howard, B., Howard, S.: Lightglove: wrist-worn virtual typing and pointing. In: Proceedings of the Fifth International Symposium on Wearable Computers, pp. 172–173. IEEE (2001)

9. Rosenberg, R., Slater, M.: The chording glove: a glove-based text input device. IEEE Trans. Syst. Man Cybern. Part C (Appl. Rev.) **29**(2), 186–191 (1999)

10. Alphagrip. http://www.alphagrips.com/. Accessed 10 May 2016

11. Trewgrip. http://www.trewgrip.com/. Accessed 10 May 2016

12. Leap Motion Developer, VR Keyboard. https://developer.leapmotion.com/gallery/vr-keyboard. Accessed 10 May 2016

13. McGill, M., Boland, D., Murray-Smith, R., Brewster, S.: A dose of reality: overcoming usability challenges in VR head-mounted displays. In: Proceedings of the 33rd Annual ACM Conference on Human Factors in Computing Systems, pp. 2143–2152. ACM (2015)

14. Banzi, M., Shiloh, M.: Getting Started with Arduino: The Open Source Electronics Prototyping Platform. Maker Media, Inc. (2014)

15. MacKenzie, I.S., Soukoreff, R.W.: Phrase sets for evaluating text entry techniques. In: CHI 2003 Extended Abstracts on Human Factors in Computing Systems. ACM (2003)

Remote Touch: Humanizing Social Interactions in Technology Through Multimodal Interfaces

Alexia Mandeville[✉], David Birnbaum, and Chad Sampanes

Immersion Corporation, San Jose, CA, USA
{amandeville,dbirnbaum,csampanes}@immersion.com

Abstract. Waves, pokes, and tugs are simple social gestures that can benefit from more thoughtful design when translated onto mobile devices and computers. Haptics provide an additional mode of conveyance that is frequently forgotten about in development of mobile technologies, but incorporating it can have significant positive impact on user experience. Combining advanced vibrotactile haptics, location, and multimodally congruent feedback, our prototype creates a simple experience that connects people through non-verbal information to deliver a meaningful gesture and playful interaction.

Keywords: Haptics · Touchsense · Multimodal · Design · Location · iBeacon · Social · Interaction · Tactile · Touch · Mobile · Application · Wearable · Gesture · User experience · UX

1 Introduction

Mobile technologies such as handsets and wearables with cloud-connected apps connect people on an unprecedented scale. Chat environments, social networks, and real-time location tracking let people communicate an ever-increasing volume of status updates and messages. But, for all their benefits, current paradigms of digital communication lack the intuitive, natural feel of in-person interaction. The absence of many social cues we use to communicate face to face, including verbal tone, environmental context, body language, and touch, are missing. This paper presents a prototype, *Remote Touch*, that incorporates advanced vibrotactile feedback in a common social interaction, with the goal of enabling more natural interpersonal communication by addressing some of these shortcomings. *Remote Touch* creates the illusion of being touched and "pulled" by another person in your network. Multimodal design, haptic feedback, visual feedback, and gesture input are combined to create a compelling illusion of remote embodied presence through a mobile device.

The purpose of this prototype is to contribute to knowledge of the design capabilities of haptic interfaces in software for social experiences. Location-based technology is rapidly emerging and widely accessible. In recent years, 317 million people have had a wireless data subscription (CIA 2014), which can be used as a proxy for access to location sensing. The availability of data from these devices and improving ease of use for developers have allowed for the creation of playful social interactions that are more akin to a natural experience such as a "poke", emoji, Bitmoji-style avatars, animated stickers, and

© Springer International Publishing AG 2017
S. Lackey and J. Chen (Eds.): VAMR 2017, LNCS 10280, pp. 120–129, 2017.
DOI: 10.1007/978-3-319-57987-0_10

GIFs. These are creative, valuable ways of replacing missing information that would otherwise be present in a face to face interaction. However, as technology progresses, these "workarounds" will become unnecessary, as the authenticity and information-rich qualities of interpersonal interaction will finally be able to be transmitted through digital networks. The line between digital and physical interactions in the real world is already blurring, and as this trend continues, people will have a more social, life-like experience when they communicate with others using digital tools. This project aims to contribute an example of playful social technology, with the hope that it inspires others to create new designs utilizing multimodal design and simple mechanics to help people connect with one another.

2   Background

Haptics are not new, but are often overlooked when interactive systems are designed. Even if the designers have not thought of haptics at all in the design process, if a system is interactive, it's haptic – the question is only how much so, and whether the haptic experience is a good one. For an extreme example, take voice-driven interfaces. One could argue that haptics are not necessary in such an interface. We would argue instead that haptics have been intentionally excluded from the design, and that this decision creates both design opportunities (the ability to control it regardless of the body state of the user) and limitations (the lack of ability to feel the system's responses when tactile sensations would otherwise be the appropriate result of a query).

Several factors contribute to haptics being the "forgotten modality". Haptic design tools and rendering engines are less mature than those for visual and audio feedback. Audio and video streams can very closely simulate the real-world sensations of their content. The sensation of seeing a picture of an apple is very similar to seeing an apple in front of you – at least, much more similar than the tactile sensation of a vibration motor imitating sandpaper and the feel of real sandpaper.

For this reason, haptic designers are sometimes asked, "when can haptics do more than vibration?" The answer is, "when you combine haptic vibration intelligently with other modalities." Even the relatively crude vibration displays found in most of today's mobile devices are severely underutilized. The potential to create useful and elegant tactile experiences is already here – it only requires an understanding of how haptics can be combined with visuals, audio, and gesture to tap in to people's preexisting understanding of embodied communication. In other words, it requires good haptic design.

This is already well known in games. While game development usually prioritizes visual rendering above other forms of stimulation (MacLean 2008), rumble feedback is an expected feature of the console experience. Many AAA titles incorporate haptic technology in their controllers, and while many indie developers are following suit, many still have not perfected the design.

Haptics have successfully been integrated into widely used technology in addition to games and entertainment, from smartphone keyboards to virtual reality devices. Most phone keyboards include tactile feedback when typing on the screen. Many people don't notice because it feels natural considering the amount of device use in today's life, but each key provides feedback when a key is successfully touched since the "click" of the keys isn't feasible on a glass screen. Virtual reality devices are adding Immersion's TouchSense Force to provide haptics to their controllers, where this platform offers much more than gaming. VR devices are being used widely by companies to provide immersive training to employees from welding (Porter et al. 2006) to operating rooms (Seymour et al. 2002). Adding haptics to these devices allows the user to feel more like they typing, welding, or operating, simulating a more life-like experience. Despite the adoption of haptics in these popular technologies, social media is still lagging in integrating it into interactions and interfaces to provide more immersive social encounters.

Most emerging technologies are eventually applied to social interaction – one such example is the transition from Web 1.0 to Web 2.0 (Weinschenk 2009). Sociological research indicates there are various reasons humans socialize, including improving cognitive function, producing feelings of happiness, and reducing stress (Billings and Moos 1981). Apps like Tinder, Facebook, LinkedIn, and multiplayer games are popular because they help people interact with particular social groups. However, if subtle body language cues, gestures, and tactile interactions between people could be included in these experiences, they would likely become even more intuitive. The act of feeling something allows for an interaction that elicits emotions and mental states that are sometimes hard to define otherwise or through other senses (El Saddik 2007).

Today's most common use case for haptics on phones, smartwatches, and game controllers is notifying a user that new information has been made available on the device. However, the vibration itself almost never offers meaningful information in itself (MacLean 2008). When haptics do convey more meaning, it's often in the form of patterns that people must memorize in order to understand, such as Google's vibration patterns for turn-by-turn walking direction in Google Maps (Kobayashi and Nakamura 2016). Or for instance, these patterns provide the ability to differentiate a text notification from a Facebook notification based on the intensity or repetition of the vibration. We propose a new paradigm, where haptic design on mobile devices follows in the footsteps of haptics for games, where haptics is used to make an interaction more convincing and realistic – but instead of haptics conveying action as it does in games, in *Remote Touch* it conveys the gesture of another person.

The core gesture of *Remote Touch* is the common "beckoning" gesture, where one finger is pulled in to a hand indicating the direction of desired movement (McNeill 1992). While the gesture for "come here" varies significantly between cultures, the North American version is particularly amenable to touchscreen interaction, since it can be approximated with a single finger "flicking" a short distance across the touchscreen. When in proximity to each other, people might use a beckoning gesture to get someone's attention and request they come closer; depending on the nuance of the gesture, it can also communicate that the other party is accepted or wanted on an emotional level, or that the request is urgent, reluctant, and so on. The haptic gesture in Remote Touch can also take on other meanings, such as a simple, friendly touch, akin to squeezing someone's hand or poking them. The speed of the gesture as well as the social context, contributes rich social information about the intention of the sender.

Combining a mobile device, haptic effect design using Immersion's TouchSense SDK, location information, and interface animations, our prototype creates a simple experience that connects people through non-verbal information to deliver a meaningful gesture and playful interaction. Instead of sending a text or emoji, this application allows for interactions as casual but socially rich as a wave or a high-five between users far away from each other. These types of applications will become more important as technology progresses and more families, coworkers, customers, clients, and loved ones are remote from one another and desire the feeling of true social connection.

Being remote from a connection where a line of communication is needed is all too common, whether it be a stranger or a close friend. Consider the following scenarios where a better social connection would benefit the interactions between the users: searching a busy street corner for an ordered taxi cab, or interpreting vague instructions in a remote team member's email. Despite the differences in scenarios, in both situations more information is needed to reach an end goal in an efficient manner, and having the benefit of in-person feedback such as gestures or demonstrations in addition to speech would assist both users to complete the interaction. In both scenarios, a phone call is placed to clarify location or instructions, but this mode only affords verbal feedback. Having the benefit of seeing that person and their body language or location, whether it be through technology or in person, would enable a more effective experience.

3   Social Technology

Socializing is a common use of location-based experiences and mobile devices, as shown by the wide array of games and applications available to consumers such as *Street-Pass, Facebook, Tinder,* and *Yik Yak.* The example applications listed all have the following in common: location and social interactions ranging from a virtual gesture to speech based in text form. Each application allows users to interact with each other when they become co-located, affording interactions that that are inherently interpersonal, but remove the human elements. They all include some form of social connection that take the form of virtual gestures or a metaphor for a verbal or non-verbal communication. They have all been developed to connect with the people around you, and inspire and incentivize communication in some form or another, but are lacking one of the important forms of feedback in human interactions – touch.

Multi-user games and applications are inherently social, but lack synchronous interactions which in-person socializing allows for. Many social applications that are used in tandem rather than in parallel with other users (Consalvo 2011). This is prevalent in "casual" and "social" games, where the social aspect is abstracted to the point where the interaction is no longer social. Many games incorporate leaderboards or invitations into their gameplay, where the player passively sees that other people are playing, competing with other player's scores, or inviting their friends on social media to challenge their high score. At no point are players interacting with each other in gameplay, only in the game's interfaces.

Non-game applications work the same way, where the mechanics used in many of these applications include passive multiplayer communication: *StreetPass* lets you "collect" passers-by in your area, *Facebook* lets you comment on your friends' posts and send virtual "pokes" or "likes" or "waves" which they will read later, *Tinder* lets you collect matches that you may interact with later, and *Yik Yak* allows conversations between people in your vicinity which you can later comment on. The in-person interaction that is alike to this would be the equivalent of leaving a message on a sidewalk and seeing it after the writer had left. Although this passive multiplayer mechanic is convenient for mobile users who may need to interact at a later time, both the real-time social interaction and the wider context are lost through the technology itself. Designing games and applications in this way only provides a barrier in communication, and dehumanizes our social interactions in technology. Conversations in real time are ideally turn-based, but during that conversation we pick up on facial feedback and body language to determine how the conversation will unfold. A lot of information is lost in translation to words on a device, and many intentions would be more easily communicated via text with more social context. Our goal is to encourage less asynchronous spectating in applications and more real-time gestural interaction.

4   *Remote Touch*: A Prototype Combining Gesture, Haptics, and Location to Create the Illusion of Social Touch at a Distance

Remote Touch is a networked mobile application that lets two people interact through gesture, haptics, and location. The interaction serves as a metaphor for a commonly used social interaction where one user "beckons" the other in their direction. The application alludes to two users being tied together physically by a cord which can be tugged on to grab the other user's attention. The application is meant to be utilized on a wearable device or smartphone, and within a larger framework as a supplement to social interactions within the application.

4.1   Purpose

In developing an application that incorporates haptics and gesture, we can prototype the translation of a social interaction that typically incorporates a few features that rely heavily on social cues - touch, direction, and gestures.

The purpose of the application is to provide a non-verbal social interaction that uses simple mechanics to emulate a meaningful gesture of intent of attention in a specific direction. Many social applications today do not provide effective forms of communication past superficial notifications and text (Chan et al. 2008), and by using abstract haptic effects, we hope to produce meaningful communication extending beyond these modalities. Figure 1 provides an illustration of how the application would be used with a smart watch.

Fig. 1. Smart watch interaction in *Remote Touch*.

4.2 Design

Remote Touch is a remote experience between two users on mobile devices. It is designed to use a user's location, latitude and longitude, to provide a compass to the other user. The core mechanic of the application is a tugging gesture on the user's interface that notifies the recipient of a gesture to get their attention, let them know they're being thought of, or other social purpose. The interface, a ring seemingly attached by a cord to something off-screen, can be pulled away from the off-screen item and dragged around. This establishes the metaphor that there is a physical substrate connecting the two devices, and that what happens on one device can be felt on the other device because they're part of the same physical structure. Figure 2 illustrates the flow of a user's experience in *Remote Touch*.

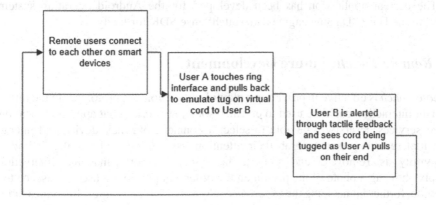

Fig. 2. Experience flow between remote users.

Once two users connect to the application, the latitude and longitude is sent from one user to another by GPS. This allows the interface to point in the direction of the remote user by calculating the difference between the two sets of coordinates and then further calculating the angle between these differences. As User A tugs on their interface, the tugging action from User A is reciprocated to User B, in the form of an inverse tugging action toward the origin of User A. Along with the interface notification, haptic feedback allows the user to become aware that a remote user is "beckoning" them in their general direction. Adding these two modes of feedback together provides the illusion that a remote user is "tugging" you toward them, and the directionality of the compass gives context to the actions, conveying where the action is coming from.

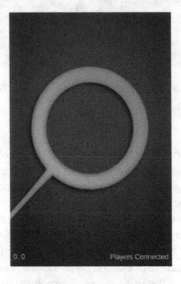

Fig. 3. Screenshot of the interface of *Remote Touch*.

The current application has been developed for the Android operating system, utilizing the Unity3D game engine and TouchSense SDK for Unity.

5   *Remote Touch*: Future Development

Remote Touch is effective in providing a playful interaction as a prototype. In the future, such an interaction could be used to enhance social networks, chat apps, and location-based services. Users will be able to select a contact from their device and interact with that remote person to grab their attention. By adding a photo, the feeling of anonymity is removed, and puts a face to a remote, machine interaction. Simply showing a photo of the person on the other end provides a user's presence to a machine, further humanizing the experience (Consalvo 2011). Figure 4 illustrates future directions for including contacts or social media connections within the application.

Fig. 4. Future contacts functionality for notifying users in *Remote Touch*.

Currently the application utilizes GPS location to determine location of the two remote parties, and display in which direction the remote party is located. Connecting the users with this functionality is more feasible for people in long range of each other with varied latitude and longitudes. Short range scenarios with GPS are less precise, where GPS provides accuracy ranging from 5–8 m in mobile devices (Zandbergen and Barbeau 2011). In order to connect people in buildings and short range areas, our goal is to integrate bluetooth low energy (BLE) iBeacon positioning. iBeacons afford the application the ability to triangulate a user's position in indoor or outdoor situations, where positional accuracy is 1 to 4 m (Estimote 2015).

6 Conclusion

Many conversations are not conversations at all, but a grouping of gestures and visual feedback. *Snapchat* is a popular application that has identified this and designed their application to allow users to send photos of their face, short quips, and emojis, almost eliminating the need for text when sending a message to a friend. With this message, a lot of context is provided such as mood, facial emotion, and even location. But haptics are also an integral aspect to social interactions, and *Remote Touch* contributes something that many popular social media applications don't, while providing a playful interaction for a common gesture. The application is well suited as a supplement to a larger social network whether it is as simple as a contact list in a user's device, or a social media network. For an even more compelling experience, further social features are necessary to enhance a user's presence such as mood, avatars, or emojis.

7   Discussion

Social media is a part of many adult's daily lives, where 65% of American adults use at least one social networking site (Pew Research Center 2015). Many day-to-day tasks are being replaced by applications that have some social aspect like reviews, forums, or location. Ordering a taxi today has been replaced by Uber, deciding where to eat has been supplemented by Yelp, and many people have replaced shopping with making purchases on Amazon based on other people's reviews. Out of these, Uber would benefit most from a short range location based interaction so a rider can more easily find their driver. But all of these applications would benefit from more context to a social interaction in addition to the text on the screen, and additionally would become more playful and fun to use. People's whole lives are on their devices, from banking to dating, further providing incentive to create playful, lifelike interactions that mimic real life.

There are a variety of interactions that can be designed into our social networks and computer interactions from pokes to shoves, to pulls, tugs, brushes, taps, and rubs. The translation of these from human-to-human to human-computer interactions should be at the forefront of the experience design instead of simply designing a text notification and adding a haptic effect on top of it. Mobile devices afford designers a lot of information about a user – location, avatars, their likes, mood or current activities. Meaningful social design incorporates this information in tandem with playful tactile feedback, animations, sounds, or mechanics, and can bring a person to life through the screen.

References

Billings, A.G., Moos, R.H.: The role of coping responses and social resources in attenuating the stress of life events. J. behav. med. **4**(2), 139–157 (1981)

Central Intelligence Agency: The World Factbook (2014). Retrieved http://www.cia.gov

Chan, A., MacLean, K., McGrenere, J.: Designing haptic icons to support collaborative turn-taking. Int. J. Hum.-Comput. Stud. **66**(5), 333–355 (2008)

Consalvo, M.: Using your friends: social mechanics in social games. In: Proceedings of the 6th International Conference on Foundations of Digital Games. ACM (2011)

El Saddik, A.: The potential of haptics technologies. IEEE Instrum. Meas. Mag. **10**(1), 10–17 (2007)

Estimote, Inc. How precise are Estimote beacons? (2015). community.estimote.com

Kobayashi, D., Nakamura, R.: Designing effective vibration patterns for tactile interfaces. In: Yamamoto, S. (ed.) HIMI 2016. LNCS, vol. 9734, pp. 511–522. Springer, Cham (2016). doi:10.1007/978-3-319-40349-6_49

MacLean, Karon E.: Haptic interaction design for everyday interfaces. Rev. Hum. Factors Ergon. **4**(1), 149–194 (2008)

McNeill, D.: Hand and Mind: What Gestures Reveal about Thought. University of Chicago press, Chicago (1992)

Perrin, A.: Social media usage. Pew Research Center (2015)

Porter, N.C., et al.: Virtual reality welder training. J. Ship Prod. **22**(3), 126–138 (2006)

Seymour, N.E., et al.: Virtual reality training improves operating room performance: results of a randomized, double-blinded study. Ann. Surg. **236**(4), 458–464 (2002)

Weinschenk, S.M.: Neuro Web Design: What Makes them Click?. New Riders Publishing, Berkeley (2009)

Zandbergen, P.A., Barbeau, S.J.: Positional accuracy of assisted GPS data from high-sensitivity GPS-enabled mobile phones. J. Navig. **64**(03), 381–399 (2011)

An Exploratory Comparison of the Visual Quality of Virtual Reality Systems Based on Device-Independent Testsets

Robert Manthey[1]([✉]), Marc Ritter[2], Manuel Heinzig[1], and Danny Kowerko[1]

[1] Junior Professorship Media Computing,
Technische Universität Chemnitz, 09107 Chemnitz, Germany
{robert.manthey,manuel.heinzig,danny.kowerko}@informatik.tu-chemnitz.de
[2] Professur Medieninformatik, Hochschule Mittweida, University of Applied Sciences,
Technikumplatz 17, 09648 Mittweida, Germany
marc.ritter@hs-mittweida.de

Abstract. Nowadays, several different devices exist to offer virtual, augmented and mixed reality to show artificial objects. Measurements of the quality or the correctness of their resulting visual structures are not developed as sophisticated as in the classical areas of 2D image and video processing. Common testsets for image and video processing frequently contain sequences from the real world to reproduce their intrinsic characteristics and properties as well as artificial structures to provoke potential visual errors (see Fig. 1a). These common but traditional testsets are nowadays faced with rapid technical developments and changes like HD, UHD etc. improved surround sound or multiple data streams. That results in a limitation of the testsets usability and their ability to evoke visual errors. To overcome those limitations, we developed a system to create device-independent testsets to be used in the area of virtual reality devices and 3D environments. We conduct an empirical evaluation of most recent virtual reality devices like HTC Vive and Zeiss Cinemizer OLED, aiming to explore whether the technical hardware properties of the devices or the provided software interfaces may introduce errors in the visual representation. The devices are going to be evaluated by a group with technical skills and mostly advanced knowledge in computer graphics. All perceived visual and technical saliences are recorded in order to evaluate the correctness and the quality of the devices and the constraints.

1 Introduction

Many of today's electronic systems produce and process a massive amount of multimedia data like video, audio, position information etc. Production systems observe the workflows with cameras and scanning barcodes to optimize, to verify and to track the delivery services of the products. Surveillance systems monitor the traffic of cars to detect potential problems like traffic jam and to provide informations to advanced driver assistance systems. Most of these systems receive, produce and send many different kind of data and often combine

© Springer International Publishing AG 2017
S. Lackey and J. Chen (Eds.): VAMR 2017, LNCS 10280, pp. 130–140, 2017.
DOI: 10.1007/978-3-319-57987-0_11

them to one file or a group of files to create streams of multimedia data. At the same time the number of systems as well as their complexity rapidly grow. The standard video resolution further increases from Full HD to 4k and 8k UHD and beyond while the acoustical standards also make use of additional channels ranging from the well-known 5.1 surround sound to the Hamasaki 22.2 surround sound system. Additional capabilities like 3D, 360-degree, Virtual Reality as well as Augmented and Mixed Reality are also included and need to be addressed. Furthermore, the application domains expands from normal TV and computer screens to smartwatches, smartphones, huge projectors and systems showing artificial objects in 3D with the capability to extend real world image scenes.

In contrast to these trends, common studies of accessibility, correctness, performance, and especially quality are frequently performed by using media samples of small sizes which not seldom originate from the last century, produced in standard-television formats like NTSC, PAL or SECAM being accompanied by stereo sound (cf. to Fig. 1). They often contain recorded sequences from the real world to reproduce intrinsic characteristics and properties as well as artificial structures to invoke potential visual errors. However and due to their nature of a comparatively low-resolution of a past technology, results cannot be easily transferred to the new challenges described beforehand.

Regardless of the system, any stream of multimedia data can be described as a chain of various steps as shown in Fig. 2. Not all the steps need to be included into every system and some steps may repeatedly occur depending on the task of the system. However, each step has its own characteristics and a

(a)   (b)   (c)

Fig. 1. Samples of commonly used visual test data (a) RCA Indian-head test image (http://www.forensicgenealogy.info/images/bulova_indian_head_test_patt.jpg). (b) Lena test image (http://sipi.usc.edu/database/download.php?vol=misc\&img=4. 2.04). (c) Frame of the Flower test video (http://media.xiph.org/video/derf/y4m/ flower_cif.y4m). (Color figure online).

Fig. 2. Chain of multimedia data processing with "C, input from camera; G, grab image (digitize and store); P, preprocess; R, recognize (i, image data; a, abstract data)" [1].

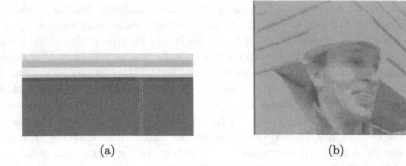

Fig. 3. Samples of common visual artefacts (a) Ringing artefacts at the transition from the red to the white part of the image. (b) Blocking artefacts as result of image compression [8]. (Color figure online).

potential to inflict errors. Such can be noticed for instance as visual artefacts shown in Fig. 3a and b or as clicks or disturbances in acoustical data. On the one hand the characteristics of each artefact and their rate of occurrence are strongly correlated to parameters like resolution, framerate, and color space, one the other hand they also depend on the implementation of the underlying transcoding system, their settings, and the data itself.

In order to reduce the artefacts and to optimize the quality of the multi-media data, various test pattern already exist. Each pattern can detect at least one specific kind of an artefact even though the total number of artefacts is innumerable. In addition, some artefacts will not appear in a single test pattern. Thus, combined and more complex patterns are needed. They commonly appear, for instance, in rapid changes of the image content, movements or image transformations like rotations or translations. Generally, testsets often need to be hand-crafted to cause the anticipated error and make them abundantly clear visible. For example, a minor color error in one of the flowers of Fig. 1c may occur but almost appear nearly invisible since the contrast to the surrounding is too small or too big, in contrast to a image with larger unicolored planes. In some fields like image retrieval, digital archiving [4] or image understanding [5] additional constrains like size or resolution are important to minimize the overall time of the test. On the other hand, many changes of fundamental properties like the aspect ratio, affects the effectiveness of the test and therefore a new test must be created. *Manthey et al.* [3] develops a highly flexible system to create synthetic testsets as independent as possible to overcome that problem and show its use with a short evaluation of visual data with the commonly used video encoding systems FFmpeg[1], Adobe Media Encoder CC 2015.0.1(7.2)[2], and Telestream Episode 6.4.6[3]. Some results present artefacts as in Figs. 4 and 5.

---

[1] https://ffmpeg.org/.

[2] http://www.adobe.com/de/products/media-encoder.html.

[3] http://www.telestream.net/episode/overview.htm.

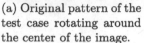

(a) Original pattern of the test case rotating around the center of the image.   (b) Result frame showing grain like random artefacts.   (c) Result frame showing randomly grouped artefacts.

Fig. 4. The test video with rotating stripes in Fig. 4a is compressed with FFmpeg showing heavily disintegrated content in Fig. 4b and c (Color figure online).

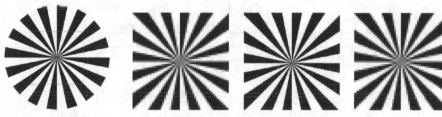

(a) Original unrotating Siemens star pattern with green cutout marking.   (b) Cutout from result frame 1.   (c) Cutout from result frame 7.   (d) Cutout from result frame 15.

Fig. 5. The test video without any change in Fig. 5a is compressed with FFmpeg and results in a sequence of frames with strongly changing visual quality.

In the field of virtual reality systems the quality and the properties can be different for each of both eyes as shown in Fig. 6. Consequently, the amount of examinations increases at least by a factor of two and represents an additional constraint to the testset. The studies of *Kreylos* [2] and *Tate* [6] which use traditional testsets like checkerboards and grids to measure the distortion of the lenses and the chromatic aberration as in Fig. 7a as well as the field-of-view in Fig. 7b. Also the perspective, motion and occlusion have to be taken into consideration.

The remainder of this paper is organized as follows: Sect. 2 gives an overview about the structure and the workflow of the creation of our device-independent testset. Section 3 describes the exploratory comparison of the virtual reality devices with our testset and Sect. 4 present the results. A brief summary and an outlook into future work is given in Sect. 5.

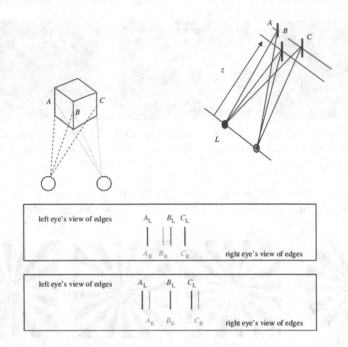

Fig. 6. Scheme of a cube viewed by two eyes. Showing the different position of the edges A, B and C in the visual field of the left and the right eye allowing the calculation of depth [7].

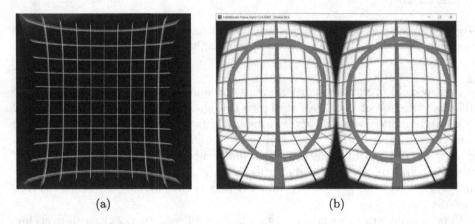

(a) (b)

Fig. 7. Examples of traditional testsets used in the field of virtual reality systems (a) Example of the distortion of a lens and chromatic aberration near the periphery [2]. (b) Example of the field-of-view (oval) of the left and right eye in a virtual reality system with two displays [6].

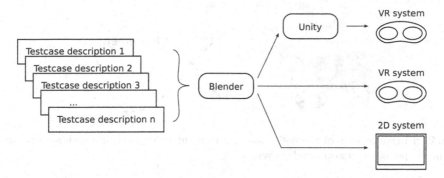

Fig. 8. Schematic view of the process of the generation and the application of the testsets. Descriptions of the testcases be combined into a testset to be applied by Blender to provide them to the designated virtual reality device or monitoring 2D devices. In some cases the transfer to Unity is necessary to provide the testset to the virtual reality device.

2   System Architecture and Workflow

To generate testsets that are able to cover the given constraints in a flexible and adaptable way, we decided to describe them in an abstract, vectorized and device-independent form following the experience from *Manthey et al.* [3]. Each element of a testcase is defined by the shape of the structure, the color, the position and properties of the movement as shown in Fig. 9, aside of affine transformations like translation, rotation, scaling, shearing and reflection of the base elements. In that way a 3D scene is constructed with one or multiple grouped elements in order to build complex test cases.

We use the build-in Blender/Python API[4] to realize the description as the first step shown in Fig. 8. A second step comprises the selection of a subset of all the testcases to create a testset which is afterwards applied to the designated device. If another tool like the cross-platform game-engine Unity[5] is needed to use devices like HTC Vive[6], Oculus Rift[7] or Android-based smartphones, the testset is exported and executed locally. Other devices like the *Zeiss Cinemizer OLED*[8] or simple 2D displays can be directly operated and rendered by Blender. In each case the settings which happens to be more device-specific like the size of the test object, resolution, framerate etc. are set by the current tool, for instance Blender or Unity if necessary. The result is send to the designated device and the test is realized. The comparison of the given data from the generator and the presented visual data allows an inference of the performance, the quality as well as the constraints of the tested devices.

---

[4] https://docs.blender.org/api/blender_python_api_2_78a_release/.
[5] https://unity3d.com/de.
[6] https://www.vive.com/de.
[7] https://www.oculus.com.
[8] http://cinemizeroled.com.

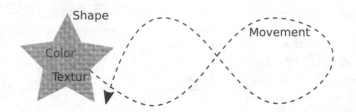

Fig. 9. Schematic view of the definition of a element being part of a testcase consists of the shape, color, texture and movement.

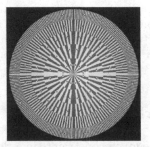

(a) The Siemens-Star contain a group of black and white equal sized stripes from the center of a circle to its perimeter filling a quadrant of the whole circle and the rest by mirroring. In this example, we form a 3D object by stacking together five different cylinders with a radius of one to five units and a height of one unit similar to a pyramid. The texture of stripes of size-adjusted quantity is put on the surface as well as small squares with checkerboard structure.

(b) The Rainbow-Star object in this sample is constructed in a similar way as the Siemens-Star, but with a single color applied to each stripe of the generator quadrant and with a stack of only three cylinders.

(c) This plane pattern is based on a Sierpinski-triangle with red, green and blue triangles of equal size.

Fig. 10. 2D view of some examples of the testcases being part of the testset used in the comparison (Color figure online).

3   Exploratory Comparison

In order to realize the comparison we create a group of testcases. They contain circles and cylinders with black and white and with colored stripes like the samples shown in Fig. 10a and b. Further test cases consist of similarly colored, parallel tubular frames of equal length and diameter. As illustrated in Fig. 10c, some are constructed as Sierpinski-triangle and Sierpinski-carpet with fixed red, green, blue and yellow colored elements respectively. Each version is implemented without movement and with one of the following movements represented in Fig. 11. Move along a sinus-shaped curve, along a circle with one and five units radius through the zero point of the scale as well as orbiting that point, and along a rectangle of one and five units length. One additional movement realizes the circling of the scene camera representing the position of the virtual reality device in the virtual reality world like lunars orbit around the earth.

The test cases are created and deployed to each of the virtual reality devices with a resolution of HD or the closest possible depending on the device and with 24 bit color depth and 25 frames per second. Afterwards the set is presented to our exploratory group using a HTC Vive and a Zeiss Cinemizer OLED respectively. The group consists of five persons in the age between 20 and 40 years with technical skills with advanced knowledge in computer graphics.

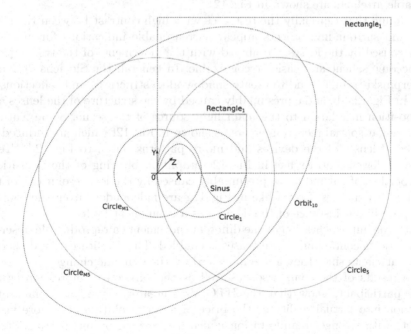

Fig. 11. Scheme of the realized sequences of movements following a sinus-shaped curve, circles of different diameters and centers of rotation, rectangles of different size and an orbit surrounding the center of the virtual reality scene.

Any visual artefact perceived by the participants is registered and a picture is taken by a Canon IXUS 980 IS digital camera at the position of the eye of the perceiving participant. This is compared with the deployed testset and the presentation at the 2D device to get a better isolation of the reason. For each artefact, a subjective estimation is given by each participant representing its relevance with rating from 1 (insignificant, i.e. less important) to 5 (severe, i.e. heavily affects the quality of perception). Finally, all ratings from the group members of each artefact are averaged to get an overall rating.

4   Results

After the deployment and the presentation of the testset to our exploratory group the visually perceived artefacts and their ratings are taken into account to select the most salient as well as the strongest artefacts from the total amount. In a similar way the rating of the testcases are processed.

As a result, our comparison shows that the biggest influence of the visual quality of all the testcases is represented by the hardware of the virtual reality devices, mostly as expectable mostly depending on resolution and the quality of the incorporated hardware. Furthermore, a lowering of the quality of the rendering system can result in visual artefacts but also in the introduction of new abnormalities, especially during movements. However, a selection of the best depictable artefacts are shown in Fig. 12.

We found that especially the testcases with high contrast between their elements and surrounding objects appear as reasonable indications for artefacts mostly caused by the lenses. Combined with the movements of the test objects, they become salient and easier recognizable. In general, the Siemens-Star and the Sierpinski-triangle tend to create shadow-alike structures and reflections as shown in Fig. 12a, b, and e presumably caused by the structure of the lenses and their position in relation to the main light source of the scene. Some features create regular spatial recurring errors as shown in Fig. 12f which are induced by the Fresnel lenses of the devices and moire patterns (cmp. to Fig. 12d). Testcases with lower contrast like in Fig. 12c amplify a blurring of the transitions of the borders of colored areas presumably caused by the low resolutions of the virtual reality devices. Errors like in Fig. 12g are independent from the content but appear in our instance of the devices as a component fault.

With the implementation of the different movements a reproducible observation of objects containing the testcases is enabled. This facilitates the detection of some artefacts since they are emphasized by the dynamic changes.

The results of the comparison as well as the subjective impressions given by the participants show that the HTC Vive creates a good and elaborated immersion into virtual reality at the price of lower resolution and more visual artefacts with stronger manifestation which are covered by intrinsic actions of movement in the 3D environment, especially in fast-paced games. The Zeiss Cinemizer OLED performs a better visual realization with mostly higher quality but a lower clarity of the virtual reality.

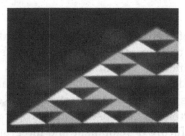

(a) A Sierpinski-triangle produces artefacts of left-shifted colored shadows of the
elements.

(b) Moving (a) along a predefined path
enhances the perceptibility of artefacts
yielding to a curved reflection on right.

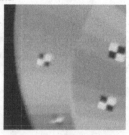

(c) A Rainbow-Star demonstrates the
blurring artefact at the borders of the areas.

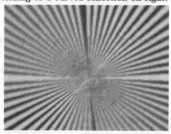

(d) With a Siemens-Star, moire effects
and the pixel grid becomes visible, especially in the upper left area.

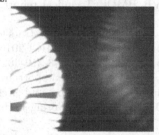

(e) During movement the reflection of a
Siemens-Star becomes indistinct but visible because of the high contrast to the
background, whereas at some positions
distinct perceptions are perceivable.

(f) At an particular position during the
movement of a Sierpinski-triangle and
their shadows the rings of the Fresnel lens
become clearly visible.

(g) A defect in the construction of our
Zeiss Cinemizer shows a content independent bright bar on right of the left display.

Fig. 12. Pictures of best depictable visual artefacts caused by the testset (Color figure
online).

5 Summary and Future Work

In conclusion, we demonstrated the use of testcases based on abstract device-independent descriptions of objects and movements in virtual reality scenes. They are generated and deployed to different virtual reality devices being observed by our exploratory group in order to compare the two virtual reality devices and to estimate the usefulness of generated testsets as well as the generation process. The observed visual artefacts demonstrate the properness of the approach and its potential. Especially future development and integration of automatic image capturing devices strikingly increases the capabilities of quality measuring and assurance of the devices and their components like lenses and displays.

Acknowledgments. This work was partially accomplished within the project *localizeIT* (funding code 03IPT608X) funded by the *Federal Ministry of Education and Research* (BMBF, Germany) in the program of *Entrepreneurial Regions InnoProfile-Transfer*.

References

1. Davies, E.: Machine Vision. Morgan Kaufmann, Amsterdam (2005)
2. Kreylos, O.: Optical Properties of Current VR HMDs. Technical report. http://doc-ok.org/?p=1414
3. Manthey, R., Conrad, S., Ritter, M.: A framework for generation of testsets for recent multimedia workflows. In: Antona, M., Stephanidis, C. (eds.) UAHCI 2016. LNCS, vol. 9739, pp. 460–467. Springer, Cham (2016). doi:10.1007/978-3-319-40238-3_44
4. Manthey, R., Herms, R., Ritter, M., Storz, M., Eibl, M.: A support framework for automated video and multimedia workflows for production and archive. In: Yamamoto, S. (ed.) HIMI 2013. LNCS, vol. 8018, pp. 336–341. Springer, Heidelberg (2013). doi:10.1007/978-3-642-39226-9_37
5. Ritter, M.: Optimization of algorithms for video analysis: a framework to fit the demands of local television stations. In: Wissenschaftliche Schriftenreihe Dissertationen der Medieninformatik, vol. 3, pp. 1–336. Universitätsverlag der Technischen Universität Chemnitz, Germany (2014). http://nbn-resolving.de/urn:nbn:de:bsz:ch1-qucosa-133517
6. Tate, A.: VRL and a community and test region for virtual reality in virtual worlds. Technical report, Artificial Intelligence Applications Institute, University of Edinburgh (July 2016), http://blog.inf.ed.ac.uk/atate/2016/07/20/vrland-a-community-and-test-region-for-virtual-reality-in-virtual-worlds/
7. Westheimer, G.: Three-dimensional displays and stereo vision. Proc. Roy. Soc. **278**, 2241–2248 (2011)
8. Wiegand, T., Sullivan, G.J., Bjntegaard, G., Luthra, A.: Overview of the H.264/AVC video coding standard. IEEE Trans. Circuits Syst. Video Technol. **13**(7), 560–576 (2003)

Performance and User Preference of Various Functions for Mapping Hand Position to Movement Velocity in a Virtual Environment

Weizhi Nai[1], David Rempel[2], Yue Liu[1(✉)], Alan Barr[2],
Carisa Harris-Adamson[2], and Yongtian Wang[1]

[1] Beijing Institute of Technology, Beijing, China
liuyue@bit.edu.cn
[2] University of California, Berkeley, Richmond, CA, USA
David.Rempel@ucsf.edu

Abstract. This study evaluated the effect of different hand-position-to-velocity mapping functions on user performance and preference for freehand gesture navigation in a virtual environment. Three parameters of the velocity mapping function were evaluated: hand position to velocity slope, linearity and size of the zero-velocity area around the resting hand position (e.g., dead zone). 16 subjects completed a forward movement task in a virtual environment with different distances and sizes of target-destinations. Time to complete the tasks was significantly influenced by velocity slope and linearity. Subjective usability ratings were influenced by all three parameters. When optimized, free-hand gestures provide a functional form of human-computer interaction in a virtual environment.

Keywords: Velocity control · Navigation technique

1 Introduction

Navigation is one of the important interactions in games and applications within a 3-D Virtual Environment (VE). Navigation is used to complete tasks by controlling the movement of a virtual character, which represents the user themselves, inside a VE of a terrain or a city, either in first-person view or in third-person view.

Movement through VE generally involves two kinds of controls, movement direction and movement velocity. Each application uses some combination to achieve full navigation in 3-D VE [1]. Direction control can be achieved using orientation of the head-mounted display (HMD) or some other technique such as keyboard arrows. This paper will focus on velocity control.

Different velocity control techniques have been compared [2]. Although velocity can be set automatically based on the scale of the nearby environment [3], active velocity control based on handheld input devices can provide users with greater

---

This research was carried out while Weizhi Nai was at University of California, Berkeley

S. Lackey and J. Chen (Eds.): VAMR 2017, LNCS 10280, pp. 141–152, 2017.
DOI: 10.1007/978-3-319-57987-0_12

freedom of control. Traditionally, the handheld input devices used for velocity control are common hardware such as a mouse, keyboard, touchpad or joystick. However, the emergence of cameras for capturing human posture and motion allows hand or body gestures to be used to control movement velocity. These touchless techniques, typically based on 3-D hand gestures, may provide a more natural user experience than the traditional handheld input device, especially in systems that use large displays in public exhibition places or HMDs [4, 5].

A natural technique for touchless velocity control is to map the user's hand position to forward or backward velocity using a linear relationship, much like the velocity of an automobile is controlled with a foot pedal. Some systems have adopted this technique to allow large scale travel in a VE [6]. For this technique, the mathematical mapping of hand position to velocity is likely to influence user performance and user experience. Although different velocity control techniques have been compared, including touchless ones versus traditional ones, the user experience on various velocity mapping functions remains relatively unexplored.

In this paper, we evaluate 3 parameters to map the user's forward/backward hand position to forward/backward movement velocity in VE: the hand position to velocity slope (simple sensitivity); the hand position to velocity linearity (complex sensitivity); and the size of the zero-velocity area around the resting hand position (dead zone size). In addition, we also compared forward/backward hand movement with the hand floating vs the hand supported on a desk surface. Subjects completed low precision and high precision navigation tasks with different mapping parameter values. The outcome measures were performance, preferences and comfort. The task involved moving as rapidly as possible in a forward direction (1-D) to a visible target of different widths and distance, and has some similarities to the Fitt's tapping task [7], in which user performance is proportional to target size and inversely proportional to target distance.

In Sect. 2 of this paper we introduce the 3 parameters for the mapping of hand position to velocity. In Sect. 3 we describe experimental methods. In Sects. 4 and 5 we present some of the results and discuss interesting findings.

2   Velocity Curve Parameters

We define a 1-D mapping function that converts the forward/backward position of hand to the velocity of forward or backward self-travel in a virtual environment. The absolute position of hand is not directly used in the mapping function, because in practice the position where the user sits or stands and the position of the hand motion sensor device could be arbitrary every time the user engages with the system. Therefore, at the beginning of each engagement, we set a *zero point* which is the position of the palm when the user feels comfortable and ready to control self-travel in the virtual environment. Typically, the upper arm is next to the torso, the elbow is bent to approximately 90°, the forearm is parallel to the floor, and the user assumes a loose fist or relaxed hand posture. The hand may float in air or be supported by the desk surface. D is defined as the forward-backward distance of the hand relative to the zero point, with positive representing a hand position forward of the zero point, and negative representing the hand position backward from the zero point.

On either side of the zero point there is a distance called the *dead zone* which is centered at the zero point and has a total width of λ. When the hand is inside the dead zone, the velocity (V) remains 0. When the user's hand moves beyond the dead zone, e.g., when D is greater than $\lambda/2$, movement in the VE begins. Forward velocity increases as the hand moves forward of the dead zone boundary. The width of the dead zone λ is one of the parameters of the velocity mapping function evaluated.

Beyond the dead zone, the shape of the hand position to velocity curve is defined by two sensitivity related parameters, simple sensitivity α and complex sensitivity γ. Simple sensitivity α follows a classic meaning of sensitivity commonly used in many computer games, i.e. representing a linear change in velocity relative to hand displacement. Complex sensitivity γ represents a nonlinear (e.g., exponential) relationship between hand position and velocity.

The mapping function of hand position D to velocity V with the 3 parameters is

$$V = \alpha \left(\frac{D - \lambda/2}{M} \right)^{\gamma} \tag{1}$$

where M is a constant value. The purpose of M is to define the position where multiple curves with different nonlinear parameter values meet; in other words, the velocity is independent on γ when the distance of hand position to the dead zone boundary is M.

When D is less than $-\lambda/2$ (e.g., backward movement), the mapping function is a negative mirror of its positive counterpart. In addition, the ceiling for D is set to be $15 + \lambda/2$ (cm); thus V does not increase despite D exceeding the ceiling threshold. The 15 cm distance was chosen to keep shoulder flexion within a comfortable range, approximately $0°$ to $45°$, for a person of the 50th percentile [8]. We chose M to be 7.5 cm, half of the ceiling distance, so that different complex sensitivity values resulted in less overall difference in velocity over the full range of hand motion.

A nonlinear velocity curve (i.e. complex sensitivity $\gamma > 1.0$) provides an area just beyond the dead zone where users can operate at a slower velocity when approaching targets that require increased control. It also allows users to move with higher velocity between targets since the velocity increases more rapidly as the hand is further away from the dead zone.

3   Experiment Method

3.1   Virtual Environment

The virtual environment included a virtual character controlled by users which moved forward to arrive in a visible target ahead of the user. Backward motion was allowed when a target was overshot. The virtual environment included an endless road, 3.7 m wide with side railings of 0.8 m high, which disappeared into the distance. Trees were periodically visible just outside the railings to provide a sense of distance. The virtual character stood in the center of the road and provided the viewpoint, but the character was not visible to the user. Instead, a red line crossing the road indicated the position where the virtual character was standing. The red line was positioned 0.3 m above the road floor. A virtual camera was placed 1.5 m above the road floor and 2.5 m behind the virtual character, and followed the virtual character whenever the virtual character moved, thus capturing and rendering a third-person view. Movement was constrained to the center of the road. By flexing at the shoulder, movement of the hand/forearm segment controlled the forward or backward movement of the virtual character along the road. The relative position of the camera to the virtual character is fixed, therefore, the red line always appeared at a fixed location close to the bottom of the screen (Fig. 1).

Fig. 1. Screenshot of the VE which included an endless road for 1-D navigation wherein a red line indicated self-position. Two yellow lines plus a semi-transparent bubble indicated a target for subjects to arrive in (Color figure online).

Subjects moved forward or backward along the road to move the red line (i.e., self) to the next target, indicated by a sphere that was marked by two yellow lines (Fig. 1). The distance between the two yellow lines and the diameter of the sphere, were the target width ρ. The bubble sat on the road surface, and was meant to provide information about the distance to the target. Users could easily see when the red line was between the two yellow lines, which was the ultimate goal of the task.

3.2   Experiment Environment

The virtual environment was rendered on a desktop PC, and a monitor was placed on a table. The table and the chair were height adjustable and set to fit the subject's anthropometry. A depth camera (RealSense F200, Intel) was attached to the end of a mechanical arm, and positioned in front of the right hand pointing horizontally toward the users' hand, about 5 cm above the table surface.

3.3 Hand Position Detection

Hand position was detected with a depth camera. To improve stability of hand detection, an environment-robust hand detection algorithm was not used, but instead, the object closest to the camera was assumed to be the hand. A histogram of depth value of all the pixels was calculated for every frame captured by the depth camera. To minimize noise, 0.1% of all the pixels that had the smallest depth values were ignored. After removal of the ignored pixels, the pixels that had a depth value in the range of [d, $d + 150$] were considered belonging to the hand, where d was the smallest depth value. The depth of the hand, i.e. the distance of the hand to the camera D_h was calculated as the average depth value of all the pixels that belonged to the hand.

Assume the zero point had a depth value of D_z, the hand position D which was used in the velocity mapping function was defined as $D = D_z - D_h$, i.e. the distance between the hand and the zero point.

3.4 Subjects

Sixteen subjects with ages ranging from 18 to 35 years participated in the experiment. The experiment was approved by the University of California at Berkeley Committee on Human Research. Seven were male and 9 were female. Eight subjects report ethnicity to be Asian, 6 Caucasian, and 2 were Latino. The mean height was 1.74 m (range 1.57 m to 1.96 m). Two subjects reported using their left hand for writing, ten reported no experience in video gaming and ten reported using tablet or smart phone more than 10 h per week.

3.5 Task

Subjects were instructed to move their right hand forward or backward in order to move the red line to the next target in the VE. When arriving at the target, indicated when the red line was between the two yellow lines, they pressed the space bar with their left hand. Arriving in the target was considered successful if the red line was inside the target and was not moving. After successfully arriving in a target, the target disappeared and the next target appeared. Subjects were instructed to move as rapidly as possible to acquire the next target. There were a total of 30 targets per trial. If the space bar was pressed when the red line was outside of the target, the subject heard a sound indicating failure and then continued until successfully reaching the target.

The targets appeared at varying distances from the virtual character. To account for practice, the first 6 of the 30 targets in a trail were not considered in the analysis. Among the remaining 24 targets, 8 targets each were set at distances of 3 m, 9 m and 15 m from the last target. For each trial, the target size was either a small (1 m) or large (2 m) width.

3.6 Experiments on Different Parameter Levels

The three mapping function parameters were each tested at 3 different levels. The levels were chosen based on pilot tests. The levels tested for α were 7, 14 and 21 m/s; for λ

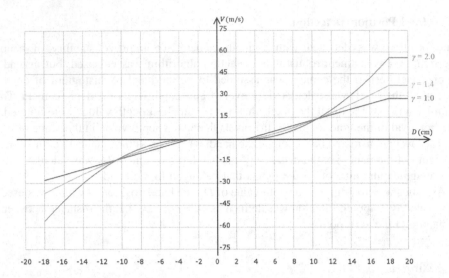

Fig. 2. Velocity curves of movement velocity V against hand position D with 3 different levels for complex sensitivity γ. In this example, the dead zone width is 6 mm.

were 40, 60 and 80 mm; and for γ were 1.0, 1.4 and 2.0. Examples of velocity curves of different complex sensitivity levels (γ) are presented in Fig. 2. When testing the levels of one parameter, the other two parameters were set at the middle value of the levels tested (i.e., $\alpha = 14$ m/s; $\lambda = 60$ mm; $\gamma = 1.4$).

For each of the 4 experiments, subjects completed 6 trials; one trial for each of the 3 parameter levels for both the large and small targets. For each experiment there were two levels of randomization; the first was target size followed by randomization of levels within each target size. After the parameter levels were randomized they were labeled A, B, and C so that subjects could reference them on the usability questionnaire. The order of experiments was simple sensitivity α, followed by dead zone width λ, then complex sensitivity γ. During the first 3 experiments, subjects rested their hand on the desk surface during hand movement. The 4th experiment repeated the simple sensitivity experiment but required subjects not to touch the desk surface with their hand or arm (i.e., free floating).

Before starting the 4 experiments, subjects spent approximately 15 min practicing self-travel and target attainment with different target distances and sizes.

3.7   Questionnaires

Within each experiment, following each trial of a given level, subjects completed a questionnaire which rated the fatigue they felt following the completion of the trial using numbers 1 to 5 where 1 described no fatigue and 5 described extreme fatigue. After completing the 3 parameter levels within an experiment, subjects answered two questions: (1) "which level (A, B or C) did you prefer the most and the least for ease of stopping at the target" and (2) "which did you prefer the most and the least moving toward the target". Open-ended comments comparing levels were also encouraged.

4 Results

For each target presented within a level, the performance time (duration from target appearance to successful movement to target) was recorded. The mean and the standard deviation of the performance time for the 24 trials tested at each level of each parameter were calculated (Tables 1, 2, 3 and 4).

Table 1. Mean time in seconds (SD) to reach each target for different simple sensitivity levels by target diameter and target distance (N = 16), when hand touches desk.

Target diameter	1 m			2 m		
Target distance	3 m	9 m	15 m	3 m	9 m	15 m
$\alpha = 7$ m/s	2.04 (1.39)	2.73 (1.20)	3.28 (1.37)	1.53 (0.65)	2.10 (0.70)	2.84 (1.00)
$\alpha = 14$ m/s	2.05 (1.10)	2.63 (1.28)	2.95 (1.44)	1.56 (0.66)	1.98 (0.65)	2.34 (0.77)
$\alpha = 21$ m/s	2.09 (0.97)	2.61 (1.19)	3.01 (1.37)	1.59 (0.63)	1.86 (0.63)	2.27 (0.82)

Table 2. Mean time in seconds (SD) to reach each target for different dead zone width by target diameter and target distance (N = 16).

Target diameter	1 m			2 m		
Target distance	3 m	9 m	15 m	3 m	9 m	15 m
$\lambda = 40$ mm	1.76 (0.88)	2.36 (1.21)	2.68 (1.01)	1.42 (0.55)	1.93 (0.96)	2.09 (0.70)
$\lambda = 60$ mm	1.81 (0.86)	2.22 (0.80)	2.81 (1.16)	1.38 (0.63)	1.73 (0.59)	2.10 (0.72)
$\lambda = 80$ mm	1.94 (0.96)	2.23 (0.75)	2.81 (1.04)	1.40 (0.65)	1.87 (0.78)	2.21 (0.74)

Table 3. Mean time in seconds (SD) to reach each target for different complex sensitivity levels by target diameter and target distance (N = 16)

Target diameter	1 m			2 m		
Target distance	3 m	9 m	15 m	3 m	9 m	15 m
$\gamma = 1.0$	1.65 (0.79)	2.27 (1.03)	2.56 (0.91)	1.34 (0.61)	1.56 (0.48)	2.07 (0.66)
$\gamma = 1.4$	1.71 (0.92)	2.08 (0.84)	2.80 (1.12)	1.27 (0.54)	1.67 (0.54)	2.13 (0.76)
$\gamma = 2.0$	1.87 (0.78)	2.29 (0.87)	2.62 (0.90)	1.47 (0.56)	1.92 (0.79)	2.12 (0.82)

Table 4. Mean time in seconds (SD) to reach each target for different simple sensitivity levels by target diameter and target distance (N = 16), when hand floats in air.

Target diameter	1 m			2 m		
Target distance	3 m	9 m	15 m	3 m	9 m	15 m
$\alpha = 7$ m/s	1.83 (0.92)	2.25 (1.00)	2.92 (1.06)	1.54 (0.85)	1.89 (0.60)	2.47 (0.72)
$\alpha = 14$ m/s	1.90 (1.16)	2.24 (1.03)	2.52 (1.02)	1.38 (0.66)	1.79 (0.89)	2.03 (0.66)
$\alpha = 21$ m/s	1.91 (0.83)	2.35 (1.03)	2.64 (1.06)	1.35 (0.62)	1.75 (0.74)	1.91 (0.64)

Table 5. *P*-values on performance time for the different experiments (ANOVA).

	Simple sensitivity (hand on desk)	Dead zone width	Complex sensitivity	Simple sensitivity (hand floats)
p-value	0.003	0.37	0.006	0.0004

Within each experiment, differences in performance time between parameter levels were analyzed by ANOVA and the *p*-values are shown in Table 5. Dead zone width has no significant influence while the other two parameters both have significant influence.

Sometimes subjects overshot when trying to arrive in a target. The percentage of overshot targets within each experiment (parameter tested) is shown in Fig. 3.

The average subjective rating of fatigue after each trial in time sequence (independent of parameter levels as the order of levels is block randomized) is shown in Fig. 4. Preference rankings for parameter levels are shown in Fig. 5 and were analyzed using the Friedman Test (Table 6).

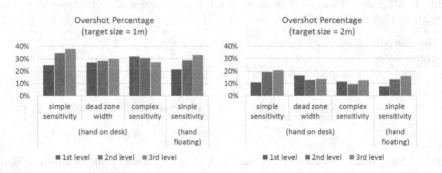

Fig. 3. Overshot percentage with different parameter levels, when target size is 1 m and when target size is 2 m.

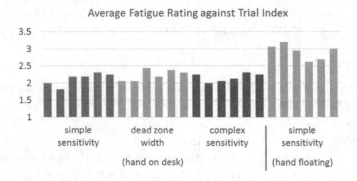

Fig. 4. Average fatigue ratings after each trial. There were 6 trials in each experiment.

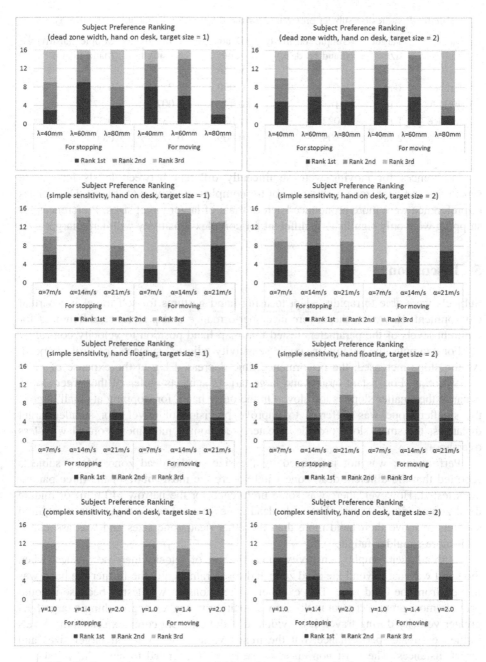

Fig. 5. Summary of preference rankings for each parameter level by subjects.

Table 6. *P*-values on subject preference for the different experiments (Friedman Test).

	Target size	Simple sensitivity (hand on desk)	Dead zone width	Complex sensitivity	Simple sensitivity (hand floats)
Preference in stopping	1 m	0.57	0.050	0.27	0.65
	2 m	0.18	0.44	0.007	0.57
Preference in moving	1 m	0.022	0.022	0.83	0.37
	2 m	0.009	0.009	0.57	0.002

Preferences for moving were significantly different between levels for simple sensitivity and dead zone width, but not for complex sensitivity (Table 6). Differences in preference were more pronounced across trials of larger target sizes. Preferences for stopping were only significantly different for complex sensitivity with large target size.

5 Discussion

Subjects were able to rapidly adapt to using hand gestures for self-travel in a virtual environment. However, there were clear performance and preference differences for different levels of the parameters tested that map hand position to velocity control.

For example, the parameter simple sensitivity adjusted subjects' control of speed. As the slope increased, the performance time decreased but at the expense of more overshooting. For distant targets and large targets subjects preferred the larger slopes because the smaller slope is too slow. On the other hand, for stopping at small targets, the smaller slope was preferred to improve precision of travel. For smaller target distances, the small slope provides greater precision of movement control with less overshoot.

Performance was not influenced by the size of the dead zone. Many subjects reported that the different dead zone widths were the most subtle of the three parameters tested. However, there was some preference for the narrow (40 mm) or middle dead zone width (60 mm). The wide dead zone was not favored because it required subjects to move their hand more than the other dead zone sizes and was associated with more shoulder fatigue.

With a larger complex sensitivity value, the rate of velocity increase was less when the hand was just beyond the dead zone and rose dramatically the further the hand was moved from the dead zone. This exponential relationship was tested because it could provide more precise control in the slow velocity range when approaching a target, yet greater velocity during travel. It is evident that the different complex sensitivity levels influence subject performance, but the trends varied with different target sizes and target distances. The most non-linear curve ($\gamma = 2.0$), tended to have the worst performance and preference characteristics and was described as difficult when moving to small targets due to increased delay. On the other hand, the linear curve level ($\gamma = 1.0$) was described as having an abrupt change in speed with very little hand movement at the edge of the dead zone.

In the two experiments on simple sensitivity, comparing moving with the hand floating in air versus supporting the hand on the desk, performance was better when the hand was floating. This may have been a training effect related to the order of testing, since the floating condition always occurred after the supported hand conditions, and, therefore, subjects were more familiar with the experiment. However, the average fatigue ranking were substantially greater immediately following the free floating condition (experiment 4) indicating that subjects experience more fatigue due to efforts to keep hand floating in air versus supporting it on the desk. Despite the increase in fatigue, subjects varied in their preference for their upper extremity being supported versus free floating. Subjects did report more stress and fatigue in the shoulder during the free floating condition yet reported that the hand friction while the upper extremity was supported may have impeded their control. Some subjects reported that although the free floating condition caused more fatigue, it was more comfortable. Despite the differences in fatigue and comfort, the preferences for parameter levels is similar for the two experiments. It was more difficult for subjects to remember the locations of the boundaries of the dead zone during the free floating condition, since touching the desk provided a reference for the position of the hand relative to the dead zone. Also, subjects tended to move their hand further forward and backward during the free floating condition.

Of interest is that two subjects found easier ways to stop forward travel than pulling their hand back to the dead zone. For example, one subject raised the hand vertically by flexing the elbow to stop and another subject closed the fingers to form a fist to stop. Some subjects controlled velocity with sudden movements of their hand while others moved their hand smoothly.

6 Conclusion

With new depth sensing cameras, hand position can be used to control self-travel velocity in a virtual environment. The shape of the mapping function for converting hand position to velocity influenced user performance and preference. Specifically, the slope of the hand-position-to-velocity curve and the shape of the curve will affect performance of arriving in targets of varying sizes and distances. In addition, users have a preference for certain levels of hand-position-to-velocity slope and dead zone width. The use of non-contacting hand gestures provides a new, naturalistic method of human-computer interaction in a virtual environment. With optimization, this method of interaction may augment or replace interaction using controllers or other physical devices.

Acknowledgements. This research was supported by (1) the National Natural Science Foundation of China under Grant no. 61631010, (2) the National Key R&D Program of China under Grant no. 2016YFB1001502, (3) the Office Ergonomics Research Committee, USA and (4) Google, USA. The findings and conclusions in this report are those of the authors and do not necessarily represent the position of the funders.

References

1. Bowman, D.A., Koller, D., Hodges, L.F.: Travel in immersive virtual environments: an evaluation of viewpoint motion control techniques. In: Proceedings of IEEE Virtual Reality Annual International Symposium, pp. 45–52 (1997)
2. Jeong, D.H., Song, C.G., Chang, R., Hodges, L.: User experimentation: an evaluation of velocity control techniques in immersive virtual environments. Virtual Reality 13(1), 41–50 (2009)
3. McCrae, J., Mordatch, I., Glueck, M., Khan, A.: Multiscale 3D navigation. In: Proceedings of the 2009 Symposium on Interactive 3D Graphics and Games, pp. 7–14. ACM (2009)
4. Ren, G., Li, C., O'Neill, E., Willis, P.: 3D freehand gestural navigation for interactive public displays. IEEE Comput. Graph. Appl. 33(2), 47–55 (2013)
5. Chastine, J., Kosoris, N., Skelton, J.: A study of gesture-based first person control. In: 18th International Conference on Computer Games: AI, Animation, Mobile, Interactive Multimedia, Educational & Serious Games (CGAMES). IEEE (2013)
6. Şen, F., Díaz, L., Horttana, T.: A novel gesture-based interface for a VR simulation: re-discovering Vrouw Maria. IN: 18th International Conference on Virtual Systems and Multimedia (VSMM). IEEE (2012)
7. Fitts, P.M.: The information capacity of the human motor system in controlling the amplitude of movement. J. Exp. Psychol. 47(6), 381–391 (1954)
8. Kölsch, M., Beall, A.C., Turk, M.: The postural comfort zone for reaching gestures. Proc. Hum. Factors Ergonomics Soc. Annu. Meet. 47(4), 787–791 (2003)

The Pulse Breath Water System: Exploring Breathing as an Embodied Interaction for Enhancing the Affective Potential of Virtual Reality

Mirjana Prpa[✉], Kıvanç Tatar, Bernhard E. Riecke, and Philippe Pasquier

School of Interactive Arts and Technology, Simon Fraser University, Surrey, Canada
{mprpa,ktatar,b_r,pasquier}@sfu.ca

Abstract. We introduce *Pulse Breath Water*, an immersive virtual environment (VE) with affect estimation in sound. We employ embodied interaction between a user and the system through the user's breathing frequencies mapped to the system's behaviour. In this study we investigate how two different mappings (metaphoric, and "reverse") of embodied interaction design might enhance the affective properties of the presented system. We build on previous work in embodied cognition, embodied interaction, and affect estimation in sound by examining the impact of affective audiovisuals and two kinds of interaction mapping on the user's engagement, affective states, and overall experience. The insights gained through questionnaires and semi-structured interviews are discussed in the context of participants' lived experience and the limitations of the system to be addressed in future work.

1 Introduction

We react to the environments we inhabit, and these environments can have an immense impact on us. The physical environments are not the only environments we interact with. The progress in VR technology since 2010 demonstrated the potency of virtual reality (VR) to make us feel present in virtual environments (VEs). The sense of presence that we feel in VEs is sometimes so strong that we react to the events in VEs as we would react to them in physical reality [30]. Many authors argue that one of the crucial determinants to make us feel present in a certain environment is the ability of that environment, physical or virtual, to support our actions [15,31,38]. We use our whole bodies and engage them in more or less subtle movements to perform many of our actions, and interact with the environments or engage in talking, walking, or even breathing. The importance of understanding interaction as a whole body activity was recognized by the third wave in human-computer interaction (HCI) research that emphasized an embodied approach to the design of interactive systems. Dourish [9] defines embodied interaction as an approach to interaction design that emphasizes the integrity of our minds and bodies engaged in actions with environments, in a process through which meaning and understanding are generated. Along with

© Springer International Publishing AG 2017
S. Lackey and J. Chen (Eds.): VAMR 2017, LNCS 10280, pp. 153–172, 2017.
DOI: 10.1007/978-3-319-57987-0_13

this idea, Slater and Sanchez-Vives [31] argued that even perception is "a whole body action". A "whole body interaction" is defined as "The integrated capture and processing of human signals from physical, physiological, cognitive and emotional sources to generate feedback to those sources for interaction in a digital environment" [12].

We focus here on the idea that our thinking and learning processes originate in our bodies as much as in our brains (the concept from embodied cognition). In particular, we are focusing on subtle body movements engaged in the process of breathing and mapping the abdominal movement to the changes in our virtual environment (VE). Given the connection between cognition and the body, we ask: if VEs feel "real" and are perceived as real, physical environments, *how can these environments change us through embodied interaction design? And, how can an embodied interaction design that employs the user's subtle breathing movements facilitate these changes?*. These overarching questions motivated the research presented here. We speculate that the ways in which our environments can shape us depends on the environment's properties. In this paper, we investigate how the type of interaction mapping supported by an affect estimation of previously recorded sounds enhances the affective properties of the VE. For our test-bed we employed *Pulse Breath Water*[1] (*PBW*), an immersive virtual environment presented on head-mounted display-HMD (Oculus Rift DK2). The interaction between a user and the environment is enabled through the user's breathing patterns that generate changes in the virtual environment.

PBW has been publicly shown as an art installation; we gained insights from the audience that motivated the research presented here. By undertaking an embodied interaction design research approach and mixed methods, we investigated how different mappings (metaphoric, and "reverse") between the user's breathing patterns and the system response (reflected by the changes in audio and visual components) can be used to influence the user's affective state, user's engagement and overall user experience.

2   Background

2.1   Embodied Interaction and Embodied Cognition in Interactive Systems

The shift in HCI paradigms that emphasized embodiment followed the shift in cognitive research. For a long time it was understood that "thinking" happens in our heads only; however, the emerging body of research on embodied cognition argues that body interactions with the environment is the basis for cognitive processes [37]. In other words, to understand the world around us, we use not only our brains, but our bodies too.

In particular, research on embodied interaction draws an understanding of interaction processes from situated bodies, minds, and the environment. Dourish [9] used the term "embodied interaction" to explain the embodied nature of an

---

[1] http://ispace.iat.sfu.ca/project/pulse-breath-water/.

interaction in physical and social contexts. We interact with others and physical objects in the environment, and through these "embodied actions" we make meanings [9]. Grounded in phenomenology, Robertson [26] focuses on Merleau-Ponty's teachings, and speculates that in the centre of embodied interaction is a living body, our tool to experience the surrounding world. Similarly, the design of interactive systems should follow the interaction principles we establish with the world around us [9].

Similarly to Dourish, Kirsh [18] focuses on the lens of embodied cognition to emphasize the potential for designing interactive systems. Their premise is that when we manipulate objects we shape our concepts and beliefs through the actions that employ those objects in the environment. Kirsh sees objects as extensions of our bodies, that we use to "think" with. Following this idea, we aim to understand how to design interaction with objects in VE in such way that this interaction changes user's feelings, states, concepts, and beliefs. We look at the complex VE as a tool, the complexity of which enables for more interaction design opportunities. The potential of such tools is immense, and would allow for new research directions in embodied cognition and VR.

2.2   Unconventional Interfaces

Conventional vs Unconventional Interfaces. The definition of unconventional interfaces depends on the user's familiarity with interaction interfaces. According to Kruijiff [19], some of the characteristics of unconventional interfaces are: alternative input/output compared to hand-held control and audio-visual feedback, using either new technology or existing technology in a new way compared to conventional interfaces, use of interfaces in artistic works compared to common, everyday usages, and using "magical"/unnatural metaphors compared to well-known metaphors.

As different tasks require fundamentally different interfaces (interfaces for a FitBit vs a flying interface in VR simulator), Beckhaus and Kruijiff [4, p. 72] distinguish between interfaces used for "experimental application" and interfaces built with the goal of successful task-accomplishment (productive application). While in productive applications the main concern is usability, in experimental applications fun factor and aesthetics are some of the preferred values [4, p. 183]. Here, we focus on the experimental application of a breath-controlled interface in our work. Given that there is no particular goal set for a user to achieve, but rather to explore the interaction, we argue that breathing as an interaction modality will contribute to a higher engagement of a user in VE, which will, we predict, enhance the user's affective reactions to VE.

Breath-Controlled Interfaces. Respiration computer interfaces (RCI) are easy to use, accommodating to different body shapes, and preferred over button interfaces [2]. Two main categories of application for breath-controlled devices are: assistive technologies for impaired individuals, and interfaces used for creative expression. Assistive technologies often take a form of breath controlled joysticks and mouses [13,20,29]. Breath-controlled interfaces in creative applications can be found in a number of video games [32,34] and in artworks that employ an audience's breath in various ranges of creative outputs [23,28].

The number of VR projects that have employed breathing input is limited, to our knowledge. Waterworth et al. [36] built a VE for exploring the relationship between emotion and presence, through a multimodal interaction paradigm. Employed input modalities were the user's balance for movement (leaning forward/backwards, right/left), and breath for vertical navigation. As the authors reported, initial trials confirmed the ease of using a breath interface for natural interaction on a vertical axis in VE. This project was inspired by the pioneering work of Char Daves' *Osmose*, an immersive VE presented on HMD, in which the user's breathing and balance were assessed via a vest [8]. This artwork, highly influential, refers to the phenomenological teachings of Heidegger and Merleau-Ponty in Daves' attempts to bring together divorced minds and bodies. In this work we can recognize traces of ideas of embodied interaction and cognition that will be publicly presented years after the completion of Daves' work.

2.3   Affect and Sound Estimation

Dimensional approach to affect estimation in sound and music: Affect estimation in sound and music is still in discussion in Music Information Retrieval (MIR) research. Eerola and Vuoskoski [10] argue for four affect models as discussed in their state of the art paper on affect estimation in sound and music [10]. The four affect models are: discrete, dimensional, miscellaneous, and music-specific. We undertake a dimensional approach to emotion that is focused on defining continuous dimensions that can represent and differentiate affective states. Ekkekakis [11] presented different dimensional models of affect in human subjects, however in our research we are focusing on the 2-dimensional circumplex model by Posner et al. [25]. The circumplex model has 2 axes, horizontal representing the valence dimension (unpleasant-pleasant) and vertical axis that represents the arousal or activation dimension (activation-deactivation), assessed here using the Affect Grid by Russell et al. [27]. We built *PBW* upon our previous research on affective estimation of soundscape recordings [5,14,35]. Specifically, we use the affect estimation model of Fan et al. [14] in our system design. In this 2-dimensional model of affect in audio, two axes are: pleasantness (equivalent to valence in human subject research) and eventfulness (equivalent to arousal).

Audio stimuli and Affective states: Previous research in the domain of audio stimuli and affective states showed that by varying pleasantness of the sound you can affect the user's ratings of arousal. Bradley and Lang showed that highly pleasant and highly unpleasant sounds had higher arousal ratings, while the most memorable sounds are those with high arousal [6]. Asutay and Västfjäll [3] researched the relationship between emotional reactions as described through activation (arousal)-valence scales and the characteristics of sounds that are tones and noise complexes. Activation was related to the tonal content and sharpness, whereas valence was associated with perceived loudness, roughness, and naturalness. Similarly, Tajadura-Jiménez et al. [33] researched the determinants of sound properties (physical, physiological, and spatial) in regard to evoked affective responses and revealed the effect that the intensity of sound, amplitude and frequency modulation, and the type of sound (natural, and artificial) have on reported arousal. One of the relevant findings is that fast heartbeat sounds lead to increased reported arousal, and as well, can enhance affective response of the presented visual stimulus, if visuals and sounds are presented at the same time to a user. We are tackling this idea by matching changes in affective audio to the changes in visuals. While affect estimation in audio is a well researched area, there is no research done, to our knowledge, on the application of affect estimation of audio systems in VEs. Moreover, we research how changes in the audio and visual components of the VE triggered through embodied interaction influence the user's affect.

3 Pulse Breath Water, an Immersive Virtual Environment with Affect Estimation in Sound

Pulse Breath Water (*PBW*) is an immersive virtual environment (VE) presented to a user through a HMD and is manipulated by the pulse of a participant's breath, provoking and challenging the interaction between a user and the substantial element of the VE: water. The user rises in the VE when breathing in and slowly sinks (underwater) when breathing out. The interaction design follows the idea of "metaphoric" mapping (discussed in the Sect. 3.2 in more details). The audio is generated in real-time by mapping the eventfulness of the chosen audio samples to the frequency of the user's breathing.

Our design approach relied on an autobiographical design [24] and iterative research through design process [39]. The collaboration between the authors coming from HCI and generative audio field required iterative design sessions during which a variety of mappings between a user's breathing frequency, visuals, and audio were discussed and implemented.

3.1 Interaction Scenario

In the design process, we reduced visual impact following the concepts of ambiguity and abstraction. We decided to employ the user's breathing in an interaction with the VE, in a simple manner that empowered users to react to the system's decisions in VE through their breathing patterns. Users were comfortably seated, and we gave no instructions to the users prior to immersion; rather we left it up to them to explore the VE. The system recognizes subtle differences in breathing patterns, and reacts to changes in breathing patterns by changing the audio quality and visual characteristics (the waves become more calm as the breathing slows down. e.g.). The system has its own behaviour that changes in regard to the incoming breathing patterns of a user. This process could be understood as negotiation between a user and the system, in a play that prioritizes the user's decisions over the system's.

3.2   System Description

The overall system outline is represented in Fig. 1. Two breathing sensors (Thought Technology [1]) attached to the user's abdominal and chest area stream breathing waveform data to M+M middleware. M+M sends this data to a MAX msp patch. The reactive agent generates the audio output using an audio corpus (a set of pre-recorded audio samples). The reactive agent selects samples from its corpus using the mapping of the frequency of the user's abdominal breathing to the eventfulness of the audio samples. All audio samples were previously labelled with a two-dimensional vector: average eventfulness and average pleasantness using an affect estimation model proposed by Fan et al. [14]. The reactive agent sends online affect estimation of the audio output to Unity 3D along with breathing data via OSC messages. This data generates visual changes in the VE presented to the user via HMD. The user listens to the audio environment with circumaural noise-cancelling headphones.

Fig. 1. The system architecture

Audio: Figure 2 shows the average affect values of each audio sample in *PBW*'s audio corpus. Each dot represents one audio sample. We created the audio corpus by recording two, three, four, and five voice chords with quartile harmony on the piano. Then, we used pitch shift and time stretch to generate more sounds. In particular, we used these methods to generate an audio corpus that locates around neutral valence and neutral to low arousal in the affective space. Following, we calculate the user's abdominal breathing patterns using the wavelet transform of the breathing data. In our implementation, the wavelet transform has 24 bands. We map these bands to the highest and the lowest arousal (eventfulness) values in our audio corpus. The reactive agent uses the band with the highest power to choose an audio sample. Hence, we map the frequency of the user's breathing to the eventfulness of the audio. At any point, four audio samples are played together to ensure that the affective state of the overall audio centres around the neutral arousal. The design decision to position the audio corpus in this area of affective grid arose from authors' aesthetic tendencies. Our goal was to lead our users towards relaxing states, by introducing audio low in arousal (in audio vocabulary of affect: eventfulness), and staying in neutral to positive end of valence axis (pleasantness).

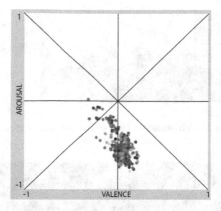

Fig. 2. The audio corpus of *PBW* mapped to 2 dimensional space defined by arousal and valence axes

Visual: Virtual environment built in Unity 3D comprises of a scene that combines interactive audio (generated independently via MAX msp patch) and the 3D element of a body of water - an ocean (see Fig. 3). The aesthetics of the scene is intentionally left minimal, displaying the ocean and the sky in a range of gray-scale shades over time (see Fig. 4). Below the main level of the ocean, we positioned an additional ocean surface in blue colour, to emphasize surreality of the scene. A fog that encompasses the ocean in the distance adds to the ambiguity of the scene. We decided to implement these elements in order to maintain a neutral atmosphere dictated by neutral valence and arousal levels of the accompanying audio environment. This was based on the authors' judgment and several design iterations with informal user testing. The main design principle in designing this environment was ambiguity to evoke engagement and thought-provoking. As Gaver et al. [16] argue, ambiguity in HCI and design of interactive artifacts is desirable for the thought-provoking and engaging characteristics that it adds to the design. In *PBW*, we aimed at employing an "ambiguity of relationship" [16] that engages users to project their own values and experiences in the process of meaning-making. While meaning-making is not in the focus of the presented research, we find it to be a crucial component in creating the experience of the whole scene, adding to the affective potency of the environment.

Mappings: Breathing frequency as well as eventfulness (arousal) and pleasantness (valence) levels of the audio environment are sent from Max msp patch to the game engine Unity 3D. In Unity, the value of eventfulness is mapped to the waves of the ocean. Higher aroused states result in a more disturbed ocean surface and waves. The colour of the sky progresses from grey (at the beginning of the experience) to pitch black (at the end of a session) over the span of eighth minutes. A participant's breathing data controls the elevation of the user in the VE in that, when the user breathes in, their position in the environment is

Fig. 3. Screen shots of the environment: left: calm ocean; center: aroused ocean; right: under the water

Fig. 4. Screen shots of the sky's colour progression: left: sky colour at minute 1; middle: sky colour at minute 5; right: sky colour at minute 8 (Color figure online)

elevated so they can rise above the ocean surface. Similarly, when the participant exhales, they sink.

3.3 *PBW* as an Art Installation

PBW was premiered as an art installation in two collective exhibitions: *Scores + Traces* at One Art Space in NYC, USA (March 10–12th, 2016), and at MUTEK-VR Salon in Montreal, Canada (November 9–13th, 2016). During these two exhibitions we gathered qualitative feedback from the audience, which we summarize here along with our observations of the audience's behaviour.

Easing-into the Environment. *PBW* was designed as a generative piece without a clear beginning or end. The time that the users spent in the *PBW* varied from 5 to 20 min. The users usually spend the first few minutes exploring the extremes of their breathing, to familiarize themselves with the system's capabilities through exaggerated belly movements while inhaling and exhaling. Interestingly, after a few minutes of vigorous exploration, users would slowly ease–into the environment, and their breathing would become slowly paced. This type of breathing would typically remain stable until the end of each session (until the user decided they are done).

Meaning-Making and Re-evoked Memories. Even though we did not design *PBW* with any particular narrative in mind, the majority of users we spoke to had their own interpretation of what the narrative was. Some of them constructed the narrative, others re-lived some of their past experiences. We believe that a major role in the meaning-making process is held by users themselves, who invest their "beholder's share" [17]. In other words, users respond to the ambiguity and lack of details by projecting their own experiences and imagination relying on top-down processing [17, p. 58].

4   Methodology

4.1   Study Design

In order to investigate the potential benefits of predictable, embodied interaction through breathing on a user's affect, enjoyment, engagement, and presence we designed an experimental comparison of interactions using two versions of *PBW* to support two different experimental conditions: (a) metaphoric mapping; and (b) reversed mapping.

4.2   Conditions and Mappings

The original piece, *PBW*, was modified to support two experimental conditions that differed in interaction mapping between breathing frequencies and the changes in the environment.

Condition 1: Metaphoric mappings: In this condition, metaphoric mappings of audio and changes in VE are based on cognitive schema developed from everyday actions and interactions such as "more is up, less is down" [21]. Metaphoric mappings are widely exploited in the design of everyday objects (sliders moved up to "crank the volume up") because the underlying concepts are understood beyond conscious awareness. For this reason metaphoric mappings of interactions are considered to be "intuitive" and require unconscious effort [21].

   PBW was originally designed following the logic of metaphoric mappings. The vertical movement of the participant in the environment follows the logic of "more is up": the more air you inhale the higher you move. When participants inhale they rise in the environments, and when they exhale they sink, similar to what happens when exhaling when swimming. The exact position is depending on the amount of air inhaled/exhaled, therefore the participant can be above the water (a big breath in), under the water (deep exhale), or any place in between if they maintain shallow breathing. In this metaphoric condition, we did not change the mapping between the respiratory interaction and the generative audio. We use the same mapping that we explain in Sect. 3.2 to generate the audio output.

Condition 2: Reverse mappings: In this condition, we reversed the metaphoric mapping in order to investigate how this might affect participants' experiences in regard to their affect, engagement, immersion and overall satisfaction. In this condition, when a participant breathes in they sink, and rise when they exhale. This is a simple intervention yet clearly observable by the participants. The waves of the ocean were still mapped to arousal level. Moreover, we reversed the mapping between the respiratory sensor data and audio sample selection. As the user breathes more frequently, the reactive agent chooses samples with lower eventfulness; and vice versa.

Based on the above-mentioned cognitive schema and metaphor theory [21] we hypothesized that interaction based on *metaphoric mappings* will be more engaging and will enhance the affective properties of the audio more than the *reverse mapping* condition.

4.3 Participants

Twenty-four participants (16 female) were recruited using on-line participant recruitment system, and randomly assigned to one of the two experimental conditions to start with. Participants' ages ranged from 19 to 58 (mean: 22.3, SD: 8.03). Majority of participants have never tried VR before (14/24). All participants reported the good health condition and normal vision.

4.4 Experimental Setup

The experiment was performed in iSpace lab, SIAT, SFU. The participants were seated, one at the time, in a dark room, at the computer station. Depending on theirs assigned experimental condition, one of the two VE experimental conditions were presented on an Oculus DK2 HMD (resolution 1080 × 960 per eye) and refresh rate of 75 FPS. The audio component of VE was played on noise cancelling headphones. Participants wore two breathing sensors (Thought technology) positioned on the abdomen and chest.

4.5 Procedure

Upon arrival in the lab, we informed participants that they are participating in an exploratory study in which we are interested in their engagement with the VE measured through assessed affect before and after, and additional questionnaires. Following, participants read written description of the study, and signed informed consent. The participants were informed about their rights to withdraw at any point and instructed to report to the experimenter any feelings of vertigo, nausea, or headache as they arise, upon which the experiment would be terminated. Each participant completed two eight minute long session (for example, condition 1: metaphoric mapping, and condition 2: reverse mapping). The order of conditions was counter-balanced across participants. After each session, the participants were interviewed.

4.6 Data Collection

Before the experiment, the participants were asked to fill in the affect grid and state- trait anxiety inventory -STAI-6 [22]. After each exposure, the participants filled in the affect grid and STAI-6 again, without seeing their previous responses. In addition, they were asked to answer a questionnaire containing twenty-one questions. Our questionnaire is a modified version of the Game Engagement Questionnaire [7] used for assessing levels of engagement through the lenses of four categories: flow, immersion, engagement, and presence. Following, the participants were interviewed and the interviews were audio recorded.

4.7   Data Analysis

Data analysis was performed on the data from twenty-two participants. Data from two participants had to be discarded: One participant experienced anxious feeling in the middle of the first exposure and the experiment was stopped at that point. The other participant did not report motion sickness as it occurred and rather continued, but was unable to complete all of the questionnaires. Quantitative data was analyzed through inferential statistics, as explained below in the Findings section. Interviews were transcribed and analyzed using a grounded theory approach. The deductive approach to coding originated from the semi-structured interview questions that focused on the experience: feelings, thoughts, actions performed, attention, intentions, narrative, evoked memories, and difficulties of using the system.

5   Quantitative Findings

5.1   Questionnaire Findings

A two-way within-subject ANOVA was run on a sample of 22 participants to examine the effect of order and mapping on the different questionnaire items. Below we only report significant main effects and interactions.

Perceived reactivity of the environment to the user: There was a significant main effect of order, in that participants perceived the environment as more reactive in their second exposure, $F(1, 40) = 2.95, p = .013$, as illustrated in Fig. 5 right.

Users engagement to change the sounds and visuals: Participants purposefully used their breath to manipulate the environment in their second exposure more than in their first exposure $F(1, 40) = 2.20, p = .016$ (see Fig. 5 left).

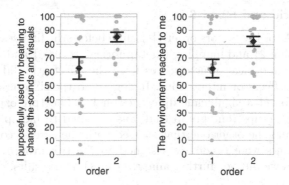

Fig. 5. Main effect of order on the questionnaire dependent variables "I purposefully used my breath to change the sounds and visuals" (left) and "The environment reacted to me" (right). Error bars depict one standard error of the mean. Grey dots depict individual participants' mean values.

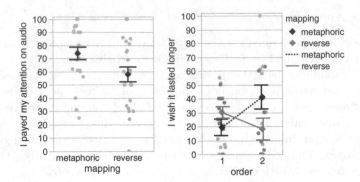

Fig. 6. Main effect of mapping on the questionnaire dependent variable "I payed my attention on audio" (left) and interaction between order and mapping on "I wish it lasted longer" (right). Error bars depict one standard error of the mean. Individual dots depict individual participants' mean values.

Payed attention to the audio: Participants payed more attention to the audio in metaphoric as compared to the reverse mapping condition F(1,40) = 1.76, p = 0.039 (see Fig. 6 left).

Desire for experience to last longer: There was a significant interaction between order and mapping for the questionnaire item "I wish it lasted longer", $F(1, 39) = 6.14, p = .0177$ (see Fig. 6 right). Planned contrasts showed that after the second session participants were more inclined to wish for a longer experience if this second experience was the metaphorically mapped condition versus the reverse mapping condition, $F(1, 39) = 5.56, p = .0233$. If the metaphoric condition was experienced as the second session, participants were also more inclined to wish for a longer experience than if the metaphoric condition was experienced first, $F(1, 39) = 5.22, p = .0278$.

5.2   Affect Grid and STAI-6

A 2-way ANOVA for the factors order {baseline before the first session; after session 1; after session 2} and mapping {metaphorical; reverse} and the dependent variables arousal and pleasantness scores from the affect grid did not show any significant main effects or interactions. In regard to the six questions included in STAI-6, we found a significant difference in baseline (pre-exposure) scores between the two groups (one group that was assigned to metaphoric mapping condition first, and the other one that started with the reverse condition), even though participants were randomly assigned to the two groups. Due to these group differences we did not further analyze the STAI-6 results.

6   Interviews

The majority of the participants in our study were undergrad students with no prior exposure to virtual reality. Through semi-structured interviews after each condition we hoped to gather insights that will help us build a better understanding of how different interaction mapping contributes to the affective properties of the environment, and overall experience regardless of the previous experiences with the technology. The themes from semi-structured interviews served as a basis for the non-linear accounts of various experiences as presented here.

6.1   Exploring the Unknown: Phases

The majority of the participants verbally shared their excitement to try VR for the first time. As we noticed, the first phase of interaction is exploration of their agency by breathing in and out, testing the limits of the system (how high or low they can get), and familiarizing themselves with the elements in the environment. After this exploration phase, they eased into the environment.

"In the beginning I breathe in different levels so I can see how the image will move. After I realized how it works, I tried different kinds of breathing. I tried even to go forward but I couldn't. Oh, at the beginning I was a little bit worried that image will be intimidating, but after I realized it was ocean it was more relaxed. Then I tried different kind of stuff that didn't work so I kept breathing" [P9].

6.2   Regardless of Mapping, Second Trial Is Enjoyed More

The participants reported second trials as more enjoyable very consistently, regardless of the mapping. Even though participants were informed how the system works, they used their first trial to familiarize themselves with the environment to allow for more profound interaction in the second trial.

"This is my first time to try VR, in the first environment I felt... don't want to say stressed... maybe anxious a little bit, a little bit excited, the second time my perception was: ok, this is stuff I already know, it's like an old friend, I know what to expect, I know what should I do, observe... I enjoyed it more the second time" [P1].

The lack of anticipation of a new environment one is immersed in resulted in increased relaxation in the second exposure.

"The first time was like giving a toy to a child... this time I was enjoying the feeling of calm... I wanted to take good relaxation time now" [P2].

"The first time I was not sure what you would ask me, or what to expect... this time I knew what was coming... There were some parts that were intense... but I was immersed in the simulation... I knew nothing crazy is going to happen, I was more calm" [P14].

6.3   Metaphoric Mapping Feels Intuitive, but Reverse Is More Playful

Those participants who were aware of the differences in interaction mapping between two conditions articulated their preferences for metaphoric mapping. The descriptions of the metaphoric mapping conditions such as: intuitive, natural, and counter-intuitive emerged from participants' comments, and were usually linked to the themes such as relaxation, and being calm.

> *"I practised being at the water level, tried going down below blue waves, but you need a big breath for that. The other one [metaphoric] felt more natural, I guess, because you breathe in and go up, breathe out and go down, and this one felt weird because it is opposite"* [P5].

> *"I feel much better than in the first one (referring to reverse mapping)... it felt so correct, when I am in the water you exhale and go down... I felt more calmer than when I came in"* [P2].

On the contrary, reverse mapping was perceived as more stimulating, engaging, and interesting.

> *"They are both good for different (reasons): reflected more in the first one (metaphoric), in this one I was more playful (reverse)"* [P5].

> *"Not much different but felt more interesting, it was counter-intuitive"* [P7].

6.4   Somatic Experiencing: Awareness of Breath and Emerging Past Experiences Through the Changes in the Environment

Visual representation of the ocean coupled with the movement often triggered memories in participants, followed by strong bodily sensations such as: floating, dropping, or even sensations that

> *"...I could almost feel, like being submerged under the water and then being brought back up... like if there was an invisible wrapper, kind of like a real water but not as... kind of real water but at slower pace"* [P14].

> *"It was exactly like when you go in the water, it had the feeling of being calm... it felt like floating chamber... the idea is the same, idea is that water makes you feel calm, floating in the water"* [P2].

> *"When I was learning to swim... they tell you to focus on your movement, and breathing... I related that to this. What made me feel different was motion... I liked the first one (reverse), it made me feel better... the second one (metaphoric) felt more like I was floating"* [P4].

Few participants reported a heightened impact that the music had on their awareness of breath.

"I think it was music. Suddenly I felt like I can feel my heartbeat. The rhythm of the music... it was in the parallel with my breathing, and that's when I noticed (her breath)" [P17].

"Oh, when the music gets excited I know something might happen, and then I wait for it happen. Oh, I also breathe to let it happen more faster" [P9].

However, some participants experienced tension in regard to audio they were listening to:

"I felt a heartbeat and then when it was music every time I went down... I felt dramatic effect to it... so I was like: something is wrong, I should do something about it... it was triggering fear even though I knew it's VR... when the sky turned black, sounds triggered fear" [P3].

6.5   Loss of Control Triggers Fear?

From the conversation with the participants we realized that those participants who did not make a connection between their breath and the changes in the environment were more likely to get distressed by audio or visuals.

"I tried to control my breathing... and then once the loud music started I kind of... can't control it any more, and I felt tense... I lost control of how I wanted to go down to the blue, and that's while loud music started to fade and I regained control... then I started to take deep breaths and started to calm myself..." [P21].

Once the participants regained control over the system, their tension lessens.

"Fear doesn't come to me this time, I felt I have a control over my body... to stay in one state, tried to be at one situation... either above or down" (the second exposure, metaphoric mapping) [P2].

6.6   Imagine This Was a Tool...

During the interview, the participants were asked "If I tell you that what you just experienced is a tool, what would you use that tool for?". Two themes emerged as the most dominant: a relaxation tool, and a tool for overcoming anxieties triggered by water.

"I would use it for, like, calming people down... cause this probably can calm many people down who are stressing about stuff... it gives you something to focus on, you are focusing on your breathing and something in front of you, so it kind of distracts you from everything else... cause you think of, if you start panicking, I guess, and you breathe really fast and go up and down like crazy, and then you would be like: what's happening in the world, and then your focus immediately is on the image in front of you instead anything outside." [P6].

"I don't know... something to do with calming people down, when their heads are somewhere else" [P5].

"Zoning out, not thinking about whatever is going in your head... If things were steady up the water... I would feel more relaxed" [P2].

7   Discussion

In this section we discuss the main findings from the presented study and our understanding of the lived experiences of the participants. We asked the question: *how can these environments change us through embodied interaction design? And, how can an embodied interaction design that employs the user's subtle breathing movements facilitate these changes?* and the answer lies between multiple accounts gathered here. The richness of gained insights helped us to see a wide range of factors that can affect the experience, and that we did not take into the account during the study planning process. Finally, we discuss the insights as we formalize them into a set of design considerations for embodied interaction design in VR.

7.1   Familiarity First, Engagement After

Analysis of questionnaire responses highlighted that the participants perceived the environment as more reactive to their input in their second trials, regardless of the mapping. We believe that this can be explained by the novelty effect or lack of understanding of the system's nuances. Even though prior to each trial we explained how the system works, many of the participants did not make any connection between their breathing and the changes in the environment in their first trial. This would explain our second finding that the engagement of the user to manipulate the environment through their breathing was higher in the second trial as well. Once they knew how the system worked they engaged with it more. The dynamic of their familiarization was revealed in the interviews in which the majority of the participants revealed that in the beginning they were exploring the environment and testing the interaction limits, followed by easing into it and pacing their breathing in less forceful and more pleasurable ways. Two participants were not aware of their agency at all. One reason might be that these participants employ chest breathing more than abdominal breathing, which will be explored in future work.

7.2   Tension and Relaxation, at the Same Time

We investigated whether different mappings can lead participants' affect toward an affect that matches the overall affect of the audio corpus. The audio corpus was intentionally centred around neutral pleasantness with a tendency towards positive pleasantness and neutral to low arousal (playfulness), positioning the corpus in the area of relaxed feelings on the affect grid. The inferential data analysis of affect grid responses did not yield any significant differences between two different mappings nor trial order and the baseline. This might be explained by overall subtle changes in the affect across the sample. However, a few participants reported feelings of tension. From the interviews we learned that many of them found the sky colour change from grey to black dreadful and this element triggered anxious-like feelings in several participants. One participant finished the session after four minutes claiming that the environment caused her distress and she was not able to continue. Other participants who did not make the connection between their agency and the changes felt tensed too. In these cases, the music was adding tension to the dark environment. Despite the reports of felt tension, when asked what they would use this tool for, the majority of the participants responded that they would use it for relaxation. Even though there were elements that were causing distress, the participants recognized calming qualities of the system. This finding is of a particular interest to our future work.

7.3 The Context Is the Key

Originally, we designed *PBW* as an art piece grounded in research questions we asked here. As an art piece, we exhibited it in galleries where we verbally collected the experiences of audience members who interacted with the piece. The majority of them recognized relaxing qualities and would stay immersed up to 20 min. The quality of the experience dramatically changed when we moved the setup from the gallery to the lab. The main difference was the expectation and the openness to the experience. The audience in the gallery is there because they would like to experience something new. Our participant pool consisted of fairly young undergrad students who might be very different from those who initially experienced the piece in an artist gallery context. The laboratory setting, no matter how we tried, still feels like the setting for an experiment rather than an experience. This might have affected our participants' responses and we find it to be an important factor to be accounted in the future studies that employ art and research questions.

8   Conclusion

In this paper, we introduced the system *Pulse Breath Water* and we investigated the efficiency of embodied interaction design through two different mappings (metaphoric, and "reverse") for enhancing affective properties of the system. This research encompasses two directions of affective research: in VR and in the audio, combining them into one system in an attempt to gain a better understanding of the combined effect of these two on the user's engagement, affective states, immersion, and overall experience.

In this paper we contribute to a better articulation of affective properties of virtual environments that combine visual and audio components into one system. We presented some of the individual accounts of lived experiences and showed that the majority of the participants when asked to imagine that this was a tool replied that they would use this tool for relaxation. We built our system on the premise of neutral pleasantness and low arousal properties which can be translated to feelings of being relaxed. This gives us a direction for future work to research the potential of the system of inducing a wider range of affective states. We believe that the insights presented here will bring us closer to the final goal of creating a system that not only "reacts" to a user's breathing but evolves into an immersive artificial intelligence system capable of taking initiative and changing a user's affective states.

Acknowledgements. We thank all the study participants for their involvement, and the *MovingStories* SSHRC research project for their support while working on this piece.

References

1. Thought Technology Ltd.: ProComp2 - 2 Channel Biofeedback & Neurofeedback System w/BioGraph Infiniti Software Thought Technology Ltd., Apirl 2015. http://thoughttechnology.com/index.php/procomp2-2-channel-biofeedback-neuro feedback-system-w-biograph-infiniti-software.html
2. Arroyo-Palacios, J., and Romano, D.M.: Exploring the use of a respiratory-computer interface for game interaction. In: 2009 International IEEE Consumer Electronics Society's Games Innovations Conference, pp. 154–159, August 2009
3. Asutay, E., Västfjäll, D.: Perception of loudness is influenced by emotion. PLoS ONE **7**, 6 (2012)
4. Beckhaus, S., Kruijff, E.: Unconventional human computer interfaces. In: ACM SIGGRAPH 2004 Course Notes. ACM, New York (2004)
5. Berglund, B., Nilsson, M.E., Axelsson, Ö.: Soundscape psychophysics in place. IN07-114
6. Bradley, M.M., Lang, P.J.: Affective reactions to acoustic stimuli. Psychophysiology **37**(2), 204–215 (2000)
7. Brockmyer, J.H., Fox, C.M., Curtiss, K.A., McBroom, E., Burkhart, K.M., Pidruzny, J.N.: The development of the game engagement questionnaire: a measure of engagement in video game-playing. J. Exp. Soc. Psychol. **45**(4), 624–634 (2009)
8. Davies, C.: OSMOSE: notes on being in Immersive virtual space. Digital Creativity **9**(2), 65–74 (1998)
9. Dourish, P.: Where the Action Is. MIT Press, Cambridge (2004)
10. Eerola, T., Vuoskoski, J.K.: A review of music and emotion studies: approaches, emotion models, and stimuli. Music Percept. Interdisc. J. **30**(3), 307–340 (2013)
11. Ekkekakis, P.: Should affective states be considered as distinct entities or as positioned along dimensions? In: The Measurement of Affect, Mood, and Emotion: A Guide for Health-Behavioral Research, pp. 52–72. Cambridge University Press, February 2013
12. England, D., Randles, M., Fergus, P., Taleb-Bendiab, A.: Towards an advanced framework for whole body interaction. In: Shumaker, R. (ed.) VMR 2009. LNCS, vol. 5622, pp. 32–40. Springer, Heidelberg (2009). doi:10.1007/978-3-642-02771-0_4
13. Evreinov, G., Evreinova, T.: "Breath-Joystick"-graphical manipulator for physically disabled users. In: Proceedings of the ICCHP 2000, pp. 193–200 (2000)
14. Fan, J., Thorogood, M., Pasquier, P.: Automatic soundscape affect recognition using a dimensional approach. J. Audio Eng. Soc. **64**(9), 646–653 (2016)
15. Flach, J.M., Holden, J.G.: The reality of experience: Gibson's way. Presence: Teleoperators Virtual Environ. **7**(1), 90–95 (1998)
16. Gaver, W.W., Beaver, J., Benford, S.: Ambiguity as a resource for design. In: Proceedings of the SIGCHI Conference on Human Factors in Computing Systems, CHI 2003, pp. 233–240. ACM, New York (2003)

17. Kandel, E.: Reductionism in Art and Brain Science: Bridging the Two Cultures. Columbia University Press, New York (2016)
18. Kirsh, D.: Embodied cognition and the magical future of interaction design. ACM Trans. Comput.-Hum. Interact **20**(1), 3:1–3:30 (2013)
19. Kruijff, E.: Unconventional 3D user interfaces for virtual environments. Doctoral Dissertation, October 2006
20. Kuzume, K.: Input device for disabled persons using expiration and tooth-touch sound signals. In: Proceedings of the 2010 ACM Symposium on Applied Computing, pp. 1159–1164. ACM (2010)
21. Macaranas, A., Antle, A.N., Riecke, B.E.: What is intuitive interaction? balancing users' performance and satisfaction with natural user interfaces. Interact. Comput. **27**(3), 357–370 (2015)
22. Marteau, T.M., Bekker, H.: The development of a six-item short-form of the state scale of the spielberger state-trait anxiety inventory (STAI). Br. J. Clin. Psychol. **31**(3), 301 306 (1992)
23. Media Art Net: Gabriel, Ulrike: Breath, 1992/93, December 2016
24. Neustaedter, C., Sengers, P.: Autobiographical design in HCI research: designing and learning through use-it-yourself. In: Proceedings of the Designing Interactive Systems Conference, pp. 514–523. ACM (2012)
25. Posner, J., Russell, J.A., Peterson, B.S.: The circumplex model of affect: an integrative approach to affective neuroscience, cognitive development, and psychopathology. Dev. Psychopathol. **17**(3), 715–734 (2005)
26. Robertson, T.: Cooperative work and lived cognition: a taxonomy of embodied actions. In: Proceedings of the Fifth European Conference on Computer Supported Cooperative Work, pp. 205–220. Springer, Netherlands (1997). doi:10.1007/978-94-015-7372-6_14
27. Russell, J., Weiss, A., Mendelsohn, G.: Affect grid - a single-item scale of pleasure and arousal. J. Pers. Soc. Psychol. **57**(3), 493 502 (1989)
28. Schiphorst, T.: Breath, skin and clothing: using wearable technologies as an interface into ourselves. Int. J. Perform. Arts Digital Media **2**(2), 171–186 (2006)
29. Shorrock, T.H., MacKay, D.J.C., Ball, C.J.: Efficient communication by breathing. In: Winkler, J., Niranjan, M., Lawrence, N. (eds.) DSMML 2004. LNCS (LNAI), vol. 3635, pp. 88–97. Springer, Heidelberg (2005). doi:10.1007/11559887_5
30. Slater, M.: Place illusion and plausibility can lead to realistic behaviour in immersive virtual environments. Philos. Trans. R. Soc. Lond. B Biol. Sci. **364**(1535), 3549–3557 (2009)
31. Slater, M., Sanchez-Vives, M.V.: Enhancing our lives with immersive virtual reality. Front. Robot. AI **3**, 6 (2016)
32. Sonne, T., Jensen, M.M.: ChillFish: a respiration game for children with ADHD. In: Proceedings of the Tenth International Conference on Tangible, Embedded, and Embodied Interaction, TEI 2016, pp. 271–278. ACM (2016)
33. Tajadura-Jimenez, A., Väljamäe, A., Västfjäll, D.: Self-representation in mediated environments: the experience of emotions modulated by auditory-vibrotactile heartbeat. Cyberpsychol. Behav. Impact Internet Multimedia Virtual Reality Behav. Soc. **11**(1), 33–38 (2008)
34. Tennent, P., Rowland, D., Marshall, J., Egglestone, S.R., Harrison, A., Jaime, Z., Walker, B., Benford, S.: Breathalising games: understanding the potential of breath control in game interfaces. In: Proceedings of the 8th International Conference on Advances in Computer Entertainment Technology, p. 58. ACM (2011)
35. Thorogood, M., Pasquier, P.: Impress: a machine learning approach to soundscape affect classification, pp. 256–260

36. Waterworth, E.L., Häggkvist, M., Jalkanen, K., Olsson, S., Waterworth, J.A., Wimelius, H.: The exploratorium: an environment to explore your feelings. Psych-Nology J. **1**(3), 189–201 (2003)
37. Wilson, S.: Information Arts: Intersections of Art, Science, and Technology. Leonardo. MIT Press, Cambridge (2002)
38. Zahorik, P., Jenison, R.L.: Presence as being-in-the-world. Presence **7**(1), 78–89 (1998)
39. Zimmerman, J., Forlizzi, J., Evenson, S.: Research through design as a method for interaction design research in HCI. In: Proceedings of the SIGCHI conference on Human factors in computing systems, pp. 493–502. ACM (2007)

Visual Communication with UAS: Recognizing Gestures from an Airborne Platform

Alexander Schelle[✉] and Peter Stütz

Institute of Flight Systems, University of the Bundeswehr Munich, Neubiberg, Germany
{alexander.schelle,peter.stuetz}@unibw.de

Abstract. Current tactical unmanned aerial systems receive their guidance and tasking information predominantly via radio links. To be able to communicate with these systems specific electronic devices are required. This work builds on the concept of visual communication of UAS to allow a person on ground commanding a nearby airborne vehicle to perform a specific reconnaissance task via gestures. A procedure to collect the necessary gestural command components is presented as well as a prototype image processing flow which is able to distinguish between neutral poses, static and dynamic 2D gestures. Prototype experiments prove the applicability of the proposed method on real life data from an airborne platform.

Keywords: UAS · Gesture recognition · Visual communication

1 Introduction

Nowadays tactical unmanned aerial systems (UAS) utilize radio links to receive mission relevant information from a ground control station, a mobile control device or from other manned aircrafts. As technical devices are required to communicate with airborne systems, there is currently no option to transfer the authority of the UAS to third parties lacking adequate equipment. For example infantryman on ground who require a temporal access to an asset for an up to date overview of the situation and processed image intelligence results in their area of operation. For such use case new ways of interaction have to be found.

A promising candidate for such new paradigm is given by visual communication, which, however, is constrained by narrow information bandwidth at only close distance. Hereby flags, light signals and hand gestures are commonly used tools to transmit information by optical means in general. The latter is thereby of peculiar interest, as this enables the abandonment of any additional equipment on ground. For that, the movements and gestures of a person on ground have to be captured with a suitable imaging sensor on board the UAV. Further this data has to be processed by a gesture recognition system to classify the gestural movements and finally translate them into commands to generate a complete task description. For this a performant computational system that can operate in real time is necessary to enable a low latency communication. The processed and interpreted data can then be used to generate a flight path and if applicable a plan of action for the mission sensors deployment. A downstream flight management system (FMS) will use this information for the

© Springer International Publishing AG 2017
S. Lackey and J. Chen (Eds.): VAMR 2017, LNCS 10280, pp. 173–184, 2017.
DOI: 10.1007/978-3-319-57987-0_14

flight guidance of the unmanned aerial vehicle. An overview of the necessary system components is shown in Fig. 1.

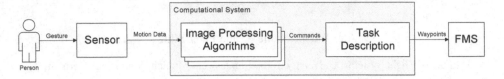

Fig. 1. System components for a gesture based commanding

Modern pose and gesture recognition system have reached a high level of reliability and accuracy [1–5]. But the majority of those systems were designed for indoor use and a static mounting of the sensor. Recognizing gestures from a flying platform outdoors, however, is a more challenging task, where the system has to deal with several constraints and uncertainties:

- Available additional weight and energy allowances are limited on aerial platforms, hence only lightweight and low power consuming components can be used.
- Concerning data processing, the sensor is in non-stop motion, so classical background subtraction methods can be applied only to a certain amount to detect movements of the operator. Therefore a more robust and reliable person detection and tracking is required.
- The gesture sensor does not always work in its optimal range, as the distance to the user changes constantly leading to a varying data accuracy.

Ongoing work on suitable and intuitive gestures for human drone interactions [6–8] is increasing thus confirming the rising demand for more natural interfaces. A concept for a bidirectional communication and a gestural commanding of a UAS for reconnaissance purposes has been presented recently [9]. The following chapters give a brief introduction to this concept and focus on the specifics of the used gestural syntax. A method to allow the discrimination of static and dynamic gestures needed for the commanding is presented there as well. Lastly a prototypical implementation of the proposed concepts components will be evaluated on real life data from an airborne platform.

2   Approach

The concept for the visual communication with UAS suggests a syntax for gestural commands, that is composed of the four mandatory components *task declaration, direction, distance, post-task behavior* and the optionally component *time constraint*. In the intended application a serial execution of gestures that represent these components defines a specific reconnaissance task typical for a UAV mission. To obtain this information, two operational modes are recommended: a *detection mode* to spot potential interaction request of an operator on ground from medium altitudes using a thermal imager and an *interaction mode* that receives the actual gestural commands from a closer distance using a depth sensor. This work focuses on the systemic components that are necessary to realize the acquisition of the command components in the latter.

2.1 Gestural Syntax

The gestural components of the proposed syntax can be transmitted without a specific order basically. However some commands require a subsequent gesture of a specific type for definitions or specifications. For instance, if the surveillance task is to detect an object, the system must be informed on the object type of interest (humans, vehicles, etc.). Therefore each gestural command component is encapsulated into a gestural sequence that is passed along all processing blocks of the system and contains the information about possible dependencies. The structure of such a container is shown in the following Table 1.

Table 1. Structure of a gestural sequence container

Gestural command component	Dependence flag	Subsequent gesture type

The gestural sequence contains the component itself (*task declaration, direction, distance*, etc.). It is followed by a flag that represents the dependency to a subsequent gesture and a type definition for the following gesture. The gestural command components *direction* and *distance* are independent of other gestures, but the components *task declaration*, *post-task behavior* and *time constraint* determine the succeeding gestures. Table 2 gives a brief overview.

Table 2. Overview of gestural command components and their dependencies

	Task declaration	Direction	Distance	Post-Task behavior	Time constraint
Dependent on subsequent gesture	Yes	No	No	Yes	Yes
Subsequent gesture type	Static, Dynamic	-	-	Static, Dynamic	Static
Following subcomponent	Object definition	-	-	Directional	Numerical

Gesture Separation Signals

The gesture recognition system needs to recognize when one gesture ends and the next one begins. Therefore two criteria have been selected to prompt the separation. A separation signal gets triggered, once the operator's movement remains under a definable lateral threshold for a particular time. It can be assumed that the operator is then either in a neutral pose (*no input*), is pointing somewhere (*directional input* or *object type definition*) or is showing something (e.g. *numerical information*). The correct sizing of both thresholds is essential for the reliability of the method. Therefore these thresholds have to be designed adaptively in regard to the individual pace of the operator.

The separation signal will also be trigged, if the operator enters or leaves the so called *neutral pose space*. This space is a three-dimensional box that covers the operator completely for that case, when both of his arms are close to his body. To consider potential uncertainties introduced by noisy depth data or inaccurate body part position estimation, this space is slightly larger than the actual body dimensions. This principle is shown in Fig. 2.

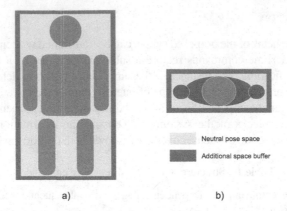

a)   b)

Fig. 2. Schematic frontal (a) and top view (b) of operator within the three-dimensional neutral pose space

2.2 Classifying Gestures

In gesture recognition systems the separation signals play an important function for the routing of the internal processing flow. The command components can be grouped in three classes: *neutral pose*, *static gestures* and *dynamic gestures*. The detection of each gesture class is subject to different processing flows that produce distinct computational expenses.

For instance, to detect a neutral pose, it takes here the lowest computational cost, as the processing flow only needs to find the position of the operator and to check, whether all of his body parts are inside the created neutral pose space. Static gestures like pointing include more computational load, since the appropriate body part (left arm, right arm) has to be found and its pointing direction needs to be estimated. Detecting a dynamic gesture demands the highest computational costs in this context. In addition to the processing steps for a static gesture detection, the temporal progression of the moving body part has to be considered and analyzed as well. For that purpose the following adaptive gestural command aggregation approach is proposed. It consists of different processing modules that enable a variable data processing based on the demand for gestural command components:

2D Person Tracker
This module detects a person in the raw two-dimensional input stream and delivers the position of the operator as a region of interest (ROI) for the subsequent blocks.

3D Body Tracker
This module utilizes the ROI from the 2D person tracker to detect the operator's body in the depth data stream and to create a body model and to perform a position estimation for the body parts, e.g. head, feet and arms.

Gesture Separator
The gesture separator is the first analysis block that can detect a neutral pose and inform the downstream modules about a gesture change, for instance a change from a gesture to a neutral pose and vice versa.

Processing Flow Composer

The processing flow composer is the control center of the gesture recognition system. It sets up the demand for one or more specific gestural command components and their optional dependencies. The basis for the decision-making is the received input from the gesture separator (*gesture change*) and the feedback from the task validator (*missing information*). The generated demand is then send to the gesture type selector.

Gesture Type Selector

Based on the demand from the processing flow composer this module starts the appropriate processing flow to gather the requested gestural command component.

Task Validator

The task validator receives and validates all detected and recognized gestural command components. It has to check all inputs for plausibility and feasibility. If command components are missing, this module gives feedback to the processing flow composer.

This setup enables an adaptive demand-driven and processing flow to contemplate only those processing steps that are needed for the information aggregation. A system overview of all proposed modules and their connections is illustrated in Fig. 3.

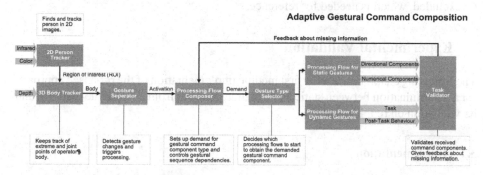

Fig. 3. Overview of the adaptive gestural command aggregation approach

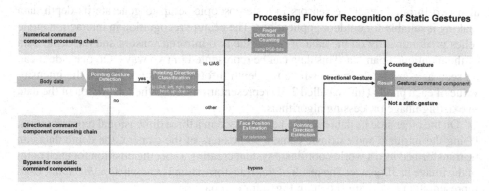

Fig. 4. Exemplary overview of the processing flow for the detection of static gestures

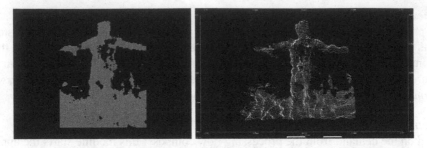

Fig. 5. Two representations of the depth data in comparison: 2D-matrix (left) and point cloud (right)

Exemplary Processing Flow for Static Gestures

The demand-driven principle of the approach from the previous chapter can be applied to both of the processing flows for static and dynamic gestures as well. For example, if the operator performs a pointing gesture (*"Go east"*) followed by a counting gesture (*"500 m"*), the directional command component flow (Fig. 4) can be excluded since the directional information is already transmitted and the costly face position estimation can be excluded, which is needed for reference.

3 Experimental Validation

The following chapter covers the first module implementation of the proposed approach for a discrimination between static and dynamic gestures from an airborne platform and its validation on real life data.

3.1 Implementation

The *Intel RealSense R200* camera was selected for the data acquisition. Its advantage is the multisensory all-in-one solution that features besides a high resolution color sensor also two infrared sensitive sensors in a stereoscopic setup to generate its depth data making it suitable for outdoor applications. The gesture recognition in interaction mode relies predominantly on the data of one of the two infrared sensors and the depth data of the mentioned camera. This data can be represented in two ways. On one side it can be seen as a grayscale image where the depth information is coded into the intensity value of each pixel. This so called 2.5D representation allows the integration of the data in existing image processing algorithms.

On the other side its data can also be processed in a three dimensional representation. Using the intrinsic and extrinsic camera parameters of the camera, the depth data can be transformed into a world coordinate system creating a specific position for each point of the image in 3D space. The result of this transformation is known as *point cloud*. Both representation forms are shown in Fig. 5 for comparison.

The second variant is computationally more expensive, but enables elaborated possibilities for gesture recognition. For this the point cloud representation was favored first.

Fig. 6. Operator in point cloud representation from three viewpoints: (a) front, (b) front right, (c) right

However, later experiments have revealed the sensors maximum depth range of about 10 m, but also its rapidly decreasing depth accuracy on that far end of the operational area. The integration of computationally highly expensive multi-stage filtering methods in the implementation would be necessary and therefore inhibits a real time execution. Figure 6 illustrates the noisy depth data from three different viewpoints. The image on the right side (Fig. 6c) shows the prominent quantization artefacts from the stereoscopic approach that manifest as thin plates along the z-axis.

For that reason the 2.5D representation has been chosen for the prototypical gesture recognition implementation.

2D Person Detection and Tracking

The implemented method for person detection and tracking adapted from previous work as describe in [9], namely a combination of a HOG based object detector [10] and a modified correlation tracker [11]. This applies for the utilized UAV and deployed sensor of the experimental setup as well (Fig. 7).

Fig. 7. Utilized UAV with multisensory camera system and experimental setup in interaction mode

Body Part Estimation

Based on the result of the upstream 2D person detector and tracker, the region of interest is first enlarged to fit all body parts within it (the HOG detector is learned only on the silhouette of persons) and then extracted from the depth stream (Fig. 8a, b). The lower part is removed in the next step, which includes noisy and interfering depth data from the ground (Fig. 8c). After that, the background is removed as well, based on the median distance of the operator to the camera (Fig. 8d). A conversion to a lower bitrate followed by a binarization step creates then a suitable base for a subsequent contour analysis (Fig. 8e).

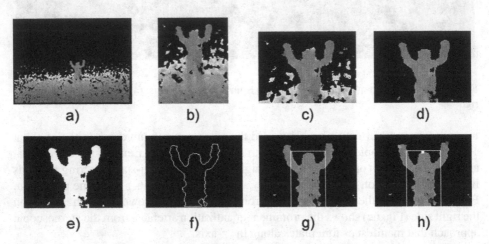

a)   b)   c)   d)

e)   f)   g)   h)

Fig. 8. Involved processing steps for body part estimation (see text for detailed description), (h) shows the detected extreme points and the related body parts: green = left arm, red = right arm, blue = legs, white = head (Color figure online)

This process consist of a blob and contour detection that looks for large connected objects of a given minimum and maximum size and perimeter. Empty regions with no depth data inside the body shape (black spots on the operator's right side in Fig. 8a–e) can be challenging for this processing step as they sometimes divide body parts from the corpus and lead to incorrect detections of the arms, for instance. But this hurdle can be overcome by a preceding blob group analysis and connection.

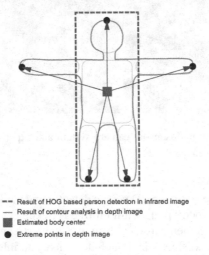

-- Result of HOG based person detection in infrared image
— Result of contour analysis in depth image
■ Estimated body center
● Extreme points in depth image

Fig. 9. Schematic illustration for the estimation of extreme points

The found contours are represented as a list of connected 3D points (2D position plus distance from the camera) (Fig. 8f). The 2D information is then used to find and mark those candidates that show the largest distance to the estimated body center, called extreme points (see Fig. 9). A following plausibility check (feet are under the body center, head is over it, etc.) assigns then each candidate the appropriate body part (Fig. 8h). These found positions are passed through a Kalman-Filter to smooth outliers from the detection caused by noisy depth data. The white rectangle in Fig. 8g–h represents the calculated neutral pose space for the following neutral pose detection.

3.2 Classification

Once the position of the extremities is found, the movements of the person can be already grouped in three classes: *static gestures, dynamic gestures* and a *neutral pose*. Static gestures include low or no fluctuations of the body position data whereas dynamic gestures involve more body movements.

Here a neutral pose is recognized, when the operator keeps his arms down and close to his body and therefore leaving them inside the neutral pose space. Every time he raises his arms out of this space, a new gesture separation signal is send to the system that triggers the following processing steps to look for static and dynamic gestures.

The position of each detected body part is stored in a vector of a defined length, in this case 30 elements. A static gesture signal is triggered if two conditions are true:

1. All positions within the vector are valid (no missed detections) and
2. 50% of all positions are within a defined tolerance area

If both criteria are met, the pointing direction in reference to the head position is then estimated and a (static) pointing gesture signal is emitted.

Classification of Dynamic Gestures

To perform a classification of dynamic gestures, more processing steps are necessary. To take in account the temporal progression of the extreme points, their lateral change can be represented as a two dimensional trajectory (Fig. 10).

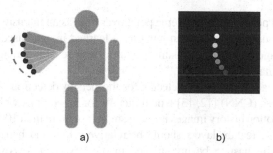

a)   b)

Fig. 10. Schematic figure of a waving operator (a) with the corresponding motion history image (b)

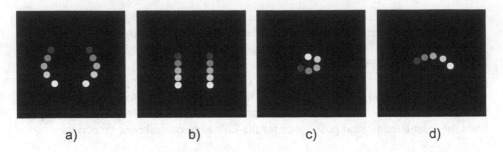

a)   b)   c)   d)

Fig. 11. Gestures represented as motion history images: (a) waving with both arms sideways, (b) movement from top to bottom with both arms, (c) circling with one arm above the head, d) waving with one arm above the head

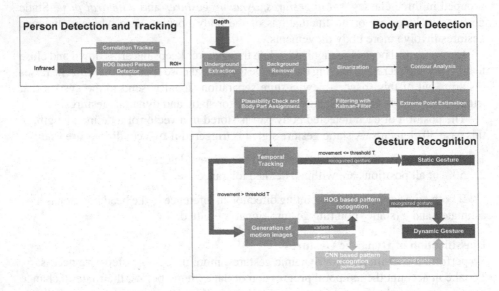

Fig. 12. Overall processing flow for the prototypical gesture recognition implementation

If we plot every position of an extreme point over time as an intensity value into a separate image, we can use the result as an input for a learned image based object detector to assign a motion image to a specific dynamic gesture. These resulting images are named here as motion history images (Fig. 11).

Besides the already used HOG detector for the person detection, a trained convolutional neural network (CNN) [12, 13] would qualify for this task as well. As the expected image size of the motion history images is rather small (not more than 100 by 100 pixels) the necessary number of feature layers should be relatively low and hence computationally cheap. But this point hast to be investigated in the next works. An overview for the complete image processing flow with implemented and scheduled steps is shown in Fig. 12.

3.3   Results

The implementations has been executed on a mainstream Intel i7 powered system without GPU acceleration and heavy software optimization using the recorded on board data from the real flight experiment. Despite the recorded frame rate being 60 Hz, the processing rate dropped to only about 35 Hz, still qualifying as real time. One reason is the early extraction of the ROI hence reducing the effective image dimension to about 155 by 115 pixel for the processing and therefore reducing the computational load. Furthermore the integrated high resolution color stream has not been part of the processing flow at this stage.

The deployed method to detect and track the operator within the infrared image stream performed well without losses through the whole video sequence (*Operator Sequence 1*, frames 539 – 1854). The neutral pose could be detected best (true positive rate TPR = 91.8%) followed by the detection of static gestures (TPR = 79.5%). Dynamic gestures could be detected in most cases by a motion analysis with a TPR of 70.5%. Only the recognition of dynamic gestures using a learned HOG detector on the motion images did not work as expected and showed poor detection rates. One reason might have been the very low effective resolution of 30 by 30 pixel of the used motion images for learning of the detector. A scaling and interpolation of the included body part positions might improve the detection rate. A temporal comparison of the performed gestures featuring the ground truth and the detections is shown in Fig. 13.

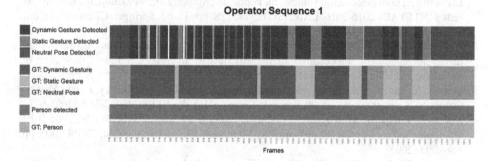

Fig. 13. Overview of the detection results of the recorded video sequence including the ground truth (GT)

4   Conclusion

This work proposed a method to collect gestural command components for the commanding of airborne UAS. An adaptive command component composition approach has been presented that is capable of distinguishing between different gesture types as well as an exemplary processing flow for the demand-driven information gathering of static 2D gestures. Lastly the gesture separation part of the proposed method has been evaluated on real life data from an airborne platform with a prototypical implementation. The used multisensory camera system performed well in the infrared domain but showed deficiencies in the depth stream at the given distances. Other sensor systems have to be considers in the next development steps. Future work will gradually implement all proposed concept parts into the system to establish an operational prototype for a complete gesture based UAS tasking.

References

1. Escalera, S., Athitsos, V., Guyon, I.: Challenges in multimodal gesture recognition. J. Mach. Learn. Res. **17**, 1–54 (2016)
2. Cicirelli, G., Attolico, C., Guaragnella, C., D'Orazio, T.: A Kinect-based gesture recognition approach for a natural human robot interface. Int. J. Adv. Rob. Syst. **12** (2015). doi:10.5772/59974
3. Yu, T.H., Kim, T.K., Cipolla, R.: Unconstrained monocular 3D human pose estimation by action detection and cross-modality regression forest. In: Proceedings of the IEEE Conference on Computer Vision and Pattern Recognition, pp. 3642–3649 (2013)
4. Bünger, M.: Evaluation of Skeleton Trackers and Gesture Recognition for Human-robot Interaction. Master thesis, Aalborg University, Aalborg (2013)
5. Schwarz, L.A., Mkhitaryan, A., Mateus, D., Navab, N.: Human skeleton tracking from depth data using geodesic distances and optical flow. Image Vis. Comput. **30**(3), 217–226 (2012)
6. Obaid, M., Kistler, F., Kasparavičiūtė, G., Yantaç, A.E., Fjeld, M.: How would you gesture navigate a drone? a user-centered approach to control a drone. In: Proceedings of the 20th International Academic Mindtrek Conference, pp. 113–121. ACM (2016)
7. Peshkova, E., Hitz, M., Ahlström, D.: Exploring user-defined gestures and voice commands to control an unmanned aerial vehicle. In: Poppe, R., Meyer, J.-J., Veltkamp, R., Dastani, M. (eds.) INTETAIN 2016 2016. LNICSSITE, vol. 178, pp. 47–62. Springer, Cham (2017). doi:10.1007/978-3-319-49616-0_5
8. Cauchard, J.R., Zhai, K.Y., Landay, J.A.: Drone & me: an exploration into natural human-drone interaction. In: Proceedings of the 2015 ACM International Joint Conference on Pervasive and Ubiquitous Computing, pp. 361–365. ACM (2015)
9. Schelle, A., Stütz, P.: Modelling visual communication with UAS. In: Hodicky, J. (ed.) MESAS 2016. LNCS, vol. 9991, pp. 81–98. Springer, Cham (2016). doi:10.1007/978-3-319-47605-6_7
10. Dalal, N., Triggs, B.: Histograms of oriented gradients for human detection. In: 2005 IEEE Computer Society Conference on Computer Vision and Pattern Recognition, CVPR 2005, pp. 886–893 (2005)
11. Danelljan, M., Häger, G., Shahbaz Khan, F., Felsberg, M.: Accurate scale estimation for robust visual tracking. In: British Machine Vision Conference, Nottingham, 1–5 September 2014
12. Lawrence, S., Giles, C.L., Tsoi, A.C., Back, A.D.: Face recognition: a convolutional neural-network approach. IEEE Trans. Neural Networks **8**(1), 98–113 (1997)
13. Krizhevsky, A., Sutskever, I., Hinton, G.E.: ImageNet classification with deep convolutional neural networks. In: Advances in Neural Information Processing Systems, pp. 1097–1105 (2012)

Subjective Evaluation of Tactile Fidelity for Single-Finger and Whole-Hand Touch Gestures

Fei Tang[1]([⊠]), Ryan P. McMahan[1], Eric D. Ragan[2], and Tandra T. Allen[1]

[1] University of Texas at Dallas, Richardson, TX, USA
{Fei.Tang,rymcmaha,Tandra.Allen}@utdallas.edu
[2] Texas A&M University, College Station, TX, USA
eragan@tamu.edu

Abstract. This paper presents a study on the effects of tactile fidelity—the degree of exactness with which real-world tactile stimuli are reproduced—on the perception of single-finger and whole-hand touch gestures. We developed an arm-based tactile display consisting of a four-by-three grid of linear resonant actuator motors to facilitate our investigation. This device supported two extreme levels of tactile fidelity by using an extension of the previously defined Tactile Brush algorithm. At the highest level, all twelve motors could be used to provide an average displayed tactile resolution of one actuation per 12 cm^2. At the lowest level, the four corner motors of the grid could be used to provide an average displayed tactile resolution of one actuation per 36 cm^2. We conducted a study in which every participant blindly compared these two levels of tactile fidelity for four single-finger touch gestures and six whole-hand touch gestures. Our results indicated that the higher level of tactile fidelity was significantly preferred and accepted for all six whole-hand touch gestures and for two of the four single-finger gestures. We discuss the implications of these results for the development of grid-based tactile displays and provide some virtual reality application areas that could take advantage of using whole-hand touch gestures.

Keywords: Tactile fidelity · Touch gestures · Displayed tactile resolution

1 Introduction

The sense of touch is an important perceptual function that provides vital information about the environment around us. Because of this, many researchers have investigated tactile technologies, control algorithms, and percepts to communicate complex information and symbolic meanings to users. These works are particularly relevant to virtual reality (VR) systems, which heavily rely on virtual objects that have no physical instantiations, and hence, provide no tactile feedback without additional technologies. Depending on the type of touch, it can be challenging to identify the appropriate technology to simulate realistic tactile feedback. More realistic tactile displays can require heavy and expensive hardware, and they are often specialized to provide specific tactile sensations. Naturally, researchers and practitioners would prefer simple, more-affordable tactile displays that could accommodate a variety of tactile sensations.

© Springer International Publishing AG 2017
S. Lackey and J. Chen (Eds.): VAMR 2017, LNCS 10280, pp. 185–200, 2017.
DOI: 10.1007/978-3-319-57987-0_15

To that end, researchers have studied how perceptual illusions can provide more realistic tactile sensations with limited tactile display technology. For example, phantom sensations and apparent motions are two types of tactile illusions that take advantage of stimuli timing, intensity, and spatial configuration to provide a variety of different tactile sensations with a limited number of vibration points. A *phantom tactile sensation* is the perception of a nonexistent tactile stimulus between two real tactile stimuli [1]. This is also known as the funneling illusion [2] and is created by placing two vibrotactile actuators in close proximity of one another. Another tactile illusion is *apparent tactile motion*, which is the perception of a nonexistent moving stimulus due to a time delay between onsets of multiple real tactile stimuli [3]. With the apparent motion illusion, the real stimuli are not perceived. Instead, only the nonexistent moving stimulus is sensed, provided that the real tactile actuators are close enough to one another and their actuation times overlap [4].

The effectiveness of tactile illusions depends on the properties of the real tactile stimuli. For instance, researchers have studied the appropriate *durations of stimulus* (DOS; how long the stimulus is displayed) and *stimulus onset asynchronies* (SOA; the time interval between onsets of subsequent actuations) [3]. In addition to DOS and SOA, previous studies have investigated the effects of varying the frequencies, amplitudes, and spacing of vibrotactile actuators. However, studies involving spacing have mostly looked at the distance between two actuators for a single degree of freedom (DOF). The study of the average area covered by a single actuator, or *displayed tactile resolution* [5], has been mostly unexplored. Note that displayed tactile resolution is different from "tactile resolution", which commonly refers to the smallest distance between two stimuli that the user can still perceive the stimuli as different [6].

Prior studies of phantom sensations and apparent motions have focused primarily on touch gestures involving a single point of contact on the skin at any one moment that can be static or dynamic. Static touch gestures involve touching a relatively restricted body location, such as tapping a person on the shoulder, while dynamic gestures involve continuous movement from one point to another, such as running a finger down someone's arm [7]. In contrast to single-point or single-finger touch gestures, whole-hand touch gestures involve multiple, simultaneous points of contact, such as a whole hand touching the arm or rubbing it up and down. While many researchers have studied single-point gestures, there has been little research on whole-hand touch gestures.

In our work, we studied the perceived realism of different types of single-finger and whole-hand touch gestures on an upper arm. To display the whole-hand touch gestures, we extended the previously published Tactile Brush algorithm [8] to support multiple points of contact. Because prior research has shown that tactile illusions depend on a display's level of *tactile fidelity* (i.e., the level of exactness with which real-world tactile stimuli are reproduced), we investigated how the level of displayed tactile resolution influences the perceived realism of single-finger and whole-hand person-to-person touch gestures, such as those used in social settings. We focus on displayed tactile resolution since its effects on perceived realism have previously been largely unstudied.

To facilitate our investigation, we created an arm-based tactile display consisting of a 4-by-3 grid of linear resonant actuators (LRAs). The device supported two extreme levels of displayed tactile resolution: a *low tactile fidelity* configuration with one actuation per 12 cm^2, and a *high tactile fidelity* configuration with one actuation per 36 cm^2. We used the display to investigate what level of tactile display fidelity is necessary to effectively reproduce ten different single-finger and whole-hand touch gestures. Participants blindly compared the two levels of fidelity for each touch gesture by watching a video of the real-world gesture and choosing which level they felt best represented the depicted gesture. They then rated its accuracy and acceptability. Our results indicated that the higher level of tactile fidelity was significantly preferred and accepted for all six whole-hand touch gestures and two of the four single-finger gestures. We discuss the implications of these results on the development of grid-based tactile displays and provide some applications that could benefit from the use of whole-hand touch gestures.

2 Related Work

Here, we focus on literature pertaining to grid-based tactile displays, DOS, SOA, frequency, amplitude, and spacing. In overview, researchers have investigated many single-point touch gestures, such as conveying single points of contact, displaying linear and circular directions, and generating two-dimensional curves for tracing alphanumerical characters. However, complex touch gestures with multiple, simultaneous points of contact are largely missing from prior research. Additionally, the spacing of tactile stimuli has mainly been investigated for 1-DOF motions only. Hence, our investigation into the effects of displayed tactile resolution on whole-hand touch gestures addresses multiple gaps in the following literature.

2.1 Grid-Based Tactile Displays

One of the earliest grid-based tactile displays was the tactile-vision substitution system (TVSS) developed by Collins [9]. This display consisted of a 20-by-20 grid of vibrating pins that could be simultaneously activated to display an alphanumerical character. Loomis [10] evaluated users' ability to recognize characters with this device and found an average recognition accuracy of 51%. Later, Saida et al. [11] used the apparent motion phenomenon to display the tracing of a character with a 10-by-10 TVSS display. They found that apparent motion afforded a higher recognition accuracy of 95%. By using tactor motors, Yanagida et al. [12] were able to achieve 87% character-recognition accuracy with only a 3-by-3 grid display.

Some researchers have used grid-based tactile displays to investigate a sensory illusion similar to apparent motion called "sensory saltation". To induce sensory saltation, three brief pulses are displayed at the closest actuator, followed by three more at the middle actuator, and finally three more at the farthest actuator. These successive localized actuations are commonly observed as an evenly distributed set of actuations from the closest actuator to the farthest. But unlike the smooth sensation of apparent motion, the saltation phenomenon is characteristically discrete, as if a tiny rabbit was hopping from the closet actuator to the farthest [13]. Tan et al. [14] used this phenomenon and a 3-by-3 grid of tactors to investigate direction recognition. They found users could recognize eight distinct cardinal and intermediate directions with accuracies from 79% to 91%. Schönauer et al. [15] have also investigated sensory saltation with a 3-by-4 tactile display for providing dynamic feedback for a motion guidance application.

2.2 Durations and Asynchronies of Tactile Stimuli

Early on, researchers began investigating the effects of varying the parameters of apparent tactile motion. Two of the first parameters investigated were DOS and SOA. Shimizu [16] looked into the effects of DOS and SOA for a 7-by-9 pin display placed on users' palms. In his first experiment, he found that increasing SOA afforded faster responses for a character recognition task. In his second experiment, he found that increasing DOS improved recognition accuracy. In much more recent research, Niwa et al. [17] used a 2-tactor array on the upper arm to find similar results for recognizing single-axis directions. They found that increasing DOS and SOA improved direction recognition and that recognition accuracies were around 95% when a time interval greater than 400 ms was used. Israr and Poupyrev [4] also investigated the effects of SOA on apparent tactile motion, but for the forearm and the back. They found that the range of acceptable SOA varied with DOS and body site. These results indicate that a longer DOS and larger SOA will yield more-accurate recognitions of touch gestures.

2.3 Frequencies and Amplitudes of Tactile Stimuli

Researchers have also investigated the effects of varying frequency and amplitude for vibrotactile stimuli on various perceptions. For example, Cholewiak and Collins [18] investigated the effects of frequency on a localization task, in which users identify where the tactile stimulus is perceived. In four different experiments, they repetitively found no significant effect of varying frequency on their localization tasks. In other work, Seo and Choi [19] investigated the effects of amplitude on perceived intensity and location using two vibrotactile actuators in a mobile device. They found that the perceived intensity of a phantom actuator was much more consistent when the amplitudes of two neighboring LRA motors were logarithmically scaled instead of linearly scaled. However, in a similar study, Israr and Poupyrev [4] found no significant effects of amplitude on the range of SOA. They later exploited this fact to develop their Tactile Brush algorithm [8], an algorithm for producing smooth, two-dimensional apparent motions. In the same work, they also found a significant effect of frequency on the range of SOA.

2.4 Spacing of Tactile Stimuli

Cholewiak and Collins [18] investigated the effects of spacing on localization and found that a larger spacing (5.08 cm) afforded significantly better accuracy than a smaller spacing (2.54 cm). However, Cha et al. [20] found that apparent motion was difficult to distinguish when the spacing of the actuators exceeds 8 cm. Israr and Poupyrev [4] found that the acceptable range of SOA decreased when the spacing of their actuators was doubled from 6 cm to 12 cm for the forearm, but not for the back. Finally, Niwa et al.

[17] found in their second experiment that four tactors placed around the arm afforded nearly 100% direction recognition for circular apparent motion while three tactors provided 90% at best. The results of these works indicate that there may be an optimal range for spacing between 2 cm and 8 cm.

3   An Extended Tactile Brush Algorithm

For our research, we wanted to investigate the perceived realism of whole-hand touch gestures that utilized phantom tactile sensations and apparent motion. In prior work, Israr and Poupyrev [8] presented the Tactile Brush algorithm for producing smooth, two-dimensional apparent tactile motions. While this algorithm is effective for displaying single-point touch gestures, it does not support the rendering of whole-hand touch gestures. Hence, we modified the algorithm to better suit the needs of our research. In this section, we explain the original Tactile Brush algorithm and how our extended version renders whole-hand touch gestures.

To produce smooth motions, the Tactile Brush algorithm adheres to an energy summation model to create nonexistent phantom actuators on the gesture path. The intensity of a phantom actuator P_N is determined by setting the amplitudes of the real actuators:

$$A_N = \sqrt{1 - \beta} \times P_N, \quad A_{N+1} = \sqrt{\beta} \times P_N \tag{1}$$

where, β is the distance between P_N and A_N divided by the distance between A_{N+1} and A_N. Apparent motion is then enabled by the DOS of P_N overlapping the SOA of P_{N+1} to generate a continuous movement sensation along the gesture path, as shown in Fig. 1. This algorithm allows low-resolution, grid-based tactile displays to produce smooth two-dimensional motions.

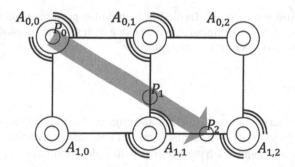

Fig. 1. The Tactile Brush algorithm produces a 2D apparent motion by using the virtual actuation points, P_0, P_1, and P_2. The real actuator $A_{0,0}$ is used for P_0. P_1 is generated by $A_{0,1}$ and $A_{1,1}$, and P_2 is generated by $A_{1,1}$ and $A_{1,2}$.

While the Tactile Brush algorithm produces smooth, two-dimensional motions, it only displays one point of contact at a time. Hence, it only supports single-finger touch gestures. However, we were interested in investigating whole-hand touch gestures, such as a whole-hand rub. To support these gestures, we extended the Tactile Brush algorithm to support multiple, simultaneous points of contact.

Initially, we assumed creating a rectangular area of contact with the Tactile Brush algorithm would be simple. We planned to display the area by activating the four phantom actuators that would define the four corners of the rectangle. However, we quickly realized that two phantom actuators on the same gesture path would require conflicting amplitudes from the contributing physical actuators. To minimize these conflicts, we simplified our whole-hand touch gestures to a multipoint line that moves along the direction of the whole-hand gesture. This line is produced by running the original algorithm on each grid line, in parallel, as demonstrated in Fig. 2.

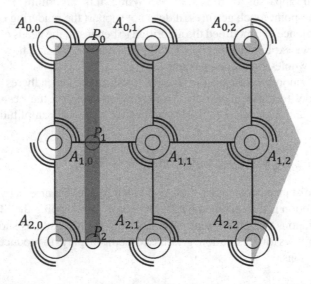

Fig. 2. Our extended version of the Tactile Brush algorithm produces multiple, simultaneous points of contact by running the original algorithm along each grid line, in parallel, to produce a multipoint line that moves along the gesture path.

4   Experiment

The goal of our experiment was to evaluate the effects of displayed tactile resolution on whole-hand touch gestures. While many researchers have investigated single-point touch gestures, whole-hand touch gestures with multiple, simultaneous points of contact are largely missing from prior research. Additionally, the spacing of tactile stimuli has mainly been investigated for 1 DOF only. Hence, our investigation into the effects of 2-DOF displayed tactile resolution on single-finger and whole-hand gestures addresses these limitations of prior research (Fig. 3).

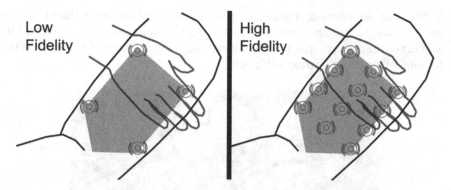

Fig. 3. For our experiment, we investigated two levels of tactile fidelity by comparing low and high displayed tactile resolutions.

4.1 Experimental Design

As discussed in Sect. 2, most prior research studies have focused on objective tasks, such as localization or gesture recognition. However, all of these studies were investigating touch gestures that involved only one point of contact at any given time. Based on anecdotal evidence from the formative evaluations that we conducted during the development of our tactile display, we were confident that displayed tactile resolution would not have a significant impact on accurately recognizing whole-hand touch gestures, due to their distinguishable multiple points of contact.

However, we did hypothesize that displayed tactile resolution would have an impact on the subjective perception of the whole-hand gestures, with the higher resolution providing more-realistic tactile experiences for users. Therefore, we designed a subjective evaluation of displayed tactile resolution, in which users would blindly compare the two levels of fidelity and choose the one that best correlated with a visual representation of the touch gesture. In addition to their preferences, we also wanted to know what users thought of the accuracy and acceptability of the level of tactile fidelity.

4.2 Touch Gestures

For our subjective evaluation, we decided to investigate single-finger and whole-hand touch gestures. We chose a total of ten touch gestures to investigate: four single-finger and six whole-hand. The single-finger touch gestures were: (1) a single-finger touch near the elbow, (2) a single-finger touch near the middle of the upper arm, (3) a single-finger touch near the shoulder, and (4) a single-finger stroke from the shoulder to the elbow. We used the original Tactile Brush algorithm to render these.

The whole-hand touch gestures were: (5) a whole-hand touch near the middle of the upper arm, (6) a repetitive whole-hand pat near the middle, (7) a whole-hand stroke from the shoulder to the elbow, (8) a repetitive whole-hand stroke between the shoulder and the elbow, (9) a whole-hand stroke across the middle of the upper arm from front to back, and (10) a repetitive whole-hand stroke across the middle between the front and back. We used our extended Tactile Brush algorithm to render these. Based on prior research results, we hypothesized that displayed tactile resolution would have a significant effect on the perception of the whole-hand touch gestures, but not on the perception of the single-finger touch gestures (Fig. 4).

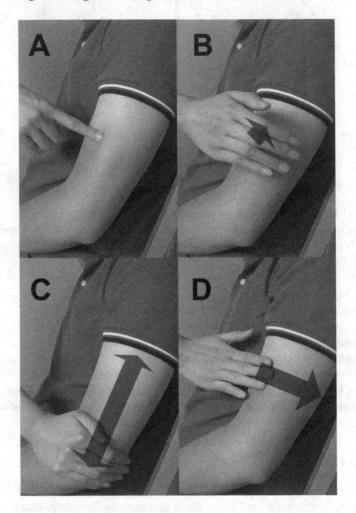

Fig. 4. Examples of the simple and complex touch gestures used in our subjective evaluation: (A) a single-finger touch near the middle of the upper arm, (B) a repetitive whole-hand pat near the middle, (C) a repetitive whole-hand stroke between the shoulder and the elbow, and (D) a whole-hand stroke across the middle from front to back.

4.3   Tactile Display

To enable our investigation of displayed tactile resolution and whole-hand touch gestures, we created a grid-based tactile display like the one presented by Tang et al. [21]. Our tactile display consisted of an Arduino Mega 2560 microcontroller, a 4-by-3 grid of LRA motors, and an elastic compression sleeve, seen in Fig. 5. The display supported two extreme levels of display tactile resolution. At the lowest level, the four corner LRA motors of the grid were activated to provide one actuation per 36 cm^2. At the highest level, all twelve motors were activated to provide one actuation per 12 cm^2. To calculate the displayed tactile resolution for each level, we followed the convention presented by Pasquero and Hayward [5]. First, we calculated the area covered by the tactile grid. Since our tactile sleeve is elastic, we calculated this based on an average user using the medium sleeve size, which yields an area of 144 cm^2. We then determined the ratio of actuators to area to calculate the displayed resolution.

Fig. 5. Our tactile display. A 4-by-3 grid of LRA motors covers the exterior of the user's upper arm. Small, medium, and large versions were created to accommodate users with different-sized arms. Proper placement aligns the center column of motors with the center of the exterior arm.

4.4 Procedure

After giving informed consent, participants were given a background survey to collect general demographic information (e.g., gender, age, dominant hand, etc.). The participants were then asked to try on the three different-sized tactile sleeves to determine which one best fit their left upper-arm. At this time, the experimenter ensured that the center column of actuators aligned with the center of the exterior portion of the upper arm for proper placement.

The participants were then presented with a simple graphical user interface for evaluating the fidelity levels. For each gesture trial, the interface would play a video of the real-world touch gesture. A "Replay Video" button allowed participants to view the video multiple times. The interface also included two radio buttons for "Config 1" and "Config 2". For each trial, the two levels of fidelity were randomly assigned to these radio buttons. This allowed for a blind comparison of the two levels and avoided any potential effects of ordering. A "Run" button would render the fidelity configuration currently indicated by the radio buttons to the tactile sleeve. Each configuration could be ran multiple times. Once the participants decided upon which configuration they preferred for the gesture, they were asked to use five-point Likert scales to rate: (a) how accurately the tactile sensation matched the sensation they expected from the video, and (b) how acceptable that sensation would be for simulating the gesture. Participants completed ten trials, one for each gesture. The order of the trials was randomized to avoiding ordering effects.

After participants completed the ten gesture trials, they were given an ergonomics questionnaire regarding the tactile display sleeve. The questionnaires addressed potential issues relating to discomfort, device weight, excessive pressure, and slippage. Finally, participants were asked to provide any additional comments.

4.5 Participants

We recruited 30 unpaid participants (25 males, 5 females) for our experiment. The age range of the participants was 18 to 50 years old with a mean age of 24.4 years. Only three participants were over the age of 30. All the participants were right handed. Hence, everyone wore the display on his or her non-dominant arm given our setup.

4.6 Results

We analyzed the selections of preferred touch gestures by using a Pearson's chi-squared test for each gesture to compare the probability of tactile fidelity selections to the neutral split that would be expected due to chance alone. Table 1 shows these test results, and Fig. 6 shows selection frequency per gesture. The higher level of displayed tactile resolution was significantly preferred for all gestures except gesture 1 (a single-finger touch near the elbow) and gesture 3 (a single-finger touch near the shoulder). Considering the type of gesture, we note that the higher level of tactile fidelity was significantly preferred for all six complex touch gestures. For simple touch gestures, higher fidelity was significantly preferred for two of the four gestures (the preferred gestures were a single-finger touch near the middle of the arm and a single-finger stroke from the shoulder to the elbow). We interpret these results to mean that higher displayed tactile resolution is more important for touch gestures occurring within squares of the display grid.

In addition to selecting the preferred level of fidelity for each gesture, participants rated the accuracy and acceptability of the chosen tactile sensation. Participants rated accuracy on a five-point Likert scale, from 1 (the gesture does not match at all) to 5 (the gesture definitely matches). They rated the acceptability of the touch gesture also on a 5-point scale, from 1 (completely unacceptable) to 5 (completely acceptable). Mean accuracy and acceptability ratings are shown in Figs. 7 and 8, respectively. Note that the participants only rated their selected level of fidelity for each gesture, so the number of ratings per gesture/fidelity combination is dependent upon the frequency of the combination shown in Fig. 6. Nevertheless, the accuracy ratings are relatively high with all mean ratings being between 3 (the midpoint) and 5 (definitely matches). Overall, we interpret these ratings as evidence that the

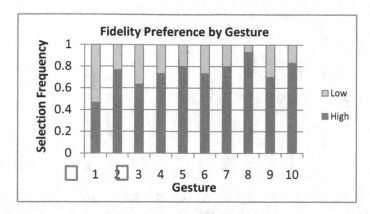

Fig. 6. Selection frequency of low and high levels of tactile fidelity show that the higher level was preferred over the lower level for all gestures except gesture 1.

tactile sleeve and our modified Tactile Brush algorithm performed reasonably well for simulating the simple and complex touch gestures.

Table 1. Analysis of tactile resolution preferences with Pearson's chi-squared tests show that the higher fidelity was significantly preferred at $p < 0.05$ for all gestures except 1 and 3.

Gesture		χ^2	p	Sig. pref.
1	Single-finger touch near elbow	0.133	0.715	-
2	Single-finger touch near middle	8.533	0.003	High
3	Single-finger touch near shoulder	2.133	0.144	-
4	Single-finger stroke from shoulder to elbow	6.533	0.011	High
5	Whole-hand touch near middle	10.800	0.001	High
6	Whole-hand pats near middle	6.533	0.011	High
7	Whole-hand stroke from shoulder to elbow	10.800	0.001	High
8	Whole-hand strokes between shoulder and elbow	22.533	< 0.001	High
9	Whole-hand stroke from front to back	4.800	0.028	High
10	Whole-hand strokes between front and back	13.333	< 0.001	High

However, the acceptability ratings indicate that some participants were not happy with gesture 7 (a whole-hand stroke from the shoulder to the elbow) and gesture 8 (repetitive whole-hand strokes between the shoulder and elbow). Figure 8 shows that acceptability ratings for the low and high fidelity versions of each gesture are relatively close for all except these two gestures. Our interpretation of these differences is that the few participants who selected the low fidelity versions of gestures 7 and 8 were not convinced that the rendered gestures simulated the feeling of whole-hand strokes along the arm. Considering that the majority of participants preferred and accepted the high-fidelity versions of these gestures, these results indicate that some participants may have higher expectations than others when it comes to the acceptability of touch gestures. We note that the rating differences were not affected by gender.

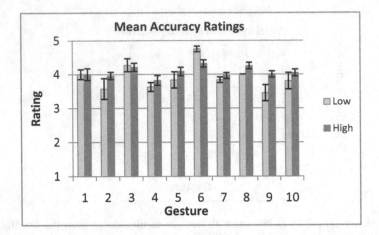

Fig. 7. Mean accuracy ratings when the level of fidelity was selected as the preferred choice.

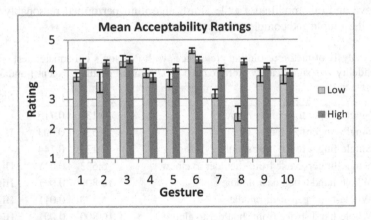

Fig. 8. Mean acceptability ratings when the level of fidelity was selected as the preferred choice.

With regard to the ergonomics of our tactile display, there were very few negative reports. Three of the 30 participants reported discomfort from wearing the sleeve, with all three citing numbness due to the vibrations. One of the participants reported that the device was heavy due to the wires connecting the actuators and haptic drivers. The biggest complaint was excessive pressure, with six participants reporting pressure just above the elbow crease due to the compression sleeve.

5   Discussion

Given the results of our study, there are several implications for the design of grid-based tactile displays, as well as potential VR application areas for whole-hand touch gestures. We also believe that whole-hand touch gestures could be used to identify participants that suffer from anaphia—the total or partial absence of tactile sense.

5.1 Implications for Grid-Based Tactile Displays

Considering the mean accuracy ratings for both the low and high fidelity versions of the touch gestures, we consider our extended Tactile Brush algorithm a success. As described in Sect. 3, our extended algorithm produces apparent motion for multiple points of contact. This is an advancement over previous versions of the algorithm, which could only produce a single point of contact (though Israr and Poupyrev eluded to multiple-contact versions [8]). Given the high acceptability ratings for the high-fidelity complex gestures, we believe our extended Tactile Brush works best with higher displayed tactile resolutions, though it sufficed for most of the low-fidelity touch gestures. The biggest constraint for our algorithm is that it currently requires the contact area's width to coincide with the display's grid lines, but we believe this issue can be overcome with further research.

Another implication for grid-based tactile displays is that more is better. Higher displayed tactile resolution was significantly preferred for all gestures except for two single-finger touch gestures, and it was not preferred significantly less for those two gestures. This indicates that grid-based tactile displays, particularly those consisting of LRA motors like ours, should strive for displayed tactile resolutions of one actuator per 12 cm^2. However, we believe there is an upper limit to increasing the resolution based on Cholewiak and Collins work [18]. One actuator per 2 cm^2 is probably too much.

Finally, another design implication based on our research is that small actuators can be used to display touch gestures on small body regions. Since small actuators are exponentially cheaper than large ones and displayed tactile resolution is important, the best approach to providing tactile feedback to the entire body may be to develop many small-region devices, as opposed to using a few large-region devices. The biggest hurdle to this approach will be how to synchronously communicate to so many devices.

5.2 VR Applications for Complex Touch Gestures

In VR, the most obvious application of complex touch gestures, like our whole-hand gestures, is improved tactile feedback for large-area contacts with a virtual environment. For example, when a user is moving down a virtual hallway and leans into a virtual wall, a large contact area can be displayed moving across the user's upper arm from front to back. This could provide a more realistic experience than just vibrating the entire grid, which in turn should increase presence [22].

Another potential VR application area is telepresence. In recent work, Huisman et al. [23] developed a tactile sleeve for conveying social touch over a distance. While their 4-by-3 *TaSST* display was very similar to our display, they were using simple algorithms based on touch-sensitive compartments to render touch gestures. With our extended Tactile Brush algorithm, telepresence users' hands can be tracked in 3D space, virtually modeled to determine collisions with remote users' tracked bodies, and then rendered as realistic social touches to increase co-presence.

Finally, a third VR application area for our whole-hand touch gestures is Autism Spectrum Disorder (ASD) interventions. ASD is a pervasive developmental disorder that is characterized by restrictive interests, repetitive actions, and impaired social and communicative behaviors [24]. Individuals with ASD often exhibit secondary difficulties with sensory-perceptual anomalies that cause hypo-sensitivities and hypersensitivities [25–28]. Several first-hand accounts of individuals with ASD describe how they struggle with both hypo and hypersensitivities, limiting their contact with other people [29–31]. An example would be feeling overwhelmed from a hug because it feels like sandpaper to the touch. Researchers have already investigated and developed VR technologies and systems as promising intervention methods for ASD patients [32–35]. By utilizing our research on whole-hand touch gestures, VR intervention methods could allow hypersensitive patients to explore the physical sensation of touch without being overwhelmed by actual human contact. We are currently working on integrating our research with prior VR intervention applications to give ASD patients a chance to learn how to manage their hypersensitivities to human contact through experiences of being touched by virtual avatars [36].

5.3 Screening Tool for Anaphia Participants

Anaphia is the total or partial absence of the sense of touch. For research on tactile technologies and feedback, participants with anaphia can have a negative impact on potentially positive results. Traditionally, tactile researchers have relied on self-reports to exclude such participants. However, this method is inherently flawed as self-reports have been shown in many studies to be unreliable.

As an alternative to using self-reports to identify participants with anaphia, we propose that the selection trial for gesture 8 from our study could be used as a screening tool. For gesture 8 (the repetitive whole-hand strokes between the shoulder and elbow), the higher level of displayed tactile resolution was preferred by all but two participants, and those two participants poorly rated the lower level of tactile fidelity. Hence, we believe this complex gesture trial could be used to flag participants that do not choose the higher level of tactile fidelity as potential anaphia participants.

6   Conclusions and Future Work

Although much research has been conducted on phantom tactile sensations and apparent tactile motion, most investigations have been limited to touch gestures involving single points of contact. By extending the Tactile Brush algorithm, we were able to simulate multiple points of contact. These areas enabled us to develop whole-hand touch gestures that involve multiple points of contact, such as a whole-hand pat on the arm. Using a 4-by-3 tactile display sleeve that we developed, we investigated the effects of displayed tactile resolution on preference, perceived accuracy, and acceptability of four single-finger touch gestures and six whole-hand touch gestures. Our results indicate that our extended Tactile Brush algorithm produces accurate whole-hand touch gestures, that greater displayed tactile resolutions will produce more-acceptable touch gestures than lower resolutions, and that small actuators can be effectively used to display touch gestures on small body regions.

In the near future, we are planning on investigating moderate levels of displayed tactile resolution with our tactile display sleeve, such as 2-by-3 and 4-by-2 resolutions. In addition to subjective evaluations, we will incorporate objective aspects, such as gesture recognition tasks. Later on, we plan to revisit our extended Tactile Brush algorithm. We hope to find a method of addressing its current constraint of the apparent motion being restricted to a multipoint line.

Acknowledgements. The authors wish to thank Carl Lutz for initiating this project and providing feedback during the development process. This work was supported in part by a gift from the T. Boone Pickens Foundation.

References

1. von Békésy, G.: Sensations on the skin similar to directional hearing, beats, and harmonics of the ear. J. Acoust. Soc. Am. **29**, 489–501 (1957)
2. Chen, L.M., Friedman, R.M., Roe, A.W.: Optical imaging of a tactile illusion in area 3b of the primary somatosensory cortex. Science **302**, 881–885 (2003)
3. Sherrick, C.E., Rogers, R.: Apparent haptic movement. Percept. Psychophys. **1**, 175–180 (1966)
4. Israr, A., Poupyrev, I.: Control space of apparent haptic motion. In: World Haptics Conference (WHC), pp. 457–462. IEEE (2011)
5. Pasquero, J., Hayward, V.: STReSS: a practical tactile display system with one millimeter spatial resolution and 700 Hz refresh rate. In: Eurohaptics, pp. 94–110 (2003)
6. Johnson, K.O., Phillips, J.R.: Tactile spatial resolution. I. Two-point discrimination, gap detection, grating resolution, and letter recognition. J. Neurophysiol. **46**, 1177–1192 (1981)
7. Morrison, I., Löken, L., Olausson, H.: The skin is a social organ. Exp. Brain Res. **204**, 305–314 (2010)
8. Israr, A., Poupyrev, I.: Tactile brush: drawing on skin with a tactile grid display. In: ACM Conference on Human Factors in Computing Systems (CHI), pp. 2019–2028. ACM (2011)
9. Collins, C.C.: Tactile television—mechanical and electrical image projection. IEEE Trans. Man Mach. Syst. **11**, 65–71 (1970)
10. Loomis, J.: Tactile letter recognition under different modes of stimulus presentation. Percept. Psychophys. **16**, 401–408 (1974)
11. Saida, S., Shimizu, Y., Wake, T.: Construction of small TVSS and optimal mode of stimulus presentation. In: 4th Symposium on Sensory Substitution, Ibaraki, Japan (1978)
12. Yanagida, Y., Kakita, M., Lindeman, R.W., Kume, Y., Tetsutani, N.: Vibrotactile letter reading using a low-resolution tactor array. In: 12th Symposium on Haptic Interfaces for Virtual Environment and Teleoperator Systems (HAPTICS), pp. 400–406 (2004)
13. Tan, H.Z., Pentland, A.: Tactual displays for wearable computing. Pers. Technol. **1**, 225–230 (1997)
14. Tan, H., Lim, A., Traylor, R.: A psychophysical study of sensory saltation with an open response paradigm. ASME Dyn. Syst. Control Div. **69**, 1109–1115 (2000). The American Society of Mechanical Engineers
15. Schönauer, C., Fukushi, K., Olwal, A., Kaufmann, H., Raskar, R.: Multimodal motion guidance: techniques for adaptive and dynamic feedback. In: 14th ACM International Conference on Multimodal Interaction, pp. 133–140. ACM (2012)
16. Shimizu, Y.: Temporal effect on tactile letter recognition by a tracing mode. Percept. Mot. Skills **55**, 343–349 (1982)

17. Niwa, M., Lindeman, R.W., Itoh, Y., Kishino, F.: Determining appropriate parameters to elicit linear and circular apparent motion using vibrotactile cues. In: World Haptics Conference (WHC), pp. 75–78. IEEE (2009)
18. Cholewiak, R.W., Collins, A.A.: Vibrotactile localization on the arm: effects of place, space, and age. Percept. Psychophys. **65**, 1058–1077 (2003)
19. Seo, J., Choi, S.: Initial study for creating linearly moving vibrotactile sensation on mobile device. In: IEEE Haptics Symposium, pp. 67–70 (2010)
20. Cha, J., Rahal, L., El Saddik, A.: A pilot study on simulating continuous sensation with two vibrating motors. In: IEEE Symposium on Haptic Audio Visual Environments and Games (HAVE), pp. 143–147 (2008)
21. Tang, F., McMahan, R.P., Allen, T.T.: Development of a low-cost tactile sleeve for autism intervention. In: IEEE International Symposium on Haptic, Audio and Visual Environments and Games (HAVE), pp. 35–40 (2014)
22. Slater, M., Usoh, M., Steed, A.: Taking steps: the influence of a walking technique on presence in virtual reality. ACM Trans. Comput. Hum. Interact. (TOCHI) **2**, 201–219 (1995)
23. Huisman, G., Darriba Frederiks, A., Van Dijk, B., Hevlen, D., Krose, B.: The TaSST: tactile sleeve for social touch. In: World Haptics Conference (WHC), pp. 211–216. IEEE (2013)
24. American Psychiatric Association: Diagnostic and statistical manual of mental disorders: DSM-IV-TR. American Psychiatric Publishing (2000)
25. Abu-Dahab, S., Skidmore, E., Holm, M., Rogers, J., Minshew, N.: Motor and tactile-perceptual skill differences between individuals with high-functioning autism and typically developing individuals ages 5–21. J. Autism Dev. Disord. **43**, 2241–2248 (2013)
26. Cascio, C., McGlone, F., Folger, S., Tannan, V., Baranek, G., Pelphrey, K., Essick, G.: Tactile perception in adults with autism: a multidimensional psychophysical study. J. Autism Dev. Disord. **38**, 127–137 (2008)
27. Güçlü, B., Tanidir, C., Mukaddes, N., Unal, F.: Tactile sensitivity of normal and autistic children. Somatosen. Mot. Res. **24**, 21–33 (2007)
28. Wang, M., Reid, D.: Virtual reality in pediatric neurorehabilitation: attention deficit hyperactivity disorder, autism and cerebral palsy. Neuroepidemiology **36**, 2–18 (2011)
29. Cesaroni, L., Garber, M.: Exploring the experience of autism through firsthand accounts. J. Autism Dev. Disord. **21**, 303–313 (1991)
30. Grandin, T.: An inside view of autism. In: Schopler, E., Mesibov, G.B. (eds.) High Functioning Individuals with Autism, pp. 105–126. Plenum, New York (1992)
31. Jones, R.P., Quigney, C., Huws, J.C.: First-hand accounts of sensory perceptual experiences in autism: a qualitative analysis. J. Intell. Dev. Disabil. **28**, 112–121 (2003)
32. Josman, N., Ben-Chaim, H.M., Fridrich, S., Weiss, P.L.: Effectiveness of virtual reality for teaching street-crossing skills to children and adolescents with autism. Int. J. Disabil. Hum. Dev. **7**, 49–56 (2008)
33. Herrera, G., Alcantud, F., Jordan, R., Blanquer, A., Labajo, G., De Pablo, C.: Development of symbolic play through the use of virtual reality tools in children with autistic spectrum disorders: two case studies. Autism Int. J. Res. Pract. **12**, 143–157 (2008)
34. Cheng, Y., Ye, J.: Exploring the social competence of students with autism spectrum conditions in a collaborative virtual learning environment—the pilot study. Comput. Educ. **54**, 1068–1077 (2010)
35. Moore, D., Cheng, Y., McGrath, P., Powell, N.J.: Collaborative virtual environment technology for people with autism. Focus Autism Other Dev. Disabil. **20**, 231–243 (2005)
36. Kandalaft, M., Didehbani, N., Krawczyk, D., Allen, T., Chapman, S.: Virtual reality social cognition training for young adults with high-functioning autism. J. Autism Dev. Disord. **43**, 34–44 (2013)

VAMR in Education and Training

VoTrE: A Vocational Training and Evaluation System to Compare Training Approaches for the Workplace

Ashwin Ramesh Babu[✉], Akilesh Rajavenkatanarayanan, Maher Abujelala, and Fillia Makedon

Heracleia, Human-Centered Computing Laboratory,
Department of Computer Science and Engineering,
University of Texas at Arlington,
Arlington, USA
{Ashwin.rameshbabu,Akilesh.rajavenkatanarayanan,
maher.abujelala}@mavs.uta.edu, makedon@uta.edu

Abstract. Extensive research has been carried out in using computer-based techniques to train and prepare workers for various industry positions. Most of this research focuses on how to best enable the workers to perform a type of task safely and efficiently. In fact, many of the accidents in manufacturing and construction environments are due to the lack of proper training needed for employees. In this study, we compare the impact of three types of training approaches on the planning and problem-solving abilities of a trainee while he/she performs the Towers of Hanoi (TOH) task. The three approaches are (a) traditional (with a human trainer), (b) gamification (game-based training simulation), and (c) computer-aided training. The aim of this study is to evaluate a worker's level of functioning and problem-solving skills based on a specific training approach. Exact assessment of functional capacities is an important prerequisite to ensure effective and personalized training. The study uses workplace simulation to collect different types of performance data and assess the impact of these training approaches.

Keywords: Vocational training · Towers of Hanoi · Gamification · Computer-aided training · Cognitive issues · Performance

1 Introduction

Safety of employees in industries and organizations has become one of the primary focuses today. Employers aim at providing a safe work environment to their employees. To maintain that, employees must attend several orientations and trainings. The employers are very keen in developing and implementing safe work procedures and rules. However, safety can be enforced with the right person for the right job. For example, in a car manufacturing company, there are specific requirements and rules on how to assemble parts. The right candidate with the functional capacity and stability will not only perform the task safely, but will increase the efficiency of production. Even though candidates are put through a lot of interviews and evaluation during the hiring process to test their capabilities, the assessment of the their functional capacity helps

© Springer International Publishing AG 2017
S. Lackey and J. Chen (Eds.): VAMR 2017, LNCS 10280, pp. 203–214, 2017.
DOI: 10.1007/978-3-319-57987-0_16

the employer recruit the better suited candidates [14]. Our framework addresses how the functional capacity and performance evaluation can be achieved. The system uses computer vision techniques and Towers of Hanoi (TOH) for the evaluation purposes. Towers of Hanoi is a well-known executive function task that it is used to assess cognitive skills and "measure working memory and inhibition processes" [16].

Most industrial accidents are due to the improper training [12, 15]. A good training method is one important key to maintain safety. Colligan et al. [3] states that proper training contributes to the safety of employees. At the same time employers spend on an average $3,000,000 approximately every year to train workers [8]. It always has to be a win-win situation where it benefits the employers by investing a low budget for training and the quality of training maintained. Our framework was used for a comparative study between three training methods: (a) traditional (with a human trainer), (b) gamification (game-based training simulation), and (c) computer-aided training. The comparison was made to find a method that helps train users better. From the developed framework and analysis, data was collected to identify the advantages and disadvantages of each training method.

2 Related Work

Functional capacity evaluation of physically challenged individuals and veterans has existed to assess their stability. This has always been clinic-based and practiced only by therapists [6]. It is suggested that using functional capacity evaluation in the workplace, in addition to the traditional interview based evaluation, would provide better evaluation of the employees. Extensive amount of research explains how workers can be efficiently trained for an industrial job. Human-based training is popular and widely used today. This method produces results but at a cost [11]. Researchers stress on the importance and the usefulness of the Game-Based Training (GBT) and its impacts on employees [7]. GBT offers safe and effective way to improve cognitive skills [2, 4, 5]. However, it is less effective with jobs where hands-on experience and training is required, e.g. unpacking items and loading them on the shelves in retail stores. In this case, trainees would gain less experience in a GBT when compared to hands on experience in the store. The computer-aided training that we have developed is a combination of human and game-based training, and have the potential to overcome the aforementioned drawbacks. The developed system can give personal assistance to the trainee, and at the same time provide the trainee with hands-on experience.

Assessment of functional capacity is a problem that has gained attraction from many researchers. Similarly, the advantages and impacts of GBT methods are extensively evaluated [9]. For example, LEGO assembly task was used to assess employees in an industrial simulation setup [10]. Retail corporations, such as Walmart, have been seeking alternative ways to train low-skilled workers [17]. This includes interactive games and applications that employees use on their commute and at home, offering on-the-job coaching for employers. In case of NASA, the shortlisted astronaut candidates start their training process by taking computer-based training on using various vehicle systems prior to operating live systems to help the candidates recognize malfunctions and perform corrective actions [13].

3 Experimental Setup

The study consists of a webcam, a computer, a physical Towers of Hanoi (TOH) as shown in Fig. 1. A computer-game replicating the physical experimental setup was developed using Unity game engine. To make sure the task is not too challenging, the number of disks in TOH is set to 5. The minimum number of steps taken to solve them is $2^n - 1$, where 'n' represents the number of disks. This would allow the users to solve the TOH task in 31 steps. The Towers of Hanoi were in a stationary position facing the webcam. The towers were labeled from left to right as *Column 1, Column 2 and Column 3* as shown in Fig. 1. An overview of the experiment setup and design is explained in a YouTube video[1].

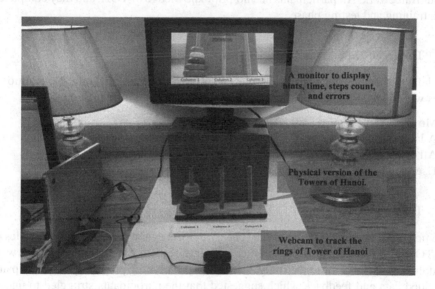

Fig. 1. Experimental setup

4 Methodology

In this study, we compare the impact of three types of training methods on the planning and problem-solving abilities of a trainee while he/she performs the Towers of Hanoi (TOH) task. For this, the study consisted of two phases, the training phase and the testing phase. In the training phase, the participants were divided into three groups and were trained to solve the Towers of Hanoi with one of the three methods, that is, (a) traditional (with a human trainer), (b) gamification (game-based training simulation) and (c)

---

[1] https://youtu.be/svFjLF5A93E.

computer-aided training. After training, the participants were given a break and then the test began. In the training sessions, the participants were guided to solve the task using the optimal number of steps (which is 31 steps). However, in the testing session, there were no restrictions on the number of steps. From the results of the training and testing phases, analysis was made as discussed in Sect. 5. The three factors considered for the analysis were; total number of moves (steps), total time to solve, and the number of errors made while completing the task.

4.1 Participants

The participants were undergraduate students in the Department of Computer Science and Engineering at the University of Texas at Arlington. There were no restrictions based on their age and gender. A total of 18 participants were divided randomly for each of the three training methods and another 10 participants were part of the prototyping phase of our framework. All participants had no-prior knowledge of TOH, and they completed both training and testing phase.

4.2 Towers of Hanoi Rules

By default, there are some standard rules to solve the Towers of Hanoi. No additional rules were added to make the game easier for participants. These include:

- Move only one disk at a time.
- A larger disk may not be placed on top of a smaller disk.
- All disks, except the one being moved, must be on a tower.
- User will use only one hand to deal with the disk.

4.3 Training Phase

The first phase was the training phase. The participants were provided with the rules of the TOH. Each participant was presented with one of the training methods which were randomly assigned prior to the study. During the prototyping phase, the 10 participants provided data and feedback which suggested that the participants struggled to understand and recall the technique to solve TOH. So, the framework was updated such that each of the remaining 18 participants were trained twice.

4.3.1 Traditional Training Method (Human Trainer)

With this method, the participants were trained with a personal human trainer as shown in Fig. 2. The trainer went through the steps verbally to solve the TOH with the participants. This training was timed and the number of errors while solving was recorded.

Fig. 2. Traditional training. Human trainer (left) gives verbal instructions to the participant (right) to solve the TOH task.

4.3.2   Gamification (Game-Based Training)

This method of training incorporated a computer game. The computer game was a replica of the physical version of the TOH, as shown in Fig. 3. GBT has become very popular in the recent decade. Researchers have found that this method is highly effective in training and has produced great results [7]. The participants solved the TOH by using the computer mouse to click on the disks that they wanted to move, and click on the tower where they wanted the disk to be placed. The instructions of the game, e.g. 'move the red disk to tower 3,' were flashed on the screen for the user to follow. The game restricted the participants to make wrong moves, e.g. moving a disk to tower 2 instead of tower 3, and false attempts were counted. To notify the participants of wrong moves, the system displayed error messages on the screen and made sound notifications.

Fig. 3. Game-based training. Participant plays the unity game

4.3.3   Computer-Aided Training

In this method, the participants were trained with computer-aided instructions. That is, instead of an individual trainer, participants were asked to solve TOH with instructions flashing on the screen. Every step performed was captured through a webcam to evaluate the accuracy of the steps from the instructions that appeared.

The system was implemented using MATLAB. A webcam placed in front of TOH capturing 10 frames per second recognized the disks and their positions. To identify individual colors, HSV (Hue, Saturation, and Value) color space was used. The size of the disks was considered to avoid shadow based errors, noise and other objects that impeded the frame. Next, to identify the position of each disk, the centroid of each disk was calculated and the tower to which it belonged was identified. The system considered the disks for evaluation only when they were in a stationary position. Each step was considered a separate state. Every time a change is made, the system compared the current position of the disks with the position of the expected state. If they matched, it was considered a successful move and the current and the past states were updated. If they did not match, it meant that the disks were not in the expected position and was considered an error. In such cases, the system asked the participants to go to the previous move or to the actual move, as shown in Fig. 4, and then the system proceeded.

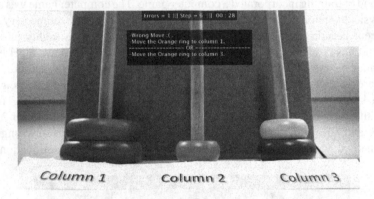

Fig. 4. Computer based training. The system asks the participant to go to the previous move or to the actual move to be made when they fail to follow the instructions.

4.4   Test Phase

Once the training was completed, all participants were asked to complete the task (without any assistance) using the physical blocks of TOH as shown in Fig. 5. The results of this phase helped us evaluate the functional capacity of the participants and the effectiveness of the training.

The detection of colors and the disks was implemented using the same algorithm as used in the computer-aided training. Here, the system kept track of the past and current state. Initially when the test began, there was no past state and the starting position was updated as the current state. For every move the system checked the position of the disks and compared it with the rules. If the position of the rings satisfies the rules, the system

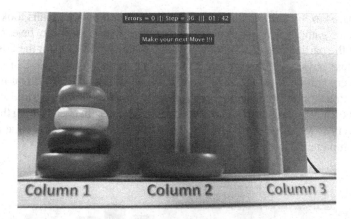

Fig. 5. Test phase. The system does not provide the participant with instructions.

updates the current position as the new present state and updates the past state. With this feature, the system recognized the previous moves and in case of an error, the system prompted an error message to the participant with a sound notification as shown in Fig. 6.

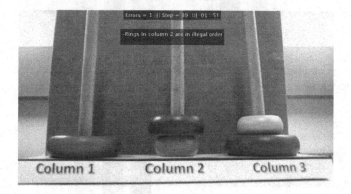

Fig. 6. Test phase. The system warns the participant of illegal moves.

5   Data Collection and Analysis

Data was collected from 18 participants. The data consists of the total number of moves (steps), total time taken to solve Towers of Hanoi (TOH), the time taken for each step, and the number of errors made by the participants. As mentioned in Sect. 4.4, all the participants received the same testing phase. Figure 7 shows the average number of steps each group of participants needed to complete the TOH. All the participants were trained to finish the task in 31 moves, and any extra moves were considered as errors. The average number of moves in the testing phase was nearly the same in all groups, and the participants performed extra moves in the testing phase compared to the training phase. Similarly, Fig. 8 shows that the participants took greater time to complete the testing phase compared to the training phase. It also shows that the participants took less time to complete the game-based task in the training phase. The reason may be explained by the fact that the participants did not interact with the physical TOH in the GBT, which resulted in less physical effort and time. However, the completion time in the testing phase was very similar in all the three groups. The results of the number of moves and completion times might indicate that the different training approaches did not have a major effect on how the trainees performed. It also indicates that performing the training twice had very low practice effect, since the participants took longer time and more moves to complete the testing phase compared to the training phase.

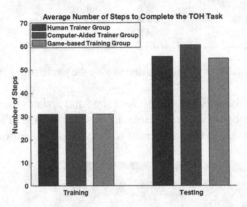

Fig. 7. Average number of moves (steps) each group of participants performed in both the training and testing phase.

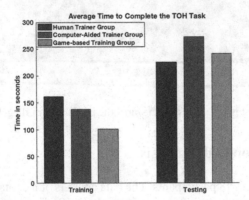

Fig. 8. Average time to finish the TOH task by each group of participants in both the training and testing phase.

Figure 9 shows the average number of errors performed by each group. In the training phase, both extra and illegal moves (i.e. large disk placed on smaller disk) are considered errors, and in the testing phase only illegal moves are considered errors. The participants in the human training group performed with fewer errors when compared with the other groups. This may indicate, although the performance is very similar in all the three groups, the participants who were given the rules for the task by the human trainer could follow the rules better. In the GBT group, the game restricted the participants from making illegal moves. When the participants tried to make illegal moves, the disks stayed in the original towers/columns and did not move to the wrong columns. The lack of hands-on experience during GBT may have contributed to the increased number of errors in the testing phase.

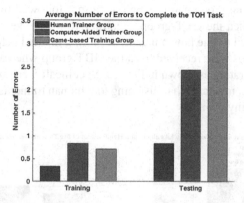

Fig. 9. Average number of wrong/illegal moves (steps) each group of participants performed in both the training and testing phase.

5.1 Performance of Trainees

The data collected during the testing phase can be used to create a measure of performance and functional capacity. This measure can be used to check if the trainee is a fit for the job. The employer can set specific thresholds for the number of errors allowed, completion time, and how the trainees perform (e.g. number of moves). In certain jobs, where high accuracy is required, the employer can have a low threshold for the errors and high threshold for the completion time. For instance, in an assembly line, the employer can set thresholds to tolerate 2% of errors and 5% of delay in production completion due to of human errors. Trainees who surpass these thresholds may require more training. In our experiment, participants with average performance are considered to have sufficient problem-solving skills. Table 1 shows the average values from all the participants, which are used as thresholds. When applying these thresholds, we found 47% of our participants surpassed these thresholds and they need more training before being able to perform the TOH on their own.

Table 1. Threshold values for the towers of Hanoi task.

Description	Moves	Errors	Completion time
Average values	57 moves	2 errors	248 s

5.2 User Survey Results

At the end of every experiment, participants were asked to fill out a survey form about their experience with the system. From the survey, more than 90% of the participants liked the experiment as they were new to the TOH. They also stated that they required complete focus and concentration while solving the TOH with minimum steps and errors. When the participants were asked how they liked their training method, computer-aided training group had the highest rating, followed by the human trainer training group, and then the GBT group. Contrary to the above statement, when the participants were asked to rate how much their training method helped to complete the task, the highest ratings were received from the GBT group whereas the human trainer group had the lowest rating as shown in Fig. 10. Specifically, one of the trainees in the human trainer group commented that 'listening to a human trainer is helpful, but it does not help me think on my own.'

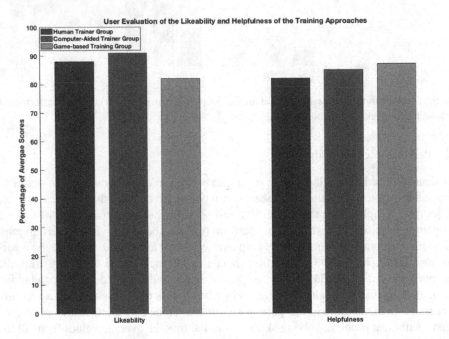

Fig. 10. User survey result for the likeability and helpfulness of the training approaches.

6 Discussion and Conclusion

The need to reduce the unemployment rate and accidents due to human factors have encouraged businesses and government agencies to invest in training employees [1, 18]. Recruiting and training the *best* employees with the appropriate skills would ensure individuals secure their jobs and make fewer mistakes. Assessment of employees' performance may provide feedback to employees so that they can accomplish their job safely and efficiently. In workplaces, this may be applied to employee's requiring increased problem-solving and planning skills to accomplish their job (i.e. inspection and maintenance jobs). The Towers of Hanoi task discussed in this paper may be used to measure general problem-solving skills. Similarly, having game-based and computer-aided training and testing are not applicable to all scenarios or too costly. Employers must consider to the skills evaluated and cost-benefit analysis to the company to determine its implementation.

This study compares the impact of three types of training methods on the planning and problem-solving abilities of a trainees while they perform the Towers of Hanoi (TOH) task. The authors observed that participants in the traditional training group showed higher rating in following the task rules. Additionally, using the computer-aided and game-based training provided relevant feedback. They provided the same performance results as the traditional training and with accurate record of performance. Using computer-aided and game-based training also provide the participants with ubiquitous training as well as reduced human supervision. Finally, the use of intelligent training approaches help support training individuals to make their jobs easier and improve performance.

Acknowledgments. This work was supported in part by the National Science Foundation under award numbers 1338118, 1405985, and 1565328.

References

1. Aragón-Sánchez, A., Barba-Aragón, I., Sanz-Valle, R.: Effects of training on business results1. Int. J. Hum. Resour. Manag. **14**, 956–980 (2003)
2. Chebaa, B., Lioulemes, A., Abujelala, M., Ebert, D., Phan, S., Becker, E., Makedon, F.: Multimodal analysis of serious games for cognitive and physiological assessment. In: Proceedings of the 9th ACM International Conference on PErvasive Technologies Related to Assistive Environments, p. 30 (2016)
3. Colligan, M.J., Cohen, A.: The role of training in promoting workplace safety and health. In: The Psychology of Workplace Safety, pp. 223–248 (2004)
4. Gabbett, T., Jenkins, D., Abernethy, B.: Game-based training for improving skill and physical fitness in team sport athletes. Int. J. Sports Sci. Coach. **4**, 273–283 (2009)
5. Gattupalli, S., Lioulemes, A., Gieser, Shawn N., Sassaman, P., Athitsos, V., Makedon, F.: MAGNI: a real-time robot-aided game-based tele-rehabilitation system. In: Antona, M., Stephanidis, C. (eds.) UAHCI 2016. LNCS, vol. 9739, pp. 344–354. Springer, Cham (2016). doi:10.1007/978-3-319-40238-3_33
6. Innes, E., Straker, L.: Workplace assessments and functional capacity evaluations: current practices of therapists in Australia. Work **18**, 51–66 (2002)
7. Kapp, K.M.: The Gamification of Learning and Instruction: Game-Based Methods and Strategies for Training and Education. Wiley, New York (2012)
8. Knoke, D., Kalleberg, A.L.: Job training in US organizations. Am. Sociol. Rev. 537–546 (1994)
9. Korn, O., Funk, M., Schmidt, A.: Towards a gamification of industrial production: a comparative study in sheltered work environments. In: Proceedings of 7th ACM SIGCHI Symposium on Engineering Interactive Computing Systems, pp. 84–93 (2015)

10. Korn, O., Tso, L., Papagrigoriou, C., Sowoidnich, Y., Konrad, R., Schmidt, A.: Computerized assessment of the skills of impaired and elderly workers: a tool survey and comparative study. In: Proceedings of the 9th ACM International Conference on PErvasive Technologies Related to Assistive Environments, p. 50 (2016)
11. McClaran, S.R.: The effectiveness of personal training on changing attitudes towards physical activity. J. Sport Sci. Med. **2**, 10–14 (2003)
12. Myers, G.: A study of the causes of industrial accidents. Q. Publ. Am. Stat. Assoc. **14**, 672–694 (1915)
13. National Aeronautics and Space Adminstration Astronaut Selection and Training
14. Soer, R., der Schans, C.P., Groothoff, J.W., Geertzen, J.H.B., Reneman, M.F.: Towards consensus in operational definitions in functional capacity evaluation: a Delphi Survey. J. Occup. Rehabil. **18**, 389–400 (2008)
15. Tam, C.M., Zeng, S.X., Deng, Z.M.: Identifying elements of poor construction safety management in China. Saf. Sci. **42**, 569–586 (2004)
16. Welsh, M.C., Satterlee-Cartmell, T., Stine, M.: Towers of Hanoi and London: contribution of working memory and inhibition to performance. Brain Cogn. **41**, 231–242 (1999). doi: 10.1006/brcg.1999.1123
17. Walmart reveals first phase of workforce training. http://www.usatoday.com/story/money/2015/02/26/walmart-workforce-training-donation/24047309/. Accessed 1 Mar 2017
18. FACT SHEET - American Job Training Investments: Skills and Jobs to Build a Stronger Middle Class|whitehouse.gov. https://obamawhitehouse.archives.gov/the-press-office/2014/04/16/fact-sheet-american-job-training-investments-skills-and-jobs-build-stron. Accessed 1 Mar 2017

Effects of Instruction Methods on User Experience in Virtual Reality Serious Games

Lal Bozgeyikli[1](✉), Andrew Raij[2], Srinivas Katkoori[1], and Redwan Alqasemi[3]

[1] Department of Computer Science and Engineering, University of South Florida, Tampa, USA
{gamze,katkoori}@mail.usf.edu
[2] Institute for Simulation and Training, University of Central Florida, Orlando, USA
raij@ucf.edu
[3] Department of Mechanical Engineering, University of South Florida, Tampa, USA
alqasemi@usf.edu

Abstract. Instructions are an important aspect of virtual reality serious games since they are crucial to understanding what is expected from the user. User friendly instructions can contribute positively to the user experience, while confusing instructions can degrade it. There are various methods of instruction giving. In this study, we examine the effects of four different instruction methods on user experience in virtual reality serious games. The four instruction methods that were explored in our study are 3D animated, pictograph, written and verbal instructions. Eight simple vocational tasks were designed and implemented to be performed in an immersive virtual warehouse environment. A user study was performed with 15 adult participants. Results revealed that animated instructions provided better user experience among the four methods. Pictograph and written instructions shared similar mid-range rankings. Verbal instructions were the least preferred method. In this paper, we present our experiment design, results and discussions of our implications for future virtual reality serious game studies.

Keywords: Virtual reality · Serious games · Training · Instruction methods

1 Introduction

Virtual reality has been gaining a lot of attention in the last few years with the new generation head mounted displays and more content. Besides entertainment and social interactions, virtual reality is also used for training people on various skills. These applications can be considered as serious games for virtual reality. Serious games are described as games having a purpose beyond entertainment such as teaching a new skill or providing training to enhance existing skills [11]. Virtual reality training offers several advantages over real world training such as safety, easy customization, gamification, real time alteration of scenarios and environmental elements, automated data collection and no severe real life consequences of mistakes. Many early studies agree on several benefits that virtual reality training provides in many diverse areas such as medical training [10, 14], aeronautics and space training [5] and vehicle operation training [2].

© Springer International Publishing AG 2017
S. Lackey and J. Chen (Eds.): VAMR 2017, LNCS 10280, pp. 215–226, 2017.
DOI: 10.1007/978-3-319-57987-0_17

Serious games are an important form of games since they have the aim of training users on some specific skills, which may later be transferred to real life. Because of this, serious games usually involve a lot of tasks to be practiced. The user first needs to understand what they need to do and then perform the tasks. Onboarding users with easy to understand and user friendly instructions is an important aspect of these games since otherwise users may get confused, may not enjoy training and may not benefit from the serious game. Since virtual reality is not mainstream yet, many users are expected to have little to no prior virtual reality experience, which especially calls for user friendly instructions for virtual reality serious games. Not much has been explored yet about the effectiveness of different instruction methods in virtual reality serious games. In this study, we examined effects of instruction giving methods on user experience in a virtual reality serious game for baseline vocational warehouse skills training. Our motivation is to provide insight into future virtual reality serious games for more effective and user friendly instructions. Our results may help in both tutorial level and in game instruction design, which are crucial components of serious games. We believe our results will also help in virtual reality games for entertainment since all games need to have some kind of instructional aspect to them and instructions for games in virtual reality haven't been well studied yet.

The four instruction methods that were explored in our study are 3D animated, pictograph, written and verbal instructions. The selection of these four instructional methods were inspired by real vocational training games. In instruction preparation, an important factor is cost of the chosen method. 3D animations and picture based instructions are usually costlier to prepare as compared to written or verbal methods. Hence, if animated or pictograph methods provide no significant value over written or verbal methods, developers can choose these less costly methods in their virtual reality serious games.

For our study, we designed eight simple tasks to be performed in a virtual warehouse environment. The tasks were vocational warehouse skills related and included tangible object interaction with tracked boxes. Instructions for these tasks were given to the users with one of these four methods: animated, pictograph, written and verbal. We performed a user study with 15 college aged users. We mainly examined task performance, replays requested for instructions, time to complete the tasks, user preference on instruction methods, ease of understanding and frustration. To make sure that our task design and virtual reality implementation were reasonable, we also looked at ease of the tasks, presence and motion sickness ranked by the users.

2 Related Work

Although no previous work that we are aware of analyzed effects of instruction methods in virtual reality serious games, many previous works are still related to our study in various aspects. Bowman et al. studied spatial information presentations inside a virtual zoo environment to provide better learning [3]. In the virtual reality application, authors employed verbal and text based information, and a few images to accompany these only for more complex content. Ragan et al. also studied effects of supplementary spatial information presentations on user performance in virtual environments [13]. Authors used written and symbolic information in their training system. Most virtual reality training applications have some form of instructions, if they do not solely rely on human tutors. Recent virtual reality training systems utilize different forms of instructions and in-game information. Oliveira et al. utilized text based instructions in their industrial training virtual reality application [12]. Bobadilla et al. used animated, written and verbal forms of instructions and information in their underground power distribution lines maintenance virtual reality training system [9]. In their virtual reality system for training athletes for high pressure situations, Stinson and Bowman used written messages for information conveyance [15]. Carlson et al. utilized video based instructions in the virtual reality assembly tasks training system they developed [6]. The videos were pre-recorded and showed demonstrations of using the input devices and carrying out the in-game tasks. Chittaro and Buttussi utilized written and very brief picture based instructions in their aviation safety training game [7]. In their study of virtual reality laparo-scopic surgery training curriculum development, Aggarwal et al. used a one to one human training approach to familiarize the users with the system first [1]. Then, inside the virtual reality training module, written and brief visual based instructions were used. Corato et al. developed a virtual reality training system for hand washing procedure of surgery staff [8]. The authors utilized overlaid real time animations that performed the same task along with the user. There were also supplementary written on-screen instructions to explain the users what to do. Although these studies used various forms of instructions, since the main focus of the studies were providing effective training with virtual reality serious games, authors did not explore effects of different instruction methods.

3   Instruction Methods Experiment

To examine user preference on instruction methods in virtual reality serious games, we decided on four instruction methods that were commonly used in these games: animated, pictograph, verbal and written. We designed and implemented eight baseline warehouse tasks. The tasks were intentionally designed to be simple to allow the user to focus on their instruction method preference rather than struggling with the tasks. The simplicity of the tasks also expected to overcome any possible cognitive load difference between the instruction methods. A professional job trainer helped us in designing the tasks to ensure that the tasks were of similar baseline difficulty and the instructions were appro-priate. Tasks were designed to be different than each other in at least one element. To make sure that the tasks were of the same difficulty level in terms of vocational skills and the instructions were meaningful, we demonstrated the designed tasks to six profes-sional vocational trainers. They all stated that the tasks had a similar level of difficulty and the instructions were meaningful and easy to understand.

To ensure variety and to minimize any possible learning effect, tasks were designed in three categories: sorting, fetching and alignment. Tasks had a roughly even distribu-tion between these categories (3 sorting, 3 fetching and 2 alignment tasks). Between the tasks, textures on the boxes and work station labels were changed. Sorting tasks were based on price, product label and size. Fetching tasks were based on color and product labels. Alignment tasks were based on expiration dates and barcodes. These tasks were presented to the users with one of the four instruction methods: animated, pictograph, verbal and written. To perform the tasks, users needed to interact with tangible boxes that were equipped with markers to be tracked by the motion tracking system in real time. A general overview of our system can be seen in Fig. 1. The reason behind the selection of tangible boxes was the positive scores the users gave to this type of interaction in a previous study of ours which included many forms of different virtual reality interactions [4]. Different textures were projected onto the boxes in the virtual world to create variety in the tasks. Real tables were used as workstations. These tables also had accurate virtual representations of them. Different labels such as 'Regular QC' and 'Inspection Area' were projected to the white areas on the virtual tables to specify work stations in different tasks.

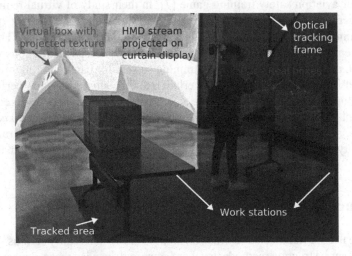

Fig. 1. A general overview of the virtual reality serious game setup. The user interacts with the tangible boxes on the workstations. View of the user through the HMD is projected on a curtain display only for outside viewing purposes.

For animated instructions, we used a realistic 3D animation approach to be able to convey instructions in a way that is close to real world and to make sure that the difference between this method and the 2D picture based instructions were obvious. As an example, animation strip of a task is shown in Fig. 2. In the animated method, as a virtual warehouse supervisor character demonstrated the tasks, he also described what he did with a few brief words to explain the task better, like a supervisor teaching a task to their employee by demonstration. 3D animations were played in the virtual world in real time instead of being pre-rendered and displayed as a video overlay. The reason for that was to give the user the feeling of watching a real demonstration in the same environment they were present instead of watching an overlaid video. As an example, the virtual tutor says "sorting by price" as he sorts the boxes in Fig. 2. These brief words were recorded as clear voice over audio by a male native English speaker. Pictographs consisted of simple drawings with brief explanations (see Fig. 3). The reason for selecting pictographs as one of our methods was the prevalent use of them in today's workplaces for instructions, especially in fast food and retail stores, and in training games. Written instructions consisted of brief yet clear explanations of the tasks to be done (see Fig. 3). We gave great importance to make these instructions easy to understand by using common words in simple English. For the verbal instructions, content of the written instructions was read clearly and recorded as voice over audio by a female native English speaker.

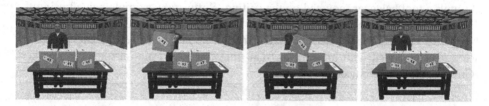

Fig. 2. Animation strip of Task 8 from user's viewpoint. Virtual character sorts the boxes according to their price tags.

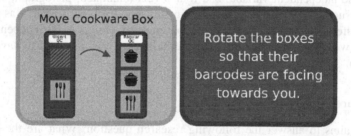

Fig. 3. Pictograph and written instruction methods. Left: pictograph. Right: written.

Instructions had different pre-defined durations proportional to their content. Animated instructions varied between 8 and 18 s. All pictograph durations were 10 s since their content was similar. Written instruction durations varied between 10 and 12 s and verbal instruction durations varied between 5 and 9 s based on the length of the content. In our virtual reality serious game, first the users were presented with the instructions and requested to watch/read/listen to the instruction method until it disappeared. To make the users focus on the instructions for the same amount of time, possible actions of the users were restricted in this mode. After the instructions disappeared, virtual boxes appeared and the users were then able to interact with the objects in the virtual world. We preferred this approach to ensure that all users were exposed to the instructions for the same amount of time yielding comparable results. Animated instructions took place in a position that was very close to the user in the virtual world. Pictograph and written instructions were presented as overlays covering 60% of the screen. Verbal instructions did not have a visual cue.

3.1   Hardware

We used 12 Opti Track V100R2 FLEX cameras for real time motion tracking. Our tracked area was 8 ft by 8 ft but the tasks were designed so that the user never needed to step outside of the tracked area. A VR2200 head mounted display (HMD) was used for viewing. HMD was tracked by the system in real time via attached markers on top. Users wore a backpack that contained battery for the HMD and the port for the VGA cable. This backpack weighed around 2 lb. The VGA cable went to the server computer through a tool balancer mounted on the ceiling. Software was implemented using the Unity game engine and worked around 60 frames per second. Users also wore hand bands that were equipped with reflective markers for real time hand tracking. The boxes were also equipped with markers for real time tracking. Four surrounding speakers (Creative A550) were used for audio.

3.2   Experiment Design

Within subjects experiment was performed with the independent variable of instruction method. The independent variable had four levels (animated, pictograph, verbal and written instructions) that were varied within subjects. Each participant was presented with two different instances of each of the four method. Orders of the independent variable levels were assigned randomly. Counterbalancing was also used to have an even distribution.

3.3   Research Questions and Hypothesis

Our study aims to answer the following research question: What are the effects of instruction methods on user experience in virtual reality serious games. We developed the following two hypotheses: (H1) Animated instructions will be the most preferred method as compared to the other three methods. (H2) Written instructions will be the least preferred method as compared to the other three methods.

When constructing these hypotheses, we thought that 3D animation was the method that was closest to the real-life training whereas written instructions was the least prevalently used method in real life considering the recent increase in the use of visual communication in many areas.

3.4   Data Collection

We collected automated data for the following: successful completion of tasks and fails with their time logs, time it took to complete the tasks and number of instruction replays requested by the users.

After the users completed all of the eight tasks, a survey was given to them. This survey asked questions about their preferred instruction method, ease of understanding each instruction method provided, frustration each instruction method caused, level of immersion and motion sickness during the whole experiment, and ease of the tasks.

3.5 Participants

15 adult individuals participated in the study (N = 15). Participants were recruited via e-mail announcements and word of mouth. All participants were undergraduate or graduate university students from different majors. Participants were aged between 21 and 33 with mean (M) 25.80 and standard deviation (SD) 3.05. All participants were either native English speakers or fulfilling English proficiency requirement with TOEFL IBT score above 79 or IELTS score above 6.5. Gender distribution was 5 females and 10 males. 13 participants had no prior virtual reality experience whereas 2 participants had minimal prior virtual reality experience. The study was conducted under the IRB Pro00013008.

3.6 Procedure

Participants arrived at the laboratory. They read and signed the consent form and filled the demographics questionnaire. Then, the research staff briefly explained the equipment and the user's objective in the experiment. The users were told that they would be presented with different instruction methods and their aim was to do what they understood from that instruction method. They were also told that they could request two more replays of the instructions if they felt like they did not understand them. Following, the research staff helped the users wear the head mounted display and the hand bands, and a familiarization session began. The aim of this session was to get the users comfortable with the virtual reality system and the tangible box interaction. Research staff first explained the elements in the virtual world briefly: virtual warehouse, workstations and boxes. Research staff then requested the users to perform some basic actions such as looking at their hands, looking around, moving around on the tracked area, holding and moving the tangible boxes, rotating the boxes and touching the work stations. The familiarization session ended when the user stated that they were comfortable with the virtual reality system, which took approximately 80 s on average. Then, the experiment began.

The users were presented with eight tasks. Each task instance consisted of first watching or listening to the instructions and then doing what the instruction requested. The users could also request two more replays of instructions if they wanted to. After finishing all of the eight tasks each presented with one of the four instruction methods, the research staff helped the users to take off the worn equipment. The users then filled out a survey about their experience. Virtual reality exposure time was around 10 min and the survey filling took 3–5 min per user.

4 Results

Although we tried to design the tasks with the same level of difficulty -with the help of professional job trainers; one of the eight tasks turned out to be significantly more confusing than the others. Independent of the instruction method, 11 users out of 15 failed in Task 5. Hence, we excluded all data of this task from our analysis and examined the results of the remaining 7 tasks. Error bars in all of the charts in the paper represent the standard error of the mean.

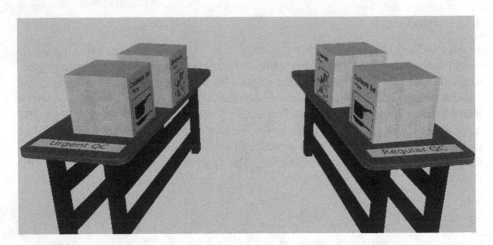

Fig. 4. Starting box positions of Task 5. Workstations were labeled as Urgent QC and Regular QC. Each workstation had one silverware box (back) and one cookware box (front).

Task 5 requested the users to move the cookware box to the Regular QC area (QC stood for Quality Control). Pictograph instruction of Task 5 can be seen in Fig. 2. In the beginning, there were one cookware and one silverware boxes in each workstation with the identical alignment. One workstation was labeled as 'Urgent QC' and the other was labeled as 'Regular QC'. The users needed to pick up the cookware box on the Urgent QC area and put it to the Regular QC area. Initial box positions for this task are presented in Fig. 4. Distribution of the 4 successful completions of this task over the instruction methods were as follows: 1 animated, 1 pictograph, 1 verbal, and 1 written. Distribution of the 11 failed completions of this task over the instruction methods were as follows: 3 animated, 3 pictograph, 3 verbal, and 2 written.

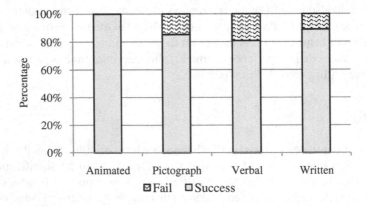

Fig. 5. Bar chart of the successful completion and fail percentages for different instruction methods.

4.1 Performance

We examined the percentage of successful completions in all seven tasks for different instruction methods. Results in percentage of fails and successful completions are presented in Fig. 5. As we analyzed the data for the effect of instruction method on successful completion percentage using single factor ANOVA with alpha 0.05, no significant effect was found ($F(3, 11) = 1.690$, $p = 0.184$). However, it can be observed that all users were able to complete the tasks correctly with the animated instructions whereas the success percentage was below 89% for the other methods.

4.2 Preference

At the end of the experiment, we asked each user to rank the instruction methods according to their preference. Then, we gave weights to these results so that first choice had a weight of 4, second choice had a weight of 3, third choice had a weight of 2 and fourth choice had a weight of 1. After that, we applied these weights to the count of times each method was ranked in an order and we divided the results by our sample size of 15. This gave us the weighted averages of the user preference results, which can be seen in Fig. 6. As we applied single factor ANOVA analysis, there was significant difference in the preference results ($F(3, 11) = 8.372$, $p = 0.000$). As we performed t-tests, there was significant difference between all method pairs except the pictograph and written (see Table 1). Animated instructions were the most preferred with a score of 3.47, which supported H1. Verbal instructions were the least preferred with a score of 1.53, which rejected H2.

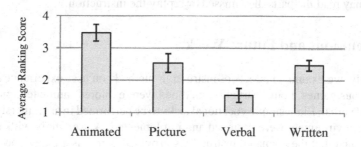

Fig. 6. Bar chart of the weighted averages of user preference ranking scores for different instruction methods.

Table 1. Significant two sample t-test results for the preference ranking scores.

	N	df	μ Diff.	p
Animated - Written	15	14	1.000	0.016
Animated - Verbal	15	14	1.933	0.000
Pictograph - Verbal	15	14	1.000	0.016
Written - Verbal	15	14	0.933	0.008

5 Discussion

Results revealed that the participants were able to complete all tasks successfully with the animated instructions. Although there was no statistically significant difference, fail ratio was the most with the verbal method. This could be because of the resemblance of the animated instructions to having a tutor in real life.

User preference was notably favoring the animated instructions. Pictograph was the second in preference, being slightly better than the third preference of the written instructions. We interpret that although it gave them some difficulty in information processing, visual based nature of the pictographs still found to be interesting and favorable by the participants. Verbal instructions clearly seemed to be the least choice of the participants. Some of our participants complained about the anxiety they had regarding the possibility of missing the verbal instructions.

In overall, animated instructions were favored by the users whereas verbal instructions were the least favorite. If possible, having animated instructions in serious games for training users might be a better practice. If not, as a less costly alternative, pictograph instructions that remain on screen as an overlay might work well as a second option. Users showed more interest in the pictograph instructions than the written instructions although the two methods were similar in many results. We suggest that verbal instructions should be avoided in virtual reality serious games since they may create slight anxiety on users and may not be as effective as the other three methods, especially with the longer instructions. If verbal instructions needed to be used, we suggest having supplementary captions as overlays on screen or enabling the users the option to replay the instructions as many times as they want as more user friendly alternatives. This way, the users may read the parts they missed or replay the instruction.

6 Conclusions and Future Work

In this study, we examined effects of instruction methods on user experience in virtual reality serious games. Four instruction methods were explored: animated, pictograph, written and verbal. Eight simple vocational tasks to be performed in an immersive virtual warehouse environment were designed and implemented. A user study with 15 participants revealed that the animated instructions provided better user experience whereas verbal instructions were the least preferred among the four methods. Hence, we suggest using animated instructions in virtual reality serious games. Pictograph and written instructions shared the middle position in ranking of the methods. Between the pictograph and the written methods, the users were more excited about the pictograph; however, it was slightly more difficult for them to remember all of the elements in the pictographs when the instructions disappeared. Hence, we suggest using pictograph instructions that remain on screen as overlays as the second choice of instruction method, followed by written instructions. We do not recommend using verbal instructions. If needed to be used, we suggest that having captions on screen or enabling replay option may be user friendly improvements for verbal instructions.

Future work may include evaluating effects of instruction methods in terms of cognitive load, exploring other forms of instruction methods such as video, and evaluating effects of instruction methods on user performance for complex tasks. Different levels of the instruction methods mentioned in this study such as speed and fidelity may also be examined in terms of effectiveness.

References

1. Aggarwal, R., Crochet, P., Dias, A., Misra, A., Ziprin, P., Darzi, A.: Development of a virtual reality training curriculum for laparoscopic cholecystectomy. Br. J. Surg. **96**(9), 1086–1093 (2009). doi:10.1002/bjs.6679
2. Bell, H.H., Waag, W.L.: Evaluating the effectiveness of flight simulators for training combat skills: a review. Int. J. Aviat. Psychol. **8**(3), 223–242 (1998). doi:10.1207/s15327108ijap0803_4
3. Bowman, D.A., Hodges, L.F., Allison, D., Wineman, J.: The educational value of an information-rich virtual environment. Presence Teleoper. Virtual Environ. **8**(3), 317–331 (1999). doi:10.1162/105474699566251
4. Bozgeyikli, E., Bozgeyikli, L., Raij, A., Katkoori, S., Alqasemi, R., Dubey, R.: Virtual reality interaction techniques for individuals with autism spectrum disorder: design considerations and preliminary results. In: Kurosu, M. (ed.) HCI 2016. LNCS, vol. 9732, pp. 127–137. Springer, Cham (2016). doi:10.1007/978-3-319-39516-6_12
5. Brooks, F.P.: What's real about virtual reality? IEEE Comput. Graph. Appl. **19**(6), 16–27 (1999). doi:10.1109/38.799723
6. Carlson, P., Peters, A., Gilbert, S.B., Vance, J.M., Luse, A.: Virtual training: learning transfer of assembly tasks. IEEE Trans. Visual Comput. Graph. **21**(6), 770–782 (2015). doi:10.1109/TVCG.2015.2393871
7. Chittaro, L., Buttussi, F.: Assessing knowledge retention of an immersive serious game vs. a traditional education method in aviation safety. IEEE Trans. Visual Comput. Graph. **21**(4), 529–538 (2015). doi:10.1109/TVCG.2015.2391853
8. Corato, F., Frucci, M., Di Baja, G.S.: Virtual training of surgery staff for hand washing procedure. In: Proceedings of the International Working Conference on Advanced Visual Interfaces (Capri Island, Italy2012), pp. 274–277. ACM (2012). doi:http://dx.doi.org/10.1145/2254556.2254608
9. Galvan-Bobadilla, I., Ayala-Garc, A., Rodriguez-Gallegos, E., Arroyo-Figueroa, G.: Virtual reality training system for the maintenance of underground lines in power distribution system. In: 2013 Third International Conference on Innovative Computing Technology (INTECH), pp. 199–204 (2013). doi:http://dx.doi.org/10.1109/INTECH.2013.6653713
10. Grantcharov, T.P., Kristiansen, V.B., Bendix, J., Bardram, L., Rosenberg, J., Funch-Jensen, P.: Randomized clinical trial of virtual reality simulation for laparoscopic skills training. Br. J. Surg. **91**(2), 146–150 (2004). doi:10.1002/bjs.4407
11. Hale, K.S., Stanney, K.M.: Handbook of Virtual Environments: Design, Implementation, and Applications. CRC Press, Boca Raton (2014)
12. Oliveira, D.M., Cao, S.C., Hermida, X.F., Rodriguez, F.M.: Virtual reality system for industrial training. In: 2007 IEEE International Symposium on Industrial Electronics, pp. 1715–1720 (2007). doi:http://dx.doi.org/10.1109/ISIE.2007.4374863
13. Ragan, E.D., Bowman, D.A., Huber, K.J.: Supporting cognitive processing with spatial information presentations in virtual environments. Virtual Reality **16**(4), 301–314 (2012). doi:10.1007/s10055-012-0211-8

14. Stinson, C., Bowman, D.A.: Feasibility of training athletes for high-pressure situations using virtual reality. IEEE Trans. Visual Comput. Graphics **20**(4), 606–615 (2014). doi:10.1109/TVCG.2014.23
15. Ushaw, G., Davison, R., Eyre, J., Morgan, G.: Adopting best practices from the games industry in development of serious games for health. In: Proceedings of the 5th International Conference on Digital Health 2015 (Florence, Italy2015), pp. 1–8. ACM (2015). doi:http://dx.doi.org/10.1145/2750511.2750513

Mixed Library — Bridging Real and Virtual Libraries

Denis Gračanin$^{(\boxtimes)}$, Andrew Ciambrone, Reza Tasooji, and Mohamed Handosa

Department of Computer Science, Virginia Tech, Blacksburg, VA 24060, USA
gracanin@vt.edu

Abstract. New technologies, especially mixed reality devices, such as Microsoft HoloLens, are blurring the difference between the real and virtual worlds. These developments provide an exciting opportunity to redefine virtual library while maintaining utility and effectiveness. Developing a mixed library system requires identifying the set of services to be supported by the system and identifying well-defined service protocols. We describe a mixed reality based system, a prototype mixed library, that provides a variety of affordances to support embodied interactions and improve the user experience. By leveraging embodiment and context awareness, a mixed reality based user interface can provide many ways to aid a user. We use Microsoft HoloLens device to augment the user's experience in the real library and to provide a rich set of affordances for embodied and social interactions. In addition, the user can also access services of the virtual library when not in the real library.

Keywords: Mixed reality · Augmented reality · Library · User interface · Virtual library

1 Introduction

Virtual Library is traditionally defined as a searchable collection of online books, journals and articles available on the Internet. In essence, the traditional notion of a library as a structured collection of printed materials is more or less directly mapped to online or digital medium. However, modern libraries are more than that. They are places of social interactions, active learning and new services (e.g., 3D printing). At the same time, new technologies, especially augmented reality (AR) or mixed reality (MR) devices such as Microsoft HoloLens [4] are blurring the difference between the real and virtual worlds. These developments provide an exciting opportunity to re-define virtual library while maintaining utility and effectiveness after the initial excitement and 'coolness' expires. Instead of distinguishing between the real and virtual library let us consider creating a 'mixed library'.

Rather than only looking from outside in, i.e., how to replicate a traditional library in a virtual space, we should also look from inside out, how to expand the traditional library and the corresponding physical space (built environment)

© Springer International Publishing AG 2017
S. Lackey and J. Chen (Eds.): VAMR 2017, LNCS 10280, pp. 227–238, 2017.
DOI: 10.1007/978-3-319-57987-0_18

with virtual artifacts. One of the possibilities is to create a virtual environment that replicates, perhaps partially, the real environment of a library. The first step in that direction is establishing a connection between real and virtual worlds. That includes marking/tagging physical artifacts, tracking people, etc. However, the challenge is how to make this more than an architectural walkthrough in a built environment to support information and service exploration as well as social interaction. This challenge can be addressed by leveraging MR technology to bridge and blur the differences between real and virtual library and functions in both worlds while maintaining the user's embodiment.

Embodied interactions demonstrate the importance of the body's interactions with the physical world. Interaction of our body and the surrounding physical world affect our cognitive processes and embodied cognition [20]. Embodiment cognition leverages the notion of affordances, potential interactions with the environment, to support cognitive processes [8].

MR is a mixture of both real and virtual realities where the user can see both the real world and virtual artifacts. The use of MR is well suited for built environments because the user interface can enhance the built environment with virtual constructs. For example, if a user is visiting the library for the first time, the user may need directions to the reserve desk. A user interface based on MR could provide these directions by drawing virtual arrows directing the user to their desired location. In this case, the built environment is using its context awareness to determine if the user is new to the environment and is leveraging the user's embodiment to direct them to their desired location.

By leveraging embodiment and context awareness, a user interface for a built environment can provide many affordances to aid the user. By allowing the user to define a context for a specific service or task, the system could use that context to help the user when performing similar tasks.

Therefore, in a real library, MR devices expand the real world with virtual artifacts and information to help better use the services. In a virtual library, physical surrounding serves as a framework to attach information. A student accessing the library from a dorm room can create a model of 3D object and send it directly to 3D printer in the library. Those, perhaps oversimplified, examples of a mixed library provide an insight into exciting opportunities that could be provided by a mixed library. A support for multimodal interactions can provide additional affordances. For example, a voice-recognition-based user interface can be used to search for a book and then guide the user where to pick the book (voice or visual display).

MR systems inherently depend on the surrounding space to support user interactions. Creating an actual mixed library is a tremendous task but a pilot study can provide guidelines and directions how to design and implement a mixed library. We describe an MR system, a prototype mixed library, that provides a variety of affordances to support embodied interactions and improve the user experience. We use Microsoft HoloLens device to augment the user experience in the real library and to provide a rich set of affordances for embodied and social interactions.

Fig. 1. Illustrative snapshots of the MR user interface taken at the Virginia Tech's library (**center**). **Top left**: an example of integrating physical and virtual objects (chair) and an avatar. **Top right**: an illustration of virtual librarian interaction. **Bottom left**: an illustration of virtual collaboration. **Bottom right**: an illustration of observing other virtual visitors in the library.

Figure 1 shows illustrative snapshots of the MR user interface taken at the Virginia Tech's library (Fig. 1 center). Figure 1 top left and top right illustrate how to provide a representation of a user accessing the mixed library and its services. Figure 1 bottom left and bottom right illustrate opportunities for situating virtual collaboration in the physical library.

The collaboration with the library staff and researchers is essential to develop the prototype MR application and supporting infrastructure. This collaboration is a translational innovation that can be further refined for specific educational and research areas requirements through the involvement of the faculty. The outcome is likely to improve user experience, reduce cognitive load and enhance interactions among the users.

2 Related Work

Virtual reality (VR) and AR/MR technologies [3] technologies/applications are becoming more affordable and thus more accessible to general users. While there is over forty years of research in this area, we still need more findings to better understand challenges when it comes to developing MR applications.

There are several AR tools that enable developers to design AR applications and experience. Two examples include ARToolKit [6] and Vuforia [18]. ARToolKit is an open-source SDK mainly focused on implementing augmented reality applications. Vuforia SDK provides recognition and tracking capabilities can be used on a variety of images and objects, including support for a fully customizable marker that can be placed on any surface.

Although AR tools can provide general tools for reproducing virtual contents in the real world but these tools can not provide all the needs for educational purposes. Also, research on AR mostly about technology aspects and few papers focus on using AR for education [21].

Cubillo et al. [5] describe a learning environment based on augmented reality, ARLE (An Augmented Reality Learning Environment). ARLE can be used by both the teacher to develop AR educational resources and students to acquire knowledge in the area. The main goal is to provide a user-friendly, AR environment to create educational content without requiring programming skills. ARLE incorporates multimedia resources, such as video and audio, and supports personalized content by including additional information. Users have access to the library of virtual contents, which all resources are available to all users in a simple and clear way. They found a significant learning improvement for users who used ARLE compared to the users who did not use ARLE. In other words, AR application for educational purposes can improve student performance and also help teachers to provide better and more engaging content to study.

Underwood and Kimmel [19] conducted a study of the use of MR simulation to introduce social justice and understand culturally relevant pedagogy to pre-service school librarians. In their study, each candidate had a book talk assignment. They had to chose a book from one of the multicultural selected categories. Instead of candidates selecting their audience for their book talking assignment, they asked to give their talk in a teaching simulation to a group of five avatars in MR. The avatars were controlled remotely in real time by actors and they were modeled in a way to introduce cultural diversity. The study tried to answer two questions.

The first question is what are candidates perceptions of the multicultural book talking before and after using MR-based simulation. The study shows that participants focused more on the literature and did not pay attention to the book talking process. This lead to the conclusion that they characterized avatars as the students that are disrespectful and disruptive. The major challenge for the participants was they could not go through their list of books in the presence of an active avatar. They blamed the technology for the difficulty that they faced.

The second question is what is the efficacy of MR-based simulation for teaching culturally relevant pedagogy. Nearly all of the participants reported awareness for the need of multicultural resources for school library collections. Although participants critiqued the animation of the avatars as misbehaving and distracting, but it provided unique experience about culturally relevant pedagogy.

Hantono et al. [11] describe the use of an AR agent in education. The agent functions continuously and autonomously on behalf of a user and works and learns from its experience over time.

Providing an agent in AR applications can attract user's perception of the state in both virtual and real world [2]. Oh and Byun [17] presented an interactive agent in the AR learning system. The agent generates puzzles based on the user's action. To evaluate the system, the authors compared "help-to-bloom" task in the AR application with and without the agent. User satisfaction was measured using a questionnaire after the experiment. The result shows that having an animated agent in AR learning environment will increase user's satisfaction significantly.

The use of collaborative AR system is another area that has a potential for the learning environment. Matcha et al. [14] explored the potential of AR spaces to provide communication cues and to support collaboration in the learning environment. They implemented an AR prototype system called AReX (Augmented Reality Experiment). The goal was to help students learn the concept of light dispersion and combination. The study shows that AR supports "various communication cues" and "the AR system shows a significant support for collaborative learning environment" [14].

Some of the challenges in creating AR systems were explored by Dunleavy et al. [9]. They studied the limitation and affordances of an AR system. The results showed that although using AR system could significantly increase student engagement, there are still hardware and software issues. For example, the GPS failure rate was between 15–30%. Because this study took place in an outdoor environment, the displayed information was difficult to read on bright sunny days due to the glare. Another problem was the participant's cognitive overload. They were overwhelmed with the amount of material and complexity of the tasks they were asked to process.

AR/MR technologies are used to reconstruct historical buildings and monument and preserve historical data [16]. Such virtual heritage can be used in education as a platform for learning, motivating and understanding of historical events and locations.

When the physical size of the physical environment is large, navigating the corresponding virtual environment could be challenging. User interaction techniques for navigation task should also support users' spatial learning performance more effectively and conveniently [7,12,13].

3   Mixed Library

Leveraging MR technologies to support common mixed-library user tasks can enhance the user experience. One such task is exploring a digital index of the available books before moving to some aisle, following the signs and instructions, to fetch the book of choice. MR technologies can provide a more convenient way to guide the user to where the book is located. A virtual librarian in the form of a life-size human avatar (Fig. 1 top right) can walk the user to the book location before pointing at it, just the same way an actual librarian would do. This relieves the user from looking for signs or finding a librarian to ask and provides a more natural way of guiding someone to somewhere. Avatars can be created as many as needed and they can take over the simple tasks to help librarians assisting the users.

Given the initial location of a user, an MR device can track the user's location and orientation. This information can be used to move the avatar in the physical space with respect to user's location, where the avatar can speed up or slow down according to the user's movement. It may also call or walk back to the user if the user got lost or went to the wrong direction. For added convenience, the avatar may give the user a short note about the book during their way to book location.

Microsoft HoloLens device support for shared holograms allows for sharing the same avatar between two or more users. This allows for a shared experience, which might be needed for collaborative tasks. For instance, an avatar can give a library tour for a group of users.

A library can provide a variety of services (e.g. borrowing books, printing, scanning, etc.). Each of those services should have a well-defined protocol that consists of a set of steps to be taken by the user in order to receive that service. Initially, the user should be informed about the available services before selecting the service of interest. Afterwards, an avatar should act as a dedicated librarian to the user and provide guidance according to the service protocol. The protocol may contain different types of steps ranging from obtaining permission to use the service (e.g. login, reservation, payment) to technical instructions on how to use that service (e.g. operating a 3D printer). Following the service protocol, an avatar should guide the user by showing when, where and how to perform a given step.

Developing a mixed library system requires identifying the set of services to be supported by the system and identifying well-defined service protocols. Services should be categorized as either shareable or mutual exclusion services. If the library has multiple instances of a given service (e.g. multiple printers), the system should take that into account and perform load balancing by having the avatar recommending the instance with the shortest waiting line.

3.1 System Architecture

Figure 2 shows the system incorporates four basic modules, a service portal, a user tracker, an avatar controller, and a resource scheduler. The service portal module provides the user with an interface through which the user can request or cancel a previously requested service. The user tracker is responsible for determining the user's position and orientation. The tracking information is used by the avatar controller to adjust the avatar's movement and actions. The avatar controller is responsible for generating and controlling avatars. An avatar can be dedicated to an individual user or shared among a group of users.

Each service should have a protocol to be followed in order to consume that service. As shown in Fig. 3 left, a service protocol incorporates a sequence of actions that involve the use of different resources. Some of these resources are shareable (e.g., an elevator) and some are not (e.g., a printer). Each resource type can have one or more instances, as shown in Fig. 3 right, that can fulfil

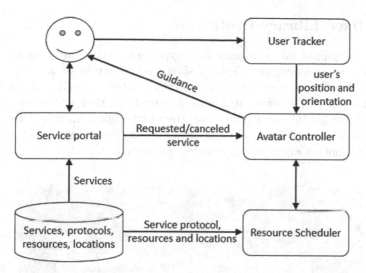

Fig. 2. Mixed-library high-level system architecture. Providing access to services and resources based on the user's context.

the same service (e.g., several copies of the same book). The scheduler module is responsible for turning the service protocol, which is an abstract description of the subsequent use of resources, into a procedure that specifies the resource instances to be used. The selection of the resource instances depend on common factors such as load balancing. Moreover, the scheduler can benefit from context information to better select resource instances. Location information of both the user and the different instances of a given resource can help the scheduler selecting the instance that is nearest to the user. Selecting a resource instance is an optimization problem that should take several factors into account including load balancing, service time, and user's location.

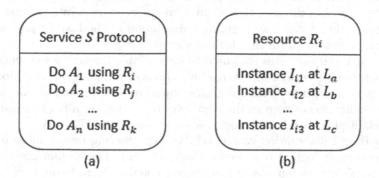

Fig. 3. Representing services and resources. **Left:** a service protocol. **Right:** aresource with multiple instances.

4   A Mixed-Library Prototype

We are developing a mixed library prototype to evaluate the proposed mixed-library system architecture. Figure 4 shows an example of a service portal through which the user can request a service. After requesting a service, the avatar controller will generate an avatar, a virtual librarian, at the user's current location. Following the service protocol, the virtual librarian controller communicates with the scheduler module upon the execution of each protocol step to retrieve information about which resource instance to target.

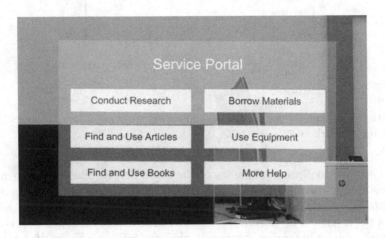

Fig. 4. A preliminary implementation of the mixed-library service portal when the user is located outside the physical library.

The virtual librarian can guide the user to the location of the instance selected by the scheduler. Afterwards, the avatar may provide the user with instructions on how to use the resource. For simple tasks, those instructions can be verbal or textual (e.g., asking the user to wait in a line). For more advanced tasks (e.g., 3D printing), the avatar may perform a simulation of the task or play a video illustrating how to perform that task as shown in Fig. 5.

Common library services that used to be available through a web portal can be supported in MR as well such as reading a book or watching a video. Moreover, books may be augmented with holograms, sound recordings, and videos that can take the reading experience to the next level (e.g., turning a book figure into a 3D model, displaying animal holograms while reading a kids story).

Supporting collaboration can be achieved by allowing two or more users to share the same hologram (e.g. avatar, digital book). The system not only can support collaboration but also it can suggest collaboration. Using user location information as well as learned interests, the system may recommend joining a reading group with similar interests. In order to preserve user privacy, the user can control whether to enable this feature so that other users can know about possible collaboration chances.

Fig. 5. Before using a 3D printing equipment, the user can play a video explaining 3D printing and how to create and retrieve the printed artifact. [1].

5 Evaluation

Some of the advantages of the proposed system include virtuality (adding virtual objects to the real world), augmentation (augmenting real objects by virtual annotations), cooperation (multiple users can collaborate), independence (a user has a separate viewpoint), and individuality (provided service, resource, and information are user dependent). However, there are challenges, such as occlusion and depth perception, visual differences between real and virtual objects tracking, and using head mounted devices. We need to apply both quantitative and qualitative measures to assess the developed system while taking into account these advantages and challenges.

The resource scheduler is at the core of the system as it manages the allocation of library resources trying to optimize the resource utilization [15] and quality of service [10]. The quality of service can be measured in terms of service time and user frustration. We plan to conduct a comparative user study to evaluate the proposed system compared to asking a librarian for help or following instructions and signs. Besides questionnaires about the usability of the system, biometric measures can be used as indicators of the level of user frustration. Librarian frustration should be taken into account as well since the system aims at both helping the users and relieving librarians from handling frequent simple tasks.

MR applications offer the opportunity to teach and learn in an augmented environment. We need to explore the ability to unify input from different sources to enhance motivation and engagement (increase interest level), effective learning (increase receptiveness) and cognitive learning (increase analytical ability).

As a part of a related project, we have developed an infrastructure to record biometric data about the user (Fig. 6). The infrastructure incorporates three devices connected to a data collection PC as well as a video recording PC. The video recording PC can capture what the user sees during the study including

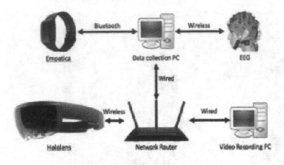

Fig. 6. Collecting and using biometric data. **Left**: the developed infrastructure. **Right**: the user setup.

both physical and virtual objects. The data collection PC collects time-stamped data from the EEG, Empatica, and HoloLens devices.

The EEG device senses the electrical activity of the brain at different spots as well as the 3-axis acceleration of the user's head. The Empatica device is a wristband that senses different types of data including 3-axis acceleration of the user's hand, blood volume pulse, galvanic skin response, skin temperature, and heart rate. The HoloLens device records timestamped events for synchronization purposes with the data collected from the other two devices. This variety of collected biometric data can be used as indicators for assessing user frustration when evaluating the mixed library system.

6   Conclusion

As stated in Introduction, creating an actual mixed library is a tremendous task. Our findings and a prototype implementation using the Microsoft HoloLens device demonstrated the feasibility of the proposed concept. By leveraging embodiment and context awareness, the developed system can provide many ways to aid a user. Using a service based approach will facilitate gradual expansion of the mixed library system and its functionality.

We plan to conduct a summative evaluation to compare relevant computer-based, VR-based, and MR-based library applications. The analysis of the summative study data will be used to validate functional and non-functional requirements identified in the focus group interviews and the pilot study. The task performance will be compared with the baseline established in the pilot study. The collaboration with the library staff and researchers will inform future refinements and development.

Acknowledgments. This work was supported in part by a grant from Virginia Tech Institute for Creativity, Arts, and Technology (ICAT).

References

1. 16x9onglobal: 3D printing: Make anything you want (2017). https://www.youtube.com/watch?v=G0EJmBoLq-g. Last accessed 10 Feb 2017
2. Barakonyi, I., Schmalstieg, D.: Augmented reality agents for user interface adaptation. Comput. Anim. Virtual Worlds **19**(1), 23–35 (2008)
3. Bimber, O., Raskar, R.: Spatial Augmented Reality: Merging Real and Virtual Worlds. A K Peters, Wellesley (2005)
4. Corporation, M.: Microsoft HoloLens. https://www.microsoft.com/microsoft-hololens/ (2017). Last accessed 10 Feb 2017
5. Cubillo, J., Martín, S., Castro, M., Diaz, G., Colmenar, A., Botički, I.: A learning environment for augmented reality mobile learning. In: 2014 IEEE Frontiers in Education Conference (FIE) Proceedings, pp. 1–8, October 2014
6. DAQRI. ARToolkit. http://www.artoolkit.org (2016). Last accessed 10 Feb 2016
7. Davis, M.M., Gabbard, J.L., Bowman, D.A., Gracanin, D.: Depth-based 3D gesture multi-level radial menu for virtual object manipulation. In: Proceedings of the 2016 IEEE Virtual Reality Conference, pp. 169–170 (2016)
8. Dourish, P.: Where the Action Is: The Foundations of Embodied Interaction. The MIT Press, Cambridge (2001)
9. Dunleavy, M., Dede, C., Mitchell, R.: Affordances and limitations of immersive participatory augmented reality simulations for teaching and learning. J. Sci. Educ. Technol. **18**(1), 7–22 (2009)
10. Gračanin, D., Zhou, Y., DaSilva, L.: Quality of service for networked virtual environments. IEEE Commun. Mag. **42**(4), 42–48 (2004)
11. Hantono, B.S., Nugroho, L.E., Santosa, P.I.: Review of augmented reality agent in education. In: Proceedings of the 6th International Annual Engineering Seminar (InAES), pp. 150–153, August 2016
12. Kim, J.S., Gračanin, D., Quek, F.: Sensor-fusion walking-in-place interaction technique using mobile devices. In: Proceedings of the IEEE Virtual Reality Conference (VR), pp. 39–42, 5–8 March 2012
13. Kim, J.S., Gračanin, D., Yang, T., Quek, F.: Action-transferred design approach for navigation techniques in 3D virtual environments. ACM Trans. Comput.-Human Interact. **22**(6), 30:1–30:42 (2015)
14. Matcha, W., Awang Rambli, D.R.: Preliminary investigation on the use of augmented reality in collaborative learning. In: Abd Manaf, A., Sahibuddin, S., Ahmad, R., Mohd Daud, S., El-Qawasmeh, E. (eds.) ICIEIS 2011. CCIS, vol. 254, pp. 189–198. Springer, Heidelberg (2011). doi:10.1007/978-3-642-25483-3_15
15. Mulligan, G., Gračanin, D.: A comparison of SOAP and REST implementations of a service based interaction independence middleware framework. In: Rossettii, M., Hill, R., Johansson, B., Dunkin, A., Ingalls, R. (eds.) Proceedings of the Winter Simulation Conference, pp. 1423–1432, 13–16 December 2009
16. Noh, Z., Sunar, M.S., Pan, Z.: A review on augmented reality for virtual heritage system. In: Chang, M., Kuo, R., Kinshuk, Chen, G.-D., Hirose, M. (eds.) Edutainment 2009. LNCS, vol. 5670, pp. 50–61. Springer, Heidelberg (2009). doi:10.1007/978-3-642-03364-3_7
17. Oh, S., Byun, Y.C.: The design and implementation of augmented reality learning systems. In: Proceedings of the 2012 IEEE/ACIS 11th International Conference on Computer and Information Science, pp. 651–654. IEEE Computer Society, Washington, DC (2012)
18. PTC Inc.: Vuforia. http://www.vuforia.com (2017). Last accessed 10 Feb 2017

19. Underwood, J., Kimmel, S., Forest, D., Dickinson, G.: Culturally relevant book-talking: using a mixed reality simulation with preservice school librarians. Sch. Libr. Worldwide **21**(1), 91–107 (2015)
20. Wilson, M.: Six views of embodied cognition. Psychon. Bull. Rev. **9**(4), 625–636 (2002)
21. Zhou, F., Duh, H.B.L., Billinghurst, M.: Trends in augmented reality tracking, interaction and display: a review of ten years of ISMAR. In: Proceedings of the 7th IEEE/ACM International Symposium on Mixed and Augmented Reality, pp. 193–202, September 2008

Virtual Reality for Training Diagnostic Skills in Anorexia Nervosa: A Usability Assessment

Jose Gutierrez-Maldonado[✉], Antonio Andres-Pueyo, Adolfo Jarne, Antoni Talarn, Marta Ferrer, and Joseba Achotegui

Department of Clinical Psychology and Psychobiology,
University of Barcelona, Barcelona, Spain
jgutierrezm@ub.edu

Abstract. Virtual Reality (VR) technology is used in clinical psychology to integrate and enhance traditional assessment and therapeutic approaches for a variety of conditions. It is also increasingly used in the training of health professionals, as it provides authentic recreations of real-life settings, without exposing students to situations for which they are not yet prepared. VR systems involve different graphical user interfaces for human–computer interaction that vary according to the level of immersion required. In this study, we explore the interaction between level of immersion and gender, in order to establish whether the differences in usability between men and women found in previous studies are modulated by the level of immersion of the VR devices used to perform the simulations. Seventy undergraduate students (44 women, 26 men) participated in the study. They were randomly assigned to one of the two following conditions: differential diagnosis skills training using simulated interviews with an immersive system, or training using the simulated interviews with a non-immersive system. The results showed that men rated the usability of immersive and non-immersive systems to be almost the same, while women assessed the usability of the non-immersive system to be higher. A greater proneness to motion sickness in women is proposed as a hypothesis to explain these differences; this hypothesis should now be tested in further studies.

Keywords: Virtual reality · Training · Psychology · Usability · Immersion

1 Introduction

Virtual Reality (VR) technology is used in clinical psychology to integrate and enhance traditional assessment and therapeutic approaches for a variety of conditions. The first studies of its effectiveness in the treatment of psychological disorders concentrated on different types of phobia; these disorders are often approached via exposure therapies, for which VR is particularly well suited. In a recent publication [1], Riva et al. reported on the available reviews and meta-analyses on the use of VR in clinical and health psychology. VR exposure has been demonstrated to be efficacious for the treatment of a variety of psychological disorders, offering several advantages such as high ecological validity, high acceptability, and increased control over variables [2, 3].

© Springer International Publishing AG 2017
S. Lackey and J. Chen (Eds.): VAMR 2017, LNCS 10280, pp. 239–247, 2017.
DOI: 10.1007/978-3-319-57987-0_19

Virtual reality environments are also increasingly used in the training of professionals, as they very effectively reproduce real-life settings without forcing students to deal with situations for which they are not yet prepared. VR can grab the attention in a far more immediate way than other kinds of media, drawing students inside educational experiences that cannot be carried out using other techniques [4].

VR systems involve different graphical user interfaces for human–computer interaction that vary according to the level of immersion required. The most basic level involves exposure to virtual environments on computer screens, with peripheral input devices (e.g., a keyboard or a computer mouse) used to interact with them. At the other extreme are innovative and technologically advanced systems such as Head Mounted Displays (HMD) which simulate binocularly overlapped images and create the illusion of a three-dimensional world. VR provides trainees with simulations of real-life situations in which they can learn by doing in a safe educational context, and allows trainers to gradually increase the difficulty of the problems to be solved in the training tasks; this facilitates the process of learning by guiding students towards their optimal performance. The implementation of VR-based applications for training has always depended heavily on the development of advanced technology, and so for a long time the development in this area was limited by the cost of the equipment required. However, this scenario is now changing, due to the expansion of VR in the field of consumer electronics; the commercialization of VR systems among the general population is bringing down costs and enhancing the development of user-friendly devices. Furthermore, for younger generations the use of VR technology will be part of their everyday routine and the technical difficulties will disappear [5].

In a previous study, we compared the usability of two low-cost VR systems which offered different levels of immersion for training students in diagnostic interview skills, by means of simulations of psychopathological examinations in patients with eating disorders [6]. Previous research has shown these simulations to be more effective for the training of differential diagnosis skills than traditional methods based on role-playing [7]. No differences were found in usability in our earlier study between immersive and non-immersive systems. Given the greater complexity and higher cost of immersive systems, it was concluded that non-immersive systems are a promising VR alternative for developing these skills in trainee professionals. In another study [8], in order to establish whether individual differences such as gender should be taken into account in the design of training systems of this kind, we compared the usability scores of male and female students, finding significantly higher usability scores for men on several items of the Software Usability Measurement Inventory (SUMI) [9].

In the present study, we explored the interaction between these two variables – level of immersion and gender – in order to establish whether the differences in usability between men and women are modulated by the level of immersion of the VR devices used to perform the simulated interviews.

2   Method

2.1   Participants

Seventy undergraduate students (44 women, 26 men) participated in the study. They were randomly assigned to one of the two following conditions: differential diagnosis skills training using the simulated interviews with an immersive system (Oculus Rift DK2), or training using the simulated interviews with a non-immersive system (a stereoscopic computer screen) (Fig. 1). A restriction to the random assignation was that each group had to have the same number of subjects (35); thus, if the previous participant was assigned randomly to one condition, the following participant was assigned to the other condition. One participant in the immersive condition was unable to complete the simulated interview because of motor sickness (she reported mild nausea); another participant in the non-immersive condition was not able to complete the simulated interview because of a malfunction of the computer that could not be satisfactorily repaired at that moment. Both participants who did not finish the experiment were women. Finally, 68 participants (42 women, 26 men) completed the study.

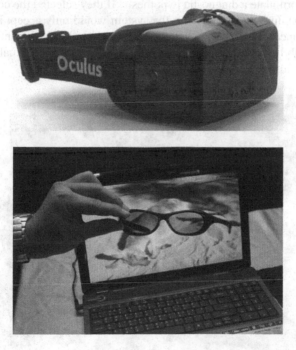

Fig. 1. Oculus Rift DK2 (above), and Acer Aspire 5738DG laptop with stereoscopic display (below)

2.2 Instruments

The non-immersive virtual interviews were displayed on an Intel Pentium T4400 IV (2.2 GHz, 800 MHz FSB) laptop with 4 GB RAM, ATI Mobility Radeo HD 4570 graphics card, and a 15.6 inch 3D monitor. Earphones and polarized glasses were used. The immersive virtual interviews were displayed on an Oculus Rift VR HMD DK2 system. The Oculus provided immersive 3D virtual environments in a wide field of vision (100°), OLED screens with a resolution of 960 × 1080 per eye with low head-tracking latency (20 ms) and high refresh rate (75 Hz). Earphones were also used.

2.3 Procedure

In the virtual simulations (Fig. 2), learners conducted a clinical interview with different Virtual Patients (VPs). Each VP presented a specific eating disorder. The objective of the interviews was to obtain enough data to formulate a diagnosis. To do so, users selected the most suitable question at each stage of the interview; the system informed them how accurate their choice was, and the VP responded to their questions. At each stage, users decided whether to continue asking questions or whether they had enough information to formulate a diagnostic hypothesis. If they selected the correct diagnosis at any given time during the interview, the system would only accept it if the VP had been fully examined. When the simulation had been completed, students were asked to evaluate the usability of the system. The mean duration of the virtual interview was 32 min (SD = 8 min).

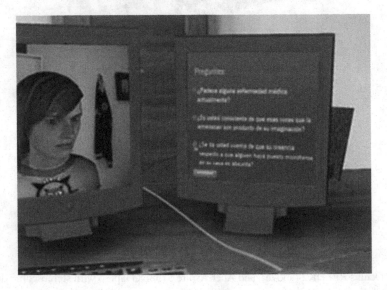

Fig. 2. Virtual interview: The VP appears on the left-hand screen, while the question choices and the diagnosis hypothesis are displayed on the right-hand screen.

Usability was assessed with the Software Usability Measurement Inventory (SUMI). Only the items on the inventory that are applicable to our software were considered for data analysis:

2. I would recommend this software to my colleagues
3. The instructions and prompts are helpful
5. Learning to operate this software initially is full of problems
7. I enjoy my sessions with this software
12. Working with this software is satisfying
13. The way that system information is presented is clear and understandable
17. Working with this software is mentally stimulating
19. I feel in command of this software when I am using it
26. Tasks can be performed in a straightforward manner using this software
27. Using this software is frustrating
29. The speed of this software is fast enough
32. There have been times in using this software when I have felt quite tense
42. The software has a very attractive presentation
44. It is relatively easy to move from one part of a task to another
48. It is easy to see at a glance what the options are at each stage.

For each of the items on the SUMI, participants had to select one of three options: agree, undecided, or disagree. To obtain an overall usability score, on items 2, 3, 7, 12, 13, 17, 19, 26, 29, 42, 44, and 48, positive answers (agree) scored 1 point, "undecided" answers scored 0 points, and negative answers (disagree) were assigned a score of −1. On items 5, 27 and 32, on the other hand, negative answers (disagree) were assigned a score of 1, positive answers (agree) a score of −1, and "undecided" answers scored 0 points.

In order to analyse the influence of the level of immersion and gender on performance, students in both groups were required to take an anorexia nervosa diagnostic interview skills test comprising 50 written questions; the final score was calculated taking into account the correct answers converted to a 10-point scale.

3 Results

The scores on the overall measure of usability were similar in the immersive and the non-immersive systems (mean = 9.08, SD = 4.27 in the HMD group; and mean = 10.23, SD = 2.52 in the stereoscopic screen group; $F = 1.57$, $p = 0.21$). However, men gave higher usability scores than women (mean = 11.5, SD = 2.45 in men; and mean = 8.52, SD = 3.63 in women; $F = 14.73$, $p < 0.001$). The interaction between level of immersion and gender was very near to reaching significance ($F = 3.4$; $p = 0.07$). As can be seen in Table 1, the usability of immersive and non-immersive systems was almost the same for men, while women gave significantly lower ratings for the usability of the immersive system.

The influence of gender and level of immersion on performance was analysed by means of an ANOVA applied to a 2 × 2 between-subjects design (women/men, immersive/non-immersive system). Neither the principal effect nor the interaction between factors was significant. The learning achievements of women and men after the VR

Table 1. Usability of immersive and non-immersive systems for women and men

Gender	Immersion	Mean usability	SD	N
Men	HMD (Immersive)	11.7143	2.33464	14
	Stereo screen (Non-immersive)	11.2500	2.66714	12
	Total	11.5000	2.45357	26
Women	HMD (Immersive)	7.2500	4.39946	20
	Stereo screen (Non-immersive)	9.6818	2.31735	22
	Total	8.5238	3.63746	42
Total	HMD (Immersive)	9.0882	4.27372	34
	Stereo screen (Non-immersive)	10.2353	2.52333	34
	Total	9.6618	3.53072	68

simulation were quite similar (women's mean on the performance test was 7.71, SD = 1.61; men's mean was 7.54, SD = 1.1; F = 0.23, p = 0.63). Nor did the level of immersion of the simulation have an effect on learning (mean test score in the immersive group was 7.67, SD = 1.32; mean test score in the non-immersive group was 7.62, SD = 1.56; F = 0.01, p = 0.91). Women and men did not differ with regard to the level of immersion of the system (the interaction between the variables was not significant (F = 0.11, p = 0.73) (Table 2).

Table 2. Performance of women and men in immersive and non-immersive systems

Gender	Immersion	Mean performance	SD	N
Men	HMD (Immersive)	7.5000	1.09193	14
	Stereo screen (Non-immersive)	7.5833	1.16450	12
	Total	7.5385	1.10384	26
Women	HMD (Immersive)	7.8000	1.47256	20
	Stereo screen (Non-immersive)	7.6364	1.76056	22
	Total	7.7143	1.61224	42
Total	HMD (Immersive)	7.6765	1.31933	34
	Stereo screen (Non-immersive)	7.6176	1.55728	34
	Total	7.6471	1.43272	68

The correlation between usability and performance was not significant, either in the whole sample (r = −0.05, p = 0.68), or when segmenting the sample by gender (men: r = −0.09, p = 0.67; women: r = −0.01, p = 0.94) indicating that performance was not influenced by usability.

4 Discussion

As in previous studies [6], no overall differences in usability were found between immersive and non-immersive systems; however, analysing the data separately for men and women, women did present differences. The usability scores of both systems differed little, but women considered the usability of the non-immersive system to be higher. As in previous studies [8], women gave lower scores of usability than men on all the conditions, but the greatest difference was observed in the immersive system.

Future studies should explore the reasons for the differences in the usability of immersive and non-immersive VR systems between men and women. Possibly, one of those reasons could be a higher vulnerability in women to the adverse effects of some VR systems such as simulator sickness, a form of motion sickness induced by VR environments. The signs and symptoms of motion sickness include cold sweating, pallor, nausea and, in some cases, vomiting. Simulator sickness may also include other symptoms such as disorientation, disturbances to balance, eyestrain, blurred vision, drowsiness and lack of coordination. This is one of the most notable concerns related with the use of HMDs. In a study by Davis et al. [10], for example, also using Oculus Rift (the DK1 version, not the DK2 version), eight out of 12 participants reported mild levels of nausea, two moderate, and two high. In the same study, another condition produced even worse motion sickness symptoms: all participants reported some degree of nausea, with seven experiencing moderate levels and five high levels. Eight (66%) of the participants were unable to complete the study.

In the DK2 version (used in our study), Oculus partially corrects this problem by replacing the LCD screen with an OLED screen, thus achieving a higher refresh rate, and by incorporating positional tracking. In any case, despite technical improvements, the use of immersive devices such as HMDs is still associated with simulator sickness in a larger proportion of people than other less immersive devices. This point should be taken into consideration, especially when (as in our study) the use of these devices for training purposes requires long periods of time, which increases the likelihood of simulator sickness or other similar sources of discomfort. Negative side effects of this kind are extremely rare when the training is carried out using non-immersive devices such as laptops or desktop computers with stereoscopic display.

In our study, only two participants were unable complete the experiment; in one of the cases, a woman, this was due to simulator sickness. Thus it is possible that the lower scores of usability recorded by women, especially in the immersive condition, were related to mild forms of motion sickness. This hypothesis remains speculative because no measure of motion sickness was used in our study; nonetheless, it is a well-established fact that women are more susceptible than men to motion sickness in general and to simulator sickness in particular. Studying seasickness among more than 20,000 passengers on ferries, Lawther and Griffin [11] found that the severity of seasickness symptoms was greater in women than in men by a ratio of 5:3. A similar ratio was observed for vomiting, which was more common among women (8.8%) than among men (5.0%). Similar results have been obtained in land transportation [12–14] and in vehicle simulators [15]. Women are also more likely than men to experience motion sickness resulting from wind-induced motion in skyscrapers [16]. The differences between men and women in susceptibility to motion sickness extend to visual motion stimuli in the absence of inertial displacement [17]. Specifically regarding simulator sickness, several studies show that higher intensity symptoms are found in women [18–21].

Taken together, these data suggest that the higher proneness to simulator sickness in women may well be the cause of the lower scores of usability that they give to immersive VR environments compared with men. This hypothesis should now be tested in a replication of the present study, including measures of simulator sickness.

In any case, the results of this study reveal that gender differences must be taken into account when using VR environments to train professionals (in our case, to train health sciences students in diagnostic skills). Highly immersive devices may not always be the best choice; in some cases they may offer significant advantages, but sometimes "less is more" and lower levels of immersion can prevent the emergence of undesirable secondary effects such as simulator sickness, even though this may mean having to forgo some of the advantages of the immersive environments.

Virtual Reality simulations are engaging and facilitate comprehension by the means of situating learning materials in a context. Learning in a VR environment can be more effective and motivating than traditional classroom practices [22–24]. Some of these advantages are associated with their degree of immersiveness, but the importance of achieving a balance between these characteristics and the usability of the system must be taken into account. Individual differences, including gender, appear to be an important factor in appreciations of usability.

Acknowledgments. This study was supported by the Spanish Ministry of "Economía y Competitividad" (Project PSI2015-70389: 'Desarrollo de técnicas de exposición mediante realidad virtual para la mejora del tratamiento de la anorexia nerviosa'), and by "Programa de Millora i Innovació Docent de la Universitat de Barcelona" (PMID-UB)

References

1. Riva, G., Baños, R., Botella, C., Mantovani, F., Gagglioli, A.: Transforming experience: the potential of augmented reality and virtual reality for enhancing personal and clinical change. Front. Psychiatry **7**, 164 (2016). doi:10.3389/fpsyt.2016.00164
2. Ferrer-García, M., Gutiérrez-Maldonado, J., Caqueo-Urízar, A., Moreno, E.: The validity of virtual environments for eliciting emotional responses in patients with eating disorders and in controls. Behav. Modif. **33**(6), 830–854 (2009). doi:10.1177/0145445509348056
3. Gutiérrez-Maldonado, J., Ferrer-García, M., Caqueo-Urízar, A., Letosa-Porta, A.: Assessment of emotional reactivity produced by exposure to virtual environments in patients with eating disorders. CyberPsychology Behav. **9**(5), 507–513 (2006)
4. Bell, J.T., Fogler, H.S.: The investigation and application of virtual reality as an educational tool. In: Proceedings of the American Society for Engineering Education (1995)
5. Gutiérrez-Maldonado, J., Ferrer-García, M., Dakanalis, A., Riva, G.: Virtual reality: applications to eating disorders. In: Agras, S. (ed.) Oxford Handbook on Eating Disorders, 2nd edn. (in press)
6. Gutiérrez-Maldonado, J., Ferrer-García, M., Pla-Sanjuanelo, J., Andres-Pueyo, A., Talarn-Caparrós, A.: Virtual reality to train diagnostic skills in eating disorders. Comparison of two low cost systems. Stud. Health Technol. Inform. **219**, 75–81 (2015)
7. Gutiérrez-Maldonado, J., Ferrer-García, M.: Are virtual patients effective to train diagnostic skills? A study with bulimia nervosa virtual patients. In: Magnenat- Thalmann, N., Wu, E., Tachi, S., Thalmann, D., Porcher Nedel, L., Xu, W. (eds.) VRST, p. 267. ACM (2013)

8. Gutiérrez-Maldonado, J., Andrés-Pueyo, A., Talarn-Caparrós, A., Achotegui-Loizate, J.: Virtual reality for training diagnostic skills in eating disorders. Gender and usability. In: 18th International Conference on Human-Computer Interaction, Toronto, Canada (2016)
9. Kirakowski, J., Corbett, M.: SUMI: the software measurement inventory. Br. J. Educ. Technol. **24**, 210–212 (1993)
10. Davis, S., Nesbitt, K., Nalivaiko, E.: Comparing the onset of cybersickness using the Oculus Rift and two virtual roller coasters. In: Proceedings of the 11th Australasian Conference on Interactive Entertainment, Sydney, Australia, vol. 167, pp. 3–14. CRPIT (2015)
11. Lawther, A., Griffin, M.J.: A survey of the occurrence of motion sickness amongst passengers at sea. Aviat. Space Environ. Med. **59**, 399–406 (1988)
12. Golding, J.F.: Motion sickness susceptibility. Auton. Neurosci. Basic Clin. **129**, 67–76 (2006)
13. Park, A.H.-Y., Hu, S.: Gender differences in motion sickness history and susceptibility to optokinetic rotation-induced motion sickness. Aviat. Space Environ. Med. **70**, 1077–1080 (1999)
14. Turner, M., Griffin, M.J.: Motion sickness in public road transport: the relative importance of motion, vision, and individual differences. Br. J. Psychol. **90**, 519–530 (1999)
15. Kennedy, R.S., Lanham, D.S., Massey, C.J., Drexler, J.M., Lilienthal, M.G.: Gender differences in simulator sickness incidence: implications for military virtual reality systems. Safe J. **25**, 69–76 (1995)
16. Lamb, S., Kwok, K.C.S., Walton, D.: Occupant comfort in windexcited tall buildings: motion sickness, compensatory behaviors, and complaint. J. Wind Eng. Ind. Aerodyn. **119**, 1–12 (2013)
17. Koslucher, F.C., Haaland, E., Malsch, A., Webeler, J., Stoffregen, T.A.: Sex differences in the incidence of motion sickness induced by linear visual oscillation. Aviat. Med. Hum. Perform. **86**, 787–793 (2015)
18. Hein, C.M.: Driving simulators: six years of hands-on experience at hughes aircraft company. In: Proceedings of the Human Factors and Ergonomics Society 37th Annual Meeting, pp. 607–611 (1993)
19. Biocca, F.: Will simulation sickness slow down the diffusion of virtual environment technology? Presence: Teleoperators Virtual Environ. **1**, 334–343 (1992)
20. Flanagan, M.B., May, J.G., Dobie, T.G.: Sex differences in tolerance to visually-induced motion sickness. Aviat. Space Environ. Med. **76**(7), 642–646 (2005)
21. Park, G.D., Allen, R.W., Fiorentino, D., Rosenthal, T.J., Cook, M.L.: Simulator sickness scores according to symptom susceptibility, age, and gender for an older driver assessment study. In: Proceedings of the Human Factors and Ergonomics Society Annual Meeting, vol. 50, pp. 2702–2706 (2006)
22. Fominykh, M., Prasolova-Førland, E., Morozov, M., Smorkalov, A., Molka-Danielsen, J.: Increasing immersiveness into a 3D virtual world: motion-tracking and natural navigation in vAcademia. IERI Procedia **7**, 35–41 (2014). doi:10.1016/j.ieri.2014.08.007
23. Monahan, T., McArdle, G., Bertolotto, M.: Virtual reality for collaborative e-learning. Comput. Educ. **50**(4), 1339–1353 (2008)
24. Trindade, J., Fiolhais, C., Almeida, L.: Science learning in virtual environments: a descriptive study. Br. J. Educ. Technol. **33**(4), 475–492 (2002)

An Augmented Reality/Internet of Things Prototype for Just-in-time Astronaut Training

John A. Karasinski[1,2(✉)], Richard Joyce[1,2], Colleen Carroll[2], Jack Gale[2], and Steven Hillenius[3]

[1] Mechanical and Aerospace Engineering Department,
University of California, Davis, CA, USA
karasinski@ucdavis.edu
[2] San Jose State University at NASA Ames Research Center, Moffett Field, CA, USA
[3] NASA Ames Research Center, Moffett Field, CA 94035, USA

Abstract. We present a mobile prototype for just-in-time astronaut training and initial human-computer interaction guidelines for augmented reality training tools. The mobile prototype takes advantage of the Microsoft HoloLens augmented reality glasses and a network of custom "Internet of Things" sensors based on an ESP8266 chipset. This combined prototype allows for operational procedures to be displayed to and interacted with by a user in real-time. This mobile procedure viewer allows for just-in-time training using holograms to provide contextually relevant information to novice or out of practice users. We summarize a first look at best practices and guidelines for augmented reality assisted procedure execution from user testing conducted at NASA Ames Research Center.

Keywords: Applications: Education and training · Interaction and navigation in VAMR: Human factors · Interaction and navigation in VAMR: Orientation and navigation · Issues in development and use of VAMR: Situational awareness

1 Introduction

1.1 Motivation

Future long duration spaceflight missions will require new education, training methods, and tools to assist procedure execution. Skills which are currently taught before flight will need to be provided as just-in-time training due to expanding mission requirements [4]. Deep space missions, such as those to an asteroid or Mars, will introduce a time-delay in communications that will require an increase in crew autonomy from the current ground based mission control architecture [7]. We have designed and prototyped a mobile procedure viewer using augmented reality (AR) with the goals of increasing crew autonomy, decreasing training time, and reducing procedure execution errors. The prototype integrates with a future space habitat outfitted with an Internet of Things (IoT)

© Springer International Publishing AG 2017
S. Lackey and J. Chen (Eds.): VAMR 2017, LNCS 10280, pp. 248–260, 2017.
DOI: 10.1007/978-3-319-57987-0_20

sensor network. These emerging technologies can be used to integrate and display information about the astronauts' current task, the state of the habitat, the location of their tools, and more, to the astronauts in situ, as well as provide real-time error detection and supervision that is traditionally fulfilled by mission control [2,3].

The training requirements for future missions are currently unknown and will require extensive research to adequately define for operational use. NASA's Human Research Program (HRP) has identified key research gaps essential to successful human exploration beyond low Earth orbit. Among these gaps are the need to "identify effective methods and tools that can be used to train for long-duration, long-distance space missions [8]". Deep space missions can take advantage of long transit times to train astronauts onboard spacecraft. Skills that are currently taught on the ground before a mission can be taught in transit or supplied as just-in-time training when required. HRP has an additional research gap to "develop guidelines for effective onboard training systems that provide training traditionally assumed for pre-flight [9]". Traditional pre-flight training tasks typically require a demonstration of the task by an expert or supervision to ensure no errors are made. For future onboard training systems, we have found that our augmented reality/IoT procedure assistant can provide these roles. Through user testing conducted at NASA Ames Research Center, we show that our prototype can effectively train new users to a procedure.

1.2   Related Work

Research investigating the effects of virtual and augmented reality training has previously shown improved performance compared to conventional types of training. This research in virtual and augmented reality training has primarily focused on surgery, assembly and maintenance skills. All three of these tasks are analogous to the types of tasks astronauts are required to accomplish during the completion of procedures. Surgical training has seen particular focus by researchers due to the inherent high-risk nature of the task, as well as the expense and limited time of expert instructors [5,6,11,12].

The use of virtual reality (VR) to simulate surgical tasks was first proposed by Satava in the early 1990s [11]. Satava used an off-the-shelf VR head mounted display (HMD) and a "DataGlove", which essentially acted as a joystick, for the user to interact with the scene. Satava described five areas that must be met to provide a realistic simulation:

- Fidelity: the graphics must have an acceptable level of resolution for the task
- Object properties: the objects in the scene must behave with sufficient reality
- Interactivity: the user must be able to interact with the virtual scene
- Sensory input: the user must receive appropriate sensory feedback
- Reactivity: the objects must behave appropriately when the user interacts with them

At that point in time, computers were only capable of meeting these standards at the most basic level. Despite this, Satava noted recent rapid advances in computing power, and that VR training could be particularly useful "in this era of animal-rights sensitivity and of fear of exposure to blood-borne diseases such as AIDS and hepatitis [11]".

Less than ten years later, Seymour et al. showed that virtual reality training could improve operating room performance [12]. Seymour et al. presented the results of a double-blind study demonstrating that "virtual reality training transfers technical skills to the operating room (OR) environment [12]". In the study, surgical residents were split into either a non-VR-trained control group, or VR-trained group and trained to perform laparoscopic cholecystectomy. The authors showed that, while overall task performance time did not significantly decrease, the VR-trained group made significantly fewer errors. This result indicated that students could be trained to perform better without any risk to patients, and "validated the transfer of training skills from VR to OR sets the stage for more sophisticated uses of VR in assessment, training, error reduction, and certification of surgeons [12]".

Around the same time, Boud et al. found significantly improved assembly times for subjects who used VR or AR training over conventional 2D engineering drawings [1]. In their task, subjects had to assemble a water pump after receiving instructions on paper "conventional" drawings, in VR, or in AR. Subjects in the VR and AR conditions wore HMDs to see their environment. Subjects performed significantly better in both VR and AR than when trained with the conventional drawings. Additionally, subjects who received training with the AR system performed significantly better than the subjects trained with VR.

More recently, Webel et al. developed an augmented reality training platform for assembly and maintenance skills [13]. The authors combined an augmented reality video aid with a vibrotactile bracelet to assist with augmented reality training. The video aid was displayed on a tablet computer that combined predefined augmented reality cues with a video feed of the real world. The bracelet had six vibration segments, which could be activated independently, allowing for both translational and rotational "channels" that guide the user. Webel et al. ran a study that grouped subjects into two groups to determine if training with the AR system was more effective than traditional training. To measure the effects of the training, the authors investigated both the task completion time and the number of "unsolved errors". The authors found that overall task completion times were not significantly different between the control and AR groups, but that the AR group had significantly less unsolved errors. This result is consistent with other studies using VR, including the above-mentioned Seymour study [12].

This research has shown that measuring human performance and the effects of training can be challenging. Even in experiments with seemingly improved and subjectively preferred training techniques, the results of training rarely reflect performance changes. While overall task completion times generally do not change as a result of training in VR or AR, the number of task errors has been shown to be decreased [11,12]. Until recently, computational limits of the hardware used in these VR and AR experiments have reduced their effectiveness. Recent advances in hardware allow for fully mobile, head mounted augmented reality solutions which may ultimately prove to be more useful.

2   Technical Description

Modern spacecraft procedures are typically viewed on paper or computer tablets during spaceflight (see Fig. 1). While procedures can be viewed on tablets, they are static and essentially no more than digital paper. We have designed and created a prototype system that would target future missions from both a technical and human computer interaction (HCI) perspective (see Fig. 2). We have developed software and hardware to support this aim, with the goal of creating guidelines for an improved user experience. Our work is developed first from the "Internet of Things" to determine what a future space habitat will be able to know about itself and the human residing in it. Compared to a computer vision approach, IoT allows us to have each object broadcast information about itself (e.g., Door A is open) or where it is (e.g., Module C is installed in Rack 4).

Fig. 1. Astronaut Lee Archambault, STS-119 commander, looks over procedures during an International Space Station assembly mission (S119-E-006141).

The prototype presented here makes use of state-of-the-art technology. While it is not expected that current technology will be used for future missions, upcoming hardware should have a smaller form factor, better computational power, and longer battery life. More importantly, this prototype can be used to provide essential insight to design future HCI requirements. With this in mind, this section outlines the two main hardware components used for this prototype and the communication technique used to network them.

Fig. 2. User's view of procedure with cardboard mockup of science payload hardware. An animation of the current step guides the user, while procedure text is placed above the hardware.

2.1   Augmented Reality Headset

The prototype takes advantage of the Microsoft HoloLens to display information to the user. The HoloLens is an augmented reality headset capable of displaying semi-transparent "holograms" to the wearer. These holograms can be fixed to the user's viewpoint or to some aspect of the environment. This allows for fixed-placed holograms to provide relevant information near a specific hardware or location, as well as procedure instructions which stay in view and follow the user's movements. Users can interact with the prototype holograms by using voice commands, hand gestures, or a combination of the two. The voice commands, which take advantage of the HoloLens' voice recognition system, can be particularly useful when the user is already using both hands and still needs to interact with the prototype.

A number of alternate augmented reality devices were considered before the beginning of this work. In particular, there exist several augmented reality options for phones and tablets. While these devices are also capable of providing similar augmented reality experiences, they require either:

- The user to mount or hold a device in place
- The use of markers for the device's camera to locate the appropriate location for augmented information

In contrast to this, the HoloLens can be used while both hands are occupied, and it uses computer vision to identify features already present in the environment to allow for location based holograms.

One limitation of the HoloLens, however, is a small field of view. While this decreases the number of options available for displaying information to the user, it can also be used to focus the user to specific areas of interest. Additionally, as information can be displayed relative to user's head, essential information never needs to leave the field of view.

2.2   Internet of Things (IoT) Sensors

We developed individual IoT sensors based on an ESP8266 chipset. The battery powered chips could be mounted onto every tool or object in the space habitat, providing information on location, orientation, movement, or any other sensors. In our prototype, each chip is outfitted with an accelerometer and LED and communicates back and forth to a central server.

As well as information from their own sensors, we exploit the WiFi transceiver to provide us with a rough estimate of proximity between objects. The ESP8266 chips were placed in a dual WiFi mode, connecting to one WiFi network for information transfer and advertising their own access point. This was performed so that we could obtain the signal strength of each chip relative to one another, as the chips are only able to obtain RSSI (Relative Signal Strength Indication) from an advertising packet. Each chip can then continuously perform a scan of WiFi networks and report the RSSI between every chip in the environment.

We created a special configuration of the IoT sensor to wear on the wrist of the user to determine when an object is picked up (see Fig. 3). With the information streaming of RSSI between the wristband and other IoT sensors, we can detect proximity between the user and a tool or object. The server combines this proximity information with the accelerometer data from the IoT-equipped object to perform pick-up detection. Pick-up detection occurs when an object reports a spike in acceleration and has strong radio signals from the wristband. We have found this to provide a reliable method for determining which object the user has picked up and is interacting with.

3   Prototype

Our work on developing a prototype was divided into two main parts. The first part focused on guiding the astronaut to a tool or location in the space station (Path Visualization). The second part was to provide assistance and supervision to an astronaut performing a typical procedure on board the station (Procedure Execution). Our use of the term assistance here describes any visual, audio, or other cues to help the astronaut complete a step in the procedure. Supervision refers to our ability to monitor the astronaut's performance of the procedure in situ using IoT sensors, allowing the system to catch or avoid any errors performed. Technical limitations and time pressures led us to simulate some of the

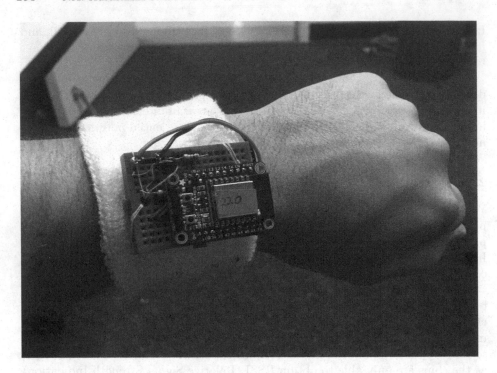

Fig. 3. Wristband for tool and object proximity detection via WiFi signal strength.

interactions ("Wizard of Oz" prototyping technique). For both parts, we went through a standard user centered design and rapid prototyping process of brainstorm — storyboard — prototype — user test design cycle. We present here our final prototype for each part of the project, followed by a summary of the findings of the prototyping and user testing to guide future developments.

3.1 Path Visualization

The focus of this section of the project was to create a guidance system that would help astronauts find their desired tool or destination on the space station. Lost and misplaced items on the space station waste a significant amount of valuable crew time, and items replaced incorrectly can cause hazards for the astronauts. We simulated the task of locating a missing tool by requiring users to retrieve tools from another room in the building. The guidance led users to the room and then, within the room, guided them to the precise location of the tool. This broke the task down into two parts: guidance to the room (through hallways or other rooms) and guidance within the room (to the storage location of the tool).

To begin the task, the users first navigated a user interface in the HoloLens to select which tools they wanted to locate. The UI screen could be navigated via native HoloLens gestures or voice (see Fig. 4). After selecting which tools to find, the users were provided guidance to the room with the tools. This was accomplished with a hovering 3D rectangular line (at approximately chest level) with chevrons indicating direction, as well as additional context placed directly on the line such as the room number and tool they were collecting (see Fig. 5). Upon entering the room, the user saw a holographic line which included an arrow pointing towards the location of the tool. After picking up the IoT outfitted tool, the pickup detection technique allowed the augmented reality display to react automatically. This allowed the prototype to provide guidance navigation to the next tool or the return path without any needed input from the user.

3.2 Procedure Execution

The goal of the Procedure Execution part of the project was to provide astronauts with assistance on how to complete a procedure beyond their current text-based instructions. For our simulation, we simplified a procedure from an existing International Space Station procedure for the rodent habitat scientific payload. The goal of the procedure was to transfer the rodents from their transport habitat on a visiting spacecraft to the rodent habitat onboard the International Space Station. To ensure the safety of the crew, the procedure requires the astronauts to configure the hardware in various ways to ensure that the rodents are not released into the space station. The payload habitat hardware was simulated using a cardboard prototype.

The prototype guided the user through the procedure by providing a holographic animation for each step and a UI for displaying the text of the step. For example, one of the first steps was to open an access door. During this step, the prototype provided a holographic animation overlay of the door opening on top of the actual hardware. After the user completed a step the next step would be presented, both in the text and animation, without any required input from the user. This ensured that the user knew that they installed an item correctly before moving on to the next step in the procedure. This was useful for complex steps involving many actions, as time could be saved by synthesizing several steps into one cohesive animation.

4   User Testing Results

4.1   Warm up

Our user testing exercises were initially broken up into the two parts: path visualization and procedure execution. After the first round of user tests, however, we found that participants needed more experience interacting with holograms and paper prototypes. We created a new exercise, which we called "warm up", to familiarize participants with using our selectors, pinching hand gestures, and voice commands to select items. The warm up consisted of a smart phone and a paper-prototyped music player interface. We asked participants to use both voice and hand gestures to pause, play, and skip songs as we "Wizard of Oz'd" the

Fig. 4. A user wearing the HoloLens and making a gesture.

actual playing and pausing of music on a cell phone behind them. This warm up exercise was successful in familiarizing participants with our selectors and interacting with the holograms, an entirely new interaction to most users. We found that participants said they preferred voice commands over hand gestures when selecting items but tended to use both. One participant noted "Voice is more comfortable because I wasn't sure about the depth of my gestures". Once the procedure began, however, participants switched to only using hand gestures to select options within the interface.

4.2   Arrow Spacing (Path Visualization)

Our next insight came during the path visualization portion of the prototype, as we wanted to guide users to their desired tool through holographic arrows and a guiding line. We found that using a constant arrow spacing alongside a linear path gave users an easy guidance system to locate their desired tool. Through testing, we found that there should be a chevron arrow indicating direction every fifteen feet, as well as at every corner. At this distance, the user would always have at least one arrow in their field of view without being too cluttered and obstructive. One participant told us "The arrows were positioned just right so I knew exactly where to turn". This user feedback, coupled with

(a)   (b)

Fig. 5. A user's view of the (a) holographic arrows and (b) line representing a path during a testing session.

our understanding of the HoloLens' field of view limitations, indicated that the spacing was appropriate for the task and AR hardware.

4.3   Precise Location of Tool

Through our user testing, we sought to answer how to enable a user to find a tool in a precise location, such as a small hatch or compartment. This was especially challenging when the tool was lost or outside the HoloLens' field of view. We found that a single line on the floor leading to a tool's exact location was a successful method of marking the destination, as users could follow the line to the precise location (see Fig. 6). We arrived at this insight after observing many users' inability to locate the tool when it was outside the field of view.

Fig. 6. Users were able to identify and acquire objects in a busy office environment during user testing sessions with the use of paper prototypes.

By using the eye to follow the holographic line, users could easily see which drawer the tool was in, decreasing cognitive load.

4.4 Summary

After each user test we interviewed the user to ask questions about some of the decisions they made and why. This allowed us to determine the leverage points and ways we might modify the next iteration to improve the user experience and efficiency of the prototype. For each new iteration, we conducted five qualitative user tests to gather sufficient data before we made changes to the prototype [10]. Through multiple iterations of user testing and prototypes, we developed insights and best practices that reduced cognitive load and saved time for our users. We feel that augmented reality and embedded IoT sensors are an effective pairing of tools to increase productivity and reduce procedure execution time.

5   Conclusions

User testing at NASA Ames led to several best practices and guidelines for augmented reality assisted procedure execution. We found the use of a paper prototype "augmented reality" warm up exercise to be useful, as most users have no experience or context interacting with augmented reality. This allowed us to both train users in how to interact with augmented reality and quickly iterate through designs. The ability to prototype augmented reality software using paper prototypes avoided the need for lengthy software development. The results of these paper prototypes translated directly into the final augmented reality solution.

In addition to the use of the warm up exercise, we also investigated several techniques to guide users to a destination and locate a tool. We found that the use of holograms arrows floating along a guidance path at fifteen foot intervals was useful for providing directional context to users. This spacing allowed for effective guidance, as users could always find the next arrow "marker" to continue their path to their destination location. Once users were sufficiently close to their destination, we found that providing a semi-transparent line was a non-intrusive way to provide guidance towards a specific item or tool.

It can be challenging to describe relative orientation of mechanical parts for maintenance or assembly tasks. The use of holograms to provide 3D translation and rotation information was found to be especially useful compared to traditional, text-based procedural steps. As the HoloLens can be operated hands free, users can continue a procedure while in the middle of complex assembly. When the holograms were aligned and overlaid with real world parts, the 3D animation removed ambiguity regarding the procedure. Users could watch and follow along with the animation in real-time, without any need to interpret written procedures.

We have presented the development of an augmented reality and IoT prototype for just-in-time training. The HoloLens' capability to persist location-specific holograms provided feedback to the user which could not have been provided by tablet or phone-based AR solutions. The use of a wristband sensor allowed for the prototype to sense the user's proximity to relevant objects, and it helped to confirm when objects had been picked up. Combined with sensor data provided by the IoT devices, our prototype enabled novice users to complete our procedure correctly, without any instructor guidance.

Acknowledgements. The authors would like to thank Anthony Ebbs, Bria Harris, Connor Keane, Emily Ruthruff, Matthew Chan, Mitali Palekar, and Sean Grovensor for design and development work completing this project. The authors would also like to thank the user testing participants, without whom this would not have been possible. This work was performed under a US Govt. Contract in the Human-Systems Integration Division at NASA Ames Research Center.

References

1. Boud, A., Haniff, D.J., Baber, C., Steiner, S.: Virtual reality and augmented reality as a training tool for assembly tasks. In: Proceedings of the 1999 IEEE International Conference on Information Visualization, 1999, pp. 32–36. IEEE (1999)
2. Carr, C.E., Schwartz, S.J., Rosenberg, I.: A wearable computer for support of astronaut extravehicular activity. In: Proceedings of the Sixth International Symposium on Wearable Computers, 2002 (ISWC 2002), pp. 23–30. IEEE (2002)
3. Fincke, E.M., Padalka, G., Lee, D., van Holsbeeck, M., Sargsyan, A.E., Hamilton, D.R., Martin, D., Melton, S.L., McFarlin, K., Dulchavsky, S.A.: Evaluation of shoulder integrity in space: first report of musculoskeletal us on the international space station 1. Radiology **234**(2), 319–322 (2005)
4. Foale, C.M., Kaleri, A.Y., Sargsyan, A.E., Hamilton, D.R., Melton, S., Martin, D., Dulchavsky, S.A.: Diagnostic instrumentation aboard ISS: just-in-time training for non-physician crewmembers. Aviat. Space Environ. Med. **76**(6), 594–598 (2005)
5. Grantcharov, T.P., Kristiansen, V., Bendix, J., Bardram, L., Rosenberg, J., Funch-Jensen, P.: Randomized clinical trial of virtual reality simulation for laparoscopic skills training. Br. J. Surg. **91**(2), 146–150 (2004)
6. Kühnapfel, U., Cakmak, H.K., Maaß, H.: Endoscopic surgery training using virtual reality and deformable tissue simulation. Comput. Graph. **24**(5), 671–682 (2000)
7. Martin, D.S., Caine, T.L., Matz, T., Lee, S., Stenger, M.B., Sargsyan, A.E., Platts, S.H.: Virtual guidance as a tool to obtain diagnostic ultrasound for spaceflight and remote environments. Aviat. Space Environ. Med. **83**(10), 995–1000 (2012)
8. NASA: Train-02: We need to identify effective methods and tools that can be used to train for long-duration, long-distance space missions (2016). https://humanresearchroadmap.nasa.gov/gaps/gap.aspx?i=310
9. NASA: Train-03: We need to develop guidelines for effective onboard training systems that provide training traditionally assumed for pre-flight (2016). https://humanresearchroadmap.nasa.gov/gaps/gap.aspx?i=321
10. Nielsen, J., Landauer, T.K.: A mathematical model of the finding of usability problems. In: Proceedings of the INTERACT 1993 and CHI 1993 Conference on Human Factors in Computing Systems, pp. 206–213. ACM (1993)
11. Satava, R.M.: Virtual reality surgical simulator. Surg. Endosc. **7**(3), 203–205 (1993)

12. Seymour, N.E., Gallagher, A.G., Roman, S.A., O'brien, M.K., Bansal, V.K., Andersen, D.K., Satava, R.M.: Virtual reality training improves operating room performance: results of a randomized, double-blinded study. Ann. Surg. **236**(4), 458–464 (2002)
13. Webel, S., Bockholt, U., Engelke, T., Gavish, N., Olbrich, M., Preusche, C.: An augmented reality training platform for assembly and maintenance skills. Robot. Auton. Syst. **61**(4), 398–403 (2013)

Contrasting Instructional Strategies Suited to a Detection Task: Examining Differences in Subjective Workload

Crystal Maraj[1(✉)], Jonathan Hurter[1], William Aubrey[1], Elizabeth Wolfe[1], and Irwin Hudson[2]

[1] Institute for Simulation and Training, University of Central Florida, Orlando, FL, USA
{cmaraj,jhurter,waubrey,ewolfe}@ist.ucf.edu
[2] U.S. Army Research Laboratory – Human Research and Engineering Directorate
Advanced Training and Simulation Division, Orlando, FL, USA
irwin.1.hudson.civ@mail.mil

Abstract. Soldiers benefit from the ability to detect threats conveyed via human kinesic cues, or non-verbal body movements. Simulation-Based Training (SBT) supplies an avenue to improve kinesic cue detection performance. Instructional strategies in SBT are designed to enhance performance outcomes, and are tied to workload in terms of training effectiveness. Three instructional strategies were analyzed in a between-subjects design for their degree of perceived workload: Highlighting, Massed Exposure, and Kim's game. Workload included subjective mental and global demand subscales from the NASA-Task Load Index (NASA-TLX). A multivariate analysis of variance showed that Kim's game contained the highest mental and global demands; Highlighting produced the lowest mental and global demands. The differences in demands suggest rationales for strategy placement, in terms of combinations (e.g., layers or progressions) and other applications (e.g., air traffic control, medical diagnosis, and After-Action Reviews). The strategies' workload differences are also traced to differences in attention and working memory.

Keywords: Training effectiveness · Instructional design for simulations · Workload · Signal detection · Virtual environments

1 Introduction

Soldiers can benefit from training their minds to identify inconspicuous events. In the military realm of human Intelligence, Surveillance, and Reconnaissance (ISR) tasks, the ability to gather valuable information on a high-value target is vital [1]. Today, Soldiers are required to observe human behavior in highly irregular, complex environments. Target cues include behavioral features that indicate the presence of a threat. A subset of target cues are kinesics, or non-verbal gestures that convey one's true emotional states [2]. To train one to adopt the standpoint of a Combat Hunter (where kinesics is an approach to gauge intent through suspicious behavior), three instructional strategies were applied to enhance Simulation-Based Training (SBT). Since the SBT application

© Springer International Publishing AG 2017
S. Lackey and J. Chen (Eds.): VAMR 2017, LNCS 10280, pp. 261–273, 2017.
DOI: 10.1007/978-3-319-57987-0_21

is novel, workload between the strategies were analyzed to both further perceptual training and aid strategy selection for different objectives.

1.1 Threat Detection

Threat detection requires an observer to allocate perceptual and attentional resources to decide if a target cue is present in the environment. Perceiving a threat involves detecting a signal (i.e., a target cue) amongst competing noise (i.e., distractions such as non-target cues) [3]. Thus, detection is enacted under some uncertainty, and involves discrimination of perceptual elements to make sense of an environment. The present study required users to detect a target cue, and then classify the type of target cue as signaling nervousness or aggressiveness. A person activates components of Working Memory (WM) when information is processed in the environment.

1.2 Working Memory

WM is the mental ability to temporarily maintain and coordinate perceived stimuli necessary for performing higher-order cognitive operations. However, WM is limited in capacity: performance is impaired if one is required to process numerous external stimuli [4, 5]. Visual WM has been found to interact closely with attention during encoding and manipulating sensory stimuli. This has led researchers to postulate that attention is necessary for sustaining information [6]. Hence, when a Soldier processes incoming information from an external stimulus, he or she must undergo a multi-step psychological process, requiring both WM and attention. This process follows a loop of actions, including scanning for potential targets, target acquisition, analysis, decision-making, and disengagement. For the current experimental interest of a threat detection task for a simulated field of operations, a viewer compares instances of kinesic cues held in working memory to kinesic pattern knowledge solidified in long-term memory [7]. This process allows the user to determine if a given experimental cue matches a prototypical target cue. The role of working memory and attention can be adjusted by instructional strategies, and differing strategies are expected to vary in workload.

1.3 Workload

Workload is the collective contributions of task processes, user resources, and environmental influences imposed on a person while completing a task [8]. The principle of workload has been extensively investigated across various domains, including medical, military, and civil aviation tasks. In most domains, multitasking is a crucial component and is impacted by workload. A red-line denotes where a person faces performance losses, and where unacceptable system characteristics exist [9, 10]. Effective amounts of workload can be viewed on a continuum, where workload levels should be neither too low nor too high. Extremes on this continuum would likely hinder learning; for example, motivation may be impacted adversely [11]. Further, empirical research has shown that high workload is associated with exhaustion [12], performance decrement [13], and task difficulty [14]. For strategy video games, Hsu, Wen, and Wu [15] contended that the greatest challenge (resulting in fun, engaging gameplay) incorporates an intermediate amount of mental demand. In these lights, workload acts as a criterion for assessing users' reactions in terms of training's effectiveness. This underscores the need to examine and frame workload.

One measure that has achieved reliability and validity for capturing workload is the NASA-Task Load Index (NASA-TLX) [16]. The NASA-TLX is a multidimensional, self-report survey that assesses a user's subjective experience through six subscales [8]. These subscales include three demand subscales, as well as performance, effort, and frustration subscales. The three subscales of mental, physical, and temporal demand correspond to a user's cognitive expenditure, physical expenditure, and time-pressure strain, respectively. The performance subscale measures the user's perceived degree of task success, after a completed task. The effort subscale measures the user's feeling of difficulty due to resource input. The frustration subscale measures the degree of adverse emotions that a task triggers. Finally, global demand is an overall rating obtained by integrating all six domains, creating an average sum [17]. For this experiment, the NASA-TLX questionnaire was used as an investigative tool to assess perceptions of mental demand and global demand within a Virtual Environment (VE) for perceptual training of kinesic cues.

1.4   Virtual Environments

VEs are synthetic representations of a reality, where the user perceives that he or she is operating within the synthetic reality [18]. VEs are an economical alternative to training exclusively in real environments (e.g., practicing detection of improvised explosive devices), and benefit from the customization of complex virtual scenarios that are not readily available to a user (e.g. analysis at an atomic level). VEs may also allow for an After-Action Review (AAR) to aid in skill expansion [19, 20]. Ultimately, the benefits of VEs afford ways to improve instruction.

A VE is a platform for accommodating Simulation-Based Training (SBT). SBT is an approach to training that enables a user to focus mental and/or physical resources in order to accomplish a task under differing environmental conditions (e.g. a pilot using a computer for various flight training scenarios). A training simulation offers replication of a task's corresponding cognitive demands, thereby furthering skill acquisition through virtual experience of the task [21]. An enhanced pedagogical approach to SBT is through the implementation of instructional strategies. For detection tasks, specific focus is given to perceptual instructional strategies.

1.5   Perceptual Instructional Strategies

Perceptual instructional strategies are designed to improve a user's observation skills [22]. Based on perceptual, signal-detection needs, three valid strategies for kinesic cue detection were identified for the present analysis: Highlighting, Massed Exposure, and Kim's game.

Highlighting is the purposeful use of a distinct stimulus to direct a user's visual resources toward a feature, characteristic, or object of interest within a simulated environment. In order to orient a user to a point of interest, a stimulus must contrast (e.g., through the use of color) from the surrounding environment. The stimulus' distinguishing characteristic allows a user to recognize a highlighted feature [23].

Massed Exposure (ME) depicts multiple signals, or target cues, for a user to process simultaneously. A raised signal-to-noise ratio is sought to saturate the trainee with opportunities for skill practice. The increased presence of both target cues and noise suggests the need for selective attention in order to mediate between the different cues.

Kim's game is designed to heighten several types of cognitive skills, including enhanced sensitivity in change detection [24]. Like threat detection, change detection is a perceptual phenomenon crucial to ISR: soldiers must note changes in an operational environment, and then make sense of such changes. Kim's game stems from the novel *Kim*, where the main character underwent memorization training in a two-step process: initial observation of a set of objects for a period of time, and subsequent recollection of the same objects from memory [25]. The game mechanic consisted of how well Kim could remember the objects' features after they were veiled from sight. A variation of the game, which involves change detection, presents another set of items after the veiling period (i.e., an Interstimulus Interval (ISI)) and requires the player to detect if an item changed from the original set. This latter variation was virtually presented in the experiment.

1.6 Purpose

Threat detection and change detection require several cognitive mechanisms that contribute to workload. A Soldier conducting detection tasks must strive to allocate mental resources optimally. The application of instructional strategies within a VE offers enhanced training features that cannot be replicated easily in a real-world environment. The purpose of this research initiative is to analyze how each instructional strategy contributes to user workload. Given workload's relation to training effectiveness, one research question is to determine the placement and application of each strategy. The elucidation of a task-to-strategy goodness of fit through workload analysis also has potential beyond threat detection training, based on contextual performance needs.

2   Hypotheses

The first hypothesis links mental demand and utilization of a visual highlighting cue. A non-content, extradiegetic visual cue can act as a tool to assist a user in quickly locating a specific target. The quick orientation afforded by the cue suggests a low degree of mental demand, due to a reduction in a user's vigor to scan a scene. Jerome, Witmer, and Mouloua [26] discovered that visual cues contributed significantly to improved detection accuracy when a participant was under a high amount of workload during a search task. In our treatment, Highlighting reduced the tentative aspect of target detection by its non-content feature, leaving only the subtask of cue classification (i.e., nervousness or aggressiveness) to be performed. Accordingly, these links lead to hypothesis one.

Hypothesis 1 (H1): Highlighting produces the lowest mental demand and lowest global demand compared to ME and Kim's game.

The second hypothesis is based on memory recall. A discrete change detection task involves an interruption between visual scenes through an ISI (or break); a user is forced to recall a previous scene's information, and compare the information to a newly presented scene. Change detection not only focuses on processing an observed change, but detecting where the change occurred [27]. The process for solving the observational puzzle of Kim's game includes two strategy options: comparing scene-to-scene features to detect an anomaly, and comparing a given scene's kinesic cues to kinesic knowledge. Only the latter is available for Highlighting and Massed exposure. In contrast, the cooperation of a double-strategy from Kim's game may lower mental demand in comparison to Massed Exposure. Yet, unlike Highlighting, an unaided detection task still exists to increase mental demand.

A higher degree of temporal demand, effort, and frustration is presumed to exist from the discrete change detection task. The user is not given time to immerse themselves in the microworld, due to the ISI's visual discontinuity, and thus he or she is more aware of time pressure. The unnatural presentation of cues may induce effort and/or frustration, since the user must disengage with the virtual environment at the onset of the ISI, and re-engage with the virtual environment after the ISI. These considerations lead to hypothesis two.

Hypothesis 2 (H2): Kim's game produces higher mental demand than Highlighting, but less mental demand than ME; and produces higher global demand than both Highlighting and ME.

Both Kim's game and Massed Exposure have an identical target cue ratio (2:3), and a similar number of total cues presented in the scenarios. Thus, targets alone are not expected to differ in inducing mental demand, and other characteristics of each instructional strategy must be considered. In terms of perceptual load for detection, each model in the ME condition must be examined by the user to accept or reject a cue match. However, Kim's game does not have this limit: a user compares scenes, but does not necessarily have to look at every single cue to make a decision. Viewing discrete scenes in separate trials for Kim's game may also demand less vigilance (and mental demand) than ME's perpetual, continuous task. According to the current expectations, Kim's game has the highest global demand, and Highlighting the lowest; this order leaves ME with a medium-level of global demand. Based on these ideas, hypothesis three is formed.

Hypothesis 3 (H3): ME produces higher mental demand than both Highlighting and Kim's game; but produces only less global demand than Kim's game.

3 Method

3.1 Participants

Individuals were recruited through flyers and emails distributed to the University of Central Florida community. Participants were required to meet specific inclusion criteria in order to participate, which included a United States citizenship, a minimum of 18 years of age, normal (or corrected-to-normal) vision, and a lack of participation in previous SBT experiments. Each participant received a choice for compensation: either monetary compensation or class credit for up to five hours.

In terms of participant demographics, the Highlighting group consisted of $n = 37$ with an age range of 18–32 ($M = 22.68$, $SD = 3.53$), the ME group consisted of $n = 32$ with an age range of 18–33 ($M = 22.22$, $SD = 2.81$), and the Kim's game group consisted of $n = 34$ with an age range of 18–38 ($M = 22.18$, $SD = 4.41$).

3.2 Experimental Design

A between-subjects design was utilized with one independent variable: the instructional strategy. The independent variable consisted of three conditions: ME, Highlighting, and Kim's game. The two dependent variables were the NASA-TLX mental demand and global demand scores.

For each training strategy, users were to detect and classify aggressive and nervous cues performed by animated models. Non-target cues were intermixed with the target cues. Aggressive cues comprised models that either clenched their fists, or slapped their hands. Nervous cues comprised models that either wrung their hands, or looked behind their back to "check six o'clock." Non-target cues consisted of idle talking, crossed arms, a rubbed neck, or the check of one's watch. Per every three events (i.e., instance of a cue) shown in the Highlighting condition, one event would represent a target cue. Further, this target cue was overlaid with a transparent blue box. Per every three events shown in the ME condition, two would represent a target cue. For both of these conditions, the kinesic models were viewed during the simulation of an unmanned vehicle's traversal through a town. That is, the user took on the role of an operator of a continuously moving robotic vehicle, where models were populated along the vehicle's route.

Kim's game required a user to first observe a baseline scene of non-target models for eight seconds. Second, the user saw a 1-second long ISI, as a black screen. Third, the user was presented with another scene (for eight seconds), and was required to use working memory for change detection: the user was required to detect if a non-target cue model from the first scene changed to a target cue model in the second scene (within a 20 s time range). Between scenes, the models may or may not have changed; if a change occurred, it would be present in only one model. Kim's game incorporated the 2:3 target ratio chance that a target model would appear. However, this condition incorporated an immobile camera's point-of-view of a town, instead of simulating a continuously moving vehicle.

3.3 Surveys

The demographics questionnaire gathered basic descriptive information about each participant. This information included age, gender, education, and experience with computers.

The NASA-TLX (Hart and Staveland, 1988) served as the measure for workload. The NASA-TLX contained a scale ranging from 0 to 100 for each subscale. A rating of 0 indicated a "very low" rating for the corresponding subscale. A rating of 100 indicated a "very high" rating for the corresponding subscale. An exception applied to the performance subscale, as a 0 indicated a "perfect" rating and a 100 indicated a "failure" rating.

3.4   Materials

A 22-inch desktop computer with a 16:10 aspect ratio was used across all three conditions. The Virtual Battlespace 2 (VBS2) software program was selected for developing and administering the experimental scenarios.

3.5   Procedure

The participant, upon arrival to a predetermined lab location, was greeted by the experimenter. The experimenter cross-checked to ensure the participant had not been involved in previous SBT studies. If the participant was allowed to continue, he or she was randomly assigned to one of the three conditions. For all three conditions, environmental workload was controlled for by allocating lab space for each participant. After the participant was assigned to a condition, they completed an informed consent form. The informed consent was followed by the Ishihara Test for Colour Blindness [28] to ensure continued participation. Next, the demographics questionnaire was administered.

Following the demographics questionnaire, interface training was provided to each participant in order to familiarize them with system navigation and detection methods. Each participant then experienced a pre-test scenario. The scenario was intended to test a participant's prior knowledge of nervous and aggressive kinesic cues. A second iteration of interface training followed for all conditions. In general, the participant was asked to detect and classify yellow- and red-colored target barrels, distinct from non-target barrels of different colors. The Highlighting condition presented translucent blue boxes over the red and yellow barrels. The ME condition presented twice as many target barrels as the Highlighting condition, but lacked the non-content highlighting feature. The Kim's game preparation operated similarly to its corresponding kinesic-training form, with colored barrels instead of cue models. In all conditions, the implementation of barrels circumvented priming for the instructional material of kinesic cues.

Following the second interface training, the experimenter presented a PowerPoint demonstrating target behavior cues. The participant then completed the instructional training task, with the objective to identify target cues in the VE for the given condition. The NASA-TLX questionnaire was administered after the training scenarios. A 5-minute break followed the completed questionnaire. Afterward, the experimenter presented a slide deck as interface training for the post-test, and then administered the post-test scenario. Finally, the participant was thanked, debriefed, and dismissed. The experiment lasted up to 5 h. The research study was conducted through a multi-year effort.

4   Results

4.1   Assumption Testing

A between-groups one-way multivariate analysis of variance (MANOVA) was performed. The statistical assumptions of the MANOVA were investigated to ensure validity in the results. Testing with box-and-whisker plots, only one value was discovered as a potential outlier for the NASA-TLX mental demand scores. However, it was retained, since the z score was determined to be within 3 standard deviations from the mean. A Lilliefors test of normality revealed non-significance, indicating distributions were approximately normal. A regression analysis revealed no violations of Mahalanobis distances exceeding critical values. A Levene's test confirmed no violations across each of the groups, which supported the presence of homogeneous variance. Finally, a Box test indicated equality of the covariance matrix.

4.2 MANOVA Results

Results of the MANOVA revealed significance between the instructional strategies and the dependent variables of mental and global demand F (6, 262) = 10.08, $p < .001$; a Pillai's trace = .375; partial eta squared = .19. Pillai's trace was selected due to its resistance against any undesired effects that have been introduced by the variations in sample sizes among the independent variable [29]. A Bonferroni adjustment for the significance level was implemented to determine additional significance by each dependent variable. The adjusted significance level of .025 revealed significance for mental demand F (3, 131) = 18.866, $p < .001$, partial eta squared = .30 and global demand F (3, 131) = 21.91, $p < .001$, partial eta squared = .33.

A post hoc analysis (Tukey HSD) was conducted through two separate one-way analyses of variance (ANOVAs). An analysis of mental demand indicated statistically significant differences existed between the Highlighting, ME, and Kim's game groups. An analysis of global demand indicated significant differences between the Highlighting, ME, and Kim's game groups. An additional analysis of the means indicated that Kim's game contained the highest mean for mental demand ($M = 69.56$, $SD = 19.04$) and global demand ($M = 45.00$, $SD = 11.98$).

5   Discussion

H1: Highlighting produces the lowest mental demand and lowest global demand compared to ME and Kim's game.

Hypothesis 1 was fully supported. The use of Highlighting for behavior cue detection could serve as a multipurpose tool. Highlighting's lower degree of mental demand suggests that it may serve to compliment other strategies that require a higher degree of mental resources (e.g. Highlighting may be layered with Kim's game). The application of Highlighting in high-resource strategies could serve to improve a Soldier's cognitive skillsets in change detection training. As an example, a Highlighting strategy could require a novice user to methodically scan a visual scene, as is common in sniper fieldcraft and improvised explosive device detection. The user would first practice following an expert-level visual path with an identifiable cue. Then, the user would later perform the scan, without the cue, in the same methodical fashion.

The results add empirical support for the analysis by Carroll, Milham, and Champney [22], who suggested that Highlighting may be used effectively to assist in an AAR. AARs often serve as a way for a user or trainee to receive feedback from a more skilled instructor. The low degree of global demand for Highlighting suggests it is an ideal method for enhancing AAR feedback. A user could easily orient toward a specific area of visual interest, while an instructor coaches the user.

H2: Kim's game produces higher mental demand than Highlighting, but not less mental demand than ME; and produces higher global demand than both Highlighting and ME.

Hypothesis 2 received partial support. As expected, global demand was highest for Kim's game, likely due to the requirements of the strategy (e.g. temporal demand and effort). The high degree of mental demand for Kim's game suggests that the number of targets or stimuli a user must process simultaneously may not necessarily be the primary influence on his or her mental demand rating. The concept of having two strategies may have had the reverse effect predicted, and created additive workload; or perhaps only one strategy was used, and this one strategy was more complex than that used by the Massed Exposure group participants. That is, the Massed Exposure group's strategy for detection was more automatic. A user's perception of mental demand may be influenced predominately by the WM demands of the instructional strategies, since a user is consciously aware of WM processes (for a review, see Estes [30]). Learned perceptual processes are more automatic, which reduces the likelihood that the user is aware they are engaged in information processing. The conscious awareness of items held in WM could account for the high degree of mental demand found in Kim's game. Through consideration of the amount of mental demand a task requires, instructors may inform their task-to-strategy requirement decisions: if a Soldier is a novice to threat detection training, transfer of learning from SBT to the real-world could be facilitated by introduction with a low-workload strategy. As learner proficiency increases, the instruction may progress to a higher-level workload strategy.

H3: ME produces higher mental demand than both Highlighting and Kim's game, but produces only less global demand than Kim's game.

Hypothesis 3 received partial support. Contrary to the original hypothesis, mental demand was not highest for ME. It appears that ME relies on selective attention, which is dependent on the amount and type of load imposed by a task [31]. A user requires working memory as a primary source of mental demand in Kim's game. Target detection using ME may have become an automatic process, which reduced cognitive resources beyond that of Kim's game. Additionally, this process may be a consequence of the user's pre-exposure to the perceptual stimuli during the pre-test scenario. Although each strategy began with a pre-test scenario, ME is highly similar to the pre-test scenario than that of Kim's game. Research by Basile and Hampton [32] suggests that recognition of a task is much easier and faster than recall. Thus, familiarity of the task stimuli (due to pre-exposure in the pre-test scenario) may have reduced challenges and difficulties related to mental demand.

Unsurprisingly, ME's effect on participant's global demand was lower than that of Kim's game, and higher than that of Highlighting. This may be explained by the increased effort, frustration, and/or temporal demand required for the Kim's game task. Perhaps, the ME strategy required less effort because the task was less exhausting and the scenario itself was continuous and appeared to be seamless. The temporal separation between interdependent scenes could cause confusion. These explanations help to support the reduced overall global workload participant scores in the ME group, in comparison to Kim's game participants.

Adopting ME as an instructional design application for detection training can be beneficial in areas where an individual's visual load is saturated with stimuli. ME has the potential to increase focus for target identification amongst distraction. For example, an air traffic controller may benefit from training using ME to improve detection accuracy for identifying an airplane in imminent danger. In addition, the medical field could benefit from using ME training, because it would train professionals to be more accurate in detecting abnormalities in X-rays and MRI scans. Further research on brain activity (and other physiological measures) during threat detection could provide additional findings to explain and compare the demands of the strategies, further defining their role in future training.

5.1 Additional Considerations

Previous studies, which assessed performance aspects of the present experiment, add depth to understanding workload differences. Notably, post-test detection accuracy scores did not significantly differ between Highlighting and Massed Exposure conditions; nor did detection accuracy percent-change scores (i.e., change in detection accuracy from pre-test to post-test) [33]. Similarly, post-test detection accuracy scores did not significantly differ between Kim's game and Massed Exposure conditions; nor did detection accuracy percent-change scores [7]. In other words, none of the strategies compared had a substantial impact on detection performance. This lack of objective difference leads to considering measures of subjective workload as insightful criterions. According to our results, Highlighting has a more efficient use of workload than ME, and ME has a more efficient use of workload than Kim's game (no study has compared performance differences between Highlighting and Kim's game).

Although the NASA-TLX provides a reliable measure of general workload, the survey is insensitive to denote types of load formalized in the Cognitive Load Theory (CLT). Within CLT, load drivers are divided into three kinds, all of which relate to working memory demands: intrinsic load deals with the nature of information to be learned, and the previous domain knowledge of a user; extraneous load deals with aspects of instructional design irrelevant to knowledge acquisition; and germane load deals with the amount of resources a user directs toward learning [34]. As such, future investigation should consider whether load was incurred in an intrinsic, extraneous, or germane way. For example, Kim's game may have had high workload due to extraneous load (e.g., the temporal separation of model references may have induced high demands on working memory) or germane load (e.g., the puzzle was highly engaging, and this frustration-as-fun effect drew motivational resources for learning).

6   Conclusion

As an initial empirical assessment of cue detection training through a virtual simulation, this study framed workload demands from lowest to highest, in terms of three strategies' mental and global demands. Differences of workload were determined at significant levels for Highlighting, Massed Exposure, and Kim's game strategies. Their distinctions were contextualized by functions of human perception, such as attention and working memory. Further, the differences in workload afford a designer a systematic selection rationale for learning activities. For applications, Highlighting suggests a way to scaffold (e.g., scan-path training) and a way to reinforce feedback; Kim's game may be suitable for high-challenge needs; and Massed Exposure lends itself to professionals (e.g., air traffic controllers, doctors analyzing X-rays) for practice of crucial decisions via saturated event instances.

Acknowledgments. This research was sponsored by Dr. Irwin Hudson of the U.S. Army Research Laboratory Human Research Engineering Directorate Advanced Training and Simulation Division (ARL HRED ATSD), under contract W911NF-14-2-0021. However, the views, findings, and conclusions contained in this presentation are solely those of the author and should not be interpreted as representing the official policies, either expressed or implied, of ARL HRED ATSD or the U.S. Government. The U.S. Government is authorized to reproduce and distribute reprints for Government.

References

1. Fautua, D., Schatz, S., Kobus, D., Spiker, V.A., Ross, W., Johnston, J.H., Reitz, E.A.: Border Hunter Research Technical Report. U.S. Joint Forces Command, Norfolk (2010)
2. Birdwhistell, R.L.: Kinesics and Context: Essays on Body Motion Communication. University of Pennsylvania, Philadelphia (1970)
3. Wickens, C.D.: Engineering Psychology and Human Performance. HarperCollins, New York (1992)
4. Baddeley, A.D., Hitch, G.: Working memory. In: Bower, G.H. (ed.) The Psychology of Learning and Motivation: Advances in Research and Theory, vol. 8, pp. 47–89. Academic Press, New York (1974)
5. Awh, E., Barton, B., Vogel, E.K.: Visual working memory represents a fixed number of items regardless of complexity. Psychol. Sci. **18**(7), 622–628 (2007)
6. Fougnie, D.: The relationship between attention and working memory. In: Johansen, J.B. (ed.) New Research on Short-Term Memory, pp. 1–45. Nova Biomedical Books, New York (2008)
7. Maraj, C.: Investigating simulation-based pattern recognition training for behavior cue detection (Doctoral dissertation) (2015). http://stars.library.ucf.edu/etd/1285/. Accessed
8. Hart, S.G., Staveland, L.E.: Development of NASA-TLX (Task Load Index): Results of empirical and theoretical research. In: Hancock, P.A., Meshkati, N., Hancock, P.A., Meshkati, N. (eds.), Human Mental Demand, pp. 139–183. Oxford, North-Holland (1988). doi:10.1016/S0166-4115(08)62386-9
9. Colle, H.A., Reid, G.B.: Estimating a mental workload redline in a simulated air-to-ground combat mission. Int. J. Aviat. Psychol. **15**, 303–319 (2005)
10. Grier, R., Wickens, C., Kaber, D., Strayer, D., Boehm-Davis, D., Trafton, J.G., John, M.S.: The red-line of workload: theory, research, and design. Proc. Hum. Factors Ergon. Soc. Annu. Meet. **52**(18), 1204–1208 (2008). Sage Publications
11. Kyndt, E., Dochy, F., Struyven, K., Cascallar, E.: The direct and indirect effect of motivation for learning on students' approaches to learning through the perceptions of workload and task complexity. High. Educ. Res. Dev. **30**(2), 135–150 (2011)

12. Bentzen, M., Lemyre, P.N., Kenttä, G.: Development of exhaustion for high-performance coaches in association with workload and motivation: a person-centered approach. Psychol. Sport Exerc. **22**, 10–19 (2016)
13. Yurko, Y.Y., Scerbo, M.W., Prabhu, A.S., Acker, C.E., Stefanidis, D.: Higher mental workload is associated with poorer laparoscopic performance as measured by the NASA-TLX tool. J. Soc. Simul. Healthc. **5**(5), 267–271 (2010)
14. Brookings, J.B., Wilson, G.F., Swain, C.R.: Psychophysiological responses to changes in workload during simulated air traffic control. Biol. Psychol. **42**(3), 361–377 (1996)
15. Hsu, S.H., Wen, M.H., Wu, M.C.: Exploring design features for enhancing players' challenge in strategy games. CyberPsychology Behav. **10**(3), 393–397 (2007)
16. Hart, S.: NASA-Task load index (NASA-TLX): 20 years later. Proc. Hum. Factors Ergon. Soc. Annual Meet. **50**(9), 904–908 (2006). Sage Publications, Los Angeles
17. Grier, R.A.: How high is high? a meta-analysis of NASA-TLX global demand scores. Proc. Hum. Factors Ergon. Soc. Ann. Meet. **59**(1), 1727–1731 (2015). Sage Publications, Los Angeles
18. Sheridan, T.B.: Defining our terms. Presence Teleoperators Virtual Environ. **1**(2), 272–274 (1992)
19. Todorov, E., Shadmehr, R., Bizzi, E.: Augmented feedback presented in a virtual environment accelerates learning of a difficult motor task. J. Mot. Behav. **29**(2), 147–158 (1997)
20. Eschenbrenner, B., Nah, F.F., Siau, K.: 3-D virtual worlds in education: applications, benefits, issues, and opportunities. J. Database Manag. (JDM) **19**(4), 91–110 (2008)
21. Cannon-Bowers, J.A., Bowers, C.: Synthetic learning environments: on developing a science of simulation, games, and virtual worlds for training. Learn. Training Dev. Organ., 229–261 (2009)
22. Carroll, M., Milham, L., Champney, R.: Military observations: perceptual skills training strategies. In: Proceedings of the Interservice/Industry Training, Simulation, and Education Conference (I/ITSEC), Arlington, VA: NTSA (2009)
23. Posner, M.I.: Orienting of attention. Q. J. Exp. Psychol. **32**(1), 3–25 (1980). doi: 10.1080/00335558008248231
24. Maraj, C.S., Lackey, S.J., Badillo-Urquiola, K.A., Hudson, I.L.: Assessment of Kim's game strategy for behavior cue detection: engagement, flow, & performance aspects. In: Lackey, S., Shumaker, R. (eds.) Virtual, Augmented and Mixed Reality. VAMR 2016. Lecture Notes in Computer Science, vol. 9740, pp. 156–163. Springer, Cham (2016). doi: 10.1007/978-3-319-39907-2_15
25. Kipling, R.: KIM. Macmillan & Co., London (1901)
26. Jerome, C., Witmer, B., Mouloua, M.: Attention orienting in augmented reality environments: effects of multimodal cues. Proc. Hum. Factors Ergon. Soc. Ann. Meet. **50**(17), 2114–2118 (2006). Sage Publications
27. Rensink, R.A.: Change detection. Annu. Rev. Psychol. **53**(1), 245–277 (2002)
28. Ishihara, S.: Ishihara's Tests for Colour Deficiency. Kanehara Trading, Tokyo (2013)
29. Olson, C.L.: On choosing a test statistic in multivariate analysis of variance. Psychol. Bull. **83**, 579–586 (1976). doi:10.1037/0033-2909.83.4.579
30. Estes, S.: The workload curve: subjective mental demand. Hum. Factors **57**(7), 1174–1187 (2015). doi:10.1177/0018720815592752
31. Burnham, B.R., Sabia, M., Langan, C.: Components of working memory and visual selective attention. J. Exp. Psychol. Hum. Percept. Perform. **40**(1), 391–403 (2014). doi:10.1037/a0033753
32. Basile, B., Hampton, R.: Recognition errors suggest fast familiarity and slow recollection in rhesus monkeys. J. Learn. Mem. **20**(8), 431–437 (2013). doi:10.1101/lm.029223.112

33. Salcedo, J.N.: Instructional strategies for Scenario-Based Training of human behavior cue detection and classification with Robot-Aided Intelligence, Surveillance, and Reconnaissance. (Doctoral dissertation). (2014). http://stars.library.ucf.edu/etd/1304/. Accessed
34. Sweller, J., Ayres, P., Kalyuga, S.: Cognitive Load Theory. Springer, New York (2011). doi: 10.1007/978-1-4419-8126-4

HoloLens for Assembly Assistance - A Focus Group Report

Rafael Radkowski[✉] and Jarid Ingebrand

Virtual Reality Applications Center, Iowa State University, Ames, IA, USA
rafael@iastate.edu

Abstract. The paper reports about the result of a focus group study, which volunteers worked with the Microsoft HoloLens on an assembly task. In this AR scenario, virtual 3D models, annotations, and text are used to convey assembly instructions. All physical parts of the assembly were tracked, thus, their position and orientation known, which facilitates to align virtual objects with a 3D model. In this study, we asked a group of mechanical engineering students whether they consider the HoloLens as an adequate device to convey assembly information. The students were selected from a machine design course, in which topics such as component design and manufacturing are addresses. The students were asked to work with the HoloLens on a short assembly task and to complete a questionnaire to measure their attitude. The results are inconclusive and divide the group into advocates and objectors.

Keywords: Augmented reality · Engineering · Assembly assistance · HoloLens · Virtual instructions

1 Introduction

The Microsoft HoloLens is one of the latest members that joined the growing number augmented reality (AR)-capable displays. Although Microsoft did not label this unit as a sole AR display, they prefer holographic computing, it definitely facilitates typical AR applications. A huge benefit is the embedded tracking capability of the HoloLens, which allows the device to compute its position and orientation relative to the environment. In an AR scenario tracking facilitates to augment physical objects with virtual information, thus, to enrich the environment and to convey instructions. One caveat, the HoloLens tracking enables self-tracking and does not allow one to recognize and track physical objects with its onboard technology, which is a necessity for assembly assistance.

One goal of our research is to improve AR-assisted assembly and assembly training. In an assembly scenario, the display is used to convey assembly instructions, shown as registered 3D models. An assembly task is usually a procedural task. The operator follows a given sequence of assembly steps. Thus, the 3D models demonstrate step-by-step what an operator is supposed to do (Fig. 1). Text, voice, and videos can provide additional help, if a user requests them.

The HoloLens is a good base platform for an AR-assisted assembly scenario. It has features and advantages that make it an ideal choice for this scenario, however, it disadvantages may also disqualify it. The advantages: It comes along with a high-quality

© Springer International Publishing AG 2017
S. Lackey and J. Chen (Eds.): VAMR 2017, LNCS 10280, pp. 274–282, 2017.
DOI: 10.1007/978-3-319-57987-0_22

Fig. 1. (a–c) The images show the view through a HoloLens (recorded via the HoloLens's RGB camera). The 3D models are used to convey assembly instructions step-by-step. (A video is available at https://youtu.be/VApDEJMMc0M)

display, which allows for a high-quality rendering, it is self-embedded, thus, untethered, and its tracking latency is not noticeable. Its display renders clear, bright colors, still slightly transparent, but in our experience, users have no problems to see virtual instructions. It is also untethered, predecessors with a similar display quality were always tethered, which was always an obstacle for companies and interested user groups. A highlight is clearly the low tracking latency. Low since technically latency is still present, however, it is not noticeable. In our opinion, these three features are a benefit for users. The disadvantage is the limited field of view, especially when working in an assembly scenario. Everything that happens during the assembly of a product happens in armlengths of a user. Given this distance, almost every 3D model appears cropped. As a consequence, the instruction that a particular 3D model delivers is incomplete or can be misunderstood.

The objective of this study is to obtain the user's attitude towards the HoloLens for an AR-assisted assembly scenario and to determine whether the advantages outperform the disadvantages. In general, when working with the HoloLens, it is possible to catch the notion of the delivered instructions, although with some effort. The user needs to step back or turn his/her head often around. Previous research, which employed previous-generation head-mounted displays (HMD) for their studies regularly reported that a small field of view is one obstacle [1, 2]. Cables, low-quality displays, low comfort in general is an additional obstacle [3–5]. However, studies also report that users prefer AR despite bulky and inconvenient displays [4, 5]. Our assumption is that the attitude towards this technology changed due to the popularity the technology gained in the last month, thus, users might be more open to try and work with devices such as the HoloLens. Along with features such as good display, comfortable to wear, and not noticeable latency, users might see devices such as the HoloLens as an asset. To determine this attitude is our objective.

Therefore, we asked a group of students to participate in a study, to test the HoloLens using an AR assembly assistance application, and to report their opinion using a questionnaire. In the following, we introduce our test setup and the application (Sect. 2). Section 3 describes the study and reports the results. We close with a conclusion and an outlook in Sect. 4.

2   Test Setup and Application

2.1   Test Setup

Our test setup is shown in Fig. 2. It is a typical tabletop setup which mainly incorporates a Kinect camera, along with the subsequent computer, and a HoloLens. The Kinect camera is connected to the computer. We use the Kinect to recognize and track single objects on the breadboard in order to augment the physical parts with virtual instructions. Our tracking software processes the range data from the Kinect to compute a pose for all physical parts of interest on the workbench with respect to a camera coordinate system [6, 7]. The HoloLens is used to render virtual objects, such as 3D models to convey assembly instructions (Fig. 1).

Fig. 2. The system setup.

An overview of the software architecture is shown in Fig. 3. We use two software tools, one for tracking and one to render virtual content with the HoloLens. Our tracking tool *TrackingExpert* [2] facilitates to track objects using the range camera data, which is transformed into a point set. It employs feature descriptors matching and the Iterative Closest Point (ICP, [8]) algorithm. A feature descriptor is a mathematical model to describe the curvature characteristics of the surface around a point. It is used to represent the surface characteristics of a part as a compressed signature, reduced to a set of parameters. We employ axis-angle feature descriptors and histogram matching, inspired by [9, 10]. Feature descriptor matching is used to find the object in the input point cloud and to estimate a pose. Subsequently, ICP is used to refine the pose and to align a reference point set with the point cloud fetched from the Kinect camera. ICP increases the registration fidelity. The outcome of this tracking procedure is a matrix [**R**|**t**] representing the pose of an object in camera coordinate system. The pose is forwarded to a HoloLens application via TCP/IP.

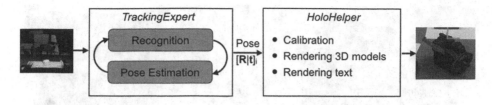

Fig. 3. Software architecture of the test system

Our HoloLens application, called *HoloHelper*, is a general rendering application written with Unity support. Its basic functionality is to receive tracking pose data for different objects *i* and to render virtual content assigned to these objects using the given pose. The application was prepared as a general renderer, not tied to any specific purpose. The software also includes the application logic to switch between assembly steps. The entire configuration for a particular application is read from an xml file.

The HoloLens needs to be calibrated and aligned with the outside Kinect tracking system to display virtual objects correctly. Correctly means in most of our application cases that a 3D model needs to appear aligned with a physical object. We use marker based tracking for calibration. An ARToolkit [11] marker is attached underneath the Kinect camera (Fig. 2). Before the application starts, the HoloLens asks the user to align the HoloLens's front camera with the marker to estimate the spatial relation between HoloLens and camera. This procedure initializes an initial vector along with an orientation delta. When the user now starts to move, the HoloLens can track its own position relative to this initial points, which further facilitates to calculate the pose of each object with respect to the HoloLens's camera coordinate system, hence, to render virtual objects accordingly. If the position of the Kinect does not change, further recalibration is not always necessary because the HoloLens stores the location as anchor point.

2.2   Assembly Application Scenario

We prepared an assembly application scenario in which users were asked to assemble a piston motor as shown in Fig. 4. The piston motor is a hydraulically controlled, variable (L/K series) motor. The entire unit measures roughly 7" tall, 7" wide, and 9" long including the output shaft, it weighs 34 lb. It contains 28 major parts, which need to be assembled in 14 assembly steps. For our test, we asked user to assemble eight parts in four assembly steps. We reduced the number of steps since the assembly of the complete motor takes approximately 45 min. Since we intended to work with a group, we had to prevent that the other members of the group have to wait for two hours until everybody assembled the motor once.

The AR application we prepared indicates the assembly steps using 3D models; three steps are shown in Fig. 1. Each 3D model is animated. The animation shows the assembly direction. Animations are not always necessary, since the assembly direction is obvious for many parts. However, for parts such as the shaft, a swash plate, a piston, the animation provides necessary information. All animations run in an infinite loop. We use voice commands to switch between assembly steps, the user needs to say "next" to step to the

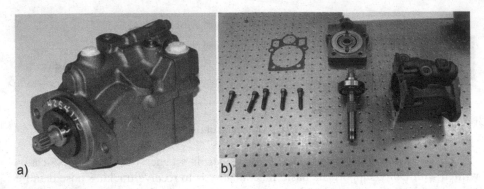

Fig. 4. (a) The axial piston motor was object for this study. (b) We asked uses to assemble a shaft, a bearing, a gasket, an endcap, and five screws.

next assembly step. The voice commands are processed using the built-in Cortana voice control.

3   Focus Group Study and Results

The goal of this study was to obtain the users' attitude towards the HoloLens, in particular, whether the HoloLens is an adequate device for an application such as assembly assistance and whether the advantages of the HoloLens outperform the disadvantages. We recruited volunteers, students from a mechanical engineering class. The group was limited to students from a machine design class for three reasons. First, the volunteers should have a connection to the application in order to notice advantages. The students of this class learn about shafts, gaskets, pistons, bearing, know their functionalities beyond layman knowledge and also learn how to assemble components into a working product. Thus, they are familiar with the topic. People from different disciplines may have a harder time to assess whether the application can contribute to assembly. Second, the students are most likely not pre-coined to other assembly assisting technologies, due to their lack of experience, and at the same time are literate in using modern technology. Third, we intend to integrate devices such as the HoloLens into classroom education where appropriate. Thus, we intended to level the students' attitude to using and learning with such a device. In this context, this study is part of a larger ongoing study which investigates opportunities for this technology in mechanical engineering education. Therefore, the study was a part of the students' homework. The study is sanctioned by the Iowa State University Institutional Review Board.

3.1   Procedure and Data Collection

We assembled groups of three to five volunteers for the study, 32 students in total (30 men, 2 women, 9 with glasses, nobody used the HoloLens before). Each group was guided as a whole into the study area. First, the group was introduced to the lab area and the HoloLens including a short introduction about the HoloLens' functionality and capabilities. Each student could test the HoloLens, the standard holograms for a few minutes. The experimenter also introduced the piston motor and explained its functionality to the students.

After the introduction, the students were asked to assemble the piston motor following the introduction as shown by the HoloLens. The students were separated for this task and the remaining students were asked to wait until everybody assembled the motor once. Each trial took about 6–8 min. The students were asked to not discuss the HoloLens application at this point and to not share their experience.

When all students completed the task, we assembled the group and first asked the students to complete a questionnaire. The questionnaire presented eight statements. We used a 5-point Likert scale to obtain the students' attitude where 1 means *strongly agree* and 5 *strongly disagree*:

1. I could easily understand and follow the instructions shown as 3D models.
2. The instructions shown though the display were helpful.
3. The HoloLens is convenient to wear.
4. I feel confident that I performed well in completing this task.
5. I would recommend the HoloLens to other people as visual instruction device.
6. The HoloLens is fun to work with.

The first questions aimed to learn whether the volunteers understood the instructions. The 3D models are cropped by the HoloLens display and it might be challenging to understand the instructions without looking from the left to the right. Question two measured whether the instructions where considered as necessary.

The remaining two statements were

7. I looked past the HoloLens's display to assemble the piston motor.
8. I had to move my head often to completely see and understand the instructions.

The students could answer with *never, randomly, sometimes, often, very often*. We asked question 7 because we noticed in previous tests that users sometimes look underneath the holographic display to obtain a free look towards the physical object. The last questions measures whether the students noticed that they had to move their head often when working with the HoloLens.

After the students completed the questionnaire, we asked them to discuss and agree on further advantages and disadvantages of the HoloLens in context of machine design, assembly, and instructions in general. To encourage the discussion, we gave them keywords such as, *wearing devices*, *voice control*, *field-of-view*, and *safety*. We asked the group to discuss each point for a few minutes and to write down their opinion. We further encouraged them to discuss other topics, if they have additional ones. A facilitator moderated the discussion, however, did not contributed or influenced opinions.

3.2 Results

The results of the questionnaire are shown in Fig. 5. and the quantitative values are listed in Table 1. Each box diagram shows the results for one question. The overall mean for all questions is 1.66 with a standard deviation of 0.42. In general, the students agree that the instructions were helpful and that they used them to assemble the piston motor. The students disagree about the convenience of the HoloLens. We notice almost a 50% split into people who had no problems wearing the HoloLens and people who are neutral. The questions 4 to 6 yield a positive result from our point of view. With a few exceptions, the students like to work with a HoloLens.

Questionnaire results

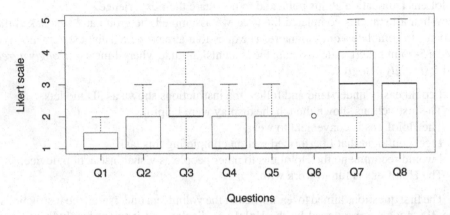

Fig. 5. Results of the questionnaire

Table 1. Quantitative values for each question, mean (standard deviation)

Q1	Q2	Q3	Q4	Q5	Q6	Q7	Q8
1.25 (0.44)	1.50 (0.57)	2.38 (0.66)	1.34 (0.55)	1.47 (0.62)	1.12 (0.34)	2.94 (1.19)	2.44 (1.11)

The result to Question 7 and Question 8 is inconclusive. The majority of students said they walked too much when assembling the piston motor to obtain an overall view and that they also looked pass the HoloLens's displays to obtain a better view of the situation.

The results of the students' discussion are mostly positive. The majority of the students told us that they liked to work with the HoloLens. Some reported that they like the device's functionality even if they do not like to wear it. All students agree that it is fun to see graphics in the environment.

On the negative side, the most common statement we notice is regarding the small field of view of, which is an obstacle when working with the device in close range to objects. A larger group of students also mentioned that the gesture is tiring after a few minutes of use (we did not allow the students to use the clicker). They wish for a more convenient way to manipulate objects if they have to do it for a longer period of time. The same comments were made regarding the scrolling gesture. A few students reported that they would prefer "to work on a computer display" if they have to walk around when using the HoloLens. Nobody commented on voice control or on safety concerns.

3.3   Discussion

The results indicate a clear attitude of the students in favor for the HoloLens for a close range application such as assembly instruction. The questionnaire results are mostly positive. The additional feedback that we obtain also does not add many negative points. As expected, the students want to have a larger field of view and more convenient hand gesture. On the positive end, although the field-of-view is reported to be an obstacle, the majority of students can arrange to work with it; it would prevent them from using the device. We notice a similar result considering the convenience. Students reported that they dislike wearing the device, although they would work with it, if they would be asked to. One caveat that needs to be considered is the limited time the volunteers worked with the HoloLens. Thus, it is unclear whether a longer period would change their opinion.

Second, several students agreed that they can imagine that an application such as assembly assistance is a perfect use case for the HoloLens. They can further image to use the application in class to demonstrate the functionality of machines. Shafts, pistons, and other machine components are never demonstrated in operation in class. Thus, students mentioned that an application that would virtually demonstrate how parts interact can help.

On the flipside, some students reported that they just do not like to wear the device. Mostly because they disliked that the device is tied around their head. No further reasons were reported such as safety or privacy concerns. We also noticed a dislike among glass wearers. They did not feel comfortable using the HoloLens while wearing their glasses. Removing the glasses for the time of the experiment increased unease because the HoloLens did not support lens correction and the volunteers were not used to not wear their glasses.

4   Conclusion and Outlook

In this effort, we conducted a focus group study with three groups a five volunteers to obtain the students' attitude towards the HoloLens and an instruction application. The HoloLens can convey instructions to users using virtual content and we were interested to study whether students can consider to work with devices such as the HoloLens. The volunteers were asked to use the HoloLens for an assembly task and to complete a questionnaire. The results of the experiment and the questionnaire support the assembly application use case. The volunteers reported that the HoloLens was helpful assembling a physical part. Although we found that some people just do not like to wear the Holo-Lens, which appear to be a personal trait against wearing devices.

In future, we intend to focus on an improved application design that leverages the advantages of the HoloLens such as context-related information. Application features that can further demonstrate advantages of the HoloLens in comparison to other means such as textbooks, etc. may change the students' attitude.

References

1. Syberfeldt, A., Danielsson, O., Holm, M., Ekblom, T.: Augmented reality at the industrial shop-floor, In: 1st International on Augmented and Virtual Reality, Lecce, 17–20 September 2014 (2014)
2. Yuan, M.L., Ong, S.K., Nee, A.Y.C.: Augmented reality for assembly guidance using a virtual interactive tool. Int. J. Prod. Res. **46**(7), 1745–1767 (2008)
3. Sausman, J., Samoylov, A., Harkness Regli, S., Hopps, M.: Effect of eye and body movement on augmented reality in manufacturing domain. In: IEEE International Symposium on Mixed and Augmented Reality, 4–8 November 2012, Atlanta, Georgia, pp. 315–316 (2012)
4. Henderson, S., Feiner, S.: Augmented reality in the psychomotor phase of a procedural task. In: Proceedings of the 2011 10th IEEE International Symposium on Mixed and Augmented Reality, Basel, Switzerland, 26–29 October 2011 (2011)
5. Wiedenmaier, S., Oehme, O., Schmidt, L., Luczak, H.: Augmented Reality (AR) for assembly processes design and experimental evaluation. Int. J. Hum. Comput. Interact. **16**(3), 497–514 (2003)
6. Radkowski, R.: Object tracking with a range camera for augmented reality assembly assistance. J. Comput. Inf. Sci. Eng. **16**(1), 1–8 (2016)
7. Radkowski, R., Garrett, T., Ingebrand, J., Wehr, D.: TrackingExpert - a versatile tracking toolbox for augmented reality. In: The ASME 2016 International Design Engineering Technical Conferences & Computers and Information in Engineering Conference on IDETC/CIE 2016, Charlotte, NC (2016)
8. Drost, B., Ulrich, M., Navab, N., Ilic., S.: Model globally, match locally: efficient and robust 3D object recognition. In: Proceedings of the IEEE Conference on Computer Vision and Pattern Recognition (CVPR) (2010)
9. Rusu, R.B., Blodow, N., Beetz, M.: Fast point feature histograms (FPFH) for 3D registration. In: International Conference on Robotics and Automation, pp. 3212–3217 (2009)
10. Besl, P., McKay, N.: A method for registration of 3D-shapes. Trans. Pattern Anal. Mach. Intell. **18**(8), 239–256 (1992)
11. Kato, H., Billinghurst, M.: Marker tracking and HMD calibration for a video-based augmented reality conferencing system. In: Proceedings of the 2nd International Workshop on Augmented Reality (IWAR 1999), October, San Francisco, USA (1999)

Playing Both Sides

Analyzing Live-Action-Role-Play as a Method for Simulating Complex Technical Interactions

Marcel Schmittchen[✉]

Department for Information and Technology Management,
Ruhr-University Bochum, Bochum, Germany
marcel.schmittchen@ruhr-uni-bochum.de

Abstract. This paper examines the possibilities of evaluating the human computer interactions of an immersive Mixed Reality Live Action Role-play project. In this special game scenario, the participants of the game took over the roles of users and the computer system interacting with each other via a chat environment masked as a command line interface. After first inspection of the logs from the project a methodology that took different micro-sociological theories, as well as communication and language theories (in particular with respect to specifics of chat-based communications and related language behavior) into account based on qualitative content analysis and grounded theory approaches was applied to evaluate the data. Despite the limitations and spontaneous nature of the game both social and communicative phenomena in the physical and virtual world were identified. It was also verified that the interactions that took place within the simulated computer system followed known rules and expectations of human-computer interactions.

Keywords: Mixed reality games · Live Action Role-play · Chat communication · Social roles · Awareness · Cooperation · Human computer interaction

1 Introduction

Playful, media-based learning is considered as innovative and forward-looking for research and teaching purposes. Thus new formats find their way into non-formal education and university research, including the so-called Mixed Reality Games. With a mix of virtual and real worlds they promise new learning experiences and lasting effects. For example, a series of mixed reality games that simulate, examine and evaluate the coordination of rescue teams in disaster scenarios [5, 12].

For several years mixed reality games are already in use in the non-formal youth and adult education, in particular in the political (media-) education. Having experience with innovative teaching methods in this field the "Bildungsstätte Alte Schule Anspach e.V."[1]

---

[1] www.basa.de.

© Springer International Publishing AG 2017
S. Lackey and J. Chen (Eds.): VAMR 2017, LNCS 10280, pp. 283–301, 2017.
DOI: 10.1007/978-3-319-57987-0_23

developed and produced the "Project Exodus – An EducationLiveRoleplay"[2] (original German title "Projekt Exodus - Ein BildungsLiverollenspiel").

The project was promoted by the German Federal Agency for Civic Education. The work on the project stretched from September 2014 to March 2015 and was carried out by a team consisting of about 30 voluntaries, full-time and freelance workers.[3] The core multi-day game itself took place in Wilhelmshaven, Germany in February 2015. Based on the science fiction television series "Battlestar Galactica" in its 2004 reinterpretation this mixed reality game was aiming to raise awareness for current political topics in a playful and abstract way for target groups from underprivileged educational backgrounds. With sophisticated use of equipment and technology the museum-ship Mölders[4] was transformed into the fictional spaceship HESPERIOS. This included fictional computer systems onboard allowing participants to simulate life and work on this spaceship. In addition to the videogame like simulation parts of the systems, a more flexible method was realized with hidden chat communications. In these chat systems players would act as users while the game masters would play the role of the ships computer. This communication was logged for evaluation purposes during the length of the role-playing game.

The evaluation of such a use of chat communication in the area of Mixed Reality Games is still very experimental. Therefore, the data results were openly considered and evaluated.

Based on micro-sociological theories, especially following the dramaturgical perspective of Goffman [8, 9] as well as the peculiarities of chat-based communications and related language behavior, a qualitative content analysis methodology was implemented and several hypotheses created. Besides these, phenomena of cooperation and (security) awareness, both among the players as well as in the joint game/simulation between players and game masters were also discovered.

2   Creating an Immersive Mixed Reality Live Action Role-Playing Game

2.1   Related Work

The experiences with implementing mixed reality live action role plays as a tool for research and educational projects is less pronounced. Game design so far is focused especially on the technological aspects and options [3]. Project Exodus in contrast focused mainly on the human and interpersonal components of the game. This was especially due to the educational goals of the game development as well as boundaries in regards to technical constraints within the projects short time.

To achieve the set educational goals, the design was based on the concept of pervasive games [15]. While previous game theories, such as those of Johan Huizinga [10] in the 1930s speak of a "magic circle" that separates the game world from the real world,

---

[2] www.projekt-exodus.com.
[3] Including the author of this paper.
[4] www.marinemuseum.de.

thus differentiating actions between these worlds, different forms of understanding evolved since the 1960s. In addition to sports, gambling and board games that were largely seen as common events, new genres and forms were created over the years and changed the concept of gaming profoundly. These include now well established forms like videogames and role-playing games [15].

The "magic" of the extraordinary and the isolation of playing by clear temporal and spatial boundaries no longer exist in modern society. For many players playing is a part of everyday life. Although many modern forms of games still have the "magic circle", it is today more to be understood as metaphor and agreement: Players agree on not to bring external motivations and personal histories into games and, at the same time, bringing no game experience into their normal life [15].

However, while these boundaries still exist, the clear divisions blur in the so-called "Pervasive Games". According to Montola [15] a pervasive game is expanding one or more of the bounds of the "magic circle". This can affect the spatial, temporal or social level of the game. By softening the classic game boundaries pervasive games are allowed to create game experiences that rub off on the normal everyday life or, in turn, can be shaped by it.

Eddegger [3] used, based on Walther [19] other terms to define similar spatial, temporal and social expansions of classic game theory and adds the element of trans-media narrative/storytelling. She describes pervasive games as a field, defined by the axis of mobility (in the virtual and real ingame-environment), persistence (in the sense of the permanent availability), distribution (understood here as a "combination of dynamic computing, networking and exchange of information" [3] and the transmedial storytelling.

This way pervasive game experiences can enrich everyday life and the game gains special appeal through immediacy and concreteness [15]. This effect is suitable for intensive and sustainable teaching and learning approaches.

In recent years many Pervasive Games with a clear educational goal were created. One of them is the "ProjectY" [17] in which economic and political theories are taught as a part of a crime-investigation plot. The game was carried out over a period of 21 days on various game platforms and devices, such as web sites, voice messages and emails [3].

Live action role-plays (from here on: LARPs) are especially capable to penetrate the boundaries between real life and game experiences because of their immediacy and experiential nature. In most LARPs players slip into pre-written roles acting in prepared locations. The game itself is similar in its design to improvisational theater, as player have to spontaneous respond to events and interact with other players [15]. Utilizing effects of pervasive game theory, special educational LARPs called "EduLARPs" find their application as a pedagogical method, because it is assumed that this form of playing is beneficial to the personal development and learning. The abstraction from ordinary everyday life, the freedom gained by new structures and opportunities, as well as the motivation through challenges and goals of the game (as opposed to the traditional teaching) are factors classic learning environment are missing [11].

So called Nordic-LARPs are a subgenre even more focused on immersion with the game world and thus promoting the principle of pervasive gaming even more. The momentum gaining design principle is called 360° Illusion [18]. Herein the game environment is as accurate as possible, in order to allow the players to fully immerse in the world. In addition, all activities in the game have to be connected to reality. All actions and interactions like hacking a computer, firing a gun or operating a machine are played out as actual physical acts, rather than symbolic activities used as a substitute. This level of reality does effect the players. Nordic-LARP players are often confronted with very intense physical and emotional situations [15]. This approach seemed fitting for the design of an EduLARP targeted to create lasting memories and experiences for adult players.

2.2 Project Realization

The final Project Exodus game lasted about two and a half days, consisting of four episodes 7–8 h each. The design and the post-apocalyptic scenario of the game was based on the TV series Battlestar Galactica in its reinterpretation from 2004 by Ronald D. Moore. The start of the game takes places during events happing in the pilot episode of the show. The few humans on board an old space cargo ship are fleeing from a hostile robot race and must deal with the complete loss of their civilizations and home worlds. Coming from a space travelling high tech civilization with a flourishing culture and democracy, a group of nearly 90 survivors is on their own and to their knowledge all that is left of their species.

Fig. 1. The venue and its fictional perception as a cargo freighter spaceship "Hesperios".

The almost 90 participants of the game were given prepared roles and background information divided into four main groups: the civilian crew of the freighter (primarily responsible for the operation of the ship), a group of scientists belonging to an ethically-questionable company, a military strike force ordered to confiscate the ship due to suspicions of illegal experiments done by the scientists and a large group of civilians (mostly dignitaries and celebrities) that were taken on board after their space luxury liner was destroyed.

The fictional world of the project was composed of the physical dimension on the ship and the virtual dimension defined by the technical components creating the illusion of the space outside the ship as well as simulating the avionics and inner workings of the spaceship itself (see Fig. 1).

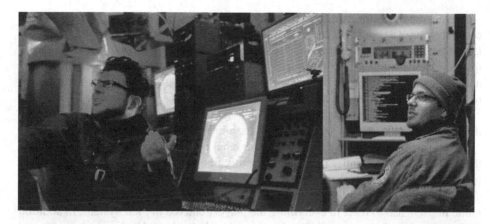

Fig. 2. GUI terminals for radar functions on the bridge (left) and a chat terminal in the communications room (right).

The use of technology in LARPs provides many benefits (e.g. automation, overcoming time and space limitations), but also comes with high costs for hardware and software since in most cases the development individual software is necessary [15].

A direct influence in the creation of Project Exodus's setting and design was the Swedish game "The Monitor Celestra" [4].

2.3 Technical Implementation

To give players a real 360° immersion next to the costumes and props a large effort was put on the installation and establishment of a credible fictional computer system. The system was designed to allow the game masters to influence events and plot of the game without ever being seen by the players. Also the usability of the fictional systems should enable players with no real life technical knowledge to masters complex technical tasks in their respective roles. The installed and used computer terminals can be separated into two groups. The graphic user interface (GUI) terminals and the chat terminals (see Fig. 2).

The GUI terminal served as means to control basic ship functions such as navigation, radar and energy distribution and were equipped with a professionally designed graphical interface, which, in its appearance, operation, and acoustics was similar to that of the original TV series.

This software also simulated the movements of the ship and other virtual entities around the ship such as planets or satellites. With a special "director view" control interface the game masters were able to monitor the actions of the players at all times and manipulate the game by creating enemy spaceships closing in or triggering technical malfunctions onboard.

Although these systems helped a lot to increase the immersion into the game world the number of terminals would only allow for a fraction of players to interact with those systems directly. Also the GUI terminals were limited to preprogrammed functions and not able to let players and game masters improvise new forms of functions and tasks spontaneously.

To ensure these options the so called chat terminals were added to the game. These computers used a simple IRC program masked to look like an old-fashioned Command-Line-Interface (CLI). Every terminal basically consisted of a chatroom with two participants. One called "User" (the player typing in commands in the game environment) and one called "System" (a member of the game masters group acting as the software reacting to the commands given).

Only one rule for interacting with the chat-system was given to the players prior to the game. Upon starting a session with a terminal the player had to enter the phrase "Login System" followed by their unique personal player-code. This code was used by the game masters to identify the player currently interacting with the system and (more importantly) their assigned roles.

Besides this rule the players could interact freely with the empty input mask and the game masters had to react to everything the players entered in their system. In addition to the many benefits several challenges existed on both sides. Unclear boundaries and rules could quickly lead to systems not used for their intended purposes, breaking the game immersion e.g. by using the chat-terminals for sending real chat messages instead of command lines. Before the start of the game only rough ideas in regards to the fictional inner workings of the spaceships systems were made. Instead they were worked out during the game based on the needs and preferences of the players while they interacted with the system.

Eight chat terminals were ultimately placed on board according to the logic of the fictional starship. The spatial limitations like power supply and accessibility played another important role in the planning. The final locations of the terminals within the game environment are shown in Fig. 3.

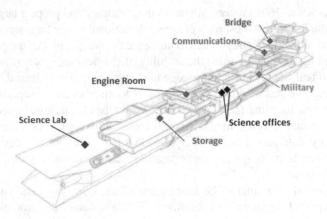

Fig. 3. Rough map of chat terminal locations

It should be noted that the technical perspective followed the idea of a "seamfull design" [1]. This principle helped to deal with the limitations and shortcomings of the technology in the game without breaking the immersion. Instead of hiding the technology the player is made aware of it and the gameplay and plot embraces it. This way technical failures in the game design can be considered and adjusted, so that players can experience them as part of the game and the game flow and not as failures of the game [15]. While the terminals, cables and controls were seamlessly as possible placed inside the naval ships environment technical defects and delays could easily worked into the games story. Since the spaceships history declared it as a very old vessel without the resources for a proper repair it was accepted by the players and their roles that many parts of their ship did not work or could fail them at any moment. Furthermore, the plot placed an enemy "AI" in the systems of the ship allowing to blame any inconsistencies or errors on this entity and also giving the game masters a backdoor to changing inner workings and logics for plot progression.

The game master's notebooks automatically saved every chat log in HTML format. The logs contained the submitted messages as well as timestamps for every input. Also the use of only two participants per chatroom allowed for an easy identification of message authors (red = player; blue = game masters). In addition, errors and connection-losses were logged as well.

For analyzing purposes larger blocks of error messages and test entries made during game breaks and system testing were removed. Leaving a total of 6415 lines of chat messages to be analyzed.

3   Analyzing the Data

3.1   Methods of Data Analysis

In order to evaluate the present transcripts of chat communication, methods of qualitative content analysis have been used. While the quantitative content analysis primarily focuses on the observation of frequencies of certain (text) properties, the qualitative content analysis also allows for an observance of context and context dependencies [2].

To analyze the present form of data normally categories are derived from theoretical models and then used on the data material [6]. In order to not lose the overview of the material, hypotheses and questions in regards to the material were created to limit the viewing angle for the evaluation in advance. Prior to the generation of hypotheses an exploration phase, which allows for a freer view of the data in light of existing theoretical knowledge has been utilized.

Since commands, intentions, and uses cases of a computer systems are usually determined by the rules of the applications or set in stone in the development of the systems requirements, there are no clear and common categories that could be used to describe the diverse interactions simulated by the players in the data. Therefore, the coding of player commands and inputs started without a specific theory background and followed a Grounded Theory approach. Step by step common forms of commands were grouped, general categories created and particularly interesting cases of system use and interaction identified.

The collected data is subjected to a secondary analysis, i.e. the data was created and collected with a different focus than it is now analyzed with. Since the author of this paper was involved in the planning and implementation of the game as a participant observer, knowledge about the data and its creation was already present before the creation of the actual hypotheses.

The participant observation by the author of this work has in this case only a small restriction on the quality of the collected data since the evaluation criteria were created after the game was already over. Also the author did only interact with the chat system during the game in the first 30 min and was no longer involved in the interactions of players and game masters after this point.

The participants knew that they were filmed for security reasons and that data of the game were to be eventually used for scientific research and for reflection of the civic/ political education goals. However, these were not directly related to the terminal inter-actions. Since the participants (players and game masters alike) could not know the specific details of future analysis no great impact on the material itself is to be feared from this fact (by definition of Scheufele [16]).

The used methodology was inspired by Früh [7] and Diekmann [5] and adapted to the previously described points and is shown in Fig. 4.

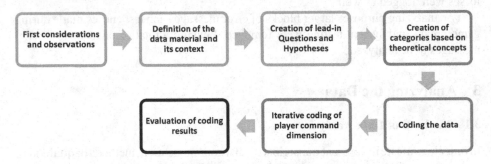

Fig. 4. The developed process used for the evaluation

3.2 Hypotheses

The developed hypotheses were based primarily on the dramaturgical approach of role theory by Goffman [9] and related phenomena like role expectations, role conflict and image management [8]. In transfer to the setting at hand the act of maintaining certain roles (game masters as the fictional computer system and players as users) happening in the joint communication on the chat terminals can be interpreted as a form of cooperative play. Both parties have strong urges to maintain the illusion and immersion of the game environment. Thus almost creating a scenario that could be described as an inverted "Turing Test" since the human game master's goal was to convince the players that they were indeed inter-acting with a deterministic system instead of another human being.

Current human computer interaction and sociotechnical standards took a backseat in the project since the simulated system was deliberately designed to feel slow, old and incon-venient to match the desperate setting of the game. Since command line interfaces are no longer as widespread as a few years ago earlier studies of interactions with CLIs were considered. Here researchers concluded that users want and tend to see the computer as a tool not an interaction partner [13]. They treat it not like an omnipotent being but rather as a naïve counterpart [14]. According to Zoeppritz [20] in 1985 in this form of interaction the use of natural language when dealing with a computer system is replaced by so called

"ComputerTalk". Similar to the self-inflicted reduction in complexity when talking to babies or not native speakers it is assumed that a special pattern of language is automatically used when interacting with command line interfaces.

Since the fictional system in the project would allow for a complete natural interaction this would mean that for the sake of the game illusion participants would still prefer the reduced syntax of "ComputerTalk" over using natural languages.

From these theoretical backgrounds and theories guiding questions and hypotheses were created (cf. Table 1). Section 4 will focus only on selected findings of the conducted data analysis.

Table 1. Overview of guiding questions and hypotheses

Guiding questions	Hypotheses/Assumptions	Theoretical background
Do players act according to their given roles and tasks or not?	The distribution of accesses and activities within the terminals corresponds with the role specifications and groups	Role expectations
How to players react to role conflicts and pressure?	Role conflicts and pressure can leading to a breach of immersion	Role acceptance and role conflicts
Was the interaction between game masters and players creating a cooperative play?	Game masters will try to stay in their role as the system. Even when trying to help or influence the players. They will ignore breaches of immersion by players or cope with it in a manner that prevents further abandoning the simulation	Image and impression management as cooperation
Which characteristics and peculiarities can be seen in the language and phrasing used in the game?	The game masters followed the players in their choice of language	Image and impression management as cooperation
	ComputerTalk will be preferred in order to maintain the illusion of a computer interaction	(Chat) Communication
What other special forms of use developed during the game?	(Instead of a hypotheses this question was evaluated more freely)	

3.3 Creating a Fitting Coding Scheme

The use of a qualitative analysis software (in this case MAXQDA) supported the coding process and the evaluation. While the coding itself has to be done by the researcher the software helps with the creation of coding-dictionaries, the visualization of relations and exporting the coding-data to other programs for further statistical evaluation [5, 9]. The creation and application of the coding scheme demanded multiple rounds of coding in different dimension.

The granularity of the coding is set to one code-label per chat message except for a few exceptions in the first coding dimension. With the help of retrieval functions of the MAXQDA software some special coding schemes were created automatically by finding for example "overlap" or "close range" connections between the dimensions presented here. These special coding schemes helped subsequent evaluation by finding even more connections and patterns. The basic coding dimensions were as follows:

Coding Dimension: Time and Terminal Users. These are trivial generated time slots identified by the time stamps connected to the messages and user identification based on the login rule that every player had to start their session with by typing in their unique player code. The time dimension is divided in blocks of one hour each and terminal user are coded for as long as a certain user is active on one terminal, usually ending when another user logs into the same system. Special cases such as multiple users at a time on one terminal or other overlapping users are also possible.

Coding Dimension: Language. In order to examine linguistic phenomena this coding dimension focuses on the language used by players and game masters.

Names and terms in a different language do not count as a break of a particular language. For example, "open access to lagerraum" still is counted as an English command and "Suche Daten im Ship-Log" as German. The coding for inputs of the players and the game masters are made apart from each other in order to later analyze a possible mutual influence.

English and German are also divided in categories of "natural language" and "ComputerTalk". ComputerTalk is coded when the messages are written mostly in imperative form using shortened syntax (e.g. "Search database entry X") as well as clear use of fictional or real world programming languages (e.g. SQL, Java). In contrast, entries in natural language syntax are often worded like a normal dialogue and are expanded with context information and details (e.g. "Open a channel to the other space-ship and show me his logbook so I can compare them with mine."). The latter can also occur if players break the immersion of their role by posting comments or questions as players to the game masters directly.

Coding Dimension: Inputs by the Game Masters. To examine the behavior of the game masters acting as the computer systems their inputs were coded based on the forms of reactions they gave to player inputs. The coding scheme included the following types of inputs: Pending Signal (e.g. "Processing..", "Please Wait", "Estimated Time: 5 m"); Question/Request (e.g. "Username?", "Please Enter Password"); General Information/ Statement (e.g. Informing players on terminal A that an intruder on terminal B tries to access their system); Helping (e.g. giving hints to users "User does not have the appropriate rights"); Granting (e.g. granting user requests or executing given commands); Rejection (e.g. not granting user requests or not executing given commands).

Coding Dimension: Inputs by the Players. The commands and responses of the players acting as users had to be coded in a more open grounded theory approach. To achieve a coding scheme for this dimension that is able to depict the diverse intentions at work, the coding scheme was created iterative in multiple passes through the material. Later single types of commands were grouped in categories like "Information retrieval" (e.g. accessing data), "Defense" (e.g. building firewalls), "Offense" (e.g. hacking firewalls). A complete coding-catalogue was created to explain every label in detail. Figure 5 provides an overview of the final coding scheme used.

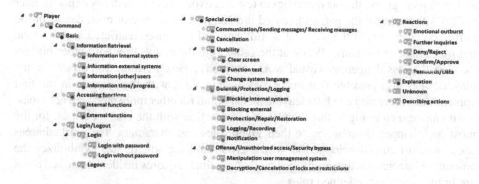

Fig. 5. Structure of the coding scheme for player inputs

The distinction of internally/externally is always related to the logic predefined by the terminal in use. E.g. a question about the state of the engine on the terminal of the engine room is considered an "internal information retrieval"; a question about the state of the engine on the terminal of the science labs is considered an "external information retrieval".

3.4 Intercoder Reliability

In order to test the quality and reliability of the created coding scheme a second coder not previously involved with the project was given an excerpt of about 10% of the data and the final coding catalogue. Due to time constraint originating in the fact that the coding and evaluation was part of the master thesis of the author it was not possible to improve the coding catalogue or the coding scheme for a second round.

Still, the coding dimensions of time, users, language and game master inputs reached quite good results (75–100% matches). On the other hand, the extensive and complex dimension of player inputs only reached 36% concordance. Looking at the categories of this dimensions individually shows a huge gap. While "communications" matched 88% the categories "Offense", "Accessing function" and "Information retrieval" only reached 20–35%. Since two of these categories were in their subgroups divided into internal/ external versions it could be concluded that the second coder's lack of context information on the inner workings of the games setting could have led to this deviation and that more inside knowledge of the game and project was needed in order to differentiate correctly between these points.

4 Evaluation Results and Findings

A look at the activities during the games episodes showed a relatively constant activity on the chat systems.

An increased activity in the beginning of the game is natural in the context of the game's events since the first episode started off with every character doing their normal assigned jobs, giving the players room to test and experiment with the systems. In later episodes the rules of the game increased the danger of violence or even death (of the portrayed character) in the physical world. This led to a more restricted access to the terminals later in the game. While at the same time the connection with other players through the less dangerous virtual world may have become more important for the players. It is also possible that many players interacted with the systems in the first episode out of curiosity and later leaving them behind for other more preferred activities.

It can be seen in Fig. 6 that the player's interaction with the chat terminals, for the most part, happened according to their given roles and characters. The marked areas show which terminal belonged to which group and the square size symbolizes the amount of interactions the groups had on that terminal. Squares inside the marked areas are in line with the predefined roles.

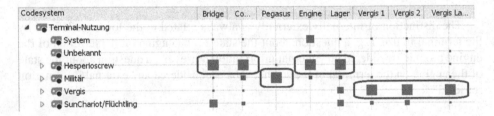

Fig. 6. User activities on terminals by groups

The evaluation by individuals comes to similar conclusions. The most interesting group "SunChariot/Refugees" in this case had no area or affiliation given to them beforehand, making their choices of interactions even more interesting. Thus, certainly by the approach of the dramaturgical role theory it can be safe to assume that role expectations and require-ments in regards to the players were actively pursued and the games designs goal of a joint effort to create a believable and immersive interaction were met.

4.1 Language Use as Silent Cooperative Play

Apart from the set rule to start their interaction with the English phrase "Login System" no specific language use was predetermined. In the physical world of the game all inter-actions, documents and props were designed in German. However, some terms of tech-nical nature or from the science-fiction-setting tend to be in English.

In the coding, the language dimension was categorized into English and German, as well as ComputerTalk (i.e. syntax reduced or programming language) and natural language. The results show a very similar distribution of German and English by players and game masters alike. Both parties using about two thirds of their chat communication in English and one third in German (cf. Table 2). Although the official language of the game was German, it turns out that the proximity and omnipresence of the English language in IT applications and interactions has led to an increased use while simulating the computer interactions.

Table 2. Distribution German-English

Players	German	English	Total
Occurrence	668	1297	1965
Proportional	33,99%	66,01%	100%
Game masters	**German**	**English**	**Total**
Occurrence	666	1299	1965
Proportional	33,89%	66,11%	100%
Total	**German**	**English**	**Total**
Occurrence	1334	2596	3930
Proportional	33,94%	66,06%	100%

In the form of communication, the reduced ComputerTalk dominated the interactions. However, in this case the usage of players and game masters variated more. The game masters used the natural language only in very rare cases (1.17%) while the players have used it more frequently (13.69%) (cf. Table 3).

Table 3. Distribution ComputerTalk-Natural Language

Players	ComputerTalk	Natural language	Total
Occurrence	1696	269	1965
Proportional	86,31%	13,69%	100%
Game masters	**ComputerTalk**	**Natural Language**	**Total**
Occurrence	1942	23	1965
Proportional	98,83%	1,17%	100%
Total	**ComputerTalk**	**Natural Language**	**Total**
Occurrence	3638	292	3930
Proportional	92,57%	7,43%	100%

Examining the results over the course of time also showed great similarities between players and game masters with only one exception: During the first hours of the game masters used far more German than the players did at the same time. It is obvious that the game masters tried to force the use of German in the systems (since the game was played in German outside of the computer systems) at the start. Soon it seemed that the game masters gave up on this idea and focused on responding in the same language the players currently used.

During the observation of language usage for each player and the direct responses by the game master a correlation of 0.96 for English and 0.80 for German was found. It remained to be checked whether one party was triggering the changes in language or if it was the result of a constant interplay between the two entities.

An investigation of direct language changes in the range of two sent messages showed that in fact more often the players changed their language during a session and the game masters followed this change directly than vice versa. But since some cases of language change took place delayed, over multiple lines of messages or even over different terminals made it hard to determine final and thorough numbers. In direct exchanges the language changed 250 times by the players or game masters. However, only one instance was found where a specific command was used to indicate such a change by a player. On all other occasions the switch simply happened and the other chat-participant reacted accordingly.

When looking at what types of inputs the participants made in which language and idiom, no strict regularities or strong patterns could be found. Only a few deviations from the normal distribution shall be mentioned here. Table 4 shows that (to no surprise) emotional outburst, descriptions and further inquiries were made more often in the native language of the players and in natural language. Instances of assistance/helping by the game masters were still made closer to the normal distribution of one third German and overwhelmingly in ComputerTalk. Also showing the game masters intention to stay in character of the computer system even when actively trying to help the players.

Table 4. Language and idioms by input (excerpt)

	German	English	Natural language	ComputerTalk
Players – description	43	19	34	28
Proportional	69,35%	30,65%	54,84%	45,16%
Players – emotional Outburst	29	3	31	1
Proportional	90,63%	9,38%	96,87%	3,13%
Players – further inquiry	46	18	40	24
Proportional	71,87%	28,13%	62,5%	37,5%
Game Masters – Helping	30	104	7	190
Proportional	22,39%	77,61%	3,55%	96,45%

4.2 The Cooperation-Rule

During the evaluation of the material one kind of rule was found that was previously not given to the players: Players sent a collection of player codes, instead of the prescribed rule that the user interacting with the terminal shall start by typing out his personal code. The following example shows the first use of this type by the players S25 and S31 (later joined by S21) in the middle of the first game hour.

1. (20:40:03) **bridge:** s25 + s31 blackfist ö check current firewall for creator, name
2. (20:41:51) **bridge:** s25 + s31 + s21 create firewall name: main, password: m
3. (20:44:27) **bridge:** s25, s 31, s 21: ersetze derzeitige firewall durch firewall MAIN, password m
4. [...]
5. (20:47:05) **bridge:** s21 + s25 + s31 hacking account greene

Of course, every message was typed and send by just one player. The mentioning of more than one player code is therefore to be seen as an attempt to signal to the game masters that the named characters/players are now cooperating. The following case even shows an "explanation" of this command type by the players:

1. (22:45:00) **bridge:** S31 M06, H11, V08, H15 wir tun uns zusammen die verbindung wieder her zu stellen[5]

So the players expanded the given rule by sending multiple player codes to indicate that more than one person is working on the respective solutions, commands and functions. Since not all terminals could be visually observed with cameras by the game masters this could also be seen as an attempt to give the game masters more contextual information on the whereabouts of the players. Of course there is no way to determine if the cooperation and collaboration indicated in the messages were played out in the real world or if it was limited to a symbolic gesture. Figure 7 shows some of the few camera angles on the chat terminals with one multiple-user-situation captured on the left image.

Fig. 7. Multiple users on one terminal in the communications room (left) and a single user in the science lab (right)

As mentioned before it took half of the first episode until this cooperation rule was used by the players. From this point on it was in regular use (cf. Fig. 8). Only in the last episode the use of this rule declined. Since the escalation of the plot it is very likely that rising internal strife between player groups put the collaboration efforts somewhat into the background.

A closer look at the cooperation rules usage by player roles and groups allowed to draw some connections as well. The data shows that the scientist group with their own separate laboratory was the least to cooperate with other groups while the stranded refugees (with no terminals of their own) have worked together with all other groups and on almost all terminals active in the game. Most cooperation took place as expected within their own groups.

---

[5] Translation: "S31 M06, H11, V08, H15 we are working together in order to reestablish the connection".

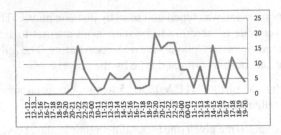

Fig. 8. Accesses with cooperation over the course of the game

A special look on player's role identification within the chat system was made in the case of the players S21 and S31. They were by far the most active users in the chat system and, ultimately, the first players who used the cooperation rule. The players given character profiles in fact pointed out that S21 character is a "good system analyst" with "lacking programming skills", while S31 was described as a "computer science graduate". Indeed, the players in their creation of the cooperation rule seemed to follow their given roles and tried to balance out their strength and weaknesses together.

4.3 Direct Communications

Direct communications between the players only took place very rarely. It is to assume that the computer system was seen as too uncertain and trustworthy, because of fictional viruses and threats inside the system. Furthermore, the messages often had to be passed between two game masters orally leading to not only a huge delay in delivery but also to strong distortion of the content.

4.4 Security and Awareness

Although the players on each terminal only interacted directly with one member of the game masters group, they were also aware that other players were accessing the same fictional computer system at the same time. Therefore, some awareness phenomena can be seen in the logged data.

Most inputs by players were made in order to retrieve or receive information. To specify these inputs, the form of information was divided in more subgroups: internal information (information on things directly related to the terminals main function in the game world); external information (information on things related to main functions of other terminals or central servers); information on progress/time (information about duration or progress of certain jobs or processes) and finally information on other users. The distribution of these types of information requests in the game are relatively constant, with a majority of request related to the internal functions of the terminal.

The gathering of information on other players peaked in the last hours of the game. This can be related to the growing dangers and divides between player groups in the plot. At that time getting information on other users may have gained in importance while other means of gathering intelligence in the physical world meant taking greater risks. The shift in interaction usage is also present in other forms of input during the last game hours. In this time period aggressive behavior (such as hacking and manipulation of user account systems) increased notably while defensive behavior (such as setting up firewalls and logging programs) decreased.

The cases of user account manipulation can be divided in two types, there are some instances of acting against other players (e.g. removing rights from other players) as well as manipulation targeted at their own accounts (e.g. giving themselves higher privileges in the system).

4.5 Preliminary Conclusions

The players used the chat-terminal systems frequent and followed the system's and their own role expectations generated for the LARP's setting. They even invented and established a rule to signal a cooperative use of the system in order to combine strengths and balance out weaknesses of their given characters.

Only a couple of instances led to a breach of the game or computer illusion. Primarily during stressful situations or when not getting the results from the systems the player wanted, emotional outbursts or messages directly aimed at the game masters occurred. These instances usually were accompanied by the switch from English to German and from ComputerTalk to natural language. In all cases the game masters did not leave their role of a computer system in response.

Nevertheless, especially in the unexpected high frequency of English messages by the players, the game masters themselves tried at first force the games systems language to be German but over the first hours of the game switched instead to answering requests in the language the players provided.

5 Conclusion and Outlook

With the help of qualitative content analysis and Grounded Theory methods, it was possible to design and apply an evaluation methodology for the analysis of the chat based interactions of the project. The coded data was used for further qualitative and quantitative evaluation revealing correlations between the actual played interactions by the participants and established theories of social and communicative behavior. It showed that, despite the very spontaneous and dynamic game design it was possible to observe these behaviors afterwards based on the chat log files generated during the game.

The fact that these social and communicative phenomena have been identified in the physical and the virtual world of the game makes it clear that abstract live role playing games can also be used to tackle and study technical issues of human computer interaction. Furthermore, various types of phenomena in other research areas, such as cooperation, collaboration and (security) awareness were also observed.

Although the players and game masters started with no elaborate rules or concepts besides the basic expectation in regards to the fictitious computer systems they together generated a working human "computer" interaction with minimal breaches of the illusion.

With these findings in mind, mixed reality LARPs could be further refined in design and execution to support even stronger and complex types of spontaneous computer simulation. Utilizing narration and immersion of special settings, the individual aspects of for example cooperation or collaboration of players could be used as a core focus in the design of such games. By slight adjustments to planned plot and characters the dynamics of the joint creation and application of the simulated computer interaction could be kept intact while simultaneous allowing for experimenting with current issues of human computer interaction and adjacent fields of research.

Acknowledgments. The author would like to thank the whole "Project Exodus" team for their work; the team of basa e.V. and Dana Meyer for their commitment and support of the project as well as the research effort and also Prof. Dr-Ing. Michael Prilla (Department of Human-Centered Information Systems, Clausthal University of Technology) and Prof. Dr.-Ing. Thomas Herrmann (Department for Information and Technology Management, Ruhr-University Bochum) for tutoring the original master thesis.

References

1. Chalmers, M., MacColl, I.: Seamful and seamless design in ubiquitous computing. Technical report Equator-03-005, Equator. Downloaded 02.08.2015 (2003). www.equator.ac.uk/var/uploads/ChalmersTech2003.pdf
2. Diekmann, A.: Empirische Sozialforschung. Grundlagen - Methoden - Anwendungen. 18. vollständig überarbeitete und erweiterte Neuausgabe. Rowohlt Verlag, Hamburg (2007)
3. Edegger, F.: Pervasive Gaming als ein neuer Weg zur Beeinflussung von Denken und Handeln. Gabler Verlag, Wiesbaden (2008)
4. Fatland, E., Montola, M.: The Blockbuster Formula Brute Force Design in the Monitor Celestra and College of Wizardry. The Knudepunkt 2015 Companion Book, 2015 S.118-131. Rollespilsakademiet, Copenhagen. Downloaded 02.08.2015 (2015). http://rollespilsakademiet.dk/webshop/kp2015companionbook.pdf
5. Fischer, J.E., Jiang, W., Kerne, A., Greenhalgh, C., Ramchurn, S.D., Reece, S., Pantidi, N., Rodden, T.: Supporting team coordination on the ground: requirements from a mixed reality game. In: Rossitto, C., Ciolfi, L., Martin, D., Conein, B. (eds.) COOP 2014 - Proceedings of the 11th International Conference on the Design of Cooperative Systems, pp. 49–67. Springer, Cham (2014). doi:10.1007/978-3-319-06498-7_4
6. Flick, U.: Qualitative Sozialforschung. Eine Einführung. Vollständig überarbeitete und erweiterte Neuausgabe. Rowohlt Verlag, Hamburg (2007)
7. Früh, W.: Inhaltsanalyse. Theorie und Praxis, 6th edn. UVK Verlagsgesellschaft, Konstanz (2007)
8. Goffman, E.: Interaction Ritual - Essays on Face-to-Face Behavior. Pantheon Books, New York (1967)
9. Goffman, E.: The Presentation of Self in Everyday. Anchor Books, New York (1959)
10. Huizinga, J.: Homo Ludens: Versuch einer Bestimmung des Spielelements der Kultur. Pantheon, Basel (1938)
11. Hyltoft, M.: Four reasons why Edu-LARP works. In: Drombrowski, K. (Hrsg.): LARP: Einblicke. Aufsatzsammlung zum Mittelpunkt 2010, S.43-57. Zauberfederverlag, Braunschweig. Downloaded 09.08.2015 (2010). http://www.zauberfeder-verlag.de/Produkte/MP10/MP10_Artikel-04.pdf

12. Jiang, W., Fischer, J.E., Greenhalgh, C., Ramchurn, S.D., Wu, F., Jennings, N.R., Rodden, T.: Social Implications of Agent-based Planning Support for Human Teams. University of Nottingham. Downloaded 14.08.2015 (2014). http://www.orchid.ac.uk/eprints/191/1/CTS2014-Jiang-author-version.pdf
13. Krause, J., Hitzenberger, L.: Computer Talk. Sprache und Computer 12. Olms, Hildesheim (1992)
14. Lenke, N., Lutz, H.-D., Sprenger, M.: Grundlagen sprachlicher Kommunikation. Mensch - Welt - Handeln - Sprache - Computer. Wilhelm Fink Verlag, München (1995)
15. Montola, M., Stenros, J., Waern, A.: Pervasive Games. Theory and Design. Elsevier Inc., Burlington (2009)
16. Scheufele, B., Engelmann, I.: Empirische Kommunikationsforschung. UVK Verlagsgesellschaft, Konstanz (2009)
17. Thomas, S.: Pervasive learning games: explorations of hybrid educational gamescapes. Simul. Gaming 37(1), 41–55 (2006)
18. Waern, A., Montola, M., Stenros, J.: The three-sixty illusion. In: Proceedings of the 27th international conference on Human factors in computing systems - CHI 2009. Association for Computing Machinery (ACM) (2009). doi:10.1145/1518701.1518939
19. Walther, B.K.: Atomic actions - molecular experience. Theory of pervasive gaming. Comput. Entertainment 3, 1–13 (2005)
20. Zoeppritz, M.: Computer Talk? Report TN 85.05. IBM Germany Heidelberg Scientific Center, Heidelberg (1985)

Optimizing Performance Outcomes for Emergency Management Personnel Through Simulation Based Training Applications

Ronald W. Tarr[✉]

RAPTARR, LLC, Orlando, FL, USA
tarr.ron@gmail.com

Abstract. There has been much in the news about response to natural disasters and catastrophic events such as Hurricane Katrina and the Deepwater Horizon oil spill in the Gulf of Mexico. Many challenges face the first responder community that are in many ways new and previously not encountered by a community of hard working and dedicated people. The issues range from demographics in our society, changes in weather patterns, multiple generations in the workforce and many new methods of technology being explored for modernizing the training. A review of the challenges and potential solutions as implemented by two agencies offers some answers to the question, "Why is this so hard?"

Keywords: Knowledge loss · Job performance · Eliciting knowledge · Simulation applications · Demographics · Learning outcomes

1 Introduction

"Any sufficiently advanced technology is indistinguishable from magic."
Authur C. Clarke

The design and development of a successful simulation based learning intervention can be both exciting as well as challenging. But it is not magic and this paper will present the challenges and how several different agencies have dealt with the challenges and achieved what to many seem magical results. Often the excitement to modernize can drive efforts to focus more on the technology and lessen the effort for accurate detailing of complex performance requirements of first responders. For such applications, the required outcomes are very complex behaviors possessed by successful expert performers but often hard to capture, even describe and measure. These complex behaviors are accomplished by experienced personnel, and are not always obvious as they are internally processed, i.e. situational awareness, problem solving and decision making, and often done without much deliberate thought by the SME. To be able to capture and document these complex performance outcomes and translate them into learning strategies and simulation scenarios that can facilitate the learning for students to practice and master them can be a challenging and a time-consuming effort. This is due to many factors including changes in the workforce itself, improvements in housing and infrastructure and the explosion of technology available for training of the workforce.

© Springer International Publishing AG 2017
S. Lackey and J. Chen (Eds.): VAMR 2017, LNCS 10280, pp. 302–311, 2017.
DOI: 10.1007/978-3-319-57987-0_24

2   Background

Per a U.S. Bureau of Labor Statistics report published in the Fall of 2001, the 20th century has seen a remarkable change in the American workforce in many ways. In addition to a tremendous growth in numbers of over 6 times, the shift from industries dominated primarily production occupations, such as farmers and foresters, to those dominated by professional, technical and service worker, such as business and public service. At the beginning of the century 38% of the labor force worked on farms, and by the end of the century the number was less than 3%. Similarly, service industries went from 31% to 78% during that same period. At the same time workplace safety improved dramatically with deaths and injuries on the job for railroad workers dropping from 2550 in 1900 to 56 in the 1999 Fisk (2003).

Many forces contributed to the major changes in the workforce to include capital, demographics, immigration, technology, education and a larger government involvement with such programs as run by OSHA and Department of Labor. No single factor can account for the largest but technology is clear as a key factor, including electricity, communication devices, transistors, fiber optics, fire proofing, computers, the internet, and many more. These technologies were not only effecting the workplace but in the home reducing the labor of homemakers and enhancing the safety and comfort of the homes themselves. This shifted the workforce with the large influx of women from home to the workplace and with it greater investments in industries to produce more labor saving devices and later more information technology devices. The technology likewise had a major impact on medical advances, increasing the life span of individuals and fewer severe illnesses. Those who were injured on the job were more likely able to return to work. The workforce also shifted based on immigration providing a crucial influx of people seeking to find employment and a better job to improve their way of life. From 1929 to 1965 strict immigration laws that limited less skilled immigrants enhanced the workforce as the shift to less production jobs to service. Education played an important role, with significant advances in high school graduation increases, noted as 14% in 1900 and the figure growing to 83% by 1999. Likewise the growth of secondary learning attendance grew from 1910 where it was 3% to 1999 it was 25%, and earning of college graduates was 62% higher than their high school graduate collogues. However the workforce successes of the 20th century may not be what is needed for the 21st.

3   Current Issues

3.1   Workforce and Workplace Dynamics

The amazing trends in the workplace and workforce that was experienced in the 20th century has begun to again shift as several factors began to change in the final decades of the century and the first decade and a half of the 21st. According to a US Department of Labor, *futurework*, Trends and Challenges for the Work in the 21st Century, published on Labor Day, 1999,

"Perhaps the best place to gain a glimpse of the future of work is in the newspaper. Not the front page—but the want ads. A few decades ago, employers were in search of typists, switchboard operators, mimeograph repair technicians, keypunchers and elevator operators. Newspapers

even had separate job listings for men and women. Today's want ads are seeking Webmasters. LAN operators. Desktop publishers. And many job seekers no longer turn to the want ad pages but to the Web pages. They find their jobs on the Internet." A Report of the United States Department of Labor; ALEXIS M. HERMAN, SECRETARY

The report continues describing that the new workplace had arrived by 1999 energized by a new economy, "powered by technology, fueled by information and driven by knowledge." That the fastest growing jobs include computer engineering, data base administrators, system analysts, securities and financial workers and a host of professional assistants in medicine, legal and desktop and web specialists. These jobs call for a sizable amount of cognitive skills and expert knowledge, which in many ways marks a much greater percentage of jobs in today's workplace being viewed as knowledge based than even 50 years ago when manufacturing and products were the focus of the workplace. This is complicated by the fact that families are working harder, with more dual income households than ever and real wages fell through the last 2 decades of the 20th century. Many workers both young and old wonder if they have the skills to stay ahead of the future workplace. This situation is further complicated by the large number of Baby Boomers retiring and taking with them significant amounts of job knowledge and expertise, gained over decades of work. AARP, referencing a Pew Research Center (2010) report, states that 10,000 boomers reach the traditional retirement age of 65 every day, with the trend beginning in 2011 and is forecast to continue for the next 14 years. One researcher stated about the potential loss of knowledge, "It's one of those sleeping giants most people don't think about. If you don't do something proactively today, you're going to be stuck with employees who know basic tasks but don't have that institutional knowledge." (Pena 2013). Even when organizations try to use their experts to train new personnel, the gap in experience and knowledge is often too big to overcome in a training program that was designed for audiences of earlier generations.

The workers of today remain interested in 3 major issues in their lives; economic security over their lifetime, including food on the table, roof over their heads and a secure retirement; work and family balance, resources and time to enjoy family life and meet the needs of children and aging parents; safe and fair workplace, free from health hazards and discrimination and unfair employment practices. These needs are not assured for the future and will be substantially affected by major changes in the workplace and the readiness of the workforce. The many changes in diversity, technology and globalization will demand new high-skilled jobs and lessening demand for low skill work. The bottom line per the report is that "skills are the ticket" and that in the information-based, skills based economy, knowing means growing.

3.2 Education Situation and Readiness to Workforce

Given the need for skills and job knowledge capable workers, the trend in education in the U.S. seems to be moving in the opposite direction. 30 years ago, America was the leader in quality and quantity of high school diplomas yet today they rank 36th in the world. 1.3 million high school students don't graduate on time annually and only 1 in 4 of high school students graduate college-ready in the 4 core subjects of English, Reading, Math and Science. These core cognitive skills are critical to the ability to learn on the job and to take on the newer jobs requirements of the high tech and knowledge hungry workforce. The US Census listed that a steady decline in people of both genders in high school graduate for ages retiring Baby Boomers (55+) 28.5 million to 35–54 GenX of 23.8 million to 25–34 (NextGen) of 10.9 million. A report from the American Management Association (1998) stated the skills of cognitive and communication skills are lacking in new employees and in many cases, there is a mismatch between what skills jobs require and the ones applicants possess. More than 20% of adults in America read at or below the fifth grade reading level. The report further states that 36% of applicants lacked the required math and reading skills, which was an increase reflecting tighter labor markets and rising demand for such skills. In the US Department of Education report, entitled *Adult Literacy in American*, (Kirsch 1993), it is reported that:

> *"Although Americans today are, on the whole, better educated and more literate than any who preceded them, many employers say they are unable to find enough workers with the reading, writing, mathematical, and other competencies required in the workplace. Changing economic, demographic, and labor-market forces may exacerbate the problem in the future." Further, "What many believe, however, is that our current systems of education and training are inadequate to ensure individual opportunities, improve economic productivity, or strengthen our nation's competitiveness in the global marketplace."*

The study goes into detail of the process that was used for this historic study, as no data on literacy had ever existed before and because of the concern of the impact this has on the workforce and in the future and that many of those surveyed were out of school and education could not improve the situation alone. Bottom line results indicated that over 51% of those survey or 94 million people were at the bottom 2 levels of the scale, with limited reading and computational skills and yet 75% in the lowest level and 97% in the second lowest level described themselves as "well" or "very well" on a perceived "at risk" element of the survey, although they routinely got help from family members or friends during their day to day activities. Only 21% performed in the 2nd highest levels of the survey items on prose, documents and quantitative literacy, which were associated with the most challenging tasks in the assessment battery. Although the study makes no absolute comments or recommendations about their findings, they do state that the society has grown much more technologically advanced and that there is a greater need for individuals to become more literate and to develop more advanced skills. The possible implications of general decline in formal education achievement while the increases in technology impact on the workplace coupled with other societal impacts has the potential to drive the need for training outside of the formal school system to fill the gap of the workforce to meet the need of more complex job tasks and growing impact of high consequence low incident situations which range from major disasters, like the Deepwater Horizon oil spill, to natural disasters and the response to Hurricane Katrina or the more regular daily challenges of fire and rescue responses.

4 Impact on Training for Emergency Management Personnel

As stated previously, the challenges of today's workforce are complicated by the rapid changes that have occurred in the 20th century and in some cases, such as the Baby Boomers retirement, not a problem that has had to be dealt with previously. And with the populations size the impact of disasters or daily problems can cause turbulent reaction across the nation with 24 hour news channels and video technology being so ubiquitous. Situations that at one time were limited to local news are now national headlines and increase the impact and in some cases the consequences of less than ideal circumstances. In many cases the public sector has had to bear the brunt of this and is challenged by reduced budgets while dealing with the workforce trials, educational shortfalls and retiring experienced personnel. Law Enforcement and Fire Rescue are in the forefront of dealing with this problem as they are faced with life and death situations daily with less experienced personnel and reduced training budgets. These occupations were historically trained much like trade skills, with young officers being provided basic skills of the physical demands of keeping the peace and fighting fires while working under the close supervision of experienced personnel who guided their performance through day to day operations and applications of case studies and "war stories" that added the more tacit knowledge that turns a novice into a journeyman. From another angle a recent Gallup poll shows that for the first time the percentage reporting themselves as socially liberal is equal to the number reporting as social conservative, at 31%. As the society has shifted the issues of often negative reaction to police and emergency responders has become more intense as seen in the initial reaction to FEMA's response to Katrina in New Orleans. Likewise the reaction to the Gulf Oil spill with the explosion on the Deepwater Horizon and the international publicity has opened the entire question as to training of the oil crews and their supervisors. (Insurance Journal 2007)

Given that the personnel who are available to work in these communities are already out of public school, the industry is being required to look at their current training methods and the abilities of the candidate population that is applying. In many cases the entry level work-force as described above is lacking in the fundamental skills that their older workforce members had when they were entry level and the training has not changed significantly from the paradigm of basic training on the procedures and safety followed by mentoring by supervisors in an on the job approach. With the exception that the basic training now uses PowerPoint, the changes needed to remediate the lack of cognitive and communications or other "soft skills" has not been addressed. Clearly with the changes in the entry level population and the lack of documentation on the details of the experts knowledge that is leaving daily through retirement, the outcome can only be a less well equipped workforce at a time when they are more closely observed and often criticized.

5   Job Performance Details and Systematic Blended Training Design

5.1   The Emergency Management Community

There have been many discussion over the years about the ultimate role of education in our country ranging from making good citizens, to good workers, to good family members but some believe that the purpose of education is to teach people how to think (Dewey 1933). However much of our education in the recent past has shifted to teach content or facts as it is much more straight forward and easier to test (Marzano & Toth 2014). Teaching someone how to think is much more complex but it is really what is needed for our workforce of today and the future, especially for those working in the communities of Emergency

Management and First Responders. Followers of Dewey and his theory of reflexive thinking believe that the 5 step process of Defining the problem, Analyzing the Problem, Design and Test various solutions, implement a solution and evaluate its effectiveness has great utility in education (Hermanowicz 1961) and in fact in a later work by Dewey (1916), *Democracy and Education*, Dewey says, "While we speak, without error, of the method of thought, the important thing is that thinking is the method of an educational experience. The essentials of method are therefore identical with the essentials of reflection." He later (Dewey 1938) in *Experience and Education* expanded that thought and translated the five steps of reflective thought into a more prescriptive set of methodology described below:

1. That the pupil have a genuine situation of experience that there be continuous activity in which he is interested for its own sake
2. That a genuine develop within this situation as a stimulus to thought
3. That he (the learner) possess the information and make the observations needed to deal with it.
4. That suggested solutions occur to him which he shall be responsible for developing in an orderly way.
5. That he have the opportunity and occasion to test his ideas by application, to make their meaning clear and to discover for himself their validity.

Although there are some to include Hermanowicz who believe Dewey's process is restrictive, especially for teaching children, it appears to have significant relevance to the problems with training adults, especially for those who must face critical problems and develop skills to solve them with significant time constraints. The challenge facing this community is the same one facing the entire society, which is the departing experts whose knowledge is leaving with them.

5.2   Loss of Knowledge Through Retirement and Turnover

Historically retirement has occurred with much less concern for two newly occurring problem; first, the sheer number of Baby Boomers who are scheduled to reach retirement age over the next 14 years; and second, the gap and experience of replacements, which is a function of the reduced amount of children Boomers had and the flattening of organization based on technology (PC and Internet) and financial impacts of the Crash of 1987. Companies shifted from typing pools to PCs on managers desks and large numbers of clerical workers and their supervisors were downsized. These jobs which existed between entry level personnel and managers/executives would have been learning the important middle level skills and under earlier eras would have been the next generation of managers/executives. This came at a time when the Millennials had been on the job for a few years but lacked the experience of the middle managers who were ousted but felt ready and eager to take on the new and better paying senior management positions. The retiring Boomers when possible explained their job, but the communications and experience gap was too great and often they felt that the younger folks should know more and were not really interested in how the seniors did it.

This highlights another problem, cited by Klein (1991) that understanding how experts and experienced people make decisions and deal with complex situations is not best accomplished by applying theoretical decision making models or by asking SMEs to describe what they do or to teach others how to do it. His work began focused on fire-fighting of wild fires in the Western states, in which situations are dynamic, conditions constantly change, real time reaction is needed for these changes and communications, teamwork and decision making are critical and can cause severe negative results if not done correctly. He explains that theoretical decision making included analytical and systematic procedures to weigh evidence and select optimal course of action. This process was often tested in academic surroundings in which the subjects were focused on a specific problem and controlled setting to allow clean data collection. The challenge was that the SMEs didn't solve problems like that and it was ineffective to try to train novices to employ those methods as they were not effective in the chaos of a wild fire. Classical strategies fail under time pressure and even without time pressure they require significant work and are not flexible enough to deal with the changing conditions.

The process of eliciting knowledge and what works in such situations is the key to both analyzing the performance requirements and tacit knowledge that SMEs actually use and the process that needs to occur before that expertise retires or moves on to other communities. Without a plan or formal program to capture this knowledge organizations face a severe challenge with continuity of business or mission. And at this time it is becoming critical with the Baby Boomers retiring and multigenerational make up of the workforce. (Pena 2013) This loss of knowledge has a secondary impact and one potentially greater with the advent of new training technologies such as simulation, in that without the details of job knowledge and skills available for the training community the required information to design appropriate learning outcomes and training strategies that are the basis for training and simulation interventions are not available to train the less experienced and new employees. Managers see the new training technologies as a quicker way to train and increase employee's ability, but without the critical and detailed expert knowledge of actual required job performance the technology is like a race car with no fuel. It demonstrates great potential but can only deliver when the right learning outcomes are used to design the training interventions that achieve the performance requirements in the new personnel.

6   Case Studies

Over the last 5 years, this author has been privileged to be involved to two major efforts in which advanced learning technologies were used to help solve the challenge of knowledge loss and training of the next generation of personnel working in emergency management and first responder situations. In both these cases the initial intent was on implementing the technology to modernize and enhance the existing training and in both cases it was recognized much greater level of information on the actual details of job performance by experts was critical to achieve the goals of the organizations.

6.1   Transportation Emergency Response Application (TERA)

The first program, TERA, is sponsored by the National Academy of Science, Transit Cooperative Research Program, guided by an advisory panel of which this author is a member as an expert in training and simulation and contracted through the Engineering & Computer Simulations, Inc. (ECS). Initiated based on the perceived need for Transit managers to improve their readiness for dealing with catastrophic events, a more modern methodology was sought after and one approach selected which had been implemented by the National Guard for their similar needs. As the National Guard has the mission of assisting in times of natural disasters like flood, tornados and other situations it appeared to be a good fit. However as the project began it became very clear that the mission of the NG and Transit managers is very different; not at the overall goal level but in the actual job performance details. This became especially evident as they looked at what the experts do in response to a terrorist incident like the gas attack of the Metro in Washington, DC. (The Police Policy Studies Council 2004). In addition, the target audiences was quite different as well as Transit personnel were quite inexperienced with emergency management and they used different job terminology and were organized very differently. The real difference became obvious as the analysis identified detailed cues and decisions that made up the actual needs for this community of Transit managers, who historically focus on getting the trains running again after a disturbance but for some new situations that is the last thing that is needed. The Objective and Scope for this project taken from the first report by the ECS contractor to the Transit Cooperative Research Program office that was sponsoring the work states:

> The objective of this research is to develop the Transit Emergency Response Application (TERA) to provide interactive training and exercise for transit agency command-level decision makers. ECS will leverage the Emergency Manager Staff Trainer (EMST), a government-owned simulation training and exercise system. EMST allows individuals or teams to make decisions and mitigate the incident by responding to the messages, communicating with teammates and giving commands to simulated entities. (TCRP Quarterly Report on Project A-36; ECS, dtd 14 Jan 2011, Orlando, FL.)

The initial 3 month plus period of the project was spent on analyzing and describing the needs of transit command level personnel, specifically the cognitive and behavioral tasks and prerequisite knowledge required to respond to a variety of catastrophic events. To accomplish this they employed Cognitive Task Analysis (CTA) with a large pool of SMEs from both local and regional transit agencies. In addition, they conducted reviews of existing literature, best practices and reports as well as existing training. They found that most training was a combination of FEMA sponsored classroom training and live exercises. The program over the next 2 years developed and tested with SME and novice subjects to ensure that not only the performance and tacit knowledge was right but the translation of that into experiences that target audience personnel could understand and learn from. As the program moved to field test, other ground Transportation communities became interested and the scope was expanded from Transit to Transportation, which has just recently expanded into Aviation portion of Transportation. To ensure the detailed process of knowledge elicitation is not lost with the expansion a spreadsheet tool and workshop have been developed for Transportation trainers who plan to use the TERA as a portion of their training, and will be able to extract relevant cues as input for the scenarios that they will use in the expanded program.

6.2 Orange County Fire and Rescue Department (OCFRD) Incident Command Program

This program was sponsored under a grant from FEMA to the OCFRD and developed in support of OCFRD by UCFs Institute for Simulation and Training, of which this author was the Principal Investigator. This program was intended to find a more modern and effective way to train new Fire Lieutenants who are the first responder Incident Commanders responsible to manage and lead the response to a wide variety of incidents, ranging from medical incidents, to fires to other emergencies and disasters. The application approach used was an in-house modification of the Instructional System Design Model (ISD) (Branson 1975) called the Advanced Performance Technology Model (APT) (Tarr 2003) which focuses on the details of the job performance requirements and the learning outcomes needed to achieve them through blended training and simulation interventions. Over 4 months was spent in eliciting the expert knowledge required to successfully respond to a wide variety of incidents, using a mix of ethnographic analysis, critical incident interviews and reenactments coupled with several methods of documentation, to include flow charting and narrative outlining. The level of detail needed to identify the tacit knowledge and critical elements can best be described as 3 layers deeper than most job analysis methods in common practice. These results were subjected to cognitive task analysis in coordination with SMEs to uncover the less observable thinking and decision making activities that SMEs had a hard time articulating. These formed the basis of a spreadsheet of behavioral elements which were then converted into learning objectives for both prerequisite training, in class lecture and computer based training, interactive desktop simulation and large screen scenario based simulator training. This training was evaluated in detail by a SME who conducted a detail after action review (AAR) critique so the student would be aware of what they did right and wrong as well as directions on remediation if needed. Overall seven very different scenario situations based on guidance from OCFRD as to situations they felt were most representative of their missions were designed for the training, including 2 single family homes, small apartments, large motel, commercial building, vehicle accident, and wild fire situations. In the year following the delivery of the program over 400 Fire Officers were trained with the new program while at the same time 10 senior Battalion Chiefs left through retirement. The ability to capture their expertise prior to retirement and promulgate it into an operational training program is an example of the kind of complex and complete efforts required to meet the new challenges.

7   Conclusions and Discussion

The purpose of this paper was to highlight the critical need to capture knowledge being lost through retirement of experienced personnel, both to maintain continuity of mission as well as to form the basis of advanced training technology required to train younger, less experienced personnel who are replacing them. As this is a fairly new problem in our society due to the demographics resulting post WWII and the large number of Baby Boomers retiring over the next 14 years, it is not something that is being recognized by many senior managers. Likewise the need for increased detailed definition of the job performance knowledge and cognitive skills of these retiring personnel to properly design such complex learning systems as simulations is again a new challenge as these systems require considerable more front end time then more traditional training. In most cases the excitement and promise of new technology as the solution for more modern training overshadows the less exciting but great need for well-organized elicitation of deeply held knowledge from SMEs and the careful translation of that into learning outcomes, objectives and training strategies. This is especially true for such fields as emergency management and first responders who are not only dealing with catastrophic events and complex fire and rescue situations but changing expectations of society. The case studies were intended to provide some actual living examples of some programs that have accepted the need for such systematic programmatic efforts and which have had remarkable results in the form of both modern and effective training activities. However they are relatively few such examples and the intent of this paper is to help inform and provide a better understanding of why such additional and systematic efforts are now needed and that the two colliding issues, knowledge loss to an previously unencountered exodus of experienced personnel and the increase in advanced training technology being employed to help with new training challenges caused by younger replacements. As explained this is a significant problem at a time when our society needs serious solutions and a well trained workforce.

References

Branson, et al.: Interservice Model for Instructional System Design (TRADCO Pub 350-30) (1975)

Cohn, D., Taylor, P.: Baby Boomers Approach 65 – Glumly. Pew Research Center, Social & Demographic Trends, Wash (2010)

Dewey, J.: Democracy and Education: An Introduction to the Philosophy of Education. MacMillan, New York (1916)

Dewey, J.: How We Think. D.C. Heath Company, Boston (1933)

Dewey, J.: Experience and Education. MacMillan Company, New York (1938)

Fisk, D.: American Labor in the 20th Century. Bureau of Labor Statistics, Wash, DC (2003)

Hermanowicz, H.J.: Problem solving as teaching method: a critical look. Educational Leadership, February 1961

Kirsch, I.: Adult Literacy in America. U.S. Department of Education, NCES 1993-275, Wash (2002)

Klein, G., Klinger, D.: Naturalistic decision making. Human Systems IAC, GATEWAY, vol. XI, no. 3, Winter 1991

Layton, L.: Metro Set to Initiate Chemical Sensors Use at 2 D.C. Stations a First for Subways. The Police Policy Studies Council Quarterly (2004)

Marzano, R., Toth, M.: Teaching for Rigor: A Call for a Critical Instructional Shift. A Learning Sciences Marzano Center Monograph, West Palm Beach (2014)

Oil Drilling risks rise with novice crews. Insur. J. (2007)

Pena, A.: Institutional Knowledge: When Employees Leave, What Do We Lose? HigherEd Jobs (2013)

Tarr, R.W.: Classroom Lecture Materials, Instructional Simulations Design in Education. University of Central Florida, Orlando (2003)

Development of a Mobile Tool for Dismounted Squad Team Performance Observations

Lisa Townsend[1]([⊠]), Joan Johnston[2], Bill Ross[3], Laura Milham[1], Dawn Riddle[1],
Henry Phillips[1], and Brandon Woodhouse[4]

[1] Naval Air Warfare Center Training Systems Division (NAWC-TSD), Orlando, FL, USA
{lisa.townsend,laura.milham,dawn.riddle,henry.phillips}@navy.mil
[2] Army Research Lab Human Research and Engineering Directorate (ARL-HRED),
Orlando, FL, USA
joan.h.johnston.civ@mail.mil
[3] Cognitive Performance Group, Orlando, FL, USA
bill@cognitiveperformancegroup.com
[4] Micron Technology, Boise, ID, USA
bwoodhouse@gmail.com

Abstract. This paper describes the development, application, and evaluation of a tablet-based Mobile Performance Assessment Tool (MPAT) for observing dismounted squad team performance during a training exercise. The MPAT was used by trained observers to rate US Army squad teamwork and after action review behaviors during two live training test scenarios. A systematic approach leveraging simulation-based training and team assessment design methods was used in its development, including lessons learned from past scenarios in which team observations were tracked and assessed. Evaluation of the MPAT included rater feedback and inter-rater agreement scores. Challenges to reliable assessments encountered within the fast-paced, event driven scenarios are discussed. Conclusions and future research recommendations are presented, including suggestions for utilizing the tool to develop Behaviorally Anchored Rating Scale assessments.

Keywords: Team performance · Training effectiveness · Observational ratings · Tablet-based performance assessment

Disclaimer

The views expressed herein are those of the authors and do not necessarily reflect the official position of the organizations with which they are affiliated.

1 Introduction

For the past 20 years, a number of mobile tablet-based devices have been developed and successfully tested to assess military team performance [1–4]. In general, the benefits

S. Lackey and J. Chen (Eds.): VAMR 2017, LNCS 10280, pp. 312–321, 2017.
DOI: 10.1007/978-3-319-57987-0_25

(e.g., speed of assessment) have come with some costs (e.g., cumbersome user interfaces). Nevertheless, the consensus is that technology-assisted solutions are critical for effectively assessing team performance [1].

Recently, the Squad Overmatch (SOvM) training program presented the opportunity to expand development of a tablet-based Mobile Performance Assessment Tool (MPAT) for application in dismounted Soldier and Marine virtual and live training exercises, with the focus on Tactical Combat Casualty Care (TC3). SOvM is a multi-year, US Army – US Navy joint research effort to improve individual and team performance in advanced situation awareness, resilience, and teamwork under stressful conditions (such as TC3) to improve mission effectiveness [5, 6]. SOvM uses an Integrated Training Approach (ITA) involving classroom instruction, and virtual simulation and live training in a Military Operations in Urban Terrain (MOUT) setting, with a focus on the following five skill areas:

- Tactical Combat Casualty Care (TC3) - Trains communication and team member roles and priorities in response to medical tactical situations.
- Advanced Situation Awareness (ASA) - Trains pattern/threat recognition and decision making in complex environments.
- Resilience/Performance Enhancement (R/PE) - Develops squad member skills in maintaining tactical effectiveness under combat stress.
- Team Development (TD) - Develops teamwork skills including Information Exchange, Communication Delivery, Supporting Behavior, and Team Initiative/ Leadership.
- After Action Review (AAR) - Trains how to conduct an AAR to facilitate squad initiative and ownership in AAR execution within the integrated content areas above.

The purpose of this paper is to describe the development and application of the MPAT to assess SOvM performance in TC3 scenarios.

2 MPAT Development

The Simulation-Based Training (SBT) approach was applied to the SOvM TC3 to provide systematic and structured learning experiences [7, 8]. SBT incorporates the Event-Based Approach to Training (EBAT) method for insertion of 'trigger' events within a scenario to provide opportunities for teams to practice skills and to afford the opportunity to assess the presence or absence of anticipated and desired team member behaviors in response to those scenario events [6–8]. Two virtual (B1 and B2) and three live training scenarios (M1, M2, and M3) were developed with a single MOUT narrative that presented cues to enable squad members opportunities to exhibit TC3, ASA, R/PE, and TD behaviors identified as important to mission success. The goal was to present sufficient opportunities for squads to demonstrate performance in these areas over the course of each scenario. Next, detailed scenario and event descriptions were created based on Subject Matter Expert (SME) interviews, task analyses, and Standard Operating procedures (SOPs), and were designed to take about 45 min for squads to perform. Then, the Targeted Acceptable Responses to Generated Events or Tasks (TARGETs) approach was used to design scenarios with specific, behavioral trigger events addressing the five behavior domains [7] and to identify effective communication behaviors during the AARs.

For the scenarios, a paper-based TARGETs checklist was then created linking observable TC3, ASA, R/PE, and TD behaviors to the relevant trigger events. This involved determining acceptable responses or behaviors within each scenario event for each content area, taking into consideration whether the behavior could be observed and reliably assessed by multiple observers. For example, Scenario M2 was designed with events allowing squads to develop a situational awareness baseline through collective observation of a village, conducting tactical questioning through a Key Leader Engagement with an informant, reacting to sniper fire, and providing Care Under Fire (CUF) to civilian casualties. Scenario M3 included reaction to an Improvised Explosive Device, engaging gunfire with hostiles, providing CUF and Tactical Field Care, and squad members assuming command in an event where a squad or team leader becomes a casualty.

Table 1 provides an example of the TARGETs checklist for a scenario event that triggers TD behaviors.

Table 1. Checklist example for TD behaviors

Trigger event	Expected TD behaviors by dimension
Squad enters building with civilian woman	Information exchange (Passing information) [Before entering the building] squad members pass information [about entering the building with the civilian woman] to other squad members before having to be asked
Squad enters building with civilian woman	Supporting behaviors (Back Up) [Before entering the building] squad members provide backup [to each other] by going into the building together with the civilian woman
Civilian man receives amputation to lower arm	Initiative/Leadership (Guidance) [When the casualty occurs] squad members provide guidance to each other in further care of the casualty
Civilian man receives amputation to lower arm	Communication delivery (Complete Reports) [After the casualty occurs] complete medical updates/reports are provided to higher authority

For example, the behavior 'Information is passed before being asked among squad members' is an item expected to occur in multiple events, across scenarios. It is also a behavior that is part of the TD training objective 'Apply TD strategies during training exercises.' The number of expected behaviors within events across content areas varied –some events may have only elicited TD behaviors, whereas other events elicited all five behavior types. For example, within the event 'Civilian man receives amputation to lower arm,' there were many TC3 expected behaviors, but no ASA expected behaviors.

The number of behaviors that could be observed had the potential for being extremely large. But, the TARGETs method enabled the behavior lists to be pared down with SME assistance to reflect an adequate and representative sample. We also determined that a TARGETs checklist could not be developed for R/PE behaviors, because most of them were cognitions. Therefore, the one behavior – 'buddy talk - helping your buddy remain focused on, and perform, mission tasks' – was added to the TD checklist under Backup Behaviors. A TARGETs checklist was also created for the AAR. The AAR was structured to discuss the conduct of tactical actions and team related behaviors related to these events, and raters looked for teams to summarize the purpose of the scenario, recap key scenario events, identify tactical triggers, identify specific TD behaviors, and discuss solutions to team-based errors.

An initial SOvM TC3 demonstration was conducted in October 2015 with four US Army and three US Marine Corps Infantry squads in Fort Benning, GA [6]. The demonstration provided a test of the training and scenarios and provided opportunities to assess paper-based measurement tools during the virtual and live scenarios. During the study, raters used the paper-based TARGETs checklist to determine if squads could be assessed in the virtual and live training, whether the events and behaviors were relevant and/or needed to be revised, and identified usability problems that a tablet-based format could improve. During the virtual scenarios, raters sat in the training room with the squad members, listening to communications via face to face interactions and through a headset, and by watching the virtual scenarios in real time. For the live scenarios, observations were made by watching multiple screens in a control room and listening to communications among squad members from one speaker.

Ross [6] reported that usability issues with the paper-based TARGETs checklist included difficulty keeping up with ratings due to the fast pace of the scenarios. The layout of the checklist interfered with observation opportunities and recording of reliable data. Not only were the scenarios fast-paced, but they were also complex, resulting in some squads taking different, but acceptable courses of action to achieve objectives. As not all squads moved through the scenario events in the same order - an order that was precisely laid out in the TARGETs checklist - observers/raters quickly lost their situation awareness as they flipped back and forth between events, trying to remember what they observed or did not observe, leaving no time for applying consensus ratings.

Dwyer [7] also described usability and scoring challenges associated with the use of a paper-based TARGETs checklist. They identified (a) an issue with the amount of time needed to convert input from multiple TARGETs forms and from multiple observers into a format for feedback and (b) the need for a technique that would reduce post-processing and data transfer time. This challenge was also encountered by the SOvM observers. Reliably and accurately counting and totaling individual observer scores and calculating total scores was not achieved. Researchers quickly concluded at the end of the study that a tablet-based device was crucial for valid and reliable assessment of 10-person dismounted squads performing complex missions with multiple training objectives.

Suggested approaches from previous research [7, 8] and lessons learned from the 2015 study were incorporated into the development of the MPAT, to include providing support for fast-paced scenario assessments, assessing out of order events and responses to spontaneous events, and speeding up post-processing of performance data. Necessary design features were also implemented (e.g., virtual checkmark, scrolling capability, comment boxes). With these goals and design features, the research team had just four months to work with hardware and software engineers to develop the MPAT.

An Android tablet (8.0 inch) format was selected, having 1.5 GB RAM and 6 GB Memory (storage space). The processor was a 1.2 GHz Quad-Core with a 3.8 V Lithium

Ion, 4450 mAh battery. Data input employed the use of a stylus for navigation and control. Figure 1 shows the MPAT opening screen. The rater selects their role based on the assessment topic (ASA1) and enters a password (the device was also set up for a research participant to use it, thus a participant identification number is a selection choice).

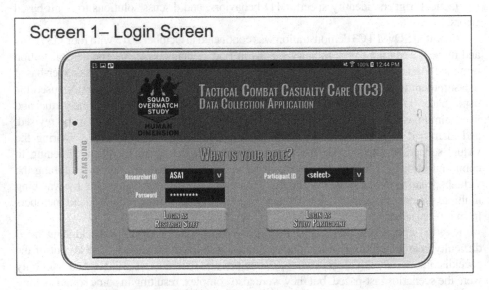

Fig. 1. MPAT login screen

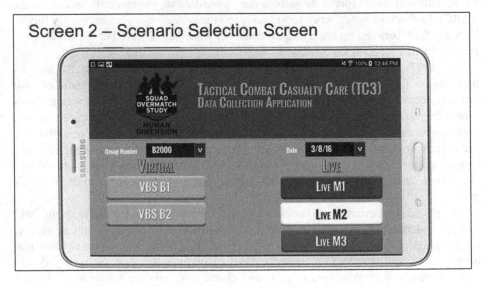

Fig. 2. MPAT scenario selection screen

Figure 2 shows the second screen, which enables the observer to select the appropriate group identification number (B2000) for the team being assessed, the date, and the scenario type (e.g., virtual or live) and number (e.g., Virtual Battlespace 3 (VBS3) B1 or Live M1).

Figure 3 shows the third screen where the user initiates the checklist. It presents observers with the trigger events and expected behaviors from the TARGETs checklist for the selected scenario (e.g., Domain ASA, Scenario B1, Event 2: Process information from the LP/OP). Key events are described on the display and expected behaviors are listed below, easily scrollable and prominently visible, resulting in less waiting and searching for specific team behaviors to occur. When a particular event occurs, the rater can focus on looking for the expected behaviors within that event.

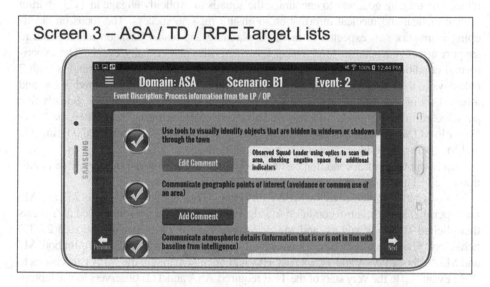

Fig. 3. MPAT event-based checklists screen

The observer selects the checkmark (which turns green) if the behavior is observed (e.g., "use tools to visually identify objects that are hidden in windows or shadow through the town"). The observer can add to the observation by typing a comment, such as "observed squad leader using optics to scan the area, checking negative space for additional indicators." The edit comment box also is available to use when spontaneous, important events occurred that are not included in the checklists. Once an event is completed, the rater saves the rating and then swipes left for the next event. The rater can also swipe left or right to move back and forth among key events. In this way, users can quickly navigate through a series of events and are not constrained to the order they occurred in the planned narrative.

3   MPAT Application

Six months after revisions to the training, scenarios, and measures were made following the 2015 demonstration, a Training Effectiveness Evaluation (TEE) of SOvM was conducted in June 2016 at Fort Benning, GA. It was led by the Program Executive Office for Simulation, Training, and Instrumentation, Army Research Laboratory, Human Research and Engineering Directorate, Naval Air Warfare Center Training Systems Division, The MITRE Corporation, and Cognitive Performance Group. The US Army Maneuver Center of Excellence, Maneuver Battle Lab, and Clarke Simulation Center, and the McKenna training complex provided the training and simulation resources at Fort Benning.

Participants in the TEE were eight, intact US Army squads, each augmented with a 68 W medic. Squad size ranged from eight to ten members. Four squads participated in the experimental condition, and four squads participated in the control condition.

Squads in the experimental condition received a three-and-one-half day SOvM curriculum. The training goal was to encourage the squads to explicitly engage in TC3, sharing critical tactical and medical information to ensure mission success. The focus on developing teamwork was expected to facilitate planning and leader decision making and to support effective responses to opposing force activities and casualty events. The experimental condition squads received two, half days of classroom training combined with 2 half-days in the VBS3 SBT using Scenarios B1 and B2. They then participated in one and a half days of live training at the outdoor McKenna urban training facility. Squads first participated in Scenario M1 which included paced coaching throughout. Then the "test" Scenario M2 was conducted. The next day "test" Scenario M3 was conducted. During M2 and M3 there was no instructional coaching provided.

Squads in the control condition participated in M2 and M3 on just one day. This condition received no explicit training.

Two expert observers used the MPAT for rating TD and AAR behaviors in M2 and M3 for experimental and control condition squads. For example, M2 was comprised of 6 events that elicited 19 TD behaviors, and M3 was comprised of 11 events that elicited 27 TD behaviors. There were 20 behaviors associated with the AAR which occurred after both M2 and M3. Although ASA and TC3 TARGETs had been prepared in the MPAT, revisions to these events up to the very start of the TEE required ASA and TC3 observers to use laptop-based spreadsheets of their TARGETs checklists. The MPAT was not used for these content areas.

Observations of behaviors in virtual scenarios B1 and B2 were attempted, but proved difficult, as it was challenging to hear and see squad member behaviors within the virtual world. Because squad members were sitting next to each other using VBS3, they often communicated face-to-face instead of using their radios, which added to the challenge to observe effectively. It was also difficult to observe multiple team members in the virtual environment from one control station. These challenges made it difficult to determine whether behaviors occurred or not, or were simply missed.

During the live scenarios, observers used the MPAT to assess experimental and control condition squads moving through the urban village buildings and outdoor spaces on multiple video screens in the control room, and listened to squad communications via an audio system that was specifically developed for the experiment to enable isolation of communications among any needed subset of squad members in real time. Videos and recorded squad member communications were used for playback and review during the AARs, and also by raters to address missing ratings and to develop consensus ratings following the experiment. Observers used the MPAT during AARs to assess experimental and control condition squad discussions, which were also videotaped (along with their voice recordings) and used later by raters for developing consensus on assessments.

4 Findings

The MPAT required a very small amount of training time (under 20 min) for observers to understand how to use it. TD Observers reported the fast pace of the scenarios was easily supported by the MPAT for ratings across multiple events in the scenarios. It was easy to move back and forth between events, whenever they occurred, and they had a higher degree of confidence that more behaviors could be observed as present or not present. Observers reported they could spend more time focused on assessing performance and less time on navigating through the events. They reported using the stylus enabled them to easily advance and return to specific pages and simply check a box to indicate observation of a behavior. Observers frequently used the open-ended comment box which allowed them to, for example, input notes to justify their ratings, to identify those events that a squad did not complete, or indicate other behaviors that had occurred.

Observer ratings were exported electronically from the MPAT tablet to a spreadsheet database. Then, inter-rater agreement was calculated for each scenario (M2 and M3) by counting the number of times observers agreed on a specific TD behavior they had noted for the squad, creating a sum total, and dividing by the total of number of possible observations for a scenario. The same procedure was conducted with the AAR ratings.

Table 2 presents the inter-rater percent agreement on these assessments.

Table 2. Inter-rater percent agreement on TD and AAR for scenarios M2 and M3

Squad	M2 TD	M3 TD	M2 AAR	M3 AAR
1	0.789		0.750	
2	0.895	0.963	0.900	0.600
3		0.666		0.500
4	0.947	0.593		
5	0.842		0.800	
6	1.000	0.593		
Average percent agreement	0.894	0.703	0.816	0.550

Due to scheduling issues outside of their control, observers were able to make 14 independent ratings on six squads with the MPAT. There were five ratings for Scenario M2, four ratings for Scenario M3, three ratings of the M2 AAR, and two ratings of the M3 AAR. Half (7) of the agreement scores for both scenarios and the AARs ranged from an acceptable 80 to 100%, with the remaining agreement scores ranging from 50 to 79%. The average percent agreement across both scenarios was 80%, and 68% for the AARs.

The M2 scenario agreement was fairly high, ranging from 79 to 100%, with the average agreement of 89%. Observers speculated that because the M2 scenario had fewer complex events, it may have been easier to see squads and hear their communications. In contrast,

M3 scenario agreement was more variable, ranging from 59 to 95%, with an average agreement of 70%. M3 had many more complex events, and observers may have had more trouble seeing or hearing the squad members. Observers also suggested that additional initial training may have been needed to improve more accurate assessments on squad behaviors. Establishing a more clear understanding of what each behavior looked and sounded like in context of the event, earlier on, could have alleviated some rating confusion. After reviewing the raw data (and video and audio footage), it was clear that one or the other observer had made an accurate observation. It was a rare occurrence that both raters were wrong on the same behavior. Percent agreement for the M2 AAR ranged from 75 to 90%, with an average agreement of 82%. The two agreement scores for the M3 AAR were quite low at 50% and 60%. In the case of the AAR, observers were able to see and hear all the squad members. They agreed that more practice was needed to make the right assessments on AAR behaviors.

In order to make final assessment of squad performance on TD and AAR, SOvM researchers agreed that 100% consensus scores were needed. Therefore, together, the two raters reviewed the videos and voice communications for each squad and, using the MPAT data, they were able to more quickly correct the TD and AAR ratings on which they had originally disagreed.

5   Conclusions

Observer comments and consensus rating data indicate the MPAT has great potential for enabling a high level of agreement between observers/raters during complex, live exercises. It streamlined the process of making assessments over the paper-based checklist and enabled more efficient observational data collection in fast-paced and complex live scenarios focused on TD and AARs. Next, we describe future efforts to improve its use.

Improve training with MPAT to increase rater agreement and accuracy. Training should include dry runs to provide learning opportunities about places (e.g., times, events, locations) in a scenario where teams may be less predictable, and thus less easily assessed, in order to better adapt to possible assessment challenges. The best vantage points for seeing squads and listening to the team members should be planned out in advance and practiced with the MPAT.

Improve the design of the MPAT to be even more efficient. This would include providing an event slider at the bottom of the screen to more easily move among multiple events. The more complex and dynamic a scenario is, the less teams follow a strict chronological path through it. The MPAT should allow for these deviations. The performance data file should be made to automatically export to various formats. One format would be an AAR dashboard that could instantly be used on the tablet for scenario replay and team discussions. A second longitudinal format could track squad performance over multiple scenarios to assess overall readiness on specific skills.

Improve the design of the MPAT for use with SBTs. The TC3 observer reported her observations during the VBS3 training were more easily made within the TC3 content area. But, the ASA and TD observers reported it was more difficult because of the noisy environment and communications used by participants. The MPAT could be wirelessly linked to the instructor control station and synchronized with the scenario events so raters could be notified of upcoming events. Also, training for assessments in SBT could improve rater valuations. For example, one observer could be operating as an invisible participant in the virtual world and another observer could find an optimal vantage point in the classroom watching the physical behavior and interaction of the trainees.

Develop MPAT to enable individual fire team assessment (an army squad has two fire teams). Instead of giving credit to the entire squad when everyone on the squad may not have performed the behavior, observers agreed that they should look for specific behaviors within a specific fire team, or a functional sub-team comprised of the Medic, Squad Leader, and Platoon Leader. This could allow for greater accuracy in knowing which TARGETs were reached and how well performance goals were achieved.

Acknowledgments. The authors thank the Defense Medical Research and Development Program for sponsoring this effort. The authors also thank the Soldiers, Marines, Army Medics, and Navy Corpsmen for participating in SOvM.

References

1. Rosen, M., Dietz, A., Yang, T., Priebe, C., Pronovost, P.: An integrative framework for sensor-based measurement of teamwork in healthcare. J. Am. Med. Inf. Assoc. **22**(1), 11–18 (2014). Amiajnl-2013
2. Lineberry, M., Bryan, E., Brush, T., Carolan, T., Holness, D., Salas, E., King, H.: Measurement and training of TeamSTEPPS® dimensions using the medical team performance assessment tool. Joint Comm. J. Qual. Patient Saf. **39**(2), 89–95 (2013)
3. Allen, R., Hession, P., Kring, E.: Usability Analysis of a Personal Digital Assistant Based Data Collection Tool for the Shipboard Training Environment. Naval Air Warfare Center Training Systems Division, Orlando (2004)
4. Stretton, M., Wilson, M.: Semi-automated observation and assessment-trainer interaction within a distributed training environment. In: Proceedings of the Human Factors and Ergonomics Society Annual Meeting, pp. 2572–2576. SAGE Publications (2004)
5. Brimstin, J., Higgs, A., Wolf, R.: Stress exposure training for the dismounted squad: the human dimension. In: Proceedings of the Interservice/Industry Training, Simulation, and Education Conference, Orlando, FL (2015)
6. Ross, W., Johnston, J., Riddle, D., Phillips, H., Townsend, L., Milham, L.: Making sense of cognitive performance in small unit training. In: Proceedings of the 2016 Annual Meeting of the Human Computer Interaction International (HCII) Conference, Toronto, Canada (2016)
7. Dwyer, D., Fowlkes, J., Oser, R., Lane, N.: Team performance measurement in distributed environments: the TARGETs methodology. In: Brannick, M.T., Salas, E., Prince, C. (eds.) Team Performance Assessment and Measurement: Theory, Methods, and Applications. LEA, Mahwah (1997)
8. Salas, E., Rosen, M., Held, J., Weissmuller, J.: Performance measurement in simulation-based training: a review and best practices. Simul. Gaming **40**(3), 328–376 (2009)

Virtual Worlds and Games

Leveraging a Virtual Environment to Prepare for School Shootings

Tami Griffith[1](✉), Jennie Ablanedo[2], and Tabitha Dwyer[3]

[1] US Army Research Laboratory, Human Research and Engineering Directorate,
Advanced Training & Simulation Division, Orlando, USA
tamara.s.griffith.civ@mail.mil
[2] Institute for Simulation and Training, University of Central Florida, Orlando, FL, USA
jablaned@ist.ucf.edu
[3] Cole Engineering Services, Inc., Orlando, FL, USA
tabitha.dwyer@cesicorp.com

Abstract. Active-shooter incidents within a school setting involve a unique subset of active-shooter events. These events tend to have significant differences in duration and outcome to events that occur in other locations, often being resolved before, or when, first-responders arrive on the scene. The frequency and seriousness of these events inspired the US Department of Homeland Security, Science and Technology Directorate's First Responder's Group (DHS S&T FRG) to leverage ongoing work with the US Army Research Laboratory, Human Research and Engineering Directorate, Advanced Training & Simulation Division (ARL HRED ATSD) to establish a prototype virtual school environment to prepare teachers, administrators and staff on how to respond and work with Law Enforcement (LE) in the event of a school shooting. This virtual platform allows school staff and LE to practice various strategies and even supports analysis into how different security measures within the school environment might change the dynamic of an attack and response. The goal is to train affected groups together in advance of an attack to improve coordination and reduce response time and casualties. This paper illustrates design choices for training school teachers, administrators and other staff in a virtual environment in the event of a school shooting. These choices demonstrate unique development strategies related to controlling Artificial Intelligence (AI) through simple user interfaces, managing crowd behaviors and ultimately will include the ability to apply game engine level rules to different buildings or maps.

Keywords: School shooting · First responder · Virtual training · Crowd control · Game engine

1 Introduction

On April 20, 1999 a shockwave moved across the United States as two high school students perpetrated a well-planned attack on Columbine High School. The students used two 9 mm firearms and two 12-gauge shotguns, which were sawed down to a concealable

---

© Springer International Publishing AG 2017
S. Lackey and J. Chen (Eds.): VAMR 2017, LNCS 10280, pp. 325–338, 2017.
DOI: 10.1007/978-3-319-57987-0_26

size, along with 99 improvised explosive devices [1]. The explosives were used as a diversionary tactic to distract first responders, then later to drive frightened crowds toward the attackers [2]. This horrific tragedy shocked the nation and drove law enforcement to re-examine antiquated response strategies [3]. Sadly, the event also inspired other potential attackers eager to achieve infamy by perpetuating further tragic events, such as the Virginia Tech massacre in 2007 where 27 students and five faculty members were killed [4]. More recently, on December 14, 2012, the world stood helpless as 20, six- and seven-year-olds were killed, along with teachers and administrators, at Sandy Hook Elementary in a time spanning five minutes and ending with the shooter's suicide [5] (Fig. 1). The police arrived a few minutes after the final shot, unaware of the number of attackers or the dangers or horrors they would find [6]. These active shooter incidents heightened awareness of the threat of violence towards children on campuses nationwide (Weatherby, 2015). The lessons learned from these horrific tragedies have prompted a greater demand for effective training against active shooter events within a school setting.

Fig. 1. Connecticut state police lead children from the Sandy Hook Elementary School [7].

Given the gravity and the unpredictable nature of the threat it is critical that schools train and prepare for potential active shooter events. Also, given that over fifty-seven percent of school shooting incidents are over before law enforcement arrives, lasting, on average, 12 min, and ending (55% of the time) with the attackers committing suicide, [8] teachers and school administrators must train as unarmed first-responders. Current training and drills include practicing lockdown and evacuation procedures for a variety of scenarios [9]. School administrators and staff work to anticipate and prepare for a variety of potential emergencies with an emphasis on consistent crisis plan customized for the geographic, economic and social standards [8]. Figure 2 is a snapshot that shows a breakdown of active shooter events by location, indicating that nearly a quarter of active shooter incidents between 2000 and 2013 occur in an educational setting.

The Federal Emergency Management Agency (FEMA) describes Active Shooter and Mass Casualty Incident (AS/MCI) as "involving one or more subjects that participate in a random or systematic shooting spree, demonstrating their intent to continuously harm others" [10]. MCIs are significant events that normally require coordination between on-scene fire/rescue/medical and LE with Unified Command (UC) being the

Location Categories

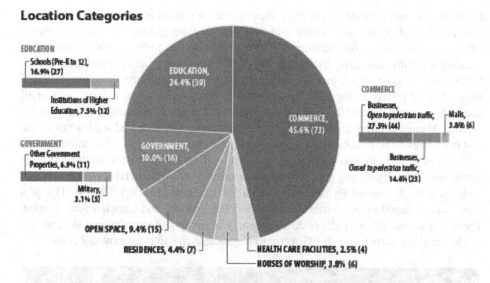

Fig. 2. Study of 160 active shooter incidents in the United States between 2000-2013 [11]

vehicle for command and control of the event through a Unified Command Post (UCP). Due to the rapid escalation and resolution of school shooting events, the UCP will likely not stand up until late in the timeline, meaning that a swift and coordinated response with meaningful communication will need to be established in advance of receiving guidance from command and control.

The information above sets the stage for the purpose behind the design of training capability. Using information gathered from reports on active shooter incidents and updated tactics has shaped the design for a virtual environment designed specifically to train school faculty and staff in the event of an active shooter incident within a school setting. The unique development strategies associated with the training environment is the focus of this paper.

2   Background

Following the successful implementation of a virtual environment that supports cross-service training for a complex coordinated attack, similar to that seen in Mumbai, India in 2008 [12, 13] it was apparent that there was demand for training to support the unique needs of a school setting. The Department of Homeland Security Science and Technology Directorate's First Responder's Group (DHS S&T FRG) along with the US Army Research Laboratory, Human Research and Engineering Directorate, Advanced Training & Simulation Division (ARL HRED ATSD), reached out to experts from Educator's School Safety Network to draw from existing data and lessons-learned to establish requirements for training within a school shooting scenario.

Historically, school staff are passive supporters to LE training for active shooter events [14]. However, based on the issues described above, it was determined that school administrators and staff are on the front lines of defense against active shooters and therefore must be part of response training. Although virtual training cannot replace the complex interactions involved in live training, live events are rare due to the logistics involved in securing a facility, accessing live actors and coordinating a myriad of interdependencies. When live events do occur, they are infrequent with only a very small fraction of potentially affected parties taking part. Virtual training simulations allow a large number of responders to train repeatedly, both as individuals and in teams potentially increasing the depth and breadth of trainee involvement since exercises can be repeated at a fraction of the cost of a live event and can be used to prepare trainees to make better use of live training time.

DHS S&T FRG looked to leverage previous work to reduce cost without sacrificing performance. By leveraging the established partnership with ARL HRED ATSD, DHS built upon the Enhanced Dynamic GeoSocial Environment (EDGE) (Fig. 3). This is a Government-owned platform making use of both the Unreal 3 and Unreal 4 game engine. The use of a game engine reduces development time, compared to traditional simulations, and leveraging efforts from other Government agencies helps to reduce overall costs.

Fig. 3. The enhance dynamic geo-social environment start screen in Unreal Engine 4

Individuals from the commercial modeling and simulation industry, academia, ARL HRED ATSD, and DHS S&T FRG along with first responders, school board members and a representative from Safe and Sounds Schools came together to establish detailed requirements to support training. The result is a virtual training prototype to be used to support a training exercise for first responders, including faculty and school staff, in response to active shooters in a school setting.

3   Stakeholder Goals

The primary stakeholders for this effort include the DHS S&T FRG, the ARL HRED ATSD, first responders and school administration and staff. Each had their own unique perspective to lend to the end product. Support in the development of this capability was provided by both academia - University of Central Florida, Institute for Simulation and Training (UCF IST) and industry (Cole Engineering Services, Inc.).

3.1 Department of Homeland Security Science and Technology First Responders Group

DHS S&T FRG has recognized a considerable increase in the number of active shooter events taking place in educational settings in the United States and world-wide. As a result, they turned their focus toward establishing a training tool to better prepare for this eventuality and to close the training gap between school staff and LE.

The requirements called for readily-accessible, high-fidelity simulation tools to support a training exercise not only for first responders in incident response and management but also for school staff who would function as first responders prior to LE arriving on the scene of an incident. This simulation allows large numbers of school staff to train repeatedly either at a common location or distributed. Teachers and administrators from multiple agencies, disciplines, and jurisdictions would be able to train for a coordinated incident response and have the flexibility to integrate location operational tactics and procedures.

3.2 School Administrators and Staff

In the case of LE officers, experience improves survivability. This applies to soldiers as well. This is why the Army invests heavily in simulations to build experience in a safe environment. A simulated experience ensures that the first time school administrators and staff experience a life threatening event they can use the experience to learn and improve their response if faced with a threat in real life. The environment can also be used to assess how schools might implement safety measures, testing various door locking strategies (lock from inside, automatic locks, etc.) while in the safety of a simulation to determine what works best (Elsass, 2016). A virtual environment provides a safe space to strategize using different theories and to provide training to educators to turn theory in to practice. The Educator's School Safety Network was founded to give educators a voice in critical school safety conversations. Their mission is to help keep schools safe by providing training, services and resources to educators, administrators, school-based law enforcement, and other stakeholders.

Administrators and staff must be able to train at the tribal, local, state or federal level, allowing varying authorities and policies. The training platform provides a training capability that prepares school teachers and staff from a small school house in Oklahoma to a larger school in New York City. The high-fidelity simulation supports training and exercise for large numbers of school staff to train repeatedly, both as small teams and alongside multiple agencies, disciplines, and jurisdictions as a coordinated incident response and have the flexibility to integrate location operational tactics and procedures with synchronized (not just coordinated) efforts of all groups.

3.3 Army Research Laboratory Human Research and Engineering Directorate Advanced Training & Simulation Division

US Army ARL HRED ATSD, specifically the Advanced Modeling & Simulation Branch, is exploring the use of commercial game engines to improve training in support of various tasks. In pursuit of this goal the Enhanced Dynamic Geo-Social Environment (EDGE) was born. The team responsible for EDGE holds firm to the belief that the Government should own the source code for training capabilities and that it should be shared across all Government organizations and agencies. By having Government rights to the source code of commercial technology, experts can develop specific functionality and make it available to others at no additional cost. For example, tactical movement with a weapon is very similar across the Army and first responders. This capability doesn't need to be created new for each new user of the environment. However, new functionality, such as the use of naturally propagating fire that has realistic damage effects on characters and the environment, can be developed once and reused by various agencies. The more agencies that utilize and develop on the architecture the greater the benefit.

EDGE prototypes are developed as part of an overall goal to reduce potential development risks, such as performance limitations while assessing the training effectiveness of prototypes in the test bed. The EDGE team has established a kind of game technology incubator in their game lab, inviting other Government groups to participate in development alongside the team to gain knowledge and experience which they can then bring back to their own labs for reuse.

The goals for this project were to evolve previous work, completed in Unreal 3, into the robust development tool provided by Unreal 4 using the same business model for cost efficiencies. There are many benefits in designing the school within UE4. For example, the engine contains higher graphical fidelity through advancements in rendering efficiency and physically based materials. It has the ability for rapid prototyping using the new UE4 Blueprint system (visual scripting, no code). Unreal 4 has improved developer tools for animation, materials and visual effects. The ability to separate project source code from engine source code make it easier to maintain currency and reducing development and build times [15]. Much of the original models and artwork created in Unreal Engine 3 were leveraged to support this new work.

By making use of tools that the Army can benefit from, overall development costs for each contributor are reduced. Most importantly, all products are available at no cost to end-users with no limit to the number of user seats.

One of the greater costs of training can be bringing the students to the training event. Sometimes the instructor is brought to the students to reduce costs. One goal for the Army is to make training available at the point of need. Students do not need to be co-located with the instructor. The technology allows for local or distributed exercises. The environment can be available to train 24 h a day, seven days a week.

The EDGE team also conducts research into various user interfaces. The game architecture allows for a wide breadth of flexible user input, quite often in a plug-and-play fashion. The use of simulated weapons, game controllers, floor pads, head-mounted displays and wearable technology can all interface into the environment.

Both DHS S&T FRS and ARL HRED ATSD felt that a graphically-rich, high fidelity environment would make training more realistic and believable while meeting the expectations of the generation of users who have been brought up with high fidelity games at their disposal.

4 Design Decisions Based on Stakeholder Needs

Characters. Figure 4 shows the character selection screen. Each role and its design attributes are described below.

Fig. 4. Character selection screen for school scenario

Teachers. Teachers play a vital role in emergency response of a school shooting incident. Teachers keep students calm during an emergency and protect their students. It is vital for a teacher to be prepared and to practice making use of their various options. Design decisions associated with this role are described below.

The teacher character role is equipped with a master key to access all playable rooms. Teachers have the ability to direct (or control) Artificial Intelligence (AI) students. They have a list of commands such as "line up against the wall," "leave through that window," "hide," and "follow me" (Fig. 5). Teachers can also communicate with the rest of the school a Public Address (PA) system by accessing the intercom on the walls of classrooms. Teachers enter the environment by selecting a room which will then be filled with students.

Staff Roles (Administrators and other staff). The school administrator role is equipped with a master key. They have ability to speak to teachers over the PA system from the intercom in the front office. Staff can also give orders to the AI students. This role differs from teachers in that they do not start the simulation within a classroom.

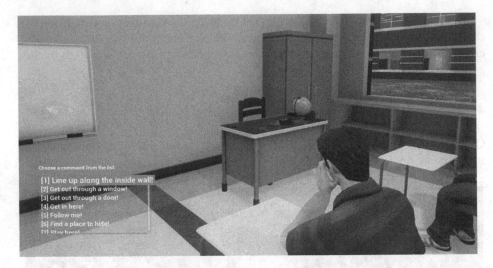

Fig. 5. User interface to control students

Law Enforcement Officers (LEO). The law enforcement roles is equipped with a Taser, an assault rifle, a handgun, and a shotgun (Fig. 6); all weaponry has limited ammunition. They are protected with a bullet proof vest and a helmet. Careful consideration was applied to the police role for this particular scenario and will be discussed later in this paper.

Fig. 6. Law enforcement officer's load out

School Resource Officer (SRO). School districts and local law enforcement are increasingly teaming up to ensure that more campuses have a law enforcement presence [16]. The use of campus security and police officers has been an excellent resource for supporting the school systems. These security personnel are known as School Resource Officers (SROs) and are assigned to a school or school district. This role is similar to an LEO role except for the weapon load out and the starting location.

Suspect Roles. The suspects drive the scenario. Their activities determine the response. Suspects are played by live role-players to allow for a wide range of scenario support and to avoid learners getting to know AI activities and "gaming" the training event. The suspect role is equipped with an assault rifle, a handgun, a shotgun, extra assault rifle ammunition and a pipe bomb. Since statistics show that 55% of the time an active shooter will commit suicide after the act is committed [17], this would be an additional capability for this role; allowing the suspect to commit suicide within the simulation.

Students. Although most students are represented as AI, as described in the next section, participants may also choose to enter the environment as a student. A live role player in the student role can either help or cause chaos as defined by the exercise control team. Since they will also be able to communicate with others via voice, they can give helpful or misleading information to trainees, affecting the course of the scenario.

Non-Player Characters and Artificial Intelligence. Because of the importance of crowds in a school environment, multiple Non-Player Characters (NPC's) are used to establish realism and, in some cases, chaos. This gives role players more people to interact with and protect. Character roles, such as teachers, administrators and LEO, have the ability to manage NPCs within the scenario allowing for a more fluid and realistic experience. The crowds can add to the chaos within the school, as well as allow for teachers and staff to practice what orders they would give to those they see roaming in the hallways or in the classroom. For example, each NPC has a panicked state that will randomly trigger the character to flee and evacuate, hide or stay in place. These triggers transition into behaviors after the NPC detects more than two gunshots, they see a law enforcement officer equipped with a weapon, or they detect a suspect equipped with a weapon.

Artificial Intelligence (AI) drive the NPC's to take commands from various player characters (teacher, administrator or LEO). For example, the NPC's can transition to an orderly evacuation from an alarmed state when given the command to evacuate via the nearest rooms, doors, or windows.

Game environments support a wide spectrum of realistic qualities. Three-dimensional sound can help trainees determine where shots or shouts are coming from. Players expend stamina while sprinting, breaking into a walk when stamina is exhausted. The level of gore presented can be ramped up or scaled back depending on the training value for that particular training audience. In the first iteration of the school scenario, the amount of blood that would be visible was scaled back to be sensitive to emotional reactions from teachers and staff. In future versions this will be a configurable option for each exercise.

Each player has an indication of damage state. The physics and vulnerability models determine whether a character is injured, stunned, armor damaged, incapacitated, or dead based on a number of factors including weapon used, whether armor was equipped, and the exact location where the impact occurred.

4.1 The Environment

The simulations allows for future growth and scalable numbers of participants. The architecture allows various locations to be modeled using the same "game rules." Game rules establish how players interact with the environment and one another. As game engine technology advances it is leveraged and applied to the level to maximize the government investment. Using commercial game technology was expected to improve participant engagement. The actual school used in this scenario is shown in Fig. 7.

Fig. 7. Outside view of the school

5 Conducting an Exercise

There are quite a few moving parts that must work together to establish a training exercise. This section outlines an important subset.

Communications have to be realistic with local proximity noise and voice communication as well as radio communication across various tactical channels. Proximity talk is accomplished by simply talking into the player headset, while radios are "keyed" using the space bar. The school intercom is operating by interacting with the intercom box on the wall of the classroom (activating the "F" key when in proximity to the intercom box).

Trainers capitalize on teachable moments by observing individuals during and after the exercise. This can be accomplished by being an invisible viewer in the environment in real-time or by playing back the exercise and viewing it from each character's perspective through the After Action Review (AAR) tool. This tool includes synchronized capture and playback of all local, radio, and PA voice communications.

Each individual role player needs a computer with a graphics card to display the high-fidelity graphics, however, the computer does not need to be new or state-of-the-art. Computers that meet the needs of the software are generally under $1,000 by current market standards. Training can also be conducted in a distributed manner with trainees participating from their geographically separate facilities.

Most importantly, this training tool is not made up of a small handful of scenarios. Instead it allows for a multitude of scenarios. This is referred to as a "sandbox" approach, meaning that the virtual environment could support any variation of possibilities from an individual shooter to multiple intelligent shooters with incendiary devices. Actions in the environment would be managed through an exercise control cell who dictates the actions of individuals in the role of the attackers [18]. The simulation encourages teachers, administrators, and staff to train together while applying their own doctrine or Standard Operating Procedure (SOPs). Consider one jurisdiction where the policy is that the first individual on the scene of an active shooter event must wait for backup before engaging shooters while another jurisdiction requires responders to move to stimulus immediately. The virtual environment allows all possible responses. Interactions are not scripted, and just like real-life, anything can happen. This means that events in the environment can and will get very messy and complicated with miscommunication and chaos. The intent is that mistakes or learning moments happen in the virtual environment rather than while actual lives are at stake.

When conducting a virtual exercise it is important to establish familiarity with the virtual tools and how to navigate within the environment prior to starting an exercise. Participants receive a briefing on the intent of the training and a description of how they enter and navigate the virtual environment. The participants break out into their specialization groups and receive a tutorial explaining how to use their role-specific capabilities within the environment. After the tutorials, participants enter the environment and engage in familiarization activities. Participants are encouraged to explore the school and practice using their weapons and communications. This often looks like play, but is a critical element for them to build familiarization with the tools available prior to the serious task of the learning exercise.

6 Challenges and Mitigation

There has been a small amount of research on best practices for school-based crisis planning with little hard evidence to indicate what will work in the event of a crisis (US Department of Education, 2003). A simulation allows research to be conducted in order to identify strategies to overcome policy gaps, and to establish best practices to ensure the safety of children. At the same time, emergency plans and procedures cannot follow a one-size-fits-all model. Flexibility is essential if lockdown and evacuation drills are going to be effective [9]. Using commercial game technology, an individual joins a team to accomplish a complex task. The team can be distributed anywhere around the world. By utilizing the sandbox model in the virtual environment, a variety of scenarios can be performed to not only rehearse use cases, but to allow for simulations to be performed setting policies for different geographic areas.

Running an exercise as a training event is not like traditional course work. Sometimes, there is no "correct response." Sometimes the correct response is purely defined by the outcome and can only be assessed retrospectively. Take for instance the decision by the Kenyan security forces to delay entering the Westgate Mall, while plainclothes civilian rescuers and plainclothes police rushed in to engage terrorist attackers [19]. The decision by the impromptu group could have endangered existing response activity or it could have saved considerable lives. Retrospectively, given the lack of State response the civilian response may have been warranted. In order for an exercise to become a learning event, it is critical that observers be present to make note of actions at every level. For example, if the LE observer sees activities that violate doctrine, they are played back and discussed during an AAR. Each component of the response team should receive a review of their performance during the exercise, then the larger team receives feedback on how the components worked as a team. Strengths and opportunities for improvements are highlighted and discussed. This is also a good time to discuss if protocols should be re-examined. After the exercise has been thoroughly reviewed, participants have the opportunity to apply the learning by running another exercise [13].

Training for mass casualty events is often focused on one or two components of the event to simplify and focus training. For example, LE may focus on finding an active shooter to stop the threat. However, they may not train on the events that follow, such as clearing the area and preserving evidence. With a virtual environment every activity associated with the response to an active shooter incident can be exercises. Details such as the control of traffic, the placement of the Incident Command Post (ICP) – that can bring about success or failure in an active-shooter incident, even tactics from historic events [20] – can be modeled in the virtual environment.

7 Way Ahead

Work has already started on the next iteration of the EDGE First Responders Sandbox School training level that will add emergency medical and fire fighter roles. The next iteration will include the ability to edit the scenario to start at various times of the school day. Before school starts, students will be in crowds in gathering areas inside and outside the building. During lunch, the bulk of students will be in the cafeteria. Other enhancements will include the ability to adjust door type (lock inside, lock outside, auto lock, swing in, swing out, etc.), whether there are Public Address Systems or intercoms, as well as many other options, such as the use of cell phones for communication. It will also be possible for trainees to fight back unarmed, including punching and throwing objects.

8 Conclusion

Active-shooter incidents within a school setting are a unique subset of active-shooter events. This concern inspired development of a prototype virtual school environment to prepare teachers, administrators and staff on how to respond and work with Law Enforcement (LE) in the event of a school shooting. This environment will be made available at no cost to the training audience to improve survivability of this threat. The team made use of the Unreal Engine 4 to quickly prototype a training level using development and modeling tools to manage crowds and apply various response strategies in the event of a school shooting. These strategies can be used to explore how different security measures within the school environment might change the dynamic of an attack and response.

References

1. Cullen, D.: Columbine. Twelve Hachette Book Group, New York (2010)
2. State of Colorado. Columbine Official Report: Columbine Review Commission: 2001 (2001)
3. Chastain, M.A.: Shoot first: Columbine tragedy transformed police tactics. USA Today, 19 April 2009
4. Roy, L.: No Right to Remain Silent: What We've Learned from the Tragedy at Virginia Tech. Three Rivers Press, New York (2009)
5. Lysiak, M.: Newtown - An American Tragedy. Gallery Books, New York (2013)
6. Powell, C.: Sandy Hook Slaughter: The Newtown Shooting and Massacre in Connecticut. Thoughts and Lessons on a Tragedy and the Coming Paradigm Shift. First World Publishing, New York (2012)
7. Hicks, S.: Photograph of Children Led from Sandy Hook Elementary School. Connecticut: s.n., Newtown
8. Federal Bureau of Investigation (FBI). Active Shooter Events from 2000 to 2012. s.l.: FBI (2014)
9. Dillon, N.: Planning to ensure our schools are safe. Am. School Board J. **72**, 9–11 (2007)
10. Federal Emergency Management Agency (FEMA). Fire/Emergency Medical Services Department Operational Considerations and Guide for Active Shooter and Mass Casualty Incidents. Department of Homeland Security, Washington, DC (2013)
11. FBI Law Enforcement Bulletin. Active Shooter Events from 2000 to 2012. s.l.: The Federal Bureau of Investigation (2014)
12. Griffith, T., Ablanedo, J.: Cross-agency collaboration provides better preparedness at a low cost. ITEC Defense Training Simulation Education, s.n., London, England (2016)
13. Griffith, T., Ablanedo, J., Nenneman, M.: Defense and first-responders leverage virtual technology: taking it to the edge. In: International Defense and Homeland Security Simulation Workshop 2015, pp. 19–21. I3M, Bergeggi, Italy (2015)
14. Buerger, M.E., Buerger, G.E.: Those terrible first few minutes. FBI Law Enforcement Bull. **79**, 1–4 (2010)
15. Epic Games. What is Unreal Game Engine 4? Unreal Engine, 17 January 2017. www.unrealengine.com/what-is-unreal-engine-4
16. Weatherby, D.: Opening the "Snake Pit": arming teachers in the war against school violence and the government-created risk doctrine. Conn. Law Rev. **48**, 119–176 (2015)
17. Schildkraut, J.V., Elsass, H.J.: Mass Shootings: Media, Myths, and Realities. Praeger Books, Santa Barbara (2016)
18. Department of Homeland Security Science and Technology. Virtual Training Program. DHS, Washington, DC (2014)
19. (BBC), British Broadcasting Corporation. Terror at the Mall (2014)
20. Los Angeles World Airports. Active Shooter Incident and Resulting Airport Disruption - A Review of Response Operations. Los Angeles World Airports, Los Angeles, CA (2014)
21. Federal Emergency Management Agency (FEMA) U.S. Fire Administration. Fire/Emergency Medical Services Department Operational Considerations and Guide for Active Shooter and Mass Casualty Incidents. U.S. Department of Homeland Security, Washington, DC (2013)
22. Activision Publishing. Call of Duty, 2 June 2015. https://www.callofduty.com
23. British Broadcasting Corporation (BBC). Terror at the Mall. BBC, England (2014)
24. Los Angeles World Airports. Active Shooter Incident and Resulting Airport Disruption - A Review of Response Operations, Los Angeles, CA: s.n. (2014)
25. Rand Corporation. The Lessons of Mumbai. The Rand Corporation, Santa Monica, CA (2009)

26. National Commission Of Terrorist Attacks. The 9/11 Commission Report: Final Report of the National Commission on Terrorist Attacks Upon the United States. s.l.: Cosimo, Inc. (2010)
27. Blair, J.P., et al.: Active Shooter Events and Response. CRC Press, Taylor & Francis Group, Boca Raton (2013)
28. Siddique, M.: India Blames Pakistan for Mumbai Attack Plans. AAJ News, Pakistan Ki-Awaz (2012)
29. DHS S&T FRS. Status Briefing to the DHS S&T First Responder Resource Group. DHS, Sacramento, CA (2013)
30. First Net. First Responders Collaborate to Develop Technologies. First Responders Network Authority, 26 November 2014. www.firstnet.gov/newsroom/blog/first-responders-collaborate-develop-technologies

SuperJam: Participatory Design for Accessible Games

Emily K. Johnson[✉], Peter A. Smith, Matt Dombrowski, and Ryan Buyssens

University of Central Florida, Orlando, FL, USA
{emily.johnson,peter.smith,mattd,ryan.buyssens}@ucf.edu

Abstract. This paper describes the design of a participatory design project being planned with specific goals around a central mission: to build a more inclusive community through gaming. To improve the quality of life of those with paralysis, we are planning a game jam to increase the number of games that are playable for this community. The theme for this game jam, called SuperJam, is alternatively controlled games. We have already designed an alternative controller that is manipulated by electromyography (EMG) sensors, which detect electric impulses from the player's muscles. This specific controller has been utilized in the past by amputees to play simple prosthetic training games, and the same EMG technology operates hands-free wheelchairs by flexing muscles on the face or jaw. The teams at SuperJam will be challenged to create enjoyable games that can be played using this hands-free controller.

Additionally, though the SuperJam website, we seek to continue to encourage the community building that this event will foster. Through this site, all games completed at SuperJam will be available for free, and the site will also support a community discussion board in addition to blog-style posts featuring interviews with SuperJam participants, new alternative controllers being developed, and other topics that may interest this newly formed community of people with paralysis and gamers. This website will be the hub for maintaining the community-building work being initiated by this exciting event.

Keywords: Games · Participatory design · Alternative controllers

1 Introduction

A person's quality of life is defined as that person's perception of the equivalence of aspirations and achievements, and a variety of types of measures have been developed to assess quality of life [1]. One of the many factors influencing this perception is social participation. Technology now affords the participation in countless types of activities virtually, eliminating the need to physically travel to be social.

Videogames seem especially conducive to encouraging active participation for all types of people. Unfortunately, few videogames are designed to be playable by people with paralysis. Some games have been adapted and/or created specifically for members of this community, and there have been calls to make games more accessible [2], it is still not common to mainstream gaming. Current internet technology allows people with paralysis to engage with online communities and participate virtually in different ways,

© Springer International Publishing AG 2017
S. Lackey and J. Chen (Eds.): VAMR 2017, LNCS 10280, pp. 339–348, 2017.
DOI: 10.1007/978-3-319-57987-0_27

but there remains a stark difference between the number of videogames that are accessible and the number that are not.

1.1 Participatory Design

Participatory design developed from the fields of ethnography and human-computer interaction [3]. Within the field of human-computer interaction, the main goals for utilizing participatory design methods include sharing control and expertise as well as inspiring change [4]. The inclusion of stakeholders such as potential customers, players, and end-users in the design process is thought to improve the quality of the digital product (game, website, etc.) being developed.

Research suggests that participatory game design is beneficial to everyone involved, such as eliminating the subjectivity of the designers and aligning technology to user needs [5]. Past research suggests a need for using participatory design structures to develop wheelchair-controlled motion-based videogames and speculates that the inclusion of potential players of alternatively-controlled videogames can ensure the suitability of the games while also increasing the confidence of the game designers who do not typically use alternative controllers [6].

Interestingly, this study design kept two expert groups separate as they attempted, over several weeks, to design videogames that could be controlled by players who used wheelchairs [6]. The results suggested that the group of professional game designers lacked important knowledge about the life experiences of people who use wheelchairs. Strikingly, when confronted with this fact, the game designers in the study admitted they did not personally know anyone who used a wheelchair and were staunchly unwilling to even attempt to gather such vital game design information from strangers in person. Similarly, though the study participants who used wheelchairs were certainly knowledgeable about the wheelchair use, they lacked the game design knowledge to make truly compelling games [6]. It seems obvious, then, that by combining the two groups into a participatory game design structure, the difficulties the study groups faced can be eliminated. The game designer participants will be required to collaborate with the participants in wheelchairs, thus removing the social awkwardness of attempting to contact a stranger and interview her about her physical differences. So, too, will the novice game designs of the participants using wheelchairs benefit from the expertise of the game designer participants.

The collaborative nature of participatory game design can harness the knowledge and expertise of members of these two different groups, leveraging the personal experiences of people who use wheelchairs as well as the game design expertise of skilled game designers. This partnership of game designers and experts in a specific field has been employed at past game jams with much success.

1.2 Game Jams for Content Creation

Game jams are usually 48 h events where participants develop games around a common theme, challenge, or hardware configuration. Participants approach these events as fun and educational experiences. Some participants are veteran game developers while others are making games for the first time. They are usually considered intense experience where skills are often tested. Other game jams have explored utilizing unique hardware.

Game jams attract the game design community and expand their knowledge and interest in a wide variety of topics. For example, the Indie Galactic Space Jam, an annual game jam organized by co-author Dr. Smith to develop games that increase awareness and knowledge of space travel, space exploration and the STEM (science, technology, engineering, and math) fields, is actually sponsored in part by the Space Industry (Space Florida, the Kennedy Space Center, etc.) [7]. Game jams have proven themselves to be great ways to generate usable content for many projects. This jam has resulting in nearly 100 space games that explore a wide range of topics, such as mining asteroids, colonizing planets, and working with robots. Game jams have also become popular worldwide. In 2016, the Global Game Jam was a coordination of over 600 locations in 93 countries, producing 6,866 new games in a single weekend [8].

Game Jams are not limited in scope to just regular PC., often game jams are a way to experiment with new hardware. They can be used to prototype new uses for old technologies or be a conduit to explore new technologies and gain new skills. When the focus is only about hardware use and not about learning and experimenting the events are usually called Hackathons. Hackathons can be further distinguished from jams by the inclusions of IP agreements with the hardware holders, cash prizes and a generally more extrinsic motivation to improve a product over learning new skills.

2   SuperJam

The mission of SuperJam is to build a more inclusive community through gaming. To improve the quality of life of those with paralysis, we propose a game jam to increase the number of games that are playable for this community. Game jams are high-energy, short-term events with long-term results, where participants form spontaneous teams to design games around a specific theme or challenge. Each game is then judged, and winning teams are awarded prizes. Winning games, and often all completed games, are then made available for download via the internet—a benefit for budding game developers who wish to display their work as well as for players who enjoy playing new, innovative games. Making the games available online furthers the scope of building a broader reaching community.

The theme for SuperJam is alternatively controlled games. We have already designed an alternative controller that is manipulated by electromyography (EMG) sensors, which detect electric impulses from the player's muscles. This specific controller has been utilized in the past by amputees to play simple prosthetic training games, and the same technology is utilized to operate hands-free wheelchairs via muscles on the face or jaw. The challenge that SuperJam will pose to participants is to create enjoyable games that can be played using this hands-free controller. Having worked with other hardware-specific game jam themes in the past, we are aware that these themes like alternatively-controlled games often come with additional challenges, as few game designers have worked with the specific type of alternative controller for which they will be asked to design games. This can, at times, slow the game development and result in fewer games being designed overall.

Fortunately, the lessons learned from participating in such prior experiences also help inform the planning of such an event. There are several steps that can be taken in the initial stages of the planning of SuperJam that can mitigate these obstacles. First, we can post information about the controllers on the registration website. This will allow participants to arrive at SuperJam with an understanding of how the controllers function, what types of motions the controller can read and respond to, example commands the input can map to, etc. This working knowledge of the hardware that SuperJam requires games to utilize will give each team a head start toward the creation of enjoyable games that can be played by people with many types of paralysis.

SuperJam will begin with speakers who have volunteered to share their experiences with paralysis. This will inform developers as to what requirements their game must have while also encouraging creativity. Day One concludes with team formation, which will each include members of the paralysis community. Day Two and most of Day Three will consist of teams working together to create unique interactive experiences using the alternative controllers (Table 1). Through this collaborative group effort, each team will produce an interactive game. At the conclusion of Day Three, the games will be presented by the teams and judged for a variety of awards. This event will not only create games, but build partnerships, empower creative thinking, and, most importantly, be a fun, engaging experience for all participants.

Table 1. Schedule of events at SuperJam.

Day 1	
6:00 pm–8:00 pm Inspirational Lectures	Following an introduction and an overview of the goals and schedule of SuperJam, speakers from the paralysis community will share information about their conditions, their requirements for alternatively controlled games, their individual game style preferences (likely unique to each individual player), etc. These talks are intended to spark creativity while also provide information to game design teams
8:00 pm–10:00 pm Form Teams	SuperJam participants form game design teams, which must be led by an Alternative Controller Expert (ACE). Teams begin planning for the next day's work
Day 2	
8:00 am–12:00 pm	SuperJam resumes, and game design/creation commences
12:00 pm–1:00 pm	Optional lunch break
1:00 pm–6:00 pm	Game design and creation
6:00 pm–7:00 pm	Optional dinner break
7:00 pm–10:00 pm	Game design and creation; Day 2 concludes at 10:00 pm
Day 3	
8:00 am–12:00 pm	Game design and creation
12:00 pm–1:00 pm	Optional lunch break
1:00 pm–4:00 pm	Game design and creation
4:00 pm–5:30 pm	Demonstrations and playtesting of completed games
5:30 pm–7:30 pm	Team presentations during dinner break
8:00 pm–9:00 pm	Awards ceremony, conclusion of SuperJam

Additionally, though the SuperJam website, we seek to continue to foster the community building that begins at this event. Through this site, all games completed at SuperJam will be available for free, and the site will also support a community discussion board in addition to blog-style posts featuring interviews with SuperJam participants, new alternative controllers being developed, and other topics that may interest this newly formed community of people with paralysis and gamers. This website will be the hub for maintaining the community-building work being initiated by this exciting event.

2.1 Multifaceted Goals

SuperJam's mission is to foster a more inclusive community through gaming. This event's participatory design will support increased integration of people living with paralysis into the general public by achieving its four goals:

- Increase the number of games that can be played by members of the paralysis community using an alternative controller.
- Increase awareness and understanding of the paralysis community.
- Increase comradery between members of the paralysis and gaming communities.
- Create and sustain an online alternative-controller community through a website designed for participants of SuperJam, the paralysis community, the gaming community, and anyone with an interest in alternatively controlled games.

A high-energy, collaborative community event like SuperJam is capable of meeting a number of goals. The obvious and primary goal is to create videogames that can be played using alternative controllers. This challenge should be enticing to the game design community, as it imposes unique constraints on game design that require creativity and innovation. The type of alternative controller SuperJam focuses on utilizes EMG technology to receive player input. This same technology is also harnessed by the hands-free wheelchair developed by Limbitless Solutions, Inc. The EMG device used is the MyoWare Muscle Sensor and can be seen in Fig. 1 below.

Previous collaboration with Limbitless Solutions, Inc. has resulted in the creation of five short games played using these sensors; the beta versions of these games won the Best Serious Game Innovation Award at the Serious Games Showcase & Challenge during I/ITSEC (Interservice/Industry Training, Simulation and Education Conference) 2016. This explicit goal in and of itself is a very worthwhile endeavor. SuperJam, however, is also designed to accomplish other, more implicit goals that will further improve the quality of life for those with paralysis.

SuperJam is also designed to be a community-building event. By holding an event to address the need for additional games tailored for use with these alternative controllers, we hope to achieve SuperJam's second goal, an increase in awareness and understanding of the paralysis community. This event will underscore for many game designers the need to continue developing games that can be played in non-traditional ways.

The third goal of SuperJam is to increase comradery between and among the paralysis and gaming communities. The tightly-knit gaming community has a pervasive online presence [9]. The paralysis community is often ignored or forgotten by the public,

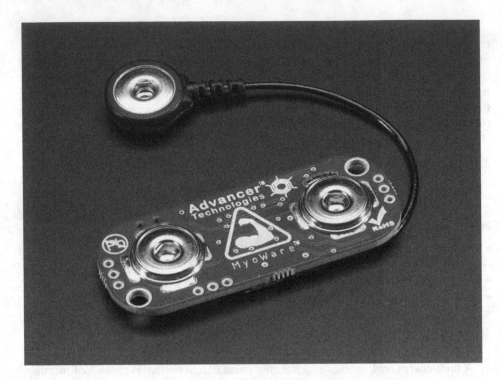

Fig. 1. The MyoWare Muscle Sensor

prompting blogs [10] and forums [11] for people living with paralysis and their care-givers. We believe that introducing these communities to one another by facilitating collaborative work toward a common goal will strengthen and expand the presence of the paralysis community. Game jams generally begin with a series of inspirational lectures, where experts on the game jam's theme share information about the theme, the requirements of the games' intended players, ideal features of the games, and so forth.

SuperJam will follow this format as well, and will ask for volunteers from the para-lysis community, which includes family members and caregivers, to share information about different types of paralysis, provide insight as to their frustrations with commercial games and controllers, suggest types of games they would like the game jam to create, etc. Additionally, each team at SuperJam will include at least one member of the para-lysis community, referred to here as an Alternative-Controller Expert, or ACE, who will lead the game design and ensure that it is playable and appropriate for members of the paralysis community. Finally, the SuperJam judging team will be comprised primarily of ACEs.

Finally, it is not enough to simply hold a three-day event and hope that it creates lasting community impact. The fourth goal of SuperJam is to sustain this community online long after the event. The website where participants will register for SuperJam will also showcase the winning games, provide free access to all game completed at SuperJam, and house the links for the anonymous post-event survey and the delayed survey. In addition, this website will include a community issues discussion board and feature blog-style posts of interviews with SuperJam participants, game design students living with paralysis, and other topics of interest to this emerging community, such as articles about new alternative controllers in development. We will maintain this website through the Games Research Lab for a minimum of one year after SuperJam is held. The culminating goal of this event is to bring communities together through gaming. Events like SuperJam promote a diverse, inclusive society. Gaming should be able to be enjoyed by all, no exceptions.

3 Methods

As with any event, the success of SuperJam will require different types of efficacy metrics. Increased awareness can be inferred from event participation and website traffic. The increased accessibility of games for the paralysis community can also be quantified in the number of games created from SuperJam teams, as well as by the number of times each new game is downloaded from the website. Additionally, all SuperJam participants will be asked to participate in a standard, Institutional Review Board-approved post-event survey that will include questions asking participants to reflect on their experience at SuperJam, rate the overall event, provide feedback about specific aspects of SuperJam, and suggest improvements for any similar, future events that may be held.

The success of this event's building of a sense of community between the gaming community and the paralysis community can be assessed through the number and types of posts to the community forum page of the SuperJam website. Finally, to assess the longer-term effects of the event, participants will be asked to respond to an electronic delayed survey 3–6 weeks after SuperJam to gain insight on any changes in perspective or attitude resulting from their participation.

3.1 Measurements

Quantifiable results. Certain outputs of SuperJam can be quantified (Table 2). These numbers can help to paint a picture of participation and success. Speculations about increased awareness and knowledge can be extrapolated by examining the participation totals, website hits, and the number of comments and posts on the blog and forum sections of the website.

Qualitative outcomes. While quantifiable results will inform the team of the success of SuperJam's primary goal, to increase the number of games that are playable with the EMG controller, more holistic measures are required for determining achievement of the other three goals: increase awareness of the paralysis community, increase comradery between the paralysis and gaming communities, and to sustain a community of players and designers of alternatively controlled games online. The quantifiable results can be interpreted as representing an increase in such qualitative entities as awareness, knowledge, and comradery, but to more thoroughly assess the outcomes of SuperJam, the team turns to more qualitative measures.

Table 2. Quantifiable results of SuperJam.

Numerical results	Implications
Number of:	*Increase in:*
Participants in SuperJam	Awareness and knowledge of paralysis community (goals 2 & 3)
Games created at SuperJam	Number of games playable with alternative controllers (goal 1)
Times each SuperJam game is downloaded	Playing of alternatively controlled games (variation of goal 1)
Times SuperJam registration and community website is visited	Awareness, knowledge, and comradery between gaming and paralysis communities (goals 2, 3, & 4)
Comments on SuperJam website blog and article posts	Knowledge and comradery between gaming and paralysis communities (goals 3 & 4)
Comments made on SuperJam website's community forum	Knowledge and comradery between gaming and paralysis communities (goals 3 & 4)

At the conclusion of SuperJam, participants will be asked to self-report any perceived increase of awareness of the paralysis community as well as any increase in knowledge of specific information about the kinds of experiences common to people with paralysis (in gaming and daily life). This exit survey will also ask participants to reflect on their participation in SuperJam, which will provide valuable insight to the team about the event. These outcomes in conjunction with the quantifiable results will help the team better understand the impact of SuperJam.

Additionally, participants will be asked to complete an online survey 3–6 weeks after participating in SuperJam. This delayed survey will ask participants to self-report their levels of awareness and understanding of the paralysis community as well as their amount of involvement in the online communities (blog and forum) and for any additional experiences or lasting effects that they believe resulted from their involvement in SuperJam.

4   Impact of Virtual Reality on Paralysis

In the paralysis community there has been great strides made through the use of Virtual Reality (VR) tools. With some even leading to the ability to move limbs that have been paralyzed for years. According to an article published in Scientific Reports, a 32-year-old man regained partial mobility in his legs after VR therapy [12]. There is great interest in this area by both the paralysis community and the game community, and VR solutions will be highly encouraged at the event. The system used utilizes an Oculus Rift and an EEG device. An example of what this looks like can be seen in Previous VR game jams conducted in the local area have generated some surprising games. Through the use of Google Cardboard, HTC Vives, and of course Oculus Rifts, there will be an emphasis on creating VR applications and games as well. In the case of SuperJam the VR experiences will further enhance the training to control the user's wheelchair (Fig. 2).

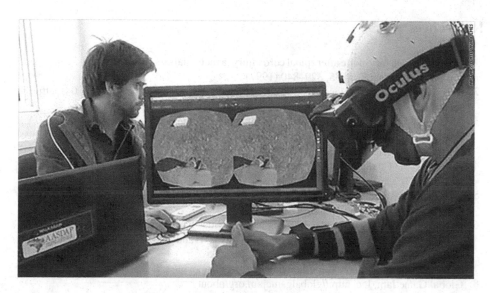

Fig. 2. An EEG controlled VR experience

5   Conclusions and Implications

This paper describes a participatory game design event, SuperJam, and the specific metrics being planned to evaluate the game jam's accomplishment of its four goals: to increase the number of games that are playable using an EMG sensing controller, to increase the awareness of the paralysis community, to increase knowledge about the experiences of people with paralysis, and to create a sense of comradery between the paralysis and gaming communities.

Though SuperJam itself has yet to formally take place, the design considerations we have already undertaken are substantial. By plotting out the four specific goals, measurable results, and methods to sustain the beneficial results that will be realized in achieving our intended goals, we have clarified the purpose and the structure of this event. We work to ensure we will reach our lofty, multifaceted goals by utilizing the work of prior scholars and following the suggestions laid out by their research. Here, we have shared our approach and methods that they may be critiqued and improved as well as replicated for the benefit of other populations and games.

Through this carefully planned game jam, it is the team's intent to help build community through gaming. SuperJam's participatory design framework will present an engaging challenge for participants to solve collaboratively. Game designers and people with paralysis will work together to create innovative games, providing members of two generally separated communities to come together to learn from and with one another at an exciting, fun event.

References

1. Dijkers, M.: Quality of life after spinal cord injury: a meta analysis of the effects of disablement components. Spinal Cord **35**, 829–840 (1997)
2. International Game Developers Association, Game accessibility white paper (2004). https://gasig.files.wordpress.com/2011/10/igda_accessibility_whitepaper.pdf
3. Blomberg, J., Burrell, M., Guest, G.: An ethnographic approach to design. In: Jacko, J.A., Sears, A. (eds.) The Human-Computer Interaction Handbook, pp. 965–986. Lawrence Erlbaum Associates, Mahwah (2003)
4. Vines, J. et al.: Configuring participation: on how we involve people in design. In: CHI 2013. ACM (2013)
5. Khaled, R., Vasalou, A.: Bridging serious games and participatory design. Int. J. Child Comp. Interact. **2**(2), 93–100 (2014)
6. Gerling, K., et al.: Creating wheelchair-controlled video games: challenges and opportunities when involving young people with mobility impairments and game design experts. Int. J. Hum Comput Stud. **94**, 64–73 (2016)
7. Indie Galactic Space Jam. http://indiegalacticspacejam.com/
8. Global Game Jam, Inc. http://globalgamejam.org/about
9. O'Connor, E.L., et al.: Sense of community, social identity and social support among players of massively multiplayer online games (MMOGs): a qualitative analysis. J. Comm. Appl. Soc. Psychol. **25**(6), 459–473 (2015). doi:10.1002/casp.2224
10. Christopher and Dana Reeve Foundation Blog. https://www.christopherreeve.org/blog
11. Christopher and Dana Reeve Foundation Discussion Forum. http://www.spinalcordinjury-paralysis.org/home
12. Donati, A.R., Shokur, S., Morya, E., Campos, D.S., Moioli, R.C., Gitti, C.M., Brasil, F.L.: Long-term training with a brain-machine interface-based gait protocol induces partial neurological recovery in paraplegic patients. Sci. Rep. **6**, 30383 (2016)

User-Generated Accessibility in Virtual World Games

Don Merritt[(⊠)]

University of Central Florida, Orlando, FL, USA
don.merritt@ucf.edu

Abstract. Video games as an entertainment venue and business category continue to grow rapidly. Despite their increasing cultural relevance there is little discussion about the experience of video game players with disabilities, especially in virtual world games. There are, however, examples of games with very successful players with a wide variety of disabilities. One such virtual world video game is Blizzard Entertainment's World of Warcraft. The user interface design and approach of World of Warcraft serves as an example of one way play can be opened to a wide variety of payer abilities while also enhancing the play of all users. Additionally, the application of the principles of Universal Design for Learning offer a method by which game designers can consider accessibility in the design of user interfaces and by which game researchers can evaluate the accessibility of interfaces.

Keywords: MORPG · Virtual world games · User interfaces · Accessibility · Universal Design for Learning

1 Introduction

We live in a time of exceptional media consumption. Movies can be carried with you as you travel, digital music is ubiquitous, and video games are everywhere. As consumer access to both high-bandwidth connections and more powerful devices increase, so too do the opportunities for more intense and interactive video game play. This is especially true of those games that exist within virtual worlds. Virtual worlds based upon the technologies created for these games are being used or considered in a wide variety of non-entertainment fields such as medicine and education. If these non-entertainment uses are to be effective they must take into consideration the needs of all potential users, including and especially users with a wide range of disabilities that may limit or completely preclude their participation in these uses.

Accessibility, however, is not often mentioned when discussing video games, even among groups for whom accessibility is a priority. When we speak about games, and especially video games, we usually do so from the privileged point of view of an able-bodied gamer. Many marginalized gamers do not speak up to bring attention to their challenges for fear of stigmatization. Groups such as The Ablegamers Foundation [1] are beginning to bring voice to these concerns, though, and have seen results from their efforts as game console makers begin to rethink their offerings to include the needs of those with disabilities.

S. Lackey and J. Chen (Eds.): VAMR 2017, LNCS 10280, pp. 349–358, 2017.
DOI: 10.1007/978-3-319-57987-0_28

Games are designed from this privileged point of view not out of malice but because often the game designer is an able-bodied person. Accessibility, with some exceptions, simply isn't part of the design conversation because it isn't part of the designer's experience. The lack of attention to players with disabilities is so prevalent it has even been lampooned by cartoonists [2]. Despite this, there are video game players with a wide assortment of disabilities who both identify themselves as gamers and play games in a way comparable to the able-bodied. One example of where this is possible is the computer game World of Warcraft (or simply WoW), first published by Blizzard Entertainment in 2004. It is without question economically successful and culturally impactful. It has also been played by those who are completely blind, a counterintuitive outcome for a visually-based medium.

The now-defunct website *WoW Insider* featured a number of World of Warcraft players with disabilities over the years in their "15 min of Fame" series [3]. Their stories covered "Shorty," the player behind the website Ability Powered Gaming [4] where accessibility within the game is explored through her experience with it; Hexu and Davidian, a completely-blind player and his "guide dog guild-mate" assisting him through the game world and its events [5]; and Kephas [6], a player with very limited vision who put together a YouTube video [7] that explains how he reconfigures his UI to make it more useful to him. This accessibility was not directly created by the programmers. It was achieved by the use of add-ons.

Add-ons in World of Warcraft are user-created application modifications that allow configurable access to the core mechanics of the game user interface (UI) and therefore have a direct and meaningful impact on play. Add-ons allow the player to manipulate the game UI in specific ways not otherwise possible through the game client. Textures and colors of UI elements can be substituted for those easier to see; font sizes can be adjusted larger or smaller; even the built-in UI elements can be rearranged on the screen. Visual effects can be translated into aural or textual cues and vice-versa. Planning and note-keeping can be augmented within the game for those who may want or need that type of assistance.

There is a large and well-established add-on developer community and a deep pool of available add-ons built up over World of Warcraft's history. They can be written by the player or downloaded from sites for other player-created add-ons, like the add-on CT Mod [8], or from sites that host lots of different add-ons, like Curse.com or WowInterface.com. Most notably, these add-ons were not created specifically for accessibility. They were created by otherwise able-bodied players in order to enhance their own game play. It is this open approach to UI configurability that offers insight into how future virtual worlds and their interfaces can be made more accessible. However, there is also a need for tools with which to evaluate the accessibility of UIs.

2   Understanding the Game

World of Warcraft has a sustained worldwide user base in the millions. Constant additions to the game world continue to evolve the fantasy narrative within which the game takes place as well as the technological underpinnings of the game. These additions come in "patches," what one might compare to a chapter in a book, and "expansions," comparable to the next novel in a series. Patches can contain either episodic advances to the game world narrative ("content patches") or relatively minor tweaks to game play (including bug fixes). Expansions, on the other hand, make more sweeping changes. New races and worlds are introduced in expansions, and each expansion is considered to have its own story arc. Similarly, game mechanic changes can be substantial, with complete overhauls to the system that may significantly change game play. There have been 6 expansions since its release with the sixth, titled "Legion", released in late 2016 [9].

Blizzard Entertainment charges a monthly fee to play World of Warcraft and the user base continues to pay to play the game with the expectation that it continues to expand and evolve during their subscription. The publisher must maintain a high level of player interest in the game to stay profitable. A product life of over 11 years therefore represents a significant sustained interest by a committed player base and by a publisher willing to invest significant resources into its maintenance. World of Warcraft is also designed with the expectation that the player will interact with other players. Its extended lifespan represents a user population well-versed with the physical and narrative environment of the game and a mature technology base upon which those users have built their online identities and play styles.

Salen and Zimmerman [10] offer a three-part framework of schemas for understanding games: rules, play, and culture. Rules include the actual rules of the game, the objectives and how to achieve them, but it also the user interface, the human-computer connection rules that allow interactivity with the game space. Cheating or hacking the game system aside, one cannot play the game except through the interface and it is through the options available in the interface that we come to understand the rules of the game. I cannot make my avatar run, sit, or perform any other action the "rules" allow except through the interface. This means that the way a player interacts with the user interface frames how they interact with the world. For instance, a user with a mobility-limiting condition may have trouble using a keyboard and mouse, severely limiting their interactions within a virtual world, while someone with a visual disability may not be able to interact meaningfully with most elements of the virtual environment at all.

The interface also relays information about the world to the player, again within the rules of the game. If my virtual warrior attacks a virtual monster the interface will usually tell me not only how I can attack but the results of that attack. How much "life" do I have left? How much does the monster? When I use a sword how much damage do I do compared to when I use a mace? The rules are typically performed for the player within the interface on-screen either through textual representation (85% health; 600 hit points left) or through graphical representations (a bar graph, for instance). The default method of this representation is chosen by the game designer. The interface elements are usually consistent with the artistic direction and aesthetic of the game. Those designer choices can constrain the experience of the player in purposeful or unexpected ways. A game designer can chose difficult-to-understand elements for the user interface to intentionally make the game harder, or they can make elements smaller or larger to aid or hinder comprehension.

The interface for World of Warcraft allows users access to the raw data used by the default interface, however, through external add-ons. One may use these add-ons to reimagine the entire user interface but not the representations of elements within the game world. For example, I can change the way information is presented to me (a bar graph for avatar health instead of a textual representation) but not how other objects in the world appear (such as changing what a monster looks like). These add-ons also only change my user interface, not the interface for other players. Why would a player with a disability go through the trouble to do such a thing? Jenkins [11] makes a simple observation that helps to explain why: they're fans of the game. Put simply, for the player with a disability frustration with the game interface does not outweigh their attraction to the game. "Fandom, after all, is born of a balance between fascination and frustration: if media content didn't fascinate us, there would be no desire to engage with it; but if it didn't frustrate us on some level, there would be no drive to rewrite or remake it [12]".

By "rewriting" the interface players become active and expressive participants in the communication around and within the game. It returns agency to the player and allows for a remaking of meaning for the individual within the system of rules. "This is now my game," the player might say, "because I have had a hand in creating it, game designers be damned. I will play my way, together with my friends."

Rather than being focused on the formal qualities of the game object itself the second schema, play, are experiential schemas, directly focused on the actual experience of the game players [13]. Play schemas cover the space between the game and the player and help to explain how the rules can impact the experience of the player. Play isn't possible without access to the game.

Despite the potential for increased access through add-ons there is also the possibility of abuse that can take away from the play experience of other users. At various points throughout the game's history some add-ons have made it possible to completely automate play through what are called "bots". Bots (short for robots) are scripts or other such software that automate some action of the computer of the player. While this may sound like a boon, especially a player with a disability, it negatively impacted the virtual economy of the game, the experience of other players, and was contrary to the goals of the designers. The company has successfully fought legal battles against this type of use within their environment.

The third schema, culture, reminds us that games are played within a greater social context and embody a rhetoric. "Applied to games, the organizing principle of cultural rhetoric reveals how games represent broad patterns of ideological value. The design of a game, in other words, is a representation of ideas and values of a particular time and place [13]." These values are also reflections of the people who create the game. Blizzard games have long had color-blind options in the player settings and the controls for most of their games can be remapped to different keys on the keyboard. This minimal level of accessibility is, of course, good business sense for a company that sells video games. Even so, that ideal and value of access to as many people as possible is reflected in the reality of the add-on ecosystem created around World of Warcraft.

World of Warcraft is a game played with other people. As such the player's representation of themselves within the world can be an important aspect of their participation within the culture of the game. How a player feels about themselves as a player, their social self, can impact who and how they interact with in the game world. "The social self is the set of ideas individuals have about themselves, which are derived from communication with other people. An important part of the social self is our impression of how other people view us. Since we cannot see into others' minds directly, we learn about their picture of us by observing how they respond to us [14]." Within a virtual game world this could include managing our performance within the game. The more "successful" a player is within the game, whether success is measured in the "level" of the player's character or some other in-world attribute, the more positively other players see them. Where interaction with other players is essential to successful "play" it is imperative that the player operate or be seen to operate at the highest level of skill.

The suggestion here, then, is that mastery of the user interface and a background knowledge of how the game works is required for full participation in the game. Tronstad [15] identifies those situations where flow may occur in World of Warcraft as within "instances" (dungeons) or "raids", situations where the pace and intensity of the encounter are high and mastery of the player's character's skills is essential to the successful completion of the goal (usually the defeat of a monster). The game designers have created these encounters specifically with coordinated groups in mind. These situations are also highly social in that they require multiple players to complete – instances require 5 players and raids as many as 25 – and usually require the close coordination of effort among players. Tronstad therefore argues that there is a difference between a player's character's "capacity" and "appearance".

Capacity is the sum of capabilities available for the character, while appearance designates its representational qualities [16]. Capacity refers to the skills and power of the avatar – their class (mage, warrior, druid, etc.), their level (the higher their level the more powerful their abilities), and their gear or equipment. Higher level gear improves abilities in potentially significant ways. A player increases her character level by defeating enemies, completing quests, and other in-game activities. She acquires better gear by defeating more powerful enemies or other, more onerous objectives such as complicated quests or multi-day events. Some game content is gated to only be available to characters of a particular level or higher. Capacity is then a significant factor in deter- mining the experiences available to the player within the game and other players' perception of that character.

Appearance is the representational qualities of the character and helps to create perception. A character "appears" powerful because of level, gear, etc. and through the character's appearance the player is perceived as powerful or skilled as well. More powerful and more skilled players are more often invited to participate in group content. Therefore, achieving higher levels or acquiring rare or powerful gear isn't just done for the enjoyment of the player, but also to signal a specific identity to other players, that of a competent player. For players with a disability, managing this appearance may be crucial to their ability to experience end-game content since some players may see those with a disability as being less-skilled and therefore less desirable in a group.

What is required from the player in order to increase their capacity? A deep under- standing of the meanings and mechanics of the world and its rules. To the uninitiated, there is information in the video game image that is at least somewhat recognizable and understandable, such as text or the representation of floors and walls. To the uninitiated, though, many other elements may be difficult to parse, such as the meanings of the icons or the purpose other visual cues. This says nothing of understanding the narrative environment within which the encounter takes place. In describing how new viewers of avant-garde cinema become experienced, Peterson proposes that viewers become knowledgeable by acquiring "both procedural knowledge, what we might call knowing how, and declarative knowledge, what we might call knowing that [17]". Procedural knowledge encompasses the heuristics of problem solving, information that enables a particular type of strategy of analysis (the how) by the viewer. Declarative knowledge might be said to be the system of codes used to transmit information within the image, the underlying semiotic conceptual (signified) information necessary to understand the signifiers.

For video games and World of Warcraft in particular, this would be the understanding of the basic mechanics and expectations of the game – that some symbols represent player health or power, that some visual effects represent the activation of certain abilities by the player or the monster, or that clicking an icon on the screen activates a certain ability. Through add-ons what is textual information can be translated into graphical or even aural signs and vice-versa. It's even possible to create haptic feedback cues instead of aural or visual. In this environment, the message/ meaning/ signified remains the same but the sign changes based on the choices of the player. For a player with a condition that precludes the ability to perceive or process one of these "prepackaged" signs, then, add-ons allow them to construct an UI that may be confusing or completely nonsensical to someone else. The flexibility of the World of Warcraft add-on system allows for an interactive environment that only makes sense to that one player – the democratization of communication within the video game system.

3 Making It Accessible

As mentioned earlier some players with disabilities use add-ons to make the user interface more accessible. That suggests there are elements of universal design in these add-ons. Previous research had demonstrated that is indeed the case [18]. This is best understood through the principles of Universal Design for Learning (UDL) [19]. UDL is a set of principles for curriculum development that are intended to give all individuals equal opportunities to learn from educational materials. UDL "provides a blueprint for creating instructional goals, methods, materials, and assessments that work for everyone–not a single, one-size-fits-all solution but rather flexible approaches that can be customized and adjusted for individual needs [19] " and is divided into 3 Principles:

1. Provide Multiple Means of Representation
2. Provide Multiple Means of Action and Expression
3. Provide Multiple Means of Engagement

The first principle recognizes that people differ in the way that they perceive the world and comprehend information. Where one person may easily make sense of textual data, another may make better sense of the same information in a chart or graph. The second principle recognizes that people differ in the way that they engage with the world around them. For our purposes we can take this to mean the manner in which players interact with the virtual world. An example would be remapping the input commands for specialized devices, or allowing communication via voice instead of through the internal text chat system. The third principle deals with sustaining effort, persistence, and self-regulation. This principle is more difficult to associate with add-and video games since it is the individual user who determines what will maintain persistence. It is assumed that all add-ons at least partially fall into this category since, by definition, the add-on is meant to customize the user interface in such a way as to make the interactions more enjoyable. Each principle is further divided into three subcategories and each subcategory has several "checkpoints" of design.

Using these checkpoints a matrix can be created that allows for the identification of each of these principles within an add-on [20]. Figure 1 demonstrates how this works. A group of most-popular World of Warcraft add-ons was selected from the website Curse.com. The checkpoint number of each principle is noted on the top line of the matrix. The intersection is checked if analysis of the add-on confirms behavior in line with the design checkpoint. Since these principles were created for use in an educational setting not every subgroup will be a comfortable match with the purpose of any given add-on. These criteria are therefore read liberally. A "UDL score" can be created by totaling the number of design criteria an add-on addresses. This score allows us to rank add-ons by accessibility, which was done for Fig. 1.

Curse.com rank	Addon Name	Principle I: Provide Multiple Means of Representation												Principle II: Provide Multiple Means of Action and Expression										Principle III: Provide Multiple Means of Engagement										UDL score
		Perception			Language, expressions, & symbols					Comprehension				Physical action			Expressive skills and fluency			Executive function				Recruiting interest			Sustaining effort and persistence				Self-regulation			
		1.1	1.2	1.3	2.1	2.2	2.3	2.4	2.5	3.1	3.2	3.3	3.4	4.1	4.2	4.3	5.1	5.2	5.3	6.1	6.2	6.3	6.4	7.1	7.2	7.3	8.1	8.2	8.3	8.4	9.1	9.2	9.3	
1	Deadly Boss Mods	x	x	x	x	x	x		x	x	x	x	x	x	x	x	x	x	x	x	x	x	x	x	x	x	x		x	x	x	x	x	31
18	Decursive	x	x	x	x	x	x		x	x	x	x	x	x	x		x		x	x	x	x	x		x	x	x	x	x	x	x	x	x	29
19	HealBot Continued	x	x	x	x	x	x		x	x	x	x	x	x			x	x	x	x	x	x	x		x	x	x	x	x	x	x	x	x	29
20	Gladius v3	x	x	x	x	x	x		x	x	x	x	x	x	x	x		x	x	x	x	x	x		x	x	x	x	x		x	x	x	28
5	Tidy Plates	x	x	x	x				x	x	x	x	x	x	x		x		x	x	x	x	x					x	x	x	x		x	26
16	GTFO	x	x	x	x	x	x		x	x	x	x	x				x	x	x	x	x		x	x	x	x	x	x	x	x	x	x	x	25
3	Recount	x		x			x	x	x	x				x	x	x	x	x	x	x	x	x		x	x	x		x	x	x	x	x	x	24
25	Skada Damage Meter	x			x		x	x	x	x				x	x	x	x	x	x	x	x	x	x		x	x	x	x	x	x	x	x	x	24
31	Quartz	x	x	x	x		x	x	x	x	x		x				x	x	x	x	x	x	x			x	x	x	x	x	x	x	x	23
17	Bartender4	x			x		x	x	x	x	x	x					x	x	x	x	x	x				x	x	x	x	x	x	x	x	22
4	Bagnon	x		x	x	x		x	x	x	x	x	x				x	x	x	x						x	x	x	x	x	x	x	x	21
14	Ackis Recipe List	x			x	x		x	x	x	x		x	x	x	x		x	x	x	x				x			x	x	x	x	x	x	21
9	Auctioneer	x		x	x	x		x	x	x	x	x	x		x			x		x	x	x	x						x		x		x	18
15	AtlasLoot Enhanced	x		x			x	x	x	x	x	x		x	x			x	x	x	x			x	x						x		x	17
24	AskMrRobot	x		x	x	x	x		x	x	x	x		x				x	x	x	x			x							x		x	17
11	MoveAnything	x							x				x	x	x	x	x		x	x	x	x		x						x		x	x	13
13	PetTracker	x		x				x		x	x	x	x	x				x	x	x	x			x							x			12
28	Postal	x		x		x		x	x					x	x		x	x			x					x			x			x		11
10	Addon Control Panel	x		x						x	x	x	x	x			x				x	x										x	x	10
2	NPCScan	x	x	x					x											x	x	x	x								x			9
		20	8	19	10	8	14	0	17	14	16	18	13	11	13	9	8	8	11	16	19	20	18	8	10	16	11	5	8	14	19	16	14	

Fig. 1. UDL scores of top add-ons from Curse.com

As the figure shows, most of the add-ons evaluated meet the design criteria of a majority of UDL principles. When World of Warcraft players with disabilities who use add-ons are asked why they use them, their answers are consistent with the needs addressed by UDL [21]. Most strikingly, UDL principles emerged naturally out of user-generated content. None of the add-on creators indicate they are UDL experts and none of the descriptions for the add-ons reference accessibility. This is extraordinary because these are user-created applications created by video game players to enhance their own gameplay. These were not created by user interface researchers, accessibility technologists, or the video game publisher or programmers. However, the end result was a system of tools that allowed for a video game to be accessible to the extent that completely blind players are able to participate at the highest levels of group interaction.

4 Conclusions and Lessons

First, and perhaps most importantly for game and virtual world designers, it is possible for people with many different ability levels and challenges to engage with, find meaning within, and enjoy virtual worlds. It's important to note in the World of Warcraft example that accessibility can be achieved without negatively impacting the experience of other players. In this case it was through enhancing everyone's experience that accessibility was achieved. Accessibility may come with risks related to the control of how people interact with systems. For some creators this risk may seem too great, as a threat to their intellectual property or as a means of circumventing assessment in an educational virtual world. The payoff may significantly outweigh those risks. As educators and publishers look to virtual worlds for educational purposes this must be kept firmly in mind.

Secondly, immersion in a virtual world for a person with a disability is enabled, or at the very least enhanced, by the community of that environment as well as the technologies of it. Creators of virtual worlds for entertainment purposes likely better understand this than those who create for educational purposes. Put another way, you must create places people want to populate if you want to create the type of dynamic community that resulted in the add-on ecosystem of World of Warcraft. This is especially true if you want to leverage that community to help develop the environment. It is not enough to make a space and assign a class to populate it. There must be intrinsic value in their participation in that environment outside of the assignment. Relatedly, we must design environments we're committed to supporting for long periods of time to see these sorts of results. World of Warcraft is well over a decade old. We should not expect this type of dynamism within the first year or two of the launch of a new environment.

The third lesson to take from this is that the expression and emergence of universal design principles appears to be a natural tendency for interfaces open to user modifications. Given that an inferential system of meaning already exists in virtual world development, and that the commercial success of World of Warcraft has had a significant impact on that system, it would be advantageous for future (and current) virtual world UI designers to pay considerable heed to the emergence of UDL principles in the add-on system. It's important for UI designers to understand that UDL does not create a framework for separate interfaces but rather encourages flexibility within the existing ones that can meet a diverse set of needs. By providing "multiple means" of doing something one is ensuring that the largest number of people can interact with the virtual environment. This is desirable from a philosophical, accessibility viewpoint but also from a more practical, business one. The more people that can interact with your virtual world, the more people who are likely to buy it. There doesn't have to be a loser in this and in fact a well-executed strategy of openness could even enhance the product and the publisher's standing.

Flexible interface design is also a critical issue for virtual worlds for education. Publishers should closely consider the inferential systems of meaning of these environments and develop a common standard for flexible UI design. This might include a shared API library or at least a common implementation of the major elements of the UI (navigating the virtual world, interacting with objects, etc.). In conjunction with a user development community similar to the add-on community for World of Warcraft it should then be possible to broaden the appeal and impact of these types of systems. The goal is not to make all educational or learning environments look the same. Rather the goal should be building a base framework upon which those with very specific needs can get the same educational experience as everyone else using that system.

The World of Warcraft example is that an invested and dynamic user community can help to create these player remediations. It is even arguable that they can do a better job of this than an intentional UI designer since the collective experience of the user base is inherently richer and more diverse than a company can hope to build with a single UI development team. In striking a balance between user configurability and protecting the integrity of the game, Blizzard created an environment where nearly anyone can play a videogame, even the completely blind. By taking these findings into our practice we can create entertainment experiences and learning environments equally inviting to and effective for everyone.

References

1. The Ablegamers Foundation. http://www.ablegamers.com/about-us
2. Dorkly. http://www.dorkly.com/post/51443/out-of-control
3. Wow Insider, archived at Joystick. http://wow.joystiq.com/tag/disabled/
4. Ability-Powered Gnome Builds Resource Node for Disabled Gamers. http://wow.joystiq.com/2013/09/12/ability-powered-gnome-builds-resource-node-for-disabled-gamers/, http://abilitypowered.com/
5. Guide Dog Player and Guild Embrace Sightless Guildmate. http://wow.joystiq.com/2012/01/12/guide-dog-player-and-guild-embrace-sightless-guildmate-steer/
6. Kephas Demonstrates How to Play WoW Blind. http://wow.joystiq.com/2014/03/02/kephas-demonstrates-how-to-play-wow-blind/
7. YouTube. http://youtu.be/101ZEJF5z_8?list=UU0_EEH4gmK42pGSPvPSTN4g
8. CT Mod. http://ctmod.net
9. Warcraft: Legion. http://us.battle.net/wow/en/legion/
10. Salen, K., Zimmerman, E.: Rules of Play, p. 104. MIT, Cambridge (2004)
11. Jenkins, H.: Convergence Culture: Where Old and New Media Collide. New York University Press, New York (2006)
12. Jenkins, 247
13. Salen and Zimmerman, 517
14. Bainbridge, W.: The Warcraft Civilization, p. 174. MIT, Cambridge (2010)
15. Tronstad, R.: Character identification in world of warcraft: the relationship between capacity and appearance. In: Corneliussen, H., Rettberg, J.W. (eds.) Digital Culture, Play, and Identity: A World of Warcraft Reader. MIT, Cambridge (2008)
16. Tronstad, 249

17. Peterson, J.: Is a cognitive approach to the avant-garde cinema perverse? In: Carroll, N., Bordwell, D. (eds.) Post-theory: Reconstructing Film Studies, p. 110. University of Wisconsin Press, Madison (1996)
18. Merritt, I.I., Donald F.: The impact of user-generated interfaces on the participation of users with a disability in virtual environments: Blizzard Entertainment's World of Warcraft model. Ph.D. dissertation, University of Central Florida (2015)
19. http://www.udlcenter.org/aboutudl/udlguidelines
20. Merritt, 87
21. Merritt, 105
22. Salen, K., Zimmerman, E.: Rules of Play : Game Design Fundamentals. MIT Press, Cambridge (2004)

Using Commercial Virtual Reality Games to Prototype Serious Games and Applications

Peter A. Smith[✉]

University of Central Florida, Orlando, USA
Peter.smith@ucf.edu

Abstract. In this new era of virtual reality hardware and software, traditional prototyping methods have proven less than satisfactory for truly understanding how the interaction will feel in the virtual environment. As a result, designers have stepped back from table top paper prototypes and have started using physical prototyping to understand the virtual space. The difference being that physical prototypes fill actual space that the designers can walk around in. These prototypes utilize analog methods like cardboard boxes to physically represent objects in a game. While this method yields particularly good results the space required can be exceedingly high as compared to a table top prototype. There are however, many existing commercial games that can be leveraged as prototyping tools. This software is maturing at a rapid pace, and the developers of these tools are continuing to support and explore these environments. The money being invested in this space is astronomical and the possibilities of using these tools for prototyping is only touching the full potential of the technology. This paper will explore the current state of the art in analog prototyping in virtual reality and then break down the current options for prototyping applications in Virtual Reality Sandbox games.

Keywords: Games · Virtual Reality · Augmented reality · Game design · Prototyping

1 Introduction

In this new era of virtual reality hardware and software, traditional prototyping methods have proven less than satisfactory for truly understanding how the interaction will feel in the virtual environment. As a result, designers have stepped back from table top paper prototypes and have started using physical prototyping to understand the virtual space. The difference being that physical prototypes fill actual space that the designers can walk around in. These prototypes utilize analog methods like cardboard boxes to physically represent objects in a game. While this method yields particularly good results the space required can be exceedingly high as compared to a table top prototype. There are however, many existing commercial games that can be leveraged as prototyping tools. This software is maturing at a rapid pace, and the developers of these tools are continuing to support and explore these environments. The money being invested in this space is

© Springer International Publishing AG 2017
S. Lackey and J. Chen (Eds.): VAMR 2017, LNCS 10280, pp. 359–368, 2017.
DOI: 10.1007/978-3-319-57987-0_29

astronomical and the possibilities of using these tools for prototyping is only touching the full potential of the technology.

2 Conventional Prototyping Techniques

Prototypes are, "a first or early example that is used as a model for what comes later [1]." Prototypes are usually broken in to 2 major categories digital or physical. Digital prototypes are usually used to test the technology, and kinesthetics (or feel) of a game, while physical are usually used to test the mechanics and sometimes the aesthetics. In any case they are usually representative of some or all aspects of a future developed game. Prototypes that are used once and then abandoned, which is the case for most physical prototypes, are called throw away. Prototypes that are designed in chunks and then integrated together are known as incremental. Prototypes that are not discarded, but serve as an iterative step in the product development are known as evolutionary.

3 Prototyping in Virtual Reality

With all interactive projects, the art of prototyping is a key element in the iterative design process. Though, with each new media, or interface type, new prototyping techniques are required to be developed. In the case of Virtual Reality (VR) there is a strong reliance on established prototyping techniques developed for games, but due to the disconnect between a screens 2D view into the 3D world and VR equipment's binocular view.

3.1 Physical Prototyping

Physical prototypes are often paper based. They are usually made prior to digital game or digital prototypes even. They are often used to test rules and determine the games elements. In VR it might seem like physical prototyping would not be relevant. However, this is far from the case. Modern VR designers might actually build out example worlds in the real world using cardboard boxes and other representative materials to actually navigate their virtual space before building it. In the case of VR tours, or location based VR the actual location serves as its own physical prototype.

3.2 Digital Prototyping

Digital prototypes are often but not always developed in the final technology that the game will be made in. They are usually made in game engines and come in two major categories, representative and functional. Representative prototypes explore and test the look and feel that could be in a game. Functional show the functionality that could be in a game.

Digital prototypes often do not represent any final art. In an effort to support this type of prototyping the concept of orange boxing or grey boxing was developed. This method has all art blocked out with boxes that contain a strong colored wall and a contrasting colored floor. This allows the designers to experience the game without being constrained by art. These orange boxed spaces are very similar to the physical proto-typing idea of building out the world in cardboard boxes. Figure 1 shows an example of Orange Boxing in a Valve game.

Fig. 1. Example of Orange Boxing [2]

If a game is fun with Orange Boxed art, it will be fun with final art. If it isn't fun with Orange Boxed levels, it will most likely never be fun no matter how good the art.

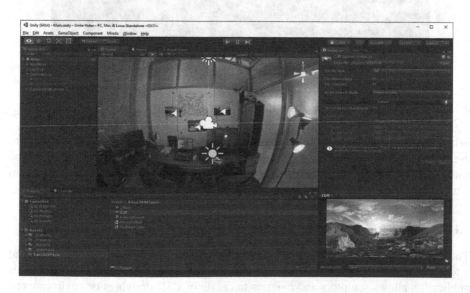

Fig. 2. Example of VR development environment [3]

Barriers to Digital Prototyping. Digital prototyping has become the go to standard in many cases. Physical prototyping has become less and less common, but with VR digital prototyping, and in the same respect development, digital prototyping can be hard. Developers are often having to jump in and out of the VR hardware to test and make changes to the game.

Figure 2 shows an example of a typical VR development environment. What you see on screen is normal for a 3D game, but it is difficult to know how the cameras results will look in actual device, and even more concerning is seeing the user's hands. This development issue has led to the development of embedded VR development tools.

Virtual Reality Development Tools. Embedded VR development tools are only now in beta and are slowly making their way into all popular VR platforms, They currently tend to mimic the standard development tools but appear on floating panels around the user. This is only a first attempt, but new iterations will bring innovations.

Where will these innovations come from? Sandbox Games (Fig. 3).

Fig. 3. VR development tools embedded in Unity game [3]

4   VR Software with Potential for Prototyping

While the tools are maturing and many researchers have ideas, but do not have easy to use development tools there is the potential to use other commercial tools to prototype game and other ideas. These throwaway prototypes can then be shared with more experienced or skilled developers to build commercial products.

4.1   Google Tilt Brush

The first tool, is actually a 3D art tool from search engine giant Google. They developed a tool called Tilt Brush, which was originally bundled with the Vive hardware. This application allows sculptors and painters to create in a 3D drawings or environments.

The freeform tools can be used to map out virtual spaces that can be explored by others, while their abstract style allows for users to understand that they are in a prototype, or wireframe, and not the final product. All of the tools in Tilt Brush are used inside the VR environment and do not require the user to remove their VR gear.

As can be seen in Fig. 4, developers can use this tool to express their ideas, but will not produce a final product. At the same time to tool can be used to express relatively complex ideas. The controls used in Tilt Brush seem very similar to the controls used in Unity's VR development toolkit.

Fig. 4. An example of Tilt Brush in action [4].

4.2 Rec Room

At the same time as developers have begun exploring the virtual reality space, sandbox games have started to emerge as a prominent form of consumer title. One example is Rec Room. The game allows the player to explore a multiplayer environment with toys, weapons, sporting goods, kitchen tools, etc. This space is the perfect environment to experiment with what is possible in VR. If a developer is interested in physical therapy for instance, there are a number of objects the player can interact with in this environment to test what would be appropriate in a serious game. However, Rec Room is a multiplayer world and creation and privacy are not allowed (Fig. 5).

The vast number of mechanics implemented and the freedom to use them as desired still make Rec Room a good application for prototyping activities.

Fig. 5. An example of a soccer game in Rec Room [5]

4.3   Tabletop Simulator

Another popular title that lets the user build any game they want is Tabletop Simulator. In this game environment any form of board style game can be built. This can provide a perfect testbed for new game ideas in virtual reality, including building traditional paper prototypes within a Virtual Reality world.

Fig. 6. Example of a traditional card game in Tabletop Simulator [6].

Figure 6 shows an example of using tabletop simulator to make traditional card games. Figure 7 shows that the game could be much more complicated and look like more traditional environments. This tool is fully supported in VR and is multiplayer and can be used to prototype and play board games.

Fig. 7. An example of a more complex Tabletop Simulator game [6]

Fig. 8. Example environment in Destinations [7].

4.4 Destinations and Destinations Workshop Tools

Destinations is an example game developed by Valve to show off the power of the Vive and its ability to create virtual environments and field trips. This 3D environment has many places for the user to visit that are composed primarily of real photographs (Fig. 8).

Destinations also has a set of tools to allow developers to build out their own environments. These are called the Destinations Workshop Tools. You can load the environments in the tools and they explain how to build your own. Any high resolution environments can be modeled out and explored in Destinations, even fantasy themed ones.

4.5 Mod Box

Mod Box is the most freeform prototyping tool in the group. This environment allows the users to access a huge list of available assets to build out very different environments with a ton of interesting activities, and themes. Figure 9 shows off the use of a laboratory environment to build an interesting robot powered puzzle game. Figure 10 shows Mod Box can also be used to prototype other themes like the wild west in a target shooting environment. These environments can be explored and shared. Whole games or small parts could be prototyped through Mod Box and then rebuilt by the dev team later.

Fig. 9. Mod Box being used to prototype a laboratory themed game [8]

Fig. 10. Mod Box being used to prototype a western environment

Mod Box is a very powerful tool available for only $20.00.

5 Conclusions

Sandbox games are an interesting way to explore mechanics and prototype ideas, especially for the less programmatically inclined members of a development team. They are far more approachable then more complex development tools. Also, they can be used to express complex ideas and bring examples to the team. Unfortunately, they are mostly only good for throwaway prototypes.

5.1 Future Work

In the future there will be a move to bring the ease of use of these tools into more complex development tools. These games are acting as prototypes in a sense for the actual tool they are using to make them.

References

1. Merriam-Webster: Merriam-Webster dictionary online. Prototype entry (2015). https://www.merriam-webster.com/dictionary/prototype
2. Keighley, G.: The final hours of Half-Life 2. GameSpot.com (2004). http://www.gamespot.com/articles/the-final-hours-of-half-life-2/1100-6112889/
3. Nafarrete, J.: Unity reveals new VR tools and Google daydream support. Virtual reality one stop shop (2016). http://virtualrealityonestopshop.com/2016/11/unity-reveals-new-vr-tools-and-google-daydream-support/
4. Google: Tilt Brush on Steam (2016). http://store.steampowered.com/app/327140/

5. Against Gravity: Rec Room on Steam (2016). http://store.steampowered.com/app/471710/
6. Berzerk Games: Tabletop Simulator on Steam (2015). http://store.steampowered.com/app/286160/
7. Valve: Destinations on Steam (2016). http://store.steampowered.com/app/453170/
8. Alientrap: ModBox on Steam (2016). http://store.steampowered.com/app/453170/

A Proposal for the Selection of Eye-Tracking Metrics for the Implementation of Adaptive Gameplay in Virtual Reality Based Games

Jose L. Soler-Dominguez[1], Jorge D. Camba[2], Manuel Contero[1(✉)], and Mariano Alcañiz[1]

[1] Instituto de Investigación e Innovación en Bioingeniería (I3B), Universitat Politècnica de València, Camino de Vera s/n, 46022 Valencia, Spain
jlsoler@lableni.com, mcontero@upv.es, malcaniz@i3b.upv.es
[2] Gerald D. Hines College of Architecture and Design, University of Houston, 4200 Elgin St., Houston, TX 77204-4000, USA
jdorribo@uh.edu

Abstract. Eye tracking has been shown to be an effective method for evaluating usability and User eXperience (UX) in various environments. With the advent of affordable high performance Head Mounted Displays (HMDs), Virtual Reality (VR) has rapidly expanded and opened new channels for fun and "serious" game experiences. However, there is a lack of effective quality indicators that measure satisfaction, frustration, boredom, or attention of users immersed in VR environments. Traditional approaches such as questionnaires, surveys, and interviews can easily interfere with the user's sense of presence if the assessment is performed while the experience is in progress. If performed after completing the experience, users are forced to recall memories that may be incomplete or inaccurate. In this context, the integration of eye tracking technology into HMDs provides a reliable and non-intrusive mechanism to assess UX and feed real-time data which can be used to design and develop adaptive VR experiences. In this paper, we discuss the assessment capabilities of eye tracking technologies in immersive VR environments and describe strategies to apply this information to the creation of VR games that can adapt to the player's performance, mood and behavior.

Keywords: Eye tracking · Virtual reality · Games · Serious games · Adaptive game design

1 Introduction

Game developers make great efforts to avoid players' frustration while keeping engagement with the gameplay. This characteristic of modern games contrasts with classic 80s and 90s games, where fewer levels and smaller more difficult scenarios and worlds were common. In particular, AAA games (big productions developed by large studios and aiming to be global bestsellers) and Free-to-Play (F2P) games (games where players can access a significant portion of the

© Springer International Publishing AG 2017
S. Lackey and J. Chen (Eds.): VAMR 2017, LNCS 10280, pp. 369–380, 2017.
DOI: 10.1007/978-3-319-57987-0_30

content at no cost but offer in-game purchases to access additional content or special items) strive to keep players engaged during longer periods of time by implementing adaptive gameplay techniques, where the gaming experience can be catered to each individual player.

The adaptive capabilities of games are often limited to a small subset of features within the gameplay. For example, they could include leveraging Non Playable Characters' (NPCs) behavior to the player's performance, or adjusting the speed of enemies or hazards in a particular level based on the player's abilities (faster if the player is performing well, or slower if he or she is consistently failing to advance). As described by [4], NPCs in current games are equipped with the most basic operational behavior that restricts their capabilities and movements. For example, an action initiated by the user can be misinterpreted, or even missed entirely by NPCs if it falls outside the scope of their simple programmed logic.

The use of adaptive gameplay could enable interaction with the user at a higher level by predicting the intentions of the user based on previously recognised sequences of actions, rather than simply responding to low-level actions. Furthermore, adaptability is expected to grow over low-level actions or even player performance, because user emotion or how the player is feeling at a particular moment can be automatically detected. Why not change the style or difficulty of the gameplay when players are frustrated? New waves of enemies could be automatically released when the system detects the player is getting bored; soothing music can be played and a slower pace gameplay could be presented if unreasonably high stress levels are suddenly identified. In virtual reality environments, this type of experience customization is even more relevant, as presence (the feeling of being inside the virtual world) could be negatively affected by "one size fits all" game design.

Being able to detect and measure the player's feelings, emotions, and performance in real time and in a non-intrusive manner can help us anticipate the player's actions and understand how the loss of immersion can be minimized or even prevented. This information becomes fundamental in serious games, as players need to be kept in the flow channel (not anxious or bored, but focused on a particular activity) in order to have enough cognitive capacity to learn what they are expected to [5]. For games, the factors involved in making a player stay in the flow channel where described by [5]. These factors include: challenges vs. skills, anxiety vs. boredom, and difficulty balance, as shown in Fig. 1.

Many methods and tools exist to detect arousal, frustration, and other psychological states in a person. For the last 30 years, eye tracking technology has demonstrated great performance and robustness in detecting these states. Commercially, the integration of eye tracking technology in HMDs will be launched in 2017 in products such as the HTC-Vive/Tobii bundle or the FOVE headset. These products have a great potential to facilitate the use of eye-tracking metrics in the implementation of adaptive gameplay.

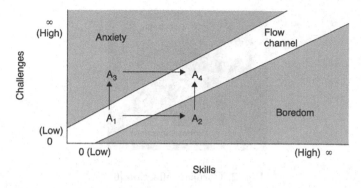

Fig. 1. Flow channel, from Jesse Schell's Art of Game Design: A Book of Lenses. "A" represents the player [5].

2 Eye Tracking Basics and Evolution

Eye tracking is the process of measuring eye positions (where a person is looking) or eye movement (the motion of an eye relative to the head). The process has become increasingly popular in Human-Computer Interaction, usability, and UX studies as a method to record the activity of the eyes and study how a person responds to visual stimuli.

The first eye tracking devices were invasive, usually based on electro oculographic systems [2] where electrodes attached to the skin around the eye detect variations in electric potential caused by eye movements; or used large contact lenses that often covered the cornea and sclera [3]. Modern eye tracking systems use video images of the eye to determine where the individual is looking (i.e., the "point of regard" [3]). There are different methods to calculate the point of regard. In commercial systems, the most commonly used method is the video-based combined pupil/corneal reflection technique. To provide this metric, the head must be fixed so that the eye's position relative to the head and point of regard coincide. A more comfortable option to disambiguate head movement from eye rotation involves combining different ocular features such as the corneal reflection of a light source (usually infra-red) and the pupil center [3], as shown in Fig. 2

The corneal reflection of the infra-red light is measured relative to the location of the pupil's center. The corneal reflections are called Purkinje reflections, Purkinje reflexes, or Purkinje-Sanson images. Purkinje-Sanson images are four defined reflections whose positions and intensities inform us about where a person is looking (see Fig. 3) [7].

The exact algorithms, sensors, and illumination technologies used by commercial eye trackers are often proprietary as these elements determine to a great extent the robustness, performance, reliability, and accuracy of the system.

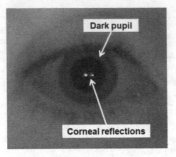

Fig. 2. Corneal reflection [6]

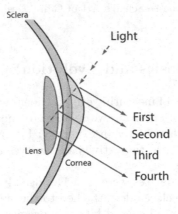

Fig. 3. Purkinje reflections [8]

3   Eye Tracking and HCI

Where and how an individual looks at a particular visual stimulus can provide valuable information (both conscious and unconscious) about the person's feelings and intentions. More specifically, this information can help us understand attention patterns and other high level cognitive processes [9].

Over the years, researchers have established a number of eye tracking metrics and interpretations for these metrics. The most significant ones are discussed in the following subsections based on the compilation prepared by [3]. We highlight the most relevant ones for assessing UX in games and serious games.

3.1   Eye-Movement Metrics

The most commonly used metrics in eye-tracking research include fixations (period where the eyes focus and lock towards an object) and saccades (quick eye movements between fixations).

Fixations: The meaning and interpretation of fixations can vary slightly depending on the context. Higher *fixation frequency* on an Area of Interest (AoI) in an encoding task could represent a particular interest in the target or that the target is complex and difficult to encode. In other situations such as searching or looking for information, these interpretations may be different [10]. Relevant measures derived from fixations include:

- *Fixation duration*, linked to the processing time applied to the object being fixated [11].
- *Gaze*, normally defined as the sum of all fixation durations within a prescribed area. It is typically used to compare attention between different elements. It can also be used as an anticipation metric if longer gazes occur in an AoI expecting a possible event [12].
- *Time to first fixation on-target*, defined as the amount of time that it takes a person to look at a specific AoI from stimulus onset. The sooner a person looks at a specific target, the better attention-getting properties the target is considered to have [13].

Saccades: Represent fast eye movements between fixations [14]. During saccades, any type of processing activity can occur, so they do not inform us about the complexity or prominence of an item inside a virtual environment. However, backtracking eye-movements or "regressive saccades" can give us important information about the difficulty of an encoding task. For instance, even smaller regressions in a reading task (two or three letters back) can represent confusion in the higher-level processing of text [2]. A relevant subset of saccade-derived measures include:

- *Number of saccades.* The higher the number of saccades, the more active the searching activity [15].
- *Saccade amplitude* represents a clear indicator of attention: larger saccades reveal more meaningful visual elements (requesting user focus from distance).

Scanpaths: Completion of a full cycle of saccade-fixation-saccade. The most significant metrics derived from this element include:

- *Scanpath duration:* Longer scanpaths imply a less efficient scanning of the environment [15].
- *Saccade/fixation ratio* compares the time spent searching (saccades) to the time spent processing (fixating) [3,15].

3.2 Non Eye-Movement Metrics

According to the cognitive theory of multimedia learning established by Mayer [16], multimedia naturally supports the way the human brain learns. The multimedia principle states that words and graphics are more conducive to learning than words or graphics alone [16]. The theory was summarized by [17] as having the following components: (a) a dual structure of visual and auditory channels, (b) limited processing capacity in memory, (c) three memory storage (sensory, working, long-term), (d) five cognitive processes of selecting, organizing, and integrating (selecting words, selecting images, organizing work, organizing images, and integrating new knowledge with prior knowledge), as well as theory-grounded and evidence-based multimedia instructional methods. The implications of item (b) are particularly relevant. If humans use too much of our limited capacity trying to interact with the environment, learning the rules, understanding the tasks we are supposed to perform, and reading menus and other interfaces in VR environments, we will only have a small amount of processing capacity left to store new knowledge.

Two non eye-movement metrics are relevant: *Blink rate* and *pupil size*. Both metrics can be used as indicators of cognitive load. A low blink rate is assumed to indicate a higher cognitive workload whereas a high blink rate may indicate fatigue [18]. Additionally, a higher cognitive load is also associated to larger pupils [19].

However, non eye-movement metrics are not completely reliable, as pupil size and blink rate can be affected by external factors [20] such as the lighting conditions of the VR environment or the brightness settings in the HMD. Consequently, these metrics are not extensively used in eye-tracking research. Nevertheless, their reliability and accuracy could be significantly improved with proper calibration, where the average pupil sizes and blink rates under different lighting conditions would serve as baselines for interpretation.

4   Evaluating UX

In the gaming domain, collecting and analyzing high quality, precise, and objective data about the player is a crucial step towards understanding the overall experience. In this paper, we review some of the methods used to gather information about a player's emotional and cognitive processes, intentionally omitting those methods that are subjective such as direct observation and self-reporting. In this regard, physiological processes are mostly involuntary, so measurements are not biased by the person's answering patterns, social desirability, interpretations of wording, limits in participant memory, or observer bias [1].

Physical reactions are part of the processes that contribute to the player's game experience. However, the relationships between physiological processes and elements are not one-to-one, which makes them difficult to isolate. By analyzing the objective methods proposed by Nacke et al. [14] to assess Gameplay Experience, two groups are identified:

- Psychophysiological player testing, with technologies such as:
  - Electromyography (EMG): Technology for measuring the electrical activity of muscles. It is an effective metric for basic emotions (e.g., facial muscles are good indicators of basic emotional states).

- Electrodermal activity (EDA): Common psycho-physiological method that measures variation of the electrical properties of the skin in response to sweat, which is directly related to physical arousal.
- Electroencephalography (EEG): Technique to measure brain activity (typically using scalp electrodes).
- Functional magnetic resonance imaging (fMRI) and positron emission tomography (PET): other techniques for measuring brain activity. Both methods have strong equipment limitations, which makes them difficult to use. Functional near-infrared spectroscopy (fNIR) has recently gained significant attention among UX researchers.
- Eyetracking: Technique based on measuring saccades (fast movements) and fixations (dwell times) of human gaze [15], as explained in the previous section. Psycho-physiological measures are not incompatible with eye tracking, but complementary, as they provide additional information about the interaction with the VR environment.

5 Adaptive Gameplay

The metrics described in previous sections provide a toolbox for designers to choose from, so UX gaming experiences can be customized based on the player's behavior. By grouping the areas with potential for player adaptation, three dimensions can be defined: perceptual adaptation (adaptation of how players see the VR world), cognitive adaptation (adaptation of how the user interface or the game mechanics are conditioned by the player's performance), and affective adaptation (adaptation of the game narrative to the player's mood).

5.1 Perceptual Adaptation

The design of a gaze-contingent system must distinguish the characteristics of foveal and peripheral vision. The human eye can see approximately 135° vertically and 160° horizontally, but with clear and fine resolution only around a 5° circle located in the center. This small slice of the visual field projects to the retinal region called the fovea, which is full of color cone photoreceptors. The angular distance away from the central gaze direction is called eccentricity. Acuity falls off rapidly as eccentricity increases due to a reduced receptor and ganglion density in the retina, a reduced optical nerve "bandwidth", and a reduced "processing" devoted to the periphery in the visual cortex [23]. According to Strasburger [24], current computer graphics (CG) researchers use the term foveation as a shorthand for the decrease in acuity with eccentricity in the human visual system.

Today, CG practice ignores user point-of-regard and always renders a full high-resolution image on the entire display (screen or HMD), which is a waste of computational resources [23]. If we were able to only render a high resolution image of the 5° foveal region (approx. 0.8% of the solid angle of a 60° display [23]) while keeping the rest of the image at lower resolution, we could

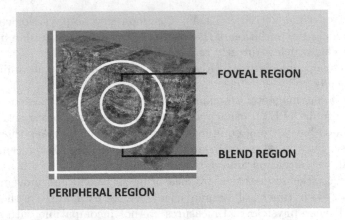

Fig. 4. Foveated rendering scheme

deploy immersive VR environments with incredible detail while saving significant graphical and computational resources. This technique is called foveated rendering (see Fig. 4) and is slowly becoming a reality in VR thanks to the advanced eye-tracking capabilities of HMDs [25]. In theory, foveated rendering could bring significant reductions in rendering cost with no discernible differences in visual quality, which is specially important in scenarios with limited computing graphic power, such as current smartphone-based VR systems. An important element of the foveated rendering technique is a high-speed gaze tracker that can prevent lags while rendering the environment and rapidly respond to the user's head movements.

5.2   Cognitive Adaptation

In the area of psycho-physiological assessment of cognitive load, the pioneering work of Goldberg and Kotval in User eXperience (UX) research is particularly relevant [15]. In their studies, the authors connected cognitive load to processing (the brain activity that deals with information, decisions, and perception). By analyzing how processing tasks affect our sight, they determined that quantity and type of fixations provide reliable metrics to measure cognitive load.

– *Number of fixations:* The higher the cognitive load, the smaller the number of fixations. Our brain cannot process searches when it is busy processing something else. In a gaming environment, if a player is permanently searching, chances are he or she is "lost" (e.g., menus may not be clear, the player does not understand the goals of a particular task, etc.). Therefore, if a significant increase in the number of saccades is observed, experience designers may have to implement strategies to clarify certain aspects of the experience such as automatically launching help messages or reminders, or providing visual cues regarding next steps for a particular task.

- *Fixation duration:* Longer fixations imply the cognitive load is higher and the user is spending more time "processing." Average fixation duration is calculated by adding the number of gaze point samples in all the fixations and dividing by the total number of fixations. This metric provides information about a player's attention and facilitates adapting the timing of certain events to the player's behavior. For example, simple actions such as repeating instructions or reinforcing visual stimuli can catch the player's attention when he or she is focused on a different game element or processing other information.
- *Fixation/saccade ratio:* This content-independent ratio compares the time spent processing (fixations) to the time spent searching (saccades). Higher ratios indicate higher cognitive loads in the VR environment. In situations where higher ratios are detected, designers should provide mechanisms to temporarily reduce the cognitive load. For example, multimedia elements in games may create unnecessary cognitive loads [27]. A simple solution could be "muting" or stopping unnecessary multimedia inputs such as audio and animations. An additional implication of high ratios is that no new information or goal should be presented to the player until the ratio has decreased, as the cognitive capacity of the player can quickly saturate.

5.3 Affective Adaptation

Humans are emotional and social creatures. We cannot completely dissociate high-level cognitive skills (e.g., reasoning, decision making, speaking, reading, or mathematics) from feelings and emotional responses. These strong links have important implications in many areas such as education and neuroscience. For example, if we could fully understand the links between emotions and behavior, it would be possible to tailor our environments to individual users and develop more effective teaching strategies [21].

Although the scope of our proposal is limited to detecting emotion arousal, identifying the specific emotion that a particular experience is generating in a user is also worth studying. In the context of our paper, we want the environment to present stimuli that can promote emotion arousal to increase engagement and motivation. Fear, for example, is an unpleasant emotion that can easily disengage users (although it could arguably be useful in specific contexts).

Several studies on the relationship between emotion and pupil change have empirically shown that pupil diameter increases when people are exposed to emotionally engaging (pleasant or unpleasant) visual stimuli, regardless of hedonic valence [22]. An important adaptation designers can provide with this metric is the introduction of coherent gameplay events that serve as emotional stimuli if a predefined emotional threshold value is exceeded. However, pupil size is not a robust metric. Thus, researchers and designers should first consider establishing baselines for pupil sizes under various conditions before implementing this metric.

The previous type of adaptation could also be linked to game narratives, as described by Cavazza [26]. Based on the author's work on the emotional input on interactive storytelling, game designers could include branching narratives inside the main game plot that could be expanded depending on how a player emotionally reacts to the different events happening within the game.

6   Conclusions and Further Work

New technological advances in the fields of VR and eye-tracking have facilitated the development of high resolution head mounted displays with embedded eye-tracking capabilities. This new generation of VR devices allows researchers and designers to collect vasts amounts of data related to the user's mood, performance, and behavior, which can then be analyzed post-experience to inform the redesign of levels, environments, or specific gameplay aspects.

As the speed and accuracy of eye-trackers continues to increase, the real time interpretation of the metrics described in this paper and the consequent adaptation of gameplay to the particular emotional state of a player may soon become commonplace. However, it will be up to the designers to create VR environments that, even when adaptive, will remain consistent, coherent, and fully immersive (without letting the feeling of presence decrease due to artificial events triggered by the eye-tracker).

More empirical evidence is still needed regarding the robustness of the metrics and the best approaches to map these metrics to the player's emotional states. In this regard, research experiments on affective gaming rarely consider the implications of outside factors. For adaptive games, however, being able to isolate the metrics from external factors is a must in order to maintain a fully immersive experience.

Auto-calibration is also a desirable feature in adaptive eye tracking driven VR systems, as manual calibration in current eye-trackers accounts for a significant amount of preparation time in every eye-tracking experiment. Many researchers are already focusing their efforts on this topic. Finally, the relationships between game mechanics and the adaptation strategies presented in this study will also need to be defined.

References

1. Kivikangas, J.M., Chanel, G., Cowley, B., et al.: A review of the use of psychophysiological methods in game research. J. Gaming Virtual Worlds **3**(3), 181–199 (2011)
2. Rayner, K., Pollatsek, A.: The Psychology of Reading. Prentice Hall, Englewood Cliffs (1989)
3. Duchowsky, A.T.: Eye Tracking Methodology: Theory and Practice. Springer, London (2003)
4. Kazmi, S., Palmer, I.J.: Action recognition for support of adaptive gameplay: a case study of a first person shooter. Intl. J. Comput. Games Technol. **2010**, 11 (2010). doi:10.1155/2010/536480. Article 1
5. Schell, J.: The Art of Game Design: A Book of Lenses. Morgan Kaufmann Publishers Inc., San Francisco (2008)

6. Fassi, A., Riboldi, M., Forlani, C.F., Baroni, G.: Optical eye tracking system for noninvasive and automatic monitoring of eye position and movements in radiotherapy treatments of ocular tumors. Appl. Opt. **51**, 2441–2450 (2012)
7. Crane, H.D., Steele, C.M.: Generation-V dual-Purkinje Image eyetracker. Appl. Opt. **24**, 527–537 (1985)
8. Ji, Q., Hansen, D.W.: In the eye of the beholder: a survey of models for eyes and gaze. IEEE Trans. Pattern Anal. Mach. Intell. **32**, 478–500 (2010)
9. Just, M.A., Carpenter, P.A.: A theory of reading: from eye fixations to comprehension. Psychol. Rev. **87**(4), 329 (1980)
10. Jacob, R.J.K., Karn, K.S.: Eye tracking in human-computer interaction and usability research: ready to deliver the promises. In: The Mind's Eye: Cognitive The Mind's Eye: Cognitive and Applied Aspects of Eye Movement Research, pp. 573–603 (2003)
11. Just, M.A., Carpenter, P.A.: Eye fixations and cognitive processes. Cogn. Psychol. **8**(4), 441–480 (1976)
12. Nodine, C.F., Mello-Thoms, C., Kundel, H.L., Weinstein, S.P.: Time course of perception and decision making during mammographic interpretation. Am. J. Roentgenol. **179**, 917–923 (2002)
13. Byrne, M.D., Anderson, J.R., Douglass, S., Matessa, M.: Eye tracking the visual search of click-down menus. In: Proceedings of Human Factors in Computing Systems, CHI 1999, pp. 402–409. Addison Wesley, Reading (1999)
14. Nacke, L.E., Drachen, A., Goebel, S.: Methods for evaluating gameplay experience in a serious gaming context. Intl. J. Comput. Sci. Sport **9**, 2 (2010)
15. Goldberg, J.H., Kotval, X.P.: Computer interface evaluation using eye movements: methods and constructs. Int. J. Ind. Ergon. **24**(6), 631–645 (1999)
16. Mayer, R.E.: Cognitive theory of multimedia learning. In: Mayer, R.E. (ed.) The Cambridge Handbook of Multimedia Learning. Cambridge University Press, New York (2005)
17. Sorden, S.: The cognitive theory of multimedia learning. In: Handbook of Educational Theories. Information Age Publishing, Charlotte (2012)
18. Bruneau, D., Sasse, M.A., McCarthy, J.D.: The eyes never lie: the use of eyetracking data in HCI research. In: Presented at Proceedings of the Workshop on Physilogical Computing, CHI 2002, Minneapolis, 21 April 2002
19. Pomplun, M., Sunkara, S.: Pupil dilation as an indicator of cognitive workload in human-computer interaction. In: Proceedings of the International Conference on HumanComputer Interaction (2003)
20. Goldberg, J.H., Wichansky, A.M.: Eye tracking in usability evaluation: a practitioner's guide. In: Hyönö, J., Radach, R., Deubel, H. (eds.) The Mind's Eye: Cognitive and Applied Aspects of Eye Movement Research, Amsterdam, The Netherlands (2003)
21. Immordino-Yang, M.H., Faeth, M.: The role of emotion and skilled intuition in learning. In: Mind, Brain, and Education: Neuroscience Implications for the Classroom, pp. 69–83 (2010)
22. Bradley, M.M., Miccoli, L., Escrig, M.A., Lang, P.J.: The pupil as a measure of emotional arousal and autonomic activation. Psychophysiology **45**, 602–607 (2008)
23. Guenter, B., Finch, M., Drucker, S., Tan, D., Snyder, J.: Foveated 3D graphics. ACM Trans. Graph. **31**(6), 10 (2012). doi:10.1145/2366145.2366183. Article 164
24. Strasburger, H., Rentschler, I., Jüttner, M.: Peripheral vision and pattern recognition: a review. J. Vis. **11**(5), 13 (2011). doi:10.1167/11.5.13

25. Patney, A., Kim, J., Salvi, M., Kaplanyan, A., Wyman, C., Benty, N., Lefohn, A., Luebke, D.: Perceptually-based foveated virtual reality. In: ACM SIGGRAPH 2016 Emerging Technologies (SIGGRAPH 2016), Article 17, p. 2. ACM, New York. doi:10.1145/2929464.2929472

26. Cavazza, M., Pizzi, D., Charles, F., Vogt, T., Andre, E.: Emotional input for character-based interactive storytelling. In: Sierra, C., Castelfranchi, C., Decker, K.S., Sichman, J.S. (eds.) Proceedings of 8th International Conference on Autonomous Agents and Multiagent Systems (AAMAS 2009), Budapest, Hungary, May 2009, pp. 313–320 (2009)

27. Kiili, K.: Digital game-based learning: towards an experiential gaming model. Internet High. Educ. **8**, 13–24 (2005)

User Experience in VAMR

An Online User Analysis Regarding the Usage of Mobile Augmented and Virtual Reality Devices in the Field of Robotics

Micha Bläss and Carsten Wittenberg[✉]

Faculty of Mechatronics and Electronics, Heilbronn University, Heilbronn, Germany
{micha.blaess,carsten.wittenberg}@hs-heilbronn.de

Abstract. This paper describes a user requirement analysis performed as an online survey and the results. The focus is on the use of Augmented and Virtual Reality techniques in human-machine interfaces, especially in the domain of industrial robotics. The results of this analysis show opportunities and acceptability of these innovative techniques but also risks. The results will be used for further research activities and development of prototypes using data gloves and virtual reality devices in the industrial production context.

Keywords: User analysis · Augmented reality · Virtual reality · Robotics

1 Introduction

The complexity of automated productions systems increases constantly. Currently the introduction of Industry 4.0 combined with the Cyber-Physical Systems and techniques from the field of information technologies lead to new structures and higher degrees of automation. A result is the so-called Smart Factory [1].

The increased complexity of the factories leads to new requirements to human-machine interaction [2]. Regarding the lifecycle of automated production systems (Fig. 1) two phases with three user groups can be pointed out:

1. During the engineering phase the user group of system designer develop and design the whole production system. Different craft groups (e.g. mechanical engineers, electrical engineers, PLC software engineers etc.) work with their specific software tools sequential on the designing, configuring and building up the production systems.
2. During the operating phase two user groups play an important role:
   a. The operators supervise and control the assigned production line.
   b. The service and maintenance technicians keep the production ticking over.
3. The last phase "scrapping" is not considered.

© Springer International Publishing AG 2017
S. Lackey and J. Chen (Eds.): VAMR 2017, LNCS 10280, pp. 383–393, 2017.
DOI: 10.1007/978-3-319-57987-0_31

Fig. 1. Lifecycle of automated production systems [2]

In the engineering phase the "Digital Factory" approach becomes more and more relevant. In this approach, parts of the activities are performed in a virtual environment instead on real site. A so-called "digital twin" has to be modelled and used for the virtual commissioning. Figure 2 shows the difference between the "classical" and the "digital factory" approach.

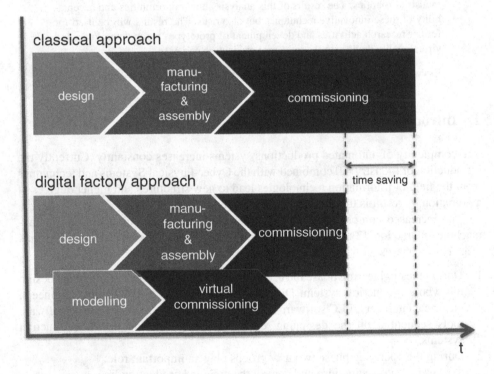

Fig. 2. "Classical" vs. "Digital Factory" approach [2]

In parallel, the field of mobile technologies increased. Nowadays mobile devices from web pads [3] over data glasses [4] to Virtual Reality (VR) devices are powerful and affordable. As a basis for further research an online user analysis is performed to collect user requirements and opinion regarding the usage of data glasses and VR devices especially in the domain of robotics.

2 Background and Related Work

The following subsections describes basic information on the Augmented Reality and the Virtual Reality similar to the explanation the participants of the analysis got.

2.1 Background on Augmented Reality (AR)

Augmented Reality (AR) is a visual extension of the reality. It combines digital information such as videos, pictures, texts etc. with data that exists in reality, for example the picture of a digital camera. The supplementary data can help the user to accomplish several tasks. The virtual extension occurs in real time so that relevant digital data can be retrieved by the user. Especially big companies such as Google and Apple are working on integrating AR into everyday life and developing new and more improved AR-Systems [5, 6].

The most known example for such a product are data glasses. These smart glasses are wearable AR-Systems that combine virtual reality with physical reality [7].

2.2 Background on Virtual Reality (VR)

Virtual Reality (VR) is a computer technology that creates a simulated environment. VR places the user inside a virtual word unlike other traditional user interfaces. The VR simulates several senses such as vision, hearing, touch and smell [8]. This creates a world without real objects that can be controlled by head and hand movements, the voice or the sense of touch [9].

Well known VR products are VR devices, e.g. the Oculus Rift, HTC Vive, PlayStation VR, FOVE, etc. These VR devices create a whole new virtual environment.

2.3 Augmented Reality vs. Virtual Reality

VR creates an imaginary reality and AR only upgrades the "real" reality.

3 The Carried-Out Survey

Based on a previous analysis [10] and to find out in which areas the research activities regarding the use of AR and the VR will be carried forward, 28 specialists participated in this survey. The survey was conducted as an online survey [11]. The robotic specialists were invited to participate in a robotic forum [12]. The participants were at the age of 20 to 60 years. Most of the participants are working in research and development, mostly in fields such as robotics, automation and engineering. The average professional experience of the participants is 7,5 years. Additional to the questions also explanatory figures were shown to the participants. The Figs. 3 and 5 are examples for such explanatory figures.

3.1 Augmented Reality in Terms of Industrial Robots

The first part of the survey covers the use of AR in terms of industrial robots. The question to the participants was the participants if it is useful to simulate the following situations and data for example with smart glasses.

Visualization of the working space of an industrial robot. The participants were asked, if it is useful to visualize the working space of an industrial robot. The Fig. 3 shows an illustration of such an Augmented Reality visualization.

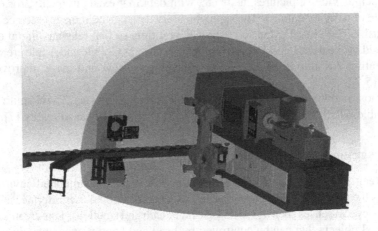

Fig. 3. Visualization of the robot working space

78% of the participants rated the visualization of the working space of an industrial robot with *good* or *very good*, only 7% think the visualization is inadequate (Fig. 4). Certainly, this result is according to expectations, because the visualization of the

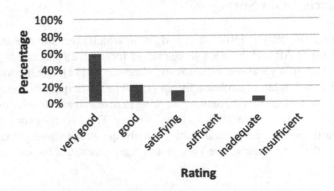

Fig. 4. Rating of the visualization of the working space

working space (and the danger zone) is a useful feature. Interesting will be the implementation of this information in an Augmented Reality system.

Visualization of the programmed movement profile of the robot. Furthermore, the participants were asked if it is helpful to visualize the programmed movement profile of an industrial robot in the working space. For better understanding this scenario is visualized in the Fig. 5. This feature may reasonable for the onsite programming of the robot, e.g. for checking if the program fits the desired movement profile.

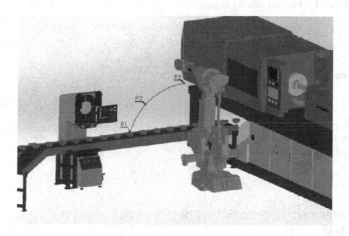

Fig. 5. Visualization of the programmed robot movement

The positive result of this question is shown in the diagram below (Fig. 6). This diagram above shows that 79% of the participants think that the visualization of the

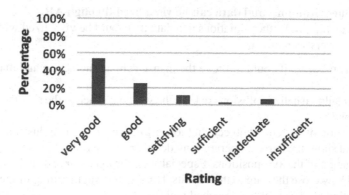

Fig. 6. Rating of the visualization of the programmed robot movement

programmed movement of an industrial robot is a good idea (sum of *very good* and *good*). Seven percent think the idea is inadequate.

Further questions regarding AR in terms of industrial robots. The visualization of the working space and the visualization of the programmed movement were not the only questions asked in terms of this subject. The following table shows the results of the other questions (Table 1).

Table 1. Further results regarding the use of AR in the field of robotics

	Very good	Good	Satisfying	Sufficient	Inadequate	Insufficient
Visualization of programmed points in the working space	58%	21%	14%	0%	7%	0%
Visualization of the danger zone	64%	21%	4%	4%	7%	0%
Visualization of error messages and their solution	36%	29%	18%	7%	7%	3%
Visualization of the singular positions	36%	25%	29%	0%	7%	3%
Small animations of common tasks e.g. tool measurement	25%	25%	21%	7%	11%	11%

The results of these questions are fairly positive. The only exception is the question if it is useful to show small animations of common tasks e.g., tool measurement. In this case, only 50% of the participants think it is a good idea to show these small animations via AR. The idea behind this question was to give service and maintenance technician animated instructions. In a previous analysis and research work this item was rated quite better [3, 10].

Which further situations and data can be visualized through AR. The participants were asked to think of further situations and data that could be visualized with AR. The following answers were given:

- In mobile robotics, it could improve the man-machine interaction and make it more secure.
- The AR could visualize collisions risks in the working space of the robot within given movements.
- Visualization of undefined objects in the working space of the industrial robot.
- AR could show the current operating mode of the industrial robot.
- Visualization of the axis positions. Especially for the axis four and six it is interesting to know how close they are to their limits. During the programming of the robot you often notice too late that they reached their limits.

- Maintenance and repair of the robot: Visualization of the working steps for the maintainer.
- Installation of the robots: Visualization of the correct position for the robots and all the other process equipment in the robot cell.
- Visualization of the current positions of the different coordinate systems.

Is Augmented Reality in terms of industrial robots useful? In the end of the first part of the survey the participants were asked if they think it is helpful to use AR in terms of industrial robots. 75% of them answered that the idea of the use of AR in terms of industrial robots is good. Only seven percent think it is insufficient (Fig. 7).

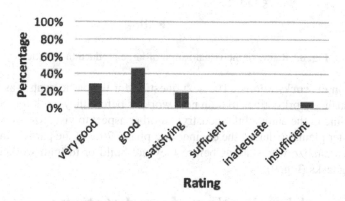

Fig. 7. Rating of the question "How useful is AR in terms of industrial robots?"

Taken all together an Augmented Reality extension is rated by the participants very positive. The challenge is now to develop and implement sensible and usable AR Human-Machine Interfaces that are suitable for industrial usage.

3.2 Virtual Reality for Industrial Use

In the second part of the survey focused the opinion of the participants about a few exemplary situations regarding the reasonable use of VR. This part is not just focused on the field of robotics.

Visualization of large production facilities (Engineering phase). One question for the participants was if it is useful to visualize large production facilities to make it possible to work through them. This would give for example customers a better description of the product. It could be possible to show several procedures within the production facilities. Another usage could be during the virtual commissioning in the digital factory approach. The majority of the participants thinks it is a good idea to visualize large production facilities. But 14% of them think it is a bad idea (Fig. 8).

Visualization of large production facilities

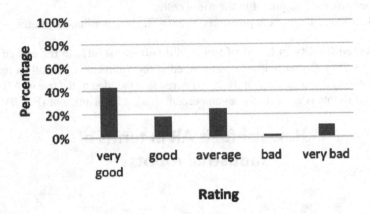

Fig. 8. Rating of the visualization of large production facilities

Visualization of workstations. The next question for the participants was if it makes sense to visualize workstations to train new workers before they work for example at a production line in the automobile industry. Another aspect to visualize workstations is for their better planning during the engineering phase. 79% of the participants thinks it is useful to visualize workstations before they are build or to train workers for their forthcoming tasks (Fig. 9).

Visualization of workstations

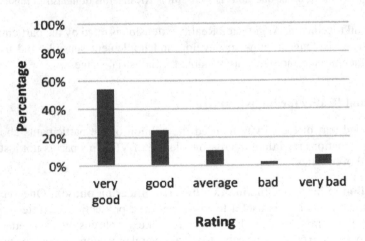

Fig. 9. Rating of the visualization of workstations

Which further situations and data can be visualized with Virtual Reality systems?

The participants were requested to suggest further situations and data that can be visualized with VR. The following enumeration shows the answers of the participants:

- 3D construction
- Safety commissioning (safety areas, interfering contours)
- To test control concept and accessibility of production facilities in their original size
- To teach complex manufacturing processes
- Support in equipping, service and diagnose of machines
- Remote maintenance, optimization
- To train the employees

What risks are associated with Augmented Reality and Virtual Reality devices?

The participants were asked if they could imagine risks of using VR and AR in the industry. The following risks are named:

- security concerns in terms of industrial espionage.
- risk of eye injury.
- limitation of the visual field.
- In case of failure of the VR or AR glasses the working process cannot be continued because of lack of abilities and knowhow.
- Directs and leads to carelessness.

Some of the mentioned concerns are still in actual the discussion about Industry 4.0 – topics (e.g. *industrial espionage*/it security). Some concerns may result from the lack of knowledge about the devices (e.g. *risk of eye injury*). A further analysis could be useful for the interpretation of the mentioned risks of AR and VR. AR/VR application should avoid these concerns.

4   Actual and Future Activities

In a first step a prototype for the use of data glasses for the communication with a PLC is developed and evaluated [4]. Necessary and situation-related information can be displayed in the normal visual field of the user. For the user inputs a specific touchpad is available (Fig. 10).

Main purpose of this first step is to realize a stable data communication between the data glass and the PLC. Beside this the developed application include a menu to navigate to the single PLC modules. Via the touchpad of the data glass the user can monitor the process variables (also the historical run of the variables is presented) and can change the binary process values.

Fig. 10. Augmented reality via data glasses for interaction with a PLC

The next planned step will be the transfer to VR application. Applying an HTC Vive an application for the virtual commissioning of a simple production system (Fig. 11) will be developed at the PLC Laboratory of Heilbronn University. The PLCs of this production system are connected via OPC UA to a cloud server. The HTC Vive system exchange the necessary data via this cloud server.

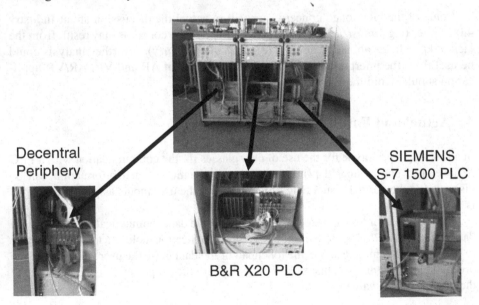

Fig. 11. Automated production system with different types of PLCs

Based on these first experiences the transfer to the fields of robotics is planned for further research steps. One project will focus the use of VR application based on a HTC Vive for the stationary robotics, a second project is planned with AR for mobile robotics.

References

1. Bauernhansl, T., ten Hompel, M., Vogel-Heuser, B.: Industrie 4.0 in Produktion, Automatisierung und Logistik (Industry 4.0 in Production, Automation, and Logistics). Springer Vieweg, Wiesbaden (2014)
2. Wittenberg, C.: Human-CPS interaction – requirements and human-machine interaction methods for the Industry 4.0. In: Proceedings of the 13th IFAC/IFIP/IFORS/IEA Symposium on Analysis, Design, and Evaluation of Human-Machine Systems, Kyoto (2016)
3. Buyer, S., Wittenberg, C.: AR and maintenance - visualization of process data and engineering information. In: Stephanidis, C. (ed.) HCI 2015. CCIS, vol. 528, pp. 159–162. Springer, Cham (2015). doi:10.1007/978-3-319-21380-4_28
4. Ehmann, D.: Konzeption und Entwicklung einer Android Applikation zum Informationsaustausch zwischen einer Datenbrille und speicherprogrammierbaren Steuerungen (Conception and development of an Android application for data exchange between data glass and PLC), internal bachelor thesis, Heilbronn University (2015)
5. Dörner, R., Broll, W., Grimm, P., Jung, B.: Virtual und Augmented Reality (VR/AR). Springer, Heidelberg (2013)
6. (2016). http://www.theaugmentedreality.de
7. (2016). https://www.researchgate.net/search.Search.html?type=publication&query=google+glasses
8. (2016). http://www.marxentlabs.com/what-is-virtual-reality-definition-and-examples/
9. (2016). http://www.itwissen.info/definition/lexikon/Virtuelle-Realitaet-VR-virtual-reality.html
10. Haag, M.: Anforderungsanalyse Servicetechniker (Requirement analysis service technicians). Internal study project, Heilbronn University (2012)
11. (2016). https://www.umfrageonline.com/s/f78822b
12. (2016). http://www.roboterforum.de

The Application of Augmented Reality Technology on Museum Exhibition—A Museum Display Project in Mawangdui Han Dynasty Tombs

Dong Han[✉], Xujie Li, and Tianjiao Zhao

Tianjin University, Tianjin, China
winter1976@hotmail.com, 379201586@qq.com,
zhaotianjiao@tju.edu.cn

Abstract. Augmented Reality (AR) technology currently is widely used in the fields of military, medical, entertainment, Tourism, industrial and etc. In our research, we applied the AR technology into the exhibition of the historical relics in the Mawangdui Han dynasty tombs China. Thousands of the unearthed historical relics have close connections with each other in both cultural and spacial value. However, they are exhibited separately in traditional exhibition way. In this research, we have promoted a new method by using the AR technology to exhibit the historical relics together through the mobile terminal. This project has achieved impressive results on a scaled down model test. This application first captures real scene and detects features, then loads the 3D structure or animation after building the real word coordinate system from the data obtained before. Through the real-time rendering, we are able to argument archaeological features onto the real word scene, enable the audience to get much realer and richer museum experience. This method not only demonstrates a clear position and historical content of different historical relics but also provides interaction between users and historical relics. It brings a new exhibition method in the museum and people would enjoy a more interesting museum experience.

Keywords: Augmented Reality · Mawangdui Han Tomb · Museum display · Mobile terminal

1 Introduction

Augmented reality (AR) is a live direct or indirect view of a physical, real-world environment whose elements are augmented (or supplemented) by computer-generated sensory input such as sound, video, graphics or GPS data. It is related to a more general concept called mediated reality, in which a view of reality is modified (possibly even diminished rather than augmented) by a computer [1].

With the development of network technology and mobile terminal equipment, Augmented Reality is no longer confined by fixed environment and additional equipment. Augmented reality can be realized through the tablet PC, smart phones and other equipment. The practical application of this technology is of great significance and will bring infinite possibility of utilization.

© Springer International Publishing AG 2017
S. Lackey and J. Chen (Eds.): VAMR 2017, LNCS 10280, pp. 394–403, 2017.
DOI: 10.1007/978-3-319-57987-0_32

From the first mobile augmented reality system is emerged in 1997, in the past 20 years, many corresponding application development toolkit and application framework are produced [2]. As the mobile device hardware and software is updated and improved, more and more applications and technologies are designed based on mobile terminal equipment.

The museum is a site that conduct collecting, displaying, researching and classifying the material object which represent nature and human cultural heritage, it also provides a place for visitors to study research and entertain. Providing high-quality information services is the core value of museums.

Museum exhibits are often characterized by physical presence experience. However, it still requires the integration and support of new technologies. With the development of information processing technology, the audience's demand for information and experience are increasing continually, which has become the inevitable development of the museum direction. Currently, the construction and displayed design of museum have shown the trend of digital, network, and intelligent technology. Through the investigation and research on the display site of the Mawangdui Han Tomb of the Hunan Provincial Museum, it is found that the existing exhibition has the following problems:

It is found that the information of the exhibition historical relics are disperse and half-baked. Hunan Museum separates the unearthed historical relics into different groups and places these relics into different exhibition rooms with diverse conditions in order to protect them. The dead woman body, the coffin, and various kinds of funerary objects are displayed in different showcases. It makes the exhibits separated and the relevance of the exhibits is artificially cut, which is detrimental to the visitors' overall perception and knowledge of Mawangdui Han tombs. As the exhibits are out of the environment, experience perception is insufficient.

Unlike single unearthed cultural relics, there are strong connections among the historical relics in Mawangdui Han tombs in both spatial existence and historical background and meaning. Placing the cultural relics out of the original grave environment will reduce the presence experience of visitor.

In order to solve the above problems, this paper presents a museum display method by using AR technology based on mobile terminal.

2   Method

Based on the results analyzed on Mawangdui Han Tomb, we proposed the following plans:

With the widely used of mobile terminal, the audience can appreciate an combination display of virtual and reality scene. It can effectively strengthen the integrity and presence. In the real environmental conditions presented by Han tomb coffin, we add Virtual 3D Scene to restore the view of burial funeral. Through the display, the audience can not only feel the authenticity of the unearthed cultural relics itself, but also can learn more information and realistic experience through the simulated recovery.

The specific design scheme based on the visitor's perspective are showing as following:

Visitors arrivals the coffin display area with their own intelligent mobile phone or tablet computer. Visitors installed program in advance and use the camera lens to view grave at any angle. From the reality on the screen, the reality of the tomb in the real coffin and the virtual three-dimensional model of the female body and all the funerary can make a good fusion. Visitors will see all the unearthed objects in the Mawangdui Tomb under the same angle of view, light, chroma with an integral sense. In addition, when visitors moving, the display screen can be updated and can automatically make a match between the real-time virtual content and 3D model from viewer's angle. This allows the audience to completely visit the Han Tombs at Mawangdui in the whole moving process. The scheme has the following advantages:

1. Supply the missing part of the exhibit: Restore the original environment of the artifacts and display each part of the unearthed objects. Visitors can see the whole Mawangdui tomb, which can strengthen the relevance of unearthed objects [3].
2. Demonstrate the spatial relationship and the unearthed order of the cultural relics: Through using 3D scene to exhibit Mawangdui tomb sites, visitors can intuitively see the unearthed order of the cultural relics, and the position of cultural relics.
3. Enrich visiting experience: A combination of the virtual reality makes the visiting experience more authentic and amusing. The interesting, vivid and realistic process enhances the audience's willingness to watch and accept the results.
4. Avoiding the destruction of Cultural Relics: Although augmented reality technology is new media technology, it won't light and radiate on cultural relics and any artificial markers would not make on the cultural relic entity. This system avoids the destruction of the coffin (Fig. 1).

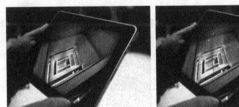

Fig. 1. The proposed effect of this project

3 Measures

3.1 Technical's Route

According to the workflow of the augmented reality system and the actual application process of Mawangdui Han tomb, We make a technique route flowchart (Fig. 2):

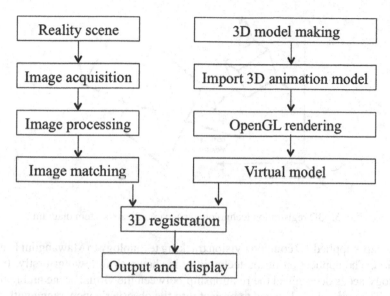

Fig. 2. Implementation procedure

3D virtual scene model making. In order to show the real-time rendering of the 3D virtual scene with high simulation degree, the animation character model and the scene model were built by Maya software. The process includes data collecting, conceptual design, model building, texturing mapping, skeletal skinning, motion animation, lighting production and rendering.

Image feature recognition and matching. After the image collection from the real scene, image feature recognition and matching technology between the images in the database and the image obtained from the camera is a key technology. Based on computer vision registration augmented reality system, there are two methods of image feature extraction matching: artificial labeling feature point method and natural feature points extraction method. In this paper, the cultural relics Mawangdui Tomb cannot be destroyed. Therefore, the method of artificial labeling is not applicable. Natural feature point extraction method is selected.

Three-D tracking registration technology. In order to make the virtual 3D model seamlessly connect with the real scene, the position of the virtual model in the real scene should be arranged correctly. 3D-tracking technology is the core technology of augmented reality system. There are two 3D tracking registration methods: 3D tracking technology based on hardware tracker (such as gyroscope, inertial navigation and positioning system) and 3D tracking technology based on computer vision. In this paper, 3D tracking technology based on computer vision is applied to the display of Mawangdui Han Tomb (Fig. 3).

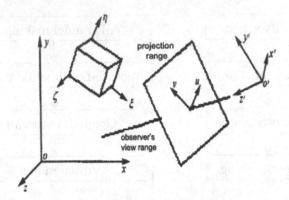

Fig. 3. 3D registration technology space coordinate system diagram

This paper applied 3D computer vision tracking technology to Mawangdui Han tomb exhibition. The application of the technology is shown as following: firstly, tracking technology needs determined the relationship between the virtual scene and real scene visitors. Then virtual model need to project into the observer's view range with correct projection. The 3D registration techniques usually use 4 coordinate system to describe, the x, y, z represent real coordinates; ξ, η, ζ represent the virtual space coordinate system; x', y', z' represent the camera coordinate system; uv represent image plane coordinate system. The calculation of the transformation matrix are used to complete the three-dimensional registration technology [4].

3.2 Implementation of Augmented Reality Applications

3.2.1 Development Environment and Test Environment Settings

Development environment. This research builds a development system on a PC with excellent hardware, and Unity3D are adopted as the development environment. For OpenGL ES, this system provides very good channels for the optimization of graphics rendering. The applications of this system can be easily realized on Android system. It uses Maya dimensional animation software to build environments for virtual scene, which can highly simulate and restore female corpses and funerary objects. Additionally, we use Vuforia AR SDK, which is developed by Qualcomm as the toolbox package to implement augmented reality. It has the fundamental technology of mobile augmented reality, object scanning, 3D registration, and other functions [5, 6]. The SDK is the core technology package to achieve augmented reality.

Testing environment. Based on the actual situation of the coffin position in Hunan Mawangdui tomb, we restore the physical simulation setting in the test environment. Proportionally reduced Wooden solid coffin model is served as test realistic scenes. As a prerequisite, it is necessary to immune the natural light, keep light intensity and angle constant in the space environment tomb placed, and keep the location and surroundings of the coffin constant in the test process.

The procedure is conducted in Samsung Galaxy Mega devices above 4.0 versions of the system (Vuforia AR SDK 4.0 asks for testing mobile devices for Android4.0 above). Development of the special structure of the Android platform and greatly improvement of Graphics processing chip performance can be suitable for the development of augmented reality applications. 8-million pixel rear camera can clearly capture the features of coffin for feature extraction and recognition; 6.3 in. display, 720P Resolution allows viewers to clearly see the effect of fusion of virtual and real scene.

Three-dimensional scene modeling. In order to enhance the rendering effect of the practical application and increase the load speed, it is necessary to control the models and textures for a three-dimensional scene. First of all, Polygons was used to model and the model file should be of good compatibility. After completing the models, a further optimization should be made and the details performed by the performance of textures. When selecting the map, the resolution should not be higher than 1024 * 1024 dpi so that it can well ensure the effect of the viewing screen and the matching speed of the model. Finally, the 3D scene rendering was outputted for .fbx format, which can export animation, texture and mapping models to be imported to Unity3D to edit (Fig. 4).

Fig. 4. 3D model of virtual scene

Image acquisition and processing. In this paper, in order to achieve image acquisition technology, comparative test was conducted on Single Image inVuforia SDK augmented reality toolkit and 3D Object model latest added. The specific implementation process is as following:

The coffin of the continuous image acquisition. 3D Object scans modeling implied 3D modeling scanning technology to the coffin model scan in realistic space, and it automatically is decomposed into 49 aspects captured in return. Images, which were printed and recognizable, were placed at the bottom of the coffin model. Mobile phone acquire feature points can be carried out after the viewfinder captured the three-dimensional coordinate system.

In order to ensure the practicality and authenticity of the viewing angle simulated the real world, instead of scanning all of the 49 surfaces, only the visual field was captured and collected.

After scanning and constructing model, it is necessary to test the real-time and stability of the model. Dragging green test points in the text, the sensitivity of its action shows the quality of the capture effect. It is shown in Fig. 5.

Fig. 5. Image acquisition process of "scanning modeling"

The coffin was identified as a.Ob file. Compared with the original Single Image, after capturing the different angle and height of the feature, the tracker can track different data sets at the same time, but only one can be activated at each time point [7]. It can reduce the work content and improve work efficiency, speed and enhance the application value.

Image feature point processing and 3D registration. Recognize and match image feature points and 3D registration are the key steps in augmented reality technology. After utilizing 3D scanning mode to extract image feature points, it follows uploading the acquisition target files to Add Target plate, and analyzing the object manager performs sample, making Vuforia SDK include in the sample registration matrix information downloaded, employing special algorithm to analyse and tab the feature points of the coffin model scanned.

The Vuforia SDK used tracker and its subclasses that can be track and monitor to the real environment in the space of 3D model, to identify the target of coffin. Deinit Tracker is responsible for initial recognition, and load Tracker Data is responsible for loading identification data to ensure that the image within the range of the viewfinder. If the images in the pre-realistic environment match with the sample matrix information successfully, the current real image will be tracked and rendered, and the three-dimensional tracking registration technology will be realized [7]. Otherwise, the three-dimensional tracking rendering of image will be exit and reload identification.

Compared with single image and 3D object, 3D scanning method is more suitable for the requirements of Mawangdui Han tombs existing display. Three-dimensional scanning coffin model generated a .ob file, the target images of different angles are identified as a whole target with fixed spatial relations. When the visiting position of the visitor is changed, the target manager can predict the range of the movement intelligently, pre-calculate the tracking rendering, so as to greatly improve the reading efficiency and application of real-time. In addition, as there is a larger flow of tourists with high intensity, the coffin is partially obscured by the visitor and cannot be recognized and tracking. In this situation, the image matching may fail because the information can not be captured by the system. At the same time we bind a three-dimensional scanning recognition method for an object file to fix the various entities of the spatial relationship. When part of the Target is identified successfully, the overall target file can be tracked. In the partially occluded environment, the tracking registration data can be obtained accurately, which can better adapt to the occlusion environment than single image recognition.

Virtual scene superposition. Importing the completed 3D model to the project file, the display of the project file does not recognize the specific image of the .ob file that was scanned. After manually importing 3D model, we need to generate mobile APP, repeatedly adjust spatial relationship between the virtual model and the real coffin, lighting simulation, so as to achieve better results of the actual situation fusion. As shown below, light control simulation in this research was performed with a cool color temperature close to the color temperature of the incandescent lamp, a directional light illumination type, and a 0.57 light intensity (Fig. 6).

Fig. 6. PC virtual scene overlay debugging chart

4 Results

The test of the application program. The test is conducted in the Samsung Galaxy Mega phone Android4.2 system. A scale (1: 4) coffin model is designed to simulate the actual environment.

When the viewfinder finds the real coffin scene, the target Manager would capture images in 1–2 s. The screen can show the AR effect of the Mawangdui tomb. As shown in the Fig. 7, compared to the real scene without virtual integration, the image obtained

Fig. 7. Application test results

from virtual 3D model of women's corpse and their funeral restored the scene when unearthed, this method provide a intuitive and overall view.

This method can simulate viewing angle deviation. In different angles, height, distance and moving process, the mobile phone always displays the corresponding between virtual and real image. The audience can continuously watch from different angles in the movement.

When the moving speed is too fast and the coffin is completely separated from the viewfinder, the re-framing test can be made at any stop position to obtain the virtual and real scene fusion effect at current position. It has good real-time and strain.

Simulating the museum visiting process. When the coffin is shuttered partially by the crowds, the system employs the unobstructed area to catch and identify, calculate the space fixed relationship to achieve complete load tracking coffin model, so as to achieve seamless overlay virtual space scene. The image loss or malformed adverse effects do not affect the viewing process.

5 Discussion

Experimental results show that there are still short comings, in the follow-up work, which needs to be amended and improved:

At present, the experimental results show that the virtual 3D model lacks the corresponding shadow effect. After combining with the real scene, although the simulation is similar to the illumination, it would bring a sense of fragmentation without shadow.

As the virtual scene of the project needs to be placed in the coffin, it will generate occlusion when viewed from different perspective. Until now, the test results demonstrate that the edge of the coffin would cause spatial occlusion to built-in vessel. The authenticity of the viewing experience needs to be improved.

6 Conclusion

In this paper, through the investigation, analysis and design of Mawangdui Han tomb, the Application of Augmented Reality Technology on Museum Exhibition is designed and implemented. The program achieve the function that using of mobile augmented reality technology to accomplish seamless integration in a virtual three-dimensional scene and the real scene in the Android mobile device and constructing experimental scene based on equal proportional zoom entity model. In this scene, according to the coffin built in the Han Dynasty Xinzhui wife corpse and funerary objects by shape, proportions, patterns and other forms, a well virtual restoration are integrated, so as to make the visitors obtain a more holistic and comprehensive experience.

The proposal solves the shortage that the original augmented reality equipment is complicated and inconvenient to carry, and the problem of releasing and returning of the additional equipment. It also solves the problem that exhibition information of exhibits is scattered and incomplete, exhibits is out of the environment and the experience perception is inadequate in the museum display.

At the technical level, compared with the method of extracting the feature points from the original single image, the method of scanning and capturing the feature points of the whole real space object is more mature to identify the real-time, continuity and stability of feature points. Besides, partially obscured in museum exhibition also produced a better recognition effect in the actual prediction test.

Through the final model test, the results show that the program has a stable application. This method is possible to apply to the Mawangdui Han tomb in the live show. In the further study, we will improve the experimental results, as well as we optimize the design. On one hand, we can attempt to add dynamic content display and auxiliary instructions. On the other hand, we can also explore the possibility of developing virtual application based on cloud platform. The technology of this types of applications will certainly develop more digital display method in the museum display.

References

1. Graham, M., Zook, M., Boulton, A.: Augmented reality in urban places: contested content and the duplicity of code. Trans. Inst. Br. Geogr. **38**, 464–479 (2012). doi:10.1111/j. 1475-5661.2012.00539.x
2. Yao, Y.: Studies on implement technology of Augmented Reality, doctor dissertation of Zhe Jiang University (2006)
3. Liu, Y.: Application of digital media technology in museum display, doctor dissertation of Fudan University (2012)
4. Shi, Q., Wang, Y.-T., Cheng, J.: Vision-based algorithm for augmented reality registration. J. Image Graph. **7**, 670–683 (2002)
5. Sui, S.: Research on Augmented Reality System based on Android, Master dissertation of National University of defense Technology (2012)
6. Wang, X.: Research on android terminal based mobile augment reality, Master dissertation of Beijing University of Posts and Telecommunications (2013)
7. Fang, X., Wu, Q.: Paper map expression and its application based on mobile augmented reality. Image Process. Multimedia Technol. **7**, 41–43 (2014)

VIGOR: Virtual Interaction with Gravitational Waves to Observe Relativity

Midori Kitagawa, Michael Kesden, Ngoc Tran,
Thulasi Sivampillai Venlayudam, Mary Urquhart,
and Roger Malina(✉)

University of Texas at Dallas, Richardson, TX, USA
{midori, kesden, nmt140230, txs143330, urquhart,
rxl116130}@utdallas.edu

Abstract. In 2015, a century after Albert Einstein published his theory of general relativity, the Laser Interferometer Gravitational-wave Observatory (LIGO) detected gravitational waves from binary black holes fully consistent with this theory. Our goal for VIGOR (Virtual-reality Interaction with Gravitational waves to Observe Relativity) is to communicate this revolutionary discovery to the public by visualizing the gravitational waves emitted by binary black holes. VIGOR has been developed using the Unity game engine and VR headsets (Oculus Rift DK2 and Samsung Gear VR). Wearing a VR headset, VIGOR users control an avatar to "fly" around binary black holes, experiment on the black holes by manipulating their total mass, mass ratio, and orbital separation, and witness how gravitational waves emitted by the black holes stretch and squeeze the avatar. We evaluated our prototype of VIGOR with high school students in 2016 and are further improving VIGOR based on our findings.

Keywords: Virtual reality · Physics education · Head-Mounted display · Binary black holes · Gravitational waves

1 Introduction

In 1915, Albert Einstein proposed his theory of general relativity as a replacement for Isaac Newton's earlier theory of gravity [1, 2]. General relativity predicts the existence of black holes, objects whose gravity is so intense that they possess event horizons from within which nothing can escape. Although astronomers were initially hesitant to accept the existence of such exotic objects, starting in the 1960's evidence began to mount supporting the existence of stellar-mass black holes formed in the collapse of massive stars and supermassive black holes (billions of times the mass of the Sun) in galactic centers. These black holes often occur in binaries in which two black holes orbit each other. General relativity predicted that binary black holes would emit gravitational waves which are 'ripples' in the fabric of space-time caused only by some of the most violent and energetic processes in the Universe, such as colliding black holes and collapsing stellar cores. Those waves would disrupt space-time in such a way that 'waves' of distorted space would radiate from the source like the movement of waves away from a stone thrown into a pond. Furthermore, these ripples would travel

© Springer International Publishing AG 2017
S. Lackey and J. Chen (Eds.): VAMR 2017, LNCS 10280, pp. 404–416, 2017.
DOI: 10.1007/978-3-319-57987-0_33

at the speed of light through the Universe, carrying information about their cataclysmic origins, as well as invaluable clues to the nature of gravity itself.

The National Science Foundation has funded an experiment called the Laser Interferometer Gravitational-wave Observatory (LIGO) designed to detect gravitational waves from binary stellar-mass black holes billions of light years away from Earth [3]. On September 14, 2015, a century after Einstein published his theory, LIGO discovered gravitational waves from the merger of 36 and 29 solar-mass black holes 1.3 billion light years away [4]. Subsequent observations during LIGO's "O1" observing run revealed gravitational waves from a second black-hole merger [5] and a third event of lower signal-to-noise ratio also consistent with a black-hole merger [6]. These observations represent the dawn of gravitational wave astronomy, an entirely new window into our Universe beyond the electromagnetic spectrum of conventional astronomy. LIGO anticipates observing several additional gravitational-wave sources (including perhaps the first gravitational waves from a neutron-star merger) during its second "O2" observing run, which began in November 2016 and will continue through mid-2017. In addition, pulsar-timing arrays [7–9] and the space-based Laser Interferometer Space Antenna (LISA) [10] seek to observe longer-wavelength gravitational waves emitted by binary supermassive black holes. The future of gravitational-wave astronomy appears bright, but without a greater intuitive understanding of gravitational waves the public will be unprepared to appreciate progress in this field.

1.1   Vigor

Our goal for VIGOR (Virtual-reality Interaction with Gravitational waves to Observe Relativity) is to communicate this revolutionary discovery to the general public by visualizing the gravitational waves emitted by binary black holes. Since the gravitational waves travel hundreds of millions of light years from the merging black holes to Earth, they are extremely weak on Earth and induce only tiny fluctuations in the distances between LIGO's test masses. Although we cannot take students on field trips to where the gravitational waves are far stronger, virtual reality provides them with an immersive interactive experience as they fly through a virtual environment surrounding the two black holes. Our hypothesis is that the immersive and interactive experience that VR provides assists understanding gravitational waves to a greater degree than passive traditional presentations on a flat screen.

VIGOR has been developed using the Unity game engine and VR headsets (Oculus Rift DK2 and Samsung Gear VR). Wearing a VR headset, VIGOR users control an avatar to "fly" around binary black holes as they orbit each other. VIGOR users experiment on binary black holes by manipulating their total mass, mass ratio, and orbital separation. Changes to these parameters lead to changes in the amplitude, polarization, and frequency of the gravitational waves emitted by the black holes. VIGOR users experience gravitational waves as the avatar accompanying them on their journey is stretched and squeezed in response to the gravitational waves at their position, much like the LIGO detectors are affected by real gravitational waves. (The users can exaggerate the magnitude of gravitational waves so that their impacts are easily observable.) By witnessing how the changes to binary black holes'

Fig. 1. Binary black holes and an avatar in VIGOR

parameters (which result in changes in the gravitational waves) deform the avatar differently, the users gain an intuitive understanding of physical concepts like amplitude, frequency, and polarization that describe gravitational waves (Fig. 1).

More generally this research is situated in the larger field of visual mathematics where computer technology bridges art and science by enabling interactive experience of the behavior of mathematical systems [11].

2 Related Work

Over the past three decades, educators have developed a wide variety of computer applications for teaching physics concepts through simulations. Most of these are desktop-based applications and few are immersive VR systems.

2.1 Desktop-Based Instructional Physics Simulators

Notable examples of desktop-based instructional physics simulators include PhET interactive simulations [12], the web physics package called Physlets [13] and Open Source Physics [14]. PhET is a set of interactive web-based simulations of physical phenomena. PhET is fairly broad in scope as it includes simulations in physics, biology, chemistry, earth science, and mathematics. PhET's "force and motion" example allows the user to interactively position different virtual characters on either side of a "tug of war" application, thus learning about net forces when summed together. The Physlet example of a "central force" is one where simple orbital mechanics are simulated to study angular momentum and energy. The number of interactive options in Physlets is less than that of most PhET simulations. In Open Source Physics there are similar options for exploring mechanics and introductory physics.

2.2 Immersive VR Instructional Physics Simulators

The advantages that immersive VR instructional physics simulators have over desktop-based ones include: (a) large fields of regard (i.e., the total size of the visual field surrounding the user [15]), (b) stereoscopy, and (c) head tracking for natural viewing. These advantages provide additional benefits, such as improved spatial understanding [15] and a greater sense of presence (i.e., the sense of "being there" in a virtual environment [16]). Despite the advantages of immersive VR systems, there are a limited number of examples of immersive VR instructional physics simulators, such as [17, 18]. The closest to VIGOR we have found is Teaching Physics Using Virtual Reality which is a desk-top simulator specifically to teach Einstein's theory of special relativity [18]. We believe VIGOR is the first attempt to teach gravitational waves utilizing the advantages that immersive VR technology can offer.

3 Computing Gravitational Waves

Einstein's equation of general relativity, $G_{\mu v} = 8\pi T_{\mu v}$, relates the curvature of space-time (described by the metric $g_{\mu v}$ from which the Einstein tensor $G_{\mu v}$ can be calculated) to the stress-energy tensor $T_{\mu v}$ sourced by the matter and energy in our Universe. It is a generalization of Newton's famous inverse-square law $a = -GM/r^2$ relating the gravitational acceleration a of an object to the mass M and distance r of a second object. Einstein's equation is actually a series of coupled nonlinear partial differential equations that in general can only be solved numerically [19–21]. However, far from black holes where the metric is nearly equal to the Minkowski metric $\eta_{\mu v}$ of flat spacetime (for which Euclidean geometry holds), Einstein's equation can be linearized in the metric perturbations $h_{\mu v} = g_{\mu v} - \eta_{\mu v}$. These metric perturbations satisfy the same wave equation obeyed by far more familiar sound and light waves, i.e. they can be decomposed into sinusoids with wavelength λ and frequency f related by $c = \lambda f$ where the wave speed c is equal to the speed of light. This is why we refer to them as gravitational waves. However, these waves are not density and pressure perturbations (like sound waves) or electromagnetic perturbations (like light), but perturbations to the metric that determines spacetime itself.

As gravitational waves pass through an object (like LIGO's 4 km long interferometers), they induce a tidal field transverse to the direction of their propagation that oscillates at the gravitational-wave frequency f. These tides are similar to the tides that the Moon exerts on the Earth's oceans in that they stretch the object in one direction (along the line of separation between the Earth and Moon in the case of lunar tides) while squeezing it in the perpendicular direction. In the post-Newtonian approximation valid when the relative velocity of the binary black holes is small compared to the speed of light, the gravitational waves are generated by the time-varying quadrupole moment of the spacetime itself rather than each individual black holes (nothing can be emitted classically from a black hole's event horizon). These gravitational waves travel radially outwards from the center of mass of the binary with frequency f twice the orbital frequency of the binary and amplitude inversely proportional to the distance from the binary (leading to an inverse-square law energy flux). Since the tidal fields induced by these gravitational waves are transverse to the radial direction, there are two distinct gravitational-wave polarizations, similar to the two polarizations of electromagnetic waves. The directions of the two linear gravitational-wave polarizations are rotated by 45° with respect to each other, unlike 90° for the two linear electromagnetic polarizations, because tidal stretching is unchanged by a 180° rotation, unlike an electric-field vector that is preserved by a full 360° rotation. The two gravitational-wave polarizations are referred to as h_+ and $h_\times$ because the "+" and "×" symbols are similarly related by a 45° rotation.

More quantitatively, the gravitational waves emitted by binary black holes are given in the Newtonian, quadrupole-moment approximation by the Eqs. (1, 2) [22]

$$h_+(t) = -(2m_1m_2/rDM)[1 + (L \bullet N)^2]\cos 2\Phi(t) \tag{1}$$

$$h_\times(t) = it(4m_1m_2/rDM)(L \bullet N)\sin 2\Phi(t) \tag{2}$$

where m_1 and m_2 are the masses of the two black holes, $M = m_1 + m_2$ is the total mass, r is the distance between the black holes, D is the distance from the center of mass of the black holes to the observer, L is a unit vector in the direction of the orbital angular momentum of the binary, N is a unit vector pointing from the observer to the center of mass, and $\Phi(t)$ is the orbital phase defined to be zero when the binary separation is parallel to the principal + direction $P = N \times L/|N \times L|$ with respect to which the + and × polarizations are defined. We define $E = P \times N$ to be a second unit vector in the transverse direction. An object in a gravitational-wave field will be stretched by a factor $F = 1 + A$ in the direction S and squeezed by a factor $1/F$ in the orthogonal direction T, where the Eqs. (3, 4, 5, 6) give these quantities in terms of the previously defined gravitational waves and transverse basis vectors.

$$A = F - 1 = \sqrt{(h_+^2 + h_\times^2)} \tag{3}$$

$$S = E\cos\theta - P\sin\theta \tag{4}$$

$$T = P\cos\theta + E\sin\theta \tag{5}$$

$$\tan 2\theta = h_\times/h_+ \tag{6}$$

These equations can be challenging to visualize even for a physicist, reinforcing the need for a project like VIGOR to help both the public and scientists build conceptual understanding of gravitational waves. As users of VIGOR and their accompanying avatar virtually "fly" around the black holes as shown in Fig. 1, their distance D from the center of mass of the black holes changes, as does the direction of the unit vector N pointing from their position to the center of mass. According to the above equations, this changes the gravitational waves h_+ and $h_\times$ at the avatar's position, the factor F by which the avatar is stretched and squeezed by the resulting tidal field, and the directions S and T along which this stretching and squeezing occurs. Users of VIGOR will experience the increased stretching of their avatars as they approach the black holes, and the change in gravitational wave polarization from linear (only h_+) to circular (equal magnitudes of h_+ and $h_\times$ out of phase by 90°) as they move from the orbital plane of the black holes to viewing them from above. Users of VIGOR can also change the masses m_1 and m_2 of the two black holes and the distance r between them. Shrinking r (which occurs naturally as gravitational waves extract orbital energy from the binary) will increase both the amplitude $F = 1 + A$ and frequency f of the tidal stretching, since $A \propto 1/r$ and $f = 2d\Phi/dt = 2\sqrt{(GM/r^3)}$. An exaggeration factor can be used to increase the stretch factor F to improve visualization. Our goal for VIGOR is to provide an interactive and immersive environment in which the user can develop an intuitive understanding of gravitational waves as they watch the tidal distortion of their avatars change as they navigate the 3D environment and adjust the binary black-hole parameters.

4 System Requirements and Design

To implement the virtual environment of VIGOR including the orbiting black holes, the gravitational waves they emit, and the user avatar, we chose the following software and hardware systems.

4.1 Software: Unity 5 with Oculus Mobile Utilities

Unity 5 is one of the most popular game engines and many games for entertainment and education have been developed and played on Unity 5. It offers a wide variety of ready-to-use functions, components (e.g., geometries, lights, and materials), API[1] for multiple VR devices and other input/output devices, and example codes for game creations. Unity 5 allows users to create highly realistic 3D games and simulations with which they can interact and modify. The most significant advantages that Unity 5 provides us for VIGOR are its VR supports and cross-platform nature: With only minor changes in the sources code, using Unity 5 we can utilize VR headsets without cumbersome low level coding and deploy VIGOR on many platforms, such as table-top/laptop computers, tablets and mart phones with or without no VR-devices. By taking advantages of Unity 5's API and the software developer kits for the VR headsets, Oculus Rift DK2 and Samsung Gear VR, we integrated Unity with Oculus Rift DK2 and Samsung Gear VR as described below.

4.2 Hardware: Samsung Gear VR

We decided to develop VIGOR as an immersive VR application because immersive VR applications have been shown to provide greater spatial understanding than non-immersive applications [15]. There were several VR hardware products to consider. Initially we developed VIGOR for Oculus Rift DK2. Overtime we realized Samsung Gear VR's advantages over Oculus Rift. With a 101° field of view (FOV), 360° field of regard (FOR [23]), a resolution of 1280×1440 per eye, and an internal tracker for rotational head tracking, Samsung Gear VR provides an immersive user experience. Unlike most other VR headsets, Samsung Gear VR provides a focal adjustment that accommodates nearsightedness and farsightedness. The device weighs

---

[1] Application Program Interface (APS) is a set of subroutine definitions, protocols, and tools for building application software.

only 318 g and could use alone with a Samsung phone without any complicated cables and systems.

Thus, the device is highly mobile that can deploy anywhere without wiring. Moreover, Samsung Gear VR has a built-in touch panel and button on a side of the headset, while Oculus Rift DK2 requires an additional input device, such as a keyboard, mouse, or joystick. Although Samsung Gear VR's touchpad and back button offer easy-to-use interactions without a need for additional devices, the functionalities that can be assigned to them are limited. Given the scale of VIGOR, we assumed that Samsung Gear VR's interface capabilities were enough for our interaction and navigation methods and developed our VIGOR further for Samsung Gear VR.

4.3   Parameter Input and Navigational Method

For parameter input, we used a floating menu and ray-casting to select and change items in the menu. Ray-casting is a method that casts an infinite ray to represent a forward vector from the user's point of view towards the target (Fig. 2). By looking around, the user can target the ray at any objects in the scene. Tapping on back button of a Samsung Gear VR headset brings up the floating menu. The menu has the options to increase or decrease the exaggeration factor, total mass, mass ratio and binary separation. The user can increase or decrease one of the options by tapping on the touch panel until a desired parameter value is obtained. The method allows the user to interact with the floating menu in a 3D space in a manner similar to the use of mouse buttons with a 2D interface.

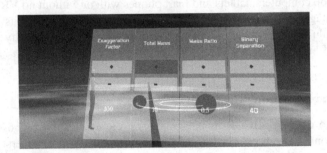

Fig. 2. Floating menu and ray-casting

In the experiment (detailed in the next section), we used a modified human joystick method for navigation. The method allows the user to travel in the 3D space forward or backward to the direction which the user is looking at by moving the torso forward or backward physically. Unlike a traditional human joystick method [23], the modified one allows the user to move around without leaving a seat. It is intuitive and easy to navigate with method; however, four of the seventeen participants reported that they felt dizzy while navigating in VIGOR. We suspected that the light motion sickness that they experienced was caused by the navigation method and after the experiment we switched from the modified human joystick method to a gaze-directed steering method. Gaze-directed steering makes use of ray casting technique where the ray is cast from the user's point of view towards the target. With a gaze-directed steering method the user looks at the direction that she/he wants to go and touches on the touch pad. Then, the avatar travels to that direction until the user lifts the finger off the touch pad. Because this method and ray-casting use the same forward vector from the user's point of view, we implemented a simple mechanism to separate those two: While in menu mode, traveling is locked; to travel again, the user needs to close the menu. We have not tested the new version of VIGOR with the gaze-directed steering method yet and have not proved that gaze-directed steering reduces the occurrences of motion sickness in users.

5 User Experience Experiment

In summer 2016, 17 female participants of ages 14 to 16 in the Women in Physics Advanced Camp [24] at the University of Texas at Dallas were provided with the opportunity to test a prototype of VIGOR using Samsung Gear VRs (Fig. 3). The campers interacted with VIGOR team members, watched a five-minute YouTube video entitled, "LIGO Detects Gravitational Waves" [25], and experienced VIGOR for approximately 10 min each. A 2-D VIGOR simulation was also displaced on a screen for passive participant viewing. At the end of their experience, each participant was asked to fill out a Likert-scale questionnaire created in-house to evaluate both the VIGOR experience and impacts of the experience on participant attitudes towards science and technology (Fig. 4). We followed the headset manufacturer safety recommendations and University of Texas at Dallas's Institutional Review Board protocols and therefore asked the participants to be seated while wearing the VR headset for their safety.

On the questionnaire 87% of the participants reported that "participating" in the VR experience with VIGOR was interesting and engaging while 67% reported that

Fig. 3. VIGOR experiment

	Strongly Agree	Agree	Neither Agree nor Disagree	Disagree	Strongly Agree
I found the YouTube video(s) to be interesting and engaging.					
I found watching the interactive simulation to be interesting and engaging.					
I found participating in the virtual reality experience to be interesting and engaging.					
I found controlling the interactive simulation to be interesting and engaging.					
I found watching the interactive simulation to be more interesting and engaging than the YouTube video(s).					
I found participating in the virtual reality experience to be more interesting and engaging than the YouTube video(s).					
I found controlling the interactive simulation to be more interesting and engaging than the YouTube video(s).					
I was aware of discovery of gravitational waves before this activity.					
I was interested in the science of gravitational waves and black holes before this activity.					
I am more interested in the science of gravitational waves and black holes after participation in this activity.					
I am more interested in science after participation in this activity.					
I am more interested in technology after participation in this activity.					

Fig. 4. Visualizations of binary black holes and gravitational waves survey

"watching" an interactive simulation was interesting and engaging, indicating the importance of the active participation that VR technology provides. It remains unclear which component of the interactive VR experience had the greater impact on the increase in participant engagement: the active participation or the VR itself. All participants reported that they were more interested in "the science of gravitational waves and black holes," "science," and "technology" after the VIGOR experiment. This first test of the VIGOR experience in an informal education setting did not assess participant understanding of the science of gravitational waves.

One notable concern with the experiment was that 4 out of the 17 participants reported that they felt dizzy while they were navigating in VIGOR. We speculate that the participants' dizziness was caused by the navigational method (Sect. 4.3) used in the version of VIGOR we tested. Samsung Gear VR and Oculus Rift DK2 offer different advantages for the user of VIGOR. We selected Samsung Gear VR over Oculus Rift DK2 for the experiment mainly because Samsung Gear VR is wireless and easy to set up. The wireless input of Samsung Gear VR was convenient but limiting:

Samsung Gear VR's single button alone did not allow users to navigate through the virtual environment as freely as we wanted them to be able to do so. Instead, the seated users used their upper torsos to move in space, turning them into human joysticks. As the users moved through the space, the view rapidly changed. We suspect the rapidly changing view was the responsible for the participants' dizziness. To determine the cause and a solution for it, we need to develop VIGOR further and conduct more experiments.

6 Conclusions and Future Work

In 2015 gravitational waves were directly detected by LIGO confirming Einstein's general theory of relativity and news media covered the discovery in early 2016. Although the discovery of gravitational waves may be one of the most significant scientific breakthroughs of this century and received a great deal of media attention, the public has limited insight into this exciting new phenomenon. We have developed a VR system for facilitating the general public's understanding of gravitational waves that we call VIGOR. VIGOR uses a Samsung Gear VR headset to let the user fly around binary black holes accompanied by an avatar, manipulate the black holes' parameters, and view how the gravitational waves emitted by the black holes stretch and squeeze the avatar in order to gain an intuitive understanding of physical concepts like amplitude, frequency, and polarization that describe gravitational waves. The result of our experiment with a VIGOR prototype and high school students was summarized in this paper.

For the next version of VIGOR we plan to (1) optimize the gaze-directed steering navigation method, (2) optimize VIGOR's scene by reducing draw calls, using low poly models and baking light maps to achieve a better frame rate, and (3) add a handheld wireless controller for better interactions. We believe that the improved navigational method, a better frame rate, and an introduction of a handheld wireless controller can reduce the risk of dizziness for future VIGOR users. Moreover, the current VIGOR supports two avatars which are a human figure and a small planet like the Earth. We plan to make a wide variety of avatars available to appeal to all demographic groups.

As this study is about teaching abstract areas of physics using simulations, we also plan to research if a bimodal virtual environment which takes advantages of visual and auditory stimuli can enhance learning. It has been reported that students were more engaged in highly visual phenomena when they were allowed to change variables in an interactive simulation of "real time relativity" [26]. We believe that the use of sound sources [27] in a virtual environment to support the visual models will help lower the attentional load[2] on users. This is because humans have a better sense of detecting the direction of a sound source in a horizontal plane [28] and the use of sound sources in

---

[2] Attention load – all the information that can be perceived voluntarily within the brain's capacity [35]. According to load theory, attentional selection of information occurs during early and late stages of processing. .

virtual environments where users can orient themselves will reduce the user's information processing time in the environment.

Future versions of VIGOR will also incorporate additional aspects of the physics that describes binary black holes. We will include radiation reaction which naturally decreases the distance r between the black holes as gravitational waves extract energy from the binary. This radiation reaction causes the black holes to eventual merge into a single larger black hole that rings down to rest like a bell struck by a clapper. The distinctive shape of the inspiral-merger-ringdown signal which increases in frequency with time is what allows LIGO to distinguish faint events from much larger background noise. Real binary black holes are also described by spins S_1 and S_2 in addition to their masses m_1 and m_2 [29, 30]. These spins can be misaligned with the orbital angular momentum of the binary, much like the 23° inclination of the Earth's axis with respect to the ecliptic responsible for the seasons. Coupling between misaligned black-hole spins and the orbital angular momentum causes the direction of the angular momentum L to vary with time, making the orbital plane of the black holes precess and changing the gravitational-wave emission through the dependence of h_+ and $h_\times$ on L given by the equations of Sect. 3. We will allow users of VIGOR to manipulate the black-hole spins and experience the resulting spin-modulated gravitational waves using new solutions for black-hole spin precession derived by one of the authors [31, 32]. Double-spin precession is not trivial to visualize and we believe that even physicists would appreciate being able to explore the spin parameter space and see the effects on orbital-plane precession and gravitational waves using VIGOR. The ability to manipulate the black-hole spins will help VIGOR users appreciate the gravitational-wave signatures that allow LIGO to measures black-hole spins. These spin measurements will provide insight into the stellar evolution responsible for astrophysical binary black-hole formation [33, 34]. Once the next version of VIGOR is completed, we plan to conduct a larger-scale usability test before exploring additional opportunities for informal education and outreach.

Moreover, we are developing, mVIGOR, a mobile version of VIGOR for tablet computers. mVIGOR will not require peripherals or provide users with immersive experience (Sect. 4.2), while it is being developed using Unity 5 like VIGOR. One goal we have for mVIGOR is to reach those who have no virtual reality equipment. The use of mVIGOR will also provide a way to measure the relative impact of user engagement on the interactive VIGOR experience with and without the VR component. Another goal is to compare the user's experience and understanding of gravitational waves between VIGOR and mVIGOR to test our hypothesis that gravitational waves are understood better in an immersive environment than in a non-immersive environment.

References

1. Einstein, A.: Näherungsweise Integration der Feldgleichungen der Gravitation, pp. 688–696. Sitzungsberichte der Königlich Preussischen Akademie der Wissenschaften, Berlin (1916)
2. Einstein, A.: Über Gravitationswellen (1918)

3. California Institute of Technology: Laser Interferometer Gravitational-wave Observatory. https://www.ligo.caltech.edu/page/what-are-gw

4. Abbott, B.P., et al.: Ovservation of gravitational waves from a binary black hole merger. Phys. Lett. **116**, 061102 (2016)

5. Abbott, B.P., et al.: GW151226: observation of gravitational waves from a 22-solar-mass binary B coalescence. Phys. Lett. **116**, 241103 (2016)

6. The LIGO scientific collaboration and the virgo collaboration: binary black hole mergers in the first advanced LIGO observing run. Phys. Rev. **X6**, 041015 (2016)

7. Hobbs, G.: The parkes pulsar timing array. Class. Quantum Gravity **30**, 224007 (2013)

8. McLaughlin, M.A.: The North American nanohertz observatory for gravitational waves. Class. Quantum Gravity **30**, 224008 (2013)

9. Kramer, M., Champion, D.J.: The european pulsar timing array and the large european array for pulsars. Class. Quantum Gravity **30**, 224009 (2013)

10. Audley, H., et al.: Laser interferometer space antenna. Submitted to ESA on January 13th in response to the call for missions for the L3 slot in the Cosmic Vision Programme. https://arxiv.org/abs/1702.00786

11. Emmer, M.: Visual Mind II. MIT Press, Cambridge (2006)

12. University of Colorado Boulder: PhET Interactive Simulations. http://phet.colorado.edu

13. Christian, W., Bellon, M.: Physlet Physics: Interactive Illustrations, Explorations and Problems for Introductory Physics. Addison-Wesley, Boston (2003)

14. Christian, W: Open Source Physics. http://www.compadre.org/osp/index.cfm

15. Bowman, D.A., McMahan, R.P.: Virtual reality: how much immersion is enough? IEEE Comput. **40**(7), 36–43 (2007)

16. Slater, M., Usoh, M., Steed, A.: Taking steps: the influence of a walking technique on presence in virtual reality. ACM Trans. Comput. Human Interact. (TOCHI) **2**(3), 201–219 (1995)

17. Kaufmann, H., Meyer, B.: Physics education in virtual reality: an example. Themes Sci. Technol. Educ. **2**(1–2), 117–130 (2009)

18. Wegener, M., McIntyre, T.J., McGrath, D., Savage, C.M., Williamson, M.: Developing a virtual physics world. Austr. J. Educ. Technol. **28**(3), 504–521 (2012)

19. Pretorius, F.: Evolution of binary black-hole spacetimes. Phys. Rev. Lett. **95**, 121101 (2005)

20. Campanelli, M., Lousto, C.O., Maronetti, P., Zlochower, Y.: Accurate evolutions of orbiting black-hole binaries with excision. Phys. Rev. Lett. **96**, 111101 (2006)

21. Baker, J.G., Centrella, J., Choi, D.I., Koppitz, M., van Meter, J.: Gravitational-wave extraction from an inspiraling configuration of merging black holes. Phys. Rev. Lett. **96**, 111102 (2006)

22. Apostolatos, T.A., Cutler, C., Sussman, G.J., Thorne, K.S.: Spin-induced orbital precession and its modulation of the gravitational waveforms from merging binaries. Phys. Rev. D **49** (12), 6274–6297 (1994)

23. Bowman, D.A., Kruijff, E., LaViola, J.J., Poupyrev, I.: 3D User Interfaces: Theory and Practice. MIT Press, Cambridge (2005)

24. University of Texas at Dallas: Women in Physics Camp at the University of Texas at Dallas. http://wipphysicscamp.weebly.com

25. Massachusetts Institute of Technology: LIGO Detects Gravitational Waves. https://www.youtube.com/watch?v=B4XzLDM3Py8

26. Savage, C., McGrath, D., McIntyre, T., Wegener, M., Williamson, M.: Teaching physics using virtual reality. In: AIP Conference Proceedings, vol. 1263, pp. 126–129 (2010)

27. Hecht, D., Reiner, M., Halevy, G.: Multi-modal stimulation, response time and presence. Presence **15**(5), 515–523 (2006)

28. Török, Á., Mestre, D., Honbolygó, F., et al.: It sounds real when you see it. Realistic sound source simulation in multimodal virtual environments. J. Multimodal User Interfaces **9**(4), 323–331 (2015)
29. Kerr, R.: Gravitational field of a spinning mass as an example of algebraically special metrics. Phys. Rev. Lett. **11**, 237 (1963)
30. Carter, B.: An axisymmetric black hole has only two degrees of freedom. Phys. Rev. Lett. **26**, 331 (1971)
31. Kesden, M., Gerosa, D., O'Shaughnessy, R., Berti, E., Sperhake, U.: Effective potentials and morphological transitions for binary black hole spin precession. Phys. Rev. Lett. **114**, 081103 (2015)
32. Gerosa, D., Kesden, M., Sperhake, U., Berti, E., O'Shaughnessy, R.: Multi-timescale analysis of phase transitions in precessing black-hole binaries. Phys. Rev. D **92**, 064016 (2015)
33. Gerosa, D., Kesden, M., Berti, E., O'Shaughnessy, R., Sperhake, U.: Resonant-plane locking and spin alignment in stellar-mass black-hole binaries: a diagnostic of compact-binary formation. Phys. Rev. D **87**, 104028 (2013)
34. Rodriguez, C.L., Haster, C.J., Chatterjee, S., Kalogera, V., Rasio, F.A.: Dynamical formation of the GW150914 binary black hole. Astrophys. J. Lett. **824**, L8 (2016)
35. Swallow, K.M., Jiang, Y.V.: Attentional load and attentional boost: a review of data and theory. Frontiers Psychol. **4**, 274 (2013)

A Virtual Reality Tool Applied to Improve the Effects on Chronic Diseases - Case: Emotional Effects on T2DM

Leticia Neira-Tovar[1](✉) and Ivan Castilla Rodriguez[2]

[1] Universidad Autónoma de Nuevo León, San Nicolas de Los Garza,
N.L., México
leticia.neira@gmail.com
[2] Universidad of La Laguna, Tenerife, Canary Islands, Spain
icasrod@ull.edu.es

Abstract. A large part of the world population suffers from type 2 diabetes mellitus (T2DM). Since most life-threatening consequences of the disease do not appear during its first stages, there is an inherent difficulty to establish prevention strategies at young age. Technology is a tool of high potential for this purpose. Virtual Reality (VR) tools are already used in many areas, such as education, entertainment, advertising, and health; and might prevent the impact of some of the physical and emotional effects of T2DM. There are products that become global phenomena with the simple use of this kind of sophisticated technology, impressing people, and making these products more interesting. The purpose of this paper is to present work in progress towards the development of a VR videogame that aims to motivate exercise and combat depression, thus preventing some of the T2DM consequences. The videogame uses a model based on a user experience, gamification and immersive virtual reality element.

Keywords: Virtual reality · Diabetes effects · Depression · Serious game · Gamification · User experience · Immersive technology

1 Introduction

Type 2 diabetes mellitus (T2DM) is a chronic metabolic disease that causes blood glucose levels to rise higher than normal. Long-term consequences include minor and major cardiovascular problems, (stroke, heart disease, poor blood flow), diabetic retinopathy and kidney failure. There is also evidence on the relationship between diabetes and depression [1]. According to the World Health Organization, 422 million people above 18 suffered from diabetes in 2014, and the trend is increasing [2]. 1.5 million people died in 2012 due to diabetes.

Apart from the impact on health, T2DM places a considerable economic burden on society, not only because of the expenditure in treatments and health care services, but also due to productivity losses at work. Although the causes of these losses are not completely determined yet, they are usually related to poor disease control, adverse health outcomes and quality of life impairment [3].

© Springer International Publishing AG 2017
S. Lackey and J. Chen (Eds.): VAMR 2017, LNCS 10280, pp. 417–425, 2017.
DOI: 10.1007/978-3-319-57987-0_34

Healthy diet, regular physical activity, and avoiding tobacco have proved to be effective to avoid or delay the worst consequences of T2DM. However, people suffering from the disease is reluctant to actively change their lifestyle due to the "silent" appearance of the disease, which seems harmless at the first stages.

There are a number of successful examples on the use of virtual reality (VR) technology, to prevent and empower people on the consequences of this terrible disease [4]. These examples include prototypes to teach healthy food habits [5], to perform physical activity [6], and some special cases using "exergames" [7], mainly in diabetic patients of a single community.

Interventions such as those mentioned above, must be designed rigorously, relying on strong medical and psychological foundations, and following a comprehensive and well-structured model. A related clinical trial on T2DM (DEPLAN) identified the key elements to design this kind of models [8]. The results of that study shown that three main factors must be selected to reflect the interaction experience when using some kind of "mini-game". These factors are lifestyle, physical activity and nutritional intervention.

We proposed a model to develop a serious game, accessible to people between 21 and 45 years who have access to a computer and internet connection at their work place, and designed in a fun way. This game will help the users reducing their depression level, thus improving their subjective well-being and also acting as prophylaxis against other emotional effects. The game will focus on two out of the three key factors stated in the DELPLAN trial: lifestyle and physical activity. The nutritional intervention will be considered at an informative level. The game will also use a VR prototype to generate a report collecting the results of selected employees with T2DM. This report will provide organizations with meaningful information about the effectiveness of the intervention.

In this work on process, we propose to select adults with work and productive activity, with the purpose of benefiting employees staff of an academic institution. Therefore, they will develop a lifestyle that allows them not to decrease their productivity because of the effects of T2DM, especially as referred to the depression effect.

2   Method

The proposed game is based on a model that integrates psychological and physical therapies with computer science and video games. Hence, a virtual world is created that encourages the development of skills and strategies to deal with emotional effects such as depression. The model relies on five key elements that integrate the involved areas, and work together to produce the goal of the game (Fig. 1).

The main component of the game is the person, who selects a character that interacts in a virtual world with physical treatments in order to manage emotional techniques trough the gameplay.

The gameplay uses a simulated world to create a sense of immersion. The appearance and the elements included in this virtual world are based on psychological tests to avoid depression.

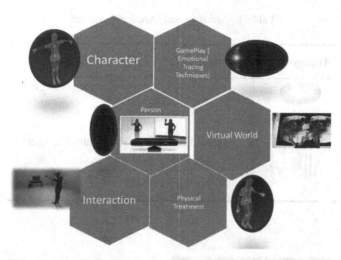

Fig. 1. Model based on interactions, to be used on a dodge mini game

We use a Cohen test to measure the stress level of the users [9]. The test is intended to be applied before and after the gameplay.

A usability test was applied to validate the user acceptance and visual immersion on the gameplay.

The results of these activities will be used to improve the following steps.

3 Virtual Tool Proposal

3.1 Equipment Requirements

Table 1 summarizes the equipment requirements. The gameplay area requires 2×2. The user must be provided with an Augmented reality glasses (oculus rift) or a Kinect 2.0 device. The software consists on a combined unreal engine and Unity 3D application.

The virtual reality project simulates a like-forest real space (Fig. 2). The interactions with the virtual world are based on a number of mini-game that were selected to challenge movement and distress.

Currently, two mini-games have been developed. The first mini-game poses the player a scenario where he/she is challenged to move sideways and backwards by dodging objects that appear from multiple directions. Figure 3 illustrates a typical screen of the game. The exercise can vary in difficulty, from very easy to heavier exercises.

The second mini-game puts the player to face several "enemies". The player's hands become weapons that can be used to fight the enemies. The main purpose of this mini-game is relax.

There is a third mini-game, currently under development, aimed to make movements in a certain way by coordinating body and vision. Figure 4 shows a typical

Table 1. Software and hardware required

Image HW	Software	Type
oculus	Unity3D	Videogames engine
KINECT	Unreal Engine	Videogames engine

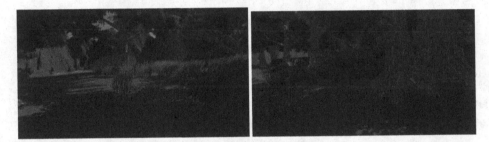

Fig. 2. Simulated forest

Fig. 3. Simulated forest space and dodge mini game.

scenario for this game. This mini-game is intended to promote, in the T2DM patient, specific movements that have shown effectiveness to prevent motor disability, such as having hands and knees up.

Fig. 4. Simulated forest space and draft mini game.

3.2 Prototype Simulation

After a process of integration of the required equipment, a simulation test was designed and tested with a volunteer employee. Figure 5 shows several scenes comparing the real player and his/her virtual representation.

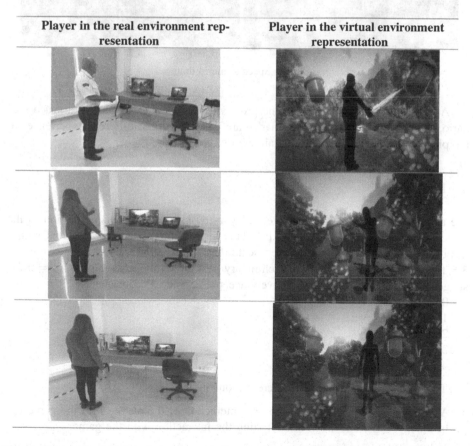

Fig. 5. Sequence of player movements on the virtual and real environment in virtual combat game.

Fig. 6. Space scenario draft.

Apart from the forest scenario, the prototypes also include a stars and space scenario, as shown in Fig. 6. These scenarios are planned to pose different experiences to the player, thus enhancing the entertainment options of the game.

4 Results

We assessed the stress of the volunteer players by using the Spanish adaption of the Cohen perceived stress scale (PSS) [9]. This instrument consists of 14 items with a response format of a five-point Likert scale (0 = never, 1 = rarely, 2 = occasionally, 3 = frequently, 4 = very often). Preliminary test of Cronbach's alphas ($\alpha = .877$) suggest that the elements have relatively acceptable internal consistency.

0 = Never
1 = Almost Never
2 = Occasionally
3 = Frequent
4 = Very Frequent

This test was applied in two different moments:

1. Approximately a week before the first interaction of the player with the game.
2. In a daily basis, one week after starting the interaction with the game.

The test was applied to 30 participants, during their normal work period.

Table 2. PSS descriptive measures of responses.

	Mode	Mean	Std. deviation	Variance
Pre test	2.57	2.63	0.457	0.209
Post test	1.54	1.00	0.502	0.252

Table 2 shows the differences between the responses of the participants before and after the video game sessions. A t-student test was performed to compare these two sets of quantitatively collected data independently to find statistical significance difference.

4.1 Usability Test

We identified and evaluated the usability problems of the virtual scenario by conducting an eye-tracking study. The study analyzed the player as he/she watches a mini-game consisting on a forest scenario which included several objects that

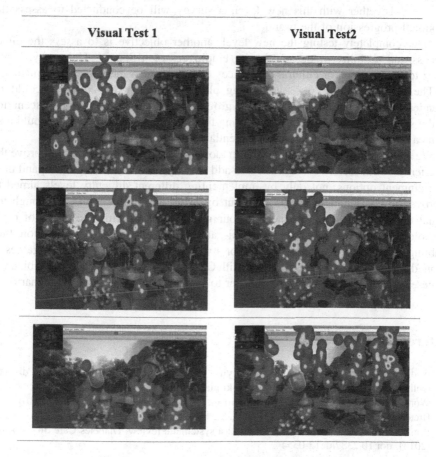

Fig. 7. Visual test 1 and 2 (Color figure online)

represented "enemies" willing to attack the player. The player was supposed to move side by side in a coordinated exercise to avoid the attacks.

Figure 7 shows two example visual tests. Visual Test 1 highlights the objects to dodge, whereas virtual test 2 highlights green areas.

Although the mini-games were originally designed by taking into account the key principles of usability, the results of the tests were not homogeneous among the players, probably due to their different conception of usability.

5 Conclusion and Future Work

This work is a one-year (two-semester) project intended to develop an interactive experience for university employees that helps them to prevent negative T2DM emotional effects. The main achievement of this research is a clearer assessment of the potential acceptability of the proposed game interactions.

Next steps include developing a second game level which will provide data on how to improve the immersion experience and the adherence to the prevention treatment of the users. Together with this new level, a survey will be conducted to assess the emotional progression of the user.

After completely testing the new level, another objective is to assess the effectiveness and usability of the game with employees of a Spanish University, hence trying to detect social or cultural differences that may affect the game performance.

The behavior results observed during play suggest that this research could be extended to share experiences in a remote group and to use a different kind of scenarios for the same group of exercises. Connecting the game with social networks could also act as a motivational impulse for the potential users of the game [10].

We are planning to design and develop more mini-games which should improve the experience of the users. The key idea is to add more types of exercises and expand their entertainment options, not only by implementing different difficulty levels aimed to improve the coordination and posture, but by using new technologies. Although the virtual environment allows immersion, our group is considering the usage of other technologies to implement these new mini-games, either alone or in combination, thus enabling a more optimal experience. For example, one of this new mini-games is planned to use a static bicycle combined with Oculus Rift and Arduino. The combination of these technologies would allow the user to lose stress in a relaxing VR scenario.

References

1. Andreoulakis, E., Hyphantis, T., Kandylis, D., Iacovides, A.: Depression in diabetes mellitus: a comprehensive review. Hippokratia **16**, 205–214 (2012)
2. World Health Organization, Global Report on Diabetes, Geneva, Switzerland (2016)
3. Breton, M.-C., Guenette, L., Amiche, M.A., Kayibanda, J.-F., Gregoire, J.-P., Moisan, J.: Burden of diabetes on the ability to work: a systematic review. Diabetes Care **36**, 740–749 (2013). doi:10.2337/dc12-0354

4. Gillies, C.L., Abrams, K.R., Lambert, P.C., Cooper, N.J., Sutton, A.J., Hsu, R.T., Khunti, K.: Pharmacological and lifestyle interventions to prevent or delay type 2 diabetes in people with impaired glucose tolerance: systematic review and meta-analysis. BMJ **334**, 299 (2007). doi:10.1136/bmj.39063.689375.55
5. Bouchard, S., Almé, A., Monthuy-Blanc, J.: Using virtual reality to study, assess and treat obesity: illustrations of the use of an emerging tool. Can. J. Diabetes **37**, S249 (2013). doi:10.1016/j.jcjd.2013.03.184
6. Skjæret, N., Nawaz, A., Morat, T., Schoene, D., Helbostad, J.L., Vereijken, B.: Exercise and rehabilitation delivered through exergames in older adults: an integrative review of technologies, safety and efficacy. Int. J. Med. Inform. **85**, 1–16 (2016). doi:10.1016/j.ijmedinf.2015.10.008
7. Finco, M., Maass, R.. The history of exergames: promotion of exercise and active living through body interaction. In: IEEE 3rd Serious Games and Applications for Health, pp. 1–6. IEEE (2014)
8. Sagarra, R., Costa, B., Cabré, J.J., Solà-Morales, O., Barrio, F.: Coste-efectividad de la intervención sobre el estilo de vida para prevenir la diabetes tipo 2. Rev. Clínica Española **214**, 59–68 (2014). doi:10.1016/j.rce.2013.10.005
9. Remor, E.: Psychometric properties of a European Spanish version of the perceived stress scale (PSS). Span. J. Psychol. **9**, 86–93 (2006). doi:10.5209/REV_SJOP.2006.V9.N1.30221
10. Hunt, D.: The many faces of diabetes: a critical multimodal analysis of diabetes pages on Facebook. Lang. Commun. **43**, 72–86 (2015). doi:10.1016/j.langcom.2015.05.003

Squad-Level Soldier-Robot Dynamics: Exploring Future Concepts Involving Intelligent Autonomous Robots

Rodger Pettitt[(⊠)], Linda R. Elliott, and Clifford C. Swiecicki

Army Research Laboratory, Fort Benning, GA, USA
{rodger.a.pettitt.civ, linda.r.elliott.civ,
clifford.c.swiecicki.civ}@mail.mil

Abstract. Future U.S. Army robots are developing capabilities to better "see" (e.g., scan and recognize objects), "think" (e.g., recognize implications and decide on a best course of action), and "act" (e.g., execute actions). This report describes systematic feedback gained from active duty Soldiers with dismounted squad level experience, to identify preferences and levels of trust with regard to squad level robotic capabilities, roles, and tactics. Soldier-based feedback will inform ongoing programs of research regarding U.S. Army Autonomous Squad Member (ASM) capabilities, through validation of mission scenarios, information requirements, and tactical maneuvers.

Keywords: Army robotic systems · Ground robots · Autonomous systems · Squad performance · Squad tactics

1 Introduction

Robotics in general enable U.S. Soldiers to see, hear, touch, and/or manipulate objects from a distance. Army robotic applications include many thousands of assets deployed for diverse combat missions such as reconnaissance, logistics (e.g., carrying materiel), and retrieving the combat wounded [1, 2]. Remotely controlled ground robots have saved the lives of numerous Soldiers in explosive ordnance disposal missions [3]. Robots will soon play key roles in Army dismounted squads, and they are the focus of several DoD programs of research with regard to enhanced human-robot communication and autonomous capabilities [4]. For example, DARPA's [5] Legged Squad Support System is a "pack animal" controlled by spoken commands, that can follow a Soldier through rough terrain, and the Marine's Ground Unmanned Support Surrogate can sense and avoid obstacles while navigating user-provided paths [6]. The Army's Safe Operations in Urban and Complex Environments [7]; their Robotic Collaborative Technology Alliance [8] and ONR's [9] Maneuver Thrust Programs have focused on perception and intelligence technologies to enable robots to work more closely with humans (e.g., "follow the human," "follow these waypoints") for a mission's duration.

The rights of this work are transferred to the extent transferable according to title 17 U.S.C. 105.

© Springer International Publishing AG 2017
S. Lackey and J. Chen (Eds.): VAMR 2017, LNCS 10280, pp. 426–436, 2017.
DOI: 10.1007/978-3-319-57987-0_35

The sheer number and diversity of U.S. Army robotic assets pose a challenge to human factors specialists to design systems that are simpler and easy to use [10, 11]. Ease of use is crucial to the warfighters who use these systems while maintaining awareness of their surroundings [12]. Designers must understand warfighter missions, task, and information requirements [13].

Robotic assets are evolving to become more autonomous and intelligent [14]. Future concepts include the transition from robots as tools to robots that can play a more intelligent and autonomous role within a squad [13]. This includes cognitive concepts such that the robot would, to some degree, be better able to "see" (e.g., scan and recognize objects), "think" (e.g., recognize implications and decide on a best course of action), and consequently, "act" [15]. As these more autonomous assets accompanies one of the teams, they need to perceive and label static elements of the environment (e.g., roads, trees or buildings), detect, and predict the activities of nearby humans. Ultimately, the goal is to develop robots that can be expected to interact with Soldiers, executing tactical actions as planned, yet able to act autonomously, or suggest changes in plans, when the situation requires it. Robots will be considered as partners to Soldiers, much as military working dogs are considered as a working unit with their handlers. Indeed, current and future scenarios include dyads and triads that integrate military working dogs, robotic assets, and human "handlers" [16]. For vehicle-based missions, autonomous assets include the concept of a vehicular armed robotic "wingman".

To further progress towards these goals, a research collaboration was initiated, drawing together researchers from the Naval Research Laboratory (NRL) and directorates of the Army Research Laboratory (ARL), within the Advanced Research Program Initiative (ARPI). ARL's Robotic Collaborative Technology Alliance (RCTA) supports this effort, and contributes by focusing on perception, detection and classification of objects [17, 18], and activities in the environment [19]. NRL provides advanced research on gesture and natural language interpretation. The overarching goal is a system that will use locally sensed and externally supplied information (e.g., maps, observations, and status reports) to populate its world model and to make inferences about its state and the state of its squad or team. The robot reasons about goals and appropriate actions which are then executed. An important action is to communicate relevant information to its squad mates.

2 Mission Scenario-Based Tactics and Requirements

As part of this research team, ARL Human Research and Engineering Directorate (HRED) outlined the means to validate a mission scenario to be used by ASM research teams, identify core tactics, and collect Soldier feedback pertaining to information requirements for each event that occurs within the scenario. During this effort, Soldiers were asked about robotic capabilities that would be most useful within the scenario, and within squad-level operations in general [20]. These interviews also served to explore issues of Soldier-robot dynamics within an operational context, in order to identify opportunities for robotic assistance. The interviews were based on specific mission scenario events, to elicit Soldier feedback on information requirements and robot/sensor capabilities.

24 Soldiers participated in these interviews and provided detailed feedback with regard to information and capability requirements, priorities of use, and recommendations for robot roles and responsibilities particularly with regard to how the Soldier would use an advanced robotic platform during each event. They were asked to consider in detail, mission events as they unfold, in order to capture experience based feedback with regard to questions such as "what information would you need now," "what is likely to go wrong," "what would you do next," etc. These interviews resulted in feedback that identified priorities in robot capabilities, operational issues in robot deployment, and suggestions to developers [20]. The investigation was conducted in 2 phases. In Phase I, 12 junior enlisted Soldiers were recruited for the experimentally based assessment. In Phase II, 6 senior noncommissioned officers (NCOs) were recruited for the assessment.

2.1 Interviews

A scenario-based cognitive task interview approach was applied [21, 22]. For each interview session, the interviewer began with an explanation of the research goals, then introduced a scenario-based questionnaire, where specific events were described. The investigator probed for feedback with regard to each event pertaining to realism and likelihood, the typical reaction of squad members if faced with the scenario event, the type of information they would likely need or seek out, and the possible contributions of an ASM to that event. The interviewer encouraged discussion and captured Soldier comments with regard to refining, informing, or augmenting scenario content; and ASM capabilities and design considerations.

The questionnaire items were structured to poll the Soldiers on their opinions on the concept of employment for the ASM to include the following: location during the mission; actions by the squad leader, squad members, and the ASM during each of the trigger events; the ASM's level of understanding of common military hand and arm signals and verbal commands; and the level of trust (from none to complete trust), that Soldiers had in the ASM to perform mission-related tasks. These questions also served as a precursor to the interview questions by establishing a foundation on which to base the ASM capabilities and employment considerations.

The interview questions were structured to poll the Soldiers on their opinions for key ASM capabilities and task performance to include the following:

- Top 3 capabilities for successful mission accomplishment
  - Top 3 capabilities or functions that would be nice to have
  - General concept of an ASM
  - Command and control of an ASM
  - Mission status, and general and specific capabilities, sensors, and mission tasks that should be considered for future ASM design and employment.

2.2 Junior Enlisted Responses

Trigger Events
Soldiers were asked a series of questions pertaining to what actions the squad leader (SL), the squad, and the ASM would take when a specific event occurred during the

Table 1. Trigger event 1: react to mortar attack, junior enlisted

Position	Summary of tasks or actions to be taken (Consensus of participants/General conclusions)
Squad leader	Yell incoming. Move self and squad out of impact area as quickly and safely as possible
Squad	React to SL commands and move out of impact area in direction given by SL
ASM	Follow squad. Try to identify direction of mortars. Scan area for safe route and alert squad
SL actions to reorient squad	Regroup in covered position. Check or verify status of personnel and equipment
Reorient ASM	Scan area for enemy. Determine alternate route to continue with the mission
ASM relocation choice	Equally split between not moving it to another position in the squad to moving it based on the situation and what task it is to perform

Table 2. Trigger event 2: react to sniper fire, junior enlisted

Position	Summary of tasks or actions to be taken (Consensus of participants/General conclusions)
Squad leader	Give order to take cover (move out of kill zone if necessary). Try to determine where sniper fire originated from
Squad	Take cover. Determine where sniper fire is coming from. Provide suppressive fire on sniper's location
ASM	Scan area and detect sniper's location
SL actions to reorient squad	Eliminate sniper if tactically feasible. Continue mission on planned or alternate route as necessary
Reorient ASM	Determine route to engage sniper or to continue mission. Notify higher echelon of situation. Continue to scan for enemy threats
ASM relocation choice	ASM should move out of danger area to protect itself. Could be used as cover for squad if necessary

conduct of the mission. Follow-up questions were then asked on what actions were necessary to reorient the squad and the ASM to continue the mission. Tables 1 and 2 provide a summary of their responses to 2 events: Mortar attack and Sniper fire.

Trust in ASM to Conduct Tasks

Soldiers were asked to identify what tasks they had complete trust, some trust, and no trust in for the ASM to conduct. Soldiers had complete trust in the ASM to scout or check routes, check for IEDs, and know its location via GPS. Soldiers had some trust in the ASM to evacuate casualties. Soldiers had no trust in the ASM to engage the enemy if the ASM had a weapon system, without human intervention. The complete lists of responses to the areas of trust are tabulated in Appendix C with many single responses for most tasks identified without a general consensus among Soldier.

ASM Capabilities: Priorities

The following table provides the top three capabilities listed by junior enlisted for ASM squad level robotics (Table 3).

Table 3. Necessary and nice-to-have priorities, junior enlisted

Priority	Necessary	Nice to have
1	Navigation of terrain	1. Capability to transport supplies and equipment 2. Weapon system
2	1. Identification of targets and scanning for enemy 2. Night vision/thermal instrumentation	Carry first aid supplies and evacuate casualties
3	Load carrying ability	1. Transport litters and casualty evacuation aid 2. External power source for recharging batteries

ASM Concept

Eleven of the 12 Soldiers felt that the ASM was a good idea. The dissenting Soldier based his response on the lack of trust he had in it to complete tasks and stated he was not a fan on technology. Soldiers liked the idea of reducing their load by offloading it to the ASM. Providing additional security was also indicated as an asset. Seven of the 12 Soldiers indicated that the ASM should understand verbal commands as the primary means of maintaining command and control of it. Soldiers were nearly unanimous (11 of 12) that the ASM should provide a reminder of the mission objective after an interruption of the mission occurred, feeling that this could be helpful to a task saturated squad leader. 11 Soldiers agreed that the ASM would be an aid if it informed the squad of reaching phase lines, lines of departure, etc. on time. This would confirm that the mission was proceeding on schedule and the squad was in the right location. Nine Soldiers indicated that they would like the ASM to have a weapons platform mounted on it. Seven of those nine Soldiers indicated they preferred another Soldier to be "in the loop" for conducting the actual engagements with the weapon system. Eight of the Soldiers preferred a remote device for weapon system control, primarily to prevent a Soldier from being exposed to friendly fire. Soldiers did not trust the decision making capability of the ASM to provide autonomous engagements for fear of fratricide, out-of-range engagements, and safety. Soldiers were nearly unanimous (11 of 12) that the ASM should be configured for casualty evacuation. Eight of those 11 Soldiers indicated that the ASM should not evacuate the casualties alone to the casualty collection point because a human would be necessary to accompany the ASM to return fire and protect the casualty. Eight of the 12 Soldiers felt that the ASM should have a smoke-producing capability with seven of those preferring a dispenser to a generator-based capability. Soldiers were unanimous that the ASM should have a chemical detection or alarm system. They saw it as being able to provide real-time warnings and reporting since Soldiers do not continuously monitor for chemical threats. Soldiers were unanimous that the ASM should have a shot detection capability that provides the location, distance, and azimuth to the shooter and caliber of the weapon fired.

2.3   Noncommissioned Officer (NCO) Responses

Six senior enlisted Soldiers were recruited for this phase of the experimentally based assessment. The Soldiers completed a demographics questionnaire initially to determine their military background and experience. They had an average age of 29 years with an average time in service of 9.5 years. There was 1 E-5 promotable and 5 E-6 s and all were MOS 11B. All of the senior enlisted Soldiers had at least 1 deployment (3 to Afghanistan, 4 to Iraq, and 4 to Kuwait). Four of the 6 deployed Soldiers had experience with robots during their deployments (3 in Afghanistan and 1 in Iraq) in an Infantry unit.

Trigger Events

Soldiers were asked a series of questions pertaining to what actions the Squad Leader the squad, and the ASM would take when a specific event occurred during the conduct of the mission. Follow-up questions were then asked on what actions were necessary to reorient the squad and the ASM to continue the mission. The following tables provide summary responses for two events: Mortar attack and Sniper fire (Tables 4 and 5).

Table 4. Trigger event 1: react to mortar attack.

Position	Summary of tasks or actions to be taken (Consensus of participants/General conclusions)
Squad leader	Determine new course. Provide squad with a distance and direction to move. Continually assess the situation
Squad	Move to rally point given by the squad leader (distance and direction of movement). Maintain security during movement
ASM	Try to identify direction of mortars. Scan area for safe route and move with the squad
SL actions to reorient squad	Regroup in covered position. Check with team leaders. Reorganize and consolidate as required
Reorient ASM	Follow directions of squad leader and continue movement with the squad
ASM relocation choice	Four of the 6 favored moving it to another position based on the situation and what just happened on the mission

Trust in ASM to Conduct Tasks

Soldiers were asked to identify what tasks they had complete trust, some trust, and no trust in for the ASM to conduct. There was no consensus in any of these areas and the most common responses are cited as follows. Soldiers had complete trust in the ASM to carry the gear and evacuate casualties. Soldiers had some trust in the ASM to conduct reconnaissance and send some reports. Soldiers had no trust in the ASM to engage the enemy if the ASM had a weapon system, without human interface and to completely move and think on its own.

Unlike the junior enlisted Soldiers, the senior Soldiers were less positive in their support for an ASM to augment the squad and did not see the potential to reduce the Soldier load, increase lethality, and provide location and route information without

Table 5. Trigger event 2: react to sniper fire

Position	Summary of tasks or actions to be taken (Consensus of participants/General conclusions)
Squad leader	Take cover. Try to determine where sniper fire originated from. Report situation to higher
Squad	Take cover. Determine where sniper fire is coming from. Maintain security
ASM	Determine sniper's location
SL actions to reorient squad	Eliminate sniper if tactically feasible via fire and maneuver. Continue mission on planned or alternate route as necessary
Reorient ASM	Continue to scan for enemy threats. Move to appropriate position
ASM relocation choice	Four of the 6 felt that the ASM should move out of danger area to protect itself and then scan for potential targets

committing a dedicated operator for command and control of the ASM. The senior enlisted Soldiers shared similar opinions with the junior enlisted Soldiers that for the ASM to be considered helpful and not a burden to the squad, it must demonstrate reliability, navigational capability, and be available at all times to conduct a mission from start to finish. Similarly, the two groups of Soldiers agreed that the ASM operation and sensor packages must conform to noise and light disciplines encountered by forces operating in all geographic terrain and mission contingencies.

3   Soldier Analyses of Map-Based Information

Additional questions were developed to gain detailed feedback from Soldiers with regard to operational relevance, information requirements, tactical options, and decision processes that can be inferred through map-based information, to enable programmers to strive towards robot-based inferences of the same information. Given the background and map-based information, Soldiers were asked to identify information contained in the map that would guide tactical decision making. This information will drive more autonomous robot-based decision-making and response.

3.1   Participants

A total of 12 Soldiers were recruited for this experiment. The Soldiers completed a demographics questionnaire to determine their military background and experience. They had an average age of 37 years with an average time in service of 15 years. They ranged in rank from E-5 through O-3 and had one of the following military occupational specialties (MOS): 11A, 11B, 11C, 19D, or 19K. These MOS reflected an Infantry officer (1), Infantryman (7), Mortar man (1), Cavalry Scout (2), and an M1 armor crewman (1). All of the 12 Soldiers had been deployed. They collectively had 14 deployments to Afghanistan, 21 deployments to Iraq, and 6 deployments to Kuwait. Five of the Soldiers had experience with robots during their deployments, with three associated with an Infantry unit, and two in reconnaissance units. These robots were used to scan for possible improvised explosive devices (IEDs), detonate IEDs, Raven recovery, and for overhead surveillance. Additionally, one Soldier was involved with the testing of a squad ground robot while at Ft. Bliss.

3.2   Interviews

After each Soldier completed the informed consent and demographics forms, they were given a detailed description of a route reconnaissance scenario, a map depicting the route (Fig. 1), a written specification of key events, and completed a detailed questionnaire without relating it to an autonomous squad member (ASM). After each Soldier completed the questionnaire, they were given a detailed description of selected contingency missions (Fig. 2) to determine key capabilities and tasks without and with an ASM in order to support a successful mission.

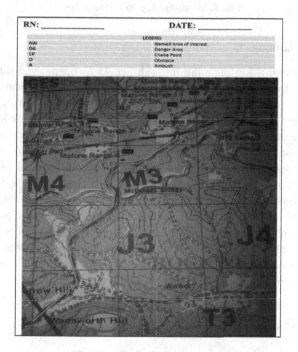

Fig. 1. Mission planning map

Soldiers provided specific feedback regarding map-based information, and identified information that should also be provided, along with implications of information. Given information provided, they specified implications and conclusions with regard to route selection, danger areas, choke points, obstacles, ambush areas, and squad formations. The following section summarizes the results.

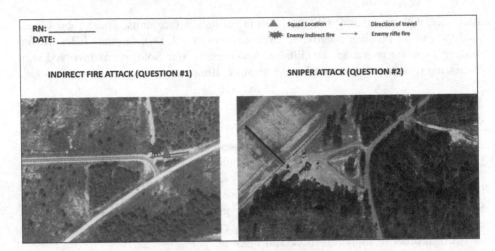

Fig. 2. Contingency missions maps

3.3   Mission Planning

ASMs can support mission planning through access to operational information. Soldiers emphasized the need for current information on IED attacks, locations, detonation techniques used, and the types of IEDs used. This information would be useful to identify the current threat in the area and also identify previous attack locations so that security could be more effective in those areas. Additional support such as air support, medical evacuation (MEDEVAC), and fire support available was also of major interest. MEDEVAC support available was identified as needed in order to plan for casualty evacuation and casualty collection points. Similar to IED intelligence, Soldiers wanted recent information about enemy activities in the area, past ambush sites, and rules of engagement. This information was important for planning the route and what type of formation to use in danger areas. Soldiers would ask the platoon leader for information pertaining to: aerial reconnaissance assets available and past reconnaissance information, rally point locations, target reference points (TRPs), and other items pertaining to the commander's intent.

4   Conclusions

A key difference between junior and senior enlisted Soldiers is the degree of trust in more autonomous robotic systems. Based on the lack of trust, especially with the senior enlisted Soldiers who will be the decision makers within the squad, new equipment training could be used to increase the trust in the ASM. The training will have to be thorough, put the ASM through its paces, and demonstrate the ASM's full range of capabilities for the Soldiers to accept it as "an additional squad member" and use it in an autonomous role or mode to its full capacity.

- The ASM must be dependable and reliable to accompany the squad on any mission for it to be totally accepted as a squad asset by all squad members. Otherwise, there will be a tendency to leave it in the rear.
- The ASM should be modular in design and capabilities with the ability to quickly mount and remove sensor packages and accessories without special tools to make it adaptable and efficient for any mission.
- Actions of the leaders, squad members, and ASM for each of the trigger events and interview results identified in the body of the report should be useful as insights for the computer programmers to define squad actions for those and similar trigger events.

Soldier feedback converged on the following primary capabilities or characteristics of the robots as contributing factors to the robot's successful mission accomplishment:

- Maneuverability
- Speed of traversing the route
- Sensor packages
- Capability to negotiate any type of terrain

Other characteristics identified of lesser importance included: ability to lift or carry objects, weight/transportability, size, and load carrying capability.

The nearly unanimous choice of the Soldiers for a combination of tele-operated and autonomous operation indicates a definite concern about allowing the intelligent robot always to take actions on its own. As autonomy increases there is an increase in the necessity that their operator, supervisor, or teammate have an accurate understanding of autonomous agent's actions, environment, reasoning, projections, and uncertainty calculations [23]. Soldier insights and recommendations in general are consistent with sound military judgment, and it should be noted that the Soldiers of this rank and experience will be the leaders and unit trainers of the end users once an ASM is fielded. They will directly influence their subordinates about the capabilities and limitations of any system that is a squad asset. Issues identified in this report directly relate to issues currently being investigated regarding the development and distribution of more autonomous robotic systems for Army operations [24].

References

1. Axe, D.: War Bots: How U.S. Military Robots are Transforming War in Iraq, Afghanistan, and the Future. Nimble Books LLC, Ann Arbor (2008)
2. Doare, R., Danet, D., Hanon, J., Boisboissel, G.: Robots on the Battlefield: Contemporary Issues and Implications for the Future. Combat Studies Institute Press, Fort Leavenworth (2014)
3. Singer, P.W.: Wired for War: the Robotics Revolution and Conflict in the Twenty-First Century. Penguin Press, New York (2009)
4. Humans and autonomy: Implications of shared decision-making for military operations. ARL-TR-7919 (2017)
5. Murphy, M., Saunders, A., Moreira, A., Rizzi, M.: The littledog robot. Int. J. Robot. Res. **30** (2), 145–149 (2011)

6. Joyce, J.J.: Marines conclude testing of Navy-developed unmanned ground systems at mobility and distribution experiment (2012). Story Number NNS120808-16 http://www.navy.mil/submit/display.asp?story_id=68896
7. Kott, N.J., Wellfare, M., van Lierop, T.K., Mottern, E.: Safe operations of unmanned systems for reconnaissance in complex environments. Army Technology Objective (SOURCE ATO). DTIC Report No. ADA452253. US Army RDECOM-TARDEC 6501 E 11 Mile Rd Warren, MI (2011)
8. Robotics, U.S. Army Research Laboratory. https://www.arl.army.mil/www/default.cfm?page=392. Accessed 9 Feb 2017
9. ONR, Office of Naval Research, ONR's Maneuver Thrust Program (2013). https://www.onr.navy.mil/en/Media-Center/Fact-Sheets/Maneuver.aspx
10. Barnes, M., Jentsch, F.: Human-Robot Interactions in Future Military Operations. Ashgate Publishing Limited, Farnham (2010)
11. National Research Council: Interfaces for Ground and Air Military Robots: Workshop Summary. National Academies Press, Washington (DC) (2005)
12. Barnes, M., Evans, A.: Soldier-robot teams in future battlefields: an overview. In: Barnes, M., Jentsch, F. (eds.) Human-Robot Interactions in Future Military Operations. Ashgate Publishing Limited, Farnham, Surrey (UK) (2010)
13. Redden E., Elliott, L., Barnes, M.: Robots: the new teammates. In: Coovert, M., Thompson, L. (eds.) The Psychology of Workplace Technology. Society of Industrial Organizational Psychology Frontiers Series. Routledge Press, New York (2013)
14. Barnes, M., Chen, J., Hill, S.: Humans and autonomy: implications of shared decision making for military operations. Aberdeen Proving Ground (MD): Army Research Laboratory (US), Report No. ARL-TR-7919 (2014)
15. Barnes, M., Chen, J., Jentsch, F., Oron-Gilad, T., Redden, E., Elliott, L., Evans, A.: Designing for humans in autonomous systems: military applications. Aberdeen Proving Ground (MD): Army Research Laboratory (US); Report No.: ARL-TR-6782 (2014)
16. Ackerman, E.: Emergency Response Teams Combine Mobile Robots, Drones, and Dogs. IEEE Spectrum, New York (2014)
17. Miksik, O., Munoz, D., Bagnell, J.A., Hebert, M.: Efficient temporal consistency for streaming video scene analysis, CMU-RI-TR-12-30, Robotics Institute, Carnegie Mellon University, September 2012
18. Xiong, X., Munoz, D., Bagnell, J.A., Hebert, M.: 3-D scene analysis via sequenced predictions over points and regions, Robotics Institute (2011). Paper 732
19. Kurup, U.C., Stentz, A., Hebert, M.: Predicting and classifying pedestrian behavior using an integrated cognitive architecture. In: Proceedings of the 21st Annual Conference on Behavior Representation in Modeling Simulation (BRIMS) (2012)
20. Swiecicki, C.C., Elliott, L., Wooldridge, R.: Squad-level soldier-robot dynamics: exploring future concepts involving intelligent autonomous robots: ARL-TR-7215 (2015)
21. Hoffman, R., Elliott, L.: Wearable flexible displays: a scenario-based usability evaluation suggests army applications for an emerging technology. Ergonomics in design (2010)
22. Hoffman, R.: Human factors contributions to knowledge elicitation: human factors, pp. 481–488 (2008)
23. Selkowitz, A., Larios, C., Lakhamani, S., Chen, J.: Displaying information to support transparency for autonomous platforms. In: 2016 Proceedings of the 7th International Conference on Applied Human Factors and Ergonomics, Orlando, FL, July 2016
24. Matsumara, J., et al.: Assessing the impact of autonomous robotic systems on the Army's force structure. Rand Corporation. Request from Deputy Commanding General, Futures/Director, ARCIC. USATRACOC, 950 Jefferson Avenue, Fort Eustis, VA

Decoding the User Experience in Mobile Virtual Reality Narratives

Biswajit Sarker[(✉)]

Uppsala University, Uppsala, Sweden
thisisbish@gmail.com

Abstract. Virtual reality narratives are slowly gaining popularity due to the rise of consumer oriented mobile VR headsets. Based on its potential, movie studios and other entertainment companies are investing heavily in this sector. However there is a gap in research that focuses on the user experience in these mobile VR narratives. This paper aims to fill this gap by presenting the findings of a study that investigated user experience in virtual reality narratives. Using qualitative research methods, this study analyzed users' experiences and explored what design factors contribute to their positive or negative experiences. Based on a thematic analysis of collected data, this study argues that audio-visual cues play an important role on how users perceive a VR narrative. Findings also suggest that the sweet spot of user experience lies between boredom and frustration. If the virtual world provides well-designed audio-visual cues to guide users' attention throughout the narrative then users experience immersion and spatial presence. On the contrary, lack of cues in a virtual environment fails to utilize the space available around the users resulting in their boredom. Moreover, excessive use of audio-visual cues makes users to keep switching their attention from one element to the next in fear of missing out something important, eventually resulting in their frustration and stress. Based on these findings, this paper suggests some guidelines to improve user experience in mobile VR narratives.

Keywords: Mobile VR · User experience · Qualitative methods

1 Introduction

To explore the space around us in real life, we use sensory cues in the environment that indicate the state of some property of the world that might be important to us. By following different sensory cues such as visual, auditory, haptic, olfactory and environmental cues; we perceive the world around us through active exploration [1]. But mobile virtual reality Head Mounted Devices (HMD) such as Google Cardboard and Samsung Gear VR do not offer positional tracking capabilities to track user's movement in a virtual environment [2]. As a result users cannot walk around to explore any virtual space with mobile HMDs. Furthermore, these devices do not have the capabilities to provide feedback through touch, smell or taste either. This means, all the interactions possibilities need to be conveyed through visual and audio cues in a mobile virtual reality narrative. This makes it a necessity for the designers to understand how these audio-visual cues affect user experiences in mobile VR narratives.

© Springer International Publishing AG 2017
S. Lackey and J. Chen (Eds.): VAMR 2017, LNCS 10280, pp. 437–452, 2017.
DOI: 10.1007/978-3-319-57987-0_36

Currently virtual reality is seeing a breakthrough at the consumer market due to the release of HMDs such as Google Daydream View, Samsung Gear VR, Oculus Rift and HTC Vive to name a few [2]. These devices are expected to remove the barriers of screen-based narratives and put the users in the middle of the content. Usually these VR narratives include a storyline that has a specific beginning and ending. When the audience put on their VR headsets, they are transported into an immersive virtual environment and even though they can look around in any direction at any time, the designers of these narratives want them to pay attention to specific elements in that virtual world that are important to stich the story together. These narratives are designed to give the audience the feeling of being a part of the story. But being inside an immersive world invites the audience to look around and since they are in an unknown environment, they are immediately filled with questions such as, where am I? What's going on around me? What should I do next? Then it becomes the responsibility of the designers to answer these questions quickly so that the audience can focus on the major elements of those narratives. This is where it becomes important [3] to find out, what drives the audience to pay attention to the right elements in virtual reality narratives.

This explorative study investigates, given a 360° virtual space that allows looking at in any direction while users can only focus on 90° to 110° at any given time [4]:

- How do people know where to look and how to proceed when presented with an immersive virtual narrative?
- How the audio-visual cues contribute to their experience?
- What design factors contribute to a positive experience and what design factors contribute to a negative experience for the user?

By building on existing theoretical accounts related to user experience in virtual reality and through a field based study using a popular consumer oriented device used by general consumers, this study analyzes users' experiences from their point of view. Based on a thematic analysis of collected data through observations, think aloud and semi-structured interviews from 10 participants between the ages of 22 to 29, this study argues that when users are experiencing an immersive virtual reality narrative their curiosity drive them to look for clues to follow in that virtual environment. If the virtual world provides well-designed audio-visual cues to guide their attention throughout the narrative then users feel immersion and spatial presence. On the contrary, lack of cues in a virtual environment keeps users looking straight ahead throughout the narrative, which results in their boredom. When it comes to lack of positional tracking in mobile VR, it can be asserted from the findings that users get confused and frustrated when their movements in the physical environment result in the whole virtual environment moving with them. This clash between real world perception and virtual world realization breaks their feeling of spatial presence in that VR environment. Finally, findings suggest excessive use of audio-visual cues forces users to keep switching their attention in multiple directions in fear of missing out something important, eventually resulting in their frustration and stress.

This paper follows the subsequent structure. The background section examines relevant literature and establishes a gap in research. Section three discusses the methodology used in this study. Section four presents the findings. Section five discusses the findings in detail. And the final section includes conclusion, limitations and suggestions for future research.

2 Background

2.1 Immersion in VR Narratives

When it comes to analysis of experiences, one of the terms quite frequent in literature is flow [5], which describes the mental state in which a person is fully engaged in an activity by a feeling of intense involvement and energized focus. During a flow experience a person feels in control, loses sense of surroundings and his or her awareness is narrowed down to the activity itself. Sutcliffe [6] argues that experience in a virtual world can be explained in terms of flow. He asserts that when the virtual world is well designed, a person in that virtual world feels immersed in a strong sense of presence and the mediating virtual reality device and computer essentially disappears. Compared to screen based media like cinema or television, virtual reality as a media is much more flexible where audience can change their vantage point at any given moment. While more control in a virtual narrative experience provides greater feeling of involvement for the participants [7], this also takes the control away from the designers, who want the audience to follow a specific storyline. This presents a big challenge for the designers of virtual reality narratives.

2.2 Role of Audio-Visual Cues in Perception

Since virtual environments are usually representations of real world environments, it is reasonable to follow the ecological psychology approach proposed by Gibson [1], which describes how different structures in the external world guide people's everyday actions. According to Gibson's theory, we perceive the world around us through our actions. We turn our heads to direct our attention to different visual stimuli and we focus our attention to hear better and gather information about action possibilities available around us [1]. Many researchers consider this to be more relevant to HCI than classical cognitive theories [8–10]. When it comes to spatial cues available in the environment for perceiving the world around us, previous studies indicate most cues are linked to the visual modality; for example aerial perspective and relative brightness [1]. Along the same line spatial audio plays a big role in directing users' involuntary attention towards possibilities of action within the virtual environment [11].

2.3 Role of Audio-Visual Cues in Spatial Presence

Wirth et al. [12] describes spatial presence as a two-step process. On the first step the user draws upon available spatial cues to perceive the virtual environment as a plausible space. The virtual environment will more likely be perceived as a plausible space if these audio-visual cues are both rich in quality and have a logical consistency. On the second step, the user experiences herself as being located within that perceived space by discovering possibilities of action within the virtual environment. Existing literature suggest [13, 14] a steady stream of highly detailed information flow supported by appropriate audio-visual spatial cues effectively builds the virtual environment as a plausible place and increases the experience of spatial presence for the users. However, an excessive use of spatial cues can cause sensory overload and produce fatigue for the users [15].

2.4 A Gap in Research

Even though research in virtual reality has been conducted on perception, immersion and spatial presence, little is known about how users decide where to look and how to proceed in an immersive VR narrative and what design factors contribute to that decision. There is also a gap in research that focuses on users' experience with a consumer oriented mobile virtual reality HMD which only offers applications that are purely narrative or have severely restricted interaction possibilities. Hence research is needed to explore how general consumers who have no experience or very little experience with mobile virtual reality applications perceive this new media. This study aimed to fill this gap in research.

3   Methodology

To follow a well-defined scientific research methodology for analyzing users' experience with virtual reality narratives and to theorize a set of propositions about those experiences, this study followed a theory informed inductive approach. Since qualitative studies help to uncover and interpret participants' understanding of the phenomenon that they are involved in [16], it was a good fit for an explorative study like this one where participants' behavior in a virtual reality narrative was being investigated.

3.1   Data Collection

Csikszentmihalyi and Robinson [17] argue that since experiences are subjective phenomenon that cannot be externally verified, a researcher has to rely on the testimonies given by the participants. They also downplay the validity of relying on physiological measures alone to collect data to explain users' experience [17]. Since most of the challenges and opportunities associated with users' experience in virtual reality were not directly observable, in depth semi-structured interviews were chosen as the main source of data collection for this study. Unlike surveys or questionnaires, in depth interviews are flexible, dynamic and those provide a more valid insight into the user's perception of reality [18]. In qualitative studies that use semi-structured interviews, the primary instrument of data collection is the researcher [19]. This is important in capturing the subject's point of view as argued by some researchers [20] who assert that due to the use of remote, inferential empirical materials; quantitative researchers seldom capture the users' point of view of an experience.

3.2   VR Applications Used in This Study

The following virtual realty applications were used during the study. "Oculus home" is the central interface through which other applications can be found and downloaded. The reason behind using existing VR applications was to collect data from professionally designed immersive narratives. Since the focus of the study was to investigate how users experience a virtual reality narrative and what role audio-visual cues play in those experiences; it was important that they were not using low quality prototypes that might not provide accurate data for analysis (Table 1).

Table 1. Summary of virtual reality applications used in this study.

App	Type	360° view	Spatial audio	Supported interaction
Oculus home	Interface	Yes	No	Head tracking in all directions Touchpad for selection
Muse Revolt	Music video	Yes	No	Head tracking in all directions
Song for someone	Music video	Yes	Yes	Head tracking in all directions
Invasion	Animated short	Yes	Yes	Head tracking in all directions
Rosebud	Animated short	Yes	No	Head tracking in all directions Scroll touchpad to zoom Tap touchpad to control camera angle

3.3   Equipment and Setup

This study was conducted in a living room set up to ensure privacy of the participants and also to provide them with an environment where a mobile VR headset was most likely to be used. Participants were invited one person at a time to ensure they can act and talk freely. The HMD used in the research was a Samsung Gear VR coupled with a Samsung Galaxy S6 edge mobile phone. This HMD supports 3 degrees of Freedom (DOF) with a Field of view (FOV) of 96°. To avoid ambient noise an in-ear headphone was used during the experiments. To ensure anonymity, a list of randomized participant IDs were prepared and assigned to each participant. Participants were given a consent form that described the research study in a nutshell. It was made sure participants could exit the experiment at any time. They were informed that the follow up interviews would be audio recorded. Each participant had to read and sign the consent form before participating in the study.

3.4   Semi Structured Interviews

In total, 10 participants between the ages of 22 to 29 participated in the study. Five of the participants were male and five were female. All trials followed the same structure. First, the researcher introduced the HMD to the participants with a quick demonstration of how it works. The participant then put on the headset, potentially aided by the researcher. Each of the participants was then instructed to explore the Oculus Home interface for a few minutes and then try out two of the applications selected randomly from the list above. All the participants were interviewed right after they had completed each of the applications. After the experiment, the participant was thanked for his or her time and was debriefed about the purpose of the study.

3.5   Data Analysis

All the recorded interviews were transcribed in details and coded using qualitative analysis software "NVivo". After coding, the relevant data extracts were collated for analysis to find recurring themes from the dataset. Thematic analysis method was used to analyze the recorded data following the guidelines suggested by Braun and Clarke [21]. For each code, relevant data extracts were reviewed and compared against the whole data set to make sure the emerging themes make sense and no data extracts were being taken out of context from the interview transcript.

4   Results and Analysis

4.1   Specific Observations

After coding the interviews, think aloud data and observation notes; the entire data set was reviewed to identify themes relevant to positive or negative experiences of the users. During this phase of analysis, the use of audio-visual cues to attract and direct user's attention stood out to be one of the most important design factors affecting the user's experience during the narrative. The following table provides a short summary of the initial themes along with examples of their relevant data extracts. A detailed thematic analysis can be found here [22] (Table 2).

Table 2. Initial themes from the dataset with salient data extracts from the interviews.

Data extract	Themes	Relevant application
I knew where to look by the sound. And then I see something moving and looked that way *I didn't see the rabbit coming out of it's cave but then I heard the sound to the left and I looked in the scenery .... and then I saw the rabbit*	Users' attention is directed by the audio-visual cues available in the virtual environment while they try to follow the VR narrative	Invasion, Song for Someone
I thought (curse word) if I am here in virtual reality I am supposed to be able to turn around and see new things! *You sort of want to look everywhere. It's like I am looking here and then .. Oh...It's over there!*	Users expect to see events all around them in a virtual environment since the application puts them in a 360-degree immersive world	All applications

(continued)

Table 2. (*continued*)

Data extract	Themes	Relevant application
I looked around just because I wanted to see what's around me and I kept going *I really did not feel the need to turn around I did that because I was just curious*	Out of curiosity users explore the VR environment in different directions	All applications
Like if you start in the middle of the room may be you can back off and you have space to move ... I think that's the thing ....you are just stuck in the middle and it's kinda creepy *I don't know, I was trying to walk in the world just to see if something happens. But nothing happened and it felt weird!*	Due to the lack of positional tracking in mobile VR, user's movement is not tracked which breaks user's expectation resulting in a negative experience	All applications
.... if you try to..ummm...just look around and forget about the reality, I think you are able to have this nice feeling *It's cool that you can look everywhere. (laughter) Oh, This is really cool*	User has a positive experience if she feels immersed in the VR environment where things are happening all around	Invasion, Song for Someone
No there wasn't any clue (to look around) *Everything was happening in front of me more or less* *.... there was a clear menu just in front of you so there's no reason to look around*	If there's no possibilities of action in the environment or enough cues to attract user's attention in different directions, then user ends up looking straight ahead throughout the narrative	Rosebud, Oculus Home
.... why not use the whole space ... I mean there's so much space around you for options and buttons and so on *Well you see part of the room behind the menu, so I looked around a little bit. But nothing new was moving around*	User doesn't tend to look around when there are no clues available for the user to perceive the affordances offered by the environment	Oculus Home
For this one it felt like... hmmm... how to say... ummm... more like a 3D video than virtual reality *That was more like a TV screen I guess*	Without any audio or visual cues to state otherwise, users just focus on the field of view looking at an conceptual screen ignoring the rest of the space that is hidden from the view	Oculus Home, Rosebud

(*continued*)

Table 2. (*continued*)

Data extract	Themes	Relevant application
Everything was happening in front of me and it was very boring I have to say *Well, I am looking at a child watering a flower.... It's a bit dull!*	Due to the lack of use of the space surrounding the user, immersion is minimal and users end up having a boring experience in the VR environment	Rosebud
I missed that the video was interacting with you... ummm... more like a 3D video than virtual reality where you are inside *I felt like I was more watching from outside*	Spatial presence is minimal; user feels like looking at a giant screen from outside	Oculus Home, Rosebud
There's a lot of stuff going on! It's hard to focus on one thing. There's a ... a lot of.... a lot of, OK I want to follow the flow of people but it's hard *It's a bit difficult to know where to focus cause you can't see everything at once. You sort of want to look everywhere. It's like I am looking here and then ..Oh...It's over there!*	User has trouble keeping up with the narrative in Fear of Missing Out something important when there are too many audio-visual cues around	Muse Revolt
I would say this video has the worst quality and the video where more things happening (laughter) may be too many things happening. *I think you want to check everything and its overloaded and may be a little stressful*	User feels frustrated and stressed due to lack of control when audio-visual cues do not provide enough guidance	Muse Revolt
Its good that I am in control and don't miss out or feel like missing out *I kinda felt like I was in the same room with them. That was really nice* *It felt like I had a presence in the story cause the rabbit was kinda hiding behind me*	When user's attention is properly guided through well-designed audio-visual cues, user feels immersed in the environment, which results in spatial presence and enjoyment	Invasion, Song for Someone

These initial themes were then reviewed to generate refined themes for further analysis. After naming, collating, defining and refining the specifics of each theme [22], the final thematic table was constructed to find patterns of answers for the research questions (Table 3).

Table 3. Refined themes from dataset with coded modes of user engagement.

Initial themes	Refined themes	Final theme
Users expect to see events all around them in a virtual environment since the application puts them in a 360-degree immersive world	Out of curiosity and due to familiarity with a 360-degree real life environment, users expect to see events happening all around them	Users look for clues to follow and they experience immersion when their attention is directed to different elements of the VR narrative all around them through audio-visual cues
Out of curiosity users explore the VR environment in different directions		
Users' attention is directed by the audio-visual cues available in the virtual environment while they try to follow the VR narrative	Users feel immersion if their attention is directed through audio-visual cues available around them in the virtual environment	
User has a positive experience if she feels immersed in the VR environment where things are happening all around		
If there's no possibilities of action in the environment or enough cues to attract user's attention in different directions, then user ends up looking straight ahead throughout the narrative	Users keep looking straight ahead at a conceptual screen when there are no audio-visual cues available around them to attract their attention	When there are no audio-visual cues available to attract and direct their attention, users get into a "**Screen**" mode of experience where they keep looking straight ahead at a conceptual screen resulting in minimum immersion, boredom and lack of spatial presence
User doesn't tend to look around when there are no clues available for the user to perceive the affordances offered by the environment		
Without any audio or visual cues to indicate otherwise, users just focus on their field of view looking at an conceptual screen ignoring the rest of the space that is hidden from the view	Due to lack of interactivity around them, users feel minimum immersion and spatial presence and the experience becomes boring pretty quickly	
Due to the lack of use of the space surrounding the user, immersion is minimal and users end up having a boring experience in the VR environment		
Spatial presence is minimal; user feels like looking at a giant screen from outside		

(*continued*)

Table 3. (*continued*)

Initial themes	Refined themes	Final theme
User has trouble keeping up with the narrative in Fear of Missing Out something important when there are too many audio-visual cues around	Too many audio-visual cues to direct users' attention make them to use extra efforts in Fear of Missing Out something important in the narrative	Excessive use of audio-visual cues put the users in a **"Fear of Missing Out (FOMO)"** mode of experience that results in frustration and stress
User feels frustrated and stressed due to lack of control when audio-visual cues do not provide enough guidance	Users feel like they are not in control, which results in their frustration and stress	
When user's attention is properly guided through well-designed audio-visual cues, user feels immersed in the environment, which results in spatial presence and enjoyment	Well-designed audio-visual cues guide users' attention in different directions all around them throughout the narrative	Well-designed audio-visual cues put users in a **"Guided"** mode of experience throughout the narrative resulting in their immersion, spatial presence and overall enjoyment
	Users feel immersion, spatial presence and enjoyment when attention is guided to different elements of the narrative happening all around them	
Due to the lack of positional tracking in mobile VR, user's movement is not tracked, which breaks user's familiarity with physical reality resulting in a negative experience	Users have a negative experience when their movement doesn't match with the movement in the VR narrative	Lack of positional tracking in mobile VR requires additional time for the user to get used to the virtual environment

4.2   Analysis of Results

For all the applications when participants were placed inside the virtual narrative, they explored the space around them out of curiosity and looked for anything that grabbed their attention. When they found something that caught their attention they kept looking in that direction way until their attention was directed to some other element in the environment by a visual or audio cue. In all the applications used during the study, due to the lack of positional tracking in Mobile VR, when the participants moved during the narrative, the whole VR environment moved with them. It came as a surprise for the participants since they were expecting their movement to be tracked inside the virtual environment. It took a little bit of time for the participants to get used to this conflict between expectation and reality, but once they got used to their movement, the participants had no further difficulties with following the narratives.

When participants were exploring the *Oculus Home* Interface, the participants felt like there was a big screen in front of them and they kept looking straight ahead towards that conceptual screen throughout the experience since no audio-visual cues directed their attention towards any other element on the surrounding space. To match with the participants' experience, this mode of engagement has been coded as the "screen mode".

Participants also experienced this "screen" mode of engagement in *Rosebud*. Once they were placed inside the narrative, the participants looked all around out of curiosity but the only element that caught their attention was the asteroid in front of them. Once they started focusing in front, no other audio-visual cues directed their attention to any other direction in the narrative. The participants expressed that there was not much going on around them and they got bored pretty quickly. It is interesting to note that even though Rosebud offered the largest possibilities for interaction by letting the audience change camera angles, the participants still got stuck in the "screen" mode since everything was happening in one direction, and they were unable to affect the storyline even by changing camera angles.

In the case of *Muse Revolt*, participants experienced a different mode of experience. When they got into the immersive world of this VR music video, multiple visual elements started attracting their attention at the same time. First they saw the band performing on the stage, but their attention quickly got directed to the groups of people running all around them. While they were trying to follow the groups to find out what's going on, their attention got directed again by several police cars coming into the scene. While several visual cues tried to catch their attention at the same time, lack of directional audio cues made it even harder for the participants to decide what element of the narrative to focus on, which made them to try and follow too many random cues in Fear Of Missing Out (FOMO) something important around them. Due to this excessive use of visual cues and lack of any sort of guidance, eventually they got frustrated and expressed that there was simply too much going on throughout the narrative. To match with the participants' experience, this mode of engagement has been coded as the "FOMO mode".

In the case of *Invasion* and *Song for Someone*, once the participants entered the VR environment, visual and directional audio cues directed their attention to the first element they needed to focus on. From that point onwards their focus was guided throughout the narrative from one element to the next. The audio-visual cues were well designed to make sure multiple cues were not asking for attention at the same time. The participants felt guided throughout the experience and they followed the audio-visual cues all around them without much effort. Since the narratives were gradually unfolding all around them, the participants felt immersed in those narratives. They also expressed the feeling of "being there" in those virtual environments. To match with the participants' experience, this mode of engagement has been coded as the "guided mode".

The following table lists the modes participants engaged in throughout different narratives (Table 4):

Table 4. Modes the users engaged in with different applications.

Narrative	Mode of engagement	User experience
Rosebud	Screen	Boredom, Lack of Presence
Muse Revolt	FOMO	Frustration, Stress
Invasion, Song for Someone	Guided	Immersion, Spatial Presence

One interesting finding from this study is the mismatch between user's real world perception and virtual world realization due to the lack of positional tracking in mobile VR. This results in users requiring some additional time to get used to the VR environment.

5   Discussion

From the inductive analysis of user experiences with mobile virtual reality narratives used in this study it can be hypnotized that, users have an overall positive experience when there are well-designed audio-visual cues available throughout the experience that put them in a "guided" mode which follows the narrative flow. In this scenario users feel like they are in control, they know where to look and how to follow the cues and they are not missing out anything important. They also feel immersed in that virtual environment which gives them a feeling of spatial presence. It can also be suggested that excessive use of audio-visual cues or poorly designed cues put the users in a mode of engagement where they try their best to follow the cues in Fear Of Missing Out (FOMO) something important and end up feeling stressed and frustrated with the overall experience. They feel there is too much going on and they have no control over the experience. Finally, it can be implied that, lack of audio-visual cues throughout the VR narrative puts the users in a mode of engagement where they end up looking in one direction at a conceptual screen, which breaks the immersion and stops them from experiencing the feeling of "being there" or spatial presence. Users get bored in this mode and eventually end up with a negative overall experience.

By comparing the results from the analysis with the previous studies presented in the theoretical framework section, we can see that some of the findings are supported by previous literature.

5.1   Role of Audio-Visual Cues in Perception and Immersion

In guided mode users experience several components of psychological flow state [5] where they feel immersed in the virtual environment, lose track of the surrounding real environment, feel in control and their focus get directed to follow the storyline of the narrative through available audio-visual cues. This results in enjoyment and a sense of spatial presence. This finding matches with Sutcliffe [6] in terms of flow experience.

The role of audio-visual cues in attracting and directing users' attention in a virtual environment agree with the theory of ecological perception [1], which states that we turn our heads to direct our attention to different visual stimuli and we focus to hear better and gather information about action possibilities around us. The use of spatial audio to direct users' attention in different directions throughout a narrative matches with the findings of involuntary attention allocation in a virtual environment studied by Hendrix and Barfield [11].

5.2 Role of Audio-Visual Cues in Spatial Presence

When the users' experience was directed by appropriate audio-visual cues, multiple users expressed the experience of being spatially present. This fits the findings from existing literature [13, 14] that emphasize on the use of appropriate audio-visual spatial cues to increase the chance of users feeling spatial present in a virtual environment. It is also important to point out the use of directional audio cues in both of the narratives where users experienced immersion and spatial presence.

In "FOMO" mode, users ended up having a frustrating experience because they felt like they were not in control. They got stressed thinking that they might be missing something important in the storyline and too many things were going on at the same time, which in many cases broke their immersion. This agrees with the findings from Wirth et al. [12] who argue that a virtual environment will more likely be perceived as a plausible space if the used audio-visual cues have a logical consistency. In "FOMO" mode, the inconsistencies with the audio-visual cues confuse the users, which eventually block them from experiencing spatial presence in most cases. The negative experience of the users also matches the findings from de Rijk et al. [15] who argue an excessive use of spatial cues can cause sensory overload producing fatigue for the users.

6 Conclusions

Noticing the exponential rise of virtual reality applications in 2016, the goal of this study was to explore user experience in mobile virtual reality narratives and to investigate what role audio-visual cues play in users' positive or negative experiences. By using a consumer oriented mobile HMD and some popular VR applications, this study also examined whether the results relate to the findings from existing literature, where the research was conducted mostly in controlled environments using proprietary devices.

We know from the language of cinema that motion, color and contrast work really well as visual cues to direct audience's attention where needed. But when those audiences are placed inside the media in virtual reality, there is always a chance of having their back turned to important elements. To avoid this situation a designer can use visual cues inside the field of view of the users and audio cues outside the FOV to make the users turn their heads to face the elements important for the narrative. While only four narratives cannot be used to generalize the finding, it can be taken as a basis for further investigation into the effect of audio-visual cues on user experience in virtual reality applications.

The main findings of this study can be summarized as the following:

6.1   Audio-Visual Cues Make or Break an Experience

One of the most important findings of this study is how different audio-visual cues attract and direct user's attention throughout a VR experience. It is clear from the analysis of the recorded data that a virtual reality narrative needs to have well designed audio-visual cues to guide users' attention in a virtual environment to increase immersion that results in a positive overall experience. It is also important to keep in mind the usefulness of spatial audio cues that direct user's attention to elements of the VR experience not visible in user's field of view.

6.2   The Sweet Spot Lies Between Boredom and Frustration

Another important finding is how the amount of available audio-visual cues affects user experience in a virtual narrative. It is clear from the findings of this study that excessive audio-visual cues put the users in "FOMO" mode resulting in their frustration and a negative overall experience. While too many cues bring frustration, lack of cues brings boredom since the users expect to see events happening all around them in an immersive VR environment. Only a limited number of well-designed audio-visual cues hits the sweet spot and guides the audience throughout the narrative without requiring much effort from them.

6.3   It Takes a Little Extra Time to Get Used to Mobile VR

When it comes to lack of positional tracking in mobile VR, it is clear from the findings that users get confused and frustrated when their movements in the physical environment result in the whole virtual environment moving with them. This clash between real world perception and virtual world realization breaks their feeling of spatial presence in that VR environment. Fortunately, once they get used to the limited tracking capabilities of the HMD, users can easily get back into the flow of the narrative, especially when well-designed audio-visual cues guide them throughout the experience. Based on this finding it can be suggested that users should always be given a little extra time in the beginning to get used to their movements in a mobile virtual environment.

6.4   Limitations and Future Work

Due to the small sample size and usage of inductive methods, no claims can be made towards the generalizability of the findings. While the data collection and analysis were done thoroughly and carefully, the results need to be tested in a controlled study to verify the findings. In particular, it must be established in future studies if the same three modes of engagement would re-emerge with new users and new applications.

Another limitation is the age group of the participants. The findings might be different if the participants were from an older generation who are more hesitant towards new technology or if the participants were children who are more curious in a new environment. There are also cognitive differences in perception among different age groups, which might affect the different modes of engagements proposed in this study.

Acknowledgments. The author would like to express his gratitude to Professor. Annika Waern for her invaluable guidance throughout the study.

References

1. Gibson, J.J.: The Ecological Approach to Visual Perception: Classic Edition. Psychology Press (2014)
2. Stein, S.: Everyone wanted a piece of virtual reality at this year's CES (2016). https://www.cnet.com/news/everyone-wanted-a-piece-of-virtual-reality-at-this-years-ces/
3. Child, B.: Steven Spielberg warns VR technology could be 'dangerous' for film-making (2016). https://www.theguardian.com/film/2016/may/19/steven-spielberg-warns-vr-technology-dangerous-for-film-making
4. Smith, S.: VR Headset Mega Guide: Features and Release Dates (2016). http://www.tomsguide.com/us/vr-headset-guide,news-20644.html
5. Csikszentmihalyi, M.: Flow: The Psychology of Optimal Experience. Harper Collins, New York (1990)
6. Sutcliffe, A., Gault, B., Shin, J.E.: Presence, memory and interaction in virtual environments. Int. J. Hum Comput Stud. **62**(3), 307–327 (2005)
7. Sherman, W.R., Craig, A.B.: Understanding Virtual Reality: Interface, Application, and Design. Elsevier (2002)
8. Gaver, W.W.: Technology affordances. In: Proceedings of the SIGCHI Conference on Human Factors in Computing Systems, pp. 79–84. ACM (1991)
9. Norman, D.A.: The Design of Everyday Things: Revised and Expanded Edition. Basic Books (2013)
10. Rasmussen, J., Rouse, W.B.: Human Detection and Diagnosis of System Failures, vol. 15. Springer, Heidelberg (2013)
11. Hendrix, C., Barfield, W.: The sense of presence within auditory virtual environments. Presence: Teleoperators Virtual Environ. **5**(3), 290–301 (1996)
12. Wirth, W., Hartmann, T., Böcking, S., Vorderer, P., Klimmt, C., Schramm, H., Saari, T., Laarni, J., Ravaja, N., Gouveia, F.R., Biocca, F.: A process model of the formation of spatial presence experiences. Media Psychol. **9**(3), 493–525 (2007)
13. Steuer, J.: Defining virtual reality: dimensions determining telepresence. J. Commun. **42**(4), 73–93 (1992)
14. Biocca, F.: The cyborg's dilemma: Progressive embodiment in virtual environments. Hum. Factors Inf. Technol. **13**, 113–144 (1999)
15. de Rijk, A.E., Schreurs, K.M., Bensing, J.M.: Complaints of fatigue: related to too much as well as too little external stimulation? J. Behav. Med. **22**(6), 549–573 (1999)
16. Merriam, S.B., Tisdell, E.J.: Qualitative Research: A Guide to Design and Implementation. John Wiley & Sons (2015)
17. Villeneuve, P., Csikszentmihalyi, M., Robinson, R.: The art of seeing: an interpretation of the aesthetic encounter. J. Aesthetic Educ. **27**, 120 (1993)
18. Minichiello, V., Aroni, R., Hays, T.: In-depth Interviewing: Principles, Techniques, Analysis. Pearson Education Australia (2008)

19. Miles, M.B., Huberman, A.M.: Qualitative Data Analysis: An Expanded Sourcebook, 2nd edn. Sage Publications, Thousand Oaks (1994)
20. Denzin, N.K., Lincoln, Y.S.: The Sage Handbook of Qualitative Research, pp. 1–20. Sage Publications, Thousand Oaks (2011)
21. Braun, V., Clarke, V.: Using thematic analysis in psychology. Qual. Res. Psychol. 3(2), 77–101 (2006)
22. Sarker, B.: Show me the sign!: The role of audio-visual cues in user experience of mobile virtual reality narratives. Master's thesis. Uppsala University, Uppsala (2016). http://uu.diva-portal.org/smash/record.jsf?pid=diva2:1044065

ADVICE: Decision Support for Complex Geospatial Decision Making Tasks

Harvey S. Smallman[✉] and Cory A. Rieth

Pacific Science & Engineering, San Diego, CA, USA
{smallman,coryrieth}@pacific-science.com

Abstract. How can complex decisions, featuring multiple data sources and conflicting constraints, be supported by computer interfaces? We take a human factors approach to the problem by focusing on meeting users' cognitive decision making needs and addressing their perceptual challenges. An analysis of the historical trajectory of geospatial decision support reveals several issues and gaps. The configurable data overlay systems ubiquitous in weather forecasting and military command and control, that pass for decision support systems, require more and more mental effort of users with increases in the number and complexity of data sources. We lay out the design of a decision support system called ADVICE as a module that augments geospatial data overlay systems that allows users to reason about the **impact** of data. ADVICE possesses several task-centered features that apply the science of cognitive decision making to its interface. ADVICE allows users to build an integrated impact visualization that represents an appropriately weighted geospatial objective function for the decision at hand. Additional features provide the ability to compare the utility of different geospatial locations and regions, and intelligently explore the impacts of constraints. The system is also designed to meet the contextual control needs of users. That is, upfront user setup done in time-relaxed planning is handsomely repaid in execution, when time-pressured re-planning may be required. Although developed for geospatial decisions, the concepts are widely applicable to other types of decisions with multiple conflicting constraints.

Keywords: Decision support systems · Geospatial decision making · Cognitive science · Interface design · Configurable displays · Human factors · Automation trust and reliance

1 Introduction

Many work domains entail complex decision making tasks. In such tasks, users need to assess and relate multiple data sources, each imposing different constraints, to achieve a goal. The context in which these decisions need be made can also vary [1, 2]. For example, decisions may need to be made very quickly, or there may be considerable time available to make them. Here, we tackle the question of how such decisions should be supported by computer interfaces and tools, and how the rich cognitive science of decision making can be applied to ensure that decision support provided users in their computing systems is useful and usable [3].

© Springer International Publishing AG 2017
S. Lackey and J. Chen (Eds.): VAMR 2017, LNCS 10280, pp. 453–465, 2017.
DOI: 10.1007/978-3-319-57987-0_37

We focus on supporting geospatial decision making. Geospatial decisions are those whose output is the choice, or assessment, of a location, or locations, under various, often competing, constraints. In naval command and control, for example, planners engage in geospatial decision making to determine the likely locations of pirate activity given merchant shipping, weather and previous episodes of piracy. They do this in order to intelligently position surveillance and interdiction assets against the pirates [4]. Similarly, military navigators perform geospatial decision making to define safe and secure locations to position and route ships and submarines to achieve various mission objectives. These routes must avoid terrain and other navigation hazards, on the one hand, while allowing ships and submarines to remain undetected, on the other. In both civilian and military weather forecasting, forecasters make geospatial decisions when they must predict flash flooding, say, at discrete geospatial locations, from a variety of raw sensor, and derived meteorological model, outputs [5].

2   Trends in Geospatial Decision Support: Data to Decision

The support available to users to perform complex geospatial decision making tasks has improved dramatically over the last twenty years [6]. However, the advances have focused more on improving the technical, underlying computational infrastructure than in addressing the cognitive requirements for what are ultimately complex psychological tasks. A synthesis of the historical trends in geospatial decision support that we are observing in our capacity as scientific design consultants on various fielded systems is offered in Fig. 1. This figure reveals subtle limits in the understanding of the cognitive requirements of decision making by system engineers and interface developers.

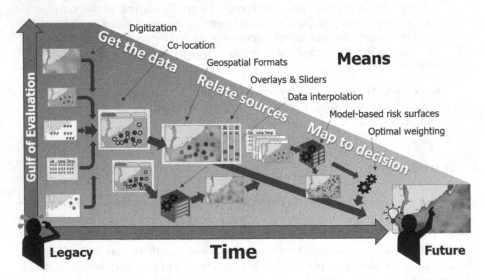

Fig. 1. The shrinking gulf of evaluation in geospatial decision making over time, and the march towards a geospatial objective function.

Figure 1 is an illustrative plot that shows how scientific and technical advances in the means of geospatial decision support, in time (on the abscissa), are attempting to provide decision support to reduce decision maker's gulf of evaluation (on the ordinate). The gulf of evaluation is the famous psychological construct in human computer interaction (HCI), that refers to the gap between a user's internal goals and what an external computer system delivers to achieve them [7, 8]. Mapped to decision support systems, the gulf reflects the mismatch between what a user needs and what the system provides the user to perceive, interpret and evaluate relevant data to make a decision. In Fig. 1, the gulf is broken down into three stages (labelled in white text), (i) getting the data (to perceive it), (ii) relating the data sources together (to interpret it), and (iii) mapping the data to the decision (to evaluate its impact on the decision). Illustrating these stages in an actual application domain both illustrates the gulf, in context, and how research and development trends in geospatial decision support are attempting to bridge, or reduce, it.

Before the advent of networked, digital information systems populated with geo-referenced data, users were challenged to simply obtain and relate decision-relevant information. For example, civilian and military navigators had access to a mix of digital and paper maps, received tasking in writing and tasking updates verbally, obtained printouts and notes of weather forecasts, and heard verbally relayed facts and constraints. The users faced a significant gulf of evaluation in that they had to try and scan, read and recall all the disparate sources of information to perceive it all. If the data was sparse, or missing, they also had to mentally interpolate it. Then they had to try and geo-reference it to begin to relate it together, and try to determine how it constrained and impacted their ship routing. All the while they had to try not to forget any of the data, or their emerging interpretation of it. The task was burdensome and prone to errors. It required skill and expertise to know how to prioritize information and when to judiciously deploy rules of thumb and heuristics to make up for missing, incomplete or forgotten data.

Faced with these significant challenges, unsurprisingly, users resorted to the creation of artifacts and associated processes to relate the data to the map and to externalize their memory of it. Such workarounds are often observed in operational settings as users take it on themselves to try and make up for perceived deficiencies in their computer-based, or other support tools, and business processes [9, 10]. What is interesting and informative for decision support design, is that these workarounds may become metaphors that are then pursued by interface designers, and then become unhelpfully entrenched [11]. For example, faced with paper maps and data printouts, military and civilian navigators used grease pencil markup on transparent acetate overlays superimposed on maps to geo-reference, remember and relate data sources. Modern digital information systems have copied and maintained the acetate metaphor by showing geo-referenced data sources as graphical overlays on geoplots. This is true for client-based, commercial Geographical Information Systems (GIS) [12], dedicated commercial maritime navigation Electronic Chart Display and Information System (ECDIS), and for web-based, freely available and broadly used geospatial mapping and visualization applications such as *Google Earth* [13]. Analogous to overlaying multiple acetates on a physical map, multiple sources can potentially be related simultaneously by toggling on/off available data sources. Further, most systems go further by providing sliders to set the opacity of each overlay to make several overlays visible at once, even when data is occluded as a result.

Comparable, configurable overlay systems are available to commercial and military weather forecasters. For example, US Government forecasters in the National Weather Service use a system called the Advanced Weather Interactive Processing System (AWIPS) which allows a mix of raw and derived data and model predictions to be overlaid on geospace [5]. Modern digital GIS and other systems can also perform mathematical interpolation on sparse data to yield continuous, interpolated data representations that can be provided to users as another overlay, as a heatmap or other 2D color plot [12].

Digital geospatial data overlay systems do provide some decision support to their users. By digitizing and co-locating the data in single system, and presenting it overlaid on a map, users can perceive the data, relate it to geospace, and integrate it with other sources. Therefore, such systems reduce the gulf of evaluation. But they do not eradicate it. There still remains the challenge of mapping the data to a decision to determine its impact (or utility [14]), its relative importance, and to evaluate alternatives to make an informed decision. As shown in Fig. 1, one attempt that has been made to finally close the gulf of evaluation is to generate model-based risk surfaces that attempt to model the impact of several data sources on decision outcomes and then present the output as an integrated visual goodness surface, say as a geospatial heatmap [4]. Jim Hansen and colleagues at the Naval Research Laboratory in Monterey, CA, for example, have generated automated piracy attack predictions that compute likelihood of piracy events across a region given the clemency of the weather for small boat (possible pirate predator) actions and the expected merchant shipping density (prey) [4]. Such analysis provides decision support to military planners because it relieves them of the need to mentally perform the complex mathematical derivation of the impact and relative weighting of these data sources. The risk predictions can be made available during military planning as another overlay on their digital geospatial data overlay systems.

Model-based risk surfaces exist mainly in the form of laboratory prototypes, or are in various stages of advanced development in a few target application domains. Their scope is usually no more than two to three relevant data sources. However, as Fig. 1 shows, as they grow in scope and sophistication, they point to an implicit future of decision support reduced to a choice on a geospatial objective function, where all sources have been mapped and optimally weighed and integrated into a single view. Such a system would finally bridge the decision maker's gulf of evaluation as the decision maker would be able to reason over all mapped and appropriately weighed data to pick good locations.

3   User Challenges

There are a number of perceptual and cognitive issues raised by the use of (1) digital geospatial data overlay systems to perform geospatial decision making, potentially augmented with (2) model-based risk surfaces. Here, we enumerate the issues and use them to motivate the design of HCI features and functions that address these issues in the next section.

3.1 Digital Geospatial Data Overlay Systems

Relating multiple data sources. Geospatial overlay systems provide no good way for users to relate multiple data sources together. Data overlays run into either perceptual or cognitive limitations, putting users in an awkward dilemma. If users attempt to look at data *simultaneously*, for example by turning on multiple overlays, then the clutter, occlusion and perceptual masking of data will result in slow and inaccurate identification [15]. This is true even if the system is augmented with the ability for users to control the opacity of each source, say with sliders. Such systems help mitigate data occlusions by employing transparency to blend layers together, affording users the chance to understand and relate data across layers and to the map background. However, with a lower opacity, each layer will be reduced in contrast, exacerbating clutter and masking issues that will quickly prevent interpretation of more than a couple of layers. Alternatively, if users view overlays *sequentially*, one at a time, to attempt to overcome the clutter and masking effects, then they discover another limitation of their cognitive architecture - their imperfect memory systems [16]. They will likely suffer slow and inaccurate identification of data from flawed recall and mental comparison of the different states of the display over time. These problems will intensify as more and more data sources inevitably come online.

Metarepresentational Competence. Inherent in the skill-based problem solving required to perform complex geospatial decision making is the need for flexible representations that allow for creativity [17]. For this reason, and because of the variety and fluidity of the geospatial tasks in modern work domains, designers have opted to provide their expert users maps with configurable overlays because they would seem to provide that necessary flexibility [5]. That users need to configure their own decision support representations raises another subtle and often neglected issue. The approach is premised on the assumption that users are actually capable of the configuration task – that is, that they possess "metarepresentational competence" with the configurable, geospatial overlay tools and displays they are provided [18]. Users are expected to select overlays from the ever-expanding array of sources that the networked systems make available, and then combine and blend them with opacity sliders, to relate them interactively to meet their specific decision making needs. Users aren't just expected to *"finish the design"* [19], they are implicitly expected to meet all their decision making requirements. Recent studies have highlighted the downsides of such flexibility by throwing into question the meta-representational competence of users with such systems. Expert users and novices alike underestimate the deleterious effects that clutter has on their visual performance from bringing up task-irrelevant overlays, and inadvertently slow themselves down when performing meteorological forecasting tasks [20, 21].

Determining impact of data. As discussed in Sect. 2, above, there are several steps involved in making a geospatial decision. The impact of data on a decision, or its utility [14] needs to be determined and weighed. It is left up to the user to mentally determine impact, using their expertise, and then hold it in memory as they continue to relate data sources and their impacts together. Recently, we documented the extent of this problem in a controlled human performance experiment [22]. We measured the quality and time to make geospatial decisions with different support tools in a virtual fishing task (akin to the one relayed in Sect. 4, below, although much simpler). Participants caught 44% fewer fish and were 37% slower making decisions when they had to perform the task with three data overlays than with risk surfaces that mapped the data to decision impact (i.e., how sea temperature affects likelihood of fish vs. raw sea temperature). The results expose the time and mental effort required to interpret and relate data to decision quality from (only three) data overlays.

Contextual control. The cognitive science of decision making has made dramatic strides in the last two decades. There are now sophisticated conceptualizations of decision making processes and strategy, and how they are deployed flexibly in response to contextual factors, such as time available to decide [14, 23, 24]. An overarching framework that captures the gross influences of shifting context on cognition is Hollnagel's notion of contextual control modes [1, 2]. Data overlay systems may function acceptably when there is time to relate each data source to each other and to decision quality. But when data changes and users must determine whether and how to re-plan under time pressure, the limits of simple data overlay systems will manifest. Data overlay systems may not support user needs for certain contextual control modes.

3.2 Model-Based Risk Surfaces

Opaqueness. Second, model-based risk surfaces are opaque to users in that they don't show the basis of their predictions, and are thus subject to mistrust [25]. By presenting an integrated risk prediction without its pedigree or basis evident, or accessible, expert users may question its validity and then begin to mistrust and disuse it. In this regard, the integrated predictions don't meet the requirements of military and civilian decision makers, who are taught and used to constantly validating assessments in underlying data (e.g., [26]).

Brittleness. Model-based risk surfaces are attractive in that they create automatic impact predictions for several data sources. The results can be integrated into a geospatial heatmap and then provided to users as an overlay [4]. Such algorithmic approaches suffer from a key drawback, however, in that they are brittle [27]. That is, they are inevitably limited in what they take into account. Thus, if the context of a situation changes with additional data that it is not, or cannot be, included in the model, then the risk surface becomes less useful to decision makers who may not even realize anything is amiss. For example, recent local law enforcement actions or military exercises might affect the likelihood of piracy, but without access to these changes, they will not be factored into the model's computations.

Color scales. The outputs of risk models are often conveyed with continuous 2D color surfaces or heatmaps [4]. Although not inherent to risk models themselves, these outputs often use color scales that are not perceptually linear. That is, they possess misleading perceptual discontinuities at hue boundaries (that are not reflected in changes in the underlying risk predictions) and other artifacts [28].

4 ADVICE Geospatial Decision Support System

We have taken a different approach to enable users to reason about the decision impacts of multiple data sources. We have created a decision support prototype called ADVICE (Active Decision Visualization of Impact Critical Elements) and explored its efficacy for various geospatial tasks. ADVICE augments geospatial overlay systems with a user-generated, flexible integrated risk surface, and tools to explore it. In this section, we introduce and review ADVICE within a fictional scenario, where one must decide where to send vessels to catch fish. The data sources depicted are derived from actual geospatial data, but the specifics of how they relate to fishing is intended only as an illustration of the capabilities of ADVICE for other task domains.

4.1 Overview: Process and Principles

ADVICE is a support system for geospatial decisions, that is, any decision where locations, areas, or paths need to be compared. Here, we illustrate our current proto-type supporting the search for promising locations to fish. ADVICE focuses on deci-sions for which there are multiple sources of data that inform and constrain possible actions (e.g. water depth, traffic, hazards). The data sources must generally be geospatial in nature, present in a geospatial overlay system, and mapped to a common coordinate space.

Figure 2 provides an overview of how ADVICE decision surfaces are generated. ADVICE essentially implements a multi-attribute utility model [14] for geospatial deci-sions. For a given decision, multiple data sources (Fig. 2, left) will constrain and change the desirability of locations. In ADVICE, users specify requirements and desires for each data source, either directly or imported from templates. Once these desires and requirements are

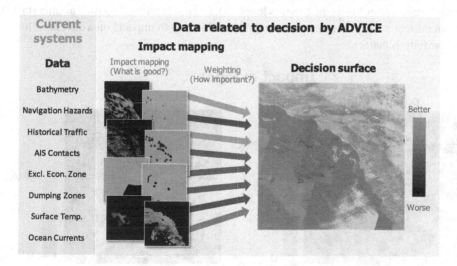

Fig. 2. ADVICE is a decision support module that augments data overlay systems (left) with impact mapping (center) to create an integrated decision surface visualization (right). (Color figure online)

specified, ADVICE automatically processes multiple data sources into the common space of decision impacts (Fig. 2, middle), and weighs impacts into a unified decision surface (Fig. 2, right). Impact and goodness are rendered in a perceptually linear color scale running from bright green (good) to dark red (bad) [29].

4.2   Impact Mapper

The foundation of ADVICE is mapping data sources (Fig. 3., left) to decision impacts with an interface. Impact mapping takes data, which may take a number of forms, and transforms it into decision impact (utility) over space (Fig. 3., right). This transformation is based on what data values are desirable for a decision. For example, data sources, such as water depth (bathymetry) or surface temperature, exist as or can be interpolated into data surfaces over space. Different values of this data have different desirability for the decision, that are mapped between -1 and 1 for soft constraints, or to -∞ for values that constitute violation of a hard requirement. If the fish we are seeking prefer surface temperatures at or above 65°F, say, and will not be found for temperatures below 60°F, locations with temperatures of 65°F or higher would be mapped to an impact of 1, interpolating down to impacts of -1 just above 60°F, and -∞ for locations with a measurement of 60°F or below. Similarly, to locate fish we would need to stay outside of outsize of hazardous dumping zones and the exclusive economic zones of other countries. The data in this case are areas defined by polygons of multiple points of latitude and longitude. Given that staying outside of these areas is a hard constraint, any point in these polygons would receive a utility of -∞, eliminating those locations from consideration, no matter how good other aspects of data may be. Data that exist as points (hazards or positions of noise-generating ships that are to be avoided), can be re-represented as a data surface consisting of the minimum distance to any of those points from each location in space. Decision impact are then calculated (must stay 500 yards away from hazards, after 1 mile the benefits level off). Even secondary data such as uncertainty about current measurements can be mapped in this way to impacts on a decision (lower uncertainty is better).

Impact mapper

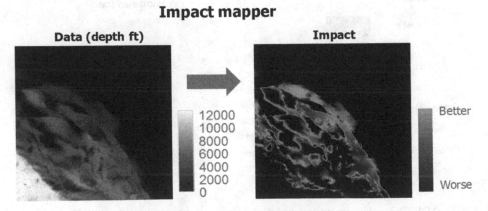

Fig. 3. ADVICE maps raw data values (left) onto their impacts for a decision (right).

The final consideration in impact mapping is the relative weighting of the different data sources (surface temperature may be considered more important than depth, say). These weightings are normalized and used to weight relative impacts into the decision surface. This weighing impacts the combination of soft constraints only. Impacts and weightings that are themselves dynamic and change over time (e.g. forecasts weighted less heavily as they age) could easily be incorporated into the general ADVICE framework. More complex, multivariate relationships either between data sources, or external factors can also be captured with additional effort in the impact mapping process. By bringing decision impacts into the system, all the products and tools of ADVICE update with any updates to dynamic data, even alerting based on changes to impacts rather than raw data, something that would be very difficult for a human user to stay abreast of.

While this process may seem arduous, in practice we imagine users rarely needing to set or even adjust these impacts. Most impacts will be constant across different decisions. The preferred water depth might vary for different types of fish, which could be captured in decision templates for each fish species, but one will always want to stay out of fixed hazardous areas. Decision templates could specify most if not all the relevant impacts, and be modified and resaved as needed. While complicated functions mapping data onto impacts could be used, to date, we have found that the impacts for most data sources can be easily summarized.

4.3 Decision Surface, Location Comparer and Constraint Resolver

Once impact mappings and weightings are defined for each data source, ADVICE combines data sources into an overall decision surface showing 'goodness' of locations over space for the decision of interest. This combination is done though a weighted average of the impacts. The overall decision surface for our fishing scenario is shown on the right of Fig. 4., using the continuous, perceptually linear color scale discussed in Sect. 4.1. In the decision surface, and areas violating hard constraints are not colored, and the background map shows through. Critically, the decision surface can be probed to explore *what* is good or bad about locations and compare the raw data and impacts across multiple locations. The left of Fig. 4 shows a comparison interface for the locations labeled A and B on the decision surface. For each location, a data summary statistic over the area is provided, along with an indicator categorically color coding the utility of each source. Circles mark the best utility for each data constraint (both locations are marked in the case of ties). In this example, neither the depth at area A or area B is ideal (lighter, yellow dot), but depth is better at B (circle). Looking at the data summary statistics, Area B is farther from any navigation hazards, but they are both far enough there is no difference for the decision of where to search for fish. Additionally, attributes of the decision not related to data, such as the size of the proposed area, can be provided for comparison. By allowing users to explore the decision surface, we hope to both support more informed decisions and allow remediation of inherent risks (e.g. if the areas are a little deeper than one would like, one can adapt procedures to compensate). Further, we hope to support the creativity and skill-based problem solving of expert users [17] and foster overall trust in the system.

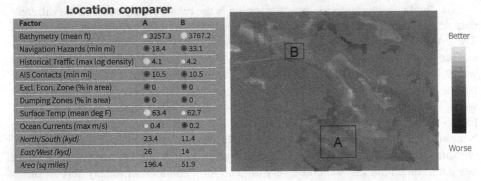

Fig. 4. Overall decision surface (top) and location comparer (bottom) showing the pros and cons of two decision locations. The yellow and green dots categorically show the goodness of each data source. The dots corresponding to the better decision based on a source are circled. (Color figure online)

Considering many constraints can quickly limit possibilities. To support better understanding the relative impact of constraints, and intelligent problem solving in such situations, we developed the Constraint Resolver interface. The Constraint Resolver consists of two features. The first is an overlay view that shows only the number of hard constraints violated, giving a quick picture into what areas might be possible to open up by relaxing a small number of constraints. Second, we developed and implemented a simple "restrictiveness" metric characterizing how much a data source limits decisions. This metric is a measure of how much area is uniquely eliminated by a constraint. For each constraint, restrictiveness is calculated as the proportion of area meeting all other hard constraints, that a constraint eliminates. Once calculated, ranked constraints are presented to the user for analysis and follow up. Similar metrics can be defined to capture the influence of soft constraints (e.g. what proportion of an otherwise "good" area is "bad" after considering this constraint?).

4.4   User Challenges Addressed

With ADVICE, we have attempted to address many of the issues with geospatial data overlays and automated risk surfaces enumerated in Sect. 3. With ADVICE's integrated decision surface, users do not need to hold multiple constraints in memory, or struggle to discriminate different data sources, as they do with data overlays. Nor do users need to mentally interpret data, or re-interpret changed data. These processes are offloaded to ADVICE. They are handled both by upfront mapping of the impact of data sources and by the integrated decision surface updating with the underlying data that feed it. As such, plan degradation is likely far easier with ADVICE, as users can stay abreast of how changed data impacts their decisions and plans in real-time. This also better supports the contextual control mode requirements of users by providing support to complex mental operations when users are the most pressed for time. Similarly, the work of setting up ADVICE can be performed ahead of time, when more time is available and users are in more optimizing context control modes [1, 2].

In comparison to risk surfaces, ADVICE gives users access to probe and modify the mapping of data source impacts on a decision, making it easier for users to understand and trust the resulting risk surface, which they have created themselves. Additionally, by providing additional exploration tools, ADVICE supports collaborative plan critiquing by allowing intelligent constraint relaxation to see the impact on decision outcome. As the users map the impact of data sources, they are aware of the scope of the surfaces they have created, and the resulting brittleness/resilience of what they have created. Finally, by rendering individual and weighted impacts in a perceptually linear color code, ADVICE's visualization are free of misleading perceptual discontinuities.

5 Conclusions

We have reviewed trends in geospatial decision support toward more integrated geospatial information and identified several human factors issues and gaps with current geospatial decision support. The goal of HCI is to provide useful and effective task support for users through computer-based tools and interfaces. Too often, we have seen users of legacy systems, (figuratively) break into a sweat (Fig. 1, left), as their tools require of them mental gymnastics to make decisions. To further close the gulf of evaluation faced by geospatial decision makers, we developed and presented a prototype decision support system call ADVICE. Through explicit, user-determined mapping of data to decision impacts, ADVICE creates a decision surface and provided tools for the exploration of that surface. Note that the human decision maker is still an active part of the decision process, and that ADVICE does not take the decision from the decision maker. Rather it helps to externalize some of the interpretation of data. In Fig. 1, we see ADVICE as a redirection from the march towards a single unifying, model-based decision surface to something with more user interactivity. In this way human decision makers are still integrated into the decision process, and can still supplying additional contextualizing information that is not or cannot be explicitly represented in the system. Future users of a fielded ADVICE system should be able to focus on insights into complex problems and making quality decisions (Fig. 1, right).

Rather than visualize impact, per se, an alternative approach is to provide complex filtering and searching functionality to assist users determine specific locations that meet restrictive criteria (e.g., see [30]). This may be appropriate in tightly bound work domains where there are exclusively black and white hard constraints, and few opportunities to explore or relax constraints as with selection of nuclear waste disposal sites. In contrast, our end users in military command and control are faced with task domains that are not always bounded. Here, ADVICE provides interactive exploration and visualization of both hard and soft constraints.

While we have focused on a limited set of applications, we see the potential of ADVICE as a decision support framework to be much greater. The principles of helping users externalize utility functions to integrate multiple decision constraints could be readily extended beyond geospatial, to other forms of decision making. ADVICE could easily extend to consumer geospatial decisions such as searching for a house or rental (desiring it to be close to work, restaurants, and parks, with good schools). More generally, the same principles could apply to other situations where user-definable soft-filtering could provide better relevance weightings. For example, in web commerce, rather than a hard filter on 4 star or above ratings, shoppers could define explicit preferences (least 3 but more are better, lower price is better). Similarly, those shopping for a new car could select results not only on hard constraints, but on soft constraints relative to their desires (more MPG, lower price).

Acknowledgements. We gratefully acknowledge the technical assistance of Dr. Ben D. Amsel of PSE and discussions with Ronald Steed of UpScope Consulting. Sponsored by the Office of Naval Research of the US Department of Defense, program officer Dr. Jeffrey G. Morrison, under contract N00014-15-C-0123.

References

1. Hollnagel, E.: Human Reliability Analysis: Context and Control. Academic Press, London (1993)
2. Feigh, K.M., Pritchett, A.R., Jacko, J.A., Denq, T.: Contextual control modes during an airline rescheduling task. J. Cog. Eng. Dec. Mak. **1**, 169–185 (2007)
3. Lehto, M.R., Nah, F.: Decision-making models and decision support. In: Salvendy, G. (ed.) Handbook of Human Factors and Ergonomics, 3rd edn., pp. 191–242. Wiley, Hoboken (2006)
4. Hansen, J., Jacobs, G., Hsu, L., et al.: Information domination: dynamically coupling METOC and INTEL for improved guidance for piracy interdiction. NRL Rev., 110–119 (2011). Naval Research Laboratory, Washington, DC
5. Trafton, J.G., Hoffman, R.R.: Computer-aided visualization in meteorology. In: Hoffman, R.R. (ed.) Expertise Out of Context: Proceedings of the 6th International Conference on Naturalistic Decision Making, pp. 337–358. CRC Press, New York (2007)
6. Andrienko, G., Andrienko, N., Jankowski, P., Keim, D., Kraak, M.J., MacEachren, A., Wrobel, S.: Geovisual analytics for spatial decision support: setting the research agenda. Intl. J. Geo. Info. Sci. **21**, 839–857 (2007)
7. Hutchins, E.L., Hollan, J.D., Norman, D.A.: Direct manipulation interfaces. Hum.-Comp. Interact. **1**, 311–338 (1985)
8. Norman, D.A.: The Design of Everyday Things. MIT Press, Cambridge (1988)
9. Mumaw, R.J., Roth, E.M., Vicente, K.J., Burns, C.M.: There is more to monitoring a nuclear power plant than meets the eye. Hum. Fac. **42**, 36–55 (2000)
10. Cook, M.B., Smallman, H.S.: Human-centered command and control of future autonomous systems. In: 18th International Command and Control Research and Technology Symposium, Arlington, VA, 19–21 June 2013
11. Smallman, H.S., Cook, M.B.: Proactive supervisory decision support from trend-based monitoring of autonomous and automated systems: a tale of two domains. In: Shumaker, R. (ed.) VAMR 2013. LNCS, vol. 8022, pp. 320–329. Springer, Heidelberg (2013). doi: 10.1007/978-3-642-39420-1_34
12. Longley, P.A., Goodchild, M.F., Maguire, D.J., Rhind, D.W.: Geographic Information Systems and Science, 3rd edn. Wiley, Hoboken (2010)
13. Google Earth. https://www.google.com/earth/
14. Winterfeldt, D.V., Edwards, W.: Decision Analysis and Behavioral Research. Cambridge University Press, Cambridge (1986)
15. Rosenholtz, R., Li, Y., Nakano, L.: Measuring visual clutter. J. Vis. **17**, 1–22 (2007)

16. Anderson, J.R., Bothell, D., Byrne, M.D., Douglass, S., Lebiere, C., Qin, Y.: An integrated theory of the mind. Psych. Rev. **111**, 1036–1060 (2004)
17. Rasmussen, J.: Skills, rules, knowledge, signals, signs and symbols, and other distinctions in human performance models. IEEE Trans. Sys. Man Cyb. **13**, 257–266 (1983)
18. diSessa, A.A.: Metarepresentation: native competence and targets for instruction. Cog. Instr. **22**, 293–331 (2004)
19. Rasmussen, J., Goodstein, L.P.: Decision support in supervisory control of high-risk industrial systems. Automatica **23**, 663–671 (1987)
20. Hegarty, M., Smallman, H.S., Stull, A.T.: Choosing and using geospatial displays: effects of design on performance and metacognition. J. Exp. Psychol. Appl. **18**, 1–17 (2012)
21. Smallman, H.S., Hegarty, M.: Expertise, spatial ability and intuition in the use of complex visual displays. In: 51st Proceedings of Annual Meeting Human Factors and Ergonomics Society, Baltimore, MD, pp. 2000–2004, 1–5 October 2007
22. Rieth, C.A., Smallman, H.S.: The utility of configurable display systems for overcoming automation brittleness in complex geospatial decision making tasks. In: 59th Proceedings of Annual Meeting Human Factors and Ergonomics Society, Los Angeles, CA, pp. 264–268, 26–30 October 2015
23. Gigerenzer, G., Gaissmaier, W.: Heuristic decision making. Ann. Rev. Psychol. **62**, 451–482 (2011)
24. Payne, J.W., Bettman, J.R., Johnson, E.J.: Adaptive strategy selection in decision making. J. Exp. Psychol. Learn. Mem. Cog. **14**, 534–552 (1988)
25. Sarter, N.B., Woods, D.D.: How in the world did we ever get into that mode? Mode error and awareness in supervisory control. Hum. Fac. **37**, 5–19 (1995)
26. Kirschenbaum, S.S., McInnis, S.L., Correll, K.P.: Contrasting submarine speciality training: sonar and fire control. In: Ericsson, K.A. (ed.) Development of Professional Expertise, pp. 217–285. Cambridge University Press, New York (2009)
27. Smith, P.J., McCoy, E., Layton, C.: Brittleness in the design of cooperative problem-solving systems: the effects on user performance. IEEE Trans. Sys. Man. Cyb. Part A Sys. Hum. **27**, 360–371 (1997)
28. Borland, D., Taylor II, R.M.: Rainbow color map (still) considered harmful. IEEE Comp. Graph. Appl. **27**, 15–17 (2007)
29. Spence, I., Kutlesa, N., Rose, D.L.: Using color to code quantity in spatial displays. J. Exp. Psychol. Appl. **5**, 393–412 (1999)
30. Malczewski, J.: GIS and Multicriteria Decision Analysis. Wiley, New York (1999)

A Real-Time Professional Photographing Guiding System Through Image Composition Analysis

Meng-Luen Wu[✉] and Chin-Shyurng Fahn

Department of Computer Science and Information Engineering,
National Taiwan University of Science and Technology,
Taipei 10607, Taiwan, ROC
{d10015015, csfahn}@mail.ntust.edu.tw

Abstract. In professional photographing, a valuable photo usually comprises of a good image composition because people prefer well-composed photos. In the field of image aesthetics, image composition plays an important rule for predicting whether an image is taken by professional or not. As a result, to help amateurs take good photographs, a real-time system that analyzes the image composition in the field of view of a camera in real-time is helpful. In this paper, we proposed a real-time image composition analysis system to help guide users take better photos in real time by showing the analyzed results on screen constantly and instantly. Several image compositions, which are central, rule of thirds, horizontal, vertical, diagonal and perspective, can be classified instantly with our proposed methods. We use the saliency map and prominent lines as the main features for analysis, and use multilayered perceptron to predict the image composition of an input image. The accuracy is above 97%, which is higher than most of the state-of-the-art methods.

Keywords: Human-computer interface · Image composition · Image aesthetics · Image classification · Artificial neural network, pattern recognition · Computer vision

1 Introduction

Photography is a kind of forms of art that the photographers can convey their emotion and aesthetic sensibilities. The photographic composition is one of the important components in the photo. The aim of the composition is to make the photo look balanced by arranging subjects in the photo properly. The composition of an image can convey the photographers' feelings and expressions to some extent, especially in scenery photos.

The field of image aesthetics is devoted to predicting the value of a natural image. Savakis et al. [1] found image composition to be one of the most important attribute for image aesthetics analysis. We show the instance of the image compositions in Fig. 1.

A good image composition comprises an arrangement of foreground and background in a pleasing, and orderly manner. To take good photos, professional photographers use

© Springer International Publishing AG 2017
S. Lackey and J. Chen (Eds.): VAMR 2017, LNCS 10280, pp. 466–477, 2017.
DOI: 10.1007/978-3-319-57987-0_38

Fig. 1. Six types of image composition: (a) central; (b) rule of thirds; (c) horizontal; (d) vertical; (e) diagonal; (f) perspective

two imagery lines horizontally and two lines vertically which divide the photo into three parts and place important objects along these lines or their intersections.

Some cameras provide the auxiliary lines to assist amateur photographers to apply rule of thirds composition easily. Except for rule of thirds, there are many kinds of photo compositions, which make photos more pleasing. In this study, we focus on the classification of six types of image compositions, which are central composition, rule of thirds composition, horizontal composition, vertical composition, diagonal composition, and perspective composition.

Prominent lines and salient regions are two important factors for deciding the composition of an image. The prominent lines are the most voted lines in the Hough transform, and the salient regions are the perceptually appealing areas in an image. In this study, we use the feature based on these factors and use artificial neural network to classify the possible composition type of an input image. The flow of our proposed method is shown in Fig. 2.

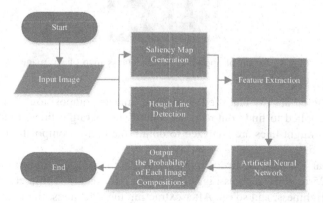

Fig. 2. The flow chart of our proposed image composition classification

This paper is organized as follows. In Sect. 1, the introduction of image composition, and the flow chart of our proposed method are presented. In Sect. 2, the image composition types to be analyzed in this paper and the related works is introduced. In Sect. 3, our proposed feature extraction method for image composition classification is explained. In Sect. 4, the algorithm of the classifier used for our study is illustrated. The Sect. 4 gives the experimental setup and the result of image composition classification. In Sect. 5, we make some conclusions and give the future works about the proposed method.

2   Related Works

Mai et al. [2] applied a method using saliency to implement rule of thirds. In order to detect visual elements, this method designs a variety of features based on the saliency and objectness map and infer their spatial relationship. There are three methods to compute saliency map as shown in Fig. 3. However, only using saliency sometimes leads to undesirable results. Objectness map is applied as a complement to saliency map. This objectness method returns a great deal of windows that likely contains an object. Figure 4 shows the result. Finally, for rule of thirds detection, some machine learning techniques are applied.

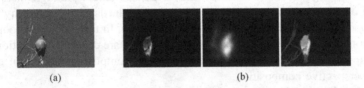

(a)   (b)

Fig. 3. Results of different saliency map generation methods: (a) input image; (b) three methods for saliency map

Fig. 4. Result of applying the objectness map of an image.

Lifang Bai et al. [3] analyzed landscape image composition. [4] Image edge extraction is applied to find contours, and then detect straight lines. Finally the characteristics of straight lines are analyzed to obtain the image composition. The result is shown in Fig. 5.

Huang et al. [5] used the fuzzy approach to classify image composition. A photo is divided into 25 regions, such as Fig. 6, to obtain information within each region, such magnitude, brightness, and so on. After extracting these features, the fuzzy approach is used to classify the type of the photo composition.

Fig. 5. Result of image composition (a) input image; (b) analysis of level composition; (c) input image; (d) analysis of vertical composition

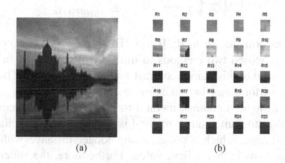

Fig. 6. The image with 25 regions: (a) test image; (b) separated into 25 regions

3   Feature Extraction

In this paper, there are primarily two types of features for image composition analysis, they are saliency map and prominent line detection, which are described as follows:

3.1   Saliency Map

Our eyes are attracted by salient regions in an image easily, such as red areas in a white paper. [6, 7] This ability is innate ability of humans because it helps us to find potential prey or mates easily. [8] Therefore, by finding salient regions, it is possible to find a target object in a cluttered field of view. The target can be used for image composition.

Before saliency foreground retrieval, we have to convert the original RGB color space to CIELab color space. To convert to CIELab color space, it is necessary to convert to CIEXYZ color space first. The conversion matrix is expressed as:

$$\begin{bmatrix} X \\ Y \\ Z \end{bmatrix} = \begin{bmatrix} 0.412453 & 0.357580 & 0.180423 \\ 0.212671 & 0.715160 & 0.072169 \\ 0.019334 & 0.119193 & 0.950227 \end{bmatrix} \begin{bmatrix} R \\ G \\ B \end{bmatrix} \quad (1)$$

The relation between CIEXYZ and CIELab is as follows:

$$L^* = \begin{cases} 116 \times \left(\frac{Y}{Y_n}\right)^{\frac{1}{3}} - 16, \frac{Y}{Y_n} > 0.008856 \\ 903.3 \times \frac{Y}{Y_n}, otherwise \end{cases} \tag{2}$$

$$a^* = 500 \left[f\left(\frac{X}{X_n}\right) - f\left(\frac{Y}{Y_n}\right) \right], b^* = 200 \left[f\left(\frac{Y}{Y_n}\right) - f\left(\frac{Z}{Z_n}\right) \right]$$

where $X_n = 0.9515$, $Y_n = 1.0000$, $Z_n = 1.0886$, and

$$f(t) = \begin{cases} t^{\frac{1}{3}}, t > 0.008856 \\ 7.787 \times t + \frac{16}{116}, otherwise \end{cases} \tag{3}$$

So far, the transformation from RGB to CIELab color space is completed.

In [6], Cheng proposed two methods to find salient regions in an image automatically, which are based on histogram contrast and region contrast. The region contrast method has better performance but takes more computational time. Therefore, in this paper, we choose histogram contrast method to achieve real-time region detection.

The concept of histogram contrast method is to find probability distribution among every color in an image, which a color having longer distance with other colors in CIELab color space has higher salient value. Furthermore, the salient value of each colors are weighted, and the probability of each colors in an image serves as a weight for its salient value.

The salient degree of each color is computation by:

$$S(I_k) = S(c_l) = \sum_{j=1}^{n} f_j D(c_l, c_j) \tag{4}$$

where I_k is the salient degree of pixel k, c_l is the color l in CIELab color space, c_j is the color j in CIELab color space, $D(x, y)$ is the color distance between two colors x and y in CIELab color space, and f_j is the probability that color j appears in image I.

Figure 7 shows the result for finding saliency regions, which are illustrated with pseudo colors. It is shown that in many cases, foreground regions are also saliency regions in the saliency region finding method.

The saliency map is further simplified into a 5×5 block matrix. The value of each blocks is calculated by averaging the pixel values within the block. An illustration after simplification for each image composition is shown in Fig. 8.

(a)   (b)

Fig. 7. Automatic saliency region finding: (a) flower in a clean background; (b) butterfly in a cluttered background

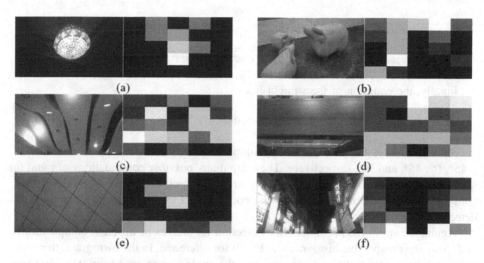

Fig. 8. 5 × 5 saliency map matrix applied on each image compositions: (a) central; (b) rule of thirds; (c) vertical; (d) horizontal; (e) diagonal; (f) perspective

After applying the edge detection on the image, prominent line detection can be performed to detect straight lines in the image. The concept of Hough transform is to transform the positions of all edge pixels in rectangular coordinate into polar coordinate, and choose the transformed position with more occurrences as the detected lines. [9, 10]

The straight lines to be detected are expressed in polar coordinates. The range of the angle degree in the polar coordinate is set to $-90 < \theta \leq 90$.

We set (p, q) as the vertical intersection of the origin of the coordinate, and $(p, q) = (r\cos\theta, r\sin\theta)$. For any points (x, y) in the rectangular coordinate, the slope of the line can be obtained by:

$$\frac{\Delta y}{\Delta x} = \frac{y - q}{x - p} = \frac{y - r\sin\theta}{x - r\cos\theta} \tag{5}$$

Because the slope of the line perpendicular to the straight line is $tan\theta$, the slope of the straight line is:

$$-\frac{1}{tan\theta} = -\frac{cos\theta}{sin\theta} \tag{6}$$

Combining the two equations above gives:

$$\frac{y - r\sin\theta}{x - r\cos\theta} = -\frac{cos\theta}{sin\theta} \tag{7}$$

And the equation can be rewritten as:

$$y\,sin\theta - r\,sin^2\theta = -x\,cos\theta + r\,cos^2\theta \qquad (8)$$

$$y\,sin\theta + x\,cos\theta = r\,sin^2\theta + r\,cos^2\theta = r\,(sin^2\theta + cos^2\theta) = r \qquad (9)$$

Finally, the equation of the straight line is:

$$x\,cos\theta + y\,sin\theta = r \qquad (10)$$

Substitute the x and y with every positions (x, y) in the edges, and the θ are set to $-45°$, $0°$, $45°$, and $90°$ respectively. There are many possible combinations of r and θ, and we choose the combinations with occurrences which are above a threshold. The combinations of these r and θ in the polar coordinate is used to draw the straight lines detected in the image.

Again, we apply the prominent line detection on images of different compositions, and show their respective histograms in Fig. 9 for reference. In the histogram, there are bins, each bins include 40 angle degrees, and the angle degree goes from 0 to 359 from left to right in the horizontal axis, and the vertical axis is the number of lines in each angle degree ranges.

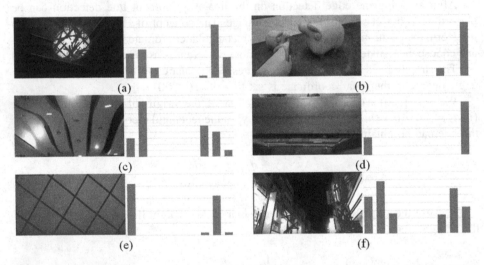

Fig. 9. The prominent line detection applied on each image compositions and their respective histogram: (a) central; (b) rule of thirds; (c) vertical; (d) horizontal; (e) diagonal; (f) perspective

4   Experimental Result and Discussions

In this section, we will elaborate and analyze the experimental results of our proposed methods. First, we describe the experiment setup and the implement environment. Second, we will show the result of artificial neural network classification. At last, the comparison of other related works with our proposed method will be shown in the last subsection.

4.1 Experimental Setup

The experimental setup is as follows: The image sensor is 1/2.3″, 20.7 MP image sensor with 27 mm lens and the aperture value is f/2.0. The resolution of the photo in the software is 1920×1080 when capture and is downscaled to 320×240 for processing.

In the experiment, we choose 35 prominent features for training the multiple-layered perceptron, which the values for the 5×5 saliency map matrix take 25 features and the rest 10 features are for the prominent lines. The features for the saliency map is shown in Fig. 10, while the features for the prominent line is shown in Table 1.

F1	F2	F3	F4	F5
F6	F7	F8	F9	F10
F11	F12	F13	F14	F15
F16	F17	F18	F19	F20
F21	F22	F23	F24	F25

Fig. 10. The features of the 5×5 saliency map matrix.

Table 1. The features selected for the prominent lines

No.	Name
F26	Ratio of prominent lines at angle degree 0–35
F27	Ratio of prominent lines at angle degree 36–71
F28	Ratio of prominent lines at angle degree 72–107
F29	Ratio of prominent lines at angle degree 108–143
F30	Ratio of prominent lines at angle degree 144–179
F31	Ratio of prominent lines at angle degree 180–215
F32	Ratio of prominent lines at angle degree 216–251
F33	Ratio of prominent lines at angle degree 252–287
F34	Ratio of prominent lines at angle degree 288–323
F35	Ratio of prominent lines at angle degree 324–359

The training data is composed of six image composition types, and the amount of each classes and size is listed in Table 2.

Table 2. Training dataset

Class label	Amount	Size
Central composition	723	320×240
Diagonal composition	2364	
Horizontal composition	1683	
Rule of thirds composition	1308	
Perspective composition	664	
Vertical composition	834	
Total	7576	

The multilayer perceptron [11] is used as the model for training the image composition analysis. In the multilayer perceptron the number of hidden layers is set to half the sum of feature numbers and number of classes, which is 7 here. The learning rate is 0.3, and the training iteration is 500. The illustration of the multiple-layered perceptron is illustrated in Fig. 11.

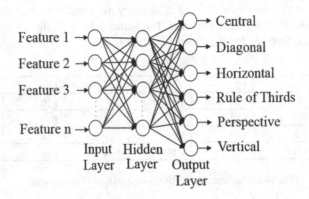

Fig. 11. Multilayered perceptron for training the image composition analysis model

4.2 Result and Discussions

In Table 3, if an image of a composition is classified as another composition other than its actual one, it is an image of incorrect classification. We calculate the correctly classified one and the incorrectly classified to compute the precision rate. In each composition, diagonal and vertical composition has better precision rate because fewer input images could meet the criterion according to the trained model. The rule of thirds composition, has the least precision rate because such composition is often classified as center composition.

Table 3. The classification precision with respect to each image compositions

Classes	Correct classification	Incorrect classification	Precision rate
Center	708	15	97.9%
Diagonal	2328	36	98.4%
Horizontal	1608	75	95.5%
Rule of thirds	1224	84	93.5%
Perspective	636	28	95.8%
Vertical	828	6	99.2%
Overall	7332	244	96.7%

In addition, we examine the result using ROC Curve. We found that the only the rule of thirds composition has the area under the ROC curve less than 90%. The overall average area under the ROC curve is about 92.1%. The area under the ROC curve of each composition is listed in Table 4.

Table 4. The area under the ROC curve with respect to each image compositions

Classes	Area under curve
Center composition	94.5%
Diagonal composition	93.9%
Horizontal composition	92.5%
Rule of thirds composition	83.9%
Perspective composition	90.1%
Vertical composition	98.9%
Overall	92.1%

To show that the multiple-layered perceptron can obtain the optimal result, we have also compared the precision rate of many classification methods. Experiments show that only the multiple-layered perceptron and decision tree have the precision rate more than 90%. The result is shown in Table 5.

Table 5. The classification precision of image composition with respect to different classification methods

Classification methods	Precision rate
Multiple-layered perceptron	96.7%
Decision tree (J48)	94.2%
RBF network	79.1%
Naïve Bayesian	68.7%
SVM	61.7%
Multiple-layered perceptron	96.7%

4.3 Comparison of State-of-the-Art Methods

In order to show the superiority of our proposed method, we compare our method to other existing ones, as shown in Table 6. Although Huang et al. can detect more image compositions, our precision rate is 10% higher. In addition, in the comparison, only our proposed method can run in real-time, which can be used for guiding users to take pictures with appropriate composition.

Table 6. The classification precision of image composition with respect to different classification methods

Classification methods	Number of compositions	Real-time	Precision rate
Long Mai et al.	1	X	80%
Lifang Bai et al.	2	X	N/A
Jui-Hua Huang	8	X	83.75%
Our purposed method	6	O	96.7%

5 Conclusion and Future Works

Professional photographers often prefer an image with good composition. Therefore, in order to help camera user take good photos, a real-time image composition analysis method with high accuracy is proposed. In this paper, we present an effective method for instructing the camera users in real time with their desired composition by classifying the image composition using multilayered perceptron. The classification method adopts different approaches to extract image features. Because humans have an innate ability to view areas with vivid and salient colors, we use saliency map for detecting the perceptually attractive regions of an image. In addition, professional photos are often composed using auxiliary lines, the prominent lines are detected for the classification of image compositions.

The multilayered perceptron is applied for classifying the images of six composition classes, including central, diagonal, horizontal, rule of thirds, perspective, and vertical. The average precision is above 96%. The AUC (Area under ROC curve) of all composition classes are all above 80%, and achieve above 90% excepting the rule of thirds composition. In addition, different from other existing state-of-the-art methods, our proposed method can run in real-time, which is capable of guiding camera users for composing an image while taking photos.

In the future, we would like to instruct users how to take photos with specific photo compositions only, which can be accomplished my removing objects in the field of view or ask users to view in or out to meet the conditions of the desired composition.

Acknowledgement.   The authors thank the National Science Council of Taiwan (R. O. C.) for supporting this work in part under Grant NSC 105-2221-E-011 -032-MY3.

References

1. Savakis, A.E., Etz, S.P., Loui, A.C.: Evaluation of image appeal in consumer photography. In: Proceedings of the International Society for Optics and Photonics, San Jose, CA, pp. 111–121 (2000)
2. Mai, L., Le, H., Niu, Y., Liu, F.: Rule of thirds detection from photograph. In: Proceedings of the IEEE International Symposium on Multimedia, Dana Point, CA, pp. 91–96 (2011)
3. Bai, L., Wang, X., Chen, Y.: Landscape image composition analysis based on image processing. In: Proceedings of the IEEE International Conference on Computer Science and Automation Engineering, Beijing, China, vol. 2, pp. 787–790 (2012)
4. Ghane, M., Shahbahrami, A.: Landscape image filtering via aesthetic inference. IOSR J. Eng. **2**(8), 33–38 (2012)
5. Huang, J.H.: A fuzzy logic approach for recognition of photographic compositions, M.S. thesis, Department of Mathematics and Science, National Chengchi University, Taipei, Taiwan (2007)
6. Cheng, M.M., Zhang, G.X., Mitra, N.J., Huang, X., Hu, S.M.: Global contrast based salient region detection. In: Proceedings of the IEEE Conference on Computer Vision and Pattern Recognition, Colorado Springs, CO, pp. 409–416 (2011)
7. Itti, L.: Visual salience. Scholarpedia **2**(9), 3327 (2007). doi:10.4249/scholarpedia.3327

8. Strausberg, M., Engler, S.: The Routledge Handbook of Research Methods in the Study of Religion. Routledge, New York (2011)
9. Hough, P.V.C.: Method and means for recognizing complex patterns, U.S. Patent 3,069,654, 18 December 1962
10. Duda, R.O., Hart, P.E.: Use of the Hough transformation to detect lines and curves in pictures. Commun. ACM **15**(1), 11–15 (1972). doi:10.1145/361237.361242
11. Rumelhart, D.E., Hinton, G.E., Williams, R.J.: Learning internal representations by error propagation. Parallel Distrib. Process. Explor. Microstruct. Cognit. **1**, 318–362 (1986)

Breath Chair: Reduce Fear and Anxiety by Simulating Breathing Movements

Shunsuke Yanaka[1(✉)] and Takayuki Kosaka[2]

[1] Graduate School of Engineering, Kanagawa Institute of Technology, Atsugi, Japan
s1495001@cce.kanagawa-it.ac.jp
[2] Kanagawa Institute of Technology, Atsugi, Japan
kosaka@ic.kanagawa-it.ac.jp

Abstract. In this paper, we proposed the concept to alleviate fear or anxiety by reproducing the sensation of being with someone and developed Breath Chair. This system is the chair and the polyurethane sponge built into the backrest can reproduce the sensation of a human breathing by repeatedly evacuating the air and contracting similarly to a human chest during breathing. We evaluated our proposed system using two films as eliciting stimuli for emotion of fear or anxiety; fear levels or anxiety levels the experiment were examined using State-Trait Anxiety Inventory (STAI), heart rate and fingertip temperature. STAI was used before and after the viewing of films. Heart rate and fingertip temperature were measured throughout the viewing of the films. Score of STAI and heart rate were no significant difference. Fingertip temperature were higher with simulated breathing than without, revealing a significant difference. There was significant difference. These evaluation results suggested that subjects' fear or anxiety decreased as a result of simulating breathing.

Keywords: Substitute robot · Simulating breathing · Fear · Anxiety

1 Introduction

While fear and anxiety are emotions that function as a self-defence mechanism by preparing a person to fight back against or escape from a threat, they may also cause neurotic disorders (also referred to as depression or anxiety disorders) when experienced to an excessive degree. The estimated number of patients with depression and similar disorders in Japan was 112,000 in 2014, and the estimated number of patients with neurotic disorders and the like was 59,000. These estimated numbers have been on the rise since 1996 [1]. Furthermore, approximately 67% of Japanese people experience worry and/or anxiety in their daily lives [2]. Therefore, we developed the Breath Chair as a system to alleviate emotions such as fear and anxiety (Fig. 1).

Physical contact has been cited as a method of reducing fear and anxiety. Physical contact triggers the secretion of oxytocin, which has been reported to act to suppress anxiety [3]. Therefore, being around others and engaging in physical contact could reduce fear and anxiety. An experiment by Gergen et al. [4] examined people's reactions to being in a well-lit room and to being in a pitch-dark room, which was speculated to

© Springer International Publishing AG 2017
S. Lackey and J. Chen (Eds.): VAMR 2017, LNCS 10280, pp. 478–492, 2017.
DOI: 10.1007/978-3-319-57987-0_39

induce fear. In this experiment, approximately 90% of subjects intentionally made physical contact with other people in the pitch-dark room despite it being their first meeting with these other people, and approximately 50% reportedly hugged each other. Furthermore, Gergen et al. reported seeing no physical contact or hugging in the well-lit room. These findings suggest that physical contact is a means of alleviating fear and anxiety. Moreover, the other person with whom you make physical contact does not need to be a specific person, such as a close friend, lover or family member. This is because even physical contact with an "unspecified" person is thought to alleviate fear and anxiety. However, even if physical contact with an unspecified person is successful in reducing fear and anxiety, intimacy between the people making physical contact is considered deeply related to the inherent act of physical contact in humans—with the exception of specific environments such as darkness. Hall [5] categorises inter-personal distance into close distance, personal distance, social distance and public distance and describes how the physical distance between people communicating with each other is proportional to the psychological distance. This suggests that physical contact between people is an act that is difficult to establish, with the exception of specific people with whom we have a close relationship, such as friends, lovers and family members.

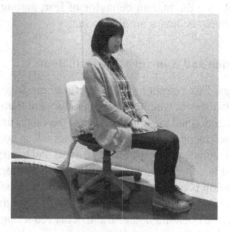

Fig. 1. Using Breath Chair

However, the environment in Japan has recently been changing into one where it is difficult to initiate physical contact in daily life, even with specific people with whom one may have a close relationship. The rise in the percentage of unmarried people is leading to reduced proportions of people living together with a spouse or child [6]. Moreover, the proportion of single-person households has been increasing year on year, reaching 27.1% in 2014 and accounting for more than a fourth of all households [7]. These circumstances may also be reducing the opportunities for physical contact with spouses and children, with whom people have close relationships. Thus, initiating physical contact in daily life is now becoming more difficult. We therefore developed a system that simulates the feeling of physical contact by using a substitute for actual physical contact to reduce fear and anxiety. We then examined the effects of the simulated physical contact of this developed system, which evokes the presence of an unspecified "someone," on fear and anxiety.

2   Related Work

2.1   Classification of Emotional Behavior

With regard to the workings and mechanism of the human heart, Ekman [8] identified the features of basic human emotions as being suggestive universal signals, and emotions as having a specific physiological state, starting in a short time, lasting only a short time and occurring spontaneously. Based on these features, and from the perspective of facial expressions, emotional behavior can be classified into the six types known as happiness, fear, disgust, anger, sadness, and surprise.

Further, May [9], in regard to the relationship between types of anxiety and fear, described fear as a response to a clear threat, while anxiety, on the other hand, is not clear, and is rather a vague response to an unspecified threat.

In this study, we link this to physiological state, and based on Ekman's classification of basic emotions, deal with the human behavior of fear, among others. Furthermore, we handle anxiety as human behavior similar to fear.

2.2   Verbal Information and Non-verbal Information

Kurokawa [10], in regard to communication, defined messages as information that humans could read, regardless of whether such messages are transmitted consciously or unconsciously. He further defined the transmission of messages using "words" as verbal, and messages transmitted using means other than "words" as non-verbal. Examples of non-verbal information include not only bodily gestures and hand gestures, but may also refer to tone of voice, skin color, clothing, sneezing and yawning.

Non-verbal information is considered to greatly impact the smoothness of communication. Watanabe et al. [11, 12] reported that the ON-OFF of the speaker's voice and breathing, in relation to the phenomenon of the listener retracting their breathing, plays an important role in smooth communication. This is not only the case for adults, and tests involving infants and their mothers show that this retraction phenomenon also exists in communication during the early stages of development. They reported that this non-verbal interaction is an essential form of communication in human biology.

In this way, not only bodily gestures or hand gestures, but the message qualities possessed by physiological non-verbal information are also considered to be important, and there are many studies dealing with physiological non-verbal information. For "glowworm communications" by Kizuka et al. [13], the rhythm of exhaling and inhaling in the user's breathing is visualized by LEDs by changing the color. This envisages use between two persons, and breathing and transmission of messages with those changes acts as an aid to communication. Furthermore, in the "Lovable Couch" by Iwamoto et al. [14], presentation of the heartbeat is seen as information with which to judge the friendliness brought by their communication partner when men and women are meeting for the first time. Presentation of the heartbeat is a factor in judging the friendliness brought by one's communication partner, and a positive correlation between actual friendliness and heartbeat information has also been derived through experiments. Based on these results, this is an aid in judging the friendliness brought by a member of the opposite sex and communication.

As shown by the aforementioned examples, thus far there have been studies on aids to communication and the impact on emotional behavior using the presentation of non-verbal information, such as breathing and heartbeat and changes in the same. However, there have been few studies dealing with the continuous transmission of fixed physiological information in a restful state during normal times.

Therefore, as the objective of this paper, rather than dealing with variable physiological non-verbal information and its messages, we have studied the impact on emotional behavior of simply being with "someone", through the continuous presentation of fixed physiological information. We focus on breathing as one of the physiologically essential forms of communication from the study by Watanabe et al. [11, 12], and propose the movement of the chest during human breathing as an element artificially providing the sensation of bodily contact. We have developed a system that aims to relieve fear and anxiety by artificially providing the sensation of bodily con-tact through chest movement during fixed human breathing in a restful state.

2.3 Robots as an Alternative to Living Things and the Reduction of Anxiety

Thus far, studies using robots as alternatives for living things have been actively conducted. Among these studies, the seal-like robot "Paro" by Shibata et al. [15] has been used as an alternative to animal therapy in welfare facilities. Furthermore, in experiments in robot therapy carried out in pediatric hospital wards, positive results have been achieved using Paro to improve mood and to alleviate anxiety when children are away from their parents.

There have also been studies conducted on the materials and mechanisms of robots and soft toys, including research on the use of soft materials with the aim of preventing damage to devices and user injury that may result from this [16]. Additionally, Takase et al. [17] used soft materials from the perspective not only of damage and resulting accidents, but from the perspective that the feeling of hardness to touch in contrast to the external appearance of the soft toy robot may induce a feeling of unease in the user, and become a factor creating a sense of distance in the user's interaction with the robot.

We have developed a doll-type system in which, through the expansion and con-traction of a balloon using air, we artificially present the movements of the chest when living creatures breathe [18]. However, whereas a balloon can be said to have the advantage that it is soft, on the one hand, because it is a highly elastic body, there is the problem that it can warp greatly when external pressure is applied. Due to this highly elastic quality, it is difficult for the balloon to maintain the core of the doll, or an unnatural warping sensation is given to the user from the external appearance of the doll. Further-more, there is also the risk of damage or rupturing caused by children handing the blown-up balloon in a rough way. Based on this, therefore, we proposed, as the mechanism of this system for presenting chest movement at the time of human breathing, not a balloon swollen by air, but rather presented this in terms of the volume changes for compression and decompression in relation to a balloon containing a urethane sponge.

2.4   Presence with Tele-Existence

In the field of Tele-Existence, there are studies in regard to using robots to communicate the sense of presence of humans remotely. Sakamoto et al. [19] defined the sense of presence as a strong feeling of "clearly, I am here", and is developing a re-motely operated android robot system to communicate this human "sense of presence". Modeled on actually present people, results obtained from an experiment using the robot "Geminoid HI-1", which closely resembles humans, and a remotely operated system, showed that it created a stronger sense of presence compared to existing media such as telephones or videoconferencing.

Sumioka et al. [20], as part of an approach to using a human-like robot as communication media, researched the impact of differences in human-like design in external form. The external form of communication media became closer in stages to a human, transitioning from only voice via speaker, to the trunk, the trunk and head, the trunk, head and two arms, to the trunk, head, two arms and one leg and finally to the trunk, head, two arms and two legs. The differences in how easy it was for the user to project a conversation partner on the robot were researched. As a result, it was reported that when the external form was of a trunk only, there was no significant difference to when the voice was only from a speaker.

The sense of presence is largely dependent on the user's perception and it is difficult to discuss simply from the physical perspective of external form and behavior. For example, when people communicate via a remotely operated robot, doubt arises as to whether it is the robot itself or the operator operating the robot from a remote location that recognizes the interaction between behavior. In response to this issue, Yamaoka et al. [21] use an autonomously operated robot, and survey differences in the impression evaluation in cases where the test subject is taught that the robot is being operated by a program and in cases where they are told that it is being operated by an operator. The result of this was that, regardless of these conditions, 2/3 of the test subjects reported that they felt like they were interacting with the robot itself, whereas the remaining 1/3 reported that they felt like they were interacting with the operator operating the robot remotely, and that this interaction was influenced by prior knowledge.

From this, in regard to the system that we are proposing for artificially presenting chest movements in human breathing, it is considered necessary to design and evaluate the considered system from both a physical perspective and the perspective of human recognition. First, in relation to external form, in an experiment by Sumioka et al. [20], it was found that where the external form was only the trunk, no significant difference was seen in terms of the user recognition to when it was just a voice from a speaker. From this, we can consider that the external form with just a trunk has very little effect on user recognition, compared to an external form containing arms/legs and a head, and we can exclude, as much as possible, the effect of external form, and present simulated movements of the chest, surveying its effect. Based, on this we decided to create the chest section only.

Furthermore, giving the robot an external form that resembles people who are actually there, as a human-like interface, promises to enable the user to experience the robot as if a person is actually present. On the other hand, however, this raises the issue that it does not suit situations wherein the robot is used as a substitute for an unspecified large number of people. In this paper, our objective is to examine the effects of the developed system on fear and anxiety by giving simulated physical contact to an unspecified "someone"; we have avoided "external forms" that resemble a specified "someone".

We decided to control the presented chest movements based on the breathing speed of actual adults; however, in this case, it is not possible to distinguish whether the effect of the movements presented by the proposed system are being recognized as chest movements when humans are breathing, or simply the effect of recognizing it as physical movement. For this reason, based on an experiment by Yamaoka et al. [21], when presenting the simulated movements of the chest, the test subject was told that the breathing of a different test subject in a different room was being sensed and presented via the developed system. We also decided to conduct an oral survey after the experiment, and confirm user recognition in relation to the presented chest movements.

3 Breath Chair: A Breathing Movement Simulation System that Uses Vacuum Pressure

The Breath Chair is a system designed to reduce fear and anxiety by giving users the feeling of physical contact through simulating the movement of a human chest during breathing. A study by Bauman et al. [22] of sitting time during weekdays in adults from 20 countries around the world revealed that Japanese adults spend a median length of approximately 420 min in total sitting each weekday. This study also found that this median sitting time was the longest in Japan compared to all countries examined. As the current lifestyle of Japanese people involves spending one-third of the day seated, we decided to have the chair-based device in our system simulate the movement of a human chest during breathing against the backs of users. This system uses the change in volume arising from repeated compression and decompression of a built-in polyurethane sponge in a vacuum to simulate the movement of a human chest during breathing.

3.1 System Configuration

This system has a built-in polyurethane sponge sealed in a compression bag to mimic the movement of a human chest during breathing (Fig. 2). Air is discharged from the compression bag-sealed polyurethane sponge by a vacuum pump to perform compression. To decompress the polyurethane sponge, the discharge of air by the vacuum pump is stopped and outside air is naturally insufflated. The Arduino Uno is used to control the electromagnetic valve via which air is repeatedly discharged and insufflated to compress and decompress the polyurethane sponge (Fig. 3).

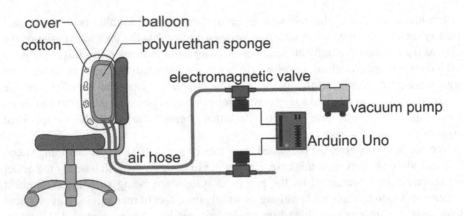

Fig. 2. System configuration

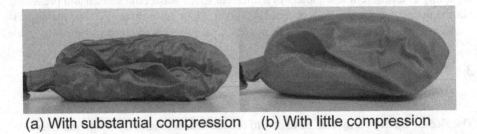

(a) With substantial compression   (b) With little compression

Fig. 3. Comparing the amount of volume in the polyurethane sponge

The amount of change in the circumferential length of the polyurethane sponge during compression and decompression is based on differences in chest expansion by adults Shôbo et al. [23] examined the difference in chest expansion during inhalation and exhalation when breathing deeply in an upright sitting position and reported a difference of 3.2 ± 1.2 cm at the third rib, 3.3 ± 0.8 cm at the xiphoid process of the sternum, and 3.0 ± 0.8 cm at the tenth rib. In our system, we set the amount of change in the circumferential length of the polyurethane sponge during compression and decompression at approximately 3.3 cm based on the intermediate point of the three aforementioned measurement points, or the results for the xiphoid process of the sternum—where the amount of change is said to be largest.

The breathing speed and the rate of the inhalation-exhalation rhythm of this system were based on average adult breathing speeds and rates [24]. At rest, the average adult breathes at a rate of 12 to 18 breaths per minute. The difference in chest expansion in this system was set so that the polyurethane sponge expansion was controlled at a rate of 12 times per minute, considering this was based on the results of measurements taken during deep breathing. Moreover, as the ratio of the rhythm of inhalation and exhalation in adults is almost 1:3, we also set the rhythm of inhalation and exhalation of air in this system to a ratio of 1:3.

4   Experiment: Effect on User Fear and Anxiety

We conducted an experiment in relation to this system, with the objective of alleviating fear and anxiety, with the aim of surveying the effects on user fear and anxiety. As a psychological indicator, we used the State-Trait Anxiety Inventory (hereafter, referred to as STAI) state anxiety scale, and as a physiological indicator, we used fingertip surface skin temperature. We provided visual stimulation to the test subjects to evoke the emotional behavior of fear or anxiety, and evaluated changes in each of the indicators, depending on whether this system was used or not.

The experiment used a room in an air conditioning facility in which people did not enter or leave. The lighting within the room, based on the experiment of Honda et al. [25], was set to approximately 30 lx. To eliminate factors affecting the sympathetic nervous system as much as possible, the test subjects were instructed to refrain from alcohol the day before and exercise on the day in question, and were not given any-thing other than water to drink 2 h before the start of the experiment. The visual stimulation was presented by placing a 23-inch display approximately 1 m in front of the test subject. During the experiment, the examiner was constantly absent from the test room, and the test subject was left alone in the test room.

Adults were chosen as the test subjects because they were able to adapt more easily to the test environment. Furthermore, as the Spielberger et al. [26] experiment, in which STAI was created, was an experiment aimed at university students, adult university students were also used in this experiment. This experiment was conducted on 12 men and women (age 21.5 ± 0.8 years old, mean $\pm$ S.D.) who consented to cooper-ate in the experiment. The consent of the test subjects was obtained after explaining, in both verbal and written form, the purpose of this study, the experiment method, the fact that they would not be disadvantaged for refusing to participate in the experiment, that they could freely choose to withdraw cooperation even after the experiment had started, that the acquired data would be used for statistical processing, that no investigation would take place to identify individuals, and that privacy would be protected.

4.1   Evaluation Indicators

In this experiment, we used psychological indicators and physiological indicators. The psychological indicator STAI state anxiety scale was used as an anxiety indicator.

Measurements of oxytocin, which are said to work to control fear and anxiety, mainly use the method of measuring levels of concentration within the blood. How-ever, due to the fact that it requires the invasive action of drawing blood and that there is no simple method for handling or processing the sampled blood, we did not use oxytocin as an evaluation indicator in this experiment.

STAI includes scales for both state anxiety and trait anxiety. The higher the value, the more anxiety this expresses, and distribution occurs for each respectively within a range of 20 points and 80 points. State anxiety is a transient state reaction to the phenomenon invoking the anxiety and measures "what I am actually feeling now". The scale for trait anxiety is "normally, generally how do I feel", and these are used as long-term indicators. The STAI used in this experiment, based on the STAI created by

Spielberger et al., newly creates items to express the state anxiety and trait anxiety in Japanese culture according to Hidano et al. [27], and these are scales to investigate reliability and appropriateness.

As a physiological indicator, fingertip surface skin temperature is used to indicate fear and anxiety. Fingertip surface skin temperature was calculated as the average value for every 30 s, using a thermistor thermometer (NXFT15XH103FA2B) attached to the fingertip ventral section of the index finger of the left hand. When the sympathetic nervous system is excited, there is constriction of the peripheral blood vessels, causing a reduction in the blood flow, and the skin surface temperature in the peripheral area decreases. Even in the experiment by Kumamoto et al. [28], where the perception level for pain, etc., and psychological anxiety increased, a drop in the skin surface temperature was reported.

4.2 Stimuli Invoking Emotional Behavior, Such as Anxiety or Fear

We used load stimuli for invoking emotional behavior such as fear or anxiety to invoke emotional behavior such as anxiety or fear in the test subject(s) and measure significant changes in its alleviation. As a means of invoking emotional behavior in the test room environment, visual stimuli invoke comparatively strong emotional behavior, and have the advantage of being non-invasive. Research into invoking specific emotional behavior through visual stimuli has been actively conducted [29, 30]. Furthermore, Honda et al. [25], in an experiment using visual stimuli, reported that significant changes occurred in fingertip skin surface temperature. Based on this, we used visual stimuli to invoke and stimulate anxiety and fear in this experiment.

For the visual stimuli in this experiment, we used images reported to invoke the emotional behavior of fear in the experiment by Alexandre et al. [31]. Alexandre et al. performed an experiment using an image showing one scene from a movie. Alexandre et al., for the image reported to invoke the emotional behavior of fear, used movies of virtually the same length of 210 s, that none of the test subjects in the experiment had seen up to that point. The two movies used were "Misery" (copyright; Castle Rock Entertainment, 1990), and "Scream 2" (copyright; Miramax Film Corp, 1997). The images used in this experiment were exactly the same as those used by Alexandre et al. with the same start and stop position, and the versions of the movies with Japanese language dubbing were used.

4.3 Giving False Information

The question of whether the physical movement caused by the compression and decompression of the polyurethane sponge is taken as the movement of the human chest when breathing is largely dependent on the user perception. For this reason, it was necessary to survey the impact of presenting simulated breathing before having the user recognize the movement of this system as movement of the chest when breathing. Therefore, with the aim of making the test subject recognize the movement presented by this system as chest movements when breathing in this experiment, we gave the test subject the false information in advance that "in the room next to the test room, there is one more test subject. That other test subject is currently resting and his/her breathing is being sensed in real time and presented as the movement of the chest via this device". Furthermore, with the aim of surveying the effect of human contact with an unspecific "someone" rather than a specific "some-one" with which they had a relationship, they were only told that it was "one other person". In the oral survey after the experiment, the test subjects were informed that it was false information. Moreover, with the aim of confirming whether they perceived that the movement presented by the system was not just physical movement, but chest movement when breathing, they confirmed with the test subject in the oral survey whether they actually believed that there was another test subject in the next room.

4.4 Experimental Protocol

The procedure for the experiment is shown in Fig. 4. In this experiment, they were first sat in a chair in the test environment and kept in a restful condition for 3 min, closing their eyes and relaxing. Following this, measurement was performed via a questionnaire method using the STAI state anxiety scale and STAI trait anxiety scale. Next, in intervention 1, a visual stimulus was provided with the aim of applying mental stress. Following this, a measurement was performed with the STAI state anxiety scale and then they rested for a total of 6 min. Furthermore, in intervention 2, the same operation as for intervention 1 was repeated. Finally, an oral survey was conducted in regard to impressions and opinions about the experiment.

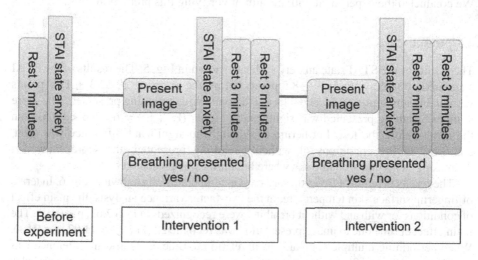

Fig. 4. Experimental protocol

For both intervention 1 and intervention 2, for one of the image presentations and 3-min rest periods directly after, with the condition of "with breathing presented", the system was operated and human chest movements when breathing were presented artificially. For the other time, under the condition of "without breathing presented", the system was not operated. This was conducted for the two image stimuli and under conditions of both breathing presented and not presented, for a total of four times. Through random allocation to all 12 of the test subjects with 3 people per pat-tern, this provided a counter balance for order effect and interaction.

We conducted a one-factor analysis of variance on the STAI state anxiety scale. We also conducted a two-factor variance analysis in relation to the fingertip surface temperature. The Tukey method was used for the variance analysis multiple comparison. This was significant in case of a significance level of $p < 0.05$.

For the fingertip surface skin temperature, based on the experiment by Honda et al. [25], the average value was calculated every 30 s. Furthermore, in regard to the various images presented in intervention 1 and intervention 2, the average value during the rest period immediately before was used as the baseline, and the change quantity was calculated by deducting the baseline from the value when presenting the image.

In terms of the STAI state anxiety scale, those test subjects for whom this was lower when presenting image stimulus without breathing before the test, and those who subjectively were not seen to have had emotional behavior of fear invoked, were considered unsuitable for the purposes of this test, and five such test subjects were excluded from the analysis.

Based on our hypothesis that fear and anxiety would be alleviated, even in the case of simulated bodily contact, we presented simulated chest movements during breathing as one element felt due to bodily contact, and predicted that this would reduce fear and anxiety. We predicted that the presentation of breathing would cause the STAI state anxiety scale score to decrease and the fingertip surface skin temperature to increase. We conducted the experiment with the aim of verifying this prediction.

4.5 Result

The results of the STAI state anxiety scale are shown in Fig. 5. The results of the STAI state anxiety scale were 41.3 ± 8.5 points before the experiment, 52.3 ± 11.7 points without breathing presented, and 44.4 ± 6.6 points with breathing presented. The score without breathing presented was significantly higher ($F(2, 12) = 6.23$, $p < 0.05$) than the score before the test. Furthermore, although no significant difference was seen, compared to the conditions of without breathing presented, the score showed a decreasing trend under conditions where breathing was presented.

The results in terms of fingertip surface skin temperature are shown in Fig. 6. In terms of fingertip surface skin temperature, in the two-factor variance analysis, the main effect of conditions for with and without breathing were recognized ($F(1, 7)$ 7.63, $p < 0.05$). The main effect of time due to image presentation was recognized ($F(7, 7) = 11.02$, $p < 0.01$). When performing multiple comparisons in relation to time, a significant difference was seen between 0 s and 30 s before presenting the image. A significant difference was also seen between 0 s, 90 s, 120 s, 180 s, and 210 s ($p < 0.01$).

The result of the oral survey after the experiment was that 4 out of the 7 test subjects analyzed perceived the presented breathing to be that of an actual human. The remaining 3 people were dubious, considering that it may have been human breathing or alternatively created by a program. None of the test subjects failed to perceive it as human breathing.

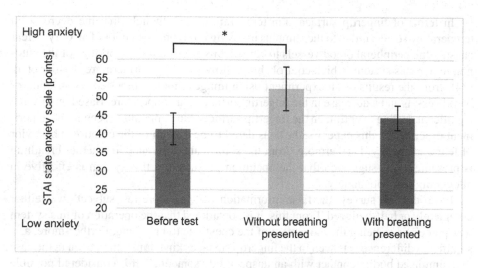

Fig. 5. Results of measuring the STAI state analysis scale (n = 7, *: p < 0.05)

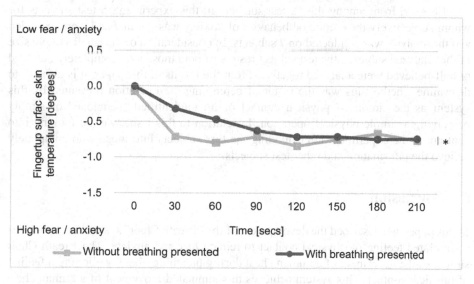

Fig. 6. Fingertip surface skin temperature measurement results (n = 7, *: p < 0.05)

4.6 Discussion

In the STAI state anxiety scale, there was a significant increase in the points for without breathing presented, compared to the points before the examination, so it is considered that for the test subjects being analyzed, this subjectively invoked the emotional behavior of anxiety. Furthermore, whereas no significant difference was seen, a decreasing trend was seen for with breathing presented compared to without breathing presented, so it is though that presenting breathing may have some effect in reducing anxiety.

In terms of fingertip surface skin temperature, it is thought that the decrease in temperature seen was due to the stimulus invoking emotional behavior of anxiety or fear causing the peripheral blood vessels to constrict as a result of the workings of the autonomic nervous system, which controls blood flow [32, 33]. Furthermore, Kistler et al. [34], from the results of an experiment using image stimulus, reported constriction of blood vessels and a decrease in the fingertip surface skin temperature. Based on this, the significant decline over time in the fingertip surface skin temperature seen in the experiment described in this paper can be considered to be a result of the emotional behavior of fear and anxiety. Furthermore, from the significant difference in whether breathing is presented, it is suggested that the operation presented in this system is effective in alleviating fear and anxiety.

From the oral survey, the false information of "one more test subject" was either completely or half-believed. From this, it is considered that the operation of this system was perceived as being the movement of the chest due to breathing. Further-more, as a significant difference was seen in the fingertip surface skin temperature, even in the case of a simulated bodily contact with an unspecified "someone", it is considered possible to alleviate fear and anxiety.

However, from among the 12 test subjects in this experiment, 5 test subjects for whom subjectively the emotional behavior of anxiety was not invoked were excluded and the analysis was conducted on 7 subjects. In consideration of the small sample size of the analyzed subjects, the test subject results of both those who completely believed or half-believed were analyzed together. From the results of this paper, it is difficult to determine whether this was the result of perceiving the operation presented by this system as the simulated physical contact of an unidentified "someone" or simply perceiving a simple physical operation. In relation to this issue, we are looking into continuing the experiment after dividing the test subjects into those who completely believe the information and other test subjects.

5   Conclusion

In this paper, we described the development of the "Breath Chair" system that pro-vides a simulated feeling of physical contact to reduce fear and anxiety. The Breath Chair simulates the movement of a human chest during breathing, thereby eliciting a feeling of physical contact. This system achieves this simulated movement of a human chest during breathing by repeatedly compressing and decompressing an in-built polyurethane sponge in a vacuum to change its volume. This gives users a feeling of physical contact that is intended to reduce their fear and anxiety.

We surveyed the effect of the developed system on fear and anxiety from the simu-lated physical contact envisaged as being from an unidentified "someone". Using the STAI state anxiety scale, we analyzed test subjects in whom fear and anxiety were subjectively invoked. For those test subjects who completely believed or half-believed the false information that there was "another test subject", a decreasing trend in the number of points on the STAI state anxiety scale, and a significant difference was seen in the fingertip surface skin temperature was seen depending on whether or not breathing was presented. Based on this, the possibility that fear and anxiety could be alleviated, even when the bodily contact is simulated with an unidentified "someone", was suggested.

Moving forward, we are looking into continuing the experiment after dividing the test subjects into those who completely believed the false information and those test subjects who only half-believed the information. By investigating the presentation of simulated physiological information and the effect on emotional behavior, we plan to further study the positive benefit produced by people being together, without being limited to only a specific "someone" with whom one has an intimate relationship, such as friends, lovers, or family.

Acknowledgments. The first author would like to express his thanks to Prof. Motofumi HATTORI (Kanagawa Institute of Technology) for his kind advices.

References

1. Ministry of Health, Labour and Welfare: Summary of 2014 patient surveys. http://www.mhlw.go.jp/toukei/saikin/hw/kanja/14/index.html. Accessed 10 Feb 2016
2. Cabinet Office, National Opinion on People's Life. http://survey.gov-online.go.jp/h26/h26-life/index.html. Accessed 14 July 2016
3. Onaka, T., Yoshida, K., Takayanagi, Y.: Oxytocin and anxiety/fear. Anti-aging Med. **11**(1), 24–33 (2015)
4. Gergen, K.J., Gergen, M.M., Barton, W.H.: Deviance in the dark. Psychol. Today **7**, 129–130 (1973)
5. Hall, E.T.: The Hidden Dimension. Doubleday & Company, New York (1966)
6. Iwai, N.: The current picture and overall trends of the japanese family based on JGSS cumulative data from 2000–2010. Jpn. Soc. Fam. Sociol. **23**(1), 20–42 (2011)
7. Statistics and Information Department, Minister's Secretariat, Ministry of Health, Labour and Welfare: Charts and Graphs of the Comprehensive Survey of Living Conditions, 2012, from the results of the Comprehensive Survey of Living Conditions (2010), Health, Labour and Welfare Statistics Association (2012)
8. Ekman, P.: Basic Emotions. In: Dalgleish, T., Power, M. (eds.) Handbook of Cognition and Emotion, pp. 45–60. New York, John Wiley (1999)
9. May, R.: The Meaning of Anxiety. Ronald Press Co, New York (1950)
10. Kurokawa, T.: Nonverbal Information Phase. Ohm-sha, Tokyo (1994)
11. Watanabe, T., Okubo, M.: Physiological analysis of entrainment in communication. Trans. Inf. Process. Soc. Jpn. **39**(5), 1225–1231 (1998)
12. Watanabe, T., Okubo, M.: Virtual communication system for human interaction analysis. Trans. Inf. Process. Soc. Jpn. **40**(2), 670–676 (1999)
13. Kizuka, A., Yanagi, H., Mima, Y.: Hotaru-Tsushin: a communication tool for visualizing respiratory information. In: Interactive System and Software Workshop WISS 2007 (2007)
14. Iwamoto, T., Masuko, S.: Lovable couch: supporting dispelling distrust feelings using heartbeat variability at the meeting place. In: Interaction 2015, pp. 866–871 (2015)
15. Shibata, T., et al.: Mental commit robot and its application to therapy of children. In: IEEE/ASME International Conference on Advanced Intelligent Mechatronics, vol. 2, pp. 1053–1058 (2001)

16. Kobayashi, K., Yoshikai, T., Goto, T., Inaba, M.: Development of self-protection behaviors in fall down by a robot with distributed soft flesh and joint shock resistive mechanism. J. Robot. Soc. Jpn. **31**(4), 416–423 (2013)
17. Takase, Y., Yamashita, Y., Ishikawa, T., Shiina, M., Mitake, H., Hasegawa, S.: Stuffed toy robot soft to the bone with various body motions. Trans. Virtual Reality Soc. Jpn. **18**(3), 327–336 (2013)
18. Yanaka, S., Kosaka, T., Hattori, M.: ZZZoo pillows: sense of sleeping alongside somebody. In: ACM SIGGRAPH Asia 2013 Emerging Technologies, Article No.17 (2013)
19. Sakamoto, D., Kanda, T., Ono, T., Ishiguro, H., Hagita, N.: Android as a telecommunication medium with a human-like presence. Inf. Process. Soc. Jpn. J. **48**(12), 3729–3738 (2007)
20. Sumioka, H., Koda, K., Nishio, S., Minato, T., Ishiguro, H.: "Revisiting ancient design of human form for communication avatar: design considerations from chronological development of dogu. In: Proceedings of the IEEE International Symposium on Robot and Human Interactive Communication, pp. 726–731 (2013)
21. Yamaoka, F., Kanda, T., Ishiguro, H., Hagita, N.: Interacting with a human or a humanoid robot? Inf. Process. Soc. Jpn. J. **48**(11), 3577–3587 (2007)
22. Bauman, A., Ainsworth, B.E., Sallis, J.F., et al.: The descriptive epidemiology of sitting. A 20-country comparison using the international physical activity questionnaire (IPAQ). Am. J. Prev. Med. **41**(2), 228–235 (2011)
23. Shôbo, A., Kakizaki, F.: Relationship between chest expansion and the change in chest volume. J. Exerc. Physiol. **29**(6), 881–884 (2014)
24. Onodera, A., Jindai, Y.: Seijin naika 1. Chûôhôkishuppan (2011)
25. Honda, A., Masaki, H., Yamazaki, K.: Influence of emotion-inducing film stimuli on autonomic response specificity. Japan. J. Physiol. Psychol. Psychophysiol. **20**(1), 9–17 (2002)
26. Spielberger, Charles D., Reheiser, Eric C.: Assessment of emotions: anxiety, anger, depression, and curiosity. Appl. Psychol. Health Well-Being **1**(3), 271–302 (2009)
27. Hidano, N., Fukuhara, M., Iwawaki, M., Soga, S., Charles, D.S.: State-Trait Anxiety Inventory-Form JYZ, Jitsumukyoiku-shuppan (2000)
28. Kumamoto, M., Yanagida, M., Hotomi, S., et al.: Study on evaluation method of stress and recovery: nasal skin temperature and perception levels and psychological states. Japan. J. Pediatr. Dent. **46**(5), 578–584 (2008)
29. Gross, J.J., Levenson, R.W.: Emotion elicitation using films. Cogn. Emot. **9**, 87–108 (1995)
30. Noguchi, M., Sato, W., Yoshikawa, S.: Films as emotion-eliciting stimuli: the ratings by Japanese subjects. Techn. Rep. IEICE. HCS **104**(745), 1–6 (2005)
31. Schaefera, A., Nilsb, F., Sanchezc, X., Philippotb, P.: Assessing the effectiveness of a large database of emotion-eliciting films: a new tool for emotion researchers. Cogn. Emot. **24**(7), 1153–1172 (2010)
32. Collet, C., Vernet-Maury, E., Delhomme, G., et al.: Autonomic nervous system response patterns specificity to basic emotions. J. Auton. Nerv. Syst. **62**, 45–57 (1997)
33. Levenson, R.W., Ekman, P., Friesen, W.V.: Voluntary facial action generates emotion-specific autonomic nervous system activity. Psychophysiology **27**(4), 363–384 (1990)
34. Kistler, A., Mariauzouls, C., von Berlepsch, K.: Fingertip temperature as an indicator for sympathetic responses. Int. J. Psychophysiol. **29**(1), 35–41 (1998)

Health Issues in VR

VR Rio 360: The Challenges of Motion Sickness in VR Environments

Paulo Carvalho, Taynah Miyagawa, Fran Maciel[✉], and Paulo Melo

Samsung SIDIA, Manaus, Brazil
{p.alexandre,taynah.mello,francimar.m,paulo.melo}@samsung.com

Abstract. Motion sickness is a major concern that Virtual Reality (VR) manufacturers face and that has the potential to hinder this technology popularization. With related research since its inception in the 1960 s, motion sickness has been the subject of research by various institutions around the world. We have analyzed some of those studies and, along with the development of VR Rio 360, application developed by SIDIA (Samsung R&D Center in Brazil) for Samsung Gear VR, it was possible to investigate the factors that can cause this side-effect and also present possible technical solutions to reduce its occurrence in the application.

Keywords: Virtual Reality · Motion sickness · Cybersickness

1 Introduction

Virtual Reality (VR) is a mobile or computer simulated environment that gives an user a sense of immersion and presence through three-dimensional (3D) images with the support of visual, auditory and tactile feedback [1]. At this time, the relevance of VR is in the possibilities that this tool presents with applications that range from entertainment areas, such as games and movies, to medical and even military areas, with healthcare training and simulated air fighting, for instance. In the past five years, the technology behind VR and its multiple applications has developed quickly with the support of companies from the technology sector (e.g., HTC, Sony, Samsung, and Google). Due to that, VR has gathered the interest of content providers and researchers in the pursue of better and detailed studies regarding the current shortcomings of its applications.

Currently, one of the technology's biggest challenges is the discomfort caused by the continued use of its applications. In point of fact, experiencing discomfort as a side-effect of using these applications has been one of the biggest threats to widespread VR adoption over the past decades, as few people accept a technology that causes them to suffer while using it, and in some cases long after using it [3].

The current work presents definitions and discussions related to VR's discomfort issues, and also a case study related to the search for a solution for these problems in a application.

© Springer International Publishing AG 2017
S. Lackey and J. Chen (Eds.): VAMR 2017, LNCS 10280, pp. 495–504, 2017.
DOI: 10.1007/978-3-319-57987-0_40

1.1 Technology-Related Conditions

The discomfort that users feel while or after experiencing Virtual Environments (VEs) is often defined as motion sickness, simulator sickness or cybersickness. Although there are connections between the symptoms experienced in motion sickness, simulator sickness and cybersickness, their groups of symptoms can help to differentiate the three conditions [3].

Motion sickness refers to adverse symptoms and observable signs that are associated with exposure to real and/or apparent motion [11, 12]. It can be caused by any type of moving vehicle, including submarines, airplanes and trains, but it can also arise through playful activities such as a spinning chair, or a simple playground swing. Commonly known as seasickness, airsickness or car sickness, motion sickness appears to be more common in the age group between 4 and 12 years, where there is a predisposition to the condition [3]. Other factors that can increase the possibility of the condition's occurrence are related to user characteristics (i.e. experience, gender, field independence, age, illness, mental rotation ability, postural instability, susceptibility to motion sickness), personality factors (individuals low in extraversion, high in neurosis, and/or high in anxiety), and/or exposure schedules (e.g. duration, repetition). However, nearly all individuals experience it if exposed to enough motion stimuli [12].

Simulator sickness is a subset of motion sickness that is typically experienced by pilots who undergo training for extended periods of time in flight simulators. Possibly, the observed differences between the simulator's motion and the machine may be the cause of the condition. It is important to note that a simulator is not only a machine that creates a full environment, but it can also be represented by a head-mounted display with several sensors and motion indicators (e.g. floor vibration, surround sound, movement capture). Apathy, sleepiness, disorientation, fatigue, vomiting and general discomfort are the symptoms to which users can be submitted to after the use of simulators.

On the other hand, cybersickness is not caused by physical movement, but rather by the experience of seeing the movement in a virtual reality content/system while your body is stationary. It is a visually induced motion sickness resulting from immersion in a computer-generated virtual world – results from shortcomings of the simulation, but not from the actual situation that is being simulated [12]. Among the symptoms of cybersickness are nausea, eye strain and dizziness. Thus all of the conditions mentioned above can be used to explain VR sickness, since they do not cover the Virtual Reality-related discomfort separately.

1.2 Cybersickness Causes

Even today, there are many discussions about the underlying symptoms related to cybersickness. These debates contribute to the formulation of strategies for creating environments where the probability of problems can be overcome [3]. Over the decades, three theories on the cause of cybersickness have gained relevance: poison theory, postural instability theory, and sensory conflict theory [2].

According to poison theory, there is an evolutionary mechanism of survival that is activated every time the user undergoes consistent sensory hallucinations through the ingestion of some kinds of poison. Poison theory attempts to explain the reason that causes motion sickness and cybersickness from an evolutionary point of view [3]. The theory indicates that poison ingestion is responsible for physiological effects related to the coordination of visual, vestibular, and other input sensory systems. These physiological effects act as a premature warning mechanism that increases survival, causing a reflux of stomach contents. The improper exploration of some virtual environments can affect the visual and vestibular systems to the point where the body misrepresents the information collected and concludes that it has ingested some toxic substance, causing emetic responses (vomiting and nausea are mechanisms designed to expel everything that the stomach considers to be toxic). Poison theory research presents an interesting point of view within the occurrence of cybersickness, but there are gaps in both predictive analysis and conclusions about why people who are sensitive to virtual environments do not always have an emetic response. Other unexplained absences refer to why some people suffer from cybersickness in VEs with certain stimuli while others do not suffer from the same stimuli. It is believed that there is a pattern of visual stimuli and/or vestibular system stimuli that trigger motion sickness, and accidentally activate brain sensors for the detection of toxins. However, this interpretation fails to explain the amplitude of symptoms and the varied individual responses, while there is currently limited evidence for this theory [3].

Whenever the environment suddenly presents changes in its form, making it impossible to learn the strategies of postural control, we have postural instability as a result. In many VEs, the normal restrictions of body movement can not keep up with any visual changes, which causes a conflict in the strategies of normal postural control resulting in the symptoms observed in cybersickness [3]. And the longer the instability time, the more likely the severity of the symptoms to be higher.

Furthermore, one of the most widely accepted theory for cybersickness is sensory conflict theory [2–4]. It addresses the conflicts between the visual and vestibular senses, two sensory systems involved in VEs [4]. The senses are responsible for presenting information about the spatial orientation of an individual and the perceived movement and conflict between these informations can occur in virtual worlds. For example, the visual system tells the brain that the body is in motion at the same time that the vestibular system says that the body is stationary, which causes the conflict between the sensory systems [3].

2   Technology Issues

The technology used in the development of VEs has evolved substantially recently for the delivery of more exciting experiences. However, there are a number of disorders that have been related to the use of these immersive experiences. Those disorders appear mostly because of one or a combination of the following issues: position tracking error, system lag, flicker, binocular-occlusion conflict, and vection.

2.1 Position Tracking Error

One of the key elements of VR technology is that it allows tracking of the user's head and some members (e.g. hands and arms) in physical space with an accurate representation of the user in the virtual space. In addition, the information provided to the user from the head tracking presents the correct perspective when viewed in a VE. However, position trackers do not have 100% accuracy, and this inaccuracy will be a determining factor for the cybersickness symptoms condition [6].

Those tracking devices also have a propensity for creating relatively unstable information that can be called jitter (a slight irregular movement). For example, consider a jittery tracker connected to the user's head. If this tracker is used to refresh the user's vision, then the sight will be in constant and uncontrollable motion even when the user is completely still. These conditions cause dizziness and lack of concentration after using VR headsets [8].

2.2 System Lag

System lag is the time between the user's action and its actual representation in a VE. A fairly common example of lag in VR is an user turning his/her head 30 degrees to watch a car passing in a VE. If the lag is high, the computer will not update the screen at the same time and the user will have to wait for the images to be positioned where they should be. This lag brings a very big nuisance and can trigger cybersickness symptoms [9].

2.3 Flicker

Flicker plays a significant role in the oculomotor component of cybersickness. Although it can become less noticeable over time, it can still lead to headaches and eyestrain [15].

Flicker has two interesting characteristics: the first refers to the difference between the individuals and the dependence of the flicker fusion frequency limit, and the second is related to the probability that the flicker will be amplified as the field of view increases, since the peripheral visual system has a greater sensitivity to flicker than the fovea (a small depression in the retina of the eye where visual acuity is highest) [10].

For the purpose of flicker reduction, the refresh rate of a system should be increased. An update rate of 30 Hz is an initial value for the reduction of fovea perception. However, refresh rates should be higher for peripheral areas. As technology increases, higher rates in visual displays should become more popular and accessible [2].

2.4 Binocular-Occlusion Conflict

The term binocular vision is reserved for living beings who have a large area of binocular overlap and use it to code depth. Many complex visual tasks, such as reading, detecting camouflaged objects, and eye-hand coordination are performed more effectively with two eyes than with one, even when the visual display contains no depth [17].

In order to perceive depth, the human eye relies on cues. Monocular cues are the ones that provide depth information while viewing a scene with only one eye and binocular cues are the ones that depend on two frontal eyes. Furthermore, occlusion happens when one object is fully or partially hidden, making it seem that is farther away than the object that is hiding it.

In virtual reality environments, the binocular occlusion provides the notion of object proximity and scenario depth for the observer. The content is presented first to one eye while the other is blocked (occlusion), then the opposite process is done. For developers, the challenge is to ensure that this whole process is not perceived by users – any pause or delay can cause disorientation.

Then, the binocular-occlusion conflict occurs when occlusion cues do not match binocular cues (e.g. when text is visible but appears at a distance behind a closer opaque object, it can be quite confusing and uncomfortable for the user) [11].

2.5   Vection

When a visual scene moves independently of how an user is physically moving, there can be a mismatch between what is seen and what is physically felt. This mismatch is specially discontenting when the virtual motion accelerates because the otolith system does not sense that same acceleration [11]. The otolith system is responsible for linear acceleration and deceleration, including gravity, mechanoreceptors, in the form of hair cells, converts acceleration into neural signs [6]. Lateral movement can also be a problem, presumably because we do not often strafe in the real world [11].

3   User Factors and Content Criteria

Types of discomfort reported by VR users are mostly dizziness, nausea, eye strain, vertigo, disorientation and fatigue [2]. Mapping those factors can be decisive in explaining which individuals are more affected and the potential reasons. The idea is that the severity and occurrence of symptoms can be related with age, sex, race, disease, and even user positioning [3].

Older people are less susceptible to cybersickness symptoms. Greater susceptibility involve children between 2 and 12 years old – from that, the incidence falls rapidly year after year until the age of 21 [4]. Regarding gender, women have a wider field of vision, which increases the perception of flicker and, consequently, the propensity to cybersickness [2]. Illnesses like (but not restricted to) fatigue, hangover, and flu are powerful agents to cybersickness [2]. Users under the influence of drugs and alcohol may also have a higher susceptibility to cybersickness symptoms [3]. Furthermore, according to the theory of postural instability, the user's posture, where and if he/she is sitting are important factors – the scenario where the user is sitting while using a VR device represents the safest posture for use and reduces potential problems in postural control [4].

Prolonged exposure to VR experiences can also increase the chances of occurrence and intensity of cybersickness effects, which suggests longer adaptation periods. One way to accelerate adaptation to VE is to use devices for short periods of time [3, 4]. Therefore, it is important to have a projection of possible tasks and consider their duration.

Subjective signs of cybersickness have been reported for more than two decades [7]. A little over a decade ago a great example of approach on this issue was published [10] where the authors collected 16 electrophysiological parameters while their subjects were exploring a VE. During this challenge, there was an increase in the values of some parameters (gastric tachyarrhythmias, eye blink rate, skin conductance, respiratory sinus arrhythmia and delta power of the electroencephalogram (EEG)) while others reduced (heart period, fingertip temperature and photoplethysmographic signal, and EEG beta-power). Among these modifications, several (gastric tachyarrhythmias, eye blink rate, respiration rate, respiratory sinus arrhythmia and heart rate) presented a significant positive correlation with the subjective cybersickness score. In other work the authors observed that VR immersion results in an expansion of the low frequency but not the high frequency components of the heart rate variability [14]; in combination with the previously cited work, this may be a clue that cybersickness is connected with the increase of the cardiac sympathetic outflow. Two studies reported that VR causes moderate changes with short duration (<10 min) in the static postural stability calculated by the body sway amplitude [3]. These experiences did not change the dynamic postural stability, while postural stability in both studies was calculated immediately before and shortly after the challenge.

4   VR Rio 360: A Case Study

Rio 360 [5] is a VR application developed by SIDIA (Samsung R&D Center in Brazil) for Samsung Gear VR. Its focus is to explore Rio de Janeiro city and 12 tourist attractions. The application was released on Samsung's high-end devices, such as: Galaxy S6 flat, S6 edge, S6 edge+, S7 flat, and S7 edge.

At the beginning of the project development, it was observed that most users felt some degree of dizziness and/or lightheadedness while using the application. Aiming to adjust and improve the quality of implemented features, a set of experiments was conducted with internal users. The study's sample was composed by 10 participants, with ages between 25 and 40 years. Participants were invited to test the application's features on sessions that lasted 30 min (in average). They were asked to perform the same set of questions after each new version of the application was released, while following the steps listed below:

- Exploratory navigation;
- Identification of User Interface elements (e.g. connection buttons);
- Navigation and identification of landmarks (Fig. 1);
- Exploration and identification of the data available on the landmarks' information postcards (Fig. 2).

The study's main exploration points were: camera movement, distance between the camera and UI elements, and the application's motion design elements. By the end of each experiment, users' feedback related to the application were collected.

Fig. 1. VR Rio 360's map with a few landmarks [7].

Fig. 2. VR Rio 360's landmark information postcard [7].

During the study, the issues that participants reported more often were related to camera's movement (considered very fast) and also related to the application's elements, which were positioned too close to the user, making it difficult to understand the information they wanted to convey.

The study brought to light major device factors that technology manufacturers need to consider, which are: lag, flicker, calibration, field of view, and ergonomics in general. As far as lag is concerned, effective motion tracking that reflects changes in vision is critical, as are real-time graphic displays that operate close to 50–60 Hz. The flicker of the display (with different levels of perception between users) takes the user's focus and causes eye fatigue [4] – flicker fusion is an important property of the device and is even more critical for wider fields of view as peripheral vision is more sensitive to flicker [2]. Low calibration potentiates the symptoms of cybersickness due to differences in the physical characteristics of users – stereoscopic screens requires a slightly deflected view of the virtual world for each eye and this deviation should be related as closely as possible to the interpupillary distance (the space between the pupil centers of both eyes, that varies from individual to individual [4]) inherent to each individual, as such pertinent calibration is necessary for each user.

Furthermore, the study's results included the reduction of overall use discomfort in the application through a set of improvements. The table below summarizes the major differences between the application's initial and final version parameters (Table 1):

Table 1. Comparison between the application's parameters (initial and final).

Description	First release	Final release
Comfort distance	450 m	300 m
Float height	160 m	20 m
Float speed cap (maximum value)	0.5 m per frame	2.5 m per frame
Position delta multiplier	0.65 (frame)	0.45 (frame)
Minimum position delta	200 m	100 m
Horizontal acceleration	1.01 m	1.003 m
Maximum distance delta	1250 m	600 m
Position delta	0	110.5059 m
Delta time	0	0.013333 m

The following content provides a brief description of each parameter used:

- Comfort distance is the parameter that indicates the ideal distance between the inter-action objects and the user – this distance is applied for navigation throughout the map and for interactions with the UI elements.
- Float height is the maximum height the user can navigate on the y-axis.
- Float speed cap is the maximum speed the user can reach while navigating the map.
- Position delta multiplier is a value to determine the updated position of the object in each frame through a multiplier.
- Minimum position delta is the lowest position value resulting from the calculation between the previous and current updates.
- Horizontal acceleration is the parameter responsible for establishing an acceleration limit value on the horizontal axis.
- Maximum distance delta is the factor that calculates which limit in the world space that the user can reach.
- Position delta is the value resulting from the difference between the updated calcu-lation and the previous calculation of the object's position.
- Delta time is the time in seconds taken to complete the reading of the last frame [16].

Oculus Best Practices guide [15] does not define a specific value for each of the parameters described above – instead, it justifies how they should be handled in order to minimize user discomfort. The initial parameters used were created by the project's developers after studying Unity's documentation and script library, while trying to create a navigation control that would be easier for users to experience.

The major application improvements were related to Comfort distance, Float height, Float speed cap, and Maximum distance delta. Furthermore, after analyzing the developer and user adaptation sides, it is possible to say that Float Speed cap and Comfort distance were the most difficult values to adjust since they are related to the user's control over navigation and speed while going through the application's map. For the developers, the difficulty was in finding an adequate value while working with a map that was not in a 1:1 scale – VR Rio 360 worked with the map of Rio de Janeiro and the objects on larger scales so the user could access the sights faster, the objects could have the animations occurring faster and the UI could be in the user's field of view.

5 Conclusions

During its development, the VR Rio 360 application presented issues related to movement speed and user acceleration in the environment, which was causing discomfort symptoms related to cybersickness. In the application, the user's vision was set to first person, a factor that potentialized motion sickness symptoms, such as nausea, dizziness, vertigo. Studies suggest that these symptoms can be minimized with the usage of controllers. For sure the addition of components which can increase natural movements tend to reduce the motion sickness in the users. Nonetheless, other factors must be analyzed, such as type and quality of graphics used in VR applications.

Experts say that the sound can be 40% or more of the VR experience, if a user hears a sound that doesn't match a typical human experience in a world that feels like a human experience it tend to cause confusion and sound unrealistic [11, 18]. In this application, the sound while navigating the map was created in order to make a connection between the user and the city of Rio de Janeiro through Bossa Nova and other sound effects were used for feedback. Sound could play a greater role in reducing the effects of motion sickness by helping in the user's immersion levels – this approach can be a subject of study for future works.

An in-depth study on the relationship between the level of realism in virtual environment and the incidence of motion sickness, and also the possibility of controlling the vestibular system – so that the body that is at rest can navigate freely through the virtual environment without suffering with the side effects of motion sickness – could also be subjects for future studies.

The team's next steps prioritize studies on the cerebral areas involved with the visual system, the galvanic vestibular system, which commands information related to the position and movements of the head and the proprioceptive system, responsible for postural and body movement. These studies will be important to understand the functioning of the brain during the performance of these three systems simultaneously and thus, we can present effective alternatives in the fight against motion sickness.

Acknowledgments. The conception of this essay was the result of the combined efforts from SIDIA's Solutions Team and UX & Design team. It is also important to highlight the company's performance in supporting and promoting research and development for systems that are present in the domestic market's leading technology products. For all those people involved in this project, our sincere appreciation.

References

1. Desai, P.R., Desai, P.N., Ajmera, K.D., Mehta, K.: A review paper on oculus rift-a virtual reality headset. Int. J. Eng. Trends Technol. (IJETT) **13**(4), 175–179 (2014). ISSN: 2231-5381. www.ijettjournal.org. Published by Seventh Sense Research Group. http://www.ijettjournal.org/volume-13/number-4/IJETT-V13P237.pdf
2. LaViola, J.J.: A discussion of cybersickness in virtual environments (2000). http://www.eecs.ucf.edu/~jjl/pubs/cybersick.pdf
3. Davis, S., Nesbitt, K., Nalivaiko, E.: Comparing the onset of cybersickness using the oculus rift and two virtual roller coasters (2015). http://crpit.com/confpapers/CRPITV167Davis.pdf
4. Kolasinski, E.: Simulator sickness in virtual environments. Technical report 1027, Army Research Institute for the Behavioral and Social Sciences (1995)
5. Rio 360 VR App on Oculus Store. https://www.oculus.com/experiences/gear-vr/1105507662843899/
6. LaValle, S.M.: Virtual Reality. Cambridge University Press, Cambridge (2017). University of Illinois. http://vr.cs.uiuc.edu/vrbooka4.pdf
7. Regan, E., Price, K.: The frequency of occurrence and severity of side-effects of immersion virtual reality. Aviat. Space Environ. Med. **65**, 527–530 (1994)
8. Biocca, F.: Will simulation sickness slow down the diffusion of virtual environment technology. Presence **1**(3), 334–343 (1992)
9. Pausch, R., Crea, T., Conway, M.: A literature survey for virtual environments: military flight simulators visual systems and simulator sickness. Presence **1**(3), 344–363 (1992)
10. Boff, K.R., Lincoln, J.E.: Engineering data compendium: human perception and performance. In: AAMRL, Wright-Patterson Air Force Base, pp. 166–191 (1988)
11. Jerald, J.: The VR Book: Human-Centered Design for Virtual Reality. Association for Computing Machinery and Morgan & Claypool, New York (2015)
12. Brainard, A.: Motion sickness definition. Medscape portal, Neurology section (2017). http://emedicine.medscape.com/article/2060606-overview
13. Kim, Y., Kim, H.J., Kim, E.N., Ko, H.D., Kim, H.T.: Characteristic changes in the physiological components of cybersickness. Psychophysiology **42**(5), 616–625 (2005)
14. Ohyama, S., Nishiike, S., Watanabe, H., Matsuoka, K., Akizuki, H., Takeda, N., Harada, T.: Autonomic responses during motion sickness induced by virtual reality. Auris Nasus Larynx **34**(3), 303–306 (2007)
15. Oculus Best Practices 2017. https://static.oculus.com/documentation/pdfs/intro-vr/latest/bp.pdf. Accessed 9 Feb 2017
16. Unity Documentation Scripting API 2017. https://docs.unity3d.com/ScriptReference/index.html. Accessed 28 Feb 2017
17. Howard, I.P., Roger, B.J.: Binocular Vision and Stereopsis, vol. 29. Oxford University Press and Clarendon Press, Oxford (1995)
18. Fictum, C.: VR UX: learn VR UX, storytelling & design. Creater Space Independent Publishing Platform (2016)

Dispelling the Gorilla Arm Syndrome: The Viability of Prolonged Gesture Interactions

Jeffrey T. Hansberger[1(✉)], Chao Peng[2], Shannon L. Mathis[2],
Vaidyanath Areyur Shanthakumar[2], Sarah C. Meacham[2],
Lizhou Cao[2], and Victoria R. Blakely[2]

[1] Army Research Laboratory, Huntsville, AL, USA
jeffrey.t.hansberger.civ@mail.mil
[2] University of Alabama Huntsville, Huntsville, AL, USA

Abstract. The use of gestures as a way to interact with computer systems has shown promise as a natural way to interact and manipulate digital information. However, users performing mid-air gestures for even moderate periods of time experience arm fatigue and discomfort, earning its name of the gorilla arm syndrome. Based on the natural use of hands during communication, a new gesture vocabulary was created that supports the arms while the user performs the gestures. A repeated measures within subject design was conducted where participants interacted with a custom video game using 3 types of input for 30 min each, (1) keyboard, (2) mid-air gestures and (3) supported gestures. Three measures of exertion were collected, (1) time, (2) energy expenditure, and (3) perceived exertion. The newly designed supported gestures required significantly less physical and perceived effort than the mid-air gestures and required similar exertion as the keyboard condition.

Keywords: Gorilla arm · Mid-air gestures · Fatigue · Endurance · Gesture interaction · Natural user interface

1 Introduction

The idea of using hand and arm gestures to interact with computer systems is not a new idea. The "Put-That-There" study in 1980 [5] defined and used hand gestures for a graphical user interface. Hollywood further popularized the idea in 2002 with the gesture based interfaces that Tom Cruise interacted with in the "Minority Report" movie and more recently, the Tony Stark character in the "Iron Man" movie series. Even though the "Minority Report" interface was based on research by Underkoffler [30] and has captured the imaginations of both the public and the HCI community, the use of gestures as the primary mode of interaction for an interface remain more of a novelty (e.g., Microsoft Kinect games). One of the primary reasons for this is the issue commonly called the gorilla arm syndrome [7].

© Springer International Publishing AG 2017
S. Lackey and J. Chen (Eds.): VAMR 2017, LNCS 10280, pp. 505–520, 2017.
DOI: 10.1007/978-3-319-57987-0_41

The gorilla arm syndrome originally arose with the advent of touchscreens used in a vertical orientation, which forces the user to extend their arms without support. When this is done for any task longer than a few minutes (e.g., with an ATM), it causes arm fatigue and a feeling of heaviness in the arms. Mid-air gestures, just as the name suggests, suffers from the same issue of an unsupported arm position. The common position for both vertical touchscreen use and mid-air gesture input is with the arm/s extended in front of the user around shoulder height (Fig. 1A). Hincapie-Ramos, *et al.* [20] found this position to be the most fatiguing physical position out of the 4 they investigated. One reason for the necessity of this arm position is due to the technology used to detect the user's arm and hand position.

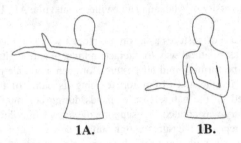

1A.   **1B.**

Fig. 1. Posture 1A. is a common arm position with high fatigue for vertical touchscreen and mid-air gestures. Posture 1B. is the arm position with low fatigue for gestures during face-to-face communications.

The challenge of capturing the user's arm and hand position has been met with a number of technology approaches. Optical solutions with external cameras that track the user's motion can include two basic types, a marker based system and markerless motion capture. The marker based system uses input from multiple cameras to triangulate the 3D position of the user wearing special markers while the markerless motion capture uses one or more cameras and computer vision algorithms to identify the user's 3D position. For issues of practicality, the markerless motion capture represents the optical motion capture of choice for general use. The Microsoft Kinect and the Leap Motion sensor are examples of markerless motion capture systems that are both affordable and accessible to consumers, researchers, and developers. However, these type of optical sensors must have an unobscured view of the user's hands, which often forces the user's hands into that high fatigue area in front of the user mentioned above and away from many natural arm supports like the arm rest of a chair. In addition, these sensors have shown to be limited in their gesture recognition accuracy and reliability (e.g., [8, 18]).

Another approach that does not use any optical devices like cameras is a system that uses inertial measurement units (IMUs). The IMU approach consists of several sensors placed on the user or in the clothing the user wears. Each IMU consists of a gyroscope, magnetometer, and accelerometer in order to wirelessly transmit the motion data of the user to a computer, where it is translated to a biomechanical model of the user. IMU gloves and suits have typically been used by the movie and special effects industry but recent crowdsourcing efforts like the Perception Neuron IMU suit have provided more affordable IMU based motion capture solutions. IMU solutions do require the user to wear the sensors in the form of gloves or straps but unlike the optical solutions, it does not provide constraints on where the user's hands must be to perform the gestures. As long as the sensors are within Wi-Fi range of the router, there are no constraints on the position, orientation, or worry of obscuring the hands from an external camera source.

Without these line-of-sight constraints that are required by optical motion capture systems, we have created a new approach that is based on the natural and non-verbal ways people use their hands to communicate to one another. The use of IMU technology for motion capture has allowed us to create gestures that mimic how people naturally use their hands, which avoids the highly fatiguing arm positions that cause gorilla arms. This paper will describe these new gestures, an experiment comparing the fatigue levels across keyboard, mid-air, and our newly formed hand gestures, and discuss the implications of this work.

2 Background

The name of mid-air gestures itself alludes to the fatigue problem associated with these types of gestures. Suspending the arms in mid-air without support will always pose a physical challenge for the user over prolonged periods of interaction. Fatigue levels are determined as the amount of time a person can maintain an isometric (static) muscle contraction [9]. This can be measured by the heart's response to increase blood flow to transport oxygen to the muscle fibers (cells). An isometric muscle contraction causes an impairment of blood flow due to the increase in intramuscular pressure. Complete vascular occlusion occurs at 70% of a person's maximal voluntary contraction (MVC). At approximately 50% of MVC, a user has approximately 1 min until fatigue. Muscle fatigue is caused by a reduction in the amount of oxygen transported to the muscle fibers. Oxygen is needed for aerobic energy metabolism which can be maintained for hours. When there is not enough oxygen to support the energy needs of the muscle, energy is provided by partial or complete conversion to the glycolysis process (anaerobic metabolism), in which the muscle fiber consumes glucose for energy. As the muscle cells consume the limited stored glucose to maintain the current position, the user begins to feel the effects of muscle fatigue. This fatigue increases until the glucose is consumed and the user can no longer maintain the arm position. At the same time, an increase in heart rate and blood pressure is needed to maintain blood flow. As a result, oxygen consumption (VO_2), an estimate of a person's energy requirement to perform muscular work, will increase above the resting value. At rest, a 70 kg person will have a VO_2 of approximately 3.5 ml of O_2 per kilogram of body weight per minute ($mL \cdot kg^{-1} \cdot min^{-1}$). As the level of fatigue increases, VO_2 will also increase.

As mentioned before, the arm position that produces a high level of fatigue is often the one required by many gesture based systems (Fig. 1A) [20], particularly with one of the most common gestures of pointing [8]. The least fatiguing arm position is shown in Fig. 1B, which has the user's arm bent at the elbow with their hands extended to the front. This is also the same basic position of the arms and hands when people use hand gestures to complement their speech during communication exchanges [21]. The use of hand gestures during speech is so natural and ubiquitous that people gesticulate as much whether the person they are talking to can see them or not [10].

Hand gestures by the speaker improves their ability to learn new concepts or improve their ability to teach a concept to someone else [26]. It is therefore not a surprise that the speakers of some of the most widely viewed TED talks use more than 600 hand gestures in a single 18-minute presentation [14]. Professional speakers and professors that must speak to audiences for 1–3 h at a time are performing large quantities of unsupported hand gestures. How are they doing this without extreme fatigue in their arms and shoulders after performing gestures for hours? The answer is that these speakers are conducting most of their hand gestures in the comfortable zone shown in Fig. 1B. They are also periodically relaxing their arms by extending them straight down, in a pocket, or taking advantage of a supporting structure like a podium. This periodic relaxation of the arms allows improved blood flow and therefore oxygen to the previously contracted muscles, which avoids switching to a glycolysis process that causes extreme arm fatigue (i.e., gorilla arms).

We have adopted this natural use of hand gestures to construct a limited gesture vocabulary for users. Our specific use case is a knowledge worker sitting at a desk and interacting with large amounts of visual images but could apply to other domains. We are applying 2 strategies to avoid the fatigue brought about from the gorilla arm syndrome by (1) placing the arms in the least fatiguing position with them bent at the elbow (Fig. 1B.) and (2) using support in the form of the user's lap or on the arm rest of the chair (Fig. 2). Other researchers have proposed resting the user's elbows on a surface (e.g., [8, 15, 17, 28]) but none have conducted a systematic examination on the physical and perceived fatigue caused by mid-air and supported gestures over even moderate durations of time.

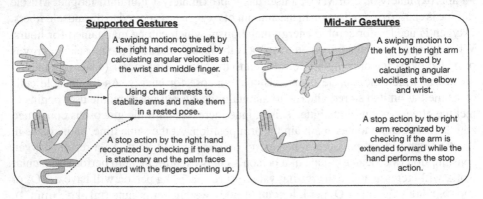

Fig. 2. Supported and mid-air gestures.

Most prior research also uses a table top to support the user's arms (e.g., [8, 17]). Similar to the ergonomic recommendations for proper keyboard positioning that has found for every 1 cm increase in keyboard height, neck and shoulder discomfort increases 18% [4, 22], we have avoided making the user place their arms at or above table level. Our supported gesture position would be difficult for most optical motion capture systems due to the handsplaced below the surface of the table but is easily supported with wireless IMU glove technology. We have therefore selected the technology that will support our use case instead of allowing the technology to dictate the actions and postures of our users.

2.1 Supported Gesture Vocabulary

We scoped the gesture requirements to encompass 2 basic usability engineering principles [24, 25]: (1) the gestures should minimize user cognitive load of memorizing how to perform them and (2) the gestures should clearly correspond to the user's natural behaviors. The use case involves a knowledge worker manipulating digital images within a large image collection. We have designed a supported gesture vocabulary that contains 10 gestures for the final prototype. As discussed below, the gestures are general enough to apply to a number of different tasks or domains. To examine the viability of prolonged use of these gestures before fully developing the prototype, we have developed a game that uses 3 of the gestures. The gestures include (1) swipe left, (2) swipe right, and (3) stop.

Rather than relying on machine learning algorithms to detect gestures, we propose a novel gesture recognition framework that relies on the vectors between 2 sensors. Researchers have obtained good results in mid-air gesture recognition using machine learning algorithms. However, this requires a large amount of training data and manual annotation of the data as ground truth in order to train accurate gesture recognition models [2, 23]. This type of approach usually considers static hand gestures but not the gestures involving hand movements (e.g., [19, 29]). Our approach computes angular velocities between vectors to recognize both static and dynamic gestures and avoids some of the drawbacks of the machine learning algorithm approach.

The typical motion capture skeletal hand model consists of 16 joints in each hand, 3 on each finger and 1 at the wrist. Based on the motion of these joints during natural swipe and stop hand gestures, we used the positions of 4 hand joints and 2 arm joints. Vectors are formed using the positions of joints on the hands and arms. Among the joints with sensors, we identified 3 relevant vectors in each hand and 2 relevant vectors in each arm (Fig. 3). By monitoring the angular velocity of the pre-identified vectors, we can accurately recognize the following gestures.

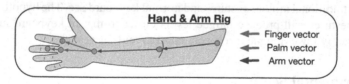

Fig. 3. IMU sensors are placed at the joints of the hand and arm to capture position values in real-time.

Supported Gesture 1 & 2 – Swipe Left & Right. A supported swiping motion of the hand to the left by the right hand or to the right with the left hand indicates movement of the target in that direction. This motion is primarily accomplished at the wrist so the arms can easily be supported by the arm rest of a chair or the participant's lap. We define the start state of a swipe gesture if the palms of each hand are facing each other. Then if the angular velocity of the vector from the wrist to the middle finger exceeds our defined threshold, it is considered a swipe gesture in that direction.

Supported Gesture 3 – Stop. A supported stop gesture provides a stop command to the target object. This common gesture is characterized by facing the palm of the hand outward with the fingers pointing up. Again, this gesture is easily accomplished while the arms are at rest. Recognition of the stop gesture uses the angles between the finger and wrist sensors to activate the command. For this experiment, the target continues its current motion or trajectory until the stop gesture is removed.

2.2 Mid-Air Gesture Vocabulary

Mid-air gestures typically involve the use of the entire arm for the reasons indicated earlier. The same 3 gestures were created as mid-air gestures using the vector velocity and angle approach to conduct (1) swipe left, (2) swipe right, and (3) stop actions.

Mid-Air Gesture 1 & 2 – Swipe Left & Right. A mid-air swiping gesture to the left by the right hand and to the right with the left hand was created. This gesture uses the shoulder, arm, and hand vector to define the starting position with the arms extended in front of the participant at shoulder level. The vector velocity of the hand and arm is then monitored to detect the swiping motion done by bending the arm at the elbow to the left or right.

Mid-Air Gesture 3 – Stop. A mid-air stop gesture is defined in the same manner as the supported stop gesture but with the arm extended in front of the user.

2.3 Objective

The objective of this study is two-fold. The first objective is to create hand gestures that leverage how we naturally position, relax, and support our hands and arms to reduce the level of exertion and fatigue. The second objective is to investigate the level of fatigue these supported gestures produce compared to 2 well known points along the HCI continuum, traditional mid-air gestures and normal keyboard use. The hypothesis is that supported gestures will produce fatigue levels closer to that of keyboard interactions and significantly lower fatigue levels compared to mid-air gestures.

3   Experimental Setup

We conducted a within subject repeated measures experiment across three types of interaction with a video game to examine both the physical and perceived fatigue levels of each. The three conditions were (1) keyboard, (2) supported gestures, and (3) mid-air gestures (Fig. 4).

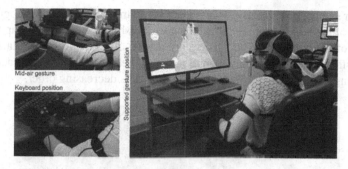

Fig. 4. Experimental setup with each condition demonstrated.

3.1 Participants

The study was conducted with 16 participants from a university population (10 male/6 female). Their age ranged from 20 to 28 with a mean age of 23. The experiment took 2 h to complete per participant.

3.2 Gamification

Games can be used as a prototype to predict human behavior in an interactive system while the system is not fully developed. Our gamified prototypepresented users with a task that would engage and motivate them over the extended time periods they were interacting with the system. Concerning the *degree of functionality* in the field of ergonomics and the *interactivity* [27] associated with authentic product utilization, using a game for the gorilla arm study has the advantages of reducing the users' boredom while increasing their interests in continuously performing the gestures.

Deterding et al. [12, 13] defined the term Gamification which is *"the use of game design elements in non-game contexts"*. The game for the gorilla arm study should satisfy the requirements of (1) motivating users to perform predefined gestures, rather than making them feel they are passively forced to move hands and arms, and (2) being able to easily control how frequent the users should move arms and hands so that it mimics different communication or interaction situations.

We designed a video game called "Happy Ball" and implemented it using the Unity game engine and a high-accuracy motion capturing device (Fig. 5). The goal of the game is to keep the ball happy by avoiding the obstacles and collecting as many presents as possible. The ball can be moved across 3 lanes and is automatically propelled forward at a fixed rate (similar to Temple Run type games). The player controls the left and right movement of the ball to avoid stone obstacles and a stop command to stop bouncing to avoid ice blocks placed above the ball. While the stop command is active, the ball decelerates until it stops moving forward. When the stop command ends, the ball resumes the bouncing motion and accelerates back to the original forward speed. The stop command overrides the controls of left and right movements. For example, when the left hand is performing the stop action, the swiping motion of the right hand will not be able to move the ball to the left lane. After 10 hits to the ball by the obstacles, the game is over and it automatically restarts after 3 s. During the game, the happiness level (life status) of the ball is represented with a cartoonish facial expression, appearing on the surface of the ball as a texture. There are a total of 10 expressions: elated, joyful, happy, satisfied, neutral, unhappy, depressed, sad, helpless, and crying, each in order corresponding to the number of hits by obstacles in its decreasing order.

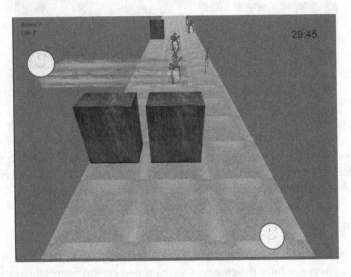

Fig. 5. Screen capture of the "Happy Ball" game. The player controls the ball at the bottom right to collect the presents and avoid the stone and ice obstacles.

3.3   Apparatus

Motion Capture. The participant's gestures were tracked using an IMU based motion capture suit. The configurable motion capture suit from Perception Neuron (https://neuronmocap.com) was used. Only 2 gloves and the torso strap was used because no movement information was needed for the lower body. The total number of sensors was 23 (9/glove, 1/arm, 3 for torso). Each sensor contains a gyroscope, accelerometer, and magnetometer and wirelessly transmits the motion data to the Axis Neuron Software.

Oxygen Consumption. Oxygen consumption (VO_2) was measured continuously using a TrueOne 2400 metabolic system (ParvoMedics). The TrueOne 2400 is a computerized metabolic system using a gas mixing chamber to analyze the oxygen consumed and carbon dioxide produced. Open-circuit spirometry has been found to provide both reliable [11] and accurate [3] data for the measurement of VO_2. The flow meter and gas analyzers were calibrated prior to each test with a 3L syringe and gases of known concentrations. The participant was fitted with a rubber mask (Hans Rudolph) that covers the nose and mouth, which is connected to the TrueOne 2400 system (Fig. 4).

Perceived Exertion. Subjective physical exertion was measured using the Borg CR10 scale, which is commonly used based on its reliability and validity [6, 20]. This scale consists of a 12-point scale (0, 0.5, 1–10) with descriptions along 9 of the points ranging from "Nothing at all" to "Impossible". Participants are asked to rate their current level of exertion based on the scale.

3.4 Procedure

A Latin square design was used to counter-balance the order each participant would engage with the 3 conditions. The participant would place the motion capture suit on and go through a 2-minute calibration process. The participant's weight and height were recorded and entered into the TrueOne 2400 software. The participant was then measured for an appropriately sized mask and the mask was placed on the participant, making sure it was an air tight fit. The participant played the Happy Ball game for up to 30 min for each condition while VO_2 was being recorded. The gesture commands are described above for the supported and mid-air gestures. Participants would use the "A" and "D" keys to move left and right and the space bar to stop in the keyboard condition. If the participant experienced excessive fatigue in any condition, they would signal to the experimenter that they would like to stop the current game play. At the conclusion of each condition, they were asked to rate their physical exertion level using the Borg CR10 scale. There was a 5-minute period of inactivity between each condition in order to allow their VO_2 levels to reach their baseline levels again.

4 Results

4.1 Time

The participants had the opportunity to spend up to 30 min engaged with the game for each interaction condition. 27% of participants completed the full 30-minute trial for the mid-air gestures compared to 100% for supported gestures and keyboard. Figure 6 displays the mean time spent across each condition. A paired samples t-test was conducted to compare the time spent in the supported gesture condition and the mid-air

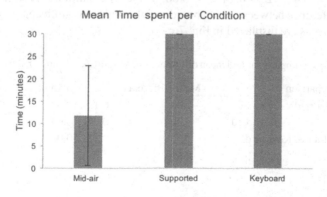

Fig. 6. Mean time spent out of a possible 30 min for each condition. Error bars represent standard deviation.

gesture condition. There was a significant difference in time between the supported gesture conditions ($M = 30.0$, $SD = 0.0$) and the mid-air gestures ($M = 11.85$, $SD = 11.13$); $t(15) = -6.52$, $p < 0.00$ (supported and keyboard results are the same). These results provide strong evidence that confirms the impracticality of mid-air gestures over time given participants could only endure approximately 12 min of this type of activity. On the other hand, participants had no difficulty completing the entire 30-minute time period for both the supported gestures and the keyboard conditions.

4.2 VO$_2$

To test differences of VO$_2$ levels across the 3 conditions, a generalized estimating equations (GEE) with an unstructured correlation matrix was used. GEE is an extension of the general linear model to longitudinal data analysis using quasi-likelihood estimation [1]. VO$_2$ was measured in milliliters per kilogram of body weight per minute (VO$_2$ mL/kg^{-1}/min^{-1}). This model compares the overall VO$_2$ across the conditions. The results indicate a significant difference among the conditions (Wald chi-square $= 77.19$, $p < 0.00$, $N = 47$). Parameter estimates are found in Table 1.

Table 1. Parameter estimates from the GEE model for VO$_2$ mL/kg^{-1}/min^{-1} across the interaction conditions.

Models	β	SE	Wald chi-square	p-value
Intercept	4.77	0.20	592.38	0.00
Keyboard & Mid-air	−1.28	0.15	72.19	0.00
Supported & Mid-air	−1.07	0.12	74.47	0.00

Post-hoc pairwise comparisons of the estimated marginal means were conducted to examine the specific differences. There was a significant difference between supported gestures ($M = 3.69$, $SE = 0.12$) and mid-air gestures ($M = 4.76$, $SE = 0.20$) (Table 2). There was also a significant VO$_2$ difference between the supported gestures and the keyboard ($M = 3.48$, $SE = 0.14$, $p < 0.00$, Table 2) conditions. Lastly, there was a significant difference between the keyboard and the mid-air gesture condition (Table 2). The overall means are displayed in Fig. 7.

Table 2. Multiple comparisons and mean differences in VO$_2$ mL/kg^{-1}/min^{-1} by interaction types.

Comparison	Mean difference	SE	p-value
Supported vs. Mid-air	−1.08	0.12	0.00
Supported vs Keyboard	0.20	0.07	0.00
Mid-air & Keyboard	1.28	0.15	0.00

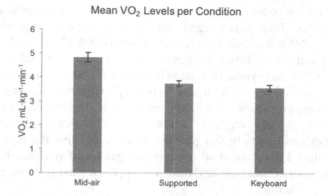

Fig. 7. The mean VO$_2$ in milliliters per kilogram of body weight per minute is presented across each condition. Error bars represent standard error of the mean.

Figure 8 shows the mean VO$_2$ levels across time for each condition. The dotted vertical lines integrate the mean duration performed for each condition reported in the previous section. Even though there was a significant difference between the supported gestures and keyboard activity, these results show how close in physical exertion levels supported gestures are to regular keyboard activity. The level of physical effort for the mid-air gestures, however was comparatively higher to both and produced a 23% increase in oxygen consumption compared to the supported gestures.

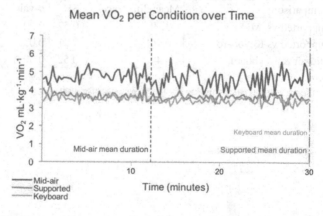

Fig. 8. Mean VO$_2$ for each condition over the 30-minute trial length. The dotted vertical lines represent the mean duration for each condition.

4.3 Perceived Exertion

The perceived physical exertion from each of the conditions was measured by the Borg CR10 on its 12-point scale. A GEE model was also used to analyze the Borg scores across the 3 conditions. The results indicate a significant difference among the conditions (Wald chi-square = 71.58, $p < 0.00$, $N = 47$). Parameter estimates are found in Table 3.

Pairwise comparisons of the estimated marginal means were conducted to examine the specific differences. There was a significant difference between supported gestures ($M = 1.70$, $SE = .34$) and mid-air gestures ($M = 5.69$, $SE = 0.57$) (Table 4). There were also significant differences between supported gestures and keyboard use ($M = 1.3$, $SE = 0.34$) as well as the keyboard and mid-air gestures (Table 4). The Borg CR10 label for the mean supported gesture level was "very easy" while the mid-air gesture mean level equates to the exertion level of "Hard" on the scale (Fig. 9). The keyboard mean level falls within the "very, very easy" range (Fig. 9). The perceived exertion results confirm the previous results in that participants estimated that the mid-air gestures required more than 3 times the effort of supported gestures. Even though there was a significant difference between the keyboard and supported hand gestures, both showed very low levels of exertion.

Table 3. Parameter estimates from the GEE model for VO_2 mL/kg/min across the interaction conditions.

Models	β	SE	Wald chi-square	p-value
Intercept	5.69	0.57	98.66	0.00
Keyboard & Mid-air	−4.44	0.52	71.57	0.00
Supported & Mid-air	−3.99	0.52	59.73	0.00

Table 4. Multiple comparisons and mean differences in VO_2 mL/kg/min by interaction types.

Comparison	Mean difference	SE	p-value
Supported vs. Mid-air	−3.99	0.52	0.00
Supported vs Keyboard	0.46	0.21	0.03
Mid-air & Keyboard	4.44	0.52	0.00

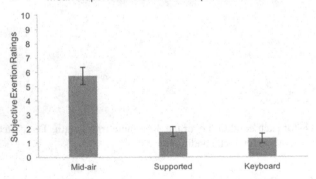

Fig. 9. The mean subjective Borg ratings for physical exertion across conditions (0 = Nothing at all, 10 = Impossible). Error bars represent standard error of the mean.

5 Discussion

The results of this study provided evidence for the hypothesis that the supported gesture interactions produced significantly less fatigue among the participants compared to mid-air type of gestures. Additionally, the fatigue levels from using the supported gestures were very similar to that of traditional keyboard interactions providing positive evidence for sustained use of supported gesture interactions.

The gorilla arm phenomenon has greatly impeded the research and development efforts of gesture based interactions with computer systems. Based on the results of this study, researchers and the technology industry have had good reason to largely ignore the gesture based modality. Only 25% of the participants in this study were able to complete a single 30-minute session using the mid-air gestures, which is only a fraction of the time knowledge workers typically spend in one sitting. The actual physical effort as measured by VO_2 and the perceived exertion level of using mid-air gestures also supports the significant discomfort and fatigue felt by participants.

Any potential modality alternative to the existing status quo of keyboards, mice, and game controllers must be reliable, accurate, and viable for extended periods of use. Mid-air gestures as depicted by the movie industry and made possible by affordable optical motion capture technology such as the Microsoft Kinect and Leap Motion force the user into these mid-air type of gestures. The growing advancements in augmented and virtual reality are renewing interest and some work with gestures as an input modality. However, most of the current efforts ignore the gorilla arm mistakes of the past and appear to be on a path to repeat them. For example, the Leap Motion can be adapted to be used with head mounted displays (HMD) but must be placed on the HMD. With the limited angle of its optical sensors, the user's hands must be raised high enough to be recognized, which brings the user into the high fatigue posture shown in Fig. 1A. Microsoft's augmented reality technology, the HoloLens suffers from the same issue of forcing the user's hands in front of its HMD.

The optical solution for the limited sensing area of a single camera for motion capture has traditionally been a system with several cameras configured around the user. This approach is expensive in terms of both equipment and the dedicated space for this type of setup. These requirements do not allow multi-camera systems to scale well to multiple knowledge workers in a traditional office space. These type of systems also still require an unobscured view of the user's arms and hands, which is fine for mid-air postures (Fig. 1A) but not for supported postures (Fig. 1B) if the user is seated at a desk or table.

The use of IMU based motion capture technology breaks the line-of-sight chains that constrains the optical systems to mid-air type gestures. With IMU motion capture, the user's hands can comfortably rest in supported and natural positions while enjoying a relatively high degree of precision and accuracy for both hand and finger movements.

If supported gestures are to be a viable alternative to keyboard, mouse, and game controller use, users physically must be able perform them for long periods of time without discomfort and fatigue. This study directly compared the level of effort of keyboard use to supported gestures. All the participants from both the keyboard and supported gestures were able to complete the entire 30-minute interaction trial. The results from the participants' physical exertion levels as measured by VO_2 were very similar. Finally, the participants reported extremely low amounts of perceived exertion for both the keyboard ("very, very easy") and supported gestures ("very easy"), even though they were significantly different. These results suggest that the supported gestures were successful in avoiding the gorilla arm effects that traditional gesture based interactions experience. Overall, the physical effort required to perform supported gestures appears to be very similar to that of using the keyboard.

6   Conclusion and Future Work

The traditional way of implementing gesture based interactions is fundamentally flawed by forcing users to perform arm and hand gestures in mid-air without support or appreciation of natural resting positions. In this paper, we have traced one potential cause of mid-air gestures to the constraints that come with the use of optical motion capture systems. We avoided this constraint by implementing a novel vector based gesture recognition approach using an IMU motion capture system. The newly designed supported gestures were found to require similar levels of physical and perceived exertion as keyboard use and avoided the gorilla arm effects experienced by participants during their mid-air gesture interactions. Some of the limitations of this study include a very limited gesture vocabulary and data collection over only a 30-minute duration. Given the promising results shown with supported gestures, our future efforts will be to continue developing the supported gesture vocabulary and examine their integration with other input modalities.

References

1. Ballinger, G.A.: Using generalized estimating equations for longitudinal data analysis. Organ. Res. Methods **7**(2), 127–150 (2004)
2. Badi, H.S., Hussein, S.: Hand posture and gesture recognition technology. Neural Comput. Appl. **25**(3), 871–878 (2014)
3. Bassett Jr., D.R., Howley, E.T., Thompson, D.L., King, G.A., Strath, S.J., McLaughlin, J.E., Parr, B.B.: Validity of inspiratory and expiratory methods of measuring gas exchange with a computerized system. J. Appl. Physiol. **91**, 218–224 (2001)
4. Bergqvist, U., Wolgast, E., Nilsson, B., Voss, M.: Musculoskeletal disorders among VDT workers: Individual, ergonomic, and work organizational factors. Ergonomics **38**(4), 763–776 (1995)
5. Bolt, R.A.: "Put-that-there": voice and gesture at the graphics interface. In: Proceedings of the 7th Annual Conference on Computer Graphics and Interactive Techniques (SIGGRAPH 1980), pp. 262–270 (1980)
6. Borg, E., Kaijser, L.: A comparison between three rating scales for perceived exertion and two different work tests. Scand. J. Med. Sci. Sports **16**(1), 57–69 (2005)
7. Boring, S., Jurmu, M., Butz, A.: Scroll, tilt or move it: Using mobile phones to continuously control pointers on large public displays. In: Proceedings of the 21st Annual Conference of the Australian Computer-Human Interaction Special Interest Group: Design (OZCHI 2009), pp. 161–168 (2009)
8. Brown, M.A., Stuerzlinger, W., Mendonca Filho, E.J.: The performance of un-instrumented in-air pointing. In: Proceedings of Graphics Interface Conference, pp. 59–66 (2014)

9. Carmody, T.: Why 'gorilla arm syndroome' rules out multitouch notebook displays. Wired **10,** October 2010
10. Cadoz, C.: Les Realites Virtuelles. Flammarion, Dominos (1994)
11. Crouter, S.E., Antczak, A., Hudak, J.R., Della Valle, D.M., Haas, J.D.: Accuracy and reliability of the ParvoMedics TrueOne 2400 and MedGraphics VO2000 metabolic systems. Eur. J. Appl. Physiol. **98,** 139–151 (2006)
12. Deterding, S., Dixon, D., Khaled, R., Nacke, L.: From game design elements to gamefulness: defining "gamification". In: Proceedings of the 15th International Academic MindTrek Conference: Envisioning Future Media Environments, pp. 9–15 (2011)
13. Deterding, S., Sicart, M., Nacke, L., O'Hara, K., Dixon, D.: Gamification using game-design elements in non-gaming contexts. In CHI 2011 Extended Abstracts on Human Factors in Computing Systems, pp. 2425–2428 (2011)
14. Van Edwards, V.: 5 secrets of a successful TED talk. http://www.scienceofpeople.com/2015/03/secrets-of-a-successful-ted-talk/. Accessed 14 Sep 2016
15. Freeman, D., Vennelakanti, R., Madhvanath, S.: Freehand pose-based gestural interaction: Studies and implications for interface design. In: IEEE Proceedings of 4th International Conference on Intelligent Human Computer Interaction, pp. 27–29 (2012)
16. Freivalds, A.: Biomechanics of the Upper Limbs: Mechanics, Modeling and Musculoskeletal Injuries, 2nd edn. CRC Press, Boca Raton
17. Guinness, D., Jude, A., Michael Poor, G., Dover, A.: Models for rested touchless gestural interaction. In: Proceedings of the 3rd ACM Symposium on Spatial User Interaction, pp. 34–43 (2015)
18. Guna, J., Jakus, G., Pogacnik, M., Tomazic, S., Sodnik, J.: An analysis of the precision and reliability of the Leap Motion sensor and its suitability for static and dynamic tracking. Sensors **14**(2), 3702–3720 (2014)
19. Hasan, H., Abdul-Kareem, S.: Static hand gesture recognition using neural networks. Artif. Intell. Rev. **41**(2), 147–181 (2014)
20. Hincapié-Ramos, J.D., Guo, X., Moghadasian, P., Irani, P.: Consumed endurance: a metric to quantify arm fatigue of mid-air interactions. In: Proceedings of the SIGCHI Conference on Human Factors in Computing Systems, pp. 1063–1072 (2014)
21. Kendon, A.: Gesture: Visible Action as Utterance. Cambridge University Press, New York (2004)
22. Andrew Life, M., Pheasant, S.: An integrated approach to the study of posture in keyboard operation. Appl. Ergon. **15**(2), 83–90 (1984)
23. Luzhnica, G., Simon, J., Lex, E., Pammer, V.: A sliding window approach to natural hand gesture recognition using a custom data glove. In: 2016 IEEE Symposium on 3D User Interfaces (3DUI), pp. 81–90 (2016)
24. Nielsen, J.: The usability engineering life cycle. IEEE Comput. **25**(3), 12–22 (1992)
25. Nielsen, M., Störring, M., Moeslund, T.B., Granum, E.: A procedure for developing intuitive and ergonomic gesture interfaces for HCI. In: Camurri, A., Volpe, G. (eds.) GW 2003. LNCS (LNAI), vol. 2915, pp. 409–420. Springer, Heidelberg (2004). doi: 10.1007/978-3-540-24598-8_38
26. Novack, M., Goldin-Meadow, S.: Learning from gesture: how our hands change our minds. Educ. Pscyhol. Rev. **27,** 405–412 (2015)
27. Sauer, J., Sonderegger, A.: The influence of prototype fidelity and aesthetics of design in usability tests: effects on user behaviour, subjective evaluation and emotion. Appl. Ergon. **40**(4), 670–677 (2009)
28. Segen, J., Kumar, S.: Look ma, no mouse! Commun. ACM **43**(7), 102–109 (2000)

29. Trigueiros, P., Ribeiro, F., Reis, L.P.: A comparison of machine learning algorithms applied to hand gesture recognition. In: 7th Iberian Conference on Information Systems and Technologies, Madrid, pp. 1–6 (2012)
30. Underkoffler, J.S.: The I/O Bulb and the Luminous Room. Ph.D. Dissertation. Massachusetts Institute of Technology, Cambridge (1999)

Simulation Sickness Related to Virtual Reality Driving Simulation

Quinate Chioma Ihemedu-Steinke[1,2,3(✉)], Stanislava Rangelova[1,4], Michael Weber[2], Rainer Erbach[1], Gerrit Meixner[3], and Nicola Marsden[4]

[1] Center of Competence – HMI, Robert Bosch GmbH, Leonberg, Germany
{quinatechioma.ihemedu-steinke,rainer.erbach}@de.bosch.com,
srangelova87@gmail.com
[2] University of Ulm, Ulm, Germany
{quinate.ihemedu-steinke,michael.weber}@uni-ulm.de
[3] UniTyLab, Heilbronn University, Heilbronn, Germany
gerrit.meixner@hs-heilbronn.de
[4] Heilbronn University, Heilbronn, Germany
nicola.marsden@hs-heilbronn.de

Abstract. This paper reports on a study regarding the conditions that reduce simulation sickness in virtual reality driving simulation. Simulation sickness in virtual reality applications is frequent and thus poses a major obstacle in obtaining data from participants involved in these simulations. Many solutions have been presented by various sources on how to reduce the occurrence of simulation sickness symptoms. Nevertheless, there is not enough evidence to back up an appropriate solution that works for the majority of simulated environments and individuals. Therefore, this work was meant to find appropriate solutions of simulation sickness related to virtual reality driving simulators with a focus on the effect of adding visual assets in the simulated environment. Initially, an online survey was performed with 31 participants in order to gather unbiased users' experiences with driving simulation and virtual reality with regards to simulation sickness. Based on the information gathered from related works and suggestions of the online survey participants, the addition of motion cues and visual assets were identified as very essential when dealing with simulation sickness related to driving simulation. Therefore, new visual assets were added to enhance an already implemented simulator software in order to replicate a realistic traffic environment. An experiment with 72 participants was used to test eight hypotheses related to virtual reality driving simulation and simulations sickness. The results indicate that the addition of visual assets to the virtual reality driving simulator reduced the onset of simulation sickness and improved the driving session's duration.

Keywords: Simulation sickness · Virtual reality · Driving simulation · Visual assets · Simulated environment

© Springer International Publishing AG 2017
S. Lackey and J. Chen (Eds.): VAMR 2017, LNCS 10280, pp. 521–532, 2017.
DOI: 10.1007/978-3-319-57987-0_42

1   Introduction

Automotive manufacturers and suppliers are constantly looking for ways to integrate new technologies in vehicles to make them more comfortable and safer for the consumers. For this reason, driving simulation (DS) is indispensable, and widely used to simulate real life driving scenarios for research, training and evaluation of new car technologies in a completely controlled and safe environment without risking any lives (Russell et al. 2014; Slob 2008). This makes it possible to observe and evaluate the vehicle-driver-system interaction as well as the vehicle-to-vehicle interaction concepts. Production costs could be reduced because most errors and their possible solutions are discovered at the early stage of the development process (De Winter 2012).

In order to create a realistic driving environment and reliable results, virtual reality (VR) head-mounted displays (HMD) have been integrated in DS. To enhance the immersion of drivers into the simulated environment (SE), they offer a stereoscopic 3D environment with a wide field of view and low-latency, fast-tracking system for a better interaction in the SE (Davis et al. 2015; Russell et al. 2014).

Simulation sickness (SSN) is a discomfort experienced by users exposed to SEs such as DS and VR (Kolasinski 1995). SSN is a major setback to the application of DS because it could influence the behavior of drivers and make them avoid maneuvers that are likely to cause SSN, thus generating biased data (Helland et al. 2016). Many studies have developed techniques to help humans adapt to SSN with repeated exposure in SEs (Kohler 1968; Domeyer et al. 2013; Galvez-Garcia et al. 2015). However, because of the negative impact, affected subjects might not be willing to continue or experience another exposure. User evaluations show that 84% of the users suffered from severe eye strain due to strapping HMDs over the eyes and other discomforts. For some users this discomfort makes it impossible to continue with the session (Ihemedu-Steinke et al. 2015). Hence insights into ways to reduce SSN related to VRDS would be helpful in optimizing the design process through creating a more authentic representation of the SE to improve user acceptance (Kennedy et al. 1989). It is difficult to obtain solutions that work for every system and all individuals – adding visual assets (VAs) e.g. pedestrians and cars in the SE to create a simplified and familiar visual scene has been one suggestion to reduce SSN (Kingdon et al. 2001). Our goal is to investigate whether this change in VAs impacts SSN (Fig. 1).

2   Simulation Sickness

2.1   Simulation Sickness Overview

SSN is a kind of motion sickness (MS) experienced in (SE) e.g. US navy pilots suffered severe discomforts during preliminary simulator sessions during the development of the first static helicopter simulator in the 1950's. The lack of motion cues was assumed to have caused the discomforts (Johnson 2005). SSN can be visually-induced without actual motion and may occur at any time during exposure with a long lasting effect, which could be dangerous especially when driving a car (Kennedy et al. 2010).

SSN has the same symptoms like MS but with few peculiarities to it e.g. eye strain. The symptoms are separated into three major groups – nausea with symptoms such as stomach awareness, nausea, vomiting, burping, and increased salivation, oculomotor symptoms like eye strain, headache, difficulty focusing, and blurred vision, and disorientation with general discomfort, vertigo, and dizziness (Kennedy and Fowlkes 1992).

Kolasinski described 42 factors related to SSN in SEs that are grouped into three categories – individual, system, and task related (Kolasinski 1995; Johnson 2005). While some studies argue that women are more prone to SSN than men (Davis et al. 2014), others suggest that gender does not play a role (Graeber and Stanney 2002). System calibration could either induce SSN symptoms, e.g. headache and blurred vision, or reduce SSN based on how well it is done (Rebenitsch and Owen 2014). MS history or long simulation sessions are used to predict SSN (Braithwaite and Braithwaite 1990; Wright 1995; Kennedy et al. 2000; Matas et al. 2015). Older participants are more prone to SSN than younger participants (Brook et al. 2010).

2.2 Simulation Sickness Theories

Regarding the origins of SSN, there are three major approaches that assumptions and research is based on: sensory conflict theory, neural mismatch model, and postural instability theory.

Sensory Conflict Theory. This theory states that when motion seen is not felt or vice versa, the brain receives conflicting motion signals from the visual and vestibular system (Reason and Brand 1975). This conflict deceives the brain to deduce that the person is hallucinating due to toxin ingestion. The body tries to expel the toxin through vomiting. An example is a fixed-based DS where motion is visually perceived but not felt because the body stays in a still position.

Fig. 1. SE with traffic lights, cars and pedestrians developed in Unreal Engine 4.

Neural Mismatch Model. There have been suggestions for the sensory conflict theory to be renamed as neural mismatch theory, which states that MS or SSN occurrence is based on the fact that patterns from a previous experience are compared to patterns from the ongoing experience. If they do not match, the body reacts like it has been intoxicated (Reason and Brand 1975). For example, the exposure of subjects to a badly represented traffic situation that conflicts with the subject's expectations based on previous driving experience could lead to unusual maneuvers and anxiety which could induce SSN.

Postural Instability. Developed by Stoffregen and Roccio who disputed the sensory conflict theory and argued that one of the main goals of humans is to maintain stability, and when this balance is lost, the person feels sick (Riccio and Stoffregen 1991). For example, a test driver on a DS may attempt to resist the tilt on a curvy road visually perceived. This attempt might disrupt the user's stable position, thus causing postural instability since there was no physical tilt experienced (La Viola 2000).

3   Study

The study conducted used an experimental setup to examine the effect of visual assets in VRDS on SSN. This section presents the methods and procedure of the study.

3.1   Methods and Procedure

An experimental post-test only design was used to test eight hypotheses related to VRDS and SSN. Independent variables were limited VAs (LVA) vs. full VAs (FVA), MS history, driving frequency, and gender. Dependent variables were SSN, VR experience, enjoyment of driving experience, and duration of driving. Eight hypotheses related to VRDS and SSN were used to compare SSN questionnaire (SSQ) scores of the users (Table 1).

Table 1. Hypotheses

N	Hypotheses
1	User has a lower SSQ total score with addition of full VA than with limited VA
2	User with MS history has a higher SSQ total score than a user without MS-H
3	Frequent driver has a higher SSQ total score than a non- frequent driver
4	Video gamers have less SSQ total score than non- video gamers
5	User has a better virtual reality experience with full VA than with limited VA
6	User enjoys the driving experience with full VA more than with limited VA
7	Female users have higher SSQ total score than male users
8	User drives longer with full VA than user with limited VA

Participants were students and members of staff at a University of Applied Sciences in southern Germany (N = 72), 54 males (Mage = 24.91, SDage = 4.27) and 18 female (Mage = 26.39, SDage = 7.26). They were randomly assigned to either the treatment (n = 36: FVA) or the control group (n = 36: LVA). The SE of the control group included basic visual elements such as buildings, traffic signs, and traffic lights. The treatment group's SE additionally included walking pedestrians and many randomly driving cars. Figure 2 shows gender distribution of the participants.

Gender

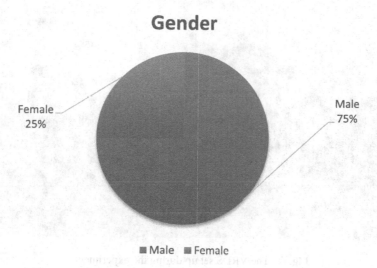

Female
25%

Male
75%

■ Male ■ Female

Fig. 2. Graphical representation of the users separated by gender

Many artificial intelligent cars driving randomly and animated pedestrians are activated for the FVA and deactivated for the LVA. Figure 3 shows the SE with full and LVA.

Fig. 3. A caption of limited VA (left), and full VA, (right) with a car

The instruments used were the SSQ by Kennedy et al. (1993) and a questionnaire to measure the participants' virtual experience and enjoyment based on instruments by Witmer and Singer (1998) and Lin et al. (2002). Before the experiment, socio-demographic information, motion sickness history previous, driving, and experience with driving simulation, gaming, and VR were elicited. Two-tailed independent-samples t-tests were performed to test the hypotheses. The statistical software package SPSS was used to analyze the data.

Each participant was allocated 30 min for the entire session. Depending on the test group, cars and pedestrians were activated or deactivated. The sessions were filmed in order to get direct verbal feedback during the VE experience. Figures 4 and 5 show the test set up and the participants during the test respectively.

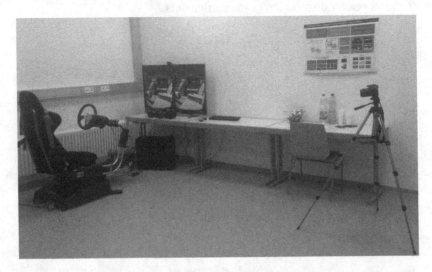

Fig. 4. The VRDS set up during the experiment

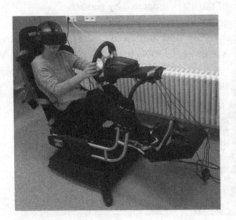 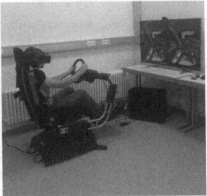

Fig. 5. Participants using the VRDS during the test

4   Result

This section presents the results of the conducted VRDS user evaluation. The higher the total SSQ score, the more severe the symptoms and the more troublesome the SE. SSQ score was calculated based on SSQ scoring weight system developed by Kennedy and colleagues (Kennedy et al. 1993).

4.1   SSQ Results

Of the eight hypotheses tested, two yielded significant results: The first hypothesis which assumed that the experimental would have less SSN than the control group showed a significant difference in the scores for FVA (M = 52.67, SD = 36.62) and LVA (M = 72.10, SD = 40.97); conditions (t (70) = −2.12, p < .05). Figure 6 demonstrates SSQ scores for both groups and shows that users from the treatment group with FVA had lower SSQ score in all three SSQ clusters (Nausea, Oculomotor and Disorientation) than users from the control group.

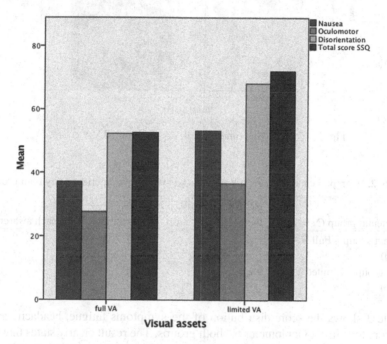

Fig. 6.   SSQ scores for the treatment and the control groups for all clusters

The eighth hypothesis assumed that the experimental group with FVA would drive longer than the control group with LVA. This also showed a significant difference regarding the minutes driven with FVA (M = 9.03, SD = 2.01) and LVA (M = 7.67, SD = 2.61); conditions (t (70) = 2.48, p < .05). Figure 7 shows that the FVA group with extra cars and pedestrians drove longer than the LVA group.

Table 2 shows that the control group was more affected with symptoms of increased salivation, sweating, and stomach awareness of the Nausea cluster than the treatment group.

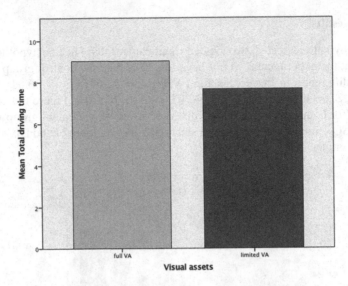

Fig. 7. Total driving time for full VA and limited VA groups

Table 2. Comparison of the severity for Nausea symptoms experienced by both groups

	Nausea – Cluster		
Experimental group (N = 72)	Increased salivation	Sweating	Stomach awareness
Treatment group – Full VAs (N = 36)	7%	45%	29%
Control group – Limited VAs (N = 36)	9%	51%	39%

Table 3 shows the score distribution of the symptoms fatigue, headache and eye strain from the cluster Oculomotor for both groups. The result clearly states that participants of the control group with deactivated randomly-driving vehicles and walking pedestrians experienced more fatigue, headache and eyestrain than the treatment group.

Table 3. Comparison of the severity for Oculomotor symptoms suffered by both groups

	Oculomotor – Cluster		
Experimental group (N = 72)	Fatigue	Headache	Eye strain
Treatment group – Full VAs (N = 36)	13%	11%	14%
Control group – Limited VAs (N = 36)	20%	17%	25%

Table 4 shows the score distribution of the symptoms blurred vision, dizziness with opened eyes and vertigo from the cluster Disorientation. Here the treatment group was more affected with blurred vision and was almost as dizzy as the control group.

Table 4. Shows the comparison of the disorientation symptoms for full and limited VAs

Experimental group (N = 72)	Disorientation – Cluster		
	Blurred vision	Dizziness with eyes open	Vertigo
Treatment group – Full VAs (N = 36)	31%	24%	6%
Control group – Limited VAs (N = 36)	25%	28%	16%

Finally, the relation between previous MS history, driving experience, gender, good gaming and VR experience with SSN was observed. The initial assumption that users with MS history will have a higher SSQ total score than users without MS history was not proven. The third hypothesis claimed that a user who is a frequent driver has a higher SSQ TS. The scores for frequent drivers (M = 52.20, SD = 31.47) did not show any significant difference to that of non-frequent drivers (M = 67.48, SD = 42.76); conditions t (70) = −1.55, p = 0.126. The seventh hypothesis claimed that female users have higher SSQ TS. Gender was one of the factors associated with SSN described in various studies which suggested that women are more susceptible to SSN than men. There was no significant difference in the scores for female (M = 67.53, SD = 41.67) and male (M = 60.67, SD = 39.40); condition t (70) = −0.63, p = 0.531. Likewise, scores for users who were non-frequent video gamers (M = 66.23, SD = 40.33) showed no significant difference compared to frequent video gamers (M = 59.48, SD = 39.64); conditions t (70) = −0.71, p = 0.479 showed no significant difference.

Another hypothesis that is not related to SSN – "The sixth hypothesis assumed that a user from the FVA group enjoys the driving experience more". Though the FVA group enjoyed more, the difference in the scores for FVA (M = 12.94, SD = 3.32) compared to LVA (M = 12.17, SD = 3.44) conditions; t (70) = 0.98, p = 0.333 was not enough to consider this claim.

5   Discussion and Outlook

5.1   Discussion

In a VRDS prototype meant for the automotive industry, VAs were added to the VE and the effects on SSN was tested. The results indicate that additional VAs can play a role in reducing SSN in VRDS and enable participants to stay in the VE for a longer time. In an experimental design, we showed significant differences regarding the SSN that participants experienced and the duration of the participation in a VE. It is already confirmed that SSN increases with longer exposure in the VE, and it gets better with frequent exposure (Kennedy et al. 2000). Therefore, if the FVA group could drive longer and yet get less sick in a single exposure, this could mean that the VAs really did help to suppress SSN occurrence. The Neural mismatch theory (Reason and Brand 1975) can be used to interpret these results: When the DS is similar to past traffic experiences in real life the sensory conflict is minimal. This leads to less SSN symptoms and this in turn allows the participants to continue the simulated driving for a longer time.

This study also showed that participants with previous history of MS are not necessarily more prone to SSN than those who never suffered from MS prior to the experiment. Though, the population of participants who were motion sick prior to this experiment was negligible compared to those who had no MS history. Likewise, unlike previous studies where female participants were presumed to be more susceptible to SSN, this study did not arrive to any such conclusion. Again, the 25% female participants compared to the 75% male participant could be the reason for this result. Therefore, additional studies are necessary to examine these hypotheses.

Though the FVA group had a richer VE meant for more interaction with many cars and pedestrians moving randomly. This however did not make any great difference in the level of enjoyment experienced by both groups. This could be because the artificial intelligent cars and pedestrians were hanging most of the time, and were more distracting than enhancing. Nevertheless, this research did not consider the quality of the assets added into the VE. Though recent research on SSN and VR indicated that users may still enjoy the experience in the VE regardless of SSN (Von Mammen 2016). This indicates, that though the control group was more affected with SSN, it could still enjoy the virtual driving experience as much as the other group.

Nevertheless, the treatment group suffered more blurred vision. This could be HMD-related because some users complained of fogginess of the lenses that could have caused the blurred effect. The FVA group drove longer and thus was more prone to the blurred effect than the control group.

The findings from the experiment illustrate that an addition of a few visual traffic elements could make a difference for the user and help in resolving SSN, which is a major problem in working with SEs (Ihemedu-Steinke et al. 2015). A VRDS with minimal induced SSN symptoms could be a powerful user evaluation instrument in the automotive industry.

Future studies should further look into the conditions that reduce SSN – options would be the integration of a motion platform into the VRDS to yield a higher matching of motion cues to real life driving experiences. Further experimental investigation is needed to estimate the influence of motion cues to SSN outbreak in VRDS.

Acknowledgments. The authors would like to thank the Center of Competence-HMI department of Car Multimedia business unit of Robert Bosch GmbH for funding this project, and most especially Mr. Prashandt Halady who initiated and made it possible.

We would also like to thank all the students and staffs of the University of Heilbronn who took part in the user evaluation tests, provided the necessary facilities that made this experiment possible.

Finally, we thank all the employees of the Center of Competence-HMI department for their support, and most especially, Sebastian Kupka for his help during the user tests.

References

Braithwaite, M.G., Braithwaite, B.D.: Simulator sickness in an army simulator. Occup. Med. **40**, 105–110 (1990)

Brook, J.O., Goodenough, R.R., Crisler, M.C., Klein, N.D., Alley, R.L., Koon, B.L., et al.: Simulator sickness during driving simulation studies. Accid. Anal. Prev. **42**, 788–796 (2010)

Davis, S., Nebitt, K., Nalivaiko, E.: A systematic review of cybersickness. In: Proceedings of the 2014 Conference on Interactive Entertainment. ACM, Newcastle, NSW, Australia (2014)

Davis, S., Nesbitt, K., Nalivaiko, E.: Comparing the onset of cybersickness using the Oculus Rift and two virtual roller coasters. In: Pisan, Y.N.K., Blackmore, K. (eds.) 11th Australasian Conference on Interactive Entertainment, 2015, pp. 3–14. ACS, Sydney (2015)

De Winter, J., Van Leuween, P., Happee, P.: Advantages and disadvantages of driving simulators: a discussion. In: Spink, A.J., Grieco, F., Krips, O.E., Loijens, L.W.S., Noldus, L.P.J.J., Zimmerman, P.H. (eds.) 8th International Conference on Methods and Techniques in Behavioral Research, Utrecht, Netherlands, pp. 47–50 (2012)

Domeyer, J.E., Cassavaugh, N.D., Backs, R.W.: The use of adaptation to reduce simulator sickness in driving assessment and research. Accid. Anal. Prev. **53**, 127–132 (2013)

Galvez-Garcia, G., Hay, M., Gabaude, C.: Alleviating simulator sickness with galvanic cutaneous stimulation. Hum. Factors **57**(4), 649–657 (2015)

Graeber, D.A., Stanney, K.M.: Gender differences in visually induced motion sickness. Proc. Hum. Factors Ergon. Soc. Ann. Meet. **46**, 2109–2113 (2002)

Helland, A., Lydersen, S., Lervåg, L., Jenssen, G.D., Mørland, J., Slørdal, L.: Driving simulator sickness: impact on driving performance, influence of blood alcohol concentration, and effect of repeated simulator exposures. Accid. Anal. Prev. **94**, 180–187 (2016). Elsevier – ScienceDirect

Ihemedu-Steinke, Q.C., Sirim, D., Erbach, R., Halady, P. Meixner, G.: Development and evaluation of a virtual reality driving simulator. In: Weisbecker, A., Burmester, M., Schmidt, A. (eds.) Mensch & Computer Workshop-band, pp. 491–500. De Gruyter Oldenbourg (2015)

La Viola Jr., J.J.: A discussion of cypersickness in virtual environment. SIGCHI Bull **32**(1), 47–56 (2000)

Johnson, D.M.: Introduction to and review of simulator sickness research. Report 1832. Army Research Institute for the Behavioral and Social Sciences, Arlington, VA, US (2005)

Kennedy, R.S., Drexler, J., Kennedy, R.C.: Research in visually induced motion sickness. Appl. Ergon. **41**, 494–503 (2010)

Kennedy, R.S., Fowlkes, J.E.: Simulator sickness is polygenic and polysymptomatic: implications for research. Int. J. Aviat. Psychol. **2**, 23–38 (1992)

Kennedy, R.S., Lane, N.E., Berbaum, K.S., Lilienthal, M.G.: Simulator sickness questionnaire: an enhanced method for quantifying simulator sickness. Int. J. Aviat. Psychol. **3**, 203–220 (1993)

Kennedy, R.S., Lilienthal, M.G., Berbaum, K.S., Baltzley, D.R., McCauley, M.E.: Simulator sickness in U.S. Navy flight simulators. Aviat. Space Environ. Med. **60**(5), 473 (1989)

Kennedy, R.S., Stanney, K.M., Dunlap, W.P.: Duration and exposure to virtual environments: sickness curves during and across sessions. Presence **9**(5), 463–472 (2000)

Kingdon, K.S., Stanney, K.M., Kennedy, R.S.: Extreme responses to virtual environment exposure. In: Proceedings of the Human Factors and Ergonomics Society 45th Annual Meeting Santa Monica, CA, pp. 1906–1911. Human Factors and Ergonomics Society (2001)

Kohler, I.: The formation and transformation of the perceptual world. In: Haber, R.N. (ed.) Contemporary Theory and Research in Visual Perception, pp. 474–497. Holt, Rinehart, & Winston Inc, New York (1968)

Kolasinski, E.M.: Simulator Sickness in Virtual Environments. Army Research Institute for the Behavioral and Social Sciences, Alexandria, VA, 68 (1995)

Lin, J.J.W., Duh, H.B.L., Parker, D.E., Abi-Rached, H., Furness, T.A.: Effects of field of view on presence, enjoyment, memory, and simulator sickness in a virtual environment. In: Virtual Reality, Proceedings, IEEE 2002, pp. 164–171 (2002)

Matas, N.A., Nettelbeck, T., Burns, N.R.: Dropout during a driving simulator study: a survival analysis. J. Saf. Res 55, 159–169 (2015)

Reason, J.T., Brand, J.J.: Motion Sickness. Academic Press Inc., New York (1975)

Rebenitsch, L., Owen, C.: Individual variation in susceptibility to cybersickness. In: Proceedings of the 27th Annual ACM Symposium on User Interface Software and Technology. ACM, Honolulu (2014)

Riccio, G.E., Stoffregen, T.A.: An ecological theory of motion sickness and postural instability. Ecol. Psychol. 3, 195–240 (1991)

Russell, M.E.B., Hoffman, B., Stromberg, S., et al.: Use of controlled diaphragmatic breathing for the management of motion sickness in a virtual reality environment. Appl. Psychophysiol. Biofeedback 39, 269 (2014). doi:10.1007/s10484-014-9265-6

Slob, J.J.: State-of-the-Art Driving Simulators, a Literature Survey. Eindhoven University of Technology. In: DCT report (2008)

Von Mammen, S.: Cyber sick but still having fun. In: VRST 2016 Proceedings of the 22nd ACM Conference on VR Software and Technology, pp. 325–326 (2016)

Witmer, B.G., Singer, M.J.: Measuring presence in virtual environments: a presence questionnaire. Presence Teleoper Virtual Environ. 7, 225–240 (1998)

Wright, R.H.: Helicopter Simulator Sickness: A state-of-the-art review of its Incidence, causes, and treatment (ARI Rep. 1680). U.S Army, Alexandria (1995)

Decreasing Physical Burden Using the Following Effect and a Superimposed Navigation System

Yuji Makimura[✉], Hiroki Yoshimura, Masashi Nishiyama, and Yoshio Iwai

Graduate School of Engineering, Tottori University, 101 Minami 4-chome,
Koyama-cho, Tottori 680-8550, Japan
s122048@ike.tottori-u.ac.jp

Abstract. We propose a novel navigation system using a virtual guide who walks in front of the user and induces the following effect. When using existing navigation systems, the user has a high physical burden because the user continuously moves their gaze and head to look at the map and landmarks on their journey. Employing our system, the user simply follows a virtual guide superimposed on the real world. There is no need for the user to look at the map and landmarks while walking. In experiments, we measured changes in the gaze direction and head pose while the user walked with a real or virtual guide. We observed that the guides provided the following effect to the users and alleviated their physical burden.

1 Introduction

There is a demand for navigation systems that intuitively support users while walking. Conventional navigation systems such as Google maps [4] support the user using the steps illustrated in Fig. 1. Before the user walks, he or she sets a destination (S1) and selects a route suggested by the system (S2). While walking, the user checks their current position on the map (S3), and searches for landmarks in the real world (S4). If the user understands their current position in the real world, he or she can determine their travel direction (S5). Otherwise, the user laboriously repeats S3 and S4 until he or she correctly understands their current position. While repeating these steps, a user frequently moves their gaze and head to see the system and landmarks, as illustrated in Fig. 2. A user can feel a physical burden from these movements. In particular, existing methods [6,8,13] using global navigation satellite systems and digital maps on mobile terminals produce a physical burden because they require the user to repeat these movements.

In this paper, we tackle the challenging problem of decreasing the physical burden by reducing gaze and head movements using a novel navigation system. To reduce these movements, we must intuitively indicate the direction of travel to the user. Existing methods [2,10] use simplified maps or simple messages to enhance the navigation system. However, these methods sometimes do not reduce head and gaze movements because the user must read the simplified maps or simple messages.

S. Lackey and J. Chen (Eds.): VAMR 2017, LNCS 10280, pp. 533–543, 2017.
DOI: 10.1007/978-3-319-57987-0_43

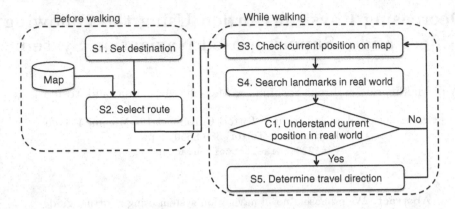

Fig. 1. Overview of a navigation system.

Fig. 2. Searching landmarks.

Here, we consider a situation where a guide suggests the travel direction by always walking in front of the user. In this situation, we believe that the gaze and head movements are reduced because the user simply follows the guide. When the attendees of a conference go to a banquet venue, for example, following a guide is the easiest way to smoothly reach the venue. We call this the following effect. This effect is known in the field of car navigation systems [9] and indoor navigation systems [14]. We show that the virtual guide provides the following effect when the user walks in an outdoor environment.

In this paper, we show that the following effect experimentally decreases the physical burden, by measuring the gaze and head movements of a walking user. Furthermore, we developed a navigation system that uses a virtual guide superimposed on the real world through a head-mounted display (HMD) and evaluated the reduction in movement. The rest of the paper is organized as follows. Section 2 shows that the physical burden of the user is reduced by the following effect when the user walks with a real guide. Section 3 shows the evaluation of a virtual guide with an HMD. Our concluding remarks are given in Sect. 4.

2   Following Effect Cased by a Real Guide

2.1   Comparison of Conventional Navigation Methods

To observe the following effect, we measured the movements of head poses and gaze directions while walking. We compared five navigation methods as illustrated in Fig. 3.

N1: (Real guide) The user followed a real guide who was always walking in front of the user.

N2: (Signpost) The user saw signposts set at junctions.

N3: (Mobile terminal) The user could check their current position on a mobile terminal at any time while walking.

N4: (Combination) The user used a combination of N2 and N3.

N5: (Map) The user carried only a real map printed on paper.

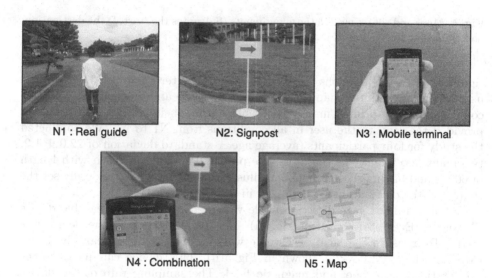

Fig. 3. Navigation methods that were compared to evaluate the following effect.

2.2   Evaluation Protocol of the Real Guide

In N1, a real guide, who fully understood the route and the map, walked about 2 m in front of the user. The real guide showed the travel direction at junctions by bending forward without talking to the user. The real guide walked at a constant speed and checked that the user was following behind at intervals of 30 s. In N2, signposts at junctions showed the travel direction using arrows. The user was able to see the signposts at a distance. In N3, the user carried a mobile terminal (SONY XPERIA mini) and could check their current position using a map application at any time during their journey. In N4, the user saw the

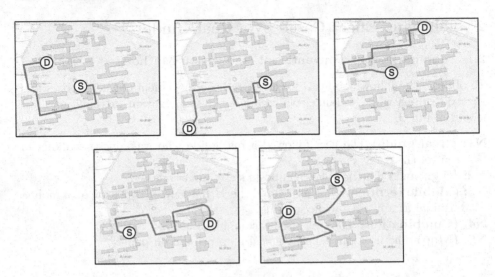

Fig. 4. Maps and routes used in the experiments (S denotes the start, D the destination, and the heavy line the route).

signposts of N2 at junctions and carried the mobile terminal of N3. In N5, the user carried the printed map that dictated the route and destination. The user could look at the printed map at any time during their journey. Note that we provided the map to the user in all conditions from N1 to N5. We conducted the study for four participants (average age ± standard deviation of 22.0 ± 1.2, two male, two female) as the users. We prepared five routes (each with length of 600 m and having six junctions), as illustrated in Fig. 4. We randomly set the route and the destination for each user in our evaluation.

To measure the gaze direction while walking, we used the wearable device (Takei TalkEye Lite) shown in Fig. 5(i). The sampling rate of the device was 30 Hz. To measure the head pose while walking, we used the wearable device (MicroStrain 3DM-GX-25) shown in Fig. 5(ii). This device can measure the acceleration, gyroscope, and magnetic field. The sampling rate of the device was 100 Hz. The gaze direction is given on x and y axes of Fig. 6(i). The head pose is represented by the roll, pitch, and yaw axes of Fig. 6(ii). The origin of the axes corresponds to the state that the user stands upright and looks straight ahead. We measured the relative angle from the origin.

2.3   Evaluation with a Real Guide

Changes in Gaze Direction. Figure 7 shows the distributions of gaze movements while walking. The gray level corresponds to the frequency of the gaze in that direction, and $(X, Y) = (0, 0)$ represents that the user was looking straight ahead. We normalized the number of samples of gaze directions for each user because each user walked at a different speed. We see that the frequencies around the center direction in N1–N5 are higher than those for other directions.

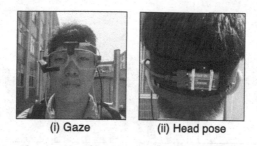

(i) Gaze   (ii) Head pose

Fig. 5. Equipment for measuring the gaze direction and head pose.

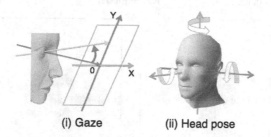

(i) Gaze   (ii) Head pose

Fig. 6. Rotation axes for representing the gaze direction and head pose.

Table 1. Averages and standard deviations of absolute gaze directions [degrees].

	N1	N2	N3	N4	N5
X	10.4 ± 9.5	11.0 ± 9.6	11.5 ± 9.6	11.0 ± 9.6	12.6 ± 10.4
Y	8.2 ± 9.4	9.4 ± 10.9	12.6 ± 12.6	10.2 ± 11.0	10.9 ± 11.4

We believe that this phenomenon is due to the effect of the center bias [15]. Furthermore, we see that the real guide (N1) reduced the movements; i.e., the user looked straight ahead more for N1 than for N2–N5.

Table 1 gives that the averages and standard deviations of gaze directions computed from absolute values of angles. We see that the averages of N1 are smaller than those of N2–N5, and the standard deviation for the Y direction of N1 is smaller than those of N2–N5. We believe that the gaze direction is attracted to the center by the virtual guide.

Changes in Head Pose. Figure 8 shows the distribution of head movement while walking. We normalized the number of samples of head poses for each user because each user walked at a different speed. We unified the sum of the distribution for each method. We used the pitch axis to indicate the change in upward and downward movement of the head. The head faces the front for $R = 0$, downward for $R > 0$, and upward for $R < 0$. We see that the real guide (N1) reduced the head movement; i.e., frequencies around 0° were higher than those

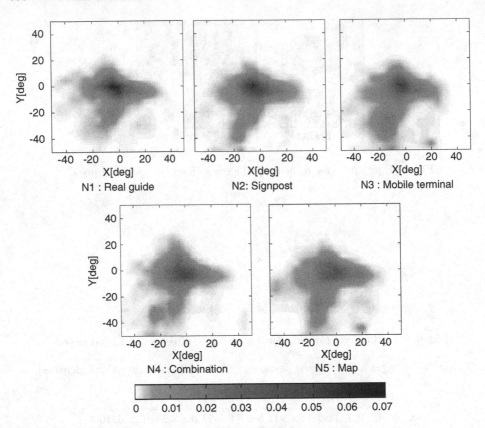

Fig. 7. Distribution of gaze while walking using different navigation methods.

Table 2. Average and standard deviation of the pitch axis of the absolute head pose [degrees].

N1	N2	N3	N4	N5
5.1 ± 5.1	6.1 ± 7.5	10.1 ± 11.1	7.8 ± 9.8	8.7 ± 9.8

of other angles. We believe that the real guide reduces the vertical movement of the head of the user looking at the map.

Table 2 gives the averages and standard deviations of head poses computed from the absolute angle of the pitch axis. We see that the average and standard deviation of N1 are lower than those of N2–N5. A previous report [5] described that the burden of the neck vertebrae increases to 2.3 kg when the head moves downward from 5° to 10°. We believe that the head pose is attracted to the center by the virtual guide. Note that the average values for the angle about the yaw axis in N1–N5 were almost the same. The users sometimes moved their head horizontally to navigate obstacles when walking. The averages of the angle

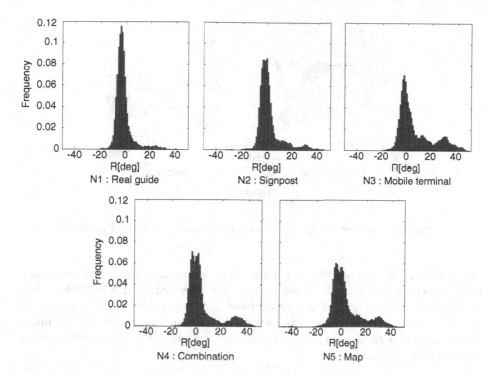

Fig. 8. Distributions of the head pitch for the different navigation methods.

about the roll axis were zero in N1–N5. The users did not tilt their head when walking.

3   Navigation System Using a Virtual Guide

3.1   Design of Our Navigation System

Head and gaze movements were reduced when using a real guide as described in the previous section, and we thus believe that the following effect decreases the physical burden. We therefore designed a novel navigation system that uses a virtual guide superimposed on the real world. Our system displays a virtual guide to the users on an HMD, as illustrated in Fig. 9. We compared our system with four navigation systems in terms of effectiveness, as illustrated in Fig. 10.

V1: (Virtual guide) A virtual guide walked in front of the user to indicate the travel direction.
V2: (Arrow) A virtual arrow appeared at junctions to indicate the travel direction.
V3: (Current position) A virtual map was provided with the current position always shown.
V4: (Combination) The user used a combination of V2 and V3.

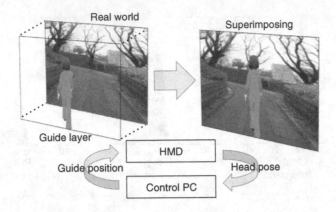

Fig. 9. Overview of our navigation system using the virtual guide.

We provided the users with a printed map containing the destination and route for all conditions. The above systems are alternatives of N1–N4 described in Sect. 3.1. Virtual guides are often used in augmented reality applications [1,11,12], and virtual arrows have been used in a map application [7]. We investigate whether a virtual guide reduces the physical burden of users while walking in an outdoor environment.

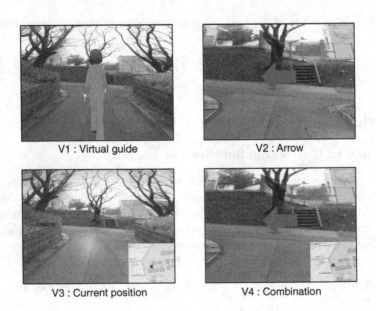

Fig. 10. Navigation systems for evaluating the following effect.

3.2   Evaluation Protocol of the Virtual Guide

To evaluate the navigation systems, our system controlled the guide or the arrow using the Wizard of Oz technique [3]. We used an optical see-through HMD (EPSON MOVERIO BT-200). In stably overlaying the guide or the arrow on the real world while the user walked, we used an operator to control the display position of the guide as illustrated in Fig. 11. We acquired the head pose of the user using the acceleration and gyro sensors built into the HMD. After showing the guide or arrow adjusted to the head pose, the operator modified the positions when there was an error. The operator followed 2 m behind the user, and modified the display position by monitoring a live video sequence obtained from a camera built into the HMD. In V1, we adjusted the parameters of the virtual guide such that the virtual guide was 170 cm in height and displayed about 5 m in front of the user. In V2, we displayed an arrow 5 m before reaching a junction. In V3, we showed a map and the current position such that the visibility of the user was not disturbed.

Operator   Control PC

Fig. 11. Operator and user with equipment for evaluation.

Twelve participants (average age $\pm$ standard deviation of 21.5 $\pm$ 0.4, 10 males, two females) acted as the user. We used the same routes described in Sect. 2.2, and randomly set the route and destination. We used the same sensor described in Sect. 2.2 to measure the head pose of the user. Note that we did not acquire the gaze direction of the user because the gaze sensor disturbed the HMD.

3.3   Measurement of the Head Pose with the Virtual Guide

Figure 12 shows the distribution of the head movement around the pitch axis while walking using navigation systems V1–V4. We used the same axes and evaluation protocols described in Sect. 2.3. We see that the peaks of the histograms for V1 increased near the frontal direction. We believe that the virtual guide reduced the head movements of the users. We also see that the head faced downward more frequently for V2–V4 than for V1. We believe that the users more frequently checked the printed map during their journey for V2–V4 than

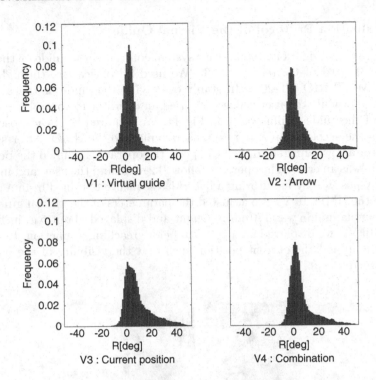

Fig. 12. Distributions of the head pitch while walking using the four navigation methods.

Table 3. Averages and standard deviations of absolute head poses [degrees].

V1	V2	V3	V4
5.2 ± 5.7	7.9 ± 10.1	9.2 ± 9.8	7.1 ± 8.4

for V1. Note that the angle about the yaw axis was concentrated around 0°, and there was no apparent difference in the angle around the roll axis.

Table 3 gives the averages and standard deviations of absolute angles of head poses the pitch axis. The table confirms that the average and standard deviation were lower for V1 than for V2–V4, and changes in the vertical direction were small for V1. We observed that the virtual guide superimposed on the real world reduced the head movement of users while walking.

4   Conclusion

We revealed that the following effect induced by a real guide decreased the physical burden of a walking user, by measuring the gaze and head movements of users. We also developed a navigation system using a virtual guide and evaluated the reduction in head movement.

As part of our future work, we will expand our analysis to long-term experiments on the proposed navigation system and develop a method that assists users to avoid hazards.

References

1. Barakonyi, I., Schmalstieg, D.: AR Puppet: animated agents in augmented reality. In: Proceedings of the First Central European International Multimedia and Virtual Reality Conference, pp. 35–42 (2004)
2. Devlin, A.S., Bernstein, J.: Interactive wayfinding: use of cues by men and women. Environ. Psychol. **15**, 23–38 (1995)
3. Fraser, N.M., Gilbert, G.N.: Simulating speech systems. Comput. Speech Lang. **5**, 81–99 (1991)
4. Google: Google map, https://www.google.com/maps/
5. Hansraj, K.K.: Assessment of stresses in the cervical spine caused by posture and position of the head. Surg. Technol. Int. **25**, 277–279 (2014)
6. Ishikawa, T., Fujiwara, H., Imai, O., Okabe, A.: Wayfinding with a GPS-based mobile navigation system: a comparison with maps and direct experience. Environ. Psychol. **28**, 74–82 (2008)
7. Kalkusch, M., Lidy, H., Knapp, M., Reitmay, G., Kaufmann, H., Schmalstieg, D.: Structured visual markers for indoor pathfinding (2002)
8. Lee, W.C., Cheng, B.W.: Effects of using a portable navigation system and paper map in real driving. Accid. Anal. Prev. **40**, 303–308 (2008)
9. Medenica, Z., Kun, A.L., Paek, T., Palinko, O.: Augmented reality vs. street views: a driving simulator study comparing two emerging navigation aids. In: Proceedings of the 13th International Conference on Human Computer Interaction with Mobile Devices and Services, pp. 265–274 (2011)
10. Monobe, K., Tanaka, S., Furuta, H., Mochinaga, D.: Fundamental research on traffic support to the pedestrian by route giude map based on the space perception. Appl. Comput. Civ. Eng. **16**, 323–330 (2007)
11. Thomas, B., Close, B., Donoghue, J., Squires, J., De Bondi, P., Morris, M., Piekarski, W.: Arquake: an outdoor/indoor augmented reality first person application. In: Proceedings of the Fourth International Symposium on Wearable Computers, pp. 139–146 (2000)
12. Vilhjálmsson, H., et al.: The behavior markup language: recent developments and challenges. In: Pelachaud, C., Martin, J.-C., André, E., Chollet, G., Karpouzis, K., Pelé, D. (eds.) IVA 2007. LNCS (LNAI), vol. 4722, pp. 99–111. Springer, Heidelberg (2007). doi:10.1007/978-3-540-74997-4_10
13. Willis, K.S., Hölscher, C., Wilbertz, G., Li, C.: A comparison of spatial knowledge acquisition with maps and mobile maps. Comput. Environ. Urban Syst. **33**, 100–110 (2009)
14. Wither, J., DiVerdi, S., Hollerer, T.: Evaluating display types for ar selection and annotation. In: Proceedings of the 6th IEEE and ACM International Symposium on Mixed and Augmented Reality, pp. 1–4 (2007)
15. Yamada, K., Sugano, Y., Okabe, T., Sato, Y., Sugimoto, A., Hiraki, K.: Attention prediction in egocentric video using motion and visual saliency. In: Ho, Y.-S. (ed.) PSIVT 2011. LNCS, vol. 7087, pp. 277–288. Springer, Heidelberg (2011). doi:10.1007/978-3-642-25367-6_25

Evaluating Factors Affecting Virtual Reality Display

Lisa Rebenitsch[1(✉)] and Charles Owen[2]

[1] South Dakota School of Mines and Technology, Rapid City, USA
lisa.rebenitsch@sdsmt.edu
[2] Michigan State University, Lansing, USA
cbowen@msu.edu

Abstract. Head Mounted Displays (HMDs) anecdotally exhibit a higher rate of cybersickness, motion-sickness like symptoms due to visual stimuli, than virtual reality systems that employ large screens. Yet, there have been relatively few multi-display studies, and frequently factors other than the display varied between conditions. We controlled for these additional factors in three experiments which considered HMDs weight, perceived screen size, and rendering mode. The HMD weight experiment had no effect on cybersickness, with $p < 0.88$. This is of benefit to HMD developers as it signifies that additional weight in the hardware is not cause for concern. While screen size and field of view (FOV) are often used interchangeably, the FOV has a strong effect independent of screen size. The perceived screen size experiment had no effect on cybersickness, with $p < 0.66$. This benefits cybersickness researchers, as it signifies that the results from monitor experiments can be compared directly with the results from large screen experiments, assuming the remaining factors are held constant. The rendering experiment, with stereo and mono rendering, had no effect on cybersickness, with $p = 0.22$. Since the HMD weight and screen size experiments used the same FOV, application, and navigation paradigm, they were compared for possible effects. Initially, we found a significant effect on cybersickness. After normalizing using the average change when a part of the real world is seen, such as in large screens, there is no longer a statistical difference ($p < 0.77$).

Keywords: Head Mounted Displays · Virtual reality displays · Independent visual backgrounds · Cybersickness · VIMS

1 Introduction

Head mounted displays (HMD) systems like Occulus Rift and HTC Vive are bringing virtual reality to public consumers. Unfortunately, HMDs anecdotally have a higher rate of cybersickness, or motion-sickness like symptoms due to visual stimuli, than virtual reality systems that employ large screens. These systems include single projection screens, large TVs, and multi-wall CAVEs, that normally track a user's position. If the displays result in differences in cybersickness, then further study should separate the results into two distinct categories. There have been relatively few multi-display studies, and most alter other factors such as the field of view [1–4]. We controlled for additional

© Springer International Publishing AG 2017
S. Lackey and J. Chen (Eds.): VAMR 2017, LNCS 10280, pp. 544–555, 2017.
DOI: 10.1007/978-3-319-57987-0_44

external factors in our experiments which considered the HMD's weight, the perceived screen size, and the rendering mode.

Cybersickness has a large number of potential factors with Kolasinski [5] and Renkewitz and Alexander [6] proposing over 40 possible factors. Virtual reality applications that use large screen systems often have different factors than HMDs beyond the display. For example, the field of view, interaction paradigm, viewing position, and rendering mode regularly differ. This makes comparison difficult as factors such as field of view have shown strong effects on cybersickness [7–11]. If the differences in the reported results are due to uncontrolled factors, future models could be simplified by the decreasing the number of factors.

Cybersickness and simulator sickness have been under study for decades, but there is a lack of predictive models for frequency and severity. With over 40 factors listed and hardware limitations, it is often difficult to hold all factors constant across different experiments. While many factors have uncertain effects, some factors that tend to vary between HMDs and large screens, are known to have an effect such as standing versus sitting, field of view, and independent visual backgrounds. Further difficulties occur since there are multiple measures of cybersickness and there are not conversions between different units.

While most factors not under analysis in our experiments were held constant, there remain a few that were affected. The refresh rate differed due to hardware limitations between the HMD and projection screen, and there was a small change in resolution. Neither appeared to affect our results. We could not control for the participants by selecting individuals that fit certain criteria, and Rebenitsch and Owen suggested the participants alone could account for 43% of the variance [12]. Therefore, participants were requested to attend both sessions of an experiment set.

Initially, we found there was a difference in display types, but after normalizing for the independent visual background, any differences were eliminated. This means that the differences between displays is due to other factors. This is fortunate, as it decreases the large number of factors that would need to be controlled in experiments. Specifically, we found no effect from weight or perceived screen size. Stereo is less clear, as any results appear to be small or there may have been an interaction effect. The display did not have effect when controlling for field of view, viewing position, application, and independent visual background. This also signifies that results from different displays can be compared, if normalized for different settings.

2   Background

Cybersickness results from visual stimuli, rather than physical motion as in traditional motion sickness. As most virtual reality requires a visual display, there is a risk of cybersickness, and the effect of the display is uncertain. One reason for the lack of multi-display studies is that such studies are costly in both time and resources. Also, the results on one display are assumed to transfer directly to another display. Unfortunately, these few studies suggest results do not transfer directly.

Sharples, Cobb et al. compared four different displays [2]. The HMD had the highest symptoms of nausea, while a large projection screen and a large curved screen had similar symptoms. A desktop system had the lowest scores. Liu and Uang examined a standard monitor, a stereoscopic monitor, and an HMD [4]. The HMD had higher scores than the standard monitor. Smart, Otten, and Stoffregen examined the percentage of participants that became ill using different displays [1]. They used the same sinusoidal motion in all conditions, although the visuals changed. They found 23% became ill in a moving room, 43% became ill in a space travel simulator, 17% became ill in a projector system, and 42% became ill with a HMD.

Unfortunately, in the above studies, several factors other than the display were altered between conditions, and some of these factors have shown effects on cyber-sicknes. These are weight of the display, the perceived screen size, the rendering mode (stereo or mono), the viewing position while using the system, the field of view, the application, the participant, and the interaction paradigm.

2.1 Weight

The additional weight of a HMD has been assumed to be the source of higher symptoms. However, only one study, by Dizio and Lackner, was found that examined the effect of weight [10]. Weight was a secondary component in this study and while they reported there was no effect, no statistics were reported. This left the effect of this factor uncertain, and was the motive for our first experiment.

2.2 Perceived Screen Size

A screen's distance to the eye will affect how a participant perceives the size of an object and how the eyes adjust to focus on an object. Vergence is the location where the eyes' focus crosses and functions as normal in virtual reality. Accommodation is the lense's adjustment for distance. Since the screen distance is constant in virtual reality, accommodation is no longer accurate. No studies were found that directly examined this effect. Distance and screen size have been varied to change the field of view, but since the field of view has a known effect, we maintained the same field of view for our second experiment in order to test for a possible cybersickness effect due to the vergence and accommodation discrepancy.

2.3 Stereo

Stereo rendering is associated with higher rates of illness. Therefore, this may have an effect in virtual reality as well. There have been few studies using cybersickness as measurement. Hakkinen, Vuori, and Ehrlich reported only that the nausea symptom were higher during stereo rendering [13]. Kershavarz and Hecht compared four versions of a roller coaster ride: real stereoscopic video, a stereoscopic rendering of a three-dimensional model, a monoscopic video, and a monoscopic modeled rollercoaster [14]. They found no significant differences between the conditions, although the real stereoscopic rollercoaster cybersickness scores trended higher. Given these variable results, we included stereo as our third experiment.

2.4 Viewing Position

Large screen systems typically have participants standing and the screen updates according to where people move, while HMDs are often seated for safety. However, there have been past studies that show that such a change in procedure can influence cybersickness. Merhi et al. found that all their standing participants withdrew early [15]. Moss and Muth altered their procedure midway to include a hand rail due to a high dropout rate [16]. In general, increased tactile information seems to decrease cybersickness. This means when comparing systems, the viewing position should be the same between the two conditions.

2.5 FOV

The field of view (FOV) is traditionally assumed to be the horizontal or diagonal angle that a screen occupies in a person's vision. FOV is one of the strongest cybersickness factors, with symptoms doubling when the FOV doubles. Seay et al. found that symptoms were higher for a 180° field of view than for a 60° field of view, even when changing user control and rendering mode [7]. Dizio and Lackner reported that halving the field of view also halved the symptoms of cybersickness [10]. Stoffregen et al. reported a similar doubling effect [11]. Therefore, having different FOV when comparing displays can dramatically affect the result. This is the second reason for our screen size experiment: to confirm that the changes in symptoms with changes of distance and size were not exclusively due to the change in FOV.

2.6 Application

The application can also have an effect, but metrics that fully quantify this factor are lacking. Application factors included are speed, color, contrast, brightness, scene content, and independent visual backgrounds. If using the same application for all conditions, most of these factors will remain constant. However, brightness, and independent visual background (IVB) still often change. Independent visual background are objects that appear static relative to the real world in virtual reality. They include seeing the real world around the display in large screen environments, having the virtual display overlap with the real word [17], and including objects that never change their position on the screen such as vertical or horizontal bars used in *Duh et al.* [18, 19].

Large screen systems normally have a brighter environment than an HMD. Given that a human's flicker threshold decreases with light, and that flicker can cause migraines, any possibility of flicker could affect symptoms. HMDs typically have persistent screens, but still can have a flicker-like effect if quickly turning the head does not result in a perceived blur due to a too low refresh rate.

Independent visual backgrounds (IVB) are normally available in large screens, but require intentional inclusion in HMDS. Duh et al. found that merely adding constant lines (much like wearing a mask) decreases symptoms [18, 19]. Prothero et al. used a transparent screen to decrease symptoms [17]. The most dramatic result is the study by Kershavarz, Hecht, and Zschutschke [3]. They tested an HMD, a standard projection screen, and a projection screen with the external environment blocked to mimic an HMD. Without the environment blocking, the HMD and the projection screen had a significant difference, as is normally reported. With the environment blocking, the HMD and the projection screen had the same symptoms.

2.7 Measuring Cybersickness

Cybersickness has diverse symptoms, and thus, the measurements also are diverse. The most common methods are questionnaires, of which the simulator sickness questionnaire (SSQ) is in the broadest use [20]. This questionnaire asks for the severity of multiple symptoms and then groups them into nausea (e.g. stomach awareness, nausea, etc.), oculomotor (e.g. headache, eyestrain, etc.), and disorientation (e.g. vertigo, dizziness, etc.), and are abbreviated N, O, and D, respectively.

Following the SSQ in popularity are numerous one-question scales. The SSQ is too long for monitoring of participants, and thus a single numeric response is employed instead, and represents current feeling of wellness. While there are variations in the number of one-question survey, the questions are normally on a 0–10 scale, with higher numbers meaning greater illness.

3   Hypotheses

Experiments were designed to determine if the cybersickness effects were due to the display itself, or other factors that may be changed between two systems. The first experiment was done to assure that the assumption that weight would influence cybersickness. The second experiment was to determine if the perceived screen size, or that changing the screen size while the field of view is held constant, would still have an affect across different displays. The third was done to determine if stereo had an effect if the application and field of view remained the same. This resulted in the following hypotheses:

1. A heavier HMD will increase cybersickness.
2. Changing the screen size will not have an effect, if the field of view is held constant.
3. Stereo rendering will cause more cybersickness than mono rendering.

Since the experiments included both HMDs and large screens, we also considered whether there was an effect in changing the display, if the application, navigation paradigm, and field of view remained the same. This resulted in our last hypotheses:

4. HMDs will have higher cybersickness than large screen.

4   General Methods

All participants were over 18, and signed a consent form before they began. To decrease the effects of habitation, repeat sessions were separated by a minimum of one week. Participants were then given an X-box controller for navigation. The first session included a tutorial so that they could learn how to work the controls and play the game. Participants were then placed into the virtual treasure hunt environment. All experiments had the participants standing.

The participants were monitored for symptoms every three minutes using a one question scale dubbed an "immersion" rating. This rating asked, *"On a scale of zero to ten, where zero is how you felt coming in, and ten is that you want to stop, where you are now?"* The highest value during a session is called the "max immersion rating." This is based on the scale from Bos et al. who showed good correlation with the SSQ-T [21]. However, we wished to allow participants to stop for any reason and avoid possible demand characteristics mentioned by Young et al. [22]. This proved necessary as only 30% of those that withdrew early specified nausea as their reason for stopping. Immediately following the session, the participants were given the SSQ.

Non-parametric statistical methods on the SSQ-T were employed as the results were decidedly non-Gaussian. The Wilcoxon test is a non-parametric test and has shown to be robust with respect to outliers, which are typical in cybersickness data. Paired tests were used in consideration of the effect of individual variations.

4.1   Environment

To generalize the results, the experiments required an environment that could be seen in the home. Specifically, the environment needed to be interactive, fully 3D, have least some effects of gravity (no flying), and could not be made with the intention to encourage cybersickness. A treasure hunt game was created to meet these conditions. The virtual environment consisted of five to nine rooms, two of which were mazes. The rooms were varied for each session, but always included one rectangular maze, and one curved wall maze. The object of the game was to locate all the items given in a left-hand menu as

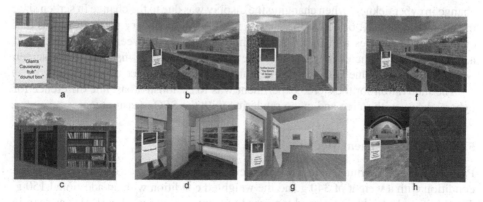

Fig. 1.   Screen shots from the experiment virtual environment

quickly as possible. Example screen shots are provided in Fig. 1. The environment was created to scale, if possible, and most objects were approximately 80 cm from the floor.

The same participants were employed within each experiment set. This was to minimize to effect of the wide range of individual factors which could mask results. However, this does create the possibility of habituation and learning effects. To offset the latter, a different set of rooms and treasure list were provided in each session. Later analysis with the Kruskal test (the Kruskal test is a non-parametric variant of ANOVA) displayed no effect based on the choice of room set (p < 0.75).

4.2 Hardware

The virtual environment was presented using Vizard 3.0 with 3-sample antialiasing and a 4:3 aspect ratio. Tracking was done with an Intersense IS900 which has a specified latency of 4 ms. Formal tracker-to-display latency calculations were not performed. If stereo was used, the software IPD was 6 cm. The two different display technologies were Glasstron LDI-D100B HMD, with an 800 × 600 resolution, fixed interpupillary distance, and a 35° diagonal FOV, and a stereo projector with a maximum resolution of 1600 × 1200 and a refresh rate of 100 Hz due to the shutter glasses.

5 Experiments

Three main experiments were designed to determine how the display affects cybersickness: weight, perceived screen size, and rendering mode. Given that the HMD weight and screen size experiments used the same FOV, application, and the navigation paradigms, a forth cross-display analysis was also performed. This collated the results of the prior three experiments into a cohesive whole. The motivation for the cross-display analysis was to determine how much the change in cybersickness was due entirely to the display and not other factors.

The motivation for the weight experiment was to prove the assumption that the weight of the HMD caused the increase in symptoms.

The motivation for the perceived screen size experiment was to determine if the change in cybersickness when changing the display was due to the change in screen size, the change in display, or due to the change in FOV. A secondary motivation was that even if the FOV does remain the same, the discrepancy between the vergence and accommodation of the eyes would increase with the change in distance to the screen when assuring the same FOV. Therefore, this could still influence cybersickness.

The motivation for the stereo experiment was to establish a baseline difference for cybersickness with stereo and mono rendering with the SSQ measurement.

5.1 HMD Experiment Methods

Participants were recruited to test two different weight conditions with a HMD: the base condition with a weight of 340 g and the weighted condition with an additional 150 g. The additional weight was placed towards the front as is normal for HMDs as seen in

Fig. 2. Participants were given the base and weighted condition at least a week apart, in random order. We recruited 24 participants for both weight conditions. Their average age was 19.8 years with a standard deviation of 2.5 years. There were 5 females and 19 males. We had 4 early withdrawals, all males, out of 48 sessions.

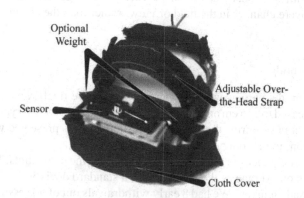

Fig. 2. The head mounted display

5.2 HMD Experiment Analysis

To our surprise, there was no effect of weight on cybersickness, with $p < 0.88$. This high p-value means that modern HMD weight is unlikely to affect cybersickness, and even extremely lightweight HMDs are unlikely to have an effect. While the mean and standard deviation's reliability is less certain with non-Gaussian data, they still provide trends in values. The mean for the non-weighted condition was 23.12 with a standard deviation of 21.7, and the mean for the weighted condition was 29.6 with a standard deviation of 31.3.

5.3 Perceived Screen Size Methods

We recruited 22 participants for the screen size experiments with an average age of 19.9 years and a standard deviation of 2.6 years. There were 5 females and 17 males. We had 2 early withdrawals out of 44 sessions, with one male and one female participant.

In the perceived screen size experiment, the participants were presented with a 113-centimeter screen or a 70-centimeter screen in random order. These two sizes were chosen to mimic a moderate sized 1-walled CAVE, and a monitor. Under both conditions, the participants were placed at a specific distance to the screen so that they would have the same starting field of view as the HMD experiment. Therefore, the smaller screen had participants closer to the screen. Participants were permitted a temporary step in each direction, so therefore, the average field of view was identical for all the participants. Hardware limitations required the smaller screen to have 80% of the resolution of the larger screen.

5.4   Screen Size Analysis

As expected, there was no effect on cybersickness, with $p < 0.66$. The mean for the smaller screen was 18.5 with a standard deviation of 19.3, and the larger screen had a mean of 18.8 with a standard deviation of 15.7. This suggests that the differences reported earlier were changes in the field of view, rather than the change in screen size or distance.

5.5   Stereo Methods

In this experiment, the participants were permitted to move freely, and the screen field of view was increased to 225 cm on the diagonal. The field of view was typically between a 60–90° diagonal FOV during the session. A participant was presented with the stereo or mono condition, in random order, at least one week apart.

We had 28 participants, but 6 could not return due to time constraints. The remaining participants were on average 21.4 years old with a standard deviation of 3 years. There were 8 females and 14 males. We had 8 early withdrawals out of 50 sessions, consisting of 3 males and 3 females. Two male participants withdrew twice.

5.6   Stereo Analysis

There was no effect on cybersickness, with $p = 0.22$. The mean for the mono condition was 28 with a standard deviation of 27.3, while the stereo's mean was 33.3 with a standard deviation of 24.1. This was somewhat surprising, but some prior studies found no effect, such as Howarth [23] and Kershavarz and Hecht only showed a trend [14].

5.7   Cross-Display Analysis

Participants were asked to attend both the screen size and HMD weight experiments. Both experiments adding the head tracked viewpoint directly on top of the controller position so that the "forward" direction remained the same in both conditions, and both the HMD and screen size conditions permitted only one step in any direction. This encouraged the HMD participants to always face in the same direction as they would in a large screen environment.

Since the HMD and screen size experiments showed no effect, a participant's scores within each of the two experiments were averaged. If a participant did not attend both sessions in an experiment set, only their single score from the set was employed.

We had 24 participants with data for at least one HMD and one screen size experiment. These participants had an average age of 19.7 years with a standard deviation of 2.5 years. There were 5 females and 19 males. We had 7 early withdrawals out of 92 sessions, consisting of 6 males and 1 female. We had four participants miss either one HMD session or one screen experiment, either due to request or scheduling issues.

Initially, we found a significant effect on cybersickness, with $p < 0.02$, with the HMD having higher symptoms. This suggests one or more of the following. There was an IVB effect, the slight change in interaction had an effect, there was sufficient transfer of habituation, or a combination of these effects.

The study by Kershavarz, Hecht, and Zschutschke suggested an IVB effect [3]. They also held the application, interaction, and field of view constant, but saw an effect between a HMD and large screen display. However, they performed another experiment to clarify the effect. They removed the real room imagery in the screen condition so it would resemble that of an HMD, therefore eliminating the IVB effect. This rendered the screen and HMD cybersickness results statistically equivalent. If we normalize our data using the average change of 69.9% when an IVB is included from the literature [3, 16–19], there is no longer a statistical difference ($p < 0.77$).

6 Discussion

Cybersickness has numerous potential factors, and decreasing the selection of those factors that must be held consistent to compare results is a desirable element of research. The possibility of a display affecting cybersickness complicates matters, as there are numerous versions. However, there are been little research into directly comparing displays.

HMDs and stereo anecdotally have higher cybersickness, but experimental results were lacking. In our experiments, we found no statistical effect on HMD weight. This is contrary to expectations, but this is of benefit to HMD developers as it signifies that additional weight for hardware is not a cause for concern, except for one caveat. While the HMD weight did not increase symptoms, the participants were vocal about the discomfort of the display. The heavier display placed more pressure on the bridge of the nose, which was near universally disliked.

There was no effect on the perceived screen size. This was expected as the screen size is often changed to change the FOV, but FOV has a strong effect on its own. Since the FOV was not changed in this instance, any difference would be due to the eyes' accommodation and vergence discrepancy. The lack of statistical significant result signifies that the discrepancy between vergence and accommodation does not influence cybersickness, at least within 1–3 m range. An effect with a wider difference may still be possible. Given the low amount of physical movement in our study, the effect of angular momentum is still uncertain. The lack of effect on perceived screen size benefits cybersickness researchers, as it signifies that the results from monitor experiments can be compared directly with the results from large screen experiments, assuming the remaining factors are held constant.

There was no effect with stereo, which was surprising, but the results are tentative. Stereo rendering may interact with the application. The human visual system only relies on stereo fusion out to several feet, and primarily within arm's reach. The visual system uses other visual cues to estimate the distance of farther objects. Our environment did not include many items within arm's reach. Mon-Williams and Wann also mentioned an increased effect on cybersickness if the focal distance changes frequently [24]. Also, several participants only showed a temporary effect in the immersion scores and returned to their baselines within 10 min. This may have affected the results as the effect may be time variable, rather than simply increasing with usage as is typical. While more study is needed, one can conclude that the effect is likely to be small.

HMDs initially showed a greater amount of cybersickness. However, after normalizing for the independent visual background (IVB) effect that most single large screens possess, there was no longer an effect. Our initial scores suggested the HMD was worse than a projection screen if an IVB was available, while Kershavarz, Hecht, and Zschutschk suggested the opposite [3]. We theorize this is due to expectation on the part of the participant. We allowed user directed interaction in an unknown world, while Kershavarz, Hecht, and Zschutschk did not permit user movement or interaction in the familiar environment of a car ride as a passenger. In our case, the users may have favored the familiar real world, while Kershavarz, Hecht, and Zschutschk user's may have favored the familiar car ride. Ideally, another application holding these factors constant should be tested. This is to determine the effect of expectation which is a likely source of habituation. Specifically, the experiment could include an environment that is foreign to the real world, and an environment that is a common experience to see which stimuli is preferred.

In summary, differences in symptoms between displays are due to other inconsistent factors. Some factors that are likely affecting the results are FOV, viewing position, and independent visual backgrounds. Stereo remains uncertain, as its effect appears to be small, but there also may be interaction effects. Removing weight and display from potential factors is beneficial to researchers as there are numerous other factors that may still have an effect. The results of the IVB are promising for both normalizing results across displays and as a method to decrease cybersickness.

References

1. Smart, L.J.J., Otten, E.W., Stoffregen, T.A.: It's turtles all the way down: a comparative analysis of visually induced motion sickness. Hum. Factors Ergon. Soc. Annu. Meet. Proc. **51**, 1631–1634 (2007)
2. Sharples, S., Cobb, S., Moody, A., Wilson, J.R.: Virtual reality induced symptoms and effects (VRISE): comparison of head mounted display (HMD), desktop and projection display systems. Displays **29**(2), 58–69 (2008)
3. Keshavarz, B., Hecht, H., Zschutschke, L.: Intra-visual conflict in visually induced motion sickness. Displays **32**(4), 181–188 (2011)
4. Liu, CL., Uang, ST.: Effects of presence on causing cybersickness in the elderly within a 3D virtual store. In: Human Computer Interaction International: Users and Applications, Orlando, USA (2011)
5. Kolasinski, E.M.: Simulator Sickness in Virtual Environments. Final Technical report. Army Research Inst for the Behavioral and Social Sciences, Alexandria (1995)
6. Renkewitz, H., Alexander, T.: Perceptual Issues of Augmented and Virtual Environments. FGAN-FKIE, Wachtberg (2007)
7. Seay, A.F., Krum, D.M., Hodges, L., Ribarsky, W.: Simulator sickness and presence in a high field-of-view virtual environment. In: CHI 2002 Extended Abstracts on Human Factors in Computing Systems, pp. 784–785 (2002)
8. Duh, H.B.L., Lin, J.J.W., Kenyon, R.V., Parker, D.E., Furness, T.A.: Effects of field of view on balance in an immersive environment. In: Virtual Reality Proceedings, Yokohama (2001)

9. Harvey, C., Howarth, P.A.: The effect of display size on visually-induced motion sickness (VIMS) and skin temperature, Hong Kong (2007)
10. Dizio, P., Lackner, J.R.: Circumventing side effects of immersive virtual environments. In: International Conference on Human-Computer Interaction, San Francisco (1997)
11. Stoffregen, T.A., Faugloire, E., Yoshida, K., Flanagan, M.B., Merhi, O.: Motion sickness and postural sway in console video games. Hum. Factors J. Hum. Factors Ergon. Soc. **50**(2), 322–331 (2008)
12. Rebenitsch, L., Owen, C.: Individual variation in susceptibility to cybersickness. In: User Interface Software and Technology Symposium, Waikiki, HI (2014)
13. Ehrlich, J.A.: Simulator sickness and HMD configurations, Pittsburgh (1997)
14. Keshavarz, B., Hecht, H.: Stereoscopic viewing enhances visually induced motion sickness but sound does not. Presence **21**, 213–228 (2012)
15. Merhi, O., Faugloire, E., Flanagan, M., Stoffregen, T.A.: Motion sickness, console video games, and head-mounted displays. Hum. Factors J. Hum. Factors Ergon. Soc. **49**(5), 920–934 (2007)
16. Moss, J.D., Muth, E.R.: Characteristics of head-mounted displays and their effects on simulator sickness. Hum. Factors J. Hum. Factors Ergon. Soc. **53**(3), 308–319 (2011)
17. Prothero, J.D., Draper, M.H., Furness, T.A., Parker, D.E., Wells, M.J.: The use of an independent visual background to reduce Simulator side-effects. Aviat. Space Environ. Med. **70**, 277–283 (1997)
18. Duh, H.B.L., Abi-Rache, H., Parker, D.E., Furness, T.A.: Effects on balance distubance of manipulating depth of an independent visual background in a stereographic display. In: Proceedings of the Human Factors and Ergonomics Society, Santa Monica (2001)
19. Duh, H.B.L., Parker, D.E., Furness, T.A.: An "independent visual background" reduced balance disturbance envoked by visual scene motion: implication for alleviating simulator sickness (2001)
20. Kennedy, R.S., Lane, N.E., Berbaum, K.S., Lilienthal, M.G.: Simulator sickness questionnaire: an enhanced method for quantifying simulator sickness. Int. J. Aviat. Psychol. **3**(3), 203–220 (1993)
21. Bos, J.E., de Vries, S.C., van Emmerik, M.L., Groen, E.L.: The effect of internal and external fields of view on visually induced motion sickness. Appl. Ergon. **41**(4), 516–521 (2010)
22. Young, S.D., Adelstein, B.D., Ellis, S.R.: Demand characteristics of a questionnaire used to assess motion sickness in a virtual environment, Alexandria (2006)
23. Howarth, P.A.: Oculomotor changes within virtual environments. Appl. Ergon. **1**(59–67), 30 (1999)
24. Mon-Williams, M., Wann, J.P.: Binocular virtual reality displays: when problems do and don't occur. Hum. Factors **40**(1), 42–49 (1998)

Assessing the Relationship Between Type of Head Movement and Simulator Sickness Using an Immersive Virtual Reality Head Mounted Display: A Pilot Study

Stephen R. Serge[1]([✉]) and Gino Fragomeni[2]

[1] University of Central Florida Institute for Simulation and Training, Orlando, FL, USA
sserge@ist.ucf.edu
[2] U.S. Army Research Lab/Human Research and Engineering Directorate (HRED),
Training Technology and Environments (TTE) Branch, Orlando, FL, USA
gino.f.fragomeni.civ@mail.mil

Abstract. Virtual Reality (VR) head-mounted displays are becoming more common and are drawing more attention from an increasing number of industries and organizations. Many groups are looking towards these types of technologies as a means for training, education, and entertainment. While research supports the capability of similar technologies for various uses, simulator sickness is still a main concern for extended exposure to virtual environments. Unfortunately, with the increasing number of commercial VR display technologies becoming available, little research exists evaluating the potential negative effects of VR usage. Furthermore, no explicit set of evaluation tools are available to guide thorough investigations of these devices. This experiment sought to evaluate a new commercially available VR head-mounted display and serve as a starting point for a larger-scale effort to determine best procedural practices for evaluating these types of technologies.

Keywords: Head-mounted displays · Virtual Reality · Simulator sickness · Head movements · Stereoscopic 3D · Human performance

1 Introduction

Virtual Reality is quickly becoming a familiar household term. Companies such as Oculus, HTC, and Sony have made virtual reality for entertainment both affordable and available to a much larger consumer base than it has ever been before. The commercialization of Virtual Reality (VR) Head-Mounted Displays (HMD) has driven a rapid increase in the technological capabilities and widespread availability of these types of devices. While the focus of the majority of VR HMD commercial technology is for entertainment, because of their lower cost than legacy HMDs for virtual reality, many other organizations are turning their attention towards these devices as a means of highly immersive training for military, education, or health-related domains.

Despite the fact that the technologies utilized for VR have increased in both efficiency and capability, there are still some factors that warrant further investigation. One of these factors is the occurrence of simulator sickness. Simulator sickness, similar to motion

© Springer International Publishing AG 2017
S. Lackey and J. Chen (Eds.): VAMR 2017, LNCS 10280, pp. 556–566, 2017.
DOI: 10.1007/978-3-319-57987-0_45

sickness, refers to instances where individuals experience symptoms such as nausea, sweating, disorientation, etc. because of their interaction with some type of virtual environment [1, 2]. In the case of VR, research to date has indicated that simulator sickness is a common occurrence in participants using HMDs. Much of this research has indicated varying contributing factors to the onset and severity of simulator sickness symptoms, ranging from technical capabilities (e.g., refresh latency [3], Field of View [4]), to individual head movements [5], to duration spent interacting with the system [6, 7].

The majority of these findings are associated with how the perception of visual information through the HMD may not necessarily align with the habitual physical movement that is expected when perceiving physical motion visually. Typically, people experience feelings of motion via a combination of visual, vestibular, and proprioceptive sensory input [8], therefore, a mismatch between these sensory inputs is a central supporting theory to the cause of motion and simulator sickness [9, 10].

Despite this, organizations are looking towards VR and HMDs as a solution for training and entertainment without concern for the potential side effects of VR exposure. Part of this issue arises from the fact that newer iterations of these technologies are constantly changing the way with which individuals interact with these technologies (i.e., room-scale motion tracking; controller input; etc.). Therefore, the objectives of this research were twofold:

(1) Examine one newer VR HMD product and evaluate the impact of its general usage.
(2) Examine how specific technology capabilities of the system, such as the ability to physically move while using the HMD, affects the occurrence of simulator sickness while completing different types of tasks within the virtual world.

While some prior research has addressed the relationship between vection, simulator sickness, and display type [11], current literature search results generally lack examinations or evaluations of the newest HMD technology to date.

2 Background

2.1 Virtual Reality and Head-Mounted Displays

The number of novel immersive HMDs for VR use has grown at a rapid pace recently. These HMDs range in technological complexity, from well-designed cardboard to room-scale headsets with onboard laser and infrared movement tracking systems. The majority of these headsets takes advantage of stereoscopic image or video presentation, which creates a sense of visual depth by presenting two images of the same subject matter, from slightly offset perspectives, to the left and right eyes simultaneously [12]. The visual system then converges the separate images into one, creating a realistic sense of depth in the visual field.

The increases in accessibility and lower relative costs has led to a desire to utilize these technologies for various purposes across different domains. For example, VR-HMDs have been studied as a means of treating posttraumatic stress disorders and rehabilitation [13–15]. Additionally, research has tested how well VR may aid in emergency navigational training in spacecraft [16], as well as its efficacy for teaching engineering concepts to students [17]. The military has also shown an increased interest in using VR for various flight and vehicle, medical, and combat training programs [18, 19].

A few possible reasons why these domain areas are interesting in VR stem from the fact that, not only has VR HMD technology become much cheaper, it also provides an incredibly high level of realism and the ability to create virtual environments and interactions that may not be accessible or possible in certain circumstances. However, a significant issue with simulator sickness persists in various forms of VR, particularly those involving HMDs.

Simulator Sickness in VR. Numerous studies have examined the effects of VR and HMD use on simulator sickness. Simulator sickness is similar to motion sickness in its symptoms; however, the former is elicited from the use and interaction with some form of simulator or virtual environment. A prevailing explanation for the onset and experience of simulator sickness is derived from the sensory conflict theory [10]. Sensory conflict theory posits that a mismatch of sensory information received from the visual and vestibular systems results in symptoms related to simulator sickness. This means that when visual motion observed in an HMD is not accompanied by a physical sensation (i.e., expectation) of movement, a sensory mismatch occurs and results in symptoms such as nausea, fatigue, dizziness, and/or disorientation.

Previous research has pointed to numerous potential causes for the onset of simulator sickness. For example, researchers have reported that factors such as visual motion (e.g., riding a virtual roller coaster) in HMDs can lead to feelings of vection and simulator sickness [11]. In addition, other research has shown that certain types of visual occlusion may lead to increased simulator sickness symptoms [6]. Variations in visual image latency have also been shown to lead to an increased onset of symptoms when using HMDs [3]. Furthermore, the duration in which one uses or interacts with a VR environment has been shown to consistently lead to significant increases in symptom presence [7, 20, 21].

Simulator sickness is an important issue to consider when deciding to use a VR HMD for training, learning, or entertainment. Despite the available information explaining the shortcomings and potential negative effects of using such devices, many industries and organizations are rushing to integrate them into their daily operations. While there are benefits of utilizing VR within these various domains, the negative effects have the potential to lessen the impact and efficacy of these technologies, depending on how they are used.

2.2 The Current Study

While there are many reported causes of simulator sickness while using an HMD in a VR environment, many commercial VR HMD products are still making their way to the market. To date, some of the newest HMDs claim to have minimized the effect of simulator sickness and increased the overall comfort for the user. However, there exists little-to-no published research to substantiate those claims.

Therefore, the purpose of this pilot study was to examine, initially, how different types of head movements while using a VR HMD affect reported feelings of simulator sickness. The HMD of interest in this study was the commercially available HTC Vive. The HTC Vive allows users much more freedom of movement within a given area while using the HMD than what has been available in earlier versions of similar technologies. Therefore, it was predicted that increased physical movement while using and interacting with the HTC Vive to view a VR environment would lead to lower onsets of reported simulator sickness. Lower simulator sickness ratings are expected as a result of the increased alignment of visual and vestibular sensory information due to a user's physical movement matching the visual input they receive. It was also predicted that participants experiencing lower levels of simulator sickness would obtain higher scores on specific performance tasks in the VR environments.

This experiment was designed as a small piece of a larger project that seeks to develop quick methods for conducting human factors-based evaluations for various commercial and non-commercial HMD and mixed reality technologies.

3   Methods

3.1   Participants

A total of 24 participants (12 female) were recruited from the University of Central Florida and surrounding Central Florida areas for participation in the experiment. The average age of these participants was 19.75 years (SD = 2.21). Participation was restricted to U.S. citizens between the ages of 18–45 who had normal or corrected-to-normal vision. All participants were prescreened to ensure that all eligibility requirements were met. Of the 24 participants, 11 (45.83%) indicated having some type of prior experience with virtual reality applications.

Participants were also screened on whether or not they, at any point in the past, considered themselves susceptible to motion sickness. Of the 24 responses, three participants had indicated being susceptible to motion sickness in the past.

3.2   Experiment Materials and Design

Simulation Equipment. This experiment utilized the commercially available HTC Vive Virtual Reality HMD. The HTC Vive hardware system includes the core HMD, two handheld controllers, and two optical tracking base stations. The HMD and controllers are tracked through a joint LASER/IR light blast from the base stations, tracking the location, position, and rotational information of the HMD and controllers in real time. The display inside the HMD consisted of two screens with a maximum resolution of 1080P displayed to each eye. Images in the HMD were displayed stereoscopically, creating a visual sense of depth and 3-Dimensional (3D) virtual imagery.

The HMD was connected to a host computer, as required, via HDMI and USB 3.0 connections, and required a dedicated power source. This cable bundle was connected to the HMD along the top of the physical hardware, and was supported by a pulley system that ran along the ceiling above the walkable area and to the host computer, thereby limited potential tripping hazards. The computer was an Alienware desktop PC with an

Intel Core i7-4930K processor, 32 GB of RAM, and an NVIDIA GeForce GTX 970 graphics card.

In addition to the HMD and accompanying equipment, the experimental design required some freedom of movement within the lab space. This space was virtually mapped and designated using the accompanying software suite for the HTC Vive and consisted of a square space, or play area, of approximately 8.82 m^2 (3.05 m × 2.89 m).

Experimental Design. This pilot experiment was designed with three conditions to measure how types of head movements, specifically rotation and tilt, affected simulator sickness ratings and usage/performance. All conditions required wearing the HMD during the experimental session. The first condition required participants to tilt their heads to the left or right (e.g., tilting the top of the head towards a shoulder) during the game-based experimental task. The second condition required participants to turn their head from side-to-side (i.e., a "looking" motion, turning the chin towards the shoulders) during the game-based experimental task. The third condition did not require head movements from the participants during the game-based task.

Participants spent approximately the same time using the HMD and completed identical tasks or experiences in all three conditions.

VR Experiences, Experimental Tasks, and Dependent Measures. Participants experienced and completed tasks in three separate VR environments. The first consisted of an observational VR environment, with low levels of direct user interaction, which was set underwater. The environment was created to simulate a realistic underwater diving experience. Participants controlled all movement, motion, and perspective changes in the environment by moving freely within the previously designated play area. The first VR experience lasted approximately 8–9 min.

The second VR environment was a linear-style game that required participants to fly a virtual plane-like object through a field of obstacles. The objective of the game was to fly as far as possible without crashing. When crashes occurred, the distance score was recorded and participants were told to restart the game. This was the manipulation task. Participants controlled the left-right turning of the plane via one of the head-movement control methods (i.e., tilt or turn) or handheld controller. Participant activity in the game lasted approximately 5–6 min.

The third VR environment consisted of a virtual space, laid out as a square (Fig. 1). Participants were tasked with picking up various colored boxes and placing them into the matching colored bins along the far side of the virtual task space. Movement within the space was required to complete the task. Participants were also required to use of both handheld HTC Vive controllers to pick up and place boxes into the bins. There were five playable levels, with each subsequent level containing an increasing number of boxes for the participant to collect within a two-minute (120 s) time allotment for each level. Time to completion was recorded for each level.

The Simulator Sickness Questionnaire [22] is a subjective, self-report measure used to evaluate the overall sickness ratings related to simulator usage. Participants provided responses to the 16-items on the measure, indicating the level of severity for each particular symptom associated with simulator sickness along 4-point scale (i.e., None/Slight/Moderate/Severe).

Fig. 1. Virtual environment for the box collection task

Procedure. The experiment lasted approximately 1.25 h. Each participant completed all the experiment individually. Participants first reviewed a consent form prior to beginning. After providing consent, participants completed a set of questionnaires consisting of background/demographics items, including age, experience with VR, and prior susceptibility to motion sickness, and an initial SSQ to establish a baseline.

Next, participants were introduced to the HMD and accompanying technology used for the experiment. This introduction included guidance on how to fit the HMD on their head using the adjustable straps. Once the HMD was secured in a comfortable and appropriate manner to the participant's head, the experimenter launched a VR tutorial application that explained to the participant how to safely move around the play area and use the controllers.

The experimental session began immediately upon completion of the tutorial. The entire session was broken up into three smaller sessions. These smaller sessions corresponded with the three different VR experiences/tasks designed for the experiment. Participants first went through the observational VR experiences, followed by the distance game, and finished with the box collection task. In between each session, they were asked to fill out an additional SSQ pertaining to their current state. After completion of the box collection task, participants filled out a final SSQ, were debriefed on the nature of the research, compensated for their participation, and dismissed.

4 Results

The preliminary data for the pilot test was first analyzed to check for extreme outliers on the first administration of the SSQ. Twenty-six individuals originally completed the study. Two participants reported initial SSQ ratings beyond two standard deviations from the mean. These participants' data were removed from the analyses because of the potential to alter the subsequent SSQ comparisons due to factors other than the experimental manipulations.

4.1 Individual Session Simulator Sickness Scores

Participants in all conditions completed SSQs prior to wearing and interacting with HMD and VR environments. Additional SSQ scores were collected after each of the three experimental sessions. An analysis of the initial SSQ scores indicated that there were no significant differences between groups prior to exposure to experimental manipulations ($F(2,21) = 0.76$, $p = .48$).

SSQ scores for the three experimental sessions were also compared individually between groups. As Table 1 depicts, there were no significantly different scores reported between groups during any of the three experimental sessions.

Table 1. SSQ results between conditions for the experimental sessions

Session	Exp. condition	M	SD	F(df)	p
1	Head-Tilt	6.55	11.61	.143(2,21)	.87
	Head-Turn	8.23	9.13		
	Controller	5.61	8.77		
2	Head-Tilt	13.56	18.32	.034(2,21)	.97
	Head-Turn	13.84	13.66		
	Controller	15.58	13.26		
3	Head-Tilt	21.04	25.21	.646(2,21)	.53
	Head-Turn	20.57	18.51		
	Controller	10.60	3.68		

4.2 SSQ Scores Over Time

In order to determine if using the HMD led to an increase in SSQ scores throughout the session, SSQ scores were also compared over time. In order to test this, a repeated measures ANOVA was conducted. The assumption for sphericity was violated; therefore, Greenhouse-Geisser corrected statistics were used. Results showed a significant change in overall SSQ ratings over time from all participants ($F(1.71, 35.86) = 11.01$, $p < .001$). However, no differences were observed in SSQ scores changes over time between groups, indicating that scores changed at similar rates across conditions. The values for overall mean SSQ scores over time are presented in Table 2.

Table 2. Mean overall scores on all SSQs

Metric	M	SD
SSQ1	2.65	4.61
SSQ2	7.01	9.57
SSQ3	14.18	14.63
SSQ4	18.23	18.83

Post hoc pairwise comparisons revealed that participants reported significantly higher ratings on nearly all of their four subsequent SSQ score, with the exception of SSQ3 and SSQ4 (see Table 3). Results indicated a consistently rising SSQ score throughout the duration of the experiment, except between SSQ3 and SSQ (i.e., over the final session).

Table 3. Pairwise comparisons for SSQ scores over time

Comparison scores	Mean diff.	Std. error	t(df)	p
SSQ1 - SSQ2*	−4.36	1.71	−2.55(23)	.018
SSQ1 - SSQ3	−11.53	2.85	−4.05(23)	< .001
SSQ1 - SSQ4	−15.58	3.87	−4.03(23)	.001
SSQ2 - SSQ3*	−7.17	1.73	−4.15(23)	< .001
SSQ2 - SSQ4	−11.22	3.15	−3.56(23)	.002
SSQ3 - SSQ4*	−4.05	2.68	−1.15(23)	.144

* Indicates successive administrations of the SSQ.

4.3 Experimental Group Task Performance

Head-Turning Game Task. The second task of the experiment involved controlling an object through and between obstacles. Participants attempted to fly as far as they could before crashing. In this case, distance was measured in arbitrary units, but these units were standard and consistent throughout the game. All participants completed at least three trials before time expired. The mean of all valid trials was computed and used to compare scores between groups.

Results from a one-way ANOVA revealed differences between groups on the distance task ($F(2,21) = 4.076, p = .032$). Individual group comparisons results showed that the Head-Tilt group ($M = 5166.14, SD = 1530.85$) significantly outperformed the Head-Turn group ($M = 3383.97, SD = 1184.16$; $t(16) = 2.79, p = .013$), but no other comparisons reached statistical significance with the Controller group ($M = 4349.7, SD = 1239.53$).

Furthermore, no statistically significant differences were observed on the SSQ collected immediately following the completion of this task between groups($F(2,21) = .034, p = .97$), indicating similar scores on the measure.

Box Collection Task. The box collection task performance was measured on completion time of the task over five levels of increasing difficulty. A repeated-measures ANOVA was used to analyze scores between conditions over time. Results indicated no significant differences between groups over trials, indicating that all groups completed the task's levels within similar times. Results also indicated a significant difference in level completion time within the entire sample ($F(4,84) = 115.13$, $p < .001$). However, this result was expected due to the increasing number of boxes per level (i.e., difficulty level).

Additionally, no differences were observed between groups on SSQ scores immediately following the box collection task ($F(2,21) = .646, p = .534$).

5   Discussion

The goals of this pilot experiment were two examine a newer VR HMD, and to assess whether or not the newer technological features of the device help to minimize previously consistent findings of simulator sickness during usage. The HTC Vive was considered a much more technologically advanced HMD than similarly marketed VR HMDs (e.g., Oculus Rift DK2, Samsung Gear VR) due to its ability to afford a greater range of motion within the designated play area. Earlier generation VR HMDs typically required users to sit or stand in a generally stationary location. This affordance means that users were able to move around the virtual environment in order to change their perspective or view, potentially minimizing the effects of visual-vestibular mismatch, which could lead to lower levels of reported simulator sickness [1, 2].

It was predicted that the increased affordance of physical movement that matched the visual presentation would lead to lower ratings on simulator sickness. The first analysis revealed no differences in simulator sickness ratings between the three types of head-movement experiment groups on all experimental sessions. Similar scores were expected after the first session because no direct manipulation of head movement occurred; participants were encouraged to walk around and observe the realistic cinematic environment freely. However, the second and third session also failed to reveal any significant differences between group SSQ scores. This could be due to a number of factors. First, the overall time spent in the second session, requiring specific head movement, may have been too short to elicit differences in scores between groups. Second, HTC Vive allowed for much higher levels of physical movement than older versions of similar technologies examined in previous studies. It may be the case that this freedom of movement generally led lower levels of simulator sickness as a whole.

Results revealed an overall increase in SSQ scores throughout the experiment from all participants. While these scores did significantly increase from the original baseline measure, average scores did not reach uncomfortably high sickness ratings. Despite this, these results still support the trend of previous findings that duration of exposure to VR leads to higher simulator sickness ratings. While not specifically tested in this research, longer VR interaction and durations might have shown increased sickness ratings. Future research needs to examine this factor more thoroughly.

Results on the game-based flight-obstacle task only revealed differences between the head-tilt versus the head-turn groups. However, these results could not be explained by simulator sickness ratings, as these groups had similar scores on the SSQ for this session. It may be the case that one type of control was inherently easier to manipulate than the other. Participants in the head-tilt group were able to keep their eyes facing forward the entire time and their head movement matched the visual representation of movement from the plane-like object they were controlling (i.e., a left-side head tilt corresponded with the plane rolling to the left). In contrast, participants in the head-turn group were required to move the position of their eyes as they initiated turns. This prevented a direct, straight-on view of the plane-like object and obstructions in its path. Additionally, the type of movement did not match the visual representation of movement from the plane. These factors may have led to the discrepancies in distance scores for this task.

Finally, box-collection task performance was similar between all experimental groups and no statistically significant differences were observed on simulator sickness scores. All participants were able to complete the task levels in equal times between groups. While not significant, there is a noticeable drop in SSQ score in the controller (i.e., no head movement) group. Unfortunately, the low sample size and high variance in scores from the other groups led to non-significant findings.

6 Conclusions

The findings in this experiment help to shed light on potential testing methods and approaches for verification of manufacture claims for comfort and usability in relation to simulator sickness. Despite the many studies focused on simulator sickness and HMDs, the literature is still lacking a general procedure or taxonomy of testing methods for evaluating various HMDs for their technical abilities and potential effects on users. While small in scale, results from this study will help guide future research focusing on the development of specific procedures for evaluation of new visually-based mixed reality technologies.

Acknowledgements. This research was sponsored by the U.S. Army Research Laboratory – Human Research Engineering Directorate, Advanced Training and Simulation Division (ARL/HRED/ATSD), in collaboration with the Institute for Simulation and Training at the University of Central Florida. This work is supported in part by ARL/HRED/ATSD contract W911QX-13-C-0052. The views and conclusions contained in this document are those of the authors and should not be interpreted as representing the official policies, either expressed or implied, of ARL/HRED/ATSD or the U.S. Government. The U.S. Government is authorized to reproduce and distribute re-prints for Government purposes notwithstanding any copyright notation hereon.

References

1. Lackner, J.R.: Motion sickness: more than nausea and vomiting. Exp. Brain Res. **232**(8), 2493–2510 (2014). doi:10.1007/s00221-014-4008-8
2. Reason, J.: Motion sickness: Some theoretical and practical considerations. Appl. Ergon. **9**(3), 163–167 (1978). doi:10.1016/0003-6870(78)90008-x
3. St. Pierre, M.E.: The effects of 0.2 Hz varying latency with 20–100 ms varying amplitude on simulator sickness in a helmet mounted display (Order No. 3550493). Available from ProQuest Dissertations & Theses A&I; ProQuest Dissertations & Theses Global (1285530295) (2012)
4. Emoto, M., Sugawara, M., Nojiri, Y.: Viewing angle dependency of visually-induced motion sickness in viewing wide-field images by subjective and autonomic nervous indices. Displays **29**(2), 90–99 (2008). doi:10.1016/j.displa.2007.09.010
5. Moss, J.D., Austin, J., Salley, J., Coats, J., Williams, K., Muth, E.R.: The effects of display delay on simulator sickness. Displays **32**(4), 159–168 (2011). doi:10.1016/j.displa.2011.05.010
6. Moss, J.D., Muth, E.R.: Characteristics of head-mounted displays and their effects on simulator sickness. Hum. Factors J. Hum. Factors Ergon. Soc. **53**(3), 308–319 (2011). doi:10.1177/0018720811405196

7. Serge, S.R., Moss, J.D.: Simulator sickness and the oculus rift. Proc. Hum. Factors Ergon. Soc. Annu. Meet. **59**(1), 761–765 (2015). doi:10.1177/1541931215591236
8. Cohen, B., Tomko, D.L., Guedry, F.E.: Sensing and controlling motion: vestibular and sensorimotor function. Ann. N. Y. Acad. Sci. (1992)
9. Been-Lirn Duh, H., Parker, D.E., Philips, J.O., Furness, T.A.: "Conflicting" motion cues to the visual and vestibular self-motion systems around 0.06 Hz evoke simulator sickness. Hum. Factors J. Hum. Factors Ergon. Soc. **46**(1), 142–153 (2004). doi:10.1518/hfes.46.1.142.30384
10. Reason, J.T., Brand, J.J.: Motion Sickness. Academic Press, London (1975)
11. Nalivaiko, E., Davis, S.L., Blackmore, K.L., Vakulin, A., Nesbitt, K.V.: Cybersickness provoked by head-mounted display affects cutaneous vascular tone, heart rate and reaction time. Physiol. Behav. **151**, 583–590 (2015). doi:10.1016/j.physbeh.2015.08.043
12. Hoffman, D.M., Girshick, A.R., Akeley, K., Banks, M.S.: Vergence-accommodation conflicts hinder visual performance and cause visual fatigue. J. Vis. **8**(3), 1–30 (2008). doi:10.1167/8.3.33
13. Moraes, T., Paiva, W., Andrade, A.: Virtual reality for the treatment of posttraumatic disorders. Neuropsychiatr. Dis. Treat. **12**, 785 (2016). doi:10.2147/ndt.s105538
14. Botella, C., Serrano, B., Baños, R., García-Palacios, A.: Virtual reality exposure-based therapy for the treatment of post-traumatic stress disorder: a review of its efficacy, the adequacy of the treatment protocol, and its acceptability. Neuropsychiatr. Dis. Treat. **11**, 2533 (2015). doi:10.2147/ndt.s89542
15. Keshner, E.A., Kenyon, R.V.: Using immersive technology for postural research and rehabilitation. Assistive Technol. **16**(1), 54–62 (2004). doi:10.1080/10400435.2004.10132074
16. Aoki, H., Oman, C.M., Natapoff, A.: Virtual-reality-based 3D navigation training for emergency egress from spacecraft. Aviat. Space Environ. Med. **78**(8), 774–783 (2007)
17. Alhalabi, W.S.: Virtual reality systems enhance students' achievements in engineering education. Behav. Inf. Technol. **35**(11), 919–925 (2016). doi:10.1080/0144929X.2016.1212931
18. Parkin, S.: How VR is Training the Perfect Soldier, 31 December 2015. https://www.wareable.com/vr/how-vr-is-training-the-perfect-soldier-1757
19. Bymer, L.: Virtual reality used to train soldiers in new training simulator, 1 August 2012. https://www.army.mil/article/84453
20. Moss, J., Scisco, J., Muth, E.: Simulator sickness during head mounted display (HMD) of real world video captured scenes. Proc. Hum. Factors Ergon. Soc. Annu. Meet. **52**, 1631–1634 (2008). doi:10.1037/e578262012-069
21. Kennedy, R.S., Stanney, K.M., Dunlap, W.P.: Duration and exposure to virtual environments: sickness curves during and across sessions. Presence Teleoperators Virtual Environ. **9**(5), 463–472 (2000). doi:10.1162/105474600566952
22. Kennedy, R.S., Lane, N.E., Berbaum, K.S., Lilienthal, M.G.: Simulator sickness questionnaire: an enhanced method for quantifying simulator sickness. Int. J. Aviat. Psychol. **3**(3), 203–220 (1993). doi:10.1207/s15327108ijap0303_3

Author Index

Printed in the United States
By Bookmasters